Introduction to Comparative Politics

BRIEF EDITION

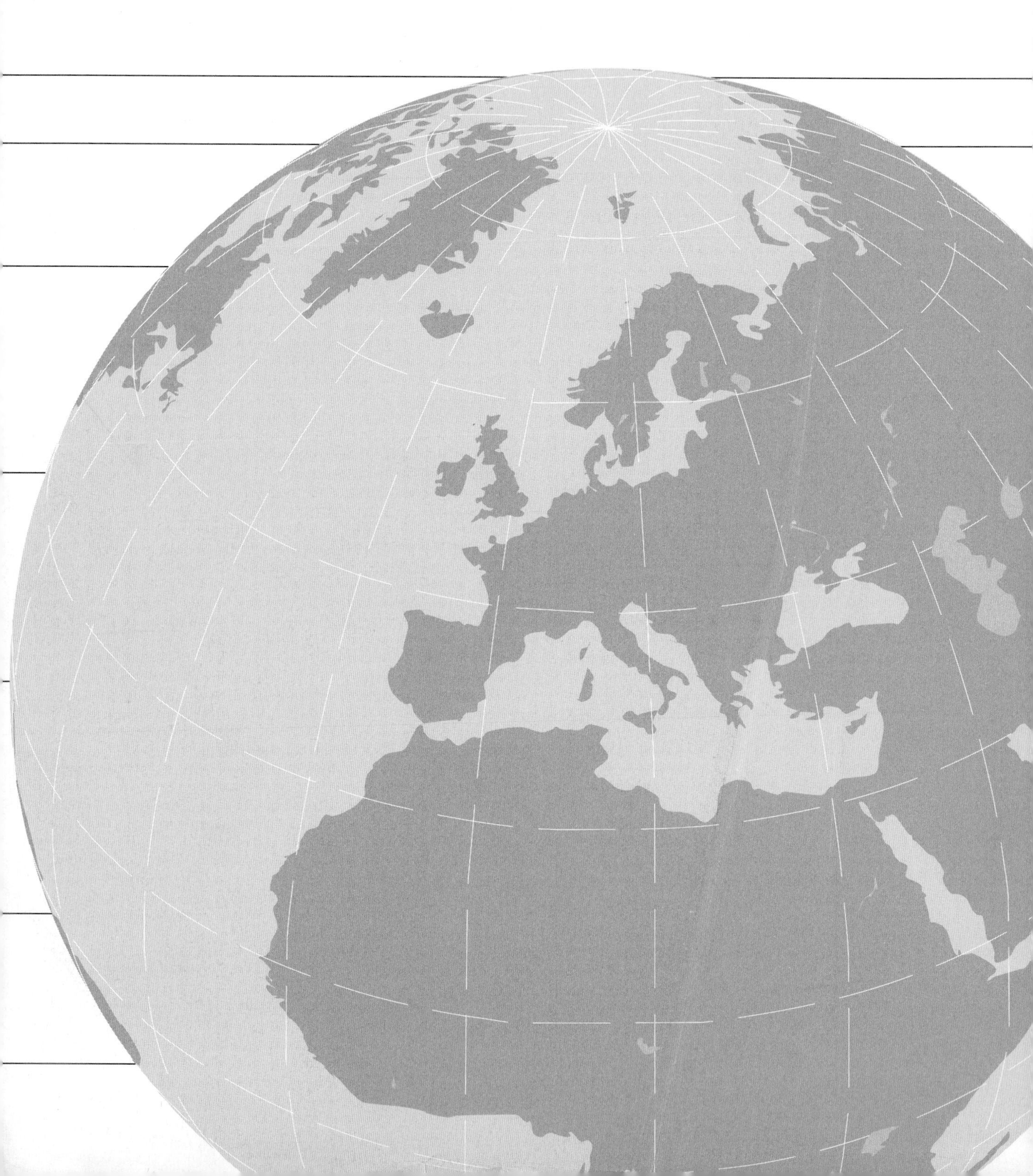

Introduction to Comparative Politics

BRIEF EDITION

Mark Kesselman
Columbia University

Joel Krieger
Wellesley College

William A. Joseph
Wellesley College

Contributors

Ervand Abrahamian
Baruch College

Amrita Basu
Amherst College

Joan DeBardeleben
Carleton University

Merilee S. Grindle
Harvard University

Atul Kohli
Princeton University

Tom Lodge
University of Limerick, Ireland

Houghton Mifflin Harcourt Publishing Company
Boston New York

To our children, who are growing up in a complex and ever more challenging world
MK—for Ishan and Javed
JK—for Nathan and Megan
WAJ—for Abigail, Hannah, and Rebecca

Publisher: Suzanne Jeans
Senior Sponsoring Editor: Traci Mueller
Marketing Manager: Edwin Hill
Discipline Product Manager: Lynn Baldridge
Senior Development Editor: Jeffrey Greene
Associate Project Editor: Carrie Parker
Senior Media Producer: Lisa Ciccolo
Content Manager: Janet Edmonds
Art and Design Manager: Jill Haber
Cover Design Manager: Anne S. Katzeff
Senior Photo Editor: Jennifer Meyer Dare
Senior Composition Buyer: Chuck Dutton
New Title Project Manager: James Lonergan
Editorial Assistant: Sareeka Rai
Marketing Assistant: Samantha Abrams
Editorial Assistant: Jill Clark

Cover image: © Ian McKinnell/Getty Images

Chapter-opening photographs: Chapter 2: Odd Anderson/AFP/Getty Images. Chapter 3: © Chris Helier/Corbis. Chapter 4: © Tom Pietrasik/Corbis. Chapter 5: AP Images. Chapter 6: © Erich Schlegel/*Dallas Morning News*/Corbis. Chapter 7: © Bettmann/Corbis. Chapter 8: © Abbas/Magnum Photos. Chapter 9: © Xiaoyang Liu/Corbis.

Printed in the U.S.A.

Library of Congress Control Number: 2008921464

ISBN-10: 0-618-86683-3
ISBN-13: 978-0-618-86683-0

1 2 3 4 5 6 7 8 9-DOW-12 11 10 09 08

Brief Contents

Contents

PART II CONSOLIDATED DEMOCRACIES

CHAPTER 2 Britain

PART IV AUTHORITARIAN REGIMES

Preface

This first edition of the brief version of *Introduction to Comparative Politics* (ICP-B) responds to requests from some instructors for a more concise version of the original text. These instructors liked the organization of ICP, especially the fact that the country chapters are organized around core themes. However, they wanted a book that, while preserving the distinctive features of ICP, was more concise and provided additional pedagogical features—more visually interesting and easier-to-read presentation of data, focus questions, and summaries at key points in each country chapter—that help guide students' learning. Many instructors were also looking for an accessible, lively writing style that supports student comprehension and a text that could be supplemented with additional readings. (For example, Mark Kesselman and Joel Krieger have edited a volume titled *Readings in Comparative Politics: Political Challenges and Changing Agendas*, published by Houghton Mifflin, whose selections reflect the organization of ICP.) We also paid close attention to instructors' suggestions about the design of this book—including current photos, adding color, and leaving ample room for marginal notes—to help encourage students in the learning process.

Structure and Approach of the Book

We have aimed to make the book accessible to students with little or no background in political science while continuing to probe the complexity of issues and events. We value readable, direct prose that is free of jargon, and we have used the same topical outline in each country chapter to facilitate cross-national comparison. We use vignettes about recent political developments in each country at the beginning of the case studies and elsewhere to engage students and underscore particular features of each country's political patterns. An array of ancillary visual materials complement the written text.

Like ICP, this brief version uses a country-by-country approach built around four core themes that strikes a balance between the richness of each country's national political development and cross-national comparative analysis. The countries included in ICP-B—Britain, France, India, Russia, Mexico, South Africa, Iran, China—have been chosen to present different types of political systems in a range of geographic and cultural settings.

Our thematic approach to comparative politics emphasizes patterns of state formation, political economy, domestic political institutions and processes, and the politics of collective identities, all within the context of globalization. We use four comparative themes to frame the presentation of each country's politics and to focus attention on the continuities and contrasts among the eight countries. We explain these themes in detail in Chapter 1 and present an intriguing "puzzle" for each to stimulate student thinking. The four themes are also highlighted in the first section of each country study and analyzed throughout the chapter.

- **A World of States** focuses on the importance of state formation, the internal organization of the state, and the interstate system for political development. In this edition, we take note of how the events of September 11 have influenced political institutions and policies.
- **Governing the Economy** emphasizes the crucial role of economic performance in determining a state's political legitimacy, analyzes state strategies for promoting economic development and competitiveness, and stresses the effects of economic globalization on domestic politics.
- **The Democratic Idea** explores the challenges posed to the state by citizens' demands for greater control and participation in both democracies and authoritarian regimes.
- **The Politics of Collective Identities** considers the political consequences of race, ethnicity, gender, religion, and nationality and their complex interplay with class-based politics.

Through our four themes, the methods of comparative analysis come alive as students examine similarities and differences among countries and within and between political systems. The thematic approach facilitates disciplined analysis of political challenges and changing agendas within countries.

Organization of Chapters

Chapter 1 explains the comparative method, analyzes the four key themes of the book, and describes core features of political institutions and processes. Each country chapter that follows consists of five sections. **Section 1** treats the historic formation of the modern state, its geographic setting, critical junctures in its political development, and the country's significance for the study of comparative politics. **Section 2** describes the political economy of past and current national development. **Section 3** outlines the major institutions of governance and policy-making. **Section 4** explains the widely varying processes of representation, participation, and contestation. Finally, **Section 5** reflects on the major issues that confront the country and are likely to shape its political future.

Several special features assist in the teaching and learning process.

- In Chapter 1, a variety of data is presented in a way that facilitates comparisons among the eight countries covered in this book and with the United States. At the beginning of each country chapter, students will find a map, data on ethnicity, religion, and language specific to that country to aid in comparing countries, and some basic information about the country's political system.

- Each major section heading in the country chapters begins with focus questions introducing students to the section that follows. Each section concludes with a brief summary of the main points covered.
- Throughout the chapters a wide array of maps, tables, charts, photographs, and political cartoons enliven the text and present key information in clear and graphic ways.
- Each country study includes several sidebar text boxes that highlight important and interesting aspects of the politics of that country. These vary chapter by chapter, and may, for example, focus on a key political leader, a distinctive institutional feature, a particularly controversial policy, unconventional forms of participation, or links between domestic and international politics. Some of the boxes make a comparison or connection between the country that is the subject of the chapter and the United States.
- Key terms are set in boldface and defined in the margin of the page where the term is first introduced and in the complete glossary at the end of the book. The glossary defines many key concepts that are used broadly in comparative politics.
- Each chapter concludes with a list of suggested readings, with an emphasis on material that we hope will be interesting and accessible to students.
- The Introduction (Chapter 1) includes a sidebar box that discusses the use of the Internet in the study of comparative politics. It notes a variety of websites where students can find more information about the countries covered in the book.

Classification of Countries

We classify the eight countries in ICP-B in three categories: *consolidated democracies* (Britain, France, India), *transitional democracies* (Mexico, Russia, South Africa), and *authoritarian regimes* (China, Iran). In the Introduction, we define these concepts and explain why they are a useful way to classify countries. In particular, we warn against assuming that there is a linear movement from authoritarian regimes to transitional democracies to consolidated democracies. Democratization is often a protracted process with ambiguous results, rather than a clearly delineated path toward completion. We call attention to "hybrid" regimes, in which the trappings and some elements of democracy co-exist with authoritarian practices. We stress that the countries we classify as transitional democracies are not on an historical escalator that mechanically leads to their becoming stable or consolidated democracies.

We also emphasize that the boundaries dividing the three groups are not airtight. For one thing, politics is a moving target. Russia is a good example of a country that is on the cusp between a transitional democracy and an authoritarian regime. Furthermore, scholars disagree about the appropriate criteria for classifying regime types as well as about how to apply the criteria to particular cases.

Indeed, instructors may find it fruitful and stimulating to organize discussion about how to best characterize the political system of a given country and about alternative conceptual schemes for classifying groups of countries.

Teaching and Learning Aids

For Instructors

Instructor Website. A website that offers a rich array of teaching and learning aids is available to support your teaching. For instructors, the website includes an image library stocked with additional images for classroom presentation, an instructor's resource manual with useful teaching tips, PowerPoint slides with figures from the text, PowerPoint slides with "clicker" questions, and useful Web links. In addition, Houghton Mifflin has partnered with the Associated Press to provide a daily news feed of national and international news that includes video clips, perfect for stimulating class discussion. We also offer a number of animations created by the Associated Press that provide some perspective on recent events.

HMTesting Instructor CD. This CD-ROM contains electronic test bank items. Through a partnership with the Brownstone Research Group, HM Testing—powered by Diploma®—provides instructors with all the tools they need to create, customize, and deliver multiple types of tests. Instructors can import questions directly from the test bank, create their own questions, or edit existing questions, all within Diploma's powerful electronic platform.

ComparingGovernments.org. This website is an online learning tool designed specifically to engage students through a variety of media, including original videos, short-form documentaries, writing excerpts, and additional resources. Students are asked to answer a series of questions in the online "Notebook," which records their answers and allows instructors to keep a record of the assignment. Correlated to the table of contents in the text, the site offers instructors four quality homework assignments per chapter and content that engages students and invigorates class discussions. In addition, to keep students current with world affairs there are news feeds from BBC World News and top stories from the United Nations News Centre.

For Students

ComparingGovernments.org. Each copy of this book includes passkey access to the valuable resources of ComparingGovernments.org, a dynamic and user-friendly website providing an array of multimedia content and web-based assignments for students. The site's video clips and interactive resources bring concepts to life and directly complement the textbook chapters. Students complete assignments on the website and submit their work to instructors with the click of a button. Students will also have access to flashcards to check their comprehension of key terms, practice tests, and the news feeds from BBC World News and the United Nations.

Acknowledgments

We are indebted to Jay Boggis, who helped shorten, enliven, and make more accessible the ICP4 country chapters that are included in ICP-B. We are also grateful to colleagues who have reviewed and critiqued ICP-B.

Linda Dolive, *Northern Kentucky University*

Walter Brown Foster, *Central Connecticut State University*

Hong N. Kim, *West Virginia University*

Christopher McDonald, *Lincoln Land Community College*

Glenn E. Perry, *Indiana State University*

Finally, our thanks to the very talented and professional staff at Houghton Mifflin who helped produce ICP-B: Traci Mueller, sponsoring editor; Jeff Greene, senior development editor; Carrie Parker, project editor; and Edwin Hill, executive marketing manager; and Alison Fields of Books by Design.

M. K.
J. K.
W. A. J.

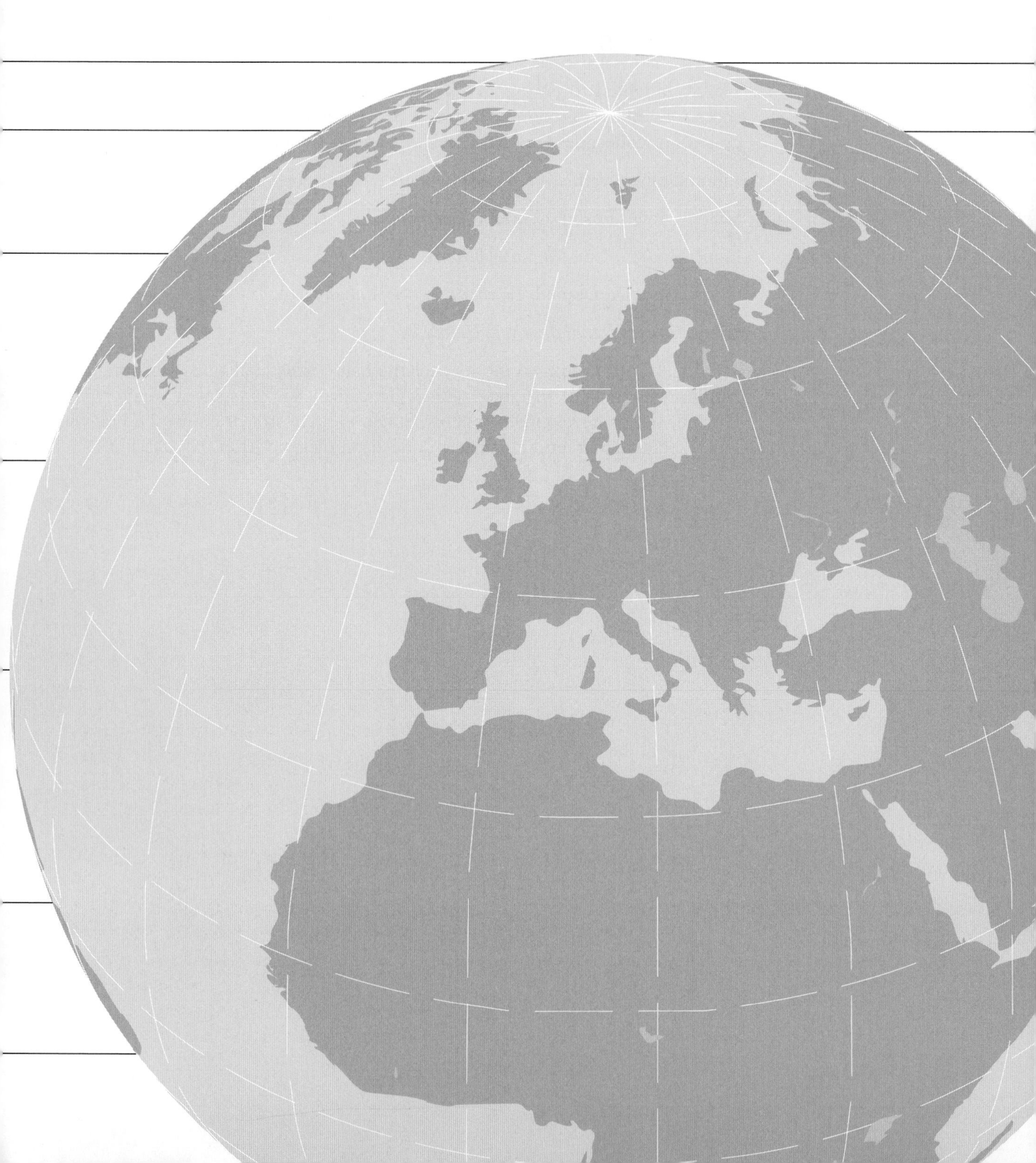

CHAPTER

1

Introducing Comparative Politics

Those who know only one country, know no country.

—Seymour Martin Lipset, *American Exceptionalism*

Mark Kesselman
Joel Krieger
William A. Joseph

When did our current political era begin? Although a precise moment is hard to identify, many people would say it began with the collapse of the Berlin Wall in 1989. Until then, the Wall separated communist-controlled East Berlin from democratic West Berlin. More broadly, it separated the two Germanies: the German Democratic Republic, allied with the Soviet Union, and the Federal Republic of Germany, allied with the United States. At the most general level, the Wall was a powerful symbol of the **Cold War**, a tense era of sometimes deadly struggle and potentially catastrophic nuclear conflict that pitted communist nations against the so-called free world. The fall of the Berlin Wall was followed by a series of mostly peaceful revolutions that overthrew the communist regimes of East Central Europe and the Soviet Union. The new governments that emerged after these revolutions were all committed to the market rather than state control of the economy and to multiparty

Cold War the hostile relations that prevailed between the United States and the Soviet Union from the late 1940s until the demise of the USSR in 1991.

Two events symbolically mark the major changes in world politics in the late twentieth and early twenty-first century: The fall of the Berlin Wall (left) in November 1989, ushered in the post–Cold War era, while the terrorist attack on the World Trade Center towers in New York City on September 11, 2001 (right), reflected a particularly violent form of the forces of globalization that now affect politics in all countries. *(Sources: (Left) Lionel Cironneau/AP Images. (Right) Gulnara Samoilova/AP Images.*

democracy rather than communist control of all political life. The Cold War was over, and the post–Cold War era, in which we now live, had begun.

While these history-shaking changes were occurring, a book with the bold title *The End of History?*[1] was published. The author, Francis Fukuyama, argued that the failure of communism signaled the end of any real alternative to the regimes of Western-style liberal democracies, that is, systems of government that combine democracy with a capitalist economy based on free markets. Was Fukuyama correct?

Clearly, history has not ended. It is still very dynamic: the period since the end of the Cold War has not been calm or without serious conflict. The years since 1989 have been turbulent and, in many ways, have dashed the hopes of those who thought the end of the Cold War would usher in extended peace and prosperity. In the most recent decades, the world has witnessed horrifying epidemics, famine, and an endless cycle of brutal clashes that have often pitted one ethnic group in a country against another. We have seen financial crises that wiped out years of economic development and the growing marginalization of whole regions of the globe. We have seen a new war, the war on terrorism, whose beginning was marked by another collapse, this time a terribly tragic one: the disintegration of the twin towers of the World Trade Center in New York City in the attacks of September 11,

2001. Since 9/11, fear of more attacks and concern for security have dominated politics within many countries and reshaped international relations. Compared to the scourge of global terrorism, the Cold War may not look so bad!

Yet there have been positive developments that suggest Fukuyama's analysis might have some merit. Today there are more democracies or countries moving in that direction than at any previous time in history. Many of the world's less developed countries, like China and India, have made impressive economic progress.

The only thing that is certain about where the world is headed politically is uncertainty! That's one of the things that can make the study of comparative politics so interesting. For example, since the 1990s, a distinctive new focus for analyzing politics both within and among countries—**globalization**—has grabbed attention and stirred debate. *Globalization* refers to the unprecedented worldwide flow of trade, investment, production, communications, technology, culture, ideas, and other influences. There is a wide range of views among political scientists, politicians, social activists, and concerned citizens about whether globalization will promote opportunity and enhance human development around the world, or whether it will only make the richer countries richer, and exclude the poorer regions from its benefits, or disadvantage them even further. These may seem like economic questions, but they are profoundly political, as well.

globalization The intensification of worldwide interconnectedness associated with the increased speed and magnitude of cross-border flows of trade, investment and finance, and processes of migration, cultural diffusion, and communication.

They are also very much at the center of the political agenda of every country in the world and they are central to framework of this book. Globalization has become such a key concept in understanding politics in the contemporary world that we devote a whole section of this chapter to it.

The attacks of 9/11 also remind us that history is full of uncertainties, surprises, and shock that have far-reaching political implications. We have to acknowledge that we can never fully explain, much less predict, politics. But this doesn't mean we should throw our hands up in the air and give up the attempt to bring order and understanding to the world of politics—just the opposite! We can best understand politics, not by getting lost in the rush of headlines and sound bites, but by using a framework that gives us a handle on what's important about politics in a particular country and points us toward similarities and differences within and between groups of countries. *Introduction to Comparative Politics* uses such a framework, based on four central themes to describe and analyze the politics of eight countries from around the world:

- *A World of States:* the historical development and political organization of individual countries and the interaction of countries within the international order
- *Governing the Economy:* the role of the government in economic management
- *The Democratic Idea:* the spread of democracy around the world and the challenges of democratization
- *The Politics of Collective Identities:* the political impact of diverse class, gender, ethnic, and religious identities.

We believe that these four themes provide valuable tools for making sense of politics in our tumultuous times. They will be more fully described later in this chapter.

The contemporary world is an amazing laboratory for the study of comparative politics, and current events give unusual significance to the subject. We turn now to explore what comparative politics actually compares and how comparative study enhances our understanding of politics in general.

SECTION 1 What—and How—Comparative Politics Compares

FOCUS QUESTIONS

What does it mean to compare things? What are two examples of how a comparison can bring to light features that might otherwise have been overlooked?

To compare and contrast is one of the most common human mental exercises. In the study of politics, the use of comparisons dates in the Western world at least from Aristotle. He categorized Greek city-states in the fourth century BCE according to their form of political rule: rule by a single individual, rule by a few, or rule by all citizens. He also distinguished "good" from "bad" versions of each type, according to whether those with power ruled in the interest of the common welfare of all citizens or only in their own interests. The modern study of comparative politics refines and systematizes the age-old practice of evaluating some feature of

What are two more examples of how comparison can distort how we look at political systems?

A by comparing it to the same feature of B in order to learn more about A than isolated study of it would permit.

comparative politics the study of the domestic politics, political institutions, and conflicts of countries.

Comparative politics is a subfield of the larger academic discipline of political science.[2] As you have probably already learned, political science is particularly concerned with the study of power: how it is gained, lost, used, abused, organized, distributed, and contested. The focus of comparative politics is the domestic, or internal, politics of different countries. In addition to comparative politics, most political science (or government) departments in the United States include courses and academic specialists in three other subfields: political theory, international relations, and American politics.

In the United States, the study of American politics is often considered a separate subfield from comparative politics. The pattern of distinguishing the study of politics at home from the study of politics abroad is also common in other countries. Students in Canada study Canadian politics as a distinct specialty, and Japanese students are expected to have particularly in-depth knowledge of Japanese politics.

comparativist a political scientist who studies the similarities and differences in the domestic politics of various countries.

However, there is no logical reason why the study of the United States should not be included within the field of comparative politics even in the United States—and many good reasons to do so. In fact, many important studies (and an increasing number of courses) integrate the study of American politics with the study of politics in other countries.[3] Comparative study can place U.S. politics into a much richer perspective and at the same time make it easier to recognize what is distinctive and most interesting about other countries. Indeed, as the prominent political scientist and **comparativist**, Seymour Martin Lipset once wrote, “Those who know only one country, know no country.”[4]

The Central Importance of Countries

country a territorial unit controlled by a single state.

We believe the best way to study comparative politics is to focus on countries. Countries comprise distinct, politically defined territories. They usually have their own political institutions, cultures, economies, and ethnic and other social identities. Most people see themselves as citizens of a particular **country**, and national citizenship is one of the most important, but not the only, source of the way people around the world connect to politics.

state the most powerful political institutions in a country, including the executive, legislative, and judicial branches of government, the police, and armed forces.

Within a given country, the most powerful cluster of institutions is referred to as the **state**. In the United States, the word *state* usually refers to the fifty states in the federal system—California, Illinois, New York, Texas, and so on. But in comparative politics, the “state” refers to the key political institutions responsible for making, implementing, enforcing, and adjudicating important policies:[5] for instance, the “German state” and the “Mexican state.” In this context, the state roughly means the same thing as the “government.” For example, we might talk about the declining role of the state (or government) in managing the economy in China over the last two or three decades.

executive the agencies of government that implement or execute policy.

The most powerful state institutions in most countries are those that are part of the national **executive** branch—usually headed by the president

cabinet the body of officials (e.g., ministers, secretaries) who direct executive departments presided over by the chief executive (e.g., prime minister, president).

bureaucracy an organization structured hierarchically, in which lower-level officials are charged with administering regulations codified in rules that specify impersonal, objective guidelines for making decisions.

and/or prime minister and the **cabinet**, which is made up of individuals who are in charge of the most important government departments and agencies. In some cases, the chief executive leader might be the head of the communist party (China), a military officer (Nigeria until 1999), or the supreme religious leader (Islamic Republic of Iran). The executive branch also includes the administrative **bureaucracy** that carries out laws and regulations. It also includes institutions that are legally allowed to use force, such as the police and military. Other important state institutions are the legislature, courts, and local governments.

All states claim the right to issue rules—notably, laws, administrative regulations, and court decisions—that people within the country must obey. Even democracies can survive only if they use force as a backup to make sure that citizens obey the law. However, in democratic regimes, representatives elected by citizens pass laws. As a result, there is by and large a much greater degree of voluntary compliance with laws in democracies than in nondemocratic states. In dictatorships, the state relies more heavily on the military and police to maintain order. But even then, long-term stability requires that the rulers have some measure of political **legitimacy**. A large percentage of the population, in particular, more influential citizens and groups, must accept that the state has the right to issue commands and to use force against those who do not obey them. Political legitimacy is a crucial concept in the study of comparative politics. It is determined by many factors, including, as we will emphasize, the state's ability to deliver satisfactory economic performance and an acceptable distribution of goods, services, and resources among its citizens.

legitimacy a belief by powerful groups and the broad citizenry that a state exercises rightful authority.

There are big differences in the ways that states are organized from one country to another. The eight country studies in this book are each written by a comparativist who specializes in studying the politics of that country. The studies devote considerable attention to the description of national political institutions and processes. Each country study begins with an analysis of **state formation**, that is, how the state has evolved historically to reach its present form.

state formation the historical development of a state, often marked by major stages, key events, or turning points (critical junctures) that influence the contemporary character of the state.

Our country studies also explore the extent to which citizens in a country share a common sense of nationhood, that is, a belief that the state's geographic boundaries coincide with citizens' **collective identities**, particularly ethnicity, language, and religion. When state boundaries and collective identities coincide, political stability is usually easier to maintain. But often they do not coincide. The result may be instability and even violence.

collective identities the groups with which people identify, including gender, class, race, region, and religion, and which are the "building blocks" for social and political action.

In some countries, nationalist movements seek to secede from the existing state and form their own state, sometimes in alliance with movements from neighboring countries with whom they claim to share a common heritage. The Kurds, for instance, have large populations in both Turkey and Iraq, and have long sought and fought to establish an independent nation-state of Kurdistan.

When a nationalist movement has distinctive ethnic, religious, and/or linguistic ties opposed to those of other groups in the country, conflicts are likely to be especially intense. Nationalist movements may pursue their separatist goal peacefully within the established political system, as has generally been the case with those who support independence for the French-majority province of Quebec from English-majority Canada. Or they may act outside established institutions and engage in illegal, sometimes violent activity. This has often happened in countries around the world, including Spain (the Basque region), Russia (Chechnya), Sri Lanka (the Tamil north), China (Tibet), and Ethiopia (Eritrea). Separatist movements tore apart the once-united country of Yugoslavia. One result of this was the "ethnic cleansing" slaughter in the Balkans region of Southern Europe.

The Comparative Approach to the Study of Politics

How do those of us who study comparative politics—we call ourselves comparativists—go about comparing? What do we compare? Because *countries* are the basic building blocks of the international system and *states* are the most significant political institutions within countries, these are the two critical units for comparative analysis. The comparativist measures and tries to explain similarities and differences among countries or states. One influential approach in comparative politics involves developing what are called **causal theories** that try to explain why "If X happens, then Y is the result." In other words, how does X (the **independent variable**) cause (or influence) Y (the **dependent variable**). This is a basic method of any study that claims to be scientific, whether in the natural, or "hard," sciences like physics and chemistry, or the social, or the "soft" sciences, which include anthropology, economics, and sociology, as well as political science.

causal theories an influential approach in comparative politics that involves trying to explain why "if X happens, then Y is the result."

independent variable an important part of social (and natural) scientific research. The cause in a cause-and-effect question.

dependent variable an important part of social (and natural) scientific research. The effect in a cause-and-effect question.

To illustrate what causal theories mean in the political science, let's say that we wanted to understand what causes conflict (Y) to intensify among various kinds of groups in a particular country. Many scholars have noted that if a country's economic pie (X) suddenly shrinks, the competition between groups for pieces of that pie will intensify, and conflict is likely to be the result. In other words, a decrease in X (economic pie) will *cause* an increase in Y (conflict). This kind of causal relationship might be tested by statistical analysis of a very large number of cases, a project facilitated in recent years by the creation of data banks that include extensive historical and contemporary data. Another way to study this issue would be to focus on one country, or several, to analyze how the relevant relationships between X and Y have varied over time and with what effect. Comparativists look at a variety of cases and try to identify similarities and differences among countries and discover significant patterns that will, hopefully, help us to better understand what causes important political outcomes.

It is important to recognize the limits on just how "scientific" political science—including comparative politics—can be. Two important differences exist between the natural and the social sciences. First, social scientists study people with free will. Because people have a margin for free choice, even if one assumes that they choose in a rational manner, their choices, attitudes, and behavior cannot be fully explained or predicted. This does not mean that people

The Internet and the Study of Comparative Politics

The Internet can be a very rich source of information about the politics of countries around the world. Following are some of the types of information you can find on the Web. We haven't included URLs since they change so often. But you should be able to find the websites easily through a key word search on Google or another search engine.

- **Current events.** Most of the world's major news organizations have excellent websites. Among those we recommend for students of comparative politics are the British Broadcasting Corporation (BBC), Cable News Network (CNN), the *New York Times*, and the *Washington Post.*
- **Elections.** Results of recent (and often past) elections, data on voter turnout, and descriptions of different types of electoral systems can be found at: the International Election Guide (IFES), Elections by country/Wikipedia, and the International Institute for Democracy and Electoral Assistance.
- **Statistics.** You can find data that is helpful both for understanding the political, economic, and social situation in individual countries and for comparing countries. Excellent sources of statistics are the Central Intelligence Agency (CIA), the Inter-parliamentary Union (IPU), the United Nations Development Program (UNDP), and the World Bank.

There are some websites that bring together data from other sources. These not only allow you to access the statistics, but also to chart or map them in a variety of ways. See, for example, Nationmaster.com and Globalis.com.

- **Rankings and Ratings.** There is a growing number of organizations that provide rankings or ratings of countries along some dimension based on comparative statistical analysis. We provide the following examples of these in the Data Charts that appear at the end of this chapter: the UNDP **Human Development Index**; the **Global Gender Gap**; the **Environmental Performance Index**; the **Corruption Perceptions Index**; and the **Freedom in the World ratings**. Others you might look are UNDP's Gender-Related Development Index (GDI) and Gender Empowerment Measure (GEM); the Global Economic Competitiveness Index; the Globalization Index; the Index of Economic Freedom; the World Audit of Freedom and Democracy; and the Press Freedom Index. *A note of caution: Some of these sites may have a certain political point of view that influences the way they collect and analyze data. As with any Web source: be sure to check out who sponsors the site and what type of organization it is.*
- **Official information and documents.** Most countries maintain websites in English. The first place to look is the website of the country's embassy in Washington, D.C., Ottawa, or London. The United Nations delegations of many countries also have websites. Governments often have English language versions of their official homepages,

Human Development Index (HDI) a composite number used by the United Nations to measure and compare levels of achievement in health, knowledge, and standard of living.

Global Gender Gap a measure of the extent to which women in 58 countries have achieved equality with men.

Environmental Performance Index a measure of how close countries come to meeting specific benchmarks for national pollution control and natural resource management.

Corruption Perceptions Index A measure developed by Transparency International that ranks countries in terms of the degree to which corruption is perceived to exist among public officials and politicians.

Freedom in the World rating an annual evaluation by Freedom House of the state of freedom in countries around the world measured according to political rights and civil liberties.

including governments with which the United States may not have official relations, such as Cuba and North Korea.

- **The United States Department of State.** The State Department's website has background notes on most countries. American embassies around the world provide information of selected topics about the country in which they are based.
- **Maps.** The Perry-Castañeda Library Map Collection at the University of Texas is probably the best currently available on-line source of worldwide maps at an educational institution.
- **General Comparative Politics.** Several American and British universities host excellent websites that provide links to a multitude of Internet resources on comparative politics (often coupled with international relations), such as those at Columbia University, Emory University, Keele University, Princeton University, Vanderbilt University, and West Virginia University. ❖

choose in a totally random fashion. We choose within the context of economic constraints, institutional dictates, and cultural prescriptions. Comparative politics systematically analyzes how such factors shape political preferences and choices; indeed, one recent study claimed that political beliefs are, to a significant degree, genetically determined,[6] that is, our political values and opinions (for example, on capital punishment or abortion) are, at least partly, inherited biologically from our parents.

A second difference between the natural and social sciences is that in the natural sciences, experimental techniques can isolate how distinct factors contribute to a particular outcome. In a laboratory setting, it is possible to change the value or magnitude of a factor—for example, the force applied to an object or mix of chemicals—and measure how the outcome has consequently changed. But political scientists and comparativists rarely have the opportunity to apply such precise experimental techniques.

Some political scientists have conducted experiments with volunteers in controlled settings to test, for example, the influence of political advertisements on voter opinions. But laboratories provide crude approximations of natural settings, since only one or a few variables can be manipulated. The real world of politics, by contrast, consists of an endless number of variables, and they cannot easily be isolated or manipulated. It simply is not possible to predict with absolute certainly how someone will vote once he or she gets into the voting booth; nor is it possible to know fully why voters cast their ballots the way they do.

Some political scientists try to get deeper into the question of cause and effect by using statistical techniques to identify the specific weight of different factors in explaining variations in political outcomes. But it is difficult to measure precisely how, for example, a person's ethnicity, gender, or income influences her or his voting choices. Nor can we ever know exactly what mix of factors—conflicts among elites, popular ideological appeals, the weakness of the state, the organizational capacity of rebel leaders, or the discontent of the masses—leads to the success or the failure of a revolution. Indeed, similar outcomes of different revolutions may result from different combinations of factors. No single theory, therefore, can explain the outcomes of all revolutions—or why people vote the way they do.

Comparative Politics and the Challenge of Globalization

FOCUS QUESTIONS

What do we mean by globalization? How does increased cross-border contact among countries and peoples affect political, social, and cultural life?

Comparative politics has traditionally focused on studying single countries or domestic institutions and processes in several countries. Comparativists considered that studying the international system fell within the subfield of international relations. However, as mentioned near the beginning of this chapter, for nearly two decades, globalization has been a critical factor in analyzing politics within and among countries. Today, business and trade, information technology, mass communications and culture, the environment, immigration and travel, as well as politics, forge deep connections—and often deep divisions—among people worldwide. To appreciate the complexity of politics in any country, comparativists now recognize that we must look beyond and across borders at the growing interdependence among nations. We have learned that we must develop a truly global perspective in order to understand the politics of individual countries and to compare them.

The terms *globalization* and *global era* identify the growing depth, extent, and diversity of today's cross-border connections. Discussion of globalization usually begins with economic activities—the great increase in international trade, finance, and overseas investment, as well as the worldwide reorganization of production and redistribution of the work force that has led to the creation of the so-called global factory in which very few manufactured products are, in fact, produced in just one country. Globalization also involves the movement of peoples through migration, employment, business, tourism, and educational opportunities.

The Internet and other new applications of technology now blur distinctions between what is around the block and what is around the world. These technologies link producers and contractors, headquarters, branch plants, suppliers, and consumers in real time anywhere in the world. Employees may be rooted in time and place, but they can take advantage of the ebb and flow of a global labor market. On the flip side: a secure job today may be gone tomorrow if an employer decides to move a business to another country.

Globalization has provoked challenges from grassroots movements in every region of the world that are concerned with its negative impact on, for example, poor people, the environment, and labor rights. Conferences convened by governments and international organizations to develop rules for global commerce have been the sites of demonstrations by coalitions of environmental, labor-based, and community activists. Activists from around the world have recently assembled in places such as Mumbai, India, and Porto Alegre, Brazil, to exchange ideas and develop alternatives to the current form of economic globalization.[7]

Globalization in its many forms challenges the ability of even the strongest countries to control their destinies. In today's world, no country can be an island unto itself and protect its national culture from outside influences, seal off its economy, or isolate its people. Many of the most important problems confronting individual states are related to globalization, including pandemics like AIDS, global climate change, financial panics, the arms trade, and international terrorism. The study of comparative politics has, in many ways, become the study of global politics.

The events of September 11, 2001, made it painfully clear that international terror networks, such as Al Qaeda, are an evil form of globalization. Terrorists, and the causes that motivate them, move around the world. They can attack anywhere. But such issues have not replaced concerns about economic globalization, which has an impact on many more countries and peoples than does terrorism. Rather these issues remind us how multifaceted globalization has become and underline the urgency of developing a more complex understanding of globalization and how it influences both politics throughout the world and the study of comparative politics.

Themes for Comparative Analysis

FOCUS QUESTIONS

Of the themes presented for comparative analysis, which one seems the most important? Why? The least important? Why?

Give an example of how, in one particular country, features of one theme can affect the features of another theme.

We have already emphasized the need to apply a clear framework to the study of comparative politics in order to make sense of major and often confusing developments that have shaped the contemporary political world. We have also explained the subject matter of comparative politics and described some of the tools of comparative analysis.

This section describes the four themes we use in *Introduction to Comparative Politics* to organize the information on state institutions and political processes in the country chapters. These themes help explain similarities and differences among countries. We also suggest a way that each theme highlights a particularly important question—or puzzle—in comparative politics.

Theme 1: A World of States

Our first theme, *a world of states*, is a bit of a play on words. It is meant to reflect the facts that individual states are the most important actors on the world stage and that all states must be understood from the perspective of their place among other states on the world stage.

For about 500 years, states have been the basic building block of global politics. International organizations (such as the United Nations) and private actors like transnational corporations (such as Microsoft)—and ordinary citizens organized in political parties and social movements—have certainly come to play a crucial role in world politics. But it is still, for the most part, states that determine the decisive outcomes in international affairs. It is the rulers of states who send armies against other states. The legal codes of states make it possible for businesses to operate within their borders and beyond. States are the main source—to greatly varying degrees—of resources for human welfare by providing assistance for the sick, poor, elderly, orphaned, or unemployed. States regulate the movement of people across borders. States negotiate and sign (or reject) treaties or agreements on the most critical issues facing individual countries and the world as a whole, be they war and peace, nuclear proliferation, trade, or pollution.

A state's position in the world of states has a powerful impact on its domestic politics. In 1796, George Washington warned the United States not to "entangle our peace and prosperity" in alliances with other nations. He believed the United States would be more successful if it could remain detached from the global power politics of the time. That kind of disengagement might have been possible then. But not today, particularly in this post–9/11 era of globalization.

Thanks to radio, television, and the Internet, people nearly everywhere can become remarkably well informed about international developments. This knowledge may lead citizens to demand that their governments intervene to stop atrocities in faraway Kosovo, Rwanda, or Dafur, or rush to aid the victims of natural disasters, as happened after the great tsunami struck South and Southeast Asia in late 2004.

Heightened global awareness may encourage citizens to hold their own government to internationally recognized standards of human rights and democracy. The recent spread of the so-called color or flower revolutions illustrates how what happens in one state can influence popular movements in other states, particularly in this era of globalized media and communications. Such movements have adopted various symbols to show their unity of purpose: the "Rose Revolution" (2003) in Georgia (a country located between Russia and Turkey, not the southern U.S. state), the "Orange Revolution" (2004) in Ukraine, the "Tulip Revolution" (2005) in Kyrgyzstan all led to the toppling of dictatorial leaders. The "Cedar Revolution" in Lebanon (2005) didn't force a change of political leadership, but it did cause the withdrawal of unpopular Syrian troops from that country, and the "Blue Revolution" in Kuwait has emerged as an important movement in support of granting women greater political rights.

failed states states in which the government no longer functions effectively.

States may collapse altogether when challenged by powerful rivals for power. And a similar outcome may occur when leaders of the state violate the rule of law and become predators, preying on their own people. Political scientist Robert Rotberg suggested the term **failed states** to describe this extreme situation, and cited as examples Sierra Leone, Somalia, and Afghanistan before and under the Taliban.[8] *Foreign Policy*, a highly respected journal on current affairs, compiles an annual ranking of failed states. In 2007, Sudan headed the list. Iraq, even under American military occupation, was ranked second.[9] The seventeenth-century English philosopher Thomas Hobbes, who lived in a time of great political disorder that included the beheading of a king, warned in his classic book, *Leviathan*, that the absence of effective state authority produces a war of every person against every other person. This desperate situation, he observed, involves "continual fear, and danger of violent death; and the life of man [is] solitary, poor, nasty, brutish, and short." For the nearly two billion people that *Foreign Policy* estimates live in states that are in serious danger of failing, Hobbes' dire warning may be all too true.

Although few states collapse into complete failure, all states today are experiencing intense pressures from external influences. But international political and economic factors do not have the same impact in all countries, and a few powerful and privileged states have the capacity to shape the international system as much as they are shaped by it. The more advantages a state possesses, the more global influence it will have. At the same time, countries with fewer advantages are more extensively molded by other states, international organizations, and transnational corporations.

Our case studies also emphasize the importance of similarities and contrasts in state formation and organization among countries. We discuss how states have developed historically: key events like colonial conquest, defeat in war, economic crises, or revolutions that had a durable impact on the character of the state.

Furthermore, the world-of-states theme draws attention to the importance of variations in the organization of states. This is the overall mix of their political institutions that distinguishes, for example, democratic from authoritarian regimes (see below for a discussion of the meaning of **authoritarianism**). This theme also highlights variations in institutions within a given regime type, such as the contrast between presidential (as in Mexico) and parliamentary (as in Britain) systems of government in democratic states.

authoritarianism a system of rule in which power depends not on popular legitimacy but on the coercive force of the political authorities.

A World-of-States Puzzle

How do states today deal with the many challenges to their authority from both internal and external forces? Increasingly, the politics and policies of states are shaped by diverse international factors from "above" often lumped together under globalization. At the same time, many states face groups within their borders who confront the power and legitimacy of central governments from "below." In reading the country case studies, try to assess how pressures from both above and below—outside and inside—affect the state in carrying out its basic functions. To what extent are even the most powerful states influenced by global and social forces that they cannot fully control? In what ways are the poorer and less powerful countries especially vulnerable to the pressures of globalization and disgruntled citizens? In this world marked by globalization and increasing interdependence, can states any longer achieve desirable outcomes on their own?

Theme 2: Governing the Economy

The success of states in maintaining the support of their people depends to a great degree on their ability to meet the economic needs and desires of their populations. An important reason for the rejection of communism and the disintegration of the Soviet Union was the poor performance of the Soviet economy. People simply became fed up with long lines to buy daily necessities, with the shoddy quality or even total lack of consumer products, crowded housing, unavailable or outrageously expensive foreign goods—to name just a few of the economic woes inflicted on its people by the Soviet state. In contrast, communist rule has survived in China in large part because of the stunning growth of the Chinese economy and the rapidly rising standard of living for the large majority of the people.

How a state organizes production and the extent and character of its intervention in the economy—that is, how it "governs the economy"[10]—reflects one of its most important functions and is a key element in its overall pattern of governance and political legitimacy. It is important to analyze, for example, how the economies of various countries differ in the balance between agricultural and industrial production, why some countries do so well in competing with other countries that offer similar products in international markets, and the relative importance of private market forces versus government direction of the economy.

political economy the study of the interaction between the state and the economy, that is, how the state and political processes affect the economy and how the organization of the economy affects political processes.

The term **political economy** refers to how government policy affects economic performance and how economic performance in turn affects a country's political processes. We believe that politics in all countries is deeply influenced by the relationship between the government and the economy and that a political economy perspective should be part of any thorough approach to the study of comparative politics.

sustainable development an approach to promoting economic growth that seeks to minimize environmental degradation and depletion of natural resources.

A Governing-the-Economy Puzzle

There is not one right way for a state to govern the economy, nor is there one single standard by which to measure economic success. There is widespread agreement that some state practices *hinder* economic development, for example, when state officials accept bribes, set tax rates so high as to discourage investment, and fail to provide public goods like education and transportation facilities that promote a productive economy. However, there is less agreement on the economic policies that states *should* adopt. As you read the country studies in this book, ask yourself: Why are some states more successful at promoting successful economic performance than others?

A related puzzle: Should economic performance be measured solely by how rapidly a country's economy grows? Or are other standards important to keep in mind, such as the quality of life of its citizens, as measured by such criteria as life expectancy, level of education, and unemployment rate? Is equality important? What about the environmental impact of economic growth? There is now much greater attention than just a few decades ago to this question, and more countries are emphasizing **sustainable development**, which promotes ecologically sound ways to modernize the economy and raise the standard of living. What do you think are the appropriate yardsticks to evaluate how well a state is governing its economy?

democracy from the Greek *demos* (the people) and *kratos* (rule). A type of political system that features the following: selection to important public offices through free and fair elections based on universal suffrage (the right of all adults to vote); political parties that are free to organize, offer their ideas, present candidates for public office, and compete in elections; an elected government that develops policy according to specified procedures that are fair and relatively open to public scrutiny; all citizens possess political rights and civil liberties; an independent judiciary (court system); civilian control of the military.

Theme 3: The Democratic Idea

One of the most important and astounding political developments in recent years has been the rapid spread of **democracy** throughout much of the world. There is overwhelming evidence of the strong appeal of the democratic idea and the desire to live in a democracy. We will define what we mean by *democracy*

How Is Economic Development Measured?

As we have already noted, we put particular importance on understanding the relationship between the political system and the economy in the study of the politics of any country and in our overall approach to comparative politics. Each of the country case studies describes and analyzes the role of the government in making economic policy. They also take special note of the impact of the global economy on national politics.

This book makes frequent reference to two commonly used measures of the overall size or power of a country's economy:

- **Gross Domestic Product (GDP):** a calculation of the total goods and services produced by the country during a given year.
- **Gross National Product (GNP):** GDP plus income earned abroad by the country's residents.

A country's GDP and GNP are different, but not hugely so. Both measure the *total output* of a country's economy. In this book, we use GDP calculated according to an increasingly popular method called **purchasing power parity (PPP)**. PPP takes into account the real cost of living in a particular country by calculating how much it would cost in the local currency to buy the same "basket of goods" in different countries. For example, how many dollars in the United States, pesos in Mexico, or rubles in Russia does it take to buy a certain amount of food or to pay for housing? Many scholars think that PPP provides a relatively reliable (and revealing) tool for comparing the size of an economy and among countries. In terms of annual total output, the world's ten largest economies are: the United States, China, Japan, India, Germany, Britain, Italy, France, Russia, and Brazil.

But a better way to measure and compare the level of economic development and the standards of living in different countries is to look at annual GDP *per capita* (per person), in other words, to look at total economic output divided by total population. Although China has the world's second-largest economy in terms of total output, from the annual GDP *per capita* perspective China ($7700) falls to 109th out of 229 countries measured between 2004–2006, and India ($3800) falls to 154th place. Luxembourg ($71,400) with its small population, ranks first while the United States is ninth ($44,000). This approach gives us a better idea of which countries in the world are rich (developed) or poor (developing).

The comparative data charts at the end of this chapter provide total GDP and GDP *per capita* as well as other economic, geographic, demographic, and social information for our eight country case studies. The data charts also provide several ways of ranking or rating countries in order to compare them along various dimensions of their economic, political, or public policy performance. One of the most important of these is the Human Development Index (HDI), which the United Nations uses to evaluate a country's level of development that considers more than just economic factors. The formula used to calculate a country's HDI takes into account *longevity* (life expectancy at birth), *knowledge* (adult literacy and average years of schooling), as well as *income* (according to PPP).

Based on this formula, countries are annually ranked and divided into three broad categories by the United Nations Development Program (UNDP): "High" "Medium," and "Low" human development. Out of 177 countries ranked according to HDI in 2006, the top three were Norway, Iceland, and Australia; the bottom three were Mali, Sierra Leone, and Niger. Look at the data charts to see how the countries in this book are ranked, and as you read the case studies try to see what connections there may be between a country's state policies, politics, and its human development ranking. ❖

gross domestic product (GDP) the total of all goods and services produced within a country that is used as a broad measure of the size of its economy.

gross national product (GNP) GDP plus income earned by the country's residents; another broad measure of the size of an economy.

purchasing power parity (PPP) a method of calculating the value of a country's money based on the actual cost of buying goods and services in that country rather than how many U.S. dollars they are worth.

TABLE 1.1

The Spread of Democracy

Year	Free Countries	Partly Free Countries	Not Free Countries
1973	43 (35%)[1]	38 (18%)	69 (47%)
1983	54 (36%)	47 (20%)	64 (44%)
1993[2]	75 (25%)	73 (44%)	38 (31%)
2006	90 (46%)	58 (17%)	45 (37%)[3]

Notes:

1. The number of countries in each category is followed by the percentage of the world population.
2. In 1993, the large increase in the number of *free* and *partly free* countries was mostly due to the collapse of communist regimes in the Soviet Union and elsewhere. The main reason that there is a significant drop in the percentage of world population living in *free* countries in 1993 is that India was classified as *partly free* from 1991 through 1997. It has been ranked as *free* since 1998.
3. The increase in the number of countries and percentage of people rated as *not free* countries in 2006 compared to 1993 reflects the fact that several countries, most notably Russia, were shifted from *partly free* to *not free*.

more precisely later in this chapter. For now, it can be taken to mean a political system in which leaders and officials are held accountable in meaningful ways to those over whom they exercise power. In democracies, citizens also have some control and influence over the decisions made by their states and governments.

Freedom House (a research organization based in the United States) annually collects and analyzes data on civil and political liberties in countries around the world and then rates them as "Free" (democratic), "Partly Free," and "Not Free." The table above is based on data from Freedom House reports[11], and shows just how dramatic the spread of democracy has been since the early 1970s.

We do not mean to claim that all countries are or inevitably will become democracies. There is a vigorous scholarly debate about whether China will democratize.[12] Furthermore, countries that have adopted democratic institutions may experience reversals. An important recent example is Russia. Following the disintegration of communist rule in the 1990s, there was a trend toward democracy. However, many democratic liberties and procedures were undermined under the rule of Vladimir Putin in the first decade of the twenty-first century. In fact, Freedom House now classifies Russia as "Not Free," although we still classify it as a "transitional democracy" (see below). Thus, a trend toward democracy is only a trend, not a certainty.

What explains why some countries become democratic? For all the attention this question has received, there is no scholarly consensus on how and why democratization occurs. Or rather, we have learned that there is not one path to democracy, just as there is not one path to economic success.

Is it possible to identify conditions that are critical for democracy to flourish? Comparativists have proposed that among such conditions are secure national boundaries, a stable state, an adequate standard of living, a large middle class, the widespread acceptance of democratic values, agreement to play by the rules of the democratic game among those who contend for power. One might extend the list, but the point should be clear. There are infinite possible factors that might explain why democratic institutions are adopted. Democracy can and has flourished in unlikely settings—for example, in India, a country with a vast population whose per capita income is among the lowest in the world. And it has failed where it might be expected to flourish—for example, in Germany in the 1930s when Hitler came to power in a country that was a very rich and modern country for the times. Democracies vary widely in terms of how they came into existence and in their specific historical, institutional, and cultural dimensions.

Toppling authoritarian regimes and then holding elections does not mean that democracy will prevail or endure. A wide gulf exists between what comparativists have termed a *transition* to democracy and the *consolidation* of democracy. A transition involves toppling an authoritarian regime and adopting the basic ingredients of a democratic state (see below); consolidation requires fuller adherence to democratic procedures, a deeper commitment to democratic values, and democratic institutions that are sturdy and durable. The process of democratic consolidation may take decades.

At the same time, the democratic idea fuels political conflicts in even the most durable democracies, because a large gap usually separates democratic ideals and the actual functioning of democratic political institutions. **Social movements** may target the democratic state because they judge that it does not respond to their demands. Such movements have organized in varied spheres including environmental regulation, reproductive rights, and race or ethnic relations. Even in countries with impressive histories of democratic institutions, citizens may demand that their government be more responsive and accountable to the ideals of democracy.

social movements large-scale grass-roots action that demands reforms of existing social practices and government policies.

A Democratic-Idea Puzzle

What is the relationship between democracy and political stability? On the one hand, democracy by its very nature permits political opposition, which can make political life in democracies turbulent and unpredictable. On the other hand, it is rarely violent. The very fact that political opposition and competition are legitimate in democracies appears to deepen support for the state, even among opponents of a particular administration. The democratic rules of the game may promote political stability by encouraging today's losers to remain in the game because they may win peacefully in future competition. As you learn about different countries, look for the stabilizing and destabilizing consequences of recent democratic transitions (Mexico, South Africa); the reasons for the reversal of democracy (Russia); the pressures (or lack of pressure) for democratization in authoritarian states (China, Iran); and the persistence of undemocratic elements even in established democracies (Britain, France, India).

A Puzzle That Combines the Democratic Idea and Governing the Economy

Is there a relationship between a democratic state and successful national economic performance? This is a question that students of political economy have long pondered—and which continues to provoke debate. All economies, even the most powerful, experience ups and downs. But the United States, Britain, and France—all long-established, durable democracies—have been notable economic success stories. Does this suggest that democracy assures economic success (that there is a causal relationship)? But, then, how do we explain that several East Asian countries, such as the Republic of Korea (South Korea), Taiwan, and Singapore, achieved remarkable development in the 1960s and 1970s while under authoritarian regimes. China is a repressive **communist party–state** ("Not Free" according to Freedom House) that has enjoyed the highest growth rate in the world since the early 1990s. It provides a vivid case of development without democracy. The fact that both South Korea and Taiwan subsequently became democracies has led some scholars to conclude that an authoritarian state may be suitable for promoting rapid economic development for a while, but that economic development itself creates pressures for democratization. China is a very interesting case study about whether that hypothesis is valid.

communist party–state a type of nation-state in which the communist party attempts to exercise a complete monopoly on political power and controls all important state institutions.

Nobel Prize–winning economist Amartya Sen has argued, "There is no clear relation between economic growth and democracy in *either* direction."[13] As you read the country studies, try to identify why some states have been more successful than others in "governing the economy," that is, fostering successful economic performance. Do you think democracy is a factor?

Theme 4: The Politics of Collective Identity

How do individuals understand who they are in political terms? National citizenship is one of the broadest sources of what we call collective political identities. On what other collective identities do people form groups to advance common political aims?

Social scientists once thought they knew. In the 1940s and 1950s, many argued that the age-old loyalties of ethnicity, religious affiliation, race, gender, and locality were on the decline and were being replaced by identities shaped by economic, political, and cultural modernization. Comparativists (as well as many others who observe and analyze society) thought that **social class**—solidarities based on the shared experience of work or, more broadly, economic position—had become the most important source of collective identity. They believed that most of the time, identity-based groups would pursue their interests in ways that were not politically destabilizing. We now know that the formation of group attachments is far more complex.

social class a group whose members share common economic status determined largely by occupation, income, and wealth.

In many long-established democracies such as the United States, Britain, and Japan, the importance of identities based on class membership has declined, although class and economic sources of collective political identity remain significant in political competition and economic organization. In many countries, identities not based on class have assumed growing, not diminishing, significance. Such affiliations may include shared language, region, religion, ethnicity, race, nationality, or gender.

The politics of collective identity involves struggles to form politically influential groups and to increase and assert their power against other groups or the state. Such politics also involves the struggle to define which groups are significant or favored players in the political process and which are marginalized, excluded, or even repressed. These issues are never fully settled, although they may rage with greater or lesser intensity in particular countries and at particular times. The issue of race relations in the United States is a powerful reminder of this basic fact of political life.

Religion is another especially important source of collective identity—as well as of severe political conflict, both within and among religious communities. Violent conflict among religious groups has recently occurred in many countries, including India, Sri Lanka, Nigeria, and Britain in Northern Ireland (an agreement in 2007 offers hope that the conflict in Northern Ireland has ended). Such conflicts may spill over national boundaries. For example, Al Qaeda claimed that the presence of non-Muslim Western forces in the sacred Islamic territory of Saudi Arabia was an important reason for its violent attacks against the United States and related targets. At the same time, we want to emphasize that the political orientation of a particular religious community is not predetermined, but is rather a product of efforts of leaders to mobilize the community to support their views. The political posture associated with Christian, Jewish, Muslim, or Hindu beliefs cannot simply be read from sacred texts of that religion. There is intense conflict *within* most religious communities—often over the meaning of the same sacred texts—that pits more liberal, secular elements against those who defend what they claim is a more orthodox, traditional interpretation.

A Collective-Identities Puzzle

distributional politics the use of power, particularly by the state, to allocate some kind of valued resource among competing groups.

How does collective identity affect a country's **distributional politics**, that is, the process of deciding how resources are distributed among different groups? Collective identities operate at both the level of symbols, attitudes, values, and beliefs and at the level of material, or economic, resources, and both are important when it comes to distributional politics.

In a situation of extreme scarcity, it may prove nearly impossible to reach any compromise among groups with conflicting material demands. But if an adequate level of material resources is available, such conflicts may be easier to resolve through distributional politics because groups can negotiate at least a minimally satisfying share of resources.

However, the nonmaterial demands of ethnic, religious, and nationalist movements may be very difficult to satisfy by distributional politics. The distributional style may be quite ineffective when, for example, a religious group demands that the government require all citizens to conform to its social practices or when a dominant linguistic group insists that a single language be used in education and government throughout the country. In such cases, political conflict tends to move from the distributive realm to the realm where compromises cannot be achieved by simply dividing the pie of material resources. As the important British weekly *The Economist* pointed out in a mid-2007 review of the crisis in the Middle East, one of the main reasons for the lack of progress in finding a solution to the Israeli-Palestinian conflict is that "What started as a national struggle between two peoples for one land is gradually, and often willfully, being transformed into a war of religion. . . ."[14] Look in the country studies for examples of identity conflicts over distributional issues that can be resolved by the normal give and take of political bargaining—and those that lead, instead, to political violence.

These four themes provide the analytic scaffold on which this book is built. With an understanding of the methods of comparative politics and the four themes in mind, we can now discuss how we have grouped the country studies that comprise *Introduction to Comparative Politics* and how the text is organized for comparative analysis.

SECTION 4 Classifying Political Systems

FOCUS QUESTIONS

What are some difficult problems involved in establishing a useful way of classifying political systems?

Can you think of another way from the one suggested in this chapter?

typology a method of classifying by using criteria that divide a group of cases into smaller numbers.

There are about 200 states in the world today, each with a political system that is distinctive in some ways. How can we classify them in a manageable fashion? It makes sense to highlight clusters of states that share important similarities, just as it is useful to identify what distinguishes one cluster of relatively similar states from other clusters. When comparativists classify a large number of cases into a smaller number of types or clusters, they call the result a **typology**.

Typologies make comparison easier both within the same type as well as between types of states. For example, Britain and the United States are long-established democracies, but they have very different institutional architecture. Britain has a parliamentary system, in which parliament (the legislature) chooses the prime minister, that is, the official who heads the executive. Parliament and the prime minister have considerable power over each other. Parliament can force the prime minister to resign by voting a motion of no confidence. And the prime minister can dissolve parliament and call new elections. The United States has a presidential system, in which the president and the legislature (Congress) are separately elected. Further, the two branches have extensive powers independent of each other. Neither branch can force the other to resign, although Congress can impeach the president. What political significance is there in the fact that Britain and the United States organize state power in such different ways? This kind of question about the different mix of state institutions within similar political systems is the kind of issue that is at the heart of comparative politics.

How do we construct typologies of states? Typologies are artificial constructs, made rather than occurring naturally. They are based on certain features that comparativists decide are important as the basis for classification. Typologies are helpful to the extent that they permit us to engage in useful comparisons that further our understanding of politics.

The typology that we use in this book classifies regimes into three groups: *consolidated democracies, transitional democracies,* and *authoritarian regimes.* This typology reveals the bedrock distinction between democratic and undemocratic regimes. To understand why we have chosen to classify countries in this fashion, it is first necessary to take a closer look at what is meant by democracy.

The Meaning—or Meanings—of Democracy

It is generally agreed by political scientists that democracy includes the following features:

- Selection to important public offices on the basis of free and fair elections based on universal suffrage (the right of all adults to vote). For an election to qualify as fair, votes must be counted accurately, with the winning candidate(s) determined according to preexisting rules about the kind of majority or plurality that is needed to gain electoral victory.
- Political parties are free to organize, offer their ideas, present candidates for public office, and compete in elections. The opposition party or parties—those not in power—enjoy adequate rights to organize and to criticize the incumbent government.
- The elected government develops policy according to specified procedures that are fair and relatively open to public scrutiny. Elected executives are held accountable for their decisions and actions at the next election, through the courts, and by the legislature. In turn, the legislature is held most directly accountable to the citizens through a system in which voters choose who will represent them in the legislature.
- All citizens possess civil and political rights—the right to participate and vote in elections periodically held to select key state officeholders—and civil liberties—the rights of free assembly, conscience, privacy, and expression, including the right to criticize the government. In theory, these rights must be available to all citizens equally.
- The political system contains a judiciary (court system) with powers independent of the executive and legislature, charged with protecting citizens' rights and liberties from violation by the state and other citizens, as well as with ensuring that governmental officials respect the constitution and other laws.
- The military must accept, without question, that it is subordinate to the elected government and that its commander-in-chief is an civilian responsible to voters.

consolidated democracies democratic political systems that have been solidly and stably established for an ample period of time and in which there is relatively consistent adherence to the core democratic principles.

transitional democracies countries that have moved from an authoritarian government to a democratic one.

Our typology of political systems distinguishes between those countries whose political regimes are democratic according to the above criteria and those that are not. The typology involves a further distinction between long-established, or **consolidated democracies**, and newly established, or **transitional democracies**. We believe that there is an important difference in kind, and not just of degree, between these two types of democratic states. We distinguish between consolidated and transitional democracies in two ways.

First, the *longevity* and *durability* of democratic institutions and practices. Have they been solidly and stably established for an ample period of time? Precisely how much time is open to question. Consolidated democracies are long-standing democracies: the countries in this book that fall in this category (Britain, France, and India) have been democracies for a minimum of about sixty years (India). There is very little likelihood that a consolidated democracy will experience a reversal and become undemocratic. Transitional democracies are those that have relatively recently adopted the essential features of democracy, and their futures as democracies may be less certain.

The second criterion for distinguishing between consolidated and transitional democracies is the *extent* of their democratic practice. In consolidated democracies, there is relatively full compliance with the democratic principles specified above. We do not mean to claim that consolidated democracies always respect democratic principles. That would be naïve. For example, police abuse and unequal treatment of citizens who are poor or from a racial or ethnic minority are all too common in democracies like Britain, France, and the United States. However consolidated democracies generally practice the democracy they preach.

The reason we highlight the extent of democracy becomes apparent when we turn to the category of transitional democracies. In such countries, formal democratic institutions and procedures often conceal informal practices that violate the checklist of core features of democracy.[15]

To be sure, there is greater legal protection of citizen rights and liberties, a more independent judiciary, and more independent political parties in transitional democracies than in authoritarian regimes—the third category that is part of our typology. But these and other democratic features are less extensive and stable than in consolidated democracies. In transitional democracies, democratic forms of governance coexist with and are often compromised by undemocratic elements. Compared to consolidated democracies, political authorities in transitional systems are much more likely to engage in corruption, control of the media, intimidation and violence against opponents, vote rigging, and other measures to make sure they get reelected. Despite what the constitution of the country may specify, the courts are often packed with judges loyal to the ruling party, and top military officers often exercise extraordinary political power behind the scenes. The countries in *Introduction to Comparative Politics* that we classify as transitional democracies are Mexico, Russia, and South Africa.

How do we define authoritarian regimes? The simplest way would be to say that they fail to meet all or most all of the characteristics of a democracy listed above. Authoritarian regimes lack meaningful procedures for selecting political leaders through competitive elections based on universal suffrage; there are no secure procedures for holding political leaders accountable to the citizens of the country; the right to criticize the government is severely restricted; people of different genders, racial groups, religions, and ethnicities do not enjoy equal rights; and the judiciary is not an independent branch of government capable of checking the power of the state or protecting the rights of citizens; and finally the military may not be effectively subject to civilian political control.

Clearly, then, authoritarian states are not democracies. But it isn't good social science to define something only by what it is not. The term *authoritarianism* refers to political systems in which power (or authority) is highly—perhaps almost totally—concentrated in a single individual, a small group of people, or a single political party or institution (such as the military). Furthermore, those with power claim an exclusive right to govern and use various means, including force, to impose their will and policies. Another way to put it: in authoritarian systems, the state is more powerful than the citizens it governs and is not accountable to them.

There is an enormous variety of authoritarian regime types: communist party–states (China and Cuba); **theocracies** in which sovereign power is held by religious leaders and law is defined in religious terms (Iran); military governments (Pakistan and Burma); absolute monarchies (Saudi Arabia); and personalistic dictatorships (Iraq under Sadaam Hussein). These types of authoritarianism differ from one another in many ways, including fundamental beliefs (**ideology**) and the degree and methods of force used to suppress opposition and control society. The countries classified as authoritarian in *Introduction to Comparative Politics* are China and Iran.

theocracy a state dominated by the clergy, who rule on the grounds that they are the only interpreters of God's will and law.

ideology a set of fundamental ideas, values, or beliefs about how a political, economic, or social system should be organized.

Although there are fundamental differences between democracy and authoritarianism, these categories are not airtight.

For example, in most authoritarian countries, there are elements of democratic practices. In Iran (a theocratic authoritarian regime), there are vigorously contested multiparty elections, although the extent of political debate and opposition is defined and limited by the Islamic clergy. For the last decade or so in China, a form of grassroots democracy has been implemented in the more than 700,000 rural villages, where a majority of the population lives. Even though the communist party still makes sure that dissent does not get out of hand, China's rural dwellers now have a real choice when they elect their local leaders, and their choices have often resulted in the ouster of corrupt and unpopular officials. Such democratic elements in Iranian and Chinese politics certainly make a difference in important ways to the citizens of those countries, but they do not fundamentally alter the essential authoritarian character of the state in these two countries.

As another example of the gray zone between democracy and nondemocracy, we consider India a consolidated democracy because it has generally respected most of the democratic procedures on our checklist since it gained independence from Britain in 1947. There is intense political competition in India, elections are usually free and fair, and the Indian judiciary is quite independent. However, India has repeatedly experienced scenes of communal violence, in which Muslim, Sikh, and Christian minorities have been brutally massacred, sometimes with the active complicity of state officials. Horrific political violence has occurred so often and sometimes on such a wide scale that India's claim to live up to the democratic idea is certainly open to question. When it comes to democracy there are many different shades of gray, but in every country a gap remains between the aims and achievements of democratic governance.

We hope that the timely information and thematic focus of this book will not only help you understand better politics in several different countries from around the world but also inspire you to explore further the comparative approach to the often troubling, sometimes inspiring, but always changing and endlessly fascinating world of politics.

SECTION 5 Organization of the Text

FOCUS QUESTIONS

If you could choose one other country to study in a comparative politics course besides the eight included in this book, what would it be? Why?

What would you like to know about politics in that country?

The core of this book consists of eight country case studies. We selected them for their significance in terms of our comparative themes and because they provide an interesting sample of types of political regimes, levels of economic development, and geographic regions. Although each of the country studies makes important comparative references, the studies primarily provide detailed descriptions and analyses of the politics of individual countries. At the same time, the country studies have common section and subsection headings to help you make comparisons and explore similar themes across the various cases. The following are brief summaries of the main issues and questions covered in the country studies.

1: The Making of the Modern State

Section 1 in each chapter provides an overview of the forces that have shaped the political development of the state up to the present. Understanding the contemporary politics of any country requires some understanding of the historical process through which its current political system took shape. Each chapter opens with a specific event to illustrate "Politics in Action" at a particularly important moment in the country's recent history and to highlight some of the critical political issues facing the country. "Geographic Setting" locates the country in its regional context and discusses the political implications of this setting. "Critical Junctures" looks at some of the major stages and decisive turning points in the state's development. This discussion shows how the country assumed its current political order and how relations between state and society have developed over time.

"Themes and Implications" explores how the past pattern of state development continues to shape the country's current political agenda. "Historical

Junctures and Political Themes" applies the text's four core themes to the making of the modern state. How has the country's political development been affected by its place in the world of states? What are the political implications of the state's approach to economic management? What has been the country's experience with the democratic idea? What are the important bases of collective identity in the country, and how do these affect the country's politics? "Implications for Comparative Politics" discusses the broader significance of the country for the study of comparative politics.

2: Political Economy and Development

Section 2 looks at the issues raised by our core theme of governing the economy and analyzes the interaction between economic development and political change. We put this section near the beginning of the country study because we believe that understanding a country's economic situation is essential for analyzing its politics. "State and Economy" discusses the basic organization of the country's economy. It emphasizes the relationship between the government and other economic actors, such as business firms and labor unions, and the state's role in managing economic life. How do the dynamics and historical timing of the country's entry into the world economy—and its current position and competitiveness within the globalized economy—affect domestic politics? This section also analyzes the state's social welfare policies, such as health care, housing, and social security programs. "Society and Economy" examines the social implications of the country's economic situation and their political impact. It asks who benefits from the state's economic policies and looks at how economic development creates or reinforces class, ethnic, gender, regional, or ideological divisions in society. "The Global Economy" considers the country's relationship to the international economy. How have patterns of trade and foreign investment changed over time? What is the country's relationship to regional and international economic organizations? How have international economic issues affected the domestic political agenda?

3: Governance and Policy-Making

Section 3 focuses on the state's major policy-making institutions and procedures. "Organization of the State" lays out the fundamental principles—reflected in the country's constitution, its dominant ideology, and its historical experience—on which the political system and the distribution of political power are based. It also sketches the basic structure of the state, including the relationship among different levels and branches of government. "The Executive" encompasses the key offices (for example, presidents, prime ministers, communist party leaders) at the top of the political system. We focus on how political leaders are selected, and how they use their power to make policy. This section also looks at the national bureaucracy and its relationship to the chief executive, and its role in policy-making. "Other State Institutions" looks at the military, the judiciary and the legal system, and at semipublic agencies, and subnational government. "The Policy-Making Process" provides an overview of how public policy gets made and implemented. It describes the roles of formal institutions and procedures, as well as informal aspects of policy-making, such as the influence of lobbyists and interest groups.

4: Representation and Participation

The relationship between a country's state and society is the topic of Section 4. How do different groups in society organize to further their political interests? How do they participate and get represented in the political system, and how do they influence policy-making? Given the importance of the U.S. Congress in policy-making, American readers might expect to find the role of the legislature described in Section 3 ("Governance and Policy-Making") rather than Section 4. But the United States is quite exceptional in having a legislature that has almost a coequal role with the executive in its policy-making role. In most other political systems, the executive dominates the policy process, even when it is ultimately responsible to the legislature, as in a parliamentary system. In these countries, the legislature functions primarily to represent and provide a forum for the political expression of various interests in government. It is only secondarily (and in some cases, such as China, only marginally) a policy-making body. Although this section does deal with the legislature's role in policy-making, its primary focus is on how the legislature represents or fails to represent different interests in society.

"Political Parties and the Party System" describes the overall organization of the country's party system and its major parties. "Elections" reviews the election process and trends in how people voted and why in recent elections. It also considers the significance of elections (or lack thereof) as a vehicle for citizen participation in politics and in bringing about changes in the government. "Political Culture, Citizenship, and Identity" examines how people perceive themselves as members of the political community: it considers such things as the nature and source of political values and attitudes, who is considered a citizen of the state, and how different groups in society understand their relationship to the state. The topics covered may include political aspects of the educational system, the media, religion, and ethnicity. "Interests, Social Movements, and Protests" discusses how various groups pursue their political interests both within and outside the political system. When do they use formal organizations (such as unions) or launch movements (such as environmental, antiglobalization, or peace movements)? What is the relationship between the state and such organizations and movements? When and how do citizens engage in acts of antistate protest? How does the state respond to such protests?

5: Politics in Transition

In Section 5, each country study returns to the book's four main themes and the major challenges reshaping the world and the study of comparative politics. "Political Challenges and Changing Agendas" lays out the major unresolved issues facing the country and assesses which are most likely to dominate in the near future. Many of the country studies address issues that have generated intense conflicts—conflicts involving globalization, collective identities, human rights and civil liberties, and the consequences of America's exercise of global power. "Politics in Comparative Perspective" highlights the implications of the country case for the study of comparative politics. How does the history—and how will the fate—of the country influence developments in a regional and global context? What does this case study tell us about politics in other countries that have similar political systems or that face similar kinds of political challenges?

Key Terms and Suggested Readings

At the end of each chapter, including this one, is a list of key terms that we think are especially important for students of comparative politics to know. Each term is in boldface the first time it appears in the text and is briefly defined on the page on which it appears and in the Glossary that appears near the end of the book. Each chapter also has a list of suggested readings: we have tried to emphasize books that we think would be both interesting and accessible to undergraduates. If you find yourself particularly interested in one or more of the countries covered in this text, we urge you to take a look at some of the suggested titles.

What's in the Comparative Data Charts?

The following charts and tables present important factual and statistical information about each of the countries included in this book, plus the United States. We hope most of this information is self-explanatory, but a few points of clarification may be helpful.

- The social and economic data largely comes from the CIA *World Factbook*, the World Bank *World Development Indicators*, and the United Nations *Human Development Report*, all of which are issued annually.
- The data presented is as up-to-date as possible. Unless otherwise indicated, it is from 2004–2007.
- Several important terms used in the data, including Gross Domestic Product (GDP), Gross National Product (GNP), Purchasing Power Parity (PPP), and Gini Index, are explained in the Glossary and/or the feature called "How Is Economic Development Measured?" on page 15.

These reports and other statistics are available from the national statistics or census agencies of individual countries and from the following websites:

- www.cia.gov/cia/publications/factbook/
- www.worldbank.org/data/
- hdr.undp.org/
- ipu.org/english/home.htm/ ❖

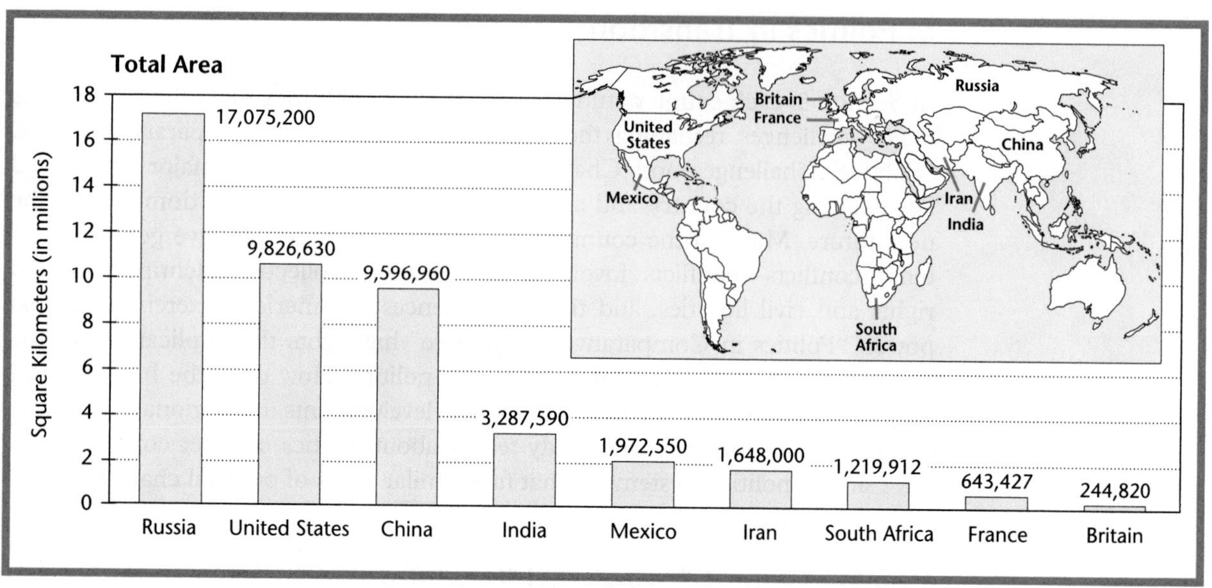

	Britain	China	France	India
Official Name	United Kingdom of Great Britain and Northern Ireland	People's Republic of China	French Republic	Republic of India
Capital	London	Beijing	Paris	New Delhi
Comparative Size	Slightly smaller than Oregon	Slightly smaller than the U.S.	Slightly smaller than Texas	Slightly smaller than one-third the size of the U.S.
Population Growth Rate (2007)	0.27%	0.61%	0.59%	1.61%
Major Ethnic Groups	White, 92.1% (comprising English, 83.6%; Scottish, 8.6%; Welsh, 4.9%; Northern Irish, 2.9%) Black, 2%; Indian, 1.8%; Pakistani, 1.3%; mixed, 1.2%; other, 1.6%	Han Chinese, 91.9%; other nationalities, 8.1% (including Zhuang, Uygur, Hui, Yi, Tibetan, Miao, Manchu, Mongol, Buyi, Korean)	French-born, 91%; other European, 3%; North African, 4% (mostly Algerian); other, 2%	Indo-Aryan, 72%; Dravidian, 25%; Mongoloid and other, 3%
Religions	Christian, 71.6% (Anglican, Roman Catholic, Presbyterian, Methodist); Muslim, 2.7%; Hindu, 1%; other, 1.6%; unspecified or none, 23.1%	Note: officially atheist; Daoist (Taoist), Buddhist, Christian, 3%–4%; Muslim, 1%–2%	Roman Catholic, 83–88%; Protestant, 2%; Jewish, 1%; Muslim, 5–10%; unaffiliated, 4%	Hindu, 80.5%; Muslim, 13.4%; Christian, 2.3%; Sikh, 1.9%; other, 1.8%; unspecified, 0.1%
Languages	English, Welsh (about 26% of the population of Wales), Scottish form of Gaelic (about 60,000 in Scotland)	Standard Chinese or Mandarin based on the Beijing dialect; other major dialects include Cantonese and Shanghaiese. Also various minority languages, such as Tibetan and Mongolian.	French	Hindi is the national language and primary tongue of 30% of the people; there are 14 other official languages. English enjoys associate status but is the most important language for national, political, and commercial communication.

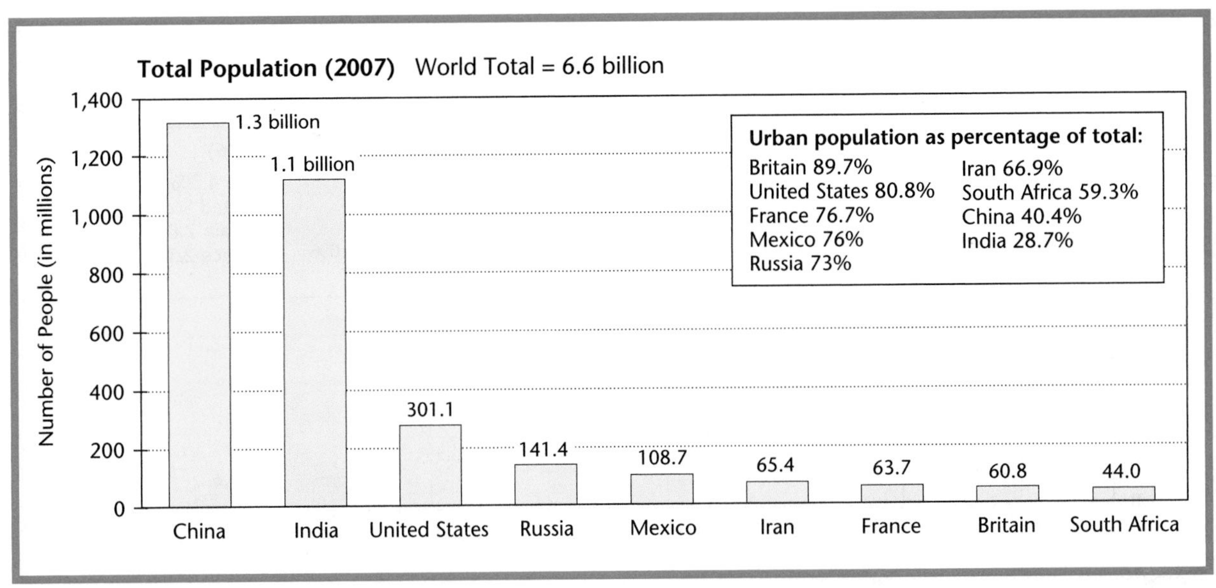

Iran	Mexico	Russia	South Africa	United States
Islamic Republic of Iran	United Mexican States	Russian Federation	Republic of South Africa	United States of America
Teheran	Mexico City	Moscow	Pretoria	Washington, D.C.
Slightly larger than Alaska	Slightly less than three times the size of Texas	Approximately 1.8 times the size of the U.S.	Slightly less than twice the size of Texas	About half the size of Russia
0.66%	1.15%	−0.48%	−0.46%	0.89%
Persian, 51%; Azeri, 24%; Gilaki and Mazandarani, 8%; Kurd, 7%; Arab, 3%; Lur, 2%; Baloch, 2%; Turkmen, 2%; other, 1%	Mestizo (Amerindian-Spanish), 60%; Amerindian or predominantly Amerindian, 30%; White, 9%; other, 1%	Russian, 79.8%; Tatar, 3.8%; Ukrainian, 2%; Bashkir, 1.2%; Chuvash, 1.1%; other/unspecified, 12.1%	Black African, 78.4%; White, 9.6%; Colored, 8.9%; Indian/Asian, 2.5%	White, 75.1%; Hispanic or Latino, 12.5%; Black/ African American, 12.3%; Asian, 3.6%; American Indian and Alaskan Native, 0.9%; Native Hawaiian and other Pacific Islander, 0.1%; some other race, 5.5%; two or more races, 2.4%
Muslim, 98% (Shi'a, 89%; Sunni, 9%); other, 2% (includes Zoroastrian, Jewish, Christian, and Baha'i)	Roman Catholic, 76.5%; Protestant, 6.3% (Pentecostal, 1.4%; Jehovah's Witnesses, 1.1%; other, 3.8%); other, 0.3%; unspecified, 13.8%; none, 3.1%	Russian Orthodox, 15–20%; Muslim, 10–15%; other Christian, 2%; large number of non-practicing believers and non-believers	Christian, 32.6% (including Anglican, Methodist, Presbyterian, Lutheran, Roman Catholic, Dutch Reformed); African Independent, 31.8%; Pentecostal/ Charismatic, 5.9%; other Christian, 9.5%; other, 3.8% (including Hindu, Muslim, Jewish); unspecified, 1.4%; none, 15.1%	Protestant, 52%; Roman Catholic, 24%; Mormon, 2%; Jewish, 1%; Muslim, 1%; other, 10%; none, 10%
Persian and Persian dialects, 58%; Turkic and Turkic dialects, 26%; Kurdish, 9%; Luri, 2%; Balochi, 1%; Arabic, 1%; Turkish, 1%; other, 2%	Spanish; various Mayan, Nahuatl, and other regional indigenous languages	Russian, many minority languages	IsiZulu, 23.8%; IsiXhosa, 17.6%; Afrikaans, 13.3%; Sepedi, 9.4%; English, 8.2%; Setswana, 8.2%; Sesotho, 7.9%; Xitsonga, 4.4%; other, 7.2%	English, 82.1%; Spanish, 10.7%; other Indo-European, 3.8%; Asian and Pacific Island, 2.7%; other, 0.7%

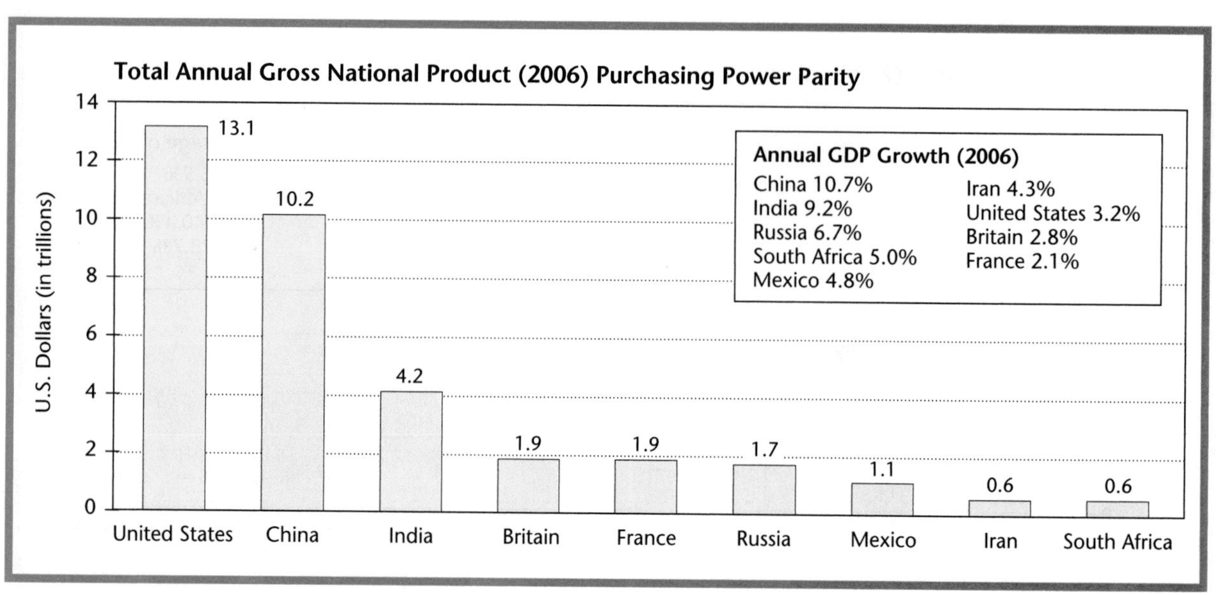

	Britain	China	France	India
GDP per capita average annual growth rate, 1990–2004	2.2%	8.9%	1.7%	4.0%
GDP by sector of the economy (2006)	Agriculture: 1% Industry: 25.6% Services: 73.4%	Agriculture: 11.9% Industry: 48.1% Services: 40%	Agriculture: 2.2% Industry: 20.6% Services: 77.2%	Agriculture: 19.9% Industry: 19.3% Services: 60.7%
Employment by sector of the economy (1999–2006)	Agriculture: 1.4% Industry: 18.2% Services: 80.4%	Agriculture: 45% Industry: 24% Services: 31%	Agriculture: 4.1% Industry: 24.4% Services: 71.5%	Agriculture: 60% Industry: 12% Services: 28%
Exports and imports as % of GDP (2004–2005)	Exports: 26.1% Imports: 30.0%	Exports: 37.5% Imports: 31.9%	Exports: 26.1% Imports: 27.1%	Exports: 20.5% Imports: 24.2%
Inequality **Share of income or consumption**				
• Poorest 20%	6.1%	4.7%	7.2%	8.9%
• Richest 20%	44.0%	50.0%	40.2%	43.3%
GINI Index (Year) *(higher = more unequal)*	36.8 (1999)	44.0 (2002)	26.7 (2002)	32.5 (2000)
Estimated income (PPP) (2004)	Male: $37,506 Female: $24,448	Male: $7,159 Female: $4,561	Male: $35,922 Female: $23,105	Male: $4,723 Female: $1,471

Economy

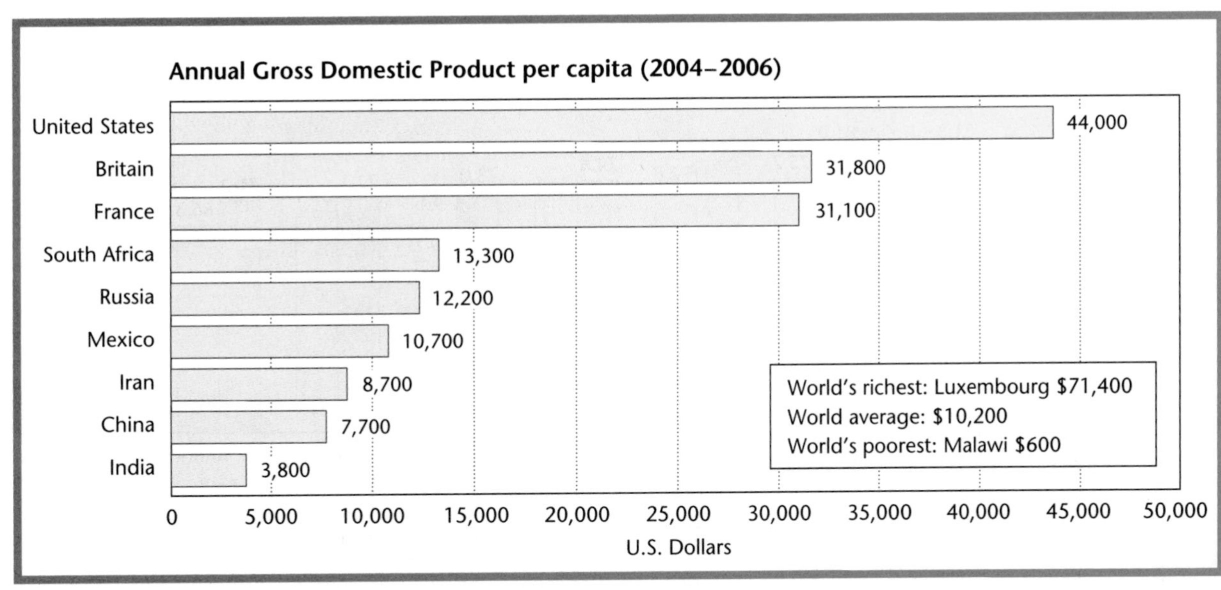

Iran	Mexico	Russia	South Africa	United States
2.3%	1.3%	−0.6%	0.6%	1.9%
Agriculture: 11.2% Industry: 41.7% Services: 47.1%	Agriculture: 3.9% Industry: 25.7% Services: 70.5%	Agriculture: 5.3% Industry: 36.6% Services: 58.2%	Agriculture: 2.6% Industry: 30.3% Services: 67.1%	Agriculture: 0.9% Industry: 20.4% Services: 78.6%
Agriculture: 30% Industry: 25% Services: 45%	Agriculture: 18% Industry: 24% Services: 58%	Agriculture: 10.8% Industry: 29.1% Services: 60.1%	Agriculture: 30% Industry: 25% Services: 45%	Agriculture: 0.7% Industry: 22.9% Services: 76.4%
Exports: 38.8% Imports: 30.2%	Exports: 29.9% Imports: 31.5%	Exports: 35.1% Imports: 21.6%	Exports: 27.1% Imports: 28.6%	Exports: 10.1% Imports: 15.4%
5.1%	4.3%	6.1%	3.5%	5.4%
49.9%	55.1%	46.6%	62.2%	45.8%
43.0 (1998)	49.5 (2002)	40.5 (2005)	57.8 (2002)	45.0 (2004)
Male: $10,830 Female: $4,122	Male: $14,202 Female: $5,594	Male: $12,401 Female: $7,735	Male: $15,521 Female: $7,014	Male: $49,075 Female: $30,581

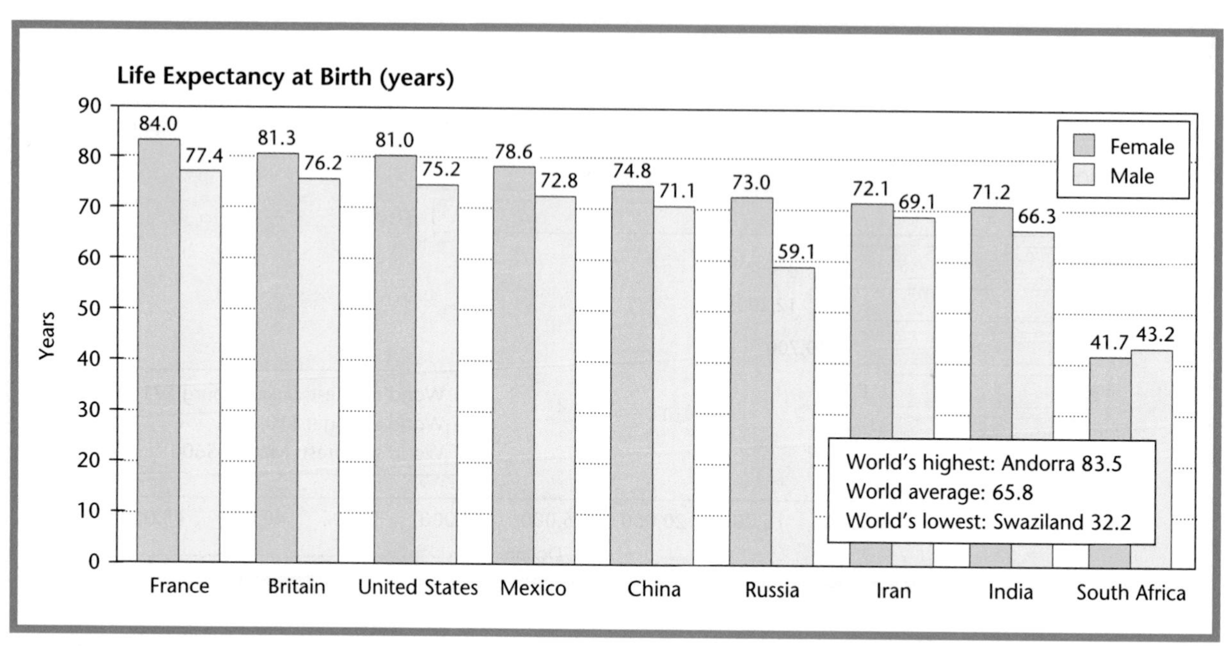

	Britain	China	France	India
Adult literacy (2002–2006)	Male: 99% Female: 99%	Male: 95.1% Female: 86.5%	Male: 99% Female: 99%	Male: 73.4% Female: 47.8%
Percentage of age-eligible population in secondary school and college	Secondary: 95.4% College: 59.7%	Secondary: 74.3% College: 20.3%	Secondary: 99.1% College: 52.8%	Secondary: 56.6% College: 11.4%
Communications and technology per 1,000 people (2004–2005)	Telephones: 528 Cell phones: 1,088 PCs: 600 Internet users: 474	Telephones: 287 Cell phones: 302 PCs: 41 Internet users: 85	Telephones: 587 Cell phones: 790 PCs: 575 Internet users: 430	Telephones: 46 Cell phones: 82 PCs: 15 Internet users: 55
Physicians (per 100,000 people) (1990–2004)	23.0	10.6	33.7	6.0
Women as percentage of national legislature	Lower: 20% Upper: 19%	Single: 20%	Lower: 12% Upper: 19%	Lower: 8% Upper: 11%

Society

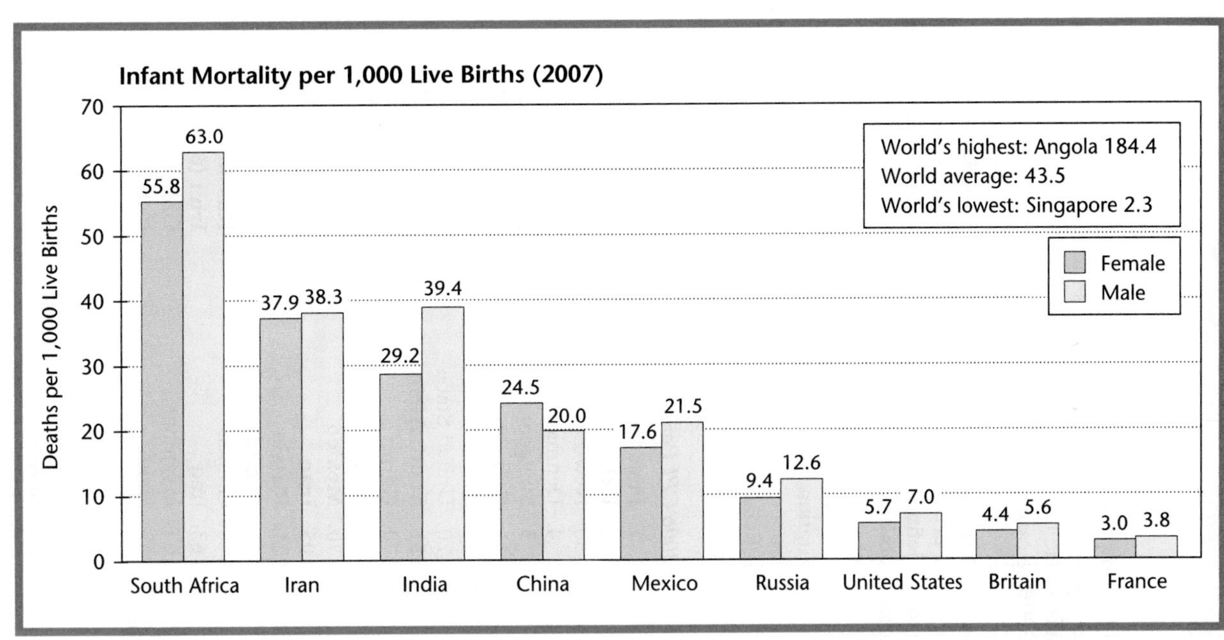

Iran	Mexico	Russia	South Africa	United States
Male: 83.5% Female: 70.4%	Male: 92.4% Female: 89.6%	Male: 99.7% Female: 99.2%	Male: 87% Female: 85.7%	Male: 99% Female: 99%
Secondary: 83.1% College: 23.9%%	Secondary: 80.2% College: 24.0%	Secondary: 91.9% College: 51.3%	Secondary: 93.4% College: 15.3%	Secondary: 94.7% College: 82.7%
Telephones: 278 Cell phones: 106 PCs: 109 Internet users: 103	Telephones: 189 Cell phones: 460 PCs: 136 Internet users: 181	Telephones: 280 Cell phones: 839 PCs: 122 Internet users: 152	Telephones: 101 Cell phones: 724 PCs: 85 Internet users: 109	Telephones: 606 Cell phones: 680 PCs: 762 Internet users: 630
4.5	19.8	42.5	7.7	25.6
Single: 4%	Lower: 23% Upper: 17%	Lower: 10% Upper: 3%	Lower: 33% Upper: 33%	Lower: 16% Upper: 16%

Comparative Rankings of Selected Categories

International organizations and research institutions have developed statistical methods to rate and rank different countries according to various categories of economic, social, political, and environmental performance. Such rankings can be controversial, but we think they provide an interesting approach to comparative analysis. Five examples of this approach are listed below. In addition to the countries included in this book and the United States, the top and bottom five countries (and in the case of the Freedom House ratings, examples of each level) are also listed.

Human Development Index (HDI) is a measure used by the United Nations to compare the overall level of well-being in countries around the world. It takes into account life expectancy, education, and the standard of living.

2006 HDI Rankings

1. Norway
2. Iceland
3. Australia
4. Ireland
5. Sweden
8. United States
16. France
18. Britain
53. Mexico
65. Russia
81. China
96. Iran
121. South Africa
126. India
173. Guinea-Bissau
174. Burkina Faso
175. Mali
176. Sierra Leone
177. Niger

Source: http://hdr.undp.org/hdr2006

Global Gender Gap measures "the extent to which women in 58 countries have achieved equality with men in five critical areas: economic participation, economic opportunity, political empowerment, educational attainment, and health and well-being."

2005 Gender Gap Rankings

1. Sweden
2. Norway
3. Iceland
4. Denmark
5. Finland
8. Britain
13. France
17. United States
31. Russia
33. China
36. South Africa
52. Mexico
53. India
54. South Korea
55. Jordan
56. Pakistan
57. Turkey
58. Egypt

Note: Iran was not included in this study, but it ranked 71 out of 75 in the UNDP's 2004 Gender Empowerment Index.
Source: www.weforum.org

Environmental Performance Index (EPI) measures how close countries come to meeting specific benchmarks for national pollution control and natural resource management.

2006 EPI Rankings

1. New Zealand
2. Sweden
3. Finland
4. Czech Republic
5. Britain
12. France
28. United States
32. Russia
53. Iran
66. Mexico
76. South Africa
94. China
118. India
129. Ethiopia
130. Mali
131. Mauritania
132. Chad
133. Niger

Source: http://www.yale.edu/epi

International Corruption Perceptions Index (CPI) defines corruption as the abuse of public office for private gain and measures the degree to which corruption is perceived to exist among a country's public officials and politicians in 163 countries.

2006 CPI Rankings

1. Finland
2. Iceland
3. New Zealand
4. Denmark
5. Singapore
11. Britain
18. France
20. United States
51. South Africa
70. China
70. India
70. Mexico
105. Iran
121. Russia
156. (4 tied)
160. Guinea
163. Iraq
163. Myanmar
163. Haiti

Source: http://www.transparency.org/
Similar numbers indicate a tie in the rankings.

Freedom in the World ratings measure how free a country is according to an analysis of its civil and political liberties. 1 = most free; 7 = least free.

2006 Freedom House Rankings

"Free" (1.0–2.5)
Britain (1.0)
France (1.0)
United States (1.0)
South Africa (1.5)
Mexico (2.0)
India (2.5)

"Partly Free" (3.0–50)
Colombia (3.0)
Tanzania (3.5)
Bangladesh (4.0)
Singapore (4.5)
Afghanistan (5.0)

"Not Free" (5.5–7.0)
Russia (5.5)
Iran (6.0)
China (6.5)
Cuba (7.0)

Source: http://www.freedomhouse.org

Key Terms

Cold War
globalization
comparative politics
comparativist
country
state
executive
cabinet
bureaucracy
legitimacy
state formation
collective identities
causal theories
independent variable
dependent variable
Human Development Index (HDI)
Global Gender Gap
Environmental Performance Index (EPI)
Corruption Perceptions Index (CPI)
Freedom in the World rating
failed states
authoritarianism
political economy
sustainable development
democracy
gross domestic product (GDP)
gross national product (GNP)
purchasing power parity (PPP)
social movements
communist party–state
social class
distributional politics
typology
consolidated democracies
transitional democracies
theocracy
ideology

Suggested Readings

Friedman, Thomas. *The World Is Flat: A Brief History of the Twenty-first Century* New York: Farrar, Straus and Giroux, 2005.

Kesselman, Mark. *The Politics of Globalization: A Reader.* Boston: Houghton Mifflin, 2006.

———. *Readings in Comparative Politics: Political Challenges and Changing Agendas.* Boston: Houghton Mifflin, 2005.

Krieger, Joel. *Globalization and State Power: A Reader.* Boston: Longman, 2005.

———. *Globalization and State Power: Who Wins When America Rules?* Boston: Longman, 2004.

Soe, Christian. *Annual Editions: Comparative Politics 07/08*, 25th ed. New York: McGraw Hill/Dushkin, 2007.

Zakaria, Fareed. *The Future of Freedom: Illiberal Democracy at Home and Abroad.* New York: W.W. Norton, 2003.

Oxford University Press (New York) publishes a series of "Very Short Introductions" that includes many books on topics related to the study of comparative politics:

- Andrew Clapham, *Human Rights* (2007)
- Bernard Crick, *Democracy* (2002)
- James Fulcher, *Capitalism* (2004)
- Steven Grosby, *Nationalism* (2005)
- Stephen Howe, *Empire* (2002)
- Khalid Koser, *International Migration* (2007)
- Robert J. McMahon, *Cold War* (2003)
- Kenneth Minogue, *Politics* (2000)
- Amrita Narlikar, *World Trade Organization* (2005)
- Michael Newman, *Socialism* (2005)

- Kevin Passmore, *Fascism (*2002)
- Malise Ruthven, *Fundamentalism* (2007)
- Manfred B. Steger, *Globalization* (2003)
- Charles Townshend, *Terrorism* (2002)

Notes

[1]Francis Fukuyama, "The End of History?" *The National Interest* 16 (Summer 1989). The article is reprinted in Mark Kesselman and Joel Krieger, eds., *Readings in Comparative Politics: Political Challenges and Changing Agendas* (Boston: Houghton Mifflin, 2006).

[2]See Philippe Schmitter, "Comparative Politics," in Joel Krieger, ed., *The Oxford Companion to Politics of the World*, 2nd ed. (New York: Oxford University Press, 2001), 160–165. For a more extended discussion and different approach, see David D. Laitin, "Comparative Politics: The State of the Subdiscipline," in Ira Katznelson and Helen V. Milner, eds., *Political Science: The State of the Discipline* (New York: Norton, 2002), 630–659. For a collection of articles in the field of comparative politics, see Kesselman and Krieger, eds., *Readings in Comparative Politics*.

[3]See Anthony Marx, *Making Race and Nation: A Comparison of the United States, South Africa, and Brazil* (Cambridge: Cambridge University Press, 1998).

[4]Seymour Martin Lipset, *American Exceptionalism: A Double-Edged Sword*. (New York: W. W. Norton, 1996), 17. Fukuyama cotaught at George Mason University with Lipset, who was first and foremost a scholar of American politics. In his appreciation of Lipset's life and work following his death in 2006, Fukuyama wrote that his colleague often began their course on American public policy with some variation on this quote; see *Journal of Democracy,* 18, no. 2 (2007) 185–188.

[5]For reviews of recent literature on the state, see Margaret Levi, "The State of the Study of the State"; Miles Kahler, "The State of the State in World Politics"; and Atul Kohli, "State, Society, and Development," in Katznelson and Milner, eds., *Political Science: State of the Discipline*, 84–117.

[6]John R. Alford, Carolyn L. Funk, and John R. Hibbin, "Are Political Orientations Genetically Transmitted?" in *American Political Science Review*, 99, no. 2 (2005), 153–167.

[7]For descriptions by sympathetic participant-observers, see John Cavanagh and Jerry Mander, eds., *Alternatives to Economic Globalization: A Better World Is Possible*, 2nd ed. (San Francisco: Berrett-Koehler, 2004); and Robin Broad, ed., *Global Backlash: Citizen Initiatives for a Just World Economy* (Lanham, Md.: Rowman & Littlefield, 2002). For spirited defenses of globalization, see Jagdish Bhagwati, *In Defense of Globalization* (New York: Oxford University Press, 2004) and Martin Wolf, *Why Globalization Works* (New Haven, Conn.: Yale University Press, 2004).

[8]Robert I. Rotberg, "Failed States in a World of Terror," *Foreign Affairs* 81, no. 4 (July–August 2002). The article is reprinted in Kesselman and Krieger, *Readings in Comparative Politics*.

[9]"The Failed State Index," www.foreignpolicy.com.

[10]This term is borrowed from Peter A. Hall, *Governing the Economy* (New York: Oxford University Press, 1986).

[11]This table is based on data from Adrian Karatnycky, "Liberty's Expansion in a Turbulent World: Thirty Years of the Survey of Freedom," *Freedom in the World, 2003: The Annual Survey of Political Rights and Civil Liberties* (Lanham, Md.: Rowman & Littlefield, 2003) and Arch Puddington, "Freedom Stagnation Amid Pushback Against Democracy," *Freedom in the World 2007: The Annual Survey of Political Rights and Civil Liberties* (Lanham, Md.: Rowman & Littlefield, 2007). Both reports are available at www.freedomhouse.org.

[12]See, for example, Bruce Gilley, *China's Democratic Future: How It Will Happen and Where It Will Lead* (New York: Columbia University Press, 2004) and Minxin Pei, *China's Trapped Transition: The Limits of Developmental Autocracy* (Cambridge, Mass.: Harvard University Press, 2006).

[13]Amartya Sen, "Democracy as a Universal Value," *Journal of Democracy* 10, no. 3 (July 1999): 3–17 (http://muse.jhu.edu/demo/jod/10.3sen.html). This article is included in Kesselman and

Krieger, *Readings in Comparative Politics*. An influential study of this question, on which Sen draws, reaches a similar conclusion: Adam Przeworski et al., *Democracy and Development: Political Institutions and Well-Being in the World, 1950–1990* (Cambridge: Cambridge University Press, 2000). For a study that reaches a different conclusion—that there is a positive correlation between democracy and economic growth—see Yi Feng, *Democracy, Governance, and Economic Performance: Theory and Evidence* (Cambridge, Mass: MIT Press, 2005).

[14]*The Economist*, May 24, 2007.

[15]See, for example, Guillermo O'Donnell, "Illusions About Consolidation," *Journal of Democracy* 7, no. 2 (April 1996): 34–51; Thomas Carothers, "The End of the Transition Paradigm," *Journal of Democracy* 13, no. 1 (January 2002): 5–21; and Steven Levitsky and Lucan A. Way, "The Rise of Competitive Authoritarianism," *Journal of Democracy* 13, no. 2 (April 2002): 51–65. All are reprinted in Kesselman and Krieger, *Readings in Comparative Politics*.

Official Name:	United Kingdom of Great Britain and Northern Ireland
Location:	Western Europe
Capital City:	London
Population (2007):	60.8 million
Size:	244,820 sq. km.; slightly smaller than Oregon

CHAPTER

2 Britain

Joel Krieger

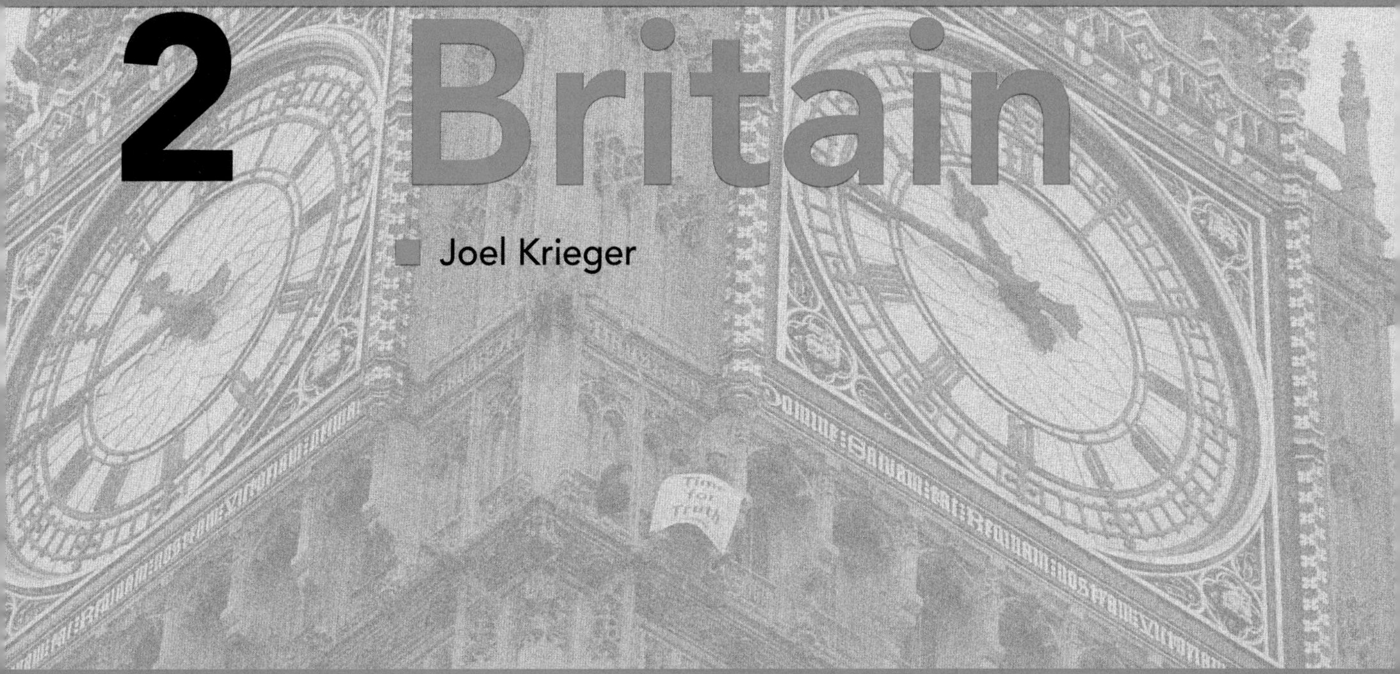

Chronology of Modern Britain's Political Development

1688	ca. 1750	1832	1837–1901	1914–1918	1929–1939	1939–1945
Glorious Revolution establishes power of Parliament	Industrial Revolution begins in Britain	Reform Act expands voting rights	Reign of Queen Victoria; height of British Empire	World War I	Great Depression	World War II

SECTION 1

The Making of the Modern British State

FOCUS QUESTIONS

How has the relationship between Gordon Brown and Tony Blair shaped the last decade of politics in Britain? Why was Blair hounded out of office?

Politics in Action

Tony Blair and Gordon Brown met innocently enough as newly elected members of parliament (MPs) after the 1983 election. They formed a friendship and shared an office: Blair charming, intuitive, telegenic; and Brown more bookish, intense, cautious, and dour. Both were rising stars in the party. Blair pushed the party to modernize and expand its political base well beyond its heritage as a labor party. Brown took on the role of shadow chancellor (the opposition party's spokesman on the economy and potential chancellor should Labour return to office).

But soon they became competitors for leadership of the party. It is universally believed (although never confirmed) that over dinner at a restaurant in 1994, as the party was selecting a new leader, Brown agreed to withdraw from the leadership contest in favor of Blair—and in return Blair promised one day to resign as in favor of Brown, who would be given unprecedented power as chancellor under Blair as prime minister. But as time dragged on and both personality and policy differences made for an increasingly testy relationship, Brown chafed at how long it was taking for Blair to make good on his promise. Increasingly, the British government began to look and feel like a dual executive, with Brown in charge of domestic policies and Blair responsible for foreign affairs.

Blair's decision to support the U.S.-led war in Iraq was very unpopular, and questions about the war hounded Blair right through the campaign leading to his third electoral victory in May 2005—a feat never before achieved by the leader of Britain's 105-year-old Labour Party. The victory was bittersweet. His parliamentary majority was slashed by nearly 100 seats. And by then, Blair and Brown were barely on speaking terms, and Brown loyalists in government had the knives sharpened and ready. Soon, a full-scale succession crisis was underway. In June 2007 Blair tendered his resignation to the Queen who immediately summoned Gordon Brown (who had run unopposed in a leadership election in the Labour Party) to become prime minister.

1945–1979	1973	1979–1990	1997–2007	2001	2007
Establishment of British welfare state; dismantling of British Empire	Britain joins the European Community	Prime Minister Margaret Thatcher promotes "enterprise culture"	Prime Minister Tony Blair and Chancellor Gordon Brown lead New Labour in government	Under Blair's leadership, Britain "stands shoulder to shoulder" with America in war against terror	Gordon Brown becomes prime minister and promises to renew the party and the nation

Blair's 2005 victory was both historic and humbling. In an image that promised to be replayed endlessly on television whenever the 2005 election was discussed, Blair visibly blanched as a defeated independent candidate, whose son died in Iraq, asked Blair to make amends to the families of those who lost loved ones in the war. *(© Jeff J. Mitchell/Reuters/Corbis)*

FOCUS QUESTION

Is Britain's geography still its destiny?

Geographic Setting

Britain is the largest of the British Isles, a group of islands off the northwest coast of Europe, and encompasses England, Scotland, and Wales. The second-largest island includes Northern Ireland and the independent Republic of Ireland. The term *Great Britain* includes England, Wales, and Scotland, but not Northern Ireland. We use the term *Britain* as shorthand for the United Kingdom of Great Britain and Northern Ireland.

Covering an area of approximately 94,000 square miles, Britain is roughly two-thirds the area of Japan, or approximately half the area of France. In 2007, the population of Britain was 60.8 million people (see Table 2.1).

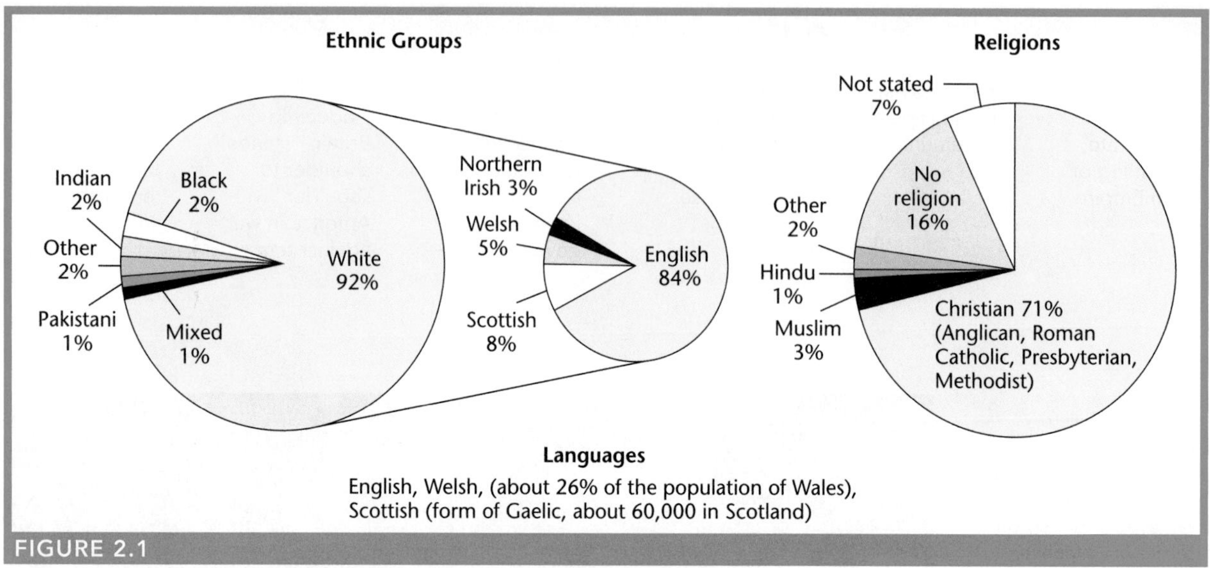

FIGURE 2.1

The British Nation at a Glance

Britain's location as an island off the shore of Europe made it less subject to invasion and conquest than its continental counterparts. This gave the country a sense of security. The geographic separation from mainland Europe has also made many Britons feel they are both apart from and a part of Europe. This feeling complicates relations with Britain's EU partners even today.

FOCUS QUESTION

How does its history of empire still shape British politics today?

Critical Junctures

Our study begins with the historical development of the modern British state. History greatly influences contemporary politics in very important ways. Once in place, institutions leave powerful legacies. Issues left unresolved in one period may create problems for the future.

The British state unified several kingdoms or crowns (hence the term *United Kingdom*). After Duke William of Normandy defeated the English in the Battle of Hastings in 1066, the Norman monarchy extended its authority throughout the British Isles, except for Scotland. The Acts of Union of 1536 and 1542 unified England and Wales legally, politically, and administratively. The unification of the Scottish and English crowns began in 1603, when James VI of Scotland ascended to the English throne as James I. Since then, England, Scotland, and Wales were known as Great Britain. Although they had the same kings, Scotland and England remained separate kingdoms, until the Act of Union of 1707. After that, a common Parliament of Great Britain replaced the two separate parliaments of Scotland and of England and Wales.

TABLE 2.1

Political Organization

Political System	Parliamentary democracy, constitutional monarchy.
Regime History	Long constitutional history, origins subject to interpretation, usually dated from the seventeenth century or earlier.
Administrative Structure	Unitary state with fusion of powers. UK parliament has supreme legislative, executive, and judicial authority. Limited powers have been transferred to representative bodies in Scotland, Wales, and Northern Ireland.
Executive	Prime minister (PM), answerable to House of Commons, subject to collective responsibility of the cabinet; member of Parliament who is leader of party that can control a majority in Commons.
Legislature	Bicameral. House of Commons elected by single-member plurality system with no fixed term but a five-year limit. Main legislative powers: to pass laws, provide for finance, scrutinize public administration and government policy. House of Lords, unelected upper house: limited powers to delay enactment of legislation and to recommend revisions; specified appeals and court functions. Recent reforms eliminated voting rights of all hereditary peers.
Judiciary	Independent but with no power to judge the constitutionality of legislation or governmental conduct. Judges appointed by Crown on recommendation of PM or lord chancellor.
Party System	Two-party dominant, with regional variation. Principal parties: Labour and Conservative; a center party (Liberal Democrat); and national parties in Scotland, Wales, and Northern Ireland.

The making of the British state also included a historic expression of constraints on monarchical rule. At first, royal control increased during the period of Norman rule after 1066, but the conduct of King John (1199–1216) fueled opposition from feudal barons. In 1215, they forced him to consent to a series of concessions that protected feudal landowners from abuses of royal power. These restrictions on royal power were embodied in the Magna Carta, a historic statement of the rights of a political community against the monarchical state. In 1236, the term *Parliament* was first used officially to refer to the gathering of feudal barons summoned by the king whenever he required their consent to special taxes. By the fifteenth century, Parliament had gained the right to make laws.

The Seventeenth-Century Settlement

The making of the British state in the sixteenth and seventeenth centuries involved a complex interplay of religious conflicts, national rivalries, and struggles between rulers and Parliament. These conflicts erupted in the civil wars of the 1640s and the forced removal of James II in 1688. The nearly bloodless political revolution of 1688, later known as the Glorious Revolution, marked the last successful revolution in British history.

The Glorious Revolution also resolved long-standing religious conflict. The replacement of the Roman Catholic James II by the Protestant William and Mary ensured the dominance of the Church of England (or Anglican Church). To this day, the Church of England remains the established (official) church, and approximately two dozen of its bishops and archbishops sit in the House of Lords, the upper house of Parliament.

By about 1700, a basic form of parliamentary democracy had emerged.

The Industrial Revolution and the British Empire

The Industrial Revolution from the mid-eighteenth century onward involved rapid expansion of manufacturing production and technological innovation. It also led to monumental social and economic transformations and created pressures for democratization. Britain's competitive edge also transformed and dominated the international order. The **Industrial Revolution** shaped the development of the British state and changed forever the British way of life.

Industrial Revolution a period of rapid and destabilizing social, economic, and political changes caused by the introduction of large-scale factory production, originating in England in the middle of the eighteenth century.

The Industrial Revolution. Despite a gradually improving standard of living in the English population in general, the effects of industrialization were often very disruptive for the people who lived through these changes. Many field laborers lost their jobs, and many small landholders were squeezed off the land. The mechanization of manufacturing upset the traditional status of skilled craft workers, made them poor, and placed them on the margins of society.

The British Empire. Britain had become an important international power during the seventeenth century, building an overseas empire and engaging actively in international trade. But it was the Industrial Revolution of the eighteenth century that established global production and exchange on a new and expanded scale, with particular consequences for the making of the British state. The manufacture of cotton cloth, the driving force behind Britain's growing industrial dominance, not only pioneered new techniques and changed labor organization, but it was also the perfect imperial industry. It relied on imported raw materials and, by the turn of the nineteenth century, already depended on overseas markets for the vast majority of its sales of finished goods. Growth depended on foreign markets rather than on domestic consumption. This export orientation fueled an expansion far more rapid than an exclusively domestic orientation would have allowed.

Because its economic might depended on overseas trade, Britain's leaders worked aggressively to secure markets and expand the empire. Britain defeated European rivals in a series of military engagements, culminating in the Napoleonic Wars (1803–1815). Backed by the unrivaled power of the British navy, international trade helped England assume the role of dominant military and economic world power.

During the reign of Queen Victoria (1837–1901), the British Empire included 25 percent of the world's population. By 1870, at the height of its glory,

TABLE 2.2

World Trade and Relative Labor Productivity

	Proportion of World Trade (%)	Relative Labor Productivity* (%)
1870	24.0	1.63
1890	18.5	1.45
1913	14.1	1.15
1938	14.0	0.92

*As compared with the average rate of productivity in other members of the world economy.

Source:

Robert O. Keohane, *After Hegemony: Cooperation and Discord in the World Economy*, p. 36. Copyright © 1984 by Princeton University Press. Reprinted by permission of Princeton University Press.

British trade represented nearly one-quarter of the world total (see Table 2.2). Britain exercised direct colonial rule over some 50 countries, including India and Nigeria. At the same time, Britain enjoyed the advantages of an extensive informal empire—a worldwide network of independent states, including China, Iran, and Brazil—whose economic fates were linked to it. Britain ruled as a **hegemonic power**, the state that controlled the pattern of alliances and terms of the international economic order. Britain often shaped domestic political developments in countries throughout the world.

hegemonic power a state that can control the pattern of alliances and terms of the international order and often shapes domestic political developments in countries throughout the world.

Overall, the making of the British state displayed a neat symmetry. Its global power helped underwrite industrial growth at home. At the same time, the reliance of domestic industry on world markets, beginning with cotton manufacture in the eighteenth century, prompted the government to project British interests overseas as forcefully as possible.

Industrial Change and the Struggle for Voting Rights. The Industrial Revolution shifted economic power from landowners to men of commerce and industry. As a result, the first critical juncture in the long process of democratization began in the late 1820s, when the "respectable opinion" of the propertied classes and increasing popular agitation pressed Parliament to expand the right to vote (the franchise). With Parliament under considerable pressure, the Reform Act of 1832 extended the franchise to a section of the (male) middle class.

In fact, the reform was very narrow and defensive. Before 1832, less than 5 percent of the adult population was entitled to vote—afterward, only about 7 percent. In extending the franchise so narrowly, the reform underscored the strict property basis for political participation and inflamed class-based tensions in Britain.

Expansion of the franchise proceeded slowly. The Representation of the People Act of 1867 increased the electorate to just over 16 percent but left cities significantly underrepresented. The Franchise Act of 1884 nearly doubled the size of the electorate, but not until the Representation of the People Act of 1918 did suffrage include nearly all adult men and women over age thirty. How slow a process was it? The franchise for men with substantial incomes dated from the fifteenth century, but women between the ages of twenty-one and thirty were not enfranchised until 1928. The voting age for both women and men was lowered to eighteen in 1969. For the most part, the struggle for extension of the franchise took place without violence, but its time horizon must be measured in centuries. This is British gradualism—at its best and worst.

World Wars, Industrial Strife, and the Depression (1914–1945)

In another sense, however, the development of the state was just beginning with the expansion of the state's direct responsibility for managing the economy and providing social welfare.

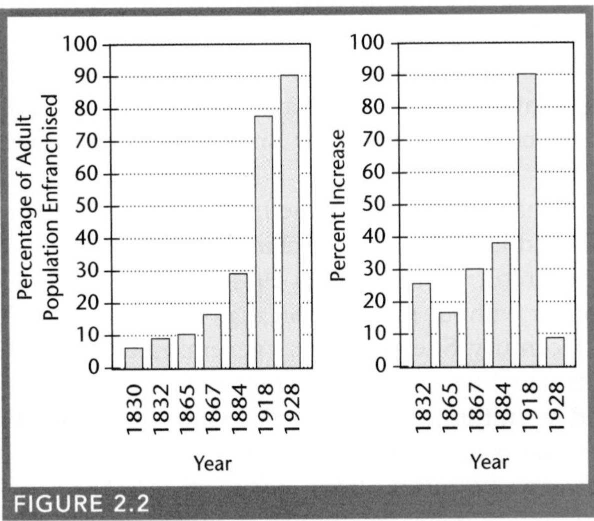

FIGURE 2.2

Expansion of Voting Rights

Expansion of the franchise in Britain was a gradual process. Despite reforms dating from the early nineteenth century, nearly universal adult suffrage was not achieved until 1928.

Source: Jorgen S. Rasmussen. *The British Political Process*, p. 151. Copyright © 1993 Wadsworth Publishing Company. Reprinted with permission of the publisher.

State involvement in the economy increased significantly during World War I (1914–1918). The state took control of a number of industries, including railways, mining, and shipping. It set prices, restricted the flow of capital abroad, and channeled resources into war production. After the war, the state remained active in managing industry, but in a rather different way. Amid tremendous industrial disputes, the state wielded its power to fragment the trade union movement and resist demands for workers' control over production. This government manipulation of the economy openly contradicted the policy of laissez-faire (minimal government interference in the operation of economic markets).

The tensions between free-market principles and interventionist practices deepened with the Great Depression—beginning in 1929 and continuing through much of the 1930s—and with the experiences of World War II (1939–1945). The fear of depression, and yearnings for a better life after the war, transformed the role of the state and ushered in a period of unusual political harmony.

welfare state a set of public policies designed to provide for citizens' needs through direct or indirect provision of pensions, health care, unemployment insurance, and assistance to the poor.

Collectivist Consensus (1945–1979)

The term *collectivism* describes the consensus that drove politics in the postwar period, when a significant majority of Britons and all major political parties agreed that governments should work to narrow the gap between rich and poor and provide for basic necessities through public education, national health care, and other policies of the **welfare state** (the set of policies designed to provide health care, pensions, unemployment benefits, and assistance to the poor). They also accepted state responsibility for economic growth and full employment. In time, however, economic downturn and political stagnation unraveled the consensus.

Margaret Thatcher and the Enterprise Culture (1979–1990)

The 1970s saw the beginning of economic stagnation and declining competitiveness of key British industries in international markets. This fueled industrial strife. Class-based tensions remained near the surface of politics. No government seemed able to manage the economy, and each party failed in turn. The Conservative government of Edward Heath (1970–1974) could not resolve the economic problems or the political tensions that resulted from the combination of increased inflation and reduced growth (stagflation). The Labour government of Harold Wilson and James Callaghan (1974–1979) fared no better. As unions became increasingly disgruntled, the country underwent a rash of strikes throughout the winter of 1978–1979, the "winter of discontent." Labour could not discipline its trade union allies, which hurt the party in the election in May 1979. The traditional centrist Conservative and Labour alternatives, within the collectivist mold, seemed exhausted. Many Britons were ready for a new policy agenda.

Margaret Thatcher met the challenge. Winning the leadership of the Conservative Party in 1975, she wasted little time in launching a set of bold policy initiatives, after the Conservatives returned to power in 1979. Reelected in 1983 and 1987, Thatcher served longer without interruption than any other British prime minister in the twentieth century. She never lost a general election.

Thatcher believed collectivism had contributed to Britain's decline by weakening British industry and permitting powerful, self-serving unions to hold the country for ransom. To reverse Britain's relative economic slide, Thatcher sought to jump-start the economy by cutting taxes, reducing social services where possible, and using government policy to stimulate competitiveness and efficiency in the private sector.

In many ways, Thatcher's leadership as prime minister (1979–1990) marks a critical dividing line in postwar British politics. She set the tone and redefined the goals of British politics like few others before her. In November 1990, a leadership challenge within Thatcher's own Conservative Party caused her sudden resignation. Her anti-EU stance and high-handed leadership style brought her down. John Major replaced her. Major served from 1990 to 1997, leading the Conservative Party to a victory in the 1992 general election before succumbing to Tony Blair's New Labour in 1997.

New Labour's Third Way

Under the leadership of Blair and Brown, the Labour Party was determined on a thorough modernization of the Labour Party. Although its official name did not change, the party was reinvented as New Labour—a party committed to modernization that promised to fundamentally recast British politics. It offered

Profile
Tony Blair

Born in 1953 to a mother from Donegal, Ireland (who moved to Glasgow after her father's death), and a father from the Clydeside shipyards, Tony Blair lacks the typical pedigree of Labour Party leaders. It is very common in the highest ranks of the Labour Party to find someone whose father or grandfather was a union official or a Labour MP. The politics in the Blair family, by contrast, were closely linked to Conservatism (as chairman of his local Conservative Party club, his father Leo had had a good chance to become a Conservative MP). Often, like Tony Blair's two predecessors—Neil Kinnock from Wales and John Smith from the West of Scotland—leaders of the Labour Party also have distinctive regional ties. In contrast, Blair moved to Durham in the north of England when he was five but spent much of his youth in boarding schools, moved south when he was old enough to set out on his own, studied law at Oxford, specialized in employment and industrial law in London—and returned to the north only to enter the House of Commons from Sedgefield in 1983. Thus, Blair has neither the traditional political or regional ties of a Labour Party leader.*

Coming of political age in opposition, Blair joined the shadow cabinet in 1988, serving in turn as shadow minister of energy, then of employment, and finally as shadow home secretary. An MP with no government experience, he easily won the contest for party leadership after his close friend and fellow modernizer John Smith died of a sudden heart attack in the summer of 1994. From the start, Blair boosted Labour Party morale and raised expectations that the party would soon regain power. As one observer put it, "The new Leader rapidly made a favorable impression on the electorate: his looks and affability of manner appealed to voters whilst his self-confidence, lucidity and clarity of mind rendered him a highly effective communicator and lent him an air of authority."† As prime minister, Blair combined firm leadership, eclectic beliefs, and bold political initiatives as he transformed the Labour Party to "New Labour."

Even before the war in Iraq, his lack of familiar roots and ideological convictions made Blair an enigmatic figure for many. His very personal decision to support the U.S.-led invasion of Iraq deepened the impression that Blair would follow his own inner voice above the preferences of party. After the 2005 election, many both within and outside the party hoped that the prime minister's inner voice would tell him to live up to his end of a deal with Gordon Brown that has been long rumored: that in exchange for Brown backing Blair for party leadership in 1994, Blair would at some point in the future resign and hand the leadership of party and country to Brown. In the end, under enormous pressure, Blair resigned in June 2007, his legacy much debated and unlikely to be settled for years to come. ❖

*See Andy McSmith, *Faces of Labour: The Inside Story* (London: Verso, 1997), pp. 7–96.

†Eric Shaw, *The Labour Party Since 1945* (Oxford: Blackwell, 1996), p. 195.

a "third-way" alternative to Thatcherism and the collectivism of traditional Labour. New Labour rejected the notion of interest-based politics, in which unions and working people naturally look to Labour and businesspeople and the more prosperous look to the Conservatives. Labour won in 1997 by drawing support from across the socioeconomic spectrum. It rejected the historic ties between Labour governments and the trade union movement. It emphasized the virtues of a partnership with business.

It also promised new approaches to economic, welfare, and social policy that emphasized the rights of citizens to assistance only if they took the responsibility to get the needed education and training; and New Labour emphasized British leadership in Europe. Blair undertook far-reaching constitutional changes to revitalize democratic participation. Labour would devolve (transfer) specified powers from the central government to Scotland, Wales, and Northern Ireland.

In the early months of his premiership, Blair displayed effective leadership after Lady Diana's death and in his aggressive efforts to achieve a potentially historic peace agreement for Northern Ireland. Soon, however, many began to suggest that Blair was better at coming up with innovative-sounding ideas than at implementing effective policy (it was said that New Labour was "more spin than substance"). In addition, Blair's popularity suffered from a set of crises—from a set of fatal train crashes beginning in 1997 to protests over the cost of petrol (gasoline) in September 2000 to an outbreak of mad cow disease in spring 2001. Nevertheless, until the war in Iraq, Blair remained a popular and charismatic leader. A few months before September 11, 2001, New Labour won what it most sought: an electoral mandate in June 2001 for a second successive term. But then its luck began to change.

special relationship refers to relations between the United States and Britain and is meant to convey not only the largely positive, mutually beneficial nature of the relationship but also the common heritage and shared values of the two countries.

After September 11. In the aftermath of the attacks on the World Trade Center, Blair decisively assumed the role of a key ally in the war on terrorism. September 11 lent new credence to the **special relationship**—a bond of language, culture, and national interests, which created an unusually close alliance—that has shaped U.S.-UK relations for 50 years. Before long, especially when the focus of the war on terrorism moved from Afghanistan to Iraq, many people in Britain

After what must have felt like an interminable wait, on June 24, 2007, Gordon Brown succeeded Tony Blair as Labour Party leader—and a few days later became prime minister. How much change would the new prime minister bring to British politics—and to the special relationship with the United States? *(Source: Paul Ellis/AFP/Getty Images)*

became disenchanted. Blair's willingness to follow the lead of President Bush locked Britain into policies over which it had little or no control. It vastly complicated Britain's relationships with France and Germany (which opposed the war) and generated hostility toward the United Kingdom in much of the Arab and Muslim world. The war in Iraq, which was very unpopular in the UK, eroded Blair's standing. In addition, many Britons believe Blair led them into war under false premises. This seems to have permanently weakened his credibility and tarnished the legacy of New Labour. One of Gordon Brown's biggest challenges as prime minister has been to distance himself from Blair's unpopular war, while keeping the support of those both within and outside the Labour Party who repeatedly voted for Blair.

FOCUS QUESTION

What are the greatest challenges facing Britain today?

Themes and Implications

Our four core themes in this book, introduced in Part I, highlight some of the most important features of British politics.

Historical Junctures and Political Themes

The first theme suggests that a country's relative position in the world of states influences its ability to manage domestic and international challenges. A weaker international standing makes it difficult for a country to control international events or insulate itself from external pressures. Britain's ability to control the terms of trade and master political alliances during the height of its imperial power in the nineteenth century confirms this maxim, but times have changed.

Through the gradual process of decolonization Britain fell to second-tier status. Its formal empire began to shrink in the interwar period (1919–1939) as the "white dominions" of Canada, Australia, and New Zealand gained independence. In Britain's Asian, Middle Eastern, and African colonies, pressure for political reforms leading to independence deepened during World War II and in the immediate postwar period. Beginning with the formal independence of India and Pakistan in 1947, an enormous empire of dependent colonies more or less dissolved in less than twenty years. Finally, in 1997, Britain returned the commercially vibrant crown colony of Hong Kong to China. The process of decolonization ended any realistic claim for Britain to be a dominant player in world politics.

Is Britain a world power or just a middle-of-the-pack country in Europe? It appears to be both. On the one hand, as a legacy of its role in World War II, Britain sits as a permanent member of the United Nations Security Council. On the other hand, Britain invariably plays second fiddle in its special relationship to the United States, a show of relative weakness that has exposed British foreign policy to extraordinary pressures, especially since September 11. In addition, British governments face persistent challenges in their dealings with the EU. Can Britain afford to remain aloof from the fast-paced changes of economic integration symbolized by the adoption of a common currency, the euro, by many countries in Europe—but not by Britain?

One year after the start of the war in Iraq, Blair's credibility was hurt as key justifications for war such as WMDs and Al Qaeda links to Iraq remained unproven. During an anniversary demonstration, two protesters reached the clock face of Big Ben and unveiled banners reading "Time for Truth." *(Source: Odd Andersen/AFP/Getty Images)*

A second theme examines the strategies employed in governing the economy. Since the dawn of Britain's Industrial Revolution, prosperity at home has relied on superior competitiveness abroad. This is even truer in today's environment of intensified international competition and global production. Will Britain's "less-is-more" **laissez-faire** approach to economic governance, invigorated by business partnerships, continue to sustain economic growth and competitiveness in a global context? Can Britain achieve a durable economic model without fuller integration into Europe?

laissez-faire a term taken from the French, which means "to let be," in other words, to allow to act freely.

A third theme is the potent political influence of the democratic idea, the universal appeal of core values associated with parliamentary democracy as practiced first in the United Kingdom. Even in Britain, issues about democratic governance, citizen participation, and constitutional reform have been renewed with considerable force.

The traditionally respected royal family has been rocked by scandal and improprieties. Few reject the monarchy outright, but questions about the role of the monarchy helped place on the agenda broader issues about citizen control over government and constitutional reform. In addition, long-settled issues about the constitutional form and unity of the state have also reemerged with unexpected force. How can the interests of England, Wales, Scotland, and Northern Ireland be balanced within a single nation-state?

Finally, we come to the fourth theme, collective identity, which considers how individuals define who they are politically in terms of group attachments, come together to pursue political goals, and face their status as political insiders or outsiders. Through the immigration of former colonial subjects to the United Kingdom, decolonization helped create a multiracial and multiethnic society.

Issues of race, ethnicity, and cultural identity have challenged the long-standing British values of tolerance and consensus. Indeed, the concept of "Britishness"—what the country stands for and who comprises the political community—has come under intense scrutiny, especially since 9/11, and in the aftermath of the bombings of the London transport system by British Muslims in July 2005.

Implications for Comparative Politics

Britain's privileged position in comparative politics textbooks follows naturally from its historical firsts. Britain was the first nation to industrialize. For much of the nineteenth century, the British Empire was the world's dominant power, with a vast network of colonies throughout the world. Britain was also the first nation to develop an effective parliamentary democracy.

For these reasons, British politics is often studied as a model of representative government. Named after the building that houses the British legislature in London, the **Westminster model** emphasizes that democracy rests on the supreme authority of a legislature—in Britain's case, the Parliament. Finally, Britain has served as a model of gradual and peaceful evolution of democratic government in a world where transitions to democracy are often turbulent, interrupted, and uncertain.

Westminster model a form of democracy based on the supreme authority of Parliament and the accountability of its elected representatives; named after the Parliament building in London.

Summary

Despite presiding over an enviable period of economic growth and exerting high-profile leadership on the world stage, Blair lost the support of his party and was forced to hand over the reins of government to Gordon Brown for one big reason: support for the war in Iraq. In addition, Britain faces many other challenges. It must try to sustain economic competitiveness and work hard to unify Britain as a multicultural, multiethnic, multinational country. And it must come to terms with its role as a European country that enjoys a particularly close alliance with the United States, but has its own distinctive national and regional perspectives and interests. Since Brown took over, everyone is watching to see how he redefines Britain's relationship to the United States and to the EU.

Political Economy and Development

The pressures of global competitiveness and the perceived advantages of a "one size fits all" style of minimalist government have encouraged the movement in many countries toward neoliberal approaches for economic management. A legacy from Thatcher's Britain, **neoliberalism** is a touchstone premise of Gordon Brown's New Labour government. Policies aim to promote free competition among firms, to interfere with entrepreneurs and managers as little as possible, and to create a business-friendly environment to attract foreign investment and spur innovation.

neoliberalism a term used to describe government policies aiming to promote free competition among business firms within the market, including reduced governmental regulation and social spending.

FOCUS QUESTION

How new is New Labour's approach to governing the economy?

The State and the Economy

Thirty years ago, there was not much to admire in the British economy. Growth was low and unemployment high. In 1976 the country received a Third World–style bailout from the International Monetary Fund to help stabilize the economy. Britain was routinely called the "sick man of Europe." But times have changed for the better. Since the mid-1990s, Britain has avoided the high unemployment and recession that have plagued many EU nations. The pattern of growth reveals the "two-track" character of the UK economy. Growth in the service sector—(especially in financial services) offsets a much weaker industrial sector. But the British economy exhibits overall strength. Although many wonder how much longer the good times will continue to roll, with low unemployment, low interest rates, low inflation, and sustained growth, the UK performance is one of the best among the leading industrial economies. In fact, in 2006 Britain ranked second among the leading industrial economies in the world in income per capita—up from fifth when New Labour took office in 1997. On the negative side, however, must be counted a productivity gap in manufacturing between the United Kingdom and key competitors, persistent deficits in the UK balance of trade, concern about low rates of domestic investment and spending on research and development, and in 2007 an uptick in inflation. Housing prices have escalated rapidly beyond the reach of many middle-class Britons. The British system of production also generates insecure jobs—without the social protections of European social and economic models. Women and ethnic minorities are significantly overrepresented in this sector.

Neoliberalism drives the economic policy of New Labour, and the economic performance of the UK economy today. But Britain's New Labour government insists that its third way—as distinct from Conservative or conventional center-left projects—can blend the dynamism of market forces with the traditional center-left concern to promote social justice and reduce inequalities. Are Britons across the board enjoying the fruits of the longest period of sustained economic growth in over 200 years? How has globalization changed the equation?

Two central dimensions, economic management and social policy, capture the new role of the state. Analysis of these policy areas also reveals how limited this new state role was in comparative terms.

Economic Management

Like all other states, whatever their commitment to free markets, the British state intervenes in economic life, sometimes with considerable force. However, the British state has generally limited its role to broad policy instruments designed to influence the economy generally (**macroeconomic policy**). How has the orientation of economic policy evolved during the postwar period? How new is New Labour?

macroeconomic policy policy intended to shape the overall economic system by concentrating on policy targets such as inflation and growth.

The Consensus Era. After World War II, the unity inspired by shared suffering and the need to rebuild the country crystallized the collectivist consensus.

The British state broadened and deepened its responsibilities for the overall performance of the economy.

The state nationalized key industries, assuming direct ownership of them. It also accepted the responsibility to secure low levels of unemployment (referred to as a policy of full employment), expand social services, maintain a steady rate of growth (increase the output or GDP), keep prices stable, and achieve desirable balance-of-payments and exchange rates. The approach is called Keynesian demand management, or **Keynesianism** (after the British economist John Maynard Keynes, 1883–1946).

Keynesianism named after British economist John Maynard Keynes, an approach to economic policy in which state economic policies are used to regulate the economy to achieve stable economic growth.

Before Thatcher became leader of the Conservative Party in 1975, Conservative leaders generally accepted the collectivist consensus. By the 1970s, however, public officials no longer saw the world they once understood. It had become a world without economic growth and with growing political discontent. Investments declined and trade union agitation increased. Industrial unrest in the winter of 1978–1979 dramatized Labour's inability to manage its allies, the trade unions. This contributed to Thatcher's electoral victory a few months later in May 1979. The winter of discontent wrote the conclusion to Britain's collectivist consensus and discredited the Keynesian welfare state.

Thatcherite Policy Orientation. In policy terms, the economic orientations of Thatcher and Major signaled a rejection of Keynesianism. In its place, **monetarism** emerged as the new economic doctrine. Monetarism assumed that there is a "natural rate of unemployment" determined by the labor market itself. State intervention to steer the economy should be limited to a few steps that would help foster appropriate rates of growth in the money supply and keep inflation low. Monetarism reflected a radical change from the postwar consensus regarding economic management. Not only was active government intervention considered unnecessary; it was seen as undesirable and destabilizing.

monetarism an approach to economic policy that assumes a natural rate of unemployment, determined by the labor market, and rejects the instrument of government spending to run budgetary deficits for stimulating the economy and creating jobs.

New Labour's Economic Policy Approach. From the start of New Labour's time in office, Gordon Brown as chancellor—and later as prime minister—insisted on establishing a "platform of stability." Above all, Brown was determined to reduce public debt. Only as he turned that debt into a surplus did the "iron chancellor" reinvent himself as a more conventional Labour chancellor. During his last few years as chancellor, Brown used economic growth to increase spending (rather than cut taxes). The money spent on the National Health Service (NHS) and on education rose dramatically from 2006 to 2008.

Does the third way represent a genuine departure in economic policy? Brown argues that since capital is international, mobile, and not subject to control, industrial policy and planning that focus on the domestic economy alone are futile. Rather, government can improve the quality of labor through education and training, maintain the labor market flexibility inherited from the Thatcher regime, and help to attract investment to Britain. Strict control of inflation and tough limits on public expenditure help promote both employment and investment opportunities. At the same time, economic policy is directed at enhancing competitive strength through government-business partnership. New Labour is very focused on designing and implementing policies to create new jobs and get people, particularly young people, into the work force.

Political Implications of Economic Policy. Today, the economic policy of New Labour is pragmatic and eclectic. Should the government intervene, work to reduce inequalities through the mildly redistributive provisions of the welfare state, and sustain the ethos of a caring society (collectivism/"Old Labour")? Should it allow the market to function competitively and thereby promote entrepreneurship, competitiveness, and individual autonomy (Thatcherism)? Or should it help secure an inclusive "stakeholder" economy in which business has the flexibility, security, and mobility to compete and workers have the skills and training to participate effectively in the global labor market (New Labour)?

Social Policy

In general, welfare state provisions interfere relatively little in the workings of the market, and policy-makers do not see the reduction of group inequalities as the proper goal of the welfare state. The NHS provides comprehensive and universal medical care and has long been championed as the jewel in the crown of the welfare state in Britain, but it remains an exception to the rule. Compared with other Western European countries, the welfare state in Britain offers few comprehensive services, and the policies are not very generous.

New Labour rejects both the cutbacks in social provisions of Conservative governments that seemed mean-spirited as well as the egalitarian traditions of Britain's collectivist era that emphasized entitlements or what in the United States is called "tax and spend liberalism." Instead, New Labour focuses its social policy on training and broader social investment as a more positive third-way alternative.

New Labour promised a modernized, leaner welfare state, in which people are actively encouraged to seek work. The reform of the welfare state emphasizes efficiencies and attempts to break welfare dependency. Positive inducements include training programs, especially targeted at youth, combined with incentives to private industry to hire new entrants to the labor market. The threats include eligibility restrictions and reductions in coverage. Referred to as the "New Deal" for the young unemployed (a policy later extended to other age groups and to working moms) welfare reform emphasized concerted efforts to create viable pathways out of dependence. This effort to identify comprehensive solutions to society's ills and reduce the tendency for government to let marginalized individuals fall by the wayside captures the third-way orientation of the New Labour project.

Nevertheless, New Labour, like all other governments in Britain and many other countries, will be accountable above all for the failure or success of more traditional social policies, especially health care and education.

FOCUS QUESTION

How have changes in social policy changed people's lives?

Society and Economy

No one can tell whether government policy creates a given distribution of resources or whether poverty increases or decreases because of a general downturn or upswing in the economy. The evidence is clear, however, that economic inequality grew in Britain during the 1980s before it stabilized or narrowed slightly in the mid-1990s, and that ethnic minorities and women continue to experience significant disadvantages.

In general, Conservative policies deepened inequalities. The economic upturn that began in 1992, combined with Major's moderating effects on the Thatcherite social policy agenda, served to narrow inequality by the mid-1990s. Attention to social exclusion in its many forms, a 1999 pledge by the prime minister to eradicate child poverty (even though Britain at the time had the highest rates of child poverty in EU Europe), and strong rates of growth are good omens for narrowing the gap between rich and poor in Britain.

But there is a long way to go. A 2007 report by UNICEF compared twenty-one wealthy countries (members of the OECD) on their success in securing the well-being of children along six dimensions. Although European countries generally achieved high scores both the United States and the United Kingdom are in the bottom third for five of the six dimensions under review. Worse still, in the summary table that presents the overall rankings, the UK comes in dead last, just behind the United States (see Figure 2.3).

Inequality and Ethnic Minorities

Poverty and diminished opportunity disproportionately characterize the situation of ethnic minorities (a term applied to peoples of non-European origin from the former British colonies in the Indian subcontinent, the Caribbean, and Africa). The ethnic minority population in the United Kingdom is considerably younger than the white population. More than one-third of the ethnic minority population is younger than age sixteen, nearly half is under age twenty-five, and more than four-fifths is under age forty-five. Ethnic minority groups are increasingly a native-born population. Thus, despite the common and often disparaging reference to ethnic minority individuals as "immigrants," the experience of members of ethnic minority groups is increasingly that of a native-born population.

Ethnic minority individuals, particularly young men, are subject to unequal treatment by the police and considerable physical harassment by citizens. They have experienced cultural isolation as well as marginalization in the educational system, job training, housing, and labor markets. There is considerable concern about the apparent rise in racially motivated crime in major metropolitan areas with significant ethnic diversity.

In general, poor rates of economic success reinforce the sense of isolation and distinct collective identities. Variations among ethnic minority communities are quite considerable, however, and there are some noteworthy success stories. For example, among men of African, Asian, Chinese, and Indian descent, the

Countries are listed here in order of their average rank for the six dimensions of child well-being that have been assessed.* A light background indicates a place in the top third of the table; midtone denotes the middle third; and a dark background the bottom third.

		Dimension 1	Dimension 2	Dimension 3	Dimension 4	Dimension 5	Dimension 6
Dimensions of Child Well-being	Average Ranking Position (for all 6 dimensions)	Material Well-being	Health and Safety	Educational Well-being	Family and Peer Relationships	Behaviors and Risks	Subjective Well-being
Netherlands	4.2	10	2	6	3	3	1
Sweden	5.0	1	1	5	15	1	7
Denmark	7.2	4	4	8	9	6	12
Finland	7.5	3	3	4	17	7	11
Spain	8.0	12	6	15	8	5	2
Switzerland	8.3	5	9	14	4	12	6
Norway	8.7	2	8	11	10	13	8
Italy	10.0	14	5	20	1	10	10
Ireland	10.2	19	19	7	7	4	5
Belgium	10.7	7	16	1	5	19	16
Germany	11.2	13	11	10	13	11	9
Canada	11.8	6	13	2	18	17	15
Greece	11.8	15	18	16	11	8	3
Poland	12.3	21	15	3	14	2	19
Czech Republic	12.5	11	10	9	19	9	17
France	13.0	9	7	18	12	14	18
Portugal	13.7	16	14	21	2	15	14
Austria	13.8	8	20	19	16	16	4
Hungary	14.5	20	17	13	6	18	13
United States	18.0	17	21	12	20	20	–
United Kingdom	18.2	18	12	17	21	21	20

*OECD countries with insufficient data to be included in the overview: Australia, Iceland, Japan, Luxembourg, Mexico, New Zealand, the Slovak Republic, South Korea, Turkey.

FIGURE 2.3

Child Well-Being in Rich Countries

Despite a strong commitment by New Labour to end child poverty, Britain comes in last in a comparison of child well-being among twenty-one wealthy countries.

Source: UNICEF, Child poverty in perspective: An overview of child well-being in rich countries. *Innocenti Report Card 7*, 2007. UNICEF Innocenti Research Centre, Florence. © The United Nations Children's Fund, 2007.

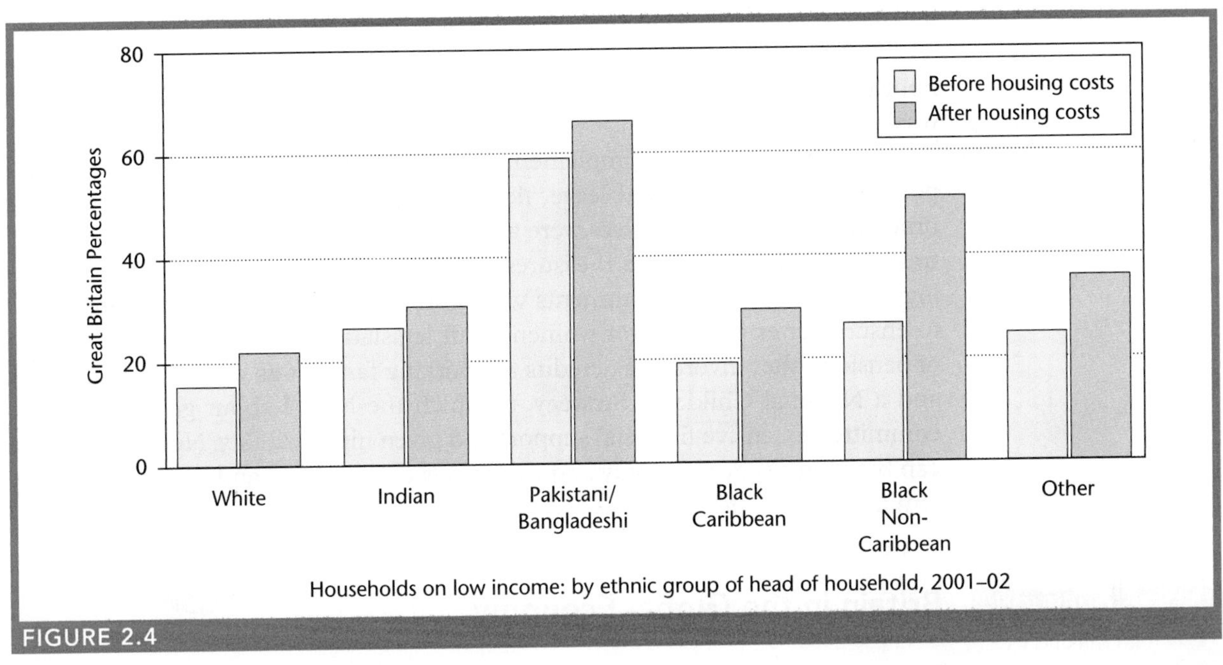

FIGURE 2.4

Low-Income Households by Ethnicity

People from Britain's ethnic minority communities are far more likely than white Britons to be in lower-income households, although there are important differences among ethnic minority groups. Nearly 60 percent of Pakistani or Bangladeshi households are low-income households, while about one-third of black Caribbean households live on low incomes.

Source: National Statistics Online: www.statistics.gov.uk/CCI/nugget.asp?ID=269&Pos=1&ColRank=2&Rank=384

proportional representation in the managerial and professional ranks is actually higher than that for white men (although they are much less likely to be senior managers in large firms). Also, Britons of South Asian, and, especially, Indian descent enjoy a high rate of entrepreneurship. Nevertheless, despite some variations, employment opportunities for women from all minority ethnic groups are limited.[1]

Inequality and Women

Women's participation in the labor market when compared to that of men also indicates marked patterns of inequality. In fact, most women in Britain work part-time, often in jobs with fewer than sixteen hours of work per week and often with fewer than eight hours (in contrast, fewer than one in every fifteen men is employed part-time). More than three-quarters of women working part-time report that they did not want a full-time job, yet more women than men (in raw numbers, not simply as a percentage) take on second jobs. Although employment conditions for women in Britain trail those of many of their EU counterparts, the gap in the differential between weekly earnings of men and women in the United Kingdom has narrowed. In fact, the **gender gap** in pay based on median hourly earnings has narrowed from 17.4 percent in 1997 to 12.6 percent

gender gap politically significant differences in social attitudes and voting behavior between men and women.

in 2006, the lowest value since records have been kept. That's the good news. The bad news is that the part-time gender pay gap (based on a comparison of the hourly wage of men working full-time and women working part-time) for 2006 was 40.2 percent.[2]

The government has implemented a set of "family-friendly" work-related policies, including parental leave, flexible working arrangements, and working times. Most of these initiatives were at the minimum EU standard as required by treaty commitments. Other measures include a commitment in principle to filling half of all public appointments with women, a review of the pension system to ensure better coverage for women, draft legislation to provide for the sharing of pensions after divorce, tax credits for working families as well as for child care, and a National Childcare Strategy, to which the New Labour government has committed extensive financial support and given high visibility. Nevertheless, the gap between childcare supply and demand is considerable and the cost for many families remains prohibitive.

FOCUS QUESTION

Is Britain making the most of globalization?

Britain in the Global Economy

foreign direct investment ownership of or investment in cross-border enterprises in which the investor plays a direct managerial role.

Britain plays a particular role within the European and international economy, one that has been reinforced by international competitive pressures in this global age. For a start, **foreign direct investment** (FDI) favors national systems, like those of Britain (and the United States), that rely more on private contractual and market-driven arrangements and less on state capacity and political or institutional arrangements. Because of such factors as low costs, political climate, government-sponsored financial incentives, reduced trade union power, and a large pool of potential nonunionized recruits, the United Kingdom is the most highly regarded location in Europe for FDI. In fact, in 2006 it placed second in the world behind the United States in FDI inflows.

In very important ways, New Labour accepted the legacy of eighteen years of Conservative assaults on trade union powers and privileges. It has chosen to modernize, but not reshape, the system of production in which nonstandard and insecure jobs without traditional social protections proliferate, a growing sector in which women and ethnic minorities are significantly overrepresented.

Still, the UK scores extremely well in international comparisons of microeconomic competitiveness and growth competitiveness. It has also achieved significant competitive success in particular pockets of science-based high technology industries. For example, the UK preserves an extremely strong position in its global market share in telecommunications equipment. The picture of UK global competitiveness remains clouded, however, by weak industrial performance—illustrated by the 2005 closure of Rover, Britain's last mass market automobile manufacturer.

Gordon Brown's Britain preaches a globalization-friendly model of flexible labor markets throughout EU Europe, and its success in boosting Britain's economic performance in comparison with the rest of Europe has won some reluctant admirers. Thus, Britain has been shaped by the international political economy in important ways and hopes to take full advantage of the economic prospects of globalization, even as it tries to reshape other European national models in its own image.

Summary

After more than a decade in office, New Labour remains a mystery to many. Blair and Brown have chalked up many successes, and yet the basic question—how new is New Labour?—is as hotly contested as ever. In the governing the economy realm there is a "back to the future" dimension to New Labour. The future of global competitiveness rests on a traditional economics of tight finance, laissez-faire, and free trade. That approach, which is anchored in business partnerships and arms-length relationships to trade unions, is certainly new for a Labour government. From economic strength, the government has attempted to tackle recurrent problems that affect people's lives. It has achieved some success in reducing child poverty and narrowing the gender gap in pay—but has done less to reduce the unequal chances faced by ethnic minorities. Globalization is a watchword of New Labour, and Britain has achieved an enviable record of growth, low inflation, and low unemployment in part because of its sustained commitment to attract foreign investment and to assume an outward-looking competitive profile.

Governance and Policy-Making

An understanding of British governance begins with consideration of Britain's constitution, which is notable for two significant features: its form and how old it is. Britain lacks a formal written constitution in the usual sense. There is no single unified and authoritative text (like the U.S. Constitution) that has special status above ordinary law and can be amended only by special procedures. Rather, the British constitution is a combination of statutory law (mainly acts of Parliament), common law, convention, and authoritative interpretations. Although it is often said that Britain has an unwritten constitution, this is not accurate. Authoritative legal treatises are written, of course, as are the much more significant acts of Parliament that define crucial elements of the British political system. These acts define the powers of Parliament and its relationship with the Crown (the monarchy), the rights governing the relationship between state and citizen, the relationship of constituent nations to the United Kingdom, the relationship of the United Kingdom to the EU, and many other rights and legal arrangements. Thus, it is probably best to say, "What distinguishes the British constitution from others is not that it is unwritten, but rather that it is part written and uncodified."[3]

It is hard to know where conventions and acts of Parliament with constitutional implications began, but they can certainly be found dating back to the seventeenth century, notably with the Bill of Rights of 1689, which helped define the relationship between the monarchy and Parliament. "Britain's constitution presents a paradox," a British scholar of constitutional history has observed. "We live in a modern world but inhabit a pre-modern, indeed, ancient, constitution."[4]

More generally, constitutional authorities have accepted the structure and principles of many areas of government for so long that appeal to convention has enormous cultural force. Thus, widely agreed-on rules of conduct, rather than law or U.S.-style checks and balances, set the limits of governmental power. This reality underscores an important aspect of British government: absolute principles of government are few. At the same time, those that exist are fundamental to the organization of the state and central to governance, policy-making, and patterns of representation.

FOCUS QUESTION

What are the three core principles of the British State? How have they evolved in recent years?

Organization of the State

The core constitutional principle of the British political system and cornerstone of the Westminster model is **parliamentary sovereignty**: Parliament can make or overturn any law; the executive, the judiciary, and the throne do not have any authority to restrict, veto, or otherwise overturn parliamentary action. In a classic **parliamentary democracy**, the prime minister is answerable to the House of Commons (the elected element of Parliament) and may be dismissed by it. That said, by passing the European Communities Act in 1972 (Britain joined the European Economic Community in 1973), Parliament accepted significant limitations on its power to act. It acknowledged that European law has force in the United Kingdom without requiring parliamentary assent and accepted the authority of the European Court of Justice (ECJ) to resolve jurisdictional disputes. To complete the circle, the ECJ has confirmed its right to suspend acts of Parliament.

parliamentary sovereignty the doctrine that grants the legislature the power to make or overturn any law and permits no veto or judicial review.

parliamentary democracy system of government in which the chief executive is answerable to the legislature and may be dismissed by it.

Second, Britain has long been a **unitary state**. By contrast to the United States, where powers not delegated to the national government are reserved for the states, no powers are reserved constitutionally for subcentral units of government in the United Kingdom. However, the Labour government of Tony Blair introduced a far-reaching program of constitutional reform that created, for the first time, a quasi-federal system in Britain. Specified powers have been delegated (the British prefer to say *devolved*) to legislative bodies in Scotland and Wales, and Northern Ireland, now that the longstanding conflict in Northern Ireland seems settled. (We will discuss the settlement in Northern Ireland and its significance in Section 5). In addition, some powers have been redistributed from the Westminster Parliament to an authority governing London with a directly elected mayor, and additional powers may be devolved to regional assemblies as well.

unitary state in contrast to a federal system, a system of government in which no powers are reserved for subnational units of government.

Third, Britain operates within a system of **fusion of powers** at the national level: Parliament is the supreme legislative, executive, and judicial authority and includes the monarch as well as the House of Commons and the House of Lords. The fusion of legislature and executive is also expressed in the function

fusion of powers a constitutional principle that merges the authority of branches of government, in contrast to the principle of separation of powers.

cabinet government a system of government in which most executive power is held by the cabinet, headed by a prime minister.

constitutional monarchy system of government in which the head of state ascends by heredity but is limited in powers and constrained by the provisions of a constitution.

and personnel of the cabinet. Whereas U.S. presidents can direct or ignore their cabinets, which have no constitutionally mandated function, the British cabinet bears enormous constitutional responsibility. Through its collective decision making, the cabinet, and not an independent prime minister, shapes, directs, and takes responsibility for government. As we will see, this core principle, **cabinet government**, may at critical junctures be observed more in principle than in practice.

Britain is a **constitutional monarchy**. The position of head of state passes by hereditary succession, but the government or state officials must exercise nearly all powers of the Crown. Taken together, parliamentary sovereignty, parliamentary democracy, and cabinet government form the core elements of the British or Westminster model of government.

FOCUS QUESTION

What are the key features of cabinet government? Has it been replaced by prime ministerial government?

The Executive

The term *cabinet government* is useful in emphasizing the key functions that the cabinet exercises: responsibility for policy-making, supreme control of government, and coordination of all government departments. However, the term does not capture the full range of executive institutions or the scale and complexity of operations. Nor does it capture the realities of a system in which power invariably flows upward to the prime minister, who is much more than a first among equals as cabinet government might imply. In addition, the executive reaches well beyond the cabinet. It extends from ministries (departments) and ministers to the civil service in one direction, and to Parliament (as we shall see in Section 4) in the other direction.

Cabinet Government

After a general election, the Crown invites the leader of the party that emerges from the election with control of a majority of seats in the House of Commons to form a government and serve as prime minister. The prime minister selects approximately two dozen ministers to constitute the cabinet. Among the most significant assignments are the Foreign Office (equivalent to the U.S. secretary of state), the Home Office (ministry of justice or attorney general), and the chancellor of the exchequer. In contrast to the French Constitution, which prohibits a cabinet minister from serving in the legislature, British constitutional tradition *requires* overlapping membership between Parliament and cabinet. (In fact, this point was made in dramatic faction when Gordon Brown elevated Mark Malloch Brown, the former UN deputy secretary general to the House of Lords, so that he could then appoint him to a new cabinet post as minister for Africa, Asia, and the United Nations.)

The cabinet room at 10 Downing Street (the prime minister's official residence) is a place of intrigue as well as deliberation. From the perspective of the prime minister, the cabinet may appear as loyal followers or as ideological combatants, potential challengers for party leadership, and parochial advocates for pet programs that run counter to the overall objectives of the government. By contrast, the convention of collective responsibility normally ensures the continuity of government by unifying the cabinet. In principle, the prime minister must gain the support of a majority of the cabinet for a range of significant decisions, notably the budget and the legislative program.

The only other constitutionally mandated mechanism for checking the prime minister is a defeat on a vote of no confidence in the House of Commons (discussed in Section 4). Since this action is rare and politically dangerous, the cabinet's role in constraining the chief executive remains the only routine check on his or her power. Does collective responsibility effectively constrain prime ministers, or does it enable them to paint "presidential" decisions with the veneer of collectivity?

A politician with strong ideological convictions and a leadership style to match, Margaret Thatcher often attempted to galvanize loyalists in the cabinet and either marginalize or expel detractors. In the end, Thatcher's treatment of the cabinet helped inspire the movement to unseat her as party leader and stretched British constitutional conventions. John Major returned to a more consultative approach, in keeping with the classic model of cabinet government.

Tony Blair, like Thatcher, narrowed the scope of collective responsibility. The prime minister, a few key cabinet members, and a handful of advisers really made policy decisions in smaller gatherings. In a striking example of this process early in the Blair premiership, right after the election when the full cabinet had not yet met, the government announced the decision to free the Bank of England to set interest rates. Under Blair, cabinet meetings were usually less than an hour and could not seriously take up (much less resolve) policy differences.

More recently, the role of cabinet in the decision to go to war in Iraq underscored its weakened capacity to exercise constitutional checks and balances. The war was often discussed in cabinet—and endlessly in bilateral meetings with key ministers and unelected policy advisers—but was never subjected to full-scale debate and formal cabinet approval. Blair and his close aides seemed skeptical about the effectiveness and centrality of the cabinet as well as cabinet committees. Blair preferred to coordinate strategically important policy areas through highly politicized special units in the Cabinet Office such as the Social Exclusion Unit, the Women's Unit, and the Prime Minister's Delivery Unit, which exerted strategic control over the delivery of public services.

How will Gordon Brown run the cabinet? Will he engage in genuinely collective deliberations? Or as many observers anticipate, based on his behavior as chancellor and domestic policy czar under Blair, will Brown rely (as did Blair) on a small cabal of trusted ministers and political advisers? The answer to this question will have important consequences for British government. If Brown continues the pattern set by Thatcher and Blair of working around the cabinet, an enduring precedent may be set and the tradition of collective responsibility may be seriously jeopardized.

On balance, cabinet government represents a durable and effective formula for governance, although the cabinet does not presently function in the role of supreme directing and controlling body it occupies in constitutional doctrine. The

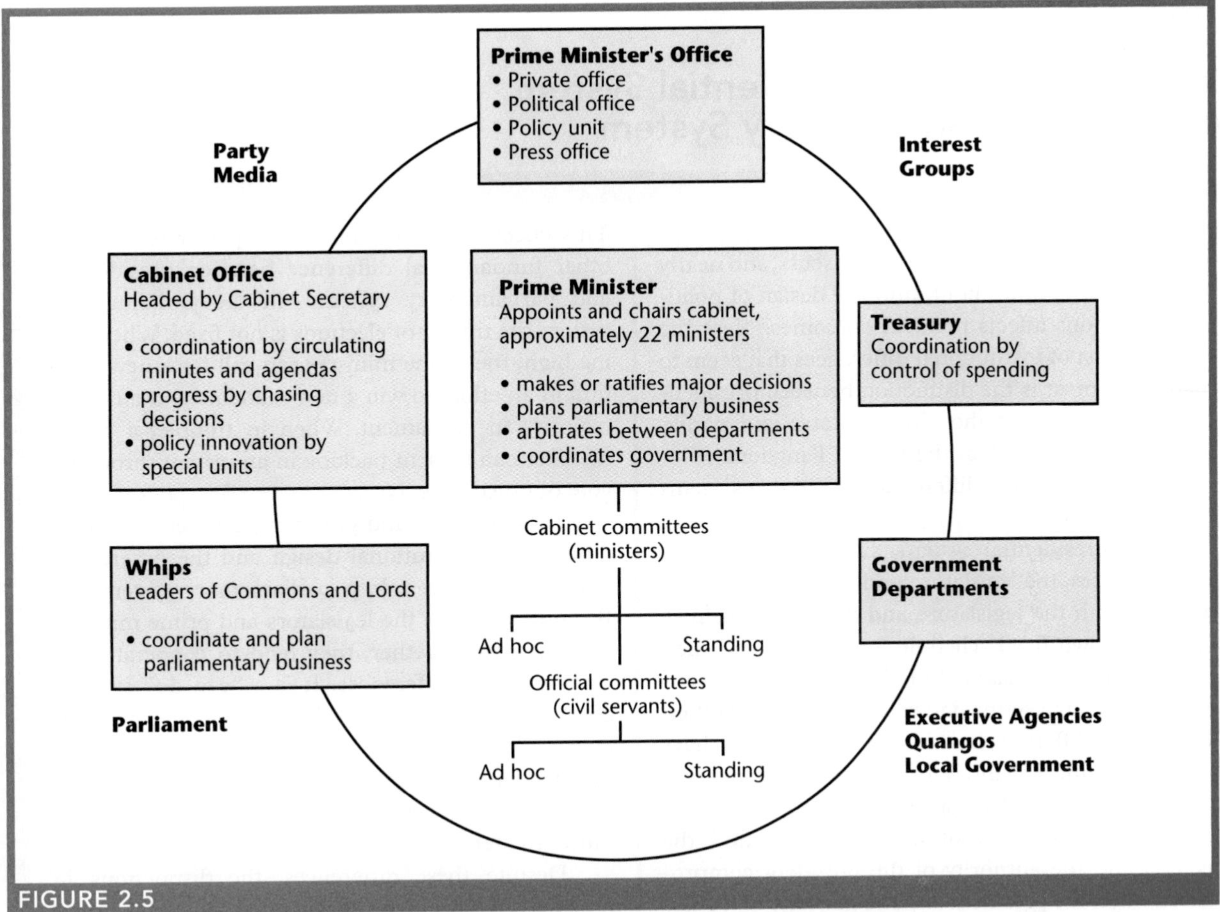

FIGURE 2.5

The Cabinet System

The cabinet is supported by a set of institutions that help formulate policy, coordinate operations, and facilitate the support for government policy. Acting within a context set by the fusion of legislature and executive, the prime minister enjoys a great opportunity for decisive leadership that is lacking in a system of checks and balances and separation of powers among the branches of government.

Source: Her Majesty's Treasury Budget Bulletin as found in *British Politics: Continuities and Change*, Third Edition, by Dennis Kavanagh, p. 251, Oxford University Press, 1996.

cabinet operates within a broader cabinet system or core executive as it is sometimes called (see Figure 2.5), and the prime minister holds or controls many of the levers of power in the core executive. Because the prime minister is the head of the cabinet, his or her office helps develop policy, coordinates operations, and functions as a liaison with the media, the party, interest groups, and Parliament.

Cabinet committees (comprising ministers) and official committees (made up of civil servants) supplement the work of the cabinet. In addition, the treasury plays an important coordinating role through its budgetary control. The cabinet office supports day-to-day operations. Leaders in both the Commons and the Lords, the *whips*, smooth the passage of legislation sponsored by the government, which is more or less guaranteed by a working majority.

The U.S. Connection

Comparing the U.S. Presidential System to the British Parliamentary System

Political scientists—especially those engaged in comparative politics—often discuss, and nearly as often argue about, how the design of political institutions affects political outcomes. Near the top of the list of institutional differences that seem to matter the most is the distinction between presidential systems such as the United States and parliamentary systems such as the United Kingdom.

What are the key differences in the two systems of government?

In a presidential system, such as that of the United States, the legislature and executive are *independent.* Both the legislature and the chief executive have their own fixed schedule for election and their own political mandate. Both legislators and presidents have won election, independently of each other. They have different constituencies and often have different political agendas. Each may even gain credibility and support by opposing the other. In presidential systems it is not uncommon to find the agenda and the authority of the president compromised when the president and the majority of legislators are from different parties—in fact this is the rule, rather than the exception, in the United States and in many other presidential systems. Stalemates on key items of legislation are common. Between presidential elections it is very difficult to remove a president, even one who has very little popular support or who is suspected of acting unconstitutionally. It requires impeachment, which, in turn, requires a finding of extraordinary misconduct and a strong opposition majority in the legislature to push through that finding.

A parliamentary system looks very different. Prime ministers must enjoy the support of the majority of the legislature to achieve office—and they must preserve that support to stay in office, since prime ministers and the governments they head can fall if they lose a vote of no confidence in the legislature. This check on prime ministerial power reveals another fundamental difference between presidential and parliamentary systems—in the parliamentary system the timing of elections is not fixed. When riding high, the prime minister can call for a new election in an effort to win a new mandate and a deeper majority in parliament. When in trouble, a prime minister can be sent packing in an instant through a vote of no confidence.

Parliamentary and presidential systems are very different in institutional design and the differences have consequences. In a parliamentary system like Britain's, because the legislators and prime minister sink or swim together, they tend to cooperate and work through differences. It is a "can do" style of government. In a presidential system like America's, because the legislature and executive are mutually independent—one can swim, while the other sinks—the tendency for finger pointing and stalemate is much greater.

Despite these differences, the distinctions in practice should not be exaggerated. Powerful prime ministers such as Thatcher and Blair were routinely criticized for being too presidential—or even dictatorial. And in Britain, the threat a prime minister faces of losing office as a consequence of a vote of no confidence has all but disappeared—it has happened only once in more than 80 years. In fact, if recent history is a good predictor of the future, an American president is more likely to face a bill of impeachment than a British prime minister is to face a serious vote of no confidence. ❖

The analysis draws heavily from Alfred Stepan, with Cindy Skatch, "Constitutional Frameworks and Democratic Consolidation: Parliamentarism versus Presidentialism," in Mark Kesselman and Joel Krieger, eds., *Readings in Comparative Politics: Political Challenges and Changing Agendas* (Boston: Houghton Mifflin, 2006), pp. 284–293.

The cabinet system and the core executive concentrate power at the top. This ensures that there is no Washington-style gridlock (the inability of legislature and executive to agree on policy) in London. The problem at the pinnacle of power in the United Kingdom is the potential for excessive concentration of power by a prime minister who is prepared to manipulate cabinet and flout the conventions of collective responsibility.

Bureaucracy and Civil Service

Policy-making at 10 Downing Street may appear to be increasingly concentrated in the prime minister's hands. When viewed from Whitehall, however, the executive may appear to be dominated by its vast administrative agencies. The range and complexity of state policy-making mean that the cabinet's authority must be shared with a vast set of unelected officials.

How is the interaction between the civil service and the cabinet ministers (and their political assistants) coordinated? A very senior career civil servant, called a permanent secretary, has chief administrative responsibility for running a department. Other senior civil servants, including deputy secretaries and undersecretaries, assist the permanent secretaries. In addition, the minister reaches into his or her department to appoint a principal private secretary, an up-and-coming civil servant who assists the minister as gatekeeper and liaison with senior civil servants.

Since nearly all legislation is introduced on behalf of the government and presented as the policy directive of a ministry, civil servants in Britain do much of the work of conceptualizing and refining legislation. (In the United States committee staffers in the Congress often do this work.) Civil servants, more than ministers, assume operational duties. Despite a certain natural level of mutual mistrust and incomprehension, the two groups must work closely together.

Since the early 1980s, the pace of change at Whitehall has been very fast. Governments have tried to cut the size of the civil service, streamline its operations, replace permanent with casual (temporary) staff, and enhance its accountability to citizens. As a result of the ongoing modernization of Whitehall (known as new public management, NPM), the civil service inherited by New Labour is very different from the civil service of thirty years ago. It has been downsized and given a new corporate structure (divided into over 120 separate executive agencies). Few at the top of these agencies (agency chief executives) are traditional career civil servants.

In recent years, many observers have expressed concern that New Labour has done—and will continue to do—whatever it can to subject the Whitehall machine to effective political and ministerial direction and control.[5] A related concern is that the centrality and impartiality of civil servants is being eroded by the growing importance of special advisers (who are both political policy advisers and civil servants). This concern came to a head as Blair made the case for war in Iraq. Key special advisers played critical roles in making the case in the famous "dodgy dossier" of September 2002 that the threat of weapons of mass destruction justified regime change in Iraq.

Public and Semipublic Institutions

Like other countries, Britain has institutionalized a set of administrative functions that expand the role of the state well beyond the traditional core executive functions and agencies. These are "semipublic" agencies. They are sanctioned by the state but without direct democratic oversight.

Nationalized Industries

The nationalization of basic industries—such as coal, iron and steel, gas and electricity supply—was a central objective of the Labour government's program during the postwar collectivist era. By the end of the Thatcher era the idea of public ownership had clearly run out of steam. For New Labour, a return to the program of public ownership of industry is unthinkable. Instead, when thinking of expanding state functions, we can look to a growing set of semipublic administrative organizations.

Nondepartmental Public Bodies

Since the 1970s, an increasing number of administrative functions have been transferred to bodies that are typically part of the government in terms of funding, function, and appointment of staff, but operate at arm's length from ministers. They are officially called nondepartmental public bodies (NDPBs) but are better known as quasi-nongovernmental organizations or **quangos**. Quangos have increasing policy influence and enjoy considerable administrative and political advantages. They take responsibility for specific functions and can combine governmental and private sector expertise. At the same time, ministers can distance themselves from controversial areas of policy.

quangos acronym for **quasi-nongovernmental organizations**, the term used in Britain for nonelected bodies that are outside traditional governmental departments or local authorities.

Despite Thatcher's attempts to reduce their number and scale back their operations, by the late 1990s, there were some six thousand quangos, 90 percent operating at the local level. They were responsible for one-third of all public spending and staffed by approximately fifty thousand people. Increasingly, the debate about NDPBs is less about the size of the public, semipublic, or private sector, and more about the effective delivery of services.

Alongside quangos, in recent years the government has looked for ways to expand the investment of the private sector in capital projects such as hospitals and schools that provide public sector goods. Thus New Labour continued the private finance initiative (PFI) it inherited from the Conservatives as a key part of its signature modernization program and as a way to revitalize public services. The results are controversial: critics and supporters disagree about the quality of services provided and whether taxpayers win or lose by the financial arrangements. In addition, the tendency of PFI initiatives to blur the line between public and private raise important and controversial issues. Do these initiatives, as Labour modernizers insist, bring welcome resources, expertise, and skills to crucial public sector provisions? Or, as critics contend, do they distort priorities in education and health care, erode vital traditions of universal provision of public goods, and chip away at the working conditions for public sector employees?[6]

FOCUS QUESTION

How has the role of the military changed under New Labour?

Other State Institutions

The Military and the Police

From the local police constable to the most senior military officer, those involved in security and law enforcement have enjoyed a rare measure of popular support in Britain. Constitutional tradition and professionalism distance the British police and military officers from politics. Nevertheless, both institutions have been placed in more politically controversial and exposed positions in recent decades.

In the case of the military, British policy since the Cold War remains focused on a gradually redefined set of North Atlantic Treaty Organization (NATO) commitments. Still ranked among the top five military powers in the world, Britain retains a global presence. In 1982, Britain soundly defeated Argentina in a war over the disputed Falkland/Malvinas Islands in the South Atlantic. In the Gulf War of 1991, Britain deployed a full armored division in the UN-sanctioned force arrayed against Iraq's Saddam Hussein. Under Blair's leadership, Britain was the sole participant alongside the United States in the aerial bombardment of Iraq in December 1998. In 1999, the United Kingdom strongly backed NATO's Kosovo campaign and pressed for ground troops. Indeed, the Kosovo campaign and Blair's "doctrine of international community," assumed an important role in Blair's justification for the war in Iraq.[7] According to Blair, global interdependence rendered isolationism obsolete and inspired a commitment to a new ethical dimension in foreign policy. Throughout the war in Iraq and its bloody aftermath, Blair persistently sought to characterize Iraq as an extension of Kosovo, an effort to liberate Muslims from brutal dictatorships, whether Serbia's Milosevic or Iraq's Saddam Hussein.

Until Blair's decision to support the American plan to shift the main venue of the war on terror from Afghanistan to Iraq, the use of the military in international conflicts generated little opposition. Indeed, even in the case of the war in Iraq, the role of the military (as distinct from the decision to go to war) generated relatively little controversy.

The police have traditionally operated as independent local forces throughout the country. Since the 1980s, the police have witnessed growth in government control, centralization, and level of political use. During the coal miners' strike of 1984–1985, the police operated to an unprecedented, perhaps unlawful, degree as a national force coordinated through Scotland Yard (London police headquarters). Police menaced strikers and hindered miners from participating in strike support activities. This partisan use of the police in an industrial dispute flew in the face of constitutional traditions and offended some police officers and officials. During the 1990s, concerns about police conduct focused on police-community relations. These included race relations, corruption, and the interrogation and treatment of people held in custody. In particular, widespread criticism of the police for mishandling their investigation into the brutal 1993 racist killing of Stephen Lawrence in South London resulted in a scathing report by a commission of inquiry in 1999.

The Judiciary

judicial review the prerogative of a high court to nullify actions by the executive and legislative branches of government that in its judgment violate the constitution.

In Britain, the principle of parliamentary sovereignty has limited the role of the judiciary. Courts have no power to judge the constitutionality of legislative acts (**judicial review**). They can only determine whether policy directives or administrative acts violate common law or an act of Parliament. Hence, the British judiciary is generally less politicized and influential than its U.S. counterpart.

Jurists, however, have participated in the wider political debate outside court. They have headed royal commissions on the conduct of industrial relations, the struggle in Northern Ireland, and riots in Britain's inner cities. Sir Richard Scott wrote a harsh report on his investigation into Britain's sales of military equipment to Iraq in the 1980s. His investigation indicates that inquiries led by judges with a streak of independence can prove highly embarrassing to the government and raise important issues for public debate. Take, for example, the inquiry by Lord Hutton, a senior jurist, into the death of David Kelly, a former UN weapons inspector and whistleblower who challenged the key tenet of Blair's case for the war in Iraq—that Iraq could launch weapons of mass destruction on forty-five minutes' notice. Such a high-profile enquiry led by a jurist confirmed this important public role of judges in the United Kingdom. The question of Hutton's independence became very controversial, however, in light of a "finding" that exonerated the prime minister.

Potentially dramatic institutional changes in law and the administration of justice are under consideration. In June 2003, Blair announced the government's intention to abolish the office of Lord Chancellor and move the law lords (who hold the ultimate authority of appeal in British law) from the House of Lords to a new "supreme court." The constitutional reform bill, introduced in 2004, faced strong opposition in the Lords (where Labour is the biggest party but does not hold a majority and must therefore rely on support from peers from other parties and from independents). The prospects for ultimate passage remain clouded.

The European dimension has also significantly influenced law and the administration of justice. As a member of the EU, Britain is bound to abide by the European Court of Justice (ECJ), as it applies and develops law as an independent institution within the EU. For example, two decisions by the ECJ led to the enactment of the Sex Discrimination Act of 1986, since previous legislation did not provide the full guarantees of women's rights in employment mandated to all members by the EU's Equal Treatment Directive. Moreover, with the passage of the Human Rights Act in 1998, Britain is required to comply with the European Convention on Human Rights (ECHR). As a sign of things to come, the adoption of the ECHR forced Britain to curtail discrimination against gays in the military. (The Ministry of Defense confirmed in 2007 that none of its initial fears about gays in the military have been justified.)

Subnational Government

The United Kingdom is a state comprising distinct nations (England, Scotland, Wales, and Northern Ireland). The distribution of powers involves two levels below the central government: national government and local (municipal) government. Because the British political framework has traditionally been unitary, not federal, no formal powers devolved to either the nation within the United Kingdom or to subnational (really subcentral or sub-UK) units as in the United States or Germany.

Although no powers have been constitutionally reserved to local governments, they historically had considerable autonomy in financial terms. They also had discretion in implementing a host of social service and related policies. The Thatcher government tightened the fiscal and political constraints on local government. In 1986, it abolished the multicultural-oriented city government (the Greater London Council, GLC) under the leadership of Ken Livingstone, as well as several other metropolitan councils. In 1989, the Thatcher government introduced a poll tax, which shifted the burden of local taxes from property owners and businesses to individuals. The poll tax proved a tremendous political liability. It maintained the local edge to national politics and helped lead to Thatcher's departure.

Much of New Labour's agenda concerning subcentral government is focused on the political role of nations within Britain. Devolution within England, however, is also part of the reform process. Regional Development Agencies (RDAs) were introduced throughout England in 1999 to facilitate economic development at the regional level. Despite the fairly low-key profile of RDAs and their limited scope (they are unelected bodies with no statutory authority), they opened the door to popular mobilization in the long term for elected regional assemblies.

In addition, the Blair government placed changes in the governance of London on the fast track. The introduction of a directly elected mayor of London in May 2000 proved embarrassing to Blair. The government's efforts to keep Livingstone out of the contest backfired, and he won handily. Livingstone has introduced an expansive agenda to spur long-term sustainable growth. He has also advanced a policy agenda that emphasizes ethnic diversity and the enhanced representation and leadership of women in London public life. In addition, London's determined effort to reduce traffic congestion by levying per day per vehicle charges within a central London zone have won widespread admiration for one of England's most controversial political leaders.

The Policy-Making Process

FOCUS QUESTION

What is the institutional focus of the policy-making practice in the UK?

Parliamentary sovereignty is the core constitutional principle of the British political system. However, when it comes to policy-making and policy implementation, the focus is not on Westminster but rather on Whitehall. In many countries, such as Japan, India, and Nigeria, personal connections and informal networks play a large role in policy-making and implementation. How different is the British system?

Unlike the U.S. system, in which policy-making is concentrated in congressional committees and subcommittees, Parliament has little direct participation in policy-making. Policy-making emerges primarily from within the executive.

There, decision making is strongly influenced by policy communities. These are informal networks with extensive knowledge, access, and personal connections to those responsible for policy. In this private hothouse environment, civil servants, ministers, and members of the policy communities work through informal ties. A cooperative style develops as the ministry becomes an advocate for key players and as civil servants come perhaps to over identify the public good with the advancement of policy within their area of responsibility.

This cozy insider-only policy process has been challenged by the delegation of more and more authority to the EU. The consequences of the European dimension are profound. Both ministers and senior civil servants spend a great deal of time in EU policy deliberations and are constrained both directly and indirectly by the EU agenda and directives. Although still effectively in charge of many areas of domestic policy, more than 80 percent of the rules governing economic life in Britain are determined by the EU. Even when the United Kingdom has opted out, as in the case of the common currency, European influences are significant. Decisions by the Council of Finance Ministers and the European Central Bank shape British macroeconomic, monetary, and fiscal policies in significant ways. Foreign and security policy are not immune from EU influences. The EU's Common Foreign and Security Policy have extended multilevel governance to these spheres. The increasing Europeanization of policy-making will be one of the most interesting and potentially transformative developments in British politics in the next decade.

Summary

In almost every institutional dimension of governance and policy-making in Britain, recent years have witnessed a significant chipping away at the key organizing principles of government. The first principle of parliamentary sovereignty remains, but in practice it is weakened by the growing power of the core executive, the subordination of the UK parliament to the ultimate authority of the EU, and the reluctance of parliament to exercise its ultimate power to remove a prime minister by a vote of no confidence (to be discussed in Section 4). The second principle of Britain as a unitary state is strained by transfer of some powers to legislative and administrative bodies in Scotland, Wales, and Northern Ireland. The third principle of fusion of powers at the national level requires the effective exercise of collective responsibility of the cabinet as a check on prime ministerial power. This principle has been compromised when powerful primes ministers—such as Thatcher and Blair—find ways to work around the cabinet. The decision by Blair to go to war in Iraq without the formal assent of the cabinet reflects a weakening of cabinet government, even as the robust use of the military to advance his doctrine of international community made the role of the military more controversial. As the policy-making process remained focused on Whitehall, we see a consistent picture of growing concentration of power in the executive.

SECTION 4

Representation and Participation

As discussed in Section 3, parliamentary sovereignty is the core constitutional principle defining the role of the legislature and, in a sense, the whole system of British government. The executive or judiciary can set no act of Parliament aside, nor is any Parliament bound by the actions of any previous Parliament. Nevertheless, in practice, the control exerted by the House of Commons (or Commons) is not unlimited. This section investigates the powers and role of Parliament, both Commons and Lords. It also looks at the party system, elections, and contemporary currents in British political culture, citizenship, and identity. We close by offering an analysis of surprising new directions in political participation and social protest.

FOCUS QUESTION

Is Parliament still as sovereign in practice as it remains in constitutional tradition?

The Legislature

From roughly the 1830s to the 1880s, it collaborated in the formulation of policy. Members amended or rejected legislation on the floor of the House of Commons. Today, the Commons does not really legislate. Its real function is to assent to government legislation, since (with rare exceptions) the governing party has a majority of the seats and requires no cross-party voting to pass bills. In addition, the balance of effective oversight of policy has shifted from the legislature to executive agencies.

The House of Commons

The House of Commons, the lower house of Parliament (with 646 seats at the time of the 2005 election), exercises the main legislative power in Britain. Along with the two unelected elements of Parliament, the Crown and the House of Lords, the Commons has three main functions: (1) to pass laws, (2) to provide finances for the state by authorizing taxation, and (3) to review and scrutinize public administration and government policy.

In practical terms, the Commons has a limited legislative function. Nevertheless, it serves a very important democratic function. It provides a highly visible arena for policy debate and the partisan collision of political worldviews. The high stakes and the flash of rhetorical skills bring drama to the historic chambers. One crucial element of drama, however, is nearly always missing. The outcome is seldom in doubt. The likelihood that the Commons will invoke its ultimate authority, to defeat a government, is very small. MPs from the governing party who consider rebelling against their leader (the prime minister) are understandably reluctant in a close and critical vote to force a general election. This would place their jobs in jeopardy. Only once since the defeat of Ramsay MacDonald's government in 1924 has a government been brought down by a defeat in the Commons (in 1979). Today, the balance of institutional power has shifted from Parliament to the governing party and the executive.

The U.S. Connection

Comparing the Commons and Congress

It may seem that the U.S. House of Representatives and the British House of Commons are broadly similar institutions. If this were so, it would come as no great surprise. The House of Representatives fashioned its original parliamentary practices after the House of Commons. And the two chambers symbolize for many the two most enduring models of representative democracy in action.

But in fact the House and the Commons have fundamentally different functions and have developed along very different lines. In its core function, the House of Commons serves as the vehicle for the formation of the government. The prime minister and members of the cabinet are drawn from the majority party or voting bloc in the Commons—and they are maintained by that bloc. The legislative role is secondary, since most bills are introduced on behalf of the government and success is all but guaranteed by the government's majority control of the Commons.

In contrast, the House of Representatives is above all a legislative forum in which outcomes are uncertain—and where the policy preferences of the representatives may or may not conform to the preferences of the government (the presidency and the executive branch). It also plays a key role as a forum for government oversight—over security preparedness before 9/11, the conduct of the war in Iraq, or the response to hurricane Katrina. (Parliamentary select committees play a more muted oversight role in the House of Commons.)

In fact, the differences in the two chambers far outweigh the similarities:

- The term of office for MPs is no more than five years, but is not otherwise fixed, while that of representatives is fixed at two years.
- A size of a parliamentary constituency is about 68,000, and that of a congressional district is approximately 670,000.
- Nine parties are represented in the Commons (after the 2005 general election), but (excluding independents) only two parties were represented in the House after the 2004 congressional elections.

What are some of the other differences between the House of Commons and the House of Representatives? In the commons, four times every week when the house is in session, Cabinet ministers (including the prime minister) respond to questions from the floor by rank-and-file MPs. Often exchanges are sharp, and dramatic impromptu debates break out. Can you imagine if the president had to answer oral questions routinely from members of Congress? Although proposals for experimental use of question periods have been offered in Congress, they have never been introduced.

When it comes to campaign spending, the contrast between the two legislative arenas could scarcely be greater. In the 2004 congressional elections the total money spent was approximately $225 million, and the average winning candidate raised over one million dollars. In the 2005 parliamentary election, by law the maximum a political party could spend per constituency was approximately $55,000 dollars. The average amount spent by individual candidates was about $7500. ❖

See Congressional Research Service, "Parliament and Congress: A Brief of the British House of Commons and the House of Representatives," www.fas.org/sgp/crs/misc/RL32206.pdf; *"Election 2005: Campaign Spending,"* www.electoralcommission.org.uk

The Legislative Process

To become law, bills must be introduced in the House of Commons and the House of Lords, although approval by the latter is not required. The procedure for developing and adopting a public bill is quite complex. The ideas for prospective legislation may come from political parties, pressure groups, think tanks, the prime minister's policy unit, or government departments. Prospective legislation is then normally drafted by civil servants, circulated within Whitehall, approved by the cabinet, and then refined by one of some thirty lawyers in the office of Parliamentary Counsel.*

According to tradition, in the House of Commons the bill usually comes to the floor three times (referred to as *readings*). The bill is formally read upon introduction (the *first reading*), printed, distributed, debated in general terms, and after an interval (from a single day to several weeks), given a *second reading*, followed by a vote. The bill is then usually sent for detailed review to a standing committee of between sixteen and fifty members chosen to reflect the overall party balance in the House. It is then subject to a report stage during which new amendments may be introduced. The *third reading* follows; normally, the bill is considered in final form (and voted on) without debate.

After the third reading, a bill passed in the House of Commons follows a parallel path in the House of Lords. There the bill is either accepted without change, amended, or rejected. According to custom, the House of Lords passes bills concerning taxation or budgetary matters without alteration, and can add technical and editorial amendments to other bills (which must be approved by the House of Commons) to add clarity in wording and precision in administration. After a bill has passed through all these stages, it is sent to the Crown for royal assent (approval by the queen or king, which is only a formality), after which it becomes law and is referred to as an Act of Parliament. ❖

*See Dennis Kavanagh, *British Politics: Continuities and Change*, 3d ed. (Oxford: Oxford University Press, 1996), 282–288.

The House of Lords

The upper chamber of Parliament, the House of Lords (or Lords), is an unelected body that comprises hereditary peers (nobility of the rank of duke, marquis, earl, viscount, or baron), life peers (appointed by the Crown on the recommendation of the prime minister), and law lords (appointed to assist the Lords in its judicial duties and who become life peers). The Lords also includes the archbishops of Canterbury and York and some two-dozen senior bishops of the Church of England. In 2007, there were roughly 750 members of the House of Lords (peers) who could vote and speak in the Lords. Labour held a plurality, but not a majority, and there was a large group of crossbenchers, or independents.

Traditionally, the House of Lords has also served as the final court of appeal for civil cases throughout Britain and for criminal cases in England, Wales, and Northern Ireland. This judicial role, performed by the law lords, drew international attention in 1998 and 1999 when a Spanish court attempted to extradite General Augusto Pinochet of Chile on charges of genocide, torture, and terrorism. As discussed in Section 3, if made into law, the constitutional reform bill, which was introduced in 2004 would transfer that function from the Lords to a new "supreme court."

In modern times, however, the Lords, which has the power to amend and delay legislation, has served mainly as a chamber of revision, providing expertise in redrafting legislation. Recently, for example, the House of Lords considered the Nationality, Immigration and Asylum Bill too harsh. The Lords battled the government for weeks and forced revisions before approving the legislation. Similarly, in 2006, the Lords persuaded the Commons—over the objections of the prime minister—to water down a bill that prohibited incitement to violence out of concerns to protect the civil liberties of British Muslims.

In 1999, the Blair government appointed a Royal Commission on the Reform of the House of Lords (the Wakeham commission). In the same year it introduced legislation to remove the right of hereditary lords to speak and vote. With the passage of House of Lords Act 1999, the number of hereditary peers was reduced to 92. In 2000, the commission recommended a partly elected second chamber, enumerating alternative models. In 2003, the Commons rejected seven options, ranging from a fully appointed chamber (Blair's preference) to an entirely elected one. The failure of a joint committee of MPs and peers to achieve consensus left reform plans in tatters. For now, the future of House of Lords reform has been consigned to the "What is Brown likely to do?" guessing game.

Reforms in Behavior and Structure

How significant are contemporary changes in the House? How far will they go to stem the tide in Parliament's much-heralded decline?

Behavioral Changes: Backbench Dissent. Since the 1970s, backbenchers (MPs of the governing party who have no governmental office and rank-and-file opposition members) have been markedly less deferential than in the past. A backbench rebellion against the Major government's EU policy took a toll on the prestige of the prime minister and weakened him considerably. The defection of some one-third of Labour MPs on key votes in February and March 2003 authorizing the use of force in Iraq represents an historic rebellion. After the 2005 election, and the bombings in London, backbench rebellion led to the first set of defeats by Blair in the Commons over new religious hate laws.

Structural Changes: Parliamentary Committees. In addition to the standing committees that routinely review bills during legislative proceedings, in 1979 the Commons revived and extended the number and responsibilities of select committees. Select committees help Parliament exert control over the executive by examining specific policies or aspects of administration.

The most controversial select committees are watchdog committees that monitor the conduct of major departments and ministries. Select committees hold hearings, take written and oral testimony, and question senior civil servants and ministers. They then issue reports that often include strong policy recommendations at odds with government policy. As one side effect of the reform, the role of the civil service has been complicated. For the first time, civil servants have been required to testify in a manner that might damage their ministers, revealing culpability or flawed judgments.

FOCUS QUESTION

What are the three main political parties—and what distinguishes them?

Political Parties and the Party System

The term *parliamentary sovereignty* conceals the reduced role of Parliament in legislation and the unmaking of governments. The term *two-party system* is also deceiving. It is true that since 1945, only leaders of the Labour or Conservative parties have served as prime ministers. Also, from 1945 through 2005, the Conservative and Labour parties each won eight general elections, with 2005 tipping the lead to Labour. Throughout the postwar period, these two parties have routinely divided at least 85 percent of the seats in the House of Commons. But since the 1980s center parties have assumed a high profile in British electoral politics, with the Liberal Democrats (Lib Dems) emerging as an important alternative to Conservative and Labour—or perhaps a coalition partner with Labour in the not too distant future. In addition, Britain has several national parties, such as the Scottish National Party (SNP) in Scotland and the Plaid Cymru in Wales as well as a roster of parties competing in Northern Ireland. (These parties are described below under "Trends in Electoral Behavior.")

The Labour Party

In the 1950s and early 1960s, those not engaged in manual labor voted Conservative three times more commonly than they did Labour. More than two out of three manual workers, by contrast, voted Labour. During this period, Britain conformed to one classic pattern of a Western European party system: a two-class/two-party system.

The period since the mid-1970s has been marked by significant changes in the party system. It has also seen growing disaffection with even the moderate social democracy associated with the Keynesian welfare state and Labourism. The party suffered from divisions between its trade unionist and parliamentary elements, constitutional wrangling over the power of trade unions to determine party policy at annual conferences, and disputes over how the leader would be selected. Divisions spilled over into foreign policy issues as well. On defense issues, there was a strong pacifist and an even stronger antinuclear sentiment within the party. Support for unilateral nuclear disarmament (the reduction and elimination of nuclear weapons systems with or without comparable developments on the Soviet side) was a decisive break with the national consensus on security policy. This contributed to the party's losses in 1983 and 1987. Unilateralism was then scrapped.

The 1980s and 1990s witnessed relative harmony within the party. Moderate trade union and parliamentary leadership agreed on major policy issues. Labour has become a moderate center-left party. Ideology now takes a back seat to performance and electoral mobilization, although divisions over the war in Iraq have inspired some soul searching about what values the party represents.

The Conservative Party

The Conservative Party dates back to the eighteenth century. Its pragmatism, flexibility, and organizational capabilities have made it one of the most successful and, at times, innovative center-right parties in Europe. Although it has fallen on hard times in recent years, it would be unwise to underestimate its potential as both an opposition and a governing party.

Wrangling among the Conservatives over Europe led to Thatcher's demise as leader and weakened Major throughout his years as prime minister. The bitter leadership contest that followed Major's resignation after the 1997 defeat only reinforced the impression of a party in turmoil. Subsequent rapid departures of party leaders after electoral defeat in 2001 and the forced resignation of the leader in 2003 created an aura of failure and self-doubt to the Conservatives.

In 2003, the combative and experienced Michael Howard took over as party leader. For a time, the Conservatives seemed revitalized. But it was not easy for Howard to translate his assured performances from the front bench in Parliament into popular support. Howard pounded Blair on the failures of intelligence in the run up to the war in Iraq and his handling of the David Kelly affair. But Conservatives gave the prime minister far less trouble on Iraq than did members of the Labour Party itself. Nor could Howard make much headway against New Labour on central social and economic policy concerns. Despite an energetic campaign in 2005, one likely to be remembered for playing the race and ethnicity card, electoral defeat led to his quick resignation. In December 2005, the Conservatives in a landslide elected David Cameron as party leader.

Cameron wasted little time in reorienting the party, modernizing its appeal, and reaching out beyond its traditional core values. Young (he was born in 1966), smart, and telegenic, Cameron acknowledged that New Labour had been right in understanding the mood of Britain and right, also, to insist on achieving both social justice and economic success. Cameron promised to reduce poverty both in Britain and globally, take on climate change as a priority, and ensure security from terrorism. He also looked for ways to retain a special relationship with America, but also promised to recalibrate British foreign policy by forging comparable special relationships with countries such as India. A testament to Blair's success, Cameron worked hard to reposition the Conservatives as a reforming more centrist party that could compete effectively with post-Blair New Labour across the economic and social spectrum. At the same time, with considerable success, Cameron encouraged the view that Brown would drift toward the discredited Old Labour left and, quite remarkably, claimed that he was the true heir to Tony Blair.[8] Cameron's unexpectedly successful performance at the Conservative Party conference in October 2007—he spun out an attractive set of proposals for tax cuts, affordable housing, and improved public services in a spirited off-the-cuff speech—placed his party in the most competitive position it had been in in more than a decade.

Liberal Democrats

Through the 1970s, the Liberal Party, a governing party before World War I and thereafter the traditional centrist third party in Britain, was the only centrist challenger to the Labour and Conservative parties. Since the 1980s, a changing roster of centrist parties has posed a potentially significant threat to the two-party dominance of Conservative and Labour. In 1981, the Social Democratic Party (SDP) formed out of a split within the Labour Party. After the Conservative victory in 1987, the Liberal Party and most of the SDP merged to form the Social and Liberal Democratic Party (now called the Liberal Democrats or Lib Dems). In recent years, the Lib Dems have become a major political player.

In the 2001 general election the party increased its vote tally by nearly one-fifth and won fifty-two seats, the most since 1929. This success positioned the party as a potentially powerful center-left critic of New Labour. That said, Labour has not made it easy for them. As the Blair government began to spend massively to improve education and health care, it narrowed the range of policy issues on which the Liberal Democrats could take on New Labour. Party leader Charles Kennedy won the political gamble in spring 2003 by opposing the war in Iraq. But it has not been easy to take electoral advantage of Blair's political weakness. Thereafter, things went downhill badly, as Kennedy resigned due to problems with alcohol, and allegations about sexual conduct plagued potential successors. The problems continued as the new leader, Menzies (Ming) Campbell, suddenly resigned, and was replaced in December 2007 by Nick Clegg, a 40-year-old ex-journalist and former member of the European Parliament.

FOCUS QUESTION

How fair is the election system in Britain?

Elections

British elections are exclusively for legislative posts. The prime minister is not elected as prime minister but as an MP from a single constituency (electoral district), averaging about 65,000 registered voters. Parliament has a maximum life of five years, with no fixed term. General elections are held after the Crown at the request of the prime minister has dissolved Parliament. Although Blair has in effect set a precedent of elections with four-year intervals, the ability to control the timing of elections is a tremendous political asset for the prime minister. This contrasts sharply with a presidential system, characteristic of the United States, with direct election of the chief executive and a fixed term of office.

The Electoral System

Election for representatives in the Commons (who are called members of Parliament, or MPs) is by a "first-past-the-post" (or winner-take-all) principle in each constituency. In this single-member plurality system, the candidate who receives the most votes is elected. There is no requirement of a majority and no element of proportional representation (a system in which each party is given a percentage of seats in a representative assembly roughly comparable to its percentage of the popular vote). Table 2.3 shows the results of the general elections from 1945 to 2005.

TABLE 2.3

British General Elections, 1945–2005

	Percentage of Popular Vote							Seats in House of Commons					
	Turnout	Conser-vative	Labour	Liberal[a]	National Parties[b]	Other	Swing[c]	Conser-vative	Labour	Liberal[a]	National Parties[b]	Other	Government Majority
1945	72.7	39.8	48.3	9.1	0.2	2.5	–12.2	213	393	12	0	22	146
1950	84.0	43.5	46.1	9.1	0.1	1.2	+3.0	299	315	9	0	2	0.5
1951	82.5	48.0	48.8	2.5	0.1	0.6	+0.9	321	295	6	0	3	17
1955	76.7	49.7	46.4	2.7	0.2	0.9	+2.1	345	277	6	0	2	60
1959	78.8	49.4	43.8	5.9	0.4	0.6	+1.2	365	258	6	0	1	100
1964	77.1	43.4	44.1	11.2	0.5	0.8	–3.2	304	317	9	0	0	4
1970	72.0	46.4	43.0	7.5	1.3	1.8	+4.7	330	288	6	1	5	30
Feb. 1974	78.7	37.8	37.1	19.3	2.6	3.2	–1.4	297	301	14	9	14	–34[d]
Oct. 1974	72.8	35.8	39.2	18.3	3.5	3.2	–2.1	277	319	13	14	12	3
1979	76.0	43.9	37.0	13.8	2.0	3.3	+5.2	339	269	11	4	12	43
1983	72.7	42.4	27.6	25.4	1.5	3.1	+4.0	397	209	23	4	17	144
1987	75.3	42.3	30.8	22.6	1.7	2.6	–1.7	376	229	22	6	17	102
1992	77.7	41.9	34.4	17.8	2.3	3.5	–2.0	336	271	20	7	17	21
1997	71.4	30.7	43.2	16.8	2.6	6.7	–10.0	165	419	46	10	19	179
2001	59.4	31.7	40.7	18.3	2.5	6.8	+1.8	166	413	52	9	19	167
2005	61.5	32.3	35.2	22.1	2.1	8.4	+3.0	197	355	62	9	22	65[e]

[a]Liberal Party, 1945–1979; Liberal/Social Democrat Alliance, 1983–1987; Liberal Democratic Party, 1992–2005.

[b]Combined vote of Scottish National Party (SNP) and Welsh National Party (Plaid Cymru).

[c]"Swing" compares the results of each election with the results of the previous election. It is calculated as the average of the winning major party's percentage point increase in its share of the vote and the losing major party's decrease in its percentage point share of the vote. In the table, a positive sign denotes a swing to the Conservatives, a negative sign a swing to Labour.

[d]Following the February 1974 election, the Labour Party was thirty-four seats short of having an overall majority. It formed a minority government until it obtained a majority in the October 1974 election.

[e]Due to the death of a candidate in one constituency, only 645 parliamentary seats were contested in the May 2005 general election, with one additional seat to be filled through a by-election.

Source:

Anthony King, ed., *New Labour Triumphs: Britain at the Polls* (Chatham, N.J.: Chatham House, 1998), p. 249. Copyright © 1998 by Chatham House. Reprinted by permission. For 2001 results, http://news.bbc.co.uk/hi/english/static/vote2001/results_constituencies/uk_breakdown/uk_full.stm. For 2005 results, http://news.bbc.co.uk/1/hi/uk_politics/vote_2005/constituencies/default.stm.

This winner-take-all electoral system tends to exaggerate the size of the victory of the largest party and to reduce the influence of regionally dispersed lesser parties. Thus, in 2005, with 35.2 percent of the popular vote, Labour won 356 seats. With 22.0 percent of the vote, the Liberal Democrats won only 62 seats. Thus, the Liberal Democrats achieved a share of the vote that was approximately two-thirds of that achieved by Labour, but won fewer than one-fifth of the seats won by Labour. Such are the benefits of the electoral system to the victor (as well as the second major party).

With a fairly stable two-and-a-half party system (Conservative, Labour, and Liberal Democrat), the British electoral system tends toward a stable single-party government. However, the electoral system raises questions about representation and fairness. The system reduces the competitiveness of smaller parties with diffuse pockets of support. In addition, the party and electoral systems have contributed to the creation of a Parliament that has been a bastion of white men. The 1997 election represented a breakthrough for women: the number of women MPs nearly doubled to 120 (18.2 percent). The 2001 election saw the number of women MPs decline to 118 (17.9 percent). But a record 128 women were elected in 2005 (19.8 percent). As a result of using women-only shortlists for the selection of candidates in many winnable seats, Labour sent far more women (94) to parliament than any other party.

In 1992, 6 ethnic minority candidates were elected, up from 4 in 1987, the first time since before World War II that Parliament included minority members. The number of ethnic minority (black and Asian) MPs rose in 1997 to 9 (1.4 percent), to 12 in 2001 (1.8 percent), and to 15 in 2005 (2.3 percent). Despite the general trend of increased representation of women and minorities, they remain substantially underrepresented in Parliament.

Trends in Electoral Behavior

Recent general elections have deepened geographic and regional fragmentation. British political scientist Ivor Crewe has referred to the emergence of two two-party systems: (1) competition between the Conservative and Labour parties dominates contests in English urban and northern seats, and (2) Conservative-center party competition dominates England's rural and southern seats.[9] In addition, a third two-party competition may be observed in Scotland, where Labour competition with the Scottish National Party dominates.

The national parties have challenged two-party dominance since the 1970s. The Scottish National Party (SNP) was founded in 1934 and its Welsh counterpart, the Plaid Cymru, in 1925. Coming in a distant second to Labour in Scotland in 1997, the SNP won 21.6 percent of the vote and six seats. In 2001, support for the SNP declined by 2 percent, and the party lost one of its seats. The 2005 election showed some interesting results in Scotland. Labour lost five seats, and the SNP gained 2 seats (for a total of 6). But the Liberal Democrats overtook the SNP's share of the vote. Both electoral and polling data indicate that Scottish voters are more inclined to support the SNP for elections to the Scottish parliament than to Westminster. Devolution may also have stemmed the rising tide of nationalism.[10] In both 1997 and 2001, the Plaid Cymru won four seats where Welsh is still spoken widely. In 2005, after an absence of eight years, three Conservative MPs were elected in Wales, as the Plaid Cymru lost one seat.

How can we come to terms with the May 2005 election? All three major parties could claim some kind of victory, but also had to face elements of failure. Blair secured an historic third term with a cautious campaign, riding a strong economy and improvements in education and health care—and recurrent images of Gordon Brown by his side—to victory. But the election nevertheless left Blair humbled, his majority slashed, his support often grudging. New Labour won by putting off tough decisions—on pension reform, public spending, climate change, Europe, and a timetable for the withdrawal of British troops from Iraq. They won, too, by locking in the middle of the electoral sentiment. They are perfectly positioned: slightly center-right on security and immigration, and slightly center-left on the economy and social policy.

Hence, the other parties couldn't lay a glove on Blair or New Labour on the core issues that drive domestic politics. The Conservatives had little to say about the government's solid economic record or about the war in Iraq (which they supported, whatever criticisms they might muster about Blair's credibility). They played the race card. As *The Economist* put it, their campaign was an "unseemly scramble for the anti-immigrant vote." The Tories could take solace in the fact that they had a net gain of 33 seats, but Michael Howard's hasty departure made it obvious that the campaign was a failure.

As in 2001, one of the most significant features of the 2005 election was the growing importance of the Liberal Democrats. They enjoyed a net gain of 11 seats. Perhaps more importantly, their share of the popular vote rose to an impressive 22 percent. On the down side, like Howard, Kennedy could not chip away at Labour's dominant position on the core economic and social policies. But he benefited from a consistent and articulate opposition to the war in Iraq. This paid dividends especially in constituencies with a strong presence of students or Muslims. As noted above, the hopes of Liberal Democrats to parlay this strong showing into a strong role in opposition and improved electoral prospects in the future soon faded.

Political Culture, Citizenship, and Identity

FOCUS QUESTION

British political cultural was once characterized by trust, pragmatism, and deference to authority. How would you characterize British culture today?

In their classic study of the ideals and values that shape political behavior, political scientists Gabriel Almond and Sidney Verba wrote that the civic (or political) culture in Britain was characterized by trust, deference to authority, and pragmatism.[11] Looking back, the 1970s appear as a crucial turning point in British political culture and group identities.

During the 1970s, the long years of economic decline culminated in economic reversals in the standard of living for many Britons. Also for many, the historic bonds of occupational and social class grew weaker. Both union membership and popularity declined. At the same time, a growing number of conservative think tanks and mass-circulation newspapers worked hard to erode support for the welfare state. New social movements such as feminism, antinuclear activism, and environmentalism, challenged basic tenets of British political culture. Identities based on race and ethnicity, gender, and sexual orientation gained significance. Thus, a combination of economic strains, ideological assaults, and changes in the social fabric of the country fragmented the political map and inspired a shift to the right.

Thatcher's ascent reflected these changes in political culture, identities, and values. To the extent that the Thatcherite worldview took hold (and the record is mixed), its new language and ethos helped transform the common sense of politics and redefined the political community. It rejected collectivism, the redistribution of resources from rich to poor, and state responsibility for full employment. Thatcherism considered individual property rights more important than the social rights claimed by all citizens in the welfare state. Thus Thatcherism set the stage in cultural terms for the new Labour consolidation of neoliberalism and the core political-cultural orientation in Britain.

Social Class

One of the key changes in political culture in Britain in the last quarter-century has been the weakening of bonds grounded in the experience of labor. During the Thatcher era, the traditional values of "an honest day's work for an honest day's pay" and solidarity among coworkers in industrial disputes were characterized as "rigidities" that reduced productivity and competitiveness. New Labour has continued to characterize social class as an impediment to competitiveness.

As many have noted, "tough on the unions" is a core premise of New Labour. This has contributed to a fundamental erosion of the ability of working people in the United Kingdom to improve their lot through collective bargaining or to exert influence over public policy through the political muscle of the trade union movement. Class still matters in the United Kingdom, but not in the dominating way that it did in the nineteenth century or in the collectivist era. It explains only about 2 percent of voting behavior.

Class still matters, but fewer workers are in unions (in December 2006 the rate of union membership for all workers in the UK was down to 25.8 percent), and unions are focused narrowly on the enforcement of individual legal rights in the workplace. Collective bargaining has been largely relegated to declining private sector industries and the public sector.[12] Strike rates in the UK have generally been below the average of both the OECD and the EU in the last decade, although there are some notable exceptions. For example, a lengthy dispute between local governments and their employees over pension rights produced a massive one-day strike in March 2006, involving between 400,000 (the estimate by employers) and one million (the estimate by union officials) workers.

The sources and relative strength of diverse group attachments have shifted in Britain in recent decades. Decolonization has created a multiethnic Britain. The fragmentation of the experiences of work makes an us-versus-them model of class interest seem outdated. National identity has become especially complicated. At the same time, gender politics has emerged as a hot-button issue.

Citizenship and National Identity

Questions about fragmented sovereignty within the context of the EU, the commingled histories of four nations (England, Scotland, Wales, and Ireland/Northern Ireland), and the interplay of race and nationality in postcolonial Britain have created doubts about British identity that run deep. Ethnicity, intra-UK territorial attachments, and the processes of Europeanization and globalization are complicating national identity. It is becoming increasingly difficult for UK residents automatically to imagine themselves Britons, constituting a resonant national community. Can Britain foster a more inclusive sense of British identity?

Ethnicity

Britain is a country of tremendous ethnic diversity. Nearly 8 percent of the people who live in Britain are of African, African-Caribbean, or Asian descent. There is the growing reality on the ground of life in a multiethnic society. The authors of a recent commission report on multiethnic Britain explained: "Many communities overlap; all affect and are affected by others. More and more people have multiple identities—they are Welsh Europeans, Pakistani Yorkshirewomen, Glaswegian Muslims, English Jews and black British. Many enjoy this complexity but also experience conflicting loyalties."[13]

While there are many success stories, ethnic minority communities have experienced police insensitivity, problems in access to the best public housing, hate crimes, and accusations that they are not truly British if they do not root for Britain's cricket team. In addition, harsh criticism is directed at immigrants and asylum seekers. Since this criticism comes in the wake of intense scrutiny of the Muslim community after September 11, it contributes to the alienation of the ethnic minority community, particularly some groups of Muslim citizens. Especially since the terror attacks by British Muslims in London in July 2005, ordinary law-abiding Muslims have experienced intensified mistrust and intimidation. But it is also true that Muslim university graduates are assuming leading roles in the professions and that more than 160 Muslim city councilors have been elected.

Gender

Historically, the issues women care about most—child care, the treatment of part-time workers, domestic violence, equal pay, and support for family caregivers—have not topped the list of policy agendas of any political party in Britain. Has New Labour significantly changed the equation?

On balance, Labour does well among women voters less because of any specific policies and more because it has made the effort to listen to concerns that women voice. Labour stalwarts insist they have addressed key concerns that women (and men) share concerning health care, crime, and education. They

Gender and Generation Gaps and Trends

The issue of a gender gap in voting behavior has long been a mainstay of British electoral studies. From 1945 to 1992, women were more likely than men to vote Conservative. In addition, since 1964 a gender-generation gap has become well established and was very clear in the 1992 election. Among younger voters (under thirty years old), women preferred Labour, while men voted strongly for the Conservatives, producing a fourteen-point gender gap favoring Labour; among older voters (over sixty-five years old), women were far more inclined to vote Conservative than were their male counterparts, creating a gender gap of eighteen points favoring the Conservatives.

The modest all-generation gender gap that favored the Tories in 1992 (6 percent) was closed in 1997 as a greater percentage of women shifted away from the Conservatives (11 percent) than did men (8 percent). As a result, women and men recorded an identical 44 percent tally for Labour. The gender-generation gap continued, however, with younger women more pro-Labour than younger men and the pattern reversing in the older generation. Moreover, one of the most striking features of the 1997 election was the generational dimension: the largest swing to Labour was among those in the age group eighteen to twenty-nine years (more than 18 percent), and among first-time voters; there was no swing to Labour among those over age sixty-five.*

After the 2001 election, analysis pointed to a generation gap in turnout. BBC exit polls revealed that young voters had the lowest turnout, most often saying the election "didn't matter." The home secretary worried aloud that youth had "switched off politics." Polling data tend to confirm the impression that there is a gender gap in the connection between citizens and mainstream politics, and that younger Britons are more divorced from politics than older ones. Three-quarters of young people aged fifteen to twenty-four have never met their local councilor, compared with just over half of those aged fifty-five or older. Also, older citizens are more than twice as likely to say that they know the name of their local councilor (46 percent compared with 20 percent of fifteen- to twenty-four-year-olds).†

That said, the unprecedented participation of British youth in the massive antiwar protests in February and March 2003 tells a different story—one of young people with strong political views and an unexpected taste for political engagement. A BBC poll of schoolchildren in February 2003 reported that 80 percent opposed the war, while Britain as a whole was more evenly divided. As part of a coordinated day of antiwar protests, thousands of teenagers across the country walked out of school and congregated in city centers, while some five hundred protested at the Houses of Parliament. "What's shocking isn't their opposition but the fact they're doing something about it," noted one electronic journalist on a youth-oriented website. "Considering that most 18–25 year olds couldn't even be bothered to put a cross in a box at the last general election this is a pretty big thing."‡ It was a big enough thing that New Labour strategists were left to ponder the consequences, knowing that the mobilization of support among young people, which was already a cause for concern, was likely to become more difficult in the aftermath of the war in Iraq.

What are the gender and generational storylines in Blair's historic third electoral victory in May 2005? The most talked about theme regarding youth was their continued disaffection from electoral politics. According to MORI, Britain's highly regarded political polling organization, only 37 percent of the possible 18–24-year-old voters turned out to vote in

*Pippa Norris, *Electoral Change in Britain Since 1945* (Oxford: Blackwell, 1997), pp. 133–135; Pippa Norris, "A Gender-Generation Gap?" in Pippa Norris and Geoffrey Norris, eds., *Critical Elections: British Parties and Voters in Long-Term Perspective* (London: Sage, 1999).

†Market & Opinion Research International, "Many Councillors 'Divorced' from the Electorate," April 30, 2002, www.mori.com/polls/2002/greenissues.shtml.

‡David Floyd, "British Youth Oppose 'Bomber Blair,'" WireTap, March 28, 2003; www.wiretapmag.org/story.html?StoryID=15505.

continued

continued

2005 (down from 39 percent in 2001). But this is only one side of the generational story. The other side is that the "gray vote" rose. Voters 55 and older made up 35 percent of the electorate in 2005 (up 2 percent from 2001), and since 75 percent voted, they represented 42 percent of those casting ballots. As for women—they delivered a very big chunk of Blair's majority.

While men split evenly between Conservatives and Labour an identical 34 percent (and 23 percent for the Lib Dems), women swung decisively to Labour, giving them a 10 percent advantage over the Conservatives (32 percent to 22 percent).[§] ❖

[§]Robert Worcester, "Women's Support Give Blair the Edge," *Guardian Unlimited*, May 8, 2005, http://politics.guardian.co.uk/election/story/0,15803,1479238,00.html#article_continue.

point with pride to the policy directions spurred by the Social Exclusion and Women's units; to the implementation of a national child-care strategy; to policies intended to help women to balance work and family commitments; and to the creation of women-only shortlists in 2005 for candidates to compete in safe Labour constituencies.

As a result, New Labour has obliterated the old gender gap in which women favored the Conservatives. It has begun to establish a new pro-Labour women's vote. This may be particularly significant, for its ability to mobilize young women (and more than a few young men, too). These developments are discussed in detail in "Gender and Generation Gaps and Trends on page 85."

FOCUS QUESTION

What would you consider the three most significant expressions of social protest in contemporary Britain?

Interests, Social Movements, and Protests

In recent years, partly in response to globalization, political protest has been on the rise. Protesters demand more accountability and transparency in the operations of powerful international trade and development agencies. London became the site of protests timed to correspond with the Seattle meeting of the World Trade Organization (WTO), which generated some 100,000 protesters in November 1999.

The intensity of environmental activism has taken off with the growing attention to genetically modified (GM) crops in the late 1990s. A newly radicalized movement worried that long-term consumption of GM food might be harmful. It also worried that GM crops—"Frankenstein food"—might cross-pollinate with "normal" plants. This captured the popular imagination. In November 1999, the government announced a ban on commercially grown GM crops in Britain.

In a movement that galvanized the country and raised critical questions about Blair's leadership, massive demonstrations that cut across constituencies and enjoyed huge popular support erupted in September 2000 to protest high fuel prices.

A quite different kind of activism spread to the countryside among a population not usually known for political protest. Farmers had been badly hurt by the "mad cow disease" crisis and saw an urban bias at play in New Labour and the growing threat to fox hunting. They launched massive protests and, even after a law banning the hunt went into effect in 2005, they kept up the heat with legal challenges.

On the far more significant matter of war in Iraq, a series of antiwar rallies were held in London. In September 2002, a huge protest rally was organized in London, led by the Stop the War Coalition and the Muslim Association of Britain. It was one of Europe's biggest antiwar rallies. Another antiwar rally in mid-February 2003 challenged Blair's stand on Iraq with at least 750,000 demonstrators.

Both within the United Kingdom and among observers of British politics and society, many still endorse the view that British culture is characterized by pragmatism, trust, and deference to authority. This may be true, but the persistence of a wide range of protest movements tells a rather different story.

Summary

When we look at representation and participation in Britain we see very clearly that even in perhaps the most enduring democracy in the world that there is much flux, uncertainty, and room for improvement. In institutional terms the declining sovereignty of parliament leaves open the prospect of an unchecked "UK presidency." A two-and-a-half party system produces stable electoral results, but also produces a built-in bias that grants a tremendous premium to the dominant party in any election and leaves the Liberal Democrats on the outside looking in—wishing for a close election in which no party has majority control of the Commons.

More broadly, Britain is grappling with diverse identities. It is not easy for Britons across the national, ethnic, gender, and class distinctions to preserve a sense of shared fates and common heritage. The divisions are reflected in the upsurge of protests across the political spectrum. Particularly in the context of massive unease over the war in Iraq and the uncertainty about the future of multiethnic Britain—and the future leadership of the country— things are more unsettled in Britain than people have come to expect.

SECTION 5 British Politics in Transition

The 1920 partition of Ireland (which separated the six counties that comprise Northern Ireland and are part of the UK from the rest of Ireland) left a legacy of mistrust and violence between the unionist Protestants, and the Catholic republicans (those who wanted an independent and unified Ireland). One of the longest festering religious, ethnic, and nationalist struggles in the world, the sectarian strife in Northern Ireland killed more than 3,500 people between 1966 and 1999, bedeviled the governments of Britain and Ireland, and shocked the conscience of the world.

At last, in the fall of 1994, cease-fire declarations made by the Irish Republican Army (IRA) and the Protestant paramilitary organizations renewed hope for a peace settlement in Northern Ireland. Then, in a dramatic new development in early spring 1995, British prime minister John Major and Irish prime minister John Bruton jointly issued a framework agreement, inspiring mounting optimism about a political settlement.

With his 1997 landslide victory, Tony Blair had political capital to spend. He invested a chunk of it on peace in Northern Ireland. Blair arranged to meet Gerry Adams, president of Sinn Fein, the party in Northern Ireland with close ties to the IRA—and shook his hand. He was the first prime minister to meet with a head of Sinn Fein since 1921.

Under deadline pressure imposed by Blair and the new Irish prime minister, Bertie Ahern, and thirty-three hours of around-the-clock talks, an agreement was reached on Good Friday 1998. It specified elections for a Northern Ireland assembly, in which Protestants and Catholics would share power. It also called for the creation of a North-South Council to facilitate "all-Ireland" cooperation on matters such as economic development, agriculture, transportation, and the environment. Both parts of Ireland voted yes in May 1998 in a referendum to approve the peace agreement. It appeared that a new era was dawning in Northern Ireland.

Handshake or not, violent turf battles within and between each camp have created fear and repeated crises in the peace process. In 2001, the IRA began disarming under the sponsorship of third-party diplomats, and yet violence rose despite cease-fires by paramilitary groups. In 2002, home rule government was suspended, and British direct rule was reimposed. On numerous occasions, Tony Blair and his Irish Republic counterpart, Bertie Ahern, pledged to redouble efforts to get Northern Ireland's faltering peace process back on track, but progress was not easy.

In January 2005 hopes for a settlement were dashed by the blockbuster announcement that linked the IRA to a $40 million bank robbery. In February, Robert McCartney, a Sinn Fein supporter, was brutally murdered by IRA members in a Belfast bar. McCartney's murder, the wall of silence the IRA imposed on some 70 witnesses, and the IRA's offer to kill the men responsible, had significant political repercussions. Despite the May 2005 election, which ousted Unionist moderate David Trimble and strengthened the hands of the more radical parties (Sinn Fein and Democratic Unionist Party), the increasingly vocal popular demands for an end to sectarian violence finally broke the deadlock. By mid-2005, the IRA had exhausted its leverage. Gerry Adams seemed ready to press for their dissolution, and—despite denials—insiders spoke of a pending settlement or even a secret deal all but agreed.

At long last, although as always in Northern Ireland, there would be detours and complications, the optimism was well founded. In March 2007, Gerry Adams and Ian Paisley, leader of the Democratic Unionist Party, sat at the same table for the first time, declaring that they would work together in a power-sharing government in Northern Ireland. This was a hard-earned crowning achievement for Prime Minister Blair, supported by chancellor Brown's commitment to a handsome "peace dividend" (a financial package of some $100 billion over a ten-year period to support development and public services, reduce

As Tony Blair beams, and Irish prime minister Bertie Ahern shows the fatigue of a very lengthy set of negotiations, sworn enemies Martin McGuinness and Ian Paisley stand side-by-side, ready to assume responsibilities as first ministers in a historic power-sharing government in Northern Ireland. *(Source: AFP/Getty Images)*

poverty and social exclusion, and spur business initiatives). In May 2007, the unimaginable came to pass. Devolution was restored to Northern Ireland. Ian Paisley became first minister of Northern Ireland and Martin McGuinness the deputy first minister and the Northern Ireland executive, although highly dependent on budgetary transfers from the UK central government, took over responsibility for regional development, health, and education.

As Ian Paisley put it in almost biblical terms on the day the power-sharing arrangement was launched, "Northern Ireland has come to a time of peace, when hate will no longer rule." Let us hope that the decades of sectarian strife ("The Troubles") in Northern Ireland are well and truly over—and nearly everyone thinks they are.

Indeed, the success in Northern Ireland was quickly heralded as the crowning achievement in Blair's legacy. Within hours of Blair's departure as prime minister, he was appointed as a Middle East envoy working on behalf of the United States, Russia, the EU, and the UN. As Blair turned his attention to the Middle East, Gordon Brown found his in box at 10 Downing Street overflowing.

FOCUS QUESTION

What do you consider New Labour's greatest achievements? What unfinished agenda items will challenge Blair's successors?

Political Challenges and Changing Agendas

As our democratic idea theme suggests, no democracy, however secure it may be, is a finished project. Even in Britain, with its centuries-old constitutional settlement and secure institutional framework, issues about democratic governance and citizens' participation remain unresolved.

Constitutional Reform

Questions about the role of the monarchy and the House of Lords have long been simmering on Britain's political agenda. "Why is the House of Commons not sovereign?" wondered one observer somewhat caustically. "Why does it have to share sovereignty with other, unelected institutions?"[14] In addition, the balance of power among constitutionally critical institutions raises important questions about a democratic deficit at the heart of the Westminster model. Britain's executive easily overpowers parliament. Its strength in relation to the legislature may be greater than in any other Western democracy. Add to these concerns the prime minister's tendency to bypass the cabinet on crucial decisions and the bias in the electoral system that privileges the two dominant parties.

Many Britons have raised questions about the accountability of the British government to its citizens and have pressed for constitutional reforms. In fact, in the heady days after Blair's 1997 election victory, amidst talk of an expanding array of constitutional reforms, it was commonplace to suggest that constitutional reform might become New Labour's most enduring legacy. But the reform agenda has been sidetracked in several areas or slowed to a crawl. For example, the Freedom of Information Act was passed in 2002, but a second stage of implementation only began in January 2005. It was also weakened by the extensive range of information it permitted ministers to withhold and by its limited provision for independent review of such ministerial decisions.[15] The Blair government began to implement far-reaching reforms of Parliament, including the removal of the right of most hereditary peers to speak and vote in the House of Lords and the redesign of the historic upper chamber. But the form of the new upper chamber has yet to take shape. In addition, the European Convention on Human Rights has been incorporated into UK law. More controversially, plans have been announced for the creation of a "supreme court," but strenuous opposition in both chambers has clouded the prospects for passage.

Despite these uncertainties, the significance of constitutional reform should not be overlooked. The power-sharing initiatives in Northern Ireland and arrangements between Westminster, the Welsh Assembly, and the Scottish Parliament represent basic modifications of UK constitutional principles. Devolution implies both an element of federalism and some compromise in the historic parliamentary sovereignty at the heart of the Westminster model. The potentially unsettling consequences feared by some have not come to pass, but neither is stability certain. In August 2007, Alex Salmond, leader of the Scottish National Party (SNP) and first minister in Scotland, promised to introduce legislation that, if passed, would likely lead to a referendum on Scottish independence by 2010.

New Labour's constitutional reform agenda confirms that even long-standing democracies face pressures to narrow the gap between government and citizens. At the same time, the relatively limited results and slowed pace of reforms, are an important reminder that democratic changes are not easy.

Identities in Flux

The relatively small scale of the ethnic minority community limits the political impact of the most divisive issues concerning collective identities. It is probably in this area that rigidities in the British political system most severely challenge tenets of democracy and tolerance. Given Britain's single-member, simple-plurality electoral system and no proportional representation, minority representation in Parliament is very low. There are deep-seated social attitudes that no government can easily transform.

The issues of immigration, refugees, and asylum still inspire a fear of multiculturalism among white Britons. Finger pointing at the Muslim community has intensified since September 11. Government policy has hardened on asylum, refuge, and immigration. By the spring of 2004, race, immigration, and asylum issues were even stealing headlines from the war in Iraq. By the start of the election campaign in April 2005, nearly one-quarter (23 percent) of the British people ranked immigration and asylum as the single most important issue facing the nation. This was nearly double the percentage who thought health care (13 percent) was the biggest issue. A strong majority thought that laws on immigration should be tougher (nine out of ten supporters of the Conservatives, but also six out of ten Labour supporters).[16]

Since the London bombings by British Muslims on 7/7 that killed 56 people, intense scrutiny has been focused on the Muslim community, which faces endless finger pointing and harassment. According to police, the number of hate crimes primarily affecting Muslims soared 600 percent in the weeks after bombings. There were 269 hate-motivated attacks in the three weeks following the bombings, compared to 40 in the same time period in 2004. In October 2006, Jack Straw, a highly visible MP and former foreign minister, sparked a controversy and angered Muslim groups, when he said that the full facial veil worn by some Muslim women had become a "visible statement of separation and difference"—and urged them to remove the veil when they came to see him in his constituency office in Blackburn. Then, in 2007, Salman Rushdie, whose book, *The Satanic Verses,* had offended many Muslims around the world and forced him into hiding in the face of a formal death threat from Iranian religious leaders, was knighted by the Queen. The honor accorded Rushdie was widely held to be an affront to the Muslim community in Britain. There is increasing concern across the political spectrum that Britain needs to find a way to deepen the ties of shared political culture and values that hold society together as well as to ensure security. Achieving this result—which is very different from making the economy run smoothly—is undoubtedly one of Gordon Brown's (and Britain's) greatest challenges.

How about other dimensions of collective identity? The situation is fluid. In political terms, the gender gap has tilted quite strongly toward Labour, as it has responded to concerns about women's employment, the disparate impact of social policy, the problems of balancing family and work responsibilities, and parliamentary representation. The electoral force of class identity has declined almost to the vanishing point in Britain. By Labour's second term and into the third, however, the country faced an upsurge in industrial action. Public sector workers such as local government staff and firefighters have led the unrest. A new generation of militant leaders in two railway unions, the postal workers' union, and the government and health workers' union has created new challenges for the government. Any downturn in the economy will likely intensify union militancy and create significant challenges for Gordon Brown.

British Politics, Terrorism, and Britain's Relationship with the United States

In the immediate aftermath of the terror attacks on the United States, Blair's decisive support for President Bush struck a resonant cord in both countries and (despite some grumbling) boosted Britain's influence in Europe. But by the spring and summer of 2002, Blair's stalwart alliance with Bush was looking more and more like a liability.

As Britons' instinctive support for America after September 11 faded, many wondered whether Tony Blair had boxed himself into a corner by aligning himself too closely with George W. Bush, without knowing where the president's foreign policy initiatives might lead in the Middle East and Asia—and in a host of policy areas from trade policy to the conduct of the continuing campaign in Afghanistan, to global warming, to the International Criminal Court. Yet, throughout the diplomatic disputes in the run-up to war in early 2003, Blair persevered in his staunch support for Bush's decision to go to war—this despite Blair's strong preference for explicit Security Council authorization for the use of force and his strong preference that significant progress in resolving the Israeli-Palestinian dispute be made before any military intervention to topple the Saddam Hussein regime.

Nonetheless, despite his inability to achieve either of these preferences, Blair refused all advice (including advice from members of his cabinet as well as his chief of defense staff) to make support of the war conditional on achievement of these ends. Blair was convinced that the threats of weapons of mass destruction (WMDs), Al Qaeda terrorism, and rogue states justified the invasion of Iraq and that Britain should and must support the United States in its leadership of a global war against terrorism. Despite initial denials by the prime minister, most Britons instinctively drew a connection between the war in Iraq and the bombs that exploded in London on 7/7. Britons who displayed enormous resolve in the face of terrorism were shaken by a set of troubling revelations—first, that the July 7th bombers were all British and, second, after a botched bombing attempt two weeks later, that London police had shot and killed an innocent man on a subway. Thus, the repercussions of Iraq continued.

There can be no doubt that when Tony Blair came to office as a modernizer offering a "third way" alternative to the tired Tory and Old Labour recipes for governing the economy, no one anticipated that he would leave office likely to be remembered most (especially in America) for his foreign policy, once the die was cast and the special relationship with the United States became the defining feature of Blair's government after 9/11. It is in Gordon Brown's interest to distinguish his premiership from Blair's in this regard and in his early months as prime minister, he began to do just that—by providing an accelerated schedule for withdrawing British troops from Iraq and through his key foreign policy appointments. As noted above, Brown appointed Mark Malloch Brown, a vociferous critic of the UK's role in the war in Iraq as a high profile minister with broad international affairs responsibilities. More importantly, Brown appointed David Miliband as foreign minister, a young rising star in the party who is known to have reservations about aspects of Blair's policy in the Middle East—and Miliband was quick to pledge his commitment to "patient as well as purposeful diplomacy," a signal that issues of development and climate change would be very high on the agenda and recourse to use of force more distant. At the same time, Brown quickly made clear that useful lessons could be learned from the experience of the war in Iraq, leaving few in doubt that he would be reluctant to repeat such an exercise anytime soon.

FOCUS QUESTION

What are the implications of New Labour's domestic model? What is its role in the world of states?

British Politics in Comparative Perspective

Until the Asian financial crisis that began in 1997, it was an axiom of comparative politics that economic success required a style of economic governance that Britain lacks. Many argued that innovation and competitiveness in the new global economy required the strategic coordination of the economy by an interventionist state. Interestingly, however, the United Kingdom escaped the recession that plagued the rest of Europe for much of the 1990s. Britain is outperforming most major world economies. It exhibits a good overall performance with low unemployment and inflation and steady growth. Britain is not an economic paradise, but there is cause for continued optimism, despite persistent poverty, weak investment, problems with productivity, trade imbalances, and the first run on a bank in over 100 years.

In many countries throughout the world, politicians are looking for an economic model that can sustain economic competitiveness while improving the plight of the socially excluded. New Labour's third way—a political orientation designed to transcend left and right in favor of practical and effective policies—has been carefully watched for more than ten years. Observers have seen in New Labour a historic intellectual and political realignment, not only in Britain, but in Clinton's America, Cardoso's (and later Lula's) Brazil, even as it was refashioning Schroeder's Germany in its own image and, in time, drawing others, such as Nigeria's Obasanjo into its orbit.

At the annual Labour Party conference in September 2007, the mood was unusually upbeat. The Blair-Brown feuds seemed a distant memory and Labour supporters felt good about the way the new prime minister had handled a set of crises that tested his early leadership, from attempted terror attacks in London and Glasgow, to horrible flooding that displaced thousands in the north of

England, to an outbreak of foot and mouth disease in cattle that created havoc for farmers in the south of England, to the collapse of one of the premier banks that provided mortgages to increasingly worried homeowners. Suddenly, with Gordon Brown at the helm, New Labour was on the upswing and the country was buzzing with talk about an early election to give Brown a proper mandate. Then, even more suddenly, Brown appeared to get cold feet and dropped plans for a snap election (none is required until spring 2010 and none now expected until 2009). The resurgent Tories made much of Brown's retreat, putting the new prime minister on the defensive not only on the timing of an election but on his decision to sign the EU reform treaty in October 2007 without committing the UK to a referendum (a promise made by Blair, before the EU constitutional treaty was rejected by French and Dutch voters in 2005).

If the third way can be sustained, through the transition from Blair to Brown, despite these setbacks, it seems destined to be even more widely emulated and assume considerable historic significance in comparative perspective. If not, for the first time in a long time, real two-party competition seems likely to return to British politics.

Summary

In the early years, it seemed that Blair and New Labour would be evaluated on the third way—and on those terms, Blair's premiership must be viewed as a notable success. But then came 9/11 and the war in Iraq, which have cast Blair's domestic successes in shadow and raised a larger comparative question. Is it time to recognize that models of government must be interpreted as much for their role in the world of states as for their efforts to govern the economy? And in those terms the record is more mixed and more controversial. A politician of convictions, Blair asserted a leading role for Britain in world affairs. His doctrine of international community raised the profile—and raised the ante—on foreign policy, as Blair took leading roles in Kosovo, Afghanistan, and Iraq. But all these missions—and especially Iraq—remain controversial. In addition Blair was never able to resolve the historic ambivalence in Britain's relationship to Europe or persuade the majority of Briton's that the "special relationship" with the United States has adequately served British national interests. For these reason's Blair's legacy is mixed, and Gordon Brown is given much of the credit for steady and sustained economic growth and the general success of New Labour and third way politics. Upon taking over as prime minister, Brown sent clear signals that his premiership will advance a more patient and less strident foreign policy. Can Brown build on his domestic policy successes as chancellor and, at the same time, find a successful formula for advancing British foreign policy interests in a purposeful and more multilateral approach? If so, he will become a formidable prime minister; and, if not, he may be little more than a footnote in the history of New Labour, as John Major was to Thatcherism.

Key Terms

Industrial Revolution
hegemonic power
welfare state
special relationship
laissez-faire
macroeconomic policy
Westminster model
neoliberalism
Keynesianism
monetarism
gender gap
foreign direct investment
parliamentary sovereignty
parliamentary democracy
unitary state
fusion of powers
cabinet government
constitutional monarchy
quangos
judicial review

Suggested Readings

Allen, Graham. *The Last Prime Minister: Being Honest About the UK Presidency.* London: Imprint Academic, 2003.

Beer, Samuel H. *Britain Against Itself: The Political Contradictions of Collectivism.* New York: Norton, 1982.

Coates, David. *Prolonged Labour.* London: Palgrave/Macmillan, 2005.

Coates, David, and Joel Krieger. *Blair's War.* Cambridge, UK, and Malden Mass.: Polity Press, 2004.

Coates, David, and Peter Lawler, eds. *New Labour in Power.* Manchester: Manchester University Press, 2000.

Cook, Robin. *The Point of Departure.* London: Simon & Schuster, 2003.

Cronin, James E. *New Labour's Pasts.* Harrow, UK: Pearson/Longman, 2004.

Driver, Stephen, and Luke Martell. *New Labour*, 3rd. ed. Cambridge: Polity, 2006.

Dunleavy, Patrick, et al. *Developments in British Politics* 7. New York: Palgrave/Macmillan, 2003.

Gamble, Andrew. *Between Europe and America: The Future of British Politics.* London: Palgrave/Macmillan, 2003.

George, Bruce. *The British Labour Party and Defense.* New York: Praeger, 1991.

Giddens, Anthony. *The Third Way: The Renewal of Social Democracy.* Cambridge: Polity Press, 1998.

Gilroy, Paul. *"There Ain't No Black in the Union Jack": The Cultural Politics of Race and Nation.* Chicago: University of Chicago Press, 1991.

Hall, Stuart, and Jacques, Martin, eds. *The Politics of Thatcherism.* London: Lawrence and Wishart, 1983.

Hobsbawm, E. J. *Industry and Empire.* Harmondsworth, UK: Penguin/Pelican, 1983.

Howell, Chris. *Trade Unions and the State: The Construction of Industrial Relations Institutions in Britain, 1890–2000.* Princeton: Princeton University Press, 2005.

Kampfner, John. *Blair's Wars.* London: Free Press, 2003.

Kavenagh, Dennis, and Anthony Seldon. *The Powers Behind the Prime Minister: The Hidden Influence of Number Ten.* London: Harper-Collins, 1999.

Keegan, William. *The Prudence of Mr Gordon Brown.* Chichester: John Wiley & Sons, 2004.

King, Anthony, ed. *Britain at the Polls, 2001.* New York and London: Chatham House, 2002.

Krieger, Joel. *British Politics in the Global Age. Can Social Democracy Survive?* New York: Oxford University Press, 1999.

Krieger, Joel. *Globalization and State Power.* New York: Pearson Longman, 2005.

Landes, David S. *The Unbound Prometheus: Technological Change and Industrial Development in Western Europe from 1750 to the Present.* Cambridge: Cambridge University Press, 1969.

Lewis, Jane, and Rebecca Surrender, eds. *Welfare State Change: Towards a Third Way?* Oxford: Oxford University Press, 2004.

Lewis, Philip. *Islamic Britain: Religion, Politics and Identity among British Muslims.* London and New York: I. B. Taurus, 2002.

Marsh, David, et al. *Postwar British Politics in Perspective.* Cambridge: Polity Press, 1999.

Marshall, Geoffrey. *Ministerial Responsibility.* Oxford: Oxford University Press, 1989.

Middlemas, Keith. *Politics in Industrial Society: The Experience of the British System Since 1911.* London: André Deutsch, 1979.

Modood, Tariq. *Multicultural Politics: Racism, Ethnicity, and Muslims in Britain.* Minneapolis: University of Minnesota Press, 2005.

Norris, Pippa. *Electoral Change in Britain Since 1945.* Oxford: Blackwell Publishers, 1997.

Parekh, Bhiku, et al., *The Future of Multi-Ethnic Britain: The Parekh Report.* London: Profile Books, 2000.

Riddell, Peter. *The Thatcher Decade.* Oxford: Basil Blackwell, 1989.

Särlvik, Bo, and Ivor Crewe. *Decade of Dealignment: The Conservative Victory of 1979 and Electoral Trends in the 1970s.* Cambridge: Cambridge University Press, 1983.

Seldon, Anthony, and Dennis Kavanagh, eds. *The Blair Effect 2001–5.* Cambridge: Cambridge University Press, 2005.

Shaw, Eric. *The Labour Party Since 1945.* Oxford: Blackwell Publishers, 1996.

Thompson, E. P. *The Making of the English Working Class.* New York: Vintage, 1966.

Thompson, Noel. *Political Economy and the Labour Party*, 2nd ed. London and New York: Routledge, 2006.

Notes

[1]Gail Lewis, "Black Women's Employment and the British Economy," in Winston James and Clive Harris, eds., *Inside Babylon: The Caribbean Diaspora in Britain* (London: Verso, 1993), pp. 73-96.

[2]Women & Equality Unit, What is the Pay Gap and Why does it Exist?" http://www.womenandequalityunit.gov.uk/pay/pay_facts.htm.

[3]See Philip Norton, *The British Polity*, 3rd ed. (New York: Longman, 1994), p. 59, for a useful discussion of the sources of the British constitution.

[4]Stephen Haseler, "Britain's Ancien Régime," *Parliamentary Affairs* 40, no. 4 (October 1990): 415.

[5]See Kevin Theakston, "Ministers and Civil Servants," in Robert Pyper and L.J. Robins, eds., *United Kingdom Governance* (London: Palgrave Macmillan, 2000), pp. 39-60.

[6]See Stephen Driver and Luke Martell, *New Labour, 2nd ed.* (Cambridge, England: Polity, 2006), pp. 125–129.

[7]Tony Blair, "Doctrine of the International Community," speech to the Economic Club of Chicago, Hilton Hotel, Chicago, April 22, 1999. For a detailed discussion of the speech and its implications for the war in Iraq, see David Coates and Joel Krieger, *Blair's War* (Malden, Mass.: Polity Press, 2004), chap. 6.

[8]See Stephen Driver and Luke Martell, *New Labour*, 2nd ed (Cambridge, England: Polity Press, 2006), pp. 8–9.

[9]Ivor Crewe, "Great Britain," in I. Crewe and D. Denver, eds., *Electoral Change in Western Democracies* (London: Croom Helm, 1985), p. 107.

[10]John Bartle, "Why Labour Won—Again," in Anthony King et al., eds., *Britain at the Polls, 2001* (New York: Chatham House, 2002), p. 171.

[11]See Gabriel A. Almond and Sidney Verba, *The Civic Culture: Political Attitudes and Democracy in Five Nations* (Princeton, N.J.: Princeton University Press, 1963); Almond and Verba, eds., *The Civic Culture Revisited* (Boston: Little, Brown, 1980); and Samuel H. Beer, *Britain Against Itself: The Political Contradictions of Collectivism* (New York: Norton, 1982), pp. 110–114.

[12]See Chris Howell, *Trade Unions and the State* (Princeton University Press, 2005), esp. Ch 6.

[13]Bhiku Parekh et al., *The Future of Multi-Ethnic Britain: The Parekh Report* (London: Profile Books, 2000), p. 10.

[14]Stephen Haseler, "Britain's Ancien Régime," *Parliamentary Affairs* 40, no. 4 (October 1990): 418.

[15]Iain Byrne and Stuart Weir, "Democratic Audit: Executive Democracy in War and Peace," *Parliamentary Affairs* 57, no. 2 (2004): 453–468.

[16]MORI, "State of the Nation," 10 April 2005 (http://www.mori.com/pubinfo/rmw/state-of-the-nation.html).

Official Name:	French Republic (*République Française*)
Location:	Western Europe
Capital City:	Paris
Population (2007):	63.7 million
Size:	634,427 sq. km.; slightly smaller than Texas

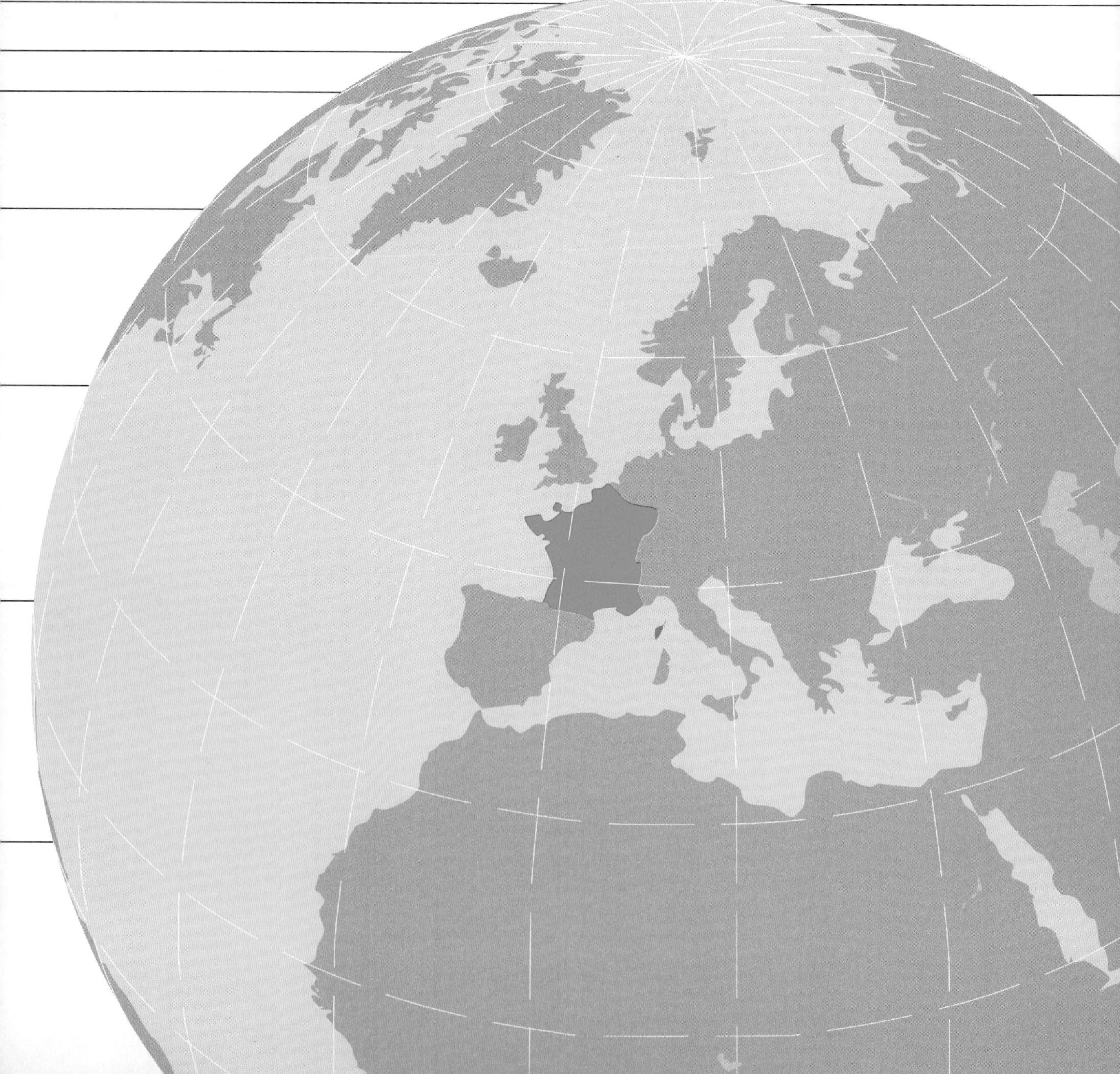

CHAPTER

3 France

Mark Kesselman

Chronology of Modern France's Political Development

Until 1789	1789–1799	1800–1814	1814–1830	1830–1848
Ancien régime (Bourbon monarchy)	Revolutionary regimes Constituent Assembly, 1789–1791 (Declaration of Rights of Man, Aug. 26, 1789) Legislative, 1791 Convention, 1792–1795: Monarchy abolished and First Republic established, 1792 Directory, 1795–1799	Consulate and First Empire (Napoleon Bonaparte)	Restoration	July Monarchy

SECTION 1

The Making of the Modern French State

FOCUS QUESTION

If you had been an adviser to Ségolène Royal, what advice might you have offered to improve her chances of winning the 2007 presidential election?

conservative the belief that existing political, social, and economic arrangements should be preserved.

socialist the doctrine stating that the state should organize and direct the economy in order to promote equality and help low-income groups.

Politics in Action

In many ways, May 2, 2007, was like any other spring day in France. And yet in one way it was very different from most others. Streets were deserted. So too were cafés, movie theaters, and restaurants. Why did France come to a halt on May 2? The reason is that a majority of French were glued to their television sets watching the only debate of the presidential campaign.

The stakes were high. According to polls, only a few percentage points separated **conservative** front-runner Nicolas Sarkozy from **Socialist** Ségolène Royal. If "Ségo" could outperform "Sarko"—or provoke him into losing his proverbially bad temper—the debate could tip the balance and alter the outcome of the election.

Unlike American presidential debates, the two candidates confronted each other directly. The result was some sharp-edged drama. As the underdog and a woman, Royal had the harder job. She needed to demonstrate that she possessed the authority and technical competence to become the first female president of France. But Sarkozy also had challenges to overcome. He needed to remain cool under fire. Further, he was the hard-line candidate of the major conservative party, and his party was the dominant party in the unpopular outgoing government. He had to demonstrate solidarity with less fortunate citizens. He also needed to persuade voters that he would make a fresh start in attacking France's ailing economy.

When the debate finally ended—it ran well over the allotted two hours—polls reported that a majority of French judged that Sarkozy was the winner. And this opinion translated into a 53 to 47 percent majority for Sarkozy in the election several days later.

Three factors explain the outcome. First, Royal was often misinformed on some basic issues involving domestic and foreign policy. Further, she dodged tough questions, for example, how she planned to finance her reform proposals. Sarkozy provided clear, persuasive, and no-nonsense answers to questions. Second, Sarkozy was supported by France's best-organized and unified party, the Union for a Popular Majority (UMP). He had been president of the UMP

1848–1851	1852–1870	1871	1871–1940	1940–1944	1946–1958	1958–Present
Second Republic	Second Empire (Louis Napoleon)	Paris Commune	Third Republic	Vichy regime	Fourth Republic	Fifth Republic

for years, and the party was solidly behind him. By contrast, many Socialist Party leaders and members gave Royal's candidacy only lukewarm support. Worse, Royal created her own campaign organization and kept the Socialist Party at arm's length. The reason was that she was involved in a bitter personal dispute with the party's director—the man who, not coincidentally, was her longtime partner. (Right after her defeat, she announced that they were separating.) Finally, a majority of voters preferred Sarkozy's vision of where he wanted to lead France. He proposed encouraging private market forces and individual initiative, rewarding hard work, deregulating the economy, downsizing government, and cracking down on crime. Royal proposed maintaining state social services and helping the needy. But she did not explain how she would revive France's ailing economy, in particular, how her program would create jobs to bring down France's distressingly high unemployment.

Will Sarkozy succeed in implementing his vision in coming years? When previous right-wing politicians proposed similar reforms, the result was nationwide protests and stalemate. To understand why, we need to study how the four major themes of *Introduction to Comparative Politics* have combined to form the exceptional pattern of French politics (see Table 3.1).

Geographic Setting

FOCUS QUESTION

What are France's favorable geographic and natural features?

France is among the world's favored countries, thanks to its temperate climate, large and fertile land area, and prosperous economy. Its natural beauty and superb architecture, culture, and cuisine make France the most popular tourist destination in the world.

France occupies a key position in Europe. It borders the Mediterranean Sea in the south and shares borders with Belgium, Switzerland, and Germany on the north and east. Spain lies to the southwest, Italy to the southeast. With a population over 60 million, France is one of the most populous countries in Western Europe. However, because of its large size—211,000 square miles—population density is low (about half that of Britain, Germany, and Italy).

France has a modern and productive economy. Most people work in the industrial and service sectors. No other French city rivals Paris, the capital, in size and influence. Lille, Lyon, and Marseille are the only other large cities in France.

TABLE 3.1

Political Organization

Political System	Unitary republic. Semipresidential system; popularly elected president, popularly elected parliament, and prime minister and government appointed by president and responsible to National Assembly (as well as informally responsible to president).
Regime History	Frequent regime changes since the French Revolution of 1789. Most recently, a dictatorial regime based on Vichy collaborated with the Nazis during World War II; the Fourth Republic existed from 1946 to 1958; and the Fifth Republic, originating in 1958, has become universally accepted.
Administrative Structure	Unitary, with 22 regions and 100 departments.
Executive	Dual executive: president (five-year term); PM appointed by president, generally leader of majority coalition in National Assembly, and responsible to National Assembly (as well as informally responsible to president).
Legislature	Bicameral. Senate (upper house) has power to delay legislation passed by lower house and to veto proposed constitutional amendments. National Assembly (lower house) can pass legislation and force government to resign by passing a censure motion.
Judiciary	A system of administrative, criminal, and civil courts. At the top, a nine-member independent Constitutional Council named for nonrenewable nine-year terms; president of republic names three members, president of each house of parliament names three. The Constitutional Council exercises right of judicial review.
Party System	Multiparty. Principal parties: Socialist Party (PS); Union for a Popular Movement (UMP); minor parties: National Front (FN); Communist Party (PCF); Green Party; and many others throughout the political spectrum.

The country's gross domestic product (GDP) is nearly $2 trillion and per capita income is $30,000. Virtually all families have a telephone, most have at least one cell phone, and four-fifths own an automobile.[1] Over half of all families own their own home. France ranked sixteenth among the 177 countries of the world included in the 2006 United Nations Development Programme's Human Development Index.

At the same time, the French have a well-earned reputation for being critical—both of others and themselves! For example, a survey examining citizen happiness around the world reported that France ranks only 64th out of 178 countries studied—far below the United States (23rd), Germany (35th), and Britain (42nd).[2]

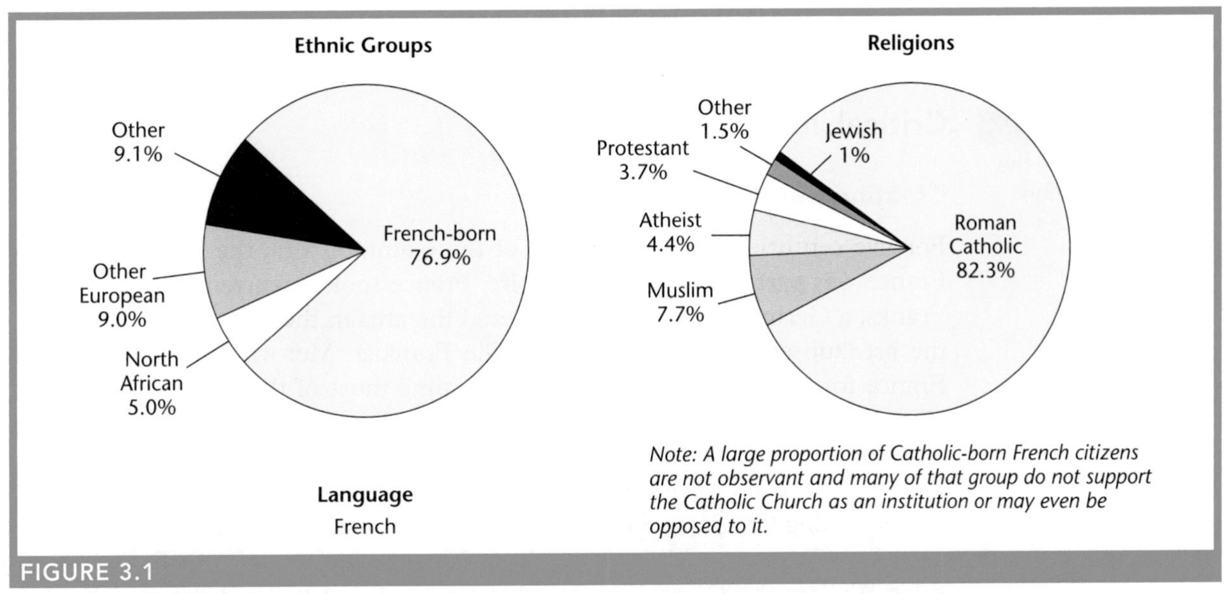

FIGURE 3.1

The French Nation at a Glance

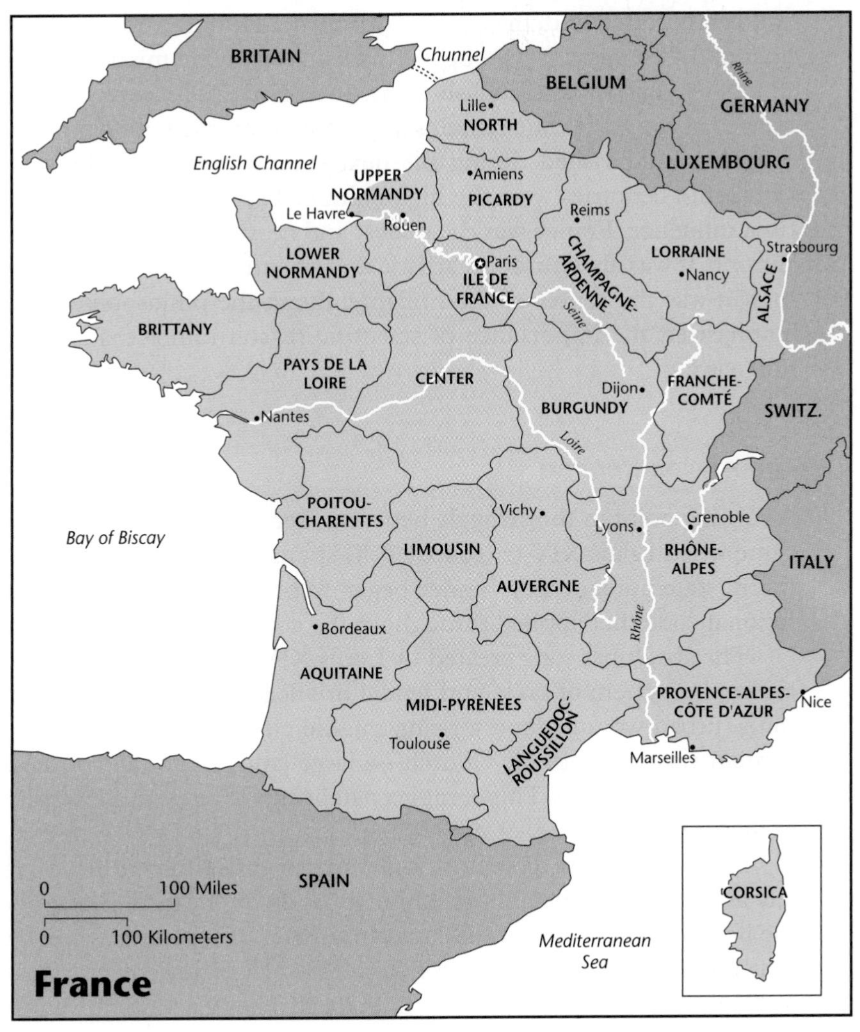

FOCUS QUESTION

What impact did the French Revolution have on France's later political development?

Critical Junctures

Creating Modern France

For five centuries at the beginning of the Common Era, the area that is now France was part of the Roman Empire. France took its current name from the Franks, a Germanic tribe that conquered the area in the fifth century AD, after the breakup of the Roman Empire. The Frankish Merovingian dynasty ruled France for several centuries. During this time most of the population became Christian. The Merovingians were succeeded by the Carolingian dynasty. Its most famous ruler, Charlemagne, became Holy Roman emperor in 800 CE and dominated much of Western Europe.

Following Charlemagne's death in 814, the empire disintegrated. Norsemen from Scandinavia established a duchy in Normandy, in northwest France. Their ruler, William the Conqueror, invaded England in 1066 and defeated English troops at the Battle of Hastings. During the next two centuries, French monarchs struggled to subdue powerful provincial rulers and groups. The English invaded, and nearly conquered, the country during the Hundred Years' War (1337–1453). Joan of Arc, a peasant who believed she had a divine mission, led French forces to victory against the English army. Joan herself, however, was captured and burned at the stake. She remains a symbol of intense national pride.

France flourished during the next several centuries. The seventeenth and eighteenth centuries were the high point of French economic, military, and cultural influence. France was the richest and most powerful country in continental Europe. It was also Europe's artistic and scientific capital. In the eighteenth century, it was the center of the Enlightenment, the philosophical movement that emphasized the importance of scientific reason rather than religious belief or folk wisdom.

The Ancien Régime

A turning point in the struggle between French monarchs and provincial rulers came when Louis XIV (r. 1643–1715) sponsored the creation of a relatively efficient state bureaucracy. France began to be administered according to a legal-rational code that applied throughout the country.

The absolutist state created by Louis XIV and his successors coexisted with a complex system of taxes and feudal privileges that weighed heavily upon peasants, urban workers, and a rising middle class. Another target of popular discontent was the Catholic Church—a large landowner, tax collector, and ally of the feudal authorities. This complex patchwork of institutions was later described as the ***ancien régime***, or old regime.

ancien régime the monarchical regime that ruled France until the Revolution of 1789, when it was toppled by a popular uprising.

From the mid-seventeenth to the mid-eighteenth century, France was usually at war with its neighbors. Unfortunately for France, Britain began to reap the benefits of the Agricultural and Industrial Revolutions while France's economy remained stagnant. As a result, the French monarchy was forced to borrow and raise taxes to compete with Britain. These economic burdens weighed especially heavily on peasants, urban workers, and members of the middle classes. In 1789, a violent reaction toppled the French monarchy and entire regime.

The Two Faces of the French Revolution, 1789–1815

revolution the process by which an established political regime is replaced (usually by force and with broad popular participation) and a new regime established that introduces radical changes throughout society.

republic in contemporary usage, a political regime in which leaders are not chosen on the basis of their inherited background (as in a monarchy).

secularism a doctrine that mandates maintaining a separation between church and state.

The Revolution of 1789 was a *political* and a *national* **revolution**. It installed a **republic** to replace the French monarchy. This meant that political offices were filled on the basis of individual talent rather than inheritance. It was an *international* revolution. It inspired national uprisings elsewhere in Europe, often promoted by French armed intervention. It was *liberal*. It championed individual liberty in the political and economic spheres, as well as **secularism** and religious freedom. It was *democratic*. It proclaimed that all citizens have the right to participate in key political decisions.

The revolutionary regime proclaimed liberty, equality, and fraternity. But it treated opponents brutally, beheading many at the guillotine. The revolution's refusal to compromise and its hostility toward organized religion, especially the Catholic Church, divided French society.

While the revolution toppled the *ancien régime*, it strengthened state institutions. Under the Emperor Napoleon Bonaparte, the brilliant revolutionary general who seized control of the state and ruled from 1799 to 1814, state institutions were created that survive to this day. Ever since the revolution, France has struggled to reconcile state autonomy—the state's independence from groups within society—with democratic participation and decision making.

Many Regimes, Slow Industrialization: 1815–1940

Between 1815 and 1958, a series of short-lived, unstable regimes ruled France. The most durable was the Third Republic. It was created after France's defeat in the Franco-Prussian War and a civil war that followed in 1871. Ever since then, democratic republics have ruled France, save for a brief period during World War II.

While during the nineteenth century regimes came and went at a dizzying pace, economic change in France was gradual. Unlike Germany, France chose economic stability over modernization. In 1800, France was the world's second economic power. By 1900 it trailed the United States, Great Britain, and Germany. The entrepreneurial spirit was relatively underdeveloped. French manufacturers excelled in custom-made luxury goods, like silk and porcelain. But these did not lend themselves to mechanized production. There were no mass markets for them. The French population grew quite slowly. This meant smaller demand and less incentive for businesses to invest.

State policies also generally aimed to assure stability. To shield farmers, manufacturers, and artisans from foreign competition, France maintained some of the highest tariff barriers in Western Europe in the nineteenth and early twentieth centuries.

The state did promote economic modernization in some respects, however. In the 1860s, it organized an efficient rail network. The government also encouraged the formation of an investment bank to finance railroad development.

Slow economic growth did not prevent political conflict. But it did contribute to France's humiliating defeat by Germany in 1940—the second such defeat in less than a century. Further, although France was on the winning side in World War I, it suffered immense losses of people and property.

Vichy France (1940–1944) and the Fourth Republic (1946–1958)

Germany overran France in 1940. Philippe Pétain, an aged World War I military hero who was prime minister at the time, destroyed the Third Republic by signing an armistice with Hitler that divided France into two. The North was under German occupation. Pétain led a regime in central and southern France that was a puppet of Nazi Germany. (It is often called the Vichy regime, since its capital was Vichy, a city in central France.) The Vichy regime collaborated with the Nazis by repressing French opposition to the Nazi regime and sending French workers to work in German factories. It was the only political regime in Western Europe that targeted Jews in areas not directly under German occupation. It rounded up about 76,000 French and foreign Jews, including 12,000 children, and sent them to Nazi death camps.

In 1945, following the Nazi defeat, the first order of business was to create a political regime for newly independent France. Charles de Gaulle, a general who had opposed the Vichy regime and led the French Resistance movement, took the lead. He considered that France's moral decline and military defeat was due to the lack of a powerful independent executive. With the memory of the **authoritarian** Vichy regime still fresh, French citizens voted to reject de Gaulle's proposal to create a regime based on strong executive leadership. He abruptly retired from politics.

authoritarianism a system of rule in which power depends not on popular legitimacy but on the coercive force of the political authorities.

The Fourth Republic (1946–1958), created after de Gaulle's departure, embodied an extreme form of parliamentary rule and weak executive. The constitution gave parliament a near monopoly of power. However, parliament was often hopelessly divided because of the large number of parties that held seats. One reason for this fragmentation was that elections to parliament were held on the basis of **proportional representation**, in which parties are awarded seats in proportion to the votes that they receive. This system compares with the single-member district first-past-the-post system used in the United States and Britain, where the party with the most votes in a given district wins the seat in that district. The single-member district system tends to favor larger parties and usually reduces the total number of parties represented in parliament. In the Fourth Republic, the many parties in parliament usually agreed on little more than dislike of the current government. As a result, they voted governments out of office about once every six months! The new regime did, however, help to reverse a century of economic stagnation by promoting economic expansion and modernization. Despite the waltz of governments, the Fourth Republic might have survived were it not for two failed attempts to hold onto France's colonial empire. First, in the 1950s, the army was unable to subdue communist forces in Vietnam that opposed France's colonial domination. Even more damaging was that the army failed to end a rebellion in Algeria, a large territory in North Africa

proportional representation (PR) a system of political representation in which seats are allocated to parties within multi-member constituencies, roughly in proportion to the votes each party receives.

that France considered part of mainland France. As the war in Algeria dragged on, some army officers threatened to invade mainland France and topple the republic. De Gaulle persuaded parliament to vote him back to power and to replace the Fourth Republic with a new regime with strong executive leadership. The Fifth Republic was created in 1958 and has lasted until now. Although periodically shaken by crises, it is relatively stable and will probably endure well into the future.

The Fifth Republic (1958 to the Present)

The Fourth Republic was all talk and no action. In the Fifth Republic, political leaders can act decisively. Too decisively, many scholars believe—the regime lacks adequate mechanisms to hold leaders accountable.

Eventually, de Gaulle's high-handed governing style provoked widespread opposition. In May 1968, students and workers engaged in the largest general strike in Western European history. Although de Gaulle regained control of the situation, he was discredited. He resigned the following year. No other president since then has rivaled de Gaulle's national and international standing.

"What!?? The president's a Socialist and the Eiffel Tower is still standing!??" "Incredible!" *(Source: Courtesy Plantu, Cartoonists and Writers Syndicate/Cartoon Arts International, Inc., from Le Monde)*

The conservative forces that took power in 1958 won every single national election until 1981. Finally, economic stagnation and divisions among conservative groups brought Socialist Party candidate François Mitterrand to power. The peaceful transition that followed demonstrated that the Fifth Republic was sturdy enough to accommodate political alternation.

The Socialist government governed in a fully democratic manner to sponsor ambitious reforms broadening state control of the economy. The centerpiece was a substantial increase of industrial firms, banks, and insurance companies in the public sector. The Socialist experiment provoked a crisis in 1983–1984, however. Political opposition became so fierce, and the reforms so costly, that Mitterrand reluctantly pulled back. Socialist governments since then have resembled conservative governments in pursuing market-friendly policies. Governments of left and right alike now agree on the need to limit inflation, budget deficits, and the public debt.

2002: The Le Pen Bombshell

Beginning in 1981, there were frequent alternations in power between governments of the center-left and center-right. The 2002 presidential elections promised to be no different. Instead, however, it revealed deep fissures in French society.

Le Monde's cartoonist compares Le Pen's attack on Chirac and Jospin to the bombing of the twin towers of the World Trade Center. *(Source: Courtesy Plantu, Cartoonists and Writers Syndicate, Cartoon Arts International, Inc., from Le Monde, April 23, 2002)*

Two rounds of elections are usually required to select a French president. Many candidates compete at the first ballot. If no candidate gains an absolute majority (over 50 percent)—the typical case—a runoff ballot is held between the two front-runners. When the 2002 election campaign opened, everyone expected that Lionel Jospin, the Socialist prime minister on the center-left, and Jacques Chirac, the conservative president on the center-right, would face off in the decisive runoff ballot. Chirac did come in first, as expected. However, to everyone's amazement a far-right candidate named Jean-Marie Le Pen nudged Jospin out of second place. Le Pen was a demagogue whose targets include Muslim immigrants, Jews, and mainstream politicians.

Nearly all supporters of Jospin and other leftist candidates swung behind Chirac in the runoff. Chirac trounced Le Pen 82 to 18 percent. But the troubling results of the first round of voting continue to raise questions about the quality of French democracy.

Five years later, in 2007, another presidential election occurred. The memory of Le Pen's success in 2002 was still fresh. Many more voters turned out to vote in 2007 than had voted in 2002. This time, Le Pen received only 10.5 percent of the first ballot vote and came in fourth. Did Le Pen perform less well because voters rejected his appeal to get tough on immigration and crime? Probably not. The main reason was probably that Nicolas Sarkozy, the candidate from the mainstream center-right party, echoed some of Le Pen's themes, such as the need to crack down on crime, limit immigration, and respect traditional conservative values. Voters may have calculated that since Sarkozy had a good chance to be elected, voting for him would be the most effective way to achieve these goals.

France after September 11

France has the largest Muslim population in West Europe. Following the terrorist attacks of September 11, 2001, the country has been deeply involved in conflicts of global politics. Although France has energetically targeted terrorism, it has strongly criticized U.S. policies. France supported the U.S. military action against Al Qaeda and the Taliban regime in Afghanistan in 2001. But it condemned the U.S. invasion of Iraq in 2003. For several years, relations between the two countries were frosty. However, the election of Nicolas Sarkozy, who has expressed great admiration for the United States, marked a turning point in relations between the two countries. When Sarkozy addressed a joint session of Congress in 2007 and lavishly praised the United States, he was given a standing ovation. Although policy differences between France and the United States will certainly arise in the future, a new era of cooperation has begun.

The French "Non"—Now or Forever?

France has traditionally been among the leading countries seeking closer cooperation among European Union (EU) countries. In 2005, France again took the lead—but this time in an opposite fashion. After two years of difficult negotiations, a commission produced an EU constitution. It streamlined decision making, increased the influence of the European parliament, and created the offices of EU president and foreign minister. EU regulations require that all member states approve changes in the EU's organization and powers. Ten member states had approved the draft constitution and no country had rejected it when French citizens voted on the constitution in a **referendum** in May 2005. However, voters turned down the constitution by 55 to 45 percent. Many French, especially those out of work, in low-paying jobs, and fearful of losing their jobs, blamed the EU for their difficulties. They were especially likely to oppose the constitution.

referendum an election in which citizens are asked to approve (or reject) a policy proposal.

Soon after President Sarkozy was elected in 2007, he tried to revive the process of European integration. Along with German Chancellor Angela Merkel, he tried to persuade other EU member states to adopt a scaled-down version of the constitution. If the plan is implemented, it will simplify EU decision making. It may also contribute to promoting economic growth within EU member countries and strengthening Europe's role on the world stage.

Themes and Implications

FOCUS QUESTIONS

What are two ways in which French political and economic patterns are distinctive?

To what extent and how have these patterns changed in recent years?

Historical Junctures and Political Themes

Analyzing the four themes that frame *Introduction to Comparative Politics* reveals dramatic changes and troubling questions about recent French politics.

France in a World of States. Although a middle-rank power, France is an important player on the world stage. It is one of the five permanent members of the UN Security Council. It has developed nuclear weapons and sophisticated military technology. It is among the world's richest, industrialized countries.

The French state has helped the country adapt to global economic competition. In recent decades, the state promoted internationally acclaimed high-tech industrial projects. It has developed high-speed rail transport. It has led the

The world's longest and tallest multispan bridge; Millau, France. *(Source: Chris Hellier/Corbis.)*

European consortium that developed the Airbus wide-bodied airplane. France also generates relatively safe and cheap nuclear-powered electricity. In 2004, the world's tallest and longest multispan bridge opened for traffic in Millau, in central France. (See photo above.) These projects may, however, represent the end of a wave of state-sponsored direction and innovation. This pattern has been called **statism**. International economic competition, EU and other treaty commitments, ideological shifts, and citizens' demands for more autonomy have resulted in a decline of the state's role in economic management.

statism the doctrine that advocates firm state direction of the economy and society.

Governing the Economy. Statism flourished after World War II. Thanks to state planning, loans and subsidies to private business, and crash programs to develop key industries, the French economy was soon rebuilt after World War II. The state went on to help modernize the relatively underdeveloped economy. However, top-down state management is less effective in a situation of rapid technological change and economic globalization. Section 2 describes how there has been a painful transition toward the state taking on a more modest role.

The Democratic Idea. France has a complicated relationship to the democratic idea. On the one hand, the statist tradition has an undemocratic aspect. Statism opposes popular participation and decision making because they prevent rational direction by qualified leaders. On the other hand, France has passionately embraced two democratic currents. The first claims that citizens should participate directly in political decisions rather than merely vote to choose leaders. This idea nourishes protest movements like that of May 1968 and more recent ones that are discussed below. A second democratic current rejects direct democracy in favor of representative or parliamentary government.

Politics of Collective Identity. French national identity has always been closely linked to state formation. The Revolution granted citizenship to everyone. But everyone had to accept dominant republican values. The approach stresses that collective identities based on religion, ethnicity, or gender should be confined to the private sphere. They should play no role in the public arena. The French generally believe that multiculturalism threatens republican unity.

At the same time, the French are deeply divided by social, economic, and cultural cleavages, as the EU referendum demonstrated. In addition, ethnic conflict and globalization have recently destabilized national identity. Jean-Marie Le Pen attracted widespread support by charging that Muslim immigrants and their children have caused unemployment, crime, and urban decay. In the past few years there has been a wave of violence by neo-Nazis and Muslim youth directed against French Jews.

Implications for Comparative Politics

French politics offers rich lessons for comparative politics. Scholars have coined the term *French exceptionalism* to highlight that French politics is distinctive. A central feature is intense ideological conflict. This in turn has fueled political instability, illustrated by frequent regime change.

Because France has continually tried to reshape its destiny by conscious political direction, it provides a natural laboratory to test the importance of variations in institutional design. To illustrate, a 1999 constitutional amendment and a law passed in 2000 requires political parties to nominate an equal number of men and women for many political offices. As a result, the number of women elected to municipal and regional councils has soared.

More generally, the French have often looked to the state to achieve important economic and political goals. In countries without a strong statist tradition (for example, the United States and Britain), private groups have to rely on their own efforts. What can we learn from comparing the two approaches?

Summary

France is celebrated for its natural beauty, rich culture, and quality of life. But the country also has a turbulent past, and deep socioeconomic and cultural divisions. For centuries, the state structured French political and social life. However, in recent decades the state has lost its preeminent role. It must now reckon with other powerful forces, including private market forces, international economic and political institutions like the EU, subnational governments, and more autonomous groups in French society. Is the state's more modest role a blessing or a handicap? Does it mean the end of French exceptionalism? Stay tuned!

Political Economy and Development

France has the world's sixth-largest economy. It has accomplished this feat by a combination of skill, state management, and favorable historical and geographic circumstances. After a lengthy period in which the French state played a key role in shaping and steering the economy, there has been a sharp increase in recent decades in the importance of markets and a corresponding decline in the state's role. Accompanying this change has been a shift from an inward-looking economic posture to an export orientation that has transformed France into a major global economic actor. Yet the French economic record is not simply a success story: France has not fared well recently in international global competition, economic benefits are unequally distributed, unemployment is at distressingly high levels, and economic fissures have produced intense political challenges.

FOCUS QUESTION

Why was there pressure to change France's traditional pattern of economic management after World War II?

The New French Revolution

During the nineteenth century, when Britain and Germany were engaged in a sweeping industrial revolution, France was less ambitious. The state's main goal was not to modernize the economy but to preserve traditional groups and contain political conflict. However, the weaknesses of this pattern were cruelly highlighted by the Third Republic's failure to meet the German threat in 1940.

When France was liberated and the Fourth Republic was created in 1946, there was widespread agreement that economic and social modernization was essential. In a few short years, the state helped to transform the French economy and society. One study described the postwar shift as "a new French Revolution. Although peaceful, this has been just as profound as that of 1789 because it has totally overhauled the moral foundations and social equilibrium of French society."[3]

dirigisme a French term denoting that the state plays a leading role in supervising the economy.

FOCUS QUESTIONS

How was the pattern of French economic management that was developed after World War II a break with the past?
How successful was the new pattern?

State and Economy

France's statist tradition of economic management could potentially be of great help in steering the economy toward modernity. But first the state had to shift its stance from guardian of the established order to sponsor of social and economic progress. This approach is called ***dirigisme***, or state direction. Partly as a result of the state's new approach, France was transformed after World War II from a relatively stagnant, rural society, to a dynamic participant in the world economy.

French-Style Economic Management

After World War II, the French developed new techniques of state economic management. The new approach placed heavy emphasis on state direction: *dirigisme*. A principal tool developed to implement the new approach was

indicative planning a term that describes a national plan identifying desirable priorities for economic and social development.

indicative planning. A national Planning Commission of civil servants identified broad national economic and social priorities for the next several years. Successive plans established maximum feasible rates of economic growth and identified social priorities, such as educational targets. They also proposed crash programs to develop particular industries and regions.

In the new scheme, the state was the chief economic player. It financed key industrial sectors. It also encouraged the creation of large firms, called "national champions." This approach is usually viewed as socialist. However, many conservative leaders in France at the time, such as Charles de Gaulle, supported *dirigisme*, as they believed it was the only way to modernize the French economy. In order to accomplish its ambitious goals, the state used the following tools:

- *Subsidies, loans, and tax write-offs.* It provided the bulk of capital for new investment, limited the outflow of French capital, and created semipublic banks for specific industries.
- *Restructuring key sectors.* These included steel, machine tools, and paper products.
- *Creating and managing entire industries.* Some state-created and state-managed firms were world-class. For example, France is a leader in designing, building, operating, and exporting nuclear power installations.

France's Economic Miracle

From 1945 to 1975, France's rate of economic growth was among the world's highest (see Table 3.2). Average yearly income nearly tripled between 1946 and 1962. France leapfrogged into the twentieth century.

TABLE 3.2

Average Growth Rates in Gross National Product, 1958–1973

Country	Rate
Japan	10.4%
France	5.5
Italy	5.3
West Germany	5.0
Belgium	4.9
Netherlands	4.2
Norway	4.2
Sweden	4.1
United States	4.1
United Kingdom	3.2

Source:
Reprinted by permission of the State University of New York Press, from *The Fifth Republic at Twenty* by William G. Andrews and Stanley Hoffmann (Eds).

Students and workers unite in a mass demonstration on the Left Bank of Paris, May 27, 1968. *(Source: Central Press/Getty Images.)*

May 1968 and Beyond: Economic Crisis and Political Conflict

Despite the dramatic economic growth of the 1950s and 1960s, economic change caused political conflict. One reason was the state's highhanded style of authority. This served as a model for a centralized style of leadership in other sectors of French society, such as universities and workplaces. Although the regime seemed stable, massive strikes and demonstrations in May 1968 revealed its weakness.

Economic Instability

New problems developed in the 1970s, when the state-centered approach had difficulty meeting the challenges of technological changes and increased global competition. These developments required economic flexibility and decentralized economic decision making—just the opposite of the centralized style that characterized *dirigisme*.

French Socialism in Practice—and Conservative Aftermath

After twenty-three years of conservative governments, Socialist candidate François Mitterrand was elected president in 1981. The Socialist Party and its allies also gained a majority in elections to the National Assembly (the more powerful legislative chamber). A new era began. The government sponsored an ambitious

France and the European Union

France has been a charter member and one of the most powerful states in the European Union since its creation in 1958. (The EU was originally known as the European Economic Community.) Before World War II, France preferred isolation to international cooperation. But three devastating wars in less than a century between France and Germany taught both countries that there was no alternative but to cooperate. The EU was a resounding success in fostering closer ties between the two countries and the other member states of the organization. (The number of members has steadily increased to twenty-seven by 2007.)

For many years, the EU enjoyed widespread support in France. It was given credit for contributing to economic prosperity and political stability. French farmers received the largest share of the EU's lavish program of agricultural subsidies. The EU helped France develop close economic relations with her West European neighbors. The EU emerged as one of the three major economic regions in the world, along with North America and East Asia.

When economic prosperity turned to stagnation in the 1980s, many began to regard the EU less as a blessing and more as a liability. Voters had a chance to demonstrate their discontent when they were asked to approve the draft EU constitution in 2005. As described in Section 1 above, President Chirac's decision to hold a referendum in France for this purpose proved a major blunder. It came at a time when unemployment in France remained at double-digit levels and when the recent enlargement of the EU was quite unpopular in France. (Polls revealed that, among all EU member countries, French public opinion was the most opposed to enlargement.)

The French vote halted forward movement within the EU. It also revealed a wide chasm between rank-and-file French voters and the governing parties, who lobbied for a yes vote. It took several years for the process of European integration to be revived. ❖

series of measures to revive the economy, create jobs, and recapture domestic markets. It hiked the minimum wage, family allowances, old-age pensions, rent subsidies, and state-mandated paid vacations. It created new jobs in the public sector. The state helped develop cutting-edge technologies in the fields of biotech, telecommunications, and aerospace. A centerpiece of its program was **nationalization**, a program in which the state purchases industrial firms and banks from private stockholders and incorporates them into the public sector. (It might be noted that in foreign policy Mitterrand was very much anti-Soviet and anticommunist.)

nationalization the policy by which the state assumes ownership and operation of private companies.

The Socialist reforms promoted social justice and helped modernize the French economy, society, and state in the long run. But in the short run, they drove France to the brink of bankruptcy. Deficits soared. International investors avoided France. International currency reserves quickly vanished.

The crisis cruelly demonstrated the limited margin of maneuver for a medium-rank power. Mitterrand reluctantly ordered an about-face in economic policy in 1983 and 1984. He set France on the conservative course that all governments since then have followed.

Critics often claim that the French Socialist government's failure in the early 1980s demonstrates that nationally based radical or democratic socialist reforms are futile. Within France, the failure dealt a body blow to the traditional *dirigiste* pattern.

France's Neoliberal Modernization Strategy

neoliberalism a term used to describe government policies that aim to promote private enterprise by reducing government economic regulation, tax rates, and social spending.

privatization the sale of state-owned enterprises to private companies or investors.

deregulation the process of dismantling state regulations that govern social and economic life.

Since 1983, the state has scaled back its commanding role. Its market-friendly "**neoliberal** modernization strategy" includes **privatization, deregulation,** and liberalization.[4] Privatization has involved selling to private investors major firms and industries formerly in the public sector, including banks, utilities, steel producers, and telecommunications companies. Deregulation has reduced the state's role in shaping prices, wage levels, allocation of credit, and production standards. Liberalization has opened the French economy to inward and outward movements of capital and goods.

France's approach to governing the economy is thus becoming similar to that of many other rich capitalist countries, such as Britain. However, while recent French governments have sponsored sweeping reforms to free market forces, they have done so in a distinctively French manner. Political scientist Vivien Schmidt observes that France has not "abandoned its statist model. . . . Governments have not stopped seeking to guide business . . . even as they engineer the retreat of the state."[5] As a result, statism remains alive (if not altogether well) in France.

Assessing French Economic Performance

The French economy faces daunting problems. For a starter, the economy has sputtered badly in recent years. During President Chirac's second term (2002–2007), economic growth was an anemic 2 percent annually. France's slippage among world-class economies is reflected in a declining share of world exports. One reason is that France devotes fewer resources than other leading countries to technological innovation. Other problems include large budget deficits, heavy public debt, and high taxes.

The unemployment rate—9 percent or more for decades—is a national disgrace. Underemployment also weighs heavily on the French economy. The average work week for full-time employed French workers is 39.1 hours, compared to 42.4 hours for British workers, and 40.3 hours for German workers.

In order to reverse economic decline, drastic reforms are needed. Nicolas Sarkozy won the 2007 presidential election because he made a convincing case for further reducing the scope of the state. He advocated unleashing free market forces, shrinking the size of the state, increasing the work week, and increasing the retirement age. Sarkozy's election, along with that of a large conservative parliamentary majority, has enabled him to implement this program. However, it has encountered stiff resistance from groups in French society asked to sacrifice long-standing benefits. And there is a risk that by shrinking and starving the state, Sarkozy will weaken its capacity to promote economic performance.

FOCUS QUESTIONS

What are the principal features of the French social model?

What are its strengths and weaknesses?

Society and Economy

France has among the world's most extensive welfare programs. Cradle-to-grave social services begin with free prenatal care. The state promotes extensive preschool facilities. All students passing a stiff high school graduation exam are entitled to virtually free university education. Extensive public housing and rent subsidies make housing affordable for most citizens. In return for moderate co-payments, most French have coverage for prescription drugs as well as excellent outpatient, specialized, and hospital care. In 2000, the World Health Organization ranked the French health care system first in the world. And the results speak for themselves. Infant mortality rates are about half those in the United States. Life expectancy is 81 years old. No wonder Michael Moore's documentary film *Sicko* (2007) praised the French public health care system so lavishly!

The standard workweek is thirty-five hours, and employees are entitled to six weeks of paid vacation annually. Those who lose their jobs receive unemployment insurance and job retraining. The long-term unemployed can participate in a minimum income program. Many citizens are eligible to retire at age 60, and pensions are nearly equal to retirees' wages or salaries.

This network of extensive social services has been dubbed the French social model. It is driven by the widely shared belief that the state should help all citizens lead healthy, secure lives. Welfare programs are designed to cover most citizens, not only the very poor.

France's sizeable social benefits come with a hefty price tag. The cost of social programs approaches one-third of the French gross domestic product. As the population ages, the costs of social benefits will further increase. Currently, there are three adults who work for every retired worker. By 2050, the ratio will drop to 1.5 employed workers for every retired worker. Critics claim that social spending slows economic growth and discourages job creation. Social mobility is low. Economic inequalities have increased. France's high unemployment has most hurt young adults seeking their first job.

Although benefits are spread broadly, some needy groups fall between the cracks. The French call this pattern of inequality *the social fracture*. On the one hand, two groups are unusually well organized and have obtained extensive social benefits: older citizens and full-time, stably employed workers (especially civil servants). For example, the lion's share of social spending pays for pensions. On the other hand, youth, women, and immigrants and their families receive fewer social benefits and are more likely to be unemployed.

Labor Relations. Stormy relations between management and labor have traditionally damaged French economic performance. Employers have viewed unions as opponents to be kept at bay. Workers have often resorted to strikes and pressured the state to obtain or safeguard gains. The labor movement has historically been quite weak. Yet unions enjoy wide public support beyond their membership. When they organize demonstrations, as has occurred often in recent years to protest proposed government cutbacks in social benefits, citizens turn out by the millions.

Inequality and Ethnic Minorities

France long prided itself on its ability to integrate ethnic minorities. Yet, as will be discussed in Section 4, this openness is flawed. The economic situation of immigrants is significantly more difficult than for native-born French. A

FIGURE 3.2

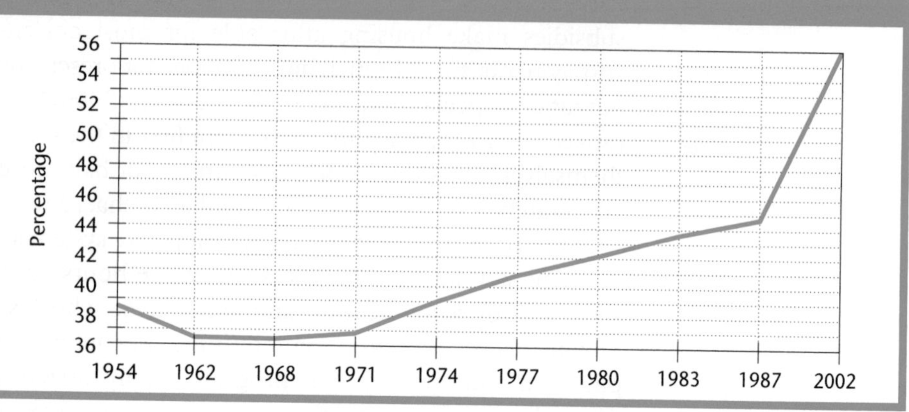

Women in the Labor Force

Source: INSEE, in Louis Dirn, *La Société Française en Tendances* (Paris: PUF, 1990), p. 108; 2002 data from INSEE, *Tableaux de l'Économie Française, 2003–2004* (Paris: INSEE, 2003), p. 77.

dramatic example was provided in a recent research project. Researchers mailed 2,000 applications for job openings using fictitious names and identical CVs. When "Thomas Lecomte" and "Guillaume Dupont" ("traditional" French names) applied for jobs, they received one invitation to a job interview for every 19 applications that were sent. When "Youssuf Belkacem" and "Karim Brahimi" (obviously, Muslim names) applied for the same jobs, they received one invitation to a job interview for every 54 applications.[6]

Inequality and Women

France has been at the forefront of providing social services, such as daycare facilities, that enable women to work outside the home. Mothers are entitled to four to six months of paid maternity leave. Fathers receive two weeks of paid paternity leave. Highly qualified teachers staff daycare facilities whose cost is low thanks to public subsidies. The availability of fine daycare has facilitated an enormous increase in female employment rates in recent decades. Laws mandate gender equality in the workplace and outlaw sexual harassment.

However, French women are far from achieving economic and social equality. France has among the lowest proportion of female managers and administrators of all industrialized countries. The wage disparity between men and women for comparable work is 20 percent.

The Generation Gap

Young adults face particular hardships. They are more than twice as likely as other citizens to be without a job. They are less likely to enjoy the benefits of a generous welfare state. Recent government measures to deregulate labor markets have proved a mixed blessing. Flexibility in scheduling work does encourage new hiring. It is especially helpful for those seeking their first job. But two-thirds of newly hired workers have temporary or part-time jobs. These jobs do not offer long-term stability, and they involve lower levels of wages and fringe benefits.

FOCUS QUESTION

What are the costs and benefits of France's participation in the global economy?

France in the Global Economy

For much of the nineteenth and twentieth centuries, France was relatively isolated from the international economy. It relied on its own resources and on trade with its colonies in North Africa, sub-Saharan Africa, and Asia. High tariff walls limited foreign competition, protected French industry, and limited technological innovation. This cozy (and, for the colonies, exploitative) pattern began to change in the 1960s. France has now become heavily integrated in the wider international economy and a major global economic player.

France and the EU

The bulk of French international trade and investment used to be with the country's former colonies in Asia and Africa. Nowadays, over 60 percent of French imports and exports are with other member states of the EU.

The Franco-German tandem has largely shaped the pace and character of European integration. The EU has helped modernize French and other European economies. In addition, French farmers have received the largest agricultural subsidies of any single group in the EU. This was because farmers are an important interest group within France, and France insisted on its farmers receiving generous help as a condition for promoting the EU.

This pattern is changing recently. The EU's decision to limit budget deficits and state subsidies challenges France's old state-led economic pattern. EU regulations prohibit states from engaging in the kind of *dirigisme* that was the hallmark of the French state in the postwar period. France has had to make greater adjustments in its style of economic management than other member countries.

France and Globalization

France became highly integrated in the global economy in the past several decades. This was an important aspect of the "new French revolution" described at the beginning of this section. Imports and exports account for over half of French GDP. Foreign investors, especially American pension funds, own nearly half of all shares traded on the Paris stock exchange. About one-third of all French workers are employed in firms that are at least partly foreign-owned. France ranks among the world's largest importers and exporters of capital. In 2003, the business magazine *Forbes* compiled a list of the world's four hundred best-performing companies. France was second only to the United States in the number of companies on the list.[7] Yet France's participation in the global economy has caused intense strains in domestic politics because the benefits of economic integration have been unequally divided. In particular, citizens with less education and job skills are more likely to be unemployed or to have lower-paying and part-time jobs. For these groups, the EU and globalization represent a threat rather than an opportunity.

Summary

Following a century of relative economic stagnation, the French economy reinvented itself after World War II. For several decades, the economy soared, and most French benefited. Central to the French economic miracle was a vigorous and effective state. The state proved the ideal agency for sponsoring large-scale industrial projects. State-sponsored development (*dirigisme*) enabled France to become a highly industrialized country.

Eventually, however, the costs of statism began to outweigh its benefits. The state has proved less effective at steering an economy that demands decentralized and flexible decision making. The French increasingly resented the state's highhanded manner. The last attempt at state-sponsored development occurred at the beginning of the Mitterrand presidency in the early 1980s. The failure of those aspects of his reform agenda that extended statism triggered a shift toward a more market-based economy. However, the break with statism has not been complete. Statism continues to play a larger role in France than in most other industrialized capitalist countries.

SECTION 3 Governance and Policy-Making

Charles de Gaulle, founding father of the Fifth Republic did his work well—too well, many now believe. He succeeded in designing the Fifth Republic to enable a strong executive to govern relatively free of parliamentary and other restraints. Yet the result has been an imbalance in power between an unchecked executive and a weak parliament. This is a design flaw in the institutional architecture of the Fifth Republic.

At the same time, fundamental changes in the character of the French state are occurring in three key respects. The first change involves the centralized state. Article 2 of the French constitution specifies, "France is a Republic, *indivisible*, secular, democratic and social." It was generally assumed that an indivisible state meant a centralized state. However, in the 1980s, the Socialist government transferred substantial governmental powers to local, departmental, and regional authorities. In 2003, a conservative government transferred additional powers to subnational governments, and a constitutional amendment was passed affirming the principle of **decentralization**. These changes involved an important reinterpretation of "indivisible." There is now a broad consensus on the value of decentralization. Most agree that the French state is more effective when subnational governments share governmental responsibilities.

decentralization policies that aim to transfer some decision-making power from higher to lower levels of government.

Second, as described in Section 2, the state's relation to the economy has shifted. Although the state continues to have an exceptionally important role, it now consults and persuades more, and commands less.

The third change involves new limits on state action. Until recently, the state that boasts the modern world's second-oldest written constitution (after

The U.S. Connection

The American Presidential System and French Semipresidential System Compared

In a presidential system, such as in the United States, the executive and the legislature are chosen separately. The two branches have independent powers. Neither one selects the other, is directly accountable to the other, or controls the other's agenda. Both institutions have fixed terms in office. This means that neither branch can force the other to resign and face new elections. The legislature can, however, impeach and force the president to resign for treason or other grave misdeeds. The French Fifth Republic has a similar impeachment procedure, although never used. An absolute majority of both houses of parliament must vote articles of impeachment. The case is then judged by a High Court of Justice comprised of twelve deputies and twelve senators elected by the two houses.

In a parliamentary system, the executive and legislature do not have powers independent of each other. The two branches are fused. The government is accountable to parliament and must resign if parliament votes no confidence. At the same time, the government has substantial control over the parliamentary agenda. It can also dissolve parliament, which triggers new elections.

In the Fifth Republic, both the president and parliament are directly elected. Unlike presidential and parliamentary systems, the French system has a dual executive. Two officials direct the executive, the president and the prime minister appointed by the president. As in parliamentary systems, the parliament can force the government to resign (but not the president) by voting no confidence. The French call this a *motion of censure*.

The Fifth Republic is a semipresidential system. The *semi* refers to the fact that the legislature and executive are not wholly separate, as they are in a pure presidential system. The government is responsible to parliament, and the government can dissolve parliament and call new elections. The system is called *semipresidential*, not *semiparliamentary*, because whenever there is deviation from a purely parliamentary or presidential model, the result strengthens the executive. The fusion of executive and legislative powers (as in parliamentary regimes) enables the executive to control the parliamentary agenda and dissolve parliament. In particular, the French parliament cannot vote censure of the president—only the less powerful prime minister.

The most important difference between the American presidential system and French semipresidential system involves executive-legislative relations. American presidents confront a proud, independent, and powerful Congress. Even when Congress is controlled by the same party as the president, senior congressional leaders have their own base of power. Further, elections to Congress occur at fixed intervals: every two years for members of the House of Representatives, every six years for members of the Senate. The president cannot alter this election calendar. Congress is very jealous of its powers. In brief, because both branches of government are independent, agreement occurs not because one branch (that is, the president) commands—but because the two bargain on nearly equal terms. By contrast, the French constitution renders the president powerful and parliament relatively humble and weak. ❖

judicial review the prerogative of a high court to nullify actions by the executive and legislative branches of government that in its judgment violate the constitution.

the United States) did not consider that the constitution should be scrupulously respected. French democratic theory held that because the government is chosen by democratic elections, it should have a free hand to govern. This too has changed. The constitution of the Fifth Republic has come to be regarded as the authoritative source for distributing power among political institutions. And the Constitutional Council has gained the vital power of **judicial review**, that is, the power to nullify legislation and sanction executive actions that it judges to be in violation of the constitution.

FOCUS QUESTIONS

Why is the Fifth Republic described as a semipresidential system?
What challenges has it overcome?

Organization of the State

The Fifth Republic is a semipresidential system. This somewhat unusual pattern combines elements of presidential and parliamentary systems. It was a product of de Gaulle's desire in 1958 to design a system that provided the executive with the power and independence that he believed was absent in the Fourth Republic.

Since the early 1980s, the Fifth Republic has overcome two daunting political challenges. The first was a shift in political control (alternation) between opposing partisan coalitions in 1981, when François Mitterrand defeated conservative incumbent president Valéry Giscard d'Estaing. The second challenge involved divided institutional control, when the president led one political coalition and parliament was controlled by a rival coalition. The French call this ***cohabitation***, or power sharing. Many feared that this would produce stalemate or crisis. The unthinkable finally occurred in 1986. Under François Mitterrand, parliamentary elections produced a conservative majority in the National Assembly. President Mitterrand immediately bowed to political realities by appointing Jacques Chirac, leader of the conservative coalition, to be prime minister. The two seasoned politicians quickly devised workable solutions for governing. As with alternation, cohabitation has occurred several times since then. However, recent changes discussed below mean that it will probably not occur again for many years.

cohabitation the term used by the French to describe the situation in the Fifth Republic when a president and prime minister belong to opposing political coalitions.

FOCUS QUESTION

What are two advantages and two disadvantages of the French executive, in which both the president and prime minister have independent powers?

The Executive

France was the first major country to adopt a semipresidential system. After the fall of communism, Russia was inspired by the French example. Other countries with semipresidential systems include Austria, Finland, Iceland, Pakistan, Portugal, Sri Lanka, and (most recently) Iraq.

The President

Most of the time, the French president possesses even more power than the U.S. president. He has command of the executive branch and is independent of the legislature. Yet he controls parliament's agenda and can dissolve parliament. When the same party coalition has won the presidential and parliamentary elections, we speak of this as united control. At these times, the president is more powerful than the chief executive in virtually any other democratic nation.

The presidency is so powerful because of (1) the towering personalities of Charles de Gaulle, the founder and first president of the Fifth Republic, and François Mitterrand, the Socialist president from 1981 to 1995; (2) the ample powers conferred on the office by the constitution; and (3) political practices of the Fifth Republic.

TABLE 3.3

Presidents of the Fifth Republic

President	Term
Charles de Gaulle	1958–1969
Georges Pompidou	1969–1974
Valéry Giscard d'Estaing	1974–1981
François Mitterrand	1981–1995
Jacques Chirac	1995–2007
Nicolas Sarkozy	2007–present

Presidential Personalities. Charles de Gaulle (1890–1970) was the most influential politician in modern France. As first president in the Fifth Republic, he set the standard for his successors. (Table 3.3 lists the Fifth Republic's presidents and their terms of office.) Thanks to his role as leader of the Resistance in World War II, he enjoyed an immense reservoir of popular support. He put his stamp on the presidential office by firm control of the government, the executive, and the entire political system. The two presidents who succeeded de Gaulle—Georges Pompidou and Valéry Giscard d'Estaing—were not noteworthy. François Mitterrand, who followed Giscard d'Estaing, further expanded presidential powers. Mitterrand was largely responsible for the Socialist government's initial radical reform agenda. He then led its right turn in 1983. He worked closely with German chancellor Helmut Kohl to promote European economic integration and monetary union. Mitterrand was president from 1981 to 1995, the longest term of any president in the Fifth Republic.

Through much of Jacques Chirac's first term as president (1995–2002), he was weakened by having to share power with his opponents. When the Socialist party won the 1997 parliamentary elections, Chirac had to appoint Socialist Party leader Lionel Jospin as prime minister. There were bitter conflicts between the two during this period. Cohabitation proved so unpopular that reforms were adopted that were designed to reduce the chances of cohabitation in the future.

In 2002, cohabitation ended. Chirac was reelected that year and his conservative allies won parliamentary elections. However, Chirac was unable to use this opportunity to exercise bold leadership or achieve noteworthy reforms. He apparently lacked a clear vision of what he wanted to accomplish, and he suffered several important setbacks during his second term in office. He failed to persuade the French to approve the 2005 referendum on the European constitution. And several massive opposition movements in 2005 and 2006, described in Section 5, stymied Chirac's reform efforts.

Will Nicolas Sarkozy, the bold leader elected president in 2007, leave a strong stamp on the presidency and France? The returns are not yet in.

Profile

President Nicolas Sarkozy

© Horacio Villalobos/epa/Corbis

Nicolas Sarkozy, elected president of France in 2007, is an audacious and controversial figure. He was born in Paris in 1955 and is the first president from an immigrant background. His parents were minor nobility who fled Hungary following the communist takeover of the country after World War II. He decided early in life to make politics his career. In 1975, at the ripe age of 20, he gained the attention of then-prime minister Jacques Chirac. Sarkozy was active in the youth movement of Chirac's conservative governing party (what is now the UMP). At a party conference in 1975, Sarkozy was designated to speak for two minutes as a representative of the party's young activists. Instead, he spoke for ten. Chirac was so impressed by Sarkozy's boldness that he invited him to lunch the next day at the prime minister's official residence in Paris!

Sarkozy swiftly rose within the ranks of the UMP. He became mayor of a posh suburb outside Paris at age twenty-eight and was elected to parliament when he was thirty-three. His political career continued to soar when he was appointed a junior minister and official spokesperson for the government five years later. He quickly established a political reputation for making waves by speaking bluntly on issues like crime and immigration in ways that his conservative supporters loved—and liberal opponents hated. At the same time, Sarkozy cultivated senior politicians like Chirac, whose help was invaluable in his rise to power.

As the 1995 presidential campaign approached, Sarkozy seemed destined to be appointed a senior cabinet minister and possibly even prime minister. But at this point he committed two blunders that might have ended his political career. The first occurred during the presidential election of 1995. Rather than supporting the presidential bid of his mentor, Jacques Chirac, Sarkozy backed Edouard Balladur, another conservative politician running for president. Chirac was furious at the betrayal. When he was elected president, he refused to name Sarkozy to the government. From that time, although both men belonged to the same conservative coalition, they became bitter rivals.

Sarkozy's second blunder occurred in 1999, four years after the first one. By that point, he had regained a position of leadership after his downfall in 1995. He was chosen to head the conservative party ticket in elections to the European Parliament that year. However, his party performed terribly, and Sarkozy was held responsible. Once again, he was back in the political wilderness.

That Sarkozy recovered from this second setback is a tribute to his burning ambition, boundless energy, oratorical skill, and knack for championing issues popular with conservative voters. He put these talents to work when he provided Chirac with valuable support during Chirac's successful bid for reelection in 2002. After the election, Sarkozy hoped to be named prime minister. He was clearly itching to gain a platform to succeed Chirac when Chirac retired. However, Chirac had not forgiven the able but erratic Sarkozy for his betrayal in 1995. He appointed Sarkozy to the senior cabinet post of minister of the interior but named a series of other conservative politicians to be prime minister. He hoped one of them could outmaneuver Sarkozy and be elected president when Chirac stepped down. Unfortunately for Chirac, every one failed utterly.

By early 2007, Sarkozy had the conservative field to himself. He easily gained his party's nomination as president and had only one other hurdle to clear: the presidential race itself. By outperforming his major opponent in 2007, Socialist candidate Ségolène Royal, Sarkozy finally gained the supreme prize in French politics. In his first year in office, President Sarkozy used the powers of the presidency to the hilt. He announced major policy initiatives, was a constant presence on television, and treated the prime minister as his personal assistant. An unanswered question is whether he will achieve his reform agenda or provoke a backlash that might destabilize France. ❖

The Constitutional Presidency. The constitution of the Fifth Republic endows the president with the ceremonial powers of head of state. He (there has not yet been a female president) resides in the resplendent Élysée Palace, in a fashionable section of Paris and represents France at international diplomatic gatherings. The fact that the president is the only political official directly chosen by the entire French electorate provides him with an enormous resource.

To run for president, one must be a French citizen at least twenty-three years old. Presidents serve a five-year term. There are no limits to how many terms a president can serve. There is no vice president in France. If a president dies in office, the president of the Senate (the upper house of parliament) acts as interim president. A new presidential election is held within a short time.

A two-ballot system of election is used for presidential elections. To win on the first ballot, a candidate must obtain an absolute majority (over 50 percent) of those voting. If no candidate receives a first-ballot majority—the case in every presidential election to date—a runoff election is held two weeks later to choose between the two front-runners.

The constitution grants the president the following political powers:

- The president names the prime minister, approves the prime minister's choice of other cabinet officials, and names high-ranking civil, military, and judicial officials.
- The president presides over meetings of the Council of Ministers (the government). Note that the constitution entrusts the president, not the prime minister, with this responsibility.
- The president conducts foreign affairs, through the power to negotiate and ratify treaties. He also names French ambassadors and accredits foreign ambassadors to France.
- The president directs the armed forces. A 1964 decree also granted the president exclusive control over France's nuclear forces.
- The president may dissolve the National Assembly and call new elections.

- The president appoints three of the nine members of the Constitutional Council, including its president. He can also refer bills passed by parliament to the Council to determine if they conform to the constitution.
- Article 16 authorizes the president to assume emergency powers in a grave crisis. The only time this power has been used was when de Gaulle faced a military uprising.
- Article 89 authorizes the president, with the approval of the prime minister, to propose constitutional amendments. To be passed, an amendment must be approved by both chambers of parliament, and then ratified either by a national referendum or by a three-fifths vote of the two houses of parliament meeting together as a congress.
- Article 11, amended in 1995, authorizes the president to organize a referendum to approve important policy initiatives or reorganize political institutions. (This procedure is distinct from the process of amending the constitution—which, as we have just seen, may also involve calling a referendum.)
- Article 5 directs the president to be an arbiter to ensure "the regular functioning of the governmental authorities, as well as the continuance of the State." The precise meaning of this clause is unclear. But the president is the sole official delegated these awesome responsibilities.

The Political President. The constitution creates a powerful office on paper. But a president must translate formal powers into actual influence. Presidential leadership hinges on whether the president commands a parliamentary majority. As we will see, the president's powers are enormously greater when his coalition controls the government and parliament.

The Prime Minister and Government

The constitution authorizes the president to appoint the prime minister. Prime ministers are usually named from the ranks of the senior politicians of the major party in the coalition with a majority in the National Assembly. This ensures parliamentary support for the prime minister and government. The prime minister in turn nominates, and the president appoints, members of the cabinet or government, a collective body under the prime minister's direction.

The reason why it matters so much for a president to enjoy a majority in parliament is that the constitution designates the government, not the president, as the preeminent policy-making institution. Article 20 states that the government "shall determine and direct the policy of the nation. It shall have at its disposal the administration and the armed forces." Article 21 authorizes the prime minister to "direct the action of the government. He [the prime minister] is responsible for national defense. He assures the execution of the laws." Thus, when prime ministers accept the president's leadership, they do so because of *political dynamics* rather than *constitutional directive*.

The relationship between the president and prime minister is a key element in the Fifth Republic. The relationship changes dramatically between periods of unified control, when the president and prime minister are political allies, as opposed to periods of cohabitation, when the two are political opponents. When the president can rely on the support of a parliamentary majority, he can name a political ally as prime minister. The result has been undisputed presidential supremacy. Loyal and effective prime ministers can provide the president with important political assets: parliamentary support for the government's policies, sympathetic media treatment, and experience in directing the state bureaucracy.

During cohabitation, the balance shifts from open displays of cooperation between president and prime minister to open displays of rivalry. Since the constitution designates the prime minister as in charge of policy-making, the president must assume the mantle of dignified and ceremonial head of state. The prime minister moves front and center to assume responsibility for leadership.

The most recent experience of cohabitation, in 1997–2002, provoked an important institutional reform. When the Socialists and their allies won the 1997 parliamentary elections, Jacques Chirac, who had been elected president only two years earlier, was forced to name Socialist leader Lionel Jospin as prime minister. Cohabitation lasted five long years—and proved highly unpopular. An attempt was made to prevent a repeat performance by reducing the president's term from seven to five years, the same length as that of the National Assembly. By holding elections for the two branches at about the same time it is probable that the same political coalition will win both elections. Nicolas Sarkozy won the presidency in 2007, and his political allies won a majority in the National Assembly. Thus, cohabitation will probably not occur again before 2012.

To summarize the complex relationship between president and prime minister: during periods of unified control, presidents have used their formal and informal powers to the hilt. Prime ministers are very much second in command. At these times, presidents have assumed the power, assigned to the prime minister by the constitution, to shape policy in virtually any domain they choose. The prime minister is responsible for translating general policies into specific programs and supervising the implementation of policy. At these times, prime ministers provide the president with important assistance. They shepherd government proposals through parliament, seek media support for the president, take the heat on controversial issues (thus sparing the president), and supervise the bureaucracy.

During cohabitation, power shifts from the president to the prime minister. Although the president retains major responsibility for overall defense and foreign policy, the prime minister assumes control over other policy areas.

Most cabinet members, also known as ministers, are senior politicians from the dominant parliamentary coalition. Cabinet ministers direct the government ministries. Positions in the cabinet are allotted to political parties in rough proportion to their strength in the majority parliamentary coalition. An attempt is also made to ensure regional balance. After his election, President Sarkozy tried to widen his base of support by appointing several Socialist politicians to the government. This bold move boosted his popularity in the electorate, although it also caused grumbling among members of his own governing coalition.

The French cabinet is not a forum for searching policy debate or collective decision making. Cabinet meetings are occasions where constitutional requirements are met. For example, the cabinet must authorize appointment of key administrative officials. The president and prime minister announce decisions. Important policies are shaped at the Élysée or Matignon (official residence of the prime minister) or by interministerial committees. These are informal working groups of ministers and high administrators directed by the president, prime minister, or their staff.

Bureaucracy and Civil Service

The bureaucracy is a large and sprawling organization that reaches far and wide to regulate French society. Some of the most powerful administrators in the French state are found in the Élysée and the Matignon, where they assist the president and prime minister. Others have offices in ornate government ministries scattered throughout Paris. An army of civil servants—approximately 2.3 million—performs the day-to-day work of the state. Another 2.7 million staff public hospitals and subnational governmental bureaucracies. About one in five employed French citizens is a civil servant!

The bureaucracy plays a key role in shaping the country's social and economic life. The Fifth Republic bolstered bureaucratic influence. It limited parliament's legislative power and extended the government's authority to issue binding regulations with the force of law. A position in the bureaucracy provides lifetime employment, considerable prestige, and, often, better pay and fringe benefits than a comparable job in the private sector.

The top positions in the bureaucracy offer among the most prestigious and powerful careers in France. Recruitment is on the basis of academic excellence: one must graduate from an elite educational establishment called a ***grande école***. Over 1 million students are enrolled in higher education at any given time (mostly public universities). But only 3,000 students attend the very best *grandes écoles*.[8] The two most prestigious ones are the École Polytechnique, which provides scientific and engineering training, and the École Nationale d'Administration, which provides training in policy analysis. Children from culturally and economically favored backgrounds have an immense advantage in the fierce competition for places in the *grandes écoles*.

grandes écoles prestigious and highly selective schools of higher education in France that train top civil servants, engineers, and business executives.

grands corps elite networks of graduates of selective training schools in France.

Students who graduate at the top of their class at a *grande école* join an even more select fraternity, a ***grand corps***. These are small, cohesive networks. Membership in a *grand corps* is for life. It guarantees a good salary, high status, and considerable power. Many members enter politics after several years in the bureaucracy. They serve in parliament or gain appointment as cabinet ministers. Over half of all prime ministers in the Fifth Republic have been members of *grands corps*, as were two presidents (Valéry Giscard d'Estaing and Jacques Chirac).

The bureaucracy is the primary organizational instrument for implementing state policies. However, the diminished scope of state activity, the increased power of the private sector, ideological changes, and the growing importance of the EU have all reduced the morale and prestige of the civil service.

Public and Semipublic Agencies

The past two decades have produced a steep decline in the number of public sector enterprises in basic industry, banking, transportation, energy, and telecommunications. Large and powerful semipublic agencies remain. For example, Electricity of France monopolizes the distribution of electricity throughout France. It has been described as a state within the state. But like the civil service, semipublic agencies no longer enjoy the prestige and power of yesteryear. Many formerly state-owned bastions like France Télécom, Air France, and the Renault automobile company have been fully or partially privatized.

Other State Institutions

FOCUS QUESTIONS

Name two checks and balances that other state institutions exercise with respect to the executive. Are the two adequate to hold the executive accountable? Why or why not?

The Judiciary

The French judicial system of Roman law, codified in the Napoleonic Code and similar codes governing industrial relations and local government, differs substantially from the pattern prevailing in Britain, the United States, and other nations inspired by the common law system. French courts accord little importance to judicial precedent; what counts are legislative texts and the codification of legislation in specific subfields. The trial system also differs from that in the United States. French judges play an active role in questioning witnesses and recommending verdicts to juries. A judicial authority, the *juge d'instruction*, is delegated responsibility for preparing the prosecution's case. Criminal defendants enjoy fewer rights than in the U.S. or British system of criminal justice.

Through much of modern French history, the judiciary had little autonomy. It was considered an arm of the executive. In the past few decades, however, this condition has changed dramatically. The powers of the Constitutional Council have grown. Independent administrative regulatory authorities now exercise extensive power in areas like broadcasting, stock market trading, and commercial competition.

The Constitutional Council. The Constitutional Council is the Cinderella of the Fifth Republic. One study observes, "Originally an obscure institution conceived to play a marginal role in the Fifth Republic, the Constitutional Council has gradually moved toward the center stage of French politics and acquired the status of a major actor in the policy-making system."[9] The council gained great independence and prominence after it successfully asserted the right of judicial review, that is, the right to strike down legislation that it judges to be in violation of the constitution or treaties. In addition, a constitutional amendment passed in 1974 authorized opposition members of parliament to refer bills for review by the council. Since then, the Constitutional Council has acted on some important occasions as a check on the legislature and, especially, the executive.

The nine members of the council serve staggered nine-year nonrenewable terms. The presidents of the National Assembly and Senate each appoint three members. The president of the republic names the remaining three members. He also designates the council's president. Members of the Constitutional Council are generally distinguished jurists or elder statesmen. The first woman became a member in 1992.

State Council. France has a system of administrative courts. Their importance comes from the great power of the bureaucracy and the wide scope of administrative regulations. Many areas regulated by laws in other democratic systems are the subject of administrative regulation in France. There are about thirty administrative courts. The most important is the *Conseil d'État* (State Council). It is a watchdog on the executive. This is especially important in the French political system, where the executive has such great autonomy.

The council decides cases brought by individuals alleging that their rights have been violated by administrative regulations and actions. It can order appropriate remedies. The State Council also advises the government about the constitutionality, legality, and coherence of proposed laws.

Subnational Government

France has three layers of subnational elected governments: municipal, departmental, and regional. There are over 36,000 municipalities. This is more than in all other Western European countries combined! The system seems unusually cumbersome. But polls suggest that citizens hold local officials in higher regard than national officeholders. Until the 1980s, local governments were quite weak. Responsibility for regulating local affairs was in the hands of nationally appointed field officers. For example, **prefects**, supervisors of civil engineering, and financial officers all represented government ministries.

prefects French administrators appointed by the minister of the interior to coordinate state agencies and programs within the one hundred French departments or localities.

The Socialist government sponsored a fundamental overhaul of local government in the 1980s. State supervision of local governments was reduced. Regional governments were created. Localities were now authorized to levy taxes. They were given important responsibility for education, transportation, social welfare, and cultural activity. A constitutional amendment in 2003 further extended the scope of decentralization. It also enshrined the principle of decentralization in the constitution. It required the national government to provide local governments with adequate tax revenues.

The reforms have brought government closer to citizens. However, decentralization has produced new problems. Some local officials have taken kickbacks from contractors who seek contracts for public works projects, questionable land development schemes, and municipal contracts. The reforms have also increased economic inequalities among localities and regions.

FOCUS QUESTIONS

Does the French policy-making process strike an adequate balance between democratic participation and coherent, energetic decision making? Name two ways that the balance could be improved.

The Policy-Making Process

The policy-making process differs substantially between periods of unified control and cohabitation. Under united control, the president formulates major policy initiatives, usually after consulting with the prime minister and powerful cabinet ministers. Government ministers, assisted by top civil servants, develop legislative proposals and administrative regulations to translate broad policy into concrete action. Under divided control (cohabitation), the prime minister has the dominant voice in most areas of policy-making. The president retreats to the political wings. However, even during cohabitation, the president retains great authority in foreign affairs.

Compared with most other democratic countries, France provides fewer opportunities for public and private actors outside government to influence policy-making. The constitution enshrines executive dominance. This comes at the expense of legislative and popular participation. The bureaucracy is large, expert, and often domineering.

France's participation in the global economy has deeply affected the executive and the French state more generally. EU commitments have limited France's freedom of action. Yet EU membership has also enabled France to leverage its power. It has a leading voice in this influential multilateral organization.

France has become more integrated within the EU and the wider global arena. But the gulf has widened between political decision makers and ordinary citizens. The result has put additional stress on the system of political representation, as we describe in Section 4.

Summary

France's semipresidential system has to a large extent achieved the goals that President de Gaulle chose when designing the Fifth Republic. However, the system has important flaws. On the one hand, during periods of unified control, there are few checks on executive power. On the other hand, during periods of cohabitation, conflict between the president and the prime minister can produce stalemate. In both cases, the result, as described in Section 4, is a wide gap between the state and civil society.

SECTION 4 Representation and Participation

Charles de Gaulle believed that political parties and parliament were too powerful in the Third and Fourth Republics and prevented vigorous executive leadership. To correct what he regarded as a dangerous imbalance, the Constitution of the Fifth Republic grants the executive an astonishing array of powers. At the same time, it sharply limits popular participation, representation, and legislative autonomy.

De Gaulle succeeded in muzzling parliament. But he completely failed to curb political parties. Ironically, however, the development of strong, well-organized, centralized parties has provided powerful support for decisive leadership and political stability. De Gaulle's decision to provide for popular election of the presidency contributed to strengthening parties. To win the all-important presidential contest, the formerly decentralized parties reorganized to become centralized, unified organizations.

The Legislature

FOCUS QUESTIONS

How effectively does the legislature represent citizens and act as a check on the executive? What are two reforms that might improve its performance?

The French parliament consists of the Senate and the more powerful National Assembly. Parliament lacks the independence that legislatures enjoy in full presidential systems. In addition, parliament cannot hold the executive fully accountable since it cannot vote a motion of no confidence in the president. In the Fifth Republic, parliament has lost power to the president, government, bureaucracy, judiciary, EU, television, and subnational governments!

The Constitution created a revolution in French constitutional law. Rather than an open-ended grant of authority, Article 34 enumerates the areas in which parliament *may* legislate and prohibits legislation on other matters. Outside these constitutionally specified areas, the executive is authorized to issue legally binding regulations and decrees without need for parliamentary approval. Even within the domain of parliamentary competence, Article 38 authorizes the government to request that parliament empower the government to issue ordinances (regulations) with the force of law. Governments have asked parliament for this authority when they wished to save time, avoid extensive parliamentary debate, or limit unwelcome amendments.

Within the limited area of lawmaking, the government has extensive powers to control legislative activity. The government initiates about 90 percent of bills passed into law. Parliament has limited control over the budget.

The executive can dissolve the National Assembly before its normal five-year term ends. The executive cannot dissolve the Senate, but this is not too significant since the Senate lacks two vital powers enjoyed by the National Assembly. It cannot pass legislation or force the government to resign by voting censure.

Additional measures bolster government control over parliament. Under Article 44, the government can call for a single vote on all or a portion of a bill. The government can select which amendments to include with the text. Governments have used (or abused) the package vote to restrict debate on many key legislative bills.

The government can curb parliament further by calling for a confidence vote in the National Assembly on either its overall policies or a specific bill (Article 49). When the government calls for a confidence vote, the measure is considered to be approved unless the National Assembly passes a censure motion by an absolute majority of all deputies within twenty-four hours. Deputies who abstain are, in effect, counted as voting with the government.

Deputies can also submit motions to censure the government on their own initiative. However, the constitution limits the number of parliament-initiated censure motions.

Because the government normally commands majority support in the National Assembly, it need not worry about censure. In fact, only one censure motion has ever passed in the entire fifty-year history of the Fifth Republic.

Parliament is widely perceived as a rubber stamp. This limits useful national debate, prevents opposition parties from airing grievances, and forces discontented groups to take to the streets rather than channel demands through parliament.

In some countries, parliamentary committees (commissions in France) play a vital role. But not in the Fifth Republic. There are six permanent commissions: Foreign Policy; Finances and Economy; Defense; Constitutional Changes, Legislation, and General Administration; Cultural, Family, and Social Affairs; and Production and Exchange. Commissions review proposed legislation. Although they may propose amendments, the government can reject those it dislikes.

The National Assembly is by far the more powerful chamber of parliament. It alone can censure the government. It also has the decisive role in passing legislation. The Senate can delay approval of legislation, and its approval is required to pass constitutional amendments.

How a Bill Becomes a Law

Following a bill's introduction in one of the two chambers (usually the National Assembly) a commission in that chamber reviews the bill. It then goes to the full house for debate, possible amendment, and vote. If approved, it is introduced in the second chamber, where the same procedure is followed.

A bill passed in identical form by the two houses becomes law (unless subsequently struck down by the Constitutional Council). If the two houses twice vote different versions of a bill (or one time each, if the government declares the bill a priority matter), a joint commission composed of members from the two houses seeks to negotiate a compromise text. If the commission reaches agreement, the revised text is debated and voted upon by both houses. If the two chambers do not pass the identical text at this reading, the government can request the National Assembly to vote once more. If the National Assembly approves the text, the measure is adopted despite the lack of senatorial approval.

Once a bill passes, the constitution authorizes the president of the republic, president of either chamber of the legislature, or sixty deputies or senators to request the Constitutional Council to review the text. The council can strike down the entire text or just those portions that it judges are in violation of the constitution. The council must be asked to rule within one month after a bill is passed. After this period, the bill becomes law and can never be reviewed by the council.

Why would the two chambers hold different positions? One reason is that they are elected by different procedures and represent different interests.

Electing the Legislature

Elections in the 577 single-member districts of the National Assembly follow a two-ballot procedure, similar to the procedure used for presidential elections. To be elected at the first ballot, a candidate must receive an absolute majority of the votes cast in the district. Some popular deputies are reelected at the first ballot. Usually, though, no candidate obtains a majority at this stage. A runoff election takes place the following week.

In presidential elections, only the two front-runners may compete at the runoff ballot. But in elections to the National Assembly, all candidates in a district who receive at least 12.5 percent of the votes at the first round can compete in the runoff. However, there are usually few of these so-called triangular races. Most second-ballot elections pit a candidate on the left against one on the right. Since party alliances typically reflect the left-right divide, the system used to elect the National Assembly contributes to polarization. It also maximizes the chances that a cohesive coalition will gain a majority in parliament. This bolsters political stability.

The procedure for selecting senators produces a chamber especially responsive to conservative, rural interests. There are 343 members of the Senate. They have six-year terms and are not chosen in general elections, but are elected by local elected officials from France's 100 *départements*. These are administrative districts into which mainland and overseas France is divided. Several overseas territories also choose senators.

The Senate is particularly responsive to the interests of small towns and villages. The reason is that senators are chosen by local elected officials, not in a general election. And rural areas have more local officials as a proportion of their population than do cities. This pattern usually results in conservative, center-right parties having a majority in the Senate. Thus, when center-right parties control the National Assembly, the two houses usually agree. When the Socialist party controls the National Assembly, conflict between the two chambers greatly increases.

Political Parties and the Party System

FOCUS QUESTION

How do electoral procedures affect the French party system?

Powerful parties, despite de Gaulle's fears, have promoted stable leadership and political alternation in office. Recently, however, with the decline in ideological distance between the center-left and center-right, many French citizens have felt unrepresented by the major parties. For example, the two largest parties—normally rivals—both called for a "yes" vote in the 2005 referendum on the European constitution. But it was resoundingly defeated. This highlights the existence of widespread citizen discontent with the major parties at the center of the political spectrum.

The Major Parties

Two parties—the center-right Union pour un mouvement populaire (UMP) and the center-left Parti socialiste (PS)—currently vie for dominance. For the past several decades, each has been the key party in a rival coalition. The two parties have alternated control of key political institutions. At the same time, each one is constantly challenged by smaller parties on its ideological flanks.

Union pour un mouvement populaire (Union for a Popular Majority). Until de Gaulle reached power in 1958, right-wing parties were numerous and fragmented. De Gaulle's allies formed a new party to support his leadership. The party proved successful in unifying many forces on the center-right. The social base of the party reflects its conservative orientation. Its electorate mostly consists of business executives, shopkeepers, professionals, the elderly, the wealthy, and the highly educated.

The party—whose name was changed to the UMP in 2002—was the keystone of the early Fifth Republic. Its fortunes flagged in the 1970s and 1980s, but it reestablished its dominance when Jacques Chirac was elected president in 1995. However, Chirac's retirement from politics in 2007 encouraged an intense succession struggle. Nicolas Sarkozy, a dynamic maverick in the UMP, gained control of the UMP, won the party's nomination for president, and was elected president in the 2007 presidential elections. The UMP also won the parliamentary elections that followed Sarkozy's victory. As a result, Sarkozy named his close ally François Fillon to become prime minister. Thus, the UMP now controls the most important institutions of the French state: the presidency, government, and parliament. It will probably remain in control of the three until at least the next presidential and parliamentary elections scheduled for 2012.

Parti socialiste (PS). A perpetual and ineffective opposition party in the early Fifth Republic, the PS became a vanguard of newly modernized France in 1981. Under François Mitterrand's leadership, it swept the presidential and parliamentary elections that year. Since then, the PS and the UMP have vied for control of French political institutions. The PS helped shape present-day France by embracing the institutions of the Fifth Republic, which parties on the left had initially opposed. As discussed in Section 2, it also sponsored an array of important political, economic, and social reforms during the early 1980s. It has promoted moderate reform since then.

The PS reached power in 1981 by advocating substantial changes. However, the party lost its ideological bearings after the right turn of 1983 described in Section 2. It suffered further damage following scandals involving Mitterrand's close personal associates. Mitterrand's own reputation was tarnished when reports surfaced that, before becoming a Resistance leader during World War II, he had been active in a far-right organization.

The U.S. Connection

French and American Political Parties Compared

An important difference between the French and American party system is the number of major parties that compete. The United States has a two-party system. Strictly speaking, this is not true, since there are many smaller parties represented on the ballot in most elections. But the vast majority of Americans vote for either the Democratic or Republican party candidate. The combined vote for "third party" candidates, that is, candidates from other parties, rarely totals 10 percent.

France has a multiparty system. Although in recent years two parties (the UMP and PS) have been the front-runners, other parties usually receive over 40 percent of the vote.

Scholars have debated the reasons for this important difference in the two countries' party systems. One frequently mentioned factor is the importance of electoral procedures. American elections are generally governed by first-past-the-post procedures, also known as the plurality system. In elections of this kind, the candidate receiving the most votes wins. French legislative and presidential elections are governed by a two-ballot system. A candidate must gain an absolute majority of votes to win at the first ballot. If no candidate does so, a runoff election is held between the front-runners to determine the winner. Why does this encourage a dispersion of the vote among many parties? Because citizens may calculate that voting for one of the smaller parties at the first ballot will not be a wasted vote. The two-ballot procedure gives them the opportunity to express a stronger preference at the first ballot knowing that they can vote "usefully" at the second ballot. Thus, this gives a boost to smaller parties.

At the same time, scholars have noted that the French party system is becoming "Americanized." This involves a trend toward main parties competing and converging toward the political center. Thus, the UMP now dominates on the center-right; the PS on the center-left. Parties that were significant players in the past now are junior partners of the two major parties. In many elections, the UMP and PS capture the lion's share of the vote at the first ballot. However, since neither of the parties' candidates gains an absolute majority, a runoff is needed.

Yet France is far from having a two-party system. For example, in the 2007 president election, 57 percent of those voting chose Sarkozy and Royal at the first ballot. The remaining 43 percent of votes, nearly half—were cast for the other ten candidates. Thus, the French party system exhibits strongly conflicting tendencies between polarization, in which competition pits the two major parties against each other, and fragmentation, involving competition among a large number of parties. ❖

Ségolène Royal, the party's nominee for president in 2007, represented a new generation of Socialists. However, her loss to Nicolas Sarkozy in the 2007 presidential race raised troubling questions about who should lead the party as well as what direction the party should take. The PS has lost the last two presidential and parliamentary elections. By the 2012 elections, it will have been out of power for a decade. To remain a major contender, the party must devise an attractive program and unite behind an effective leader.

The PS draws support from civil servants, low-income groups, and educated professionals. Its support to some extent is the mirror image of the UMP's. But in another respect the two parties are similar. Both represent the more secure strata of French society. Vulnerable and excluded groups—unskilled workers, the unemployed, and school dropouts—often support fringe parties.

Small Parties

The largest splinter parties at present are the Front national (FN), Les Verts (Greens), centrist parties that emerged from a split in 2007 in the former broad centrist party—the Union des démocrates pour la France (UDF), and the Parti communiste français (PCF). Given space limitations, we focus on only one small party here. This requires neglecting other significant parties. For example, consider the PCF. It is one of the few remaining parties in Western Europe that proclaims itself to be communist. The PCF was among the largest parties in postwar France. But it has steadily declined ever since then. At the same time, it continues to control a significant number of town halls and elected 15 deputies to parliament in 2007.

Front national (FN). The FN was among the first parties in Western Europe since World War II to promote racist themes. At first, its principal target was Muslim immigrants from North Africa, especially Algeria. The FN proposed expelling immigrants or at least depriving them of social benefits. This was its overly simple answer to troubling questions about unemployment, crime, and ethnic diversity.

Jean-Marie Le Pen, the party's demagogic leader for most of its existence, did not pretend to have the smooth, polished manner of most French politicians. Instead, he was known for his crude humor and combative style.

Le Pen broadened the party's focus in the 1990s by highlighting France's rising crime rate, the corruption of mainstream politicians, and the problems of European integration. He proposed outlawing abortion and advocated France's withdrawal from the EU. He also began to attack Jews. He cracked anti-Semitic jokes, characterized the Holocaust as an insignificant "historical detail," and declared that the Nazi occupation of France during World War II was not especially inhumane.

Le Pen ran for president in 1988 and 1995. Both times, he attracted significant electoral support—about 15 percent of the vote—and both times he came in fourth. His dramatic breakthrough was in the 2002 presidential elections. By coming in second, he made it to the runoff ballot.

The year 2002 has proven the high point of Le Pen's influence. He ran again for president in 2007. But this time his vote sank back to 10 percent, and he again came in fourth. One reason was his advanced age (seventy-eight at the time of the election). Further, Nicolas Sarkozy stole Le Pen's thunder by adopting several of his favorite themes.

However, Le Pen and the FN have had a profound influence on French politics. They have been highly successful in creating a cleavage that pits mainstream parties and values of both center-left and center-right against the party's racist, xenophobic, and homophobic platform.

FOCUS QUESTIONS

Do you agree with those scholars who speak of a crisis of the party system? Provide two pieces of evidence or arguments in favor of this claim and two that challenge the claim.

Elections

The most important elections are the legislative and presidential elections (see Tables 3.4 and 3.5). Troubling developments have led some scholars to speak of a crisis of political representation and the party system.

- There is extensive support for fringe parties not part of the select "cartel" of governmental parties.
- Voting patterns have been increasingly unstable. In every one of the six legislative elections between 1981 and 2002, the governing majority swung between the center-left and center-right parties. The 2007 parliamentary elections, won by the incumbent UMP, were the first time in thirty years that there was no alternation in power between competing coalitions.
- Voter turnout has been steadily declining in both presidential and parliamentary elections.
- Senior politicians across the political spectrum, including cabinet ministers, the president of the Constitutional Council, and prominent mayors, have been prosecuted on charges of financial corruption. During his years as president, Jacques Chirac was dogged by allegations of corruption. Although the Constitutional Court ruled that a sitting president has legal immunity, he must answer to criminal charges now that he has left office.
- Polls reveal that political leaders and institutions are held in pitifully low esteem. Between 1977 and 2006, the proportion of the French who judged that politicians "are very little or not at all concerned" with what ordinary French think, increased from 42 to 69 percent. Fewer than half the French polled during the 2007 presidential campaign judged that the election results would help improve living conditions in France. And 61 percent of those polled reported not trusting either major party to govern the country.[10]

Allegations of corruption by President Chirac. *(Photo © Phillipe Wojazer/Reuters/Corbis; cover © 2001 The Economist Newspaper Ltd. All rights reserved. Reprinted with permission. Further reproduction prohibited. www.economist.com.)*

FOCUS QUESTION

How well does French political culture achieve a balance between national unity and social diversity?

Political Culture, Citizenship, and Identity

Until the 1980s, two traditional subcultures powerfully shaped French political and cultural life. One subculture, with a predominantly working-class flavor, was structured by the French Communist Party (PCF) and the PCF's trade union ally, which dominated the labor movement. The other, a conservative subculture centered on the Catholic Church and its social organizations. The subcultures

TABLE 3.4

Electoral Results, Elections to National Assembly, 1958–2007 (percentage of those voting)

	1958	1962	1967	1968	1973	1978	1981	1986	1988	1993	1997	2002	2007
Far Left	2%	2%	2%	4%	3%	3%	1%	2%	0%	2%	2%	3%	2%
PCF	19	22	23	20	21	21	16	10	11	9	10	5	4
Socialist Party/Left Radicals	23	21	19	17	22	25	38	32	38	21	26	25	26
Ecology	—	—	—	—	—	2	1	1	1	12	8	4	3
Center	15	15	18	10	16	21*	19*		19*	19*	15*		8
Center-Right	14	14	0	4	7			42*				5*	4
UNR-RPR-UMP	18	32	38	44	24	23	21	—	19	20	17	34	40
Far Right	3	1	1	0	3	0	3	10	10	13	15	12	7
Abstentions	23	31	19	20	19	17	30	22	34	31	32	36	40

*Number represents the percentage of combined votes for Center and Center-Right parties.

Sources:

Françoise Dreyfus and François D'Arcy, *Les Institutions politiques et administratives de la France* (Paris: Economica, 1985), 54; *Le Monde*, March 18, 1986; *Le Monde*, *Les élections législatives* (Paris: *Le Monde*, 1988). Ministry of the Interior, 1993, 1997. *Le Monde*, June 11, 2002; **www.electionresources.org/fr/deputies.php?election=2007®ion=fr (accessed 6/18/2007)**.

provided members with distinctive (and opposed) political orientations and social identities. Many French citizens were not fully integrated in these subcultures. But they still identified with one or the other. In the past few decades, the two subcultures have disintegrated, and no comparably broad-based identities have developed to replace them. A related challenge involves the relationship between French citizens from immigrant backgrounds and those from the dominant French culture. The result is that France is apparently experiencing a crisis of identity.

Social Class

For centuries, class cleavages periodically fueled intense political conflict in France. With economic change and ideological reorientation, however, class identification rapidly declined in the 1970s. The most extensive decline has occurred in the ranks of manual workers. One reason is that the number of manual workers has fallen, as basic industries, including steel, shipbuilding, automobiles, and textiles, have drastically downsized the industrial work force. In addition the trade union movement has declined and changed.

Citizenship and National Identity

France's dominant approach to immigration, citizenship, and national identity is often described as the republican model. On the one hand, the inclusionary aspect of the model specifies that any immigrant who accepts French political

TABLE 3.5

Presidential Elections in the Fifth Republic (percentage of those voting)

December 1965		June 1969		May 1974		April–May 1981		April–May 1988		April–May 1995		April–May 2002		April–May 2007	
Candidate	**Ballot Percentage**	**Candidate**	**Ballot Percentage**	**Candidate**	**Ballot Percentage**	**Candidate**	**Ballot Percentage**	**Candidate**	**Ballot Percentage**	**Candidate**	**Ballot Percentage**	**Candidate**	**Ballot Percentage**	**Candidate**	**Ballot Percentage**
Extreme Right															
								Le Pen (FN)	14.4	Le Pen (FN)	15.0	Le Pen (FN)	17.0 (17.9)	Le Pen (FN)	10
														De Villiers	2
Center Right															
de Gaulle (Center-Right)	43.7 (54.5)	Pompidou (UNR)	44.0 (57.6)			Chirac (RPR)	18.0	Chirac (RPR)	19.9 (46.0)	Chirac (RPR)	20.8 (52.6)	Chirac (RPR)	19.9 (82.1)	Sarkozy (UMP)	31 (53)
Center															
Lecanuet (Opposition-Center)	15.8	Poher (Center)	23.4 (42.4)	Giscard	32.9 (50.7)	Giscard	28.3 (48.2)	Barre	16.5	Balladur (UDF)	18.9	Bayrou (UDF)	6.8	Bayrou (UDF)	19
												Saint-Josse (CNPT)	4.3	Nihous (CNPT)	1
												Madelin (PR)	3.9		
Center Left															
Mitterrand (Socialist-Communist)	32.2 (45.5)	Defferre (PS)	5.1	Mitterrand (PS)	43.4 (49.3)	Mitterrand (PS)	25.8 (51.8)	Mitterrand (PS)	34.1 (54.0)	Jospin (PS)	23.3 (47.4)	Jospin (PS)	16.1	Royal (PS)	26 (47)
												Chevènement	5.3	Voynet (Greens)	2
												Mamère (Greens)	5.3		
Left															
		Duclos (PCF)	21.5			Marchais (PCF)	15.3	Lajoinie (PCF)	6.8	Hue (PCF)	8.6	Hue (PCF)	3.4	Buffet (PCF)	2
												3 candidates (Extreme Left)	10.6	4 candidates (Extreme Left)	7
Abstentions	15.0 (15.5)		21.8 (30.9)		15.1 (12.1)		18.9 (14.1)				20.6		27.9 (19.9)		16 (16)

Note:

Numbers in parentheses indicate percentage of vote received in second ballot. Percentages of votes for candidates do not add to 100 because of minor party candidates and rounding errors.

Sources:

John R. Frears and Jean-Luc Parodi, *War Will Not Take Place: The French Parliamentary Elections of March 1978* (London: Hurst, 1976), p. 6; *Le Monde, L'Élection présidentielle: 26 avril–10 mai 1981* (Paris: Le Monde, 1981), pp. 98, 138; *Le Monde*, April 28 and May 12, 1998; *Journal officiel*, May 14, 1995; *Le Monde*, May 5–6, 2002; *Le Monde*, May 7, 2002; www.electionresources.org/fr/president.php?election=2007%region=fr. This site was accessed on June 18, 2007.

values and culture is entitled to citizenship. There are no ethnic, racial, or other ascriptive (inherited) restrictions on becoming a French citizen. On the other hand, the republican model insists that distinctive cultural identities and values should remain private. They should play no role in the public sphere. Most French regard the American conception of multiculturalism as dangerous. In the French view, it encourages "identity politics," creating conflicts among groups based on ethnic or religious affiliation.

An illustration of how the republican model can influence public policy is provided by a law passed in 2004. The law prohibited students from displaying "conspicuous signs of religious affiliation" in public schools. The principal reason for the reform was to prevent Muslim girls from wearing the *hidjab* (headscarf) in school. Girls who defied the ban were suspended. The government claimed that the law was needed to preserve religious neutrality in public schools. Banning headscarves was designed to combat Muslim **fundamentalism**. Large majorities of French citizens supported the ban. Yet a policy defended as preserving neutral public space had the effect of excluding from school Muslim girls who defied the ban.

fundamentalism a term recently popularized to describe extremist religious movements throughout the world.

France's color-blind and ethnic-blind model has often marginalized members of racial and ethnic minorities. For example, few members of ethnic minorities have been selected for membership in key political institutions, including the Constitutional Council, parliament, and government. When Nicolas Sarkozy was elected president in 2007, he made a dramatic break with this informal form of discrimination by appointing women of North African and black African backgrounds to a senior cabinet position and to two junior cabinet posts.

The French have recently been engaging in a national conversation about how to define their national identity. French school children are taught to revere the Declaration of the Rights of Man and the Citizen of 1789. The French take pride in the fact that the country is known for having championed liberty, equality, and fraternity. But these values have become the heritage of people throughout the world. They no longer serve as markers to identify what is distinctively French. And France's membership in the EU causes further confusion about what it means these days to be French.

Ethnicity and Immigration

France has traditionally attracted large numbers of immigrants. Indeed, in 1930, the proportion of immigrants in France was higher than in the United States.[11] Today, one French person in four has at least one grandparent who is foreign-born. Tensions have increased recently in part because most new immigrants are Muslims from France's former colonies in North Africa. Since the 1980s public attitudes about the meaning of citizenship have shifted dramatically. One historian suggests that "the view that immigrants represented a threat to 'national identity,' originally launched by the far right, [is now] held by large sectors of the public."[12] We can see here, once again, the impact of Le Pen's National Front.

President Sarkozy provoked a sharp controversy after being elected in 2007. He created a Ministry of Immigration and National Identity. Critics charged that the initiative implied that immigrants were responsible for the troubled state of France's national identity. They also expressed opposition to the state seeking to officially define the meaning of France's national identity.

Gender

French philosopher and novelist Simone de Beauvoir's *The Second Sex,* published after World War II, is a feminist landmark that analyzed the process by which women are assigned to a secondary role. In the 1960s and 1970s, French feminist theorists played a major role in reshaping literary studies around the world. However, there is considerable gender inequality in France. Women's movements, like many other French social movements, have been relatively weak.

Women have traditionally been highly underrepresented in the French political system. Although women are over half the electorate, there has never been a female president and only one prime minister. However, France took a giant step by amending the constitution in 1999 and passing legislation in 2000 that mandates gender parity in political representation.

parity law a French law passed in 2000 that directs political parties to nominate an equal number of men and women for most elections.

The **parity law** requires parties to nominate an equal number of male and female candidates in elections where seats are filled by proportional representation. Parties failing to do so may be disqualified. In elections held in single-member districts, parties that fail to nominate an equal number of men and women receive smaller public campaign subsidies.

The 2001 municipal elections produced a dramatic increase in women's representation. The number of women elected skyrocketed from 7,000 to 39,000. Similarly, women doubled their representation in elections to the Senate and regional councils in 2004. The proportion of women elected to the National Assembly, an institution where the parity law is less demanding, increased from 12 to 19 percent in 2007.

The parity law does not apply to presidential elections. Nonetheless, it may have informally had an influence in the 2007 presidential election, the first time in the Fifth Republic that a woman was a major presidential candidate. As discussed at the opening of this chapter, Ségolène Royal, president of a regional council and a leader of the Socialist party, received a respectable 47 percent of the vote in the runoff ballot.

Following his election as president in 2007, Nicolas Sarkozy appointed an unprecedented number of female cabinet ministers. Seven of fifteen senior cabinet posts went to women and four of twelve junior cabinet positions. Moreover, for the first time women were named ministers of the Interior and of Economy, Finance, and Employment, among the most powerful departments.

FOCUS QUESTION

What are two ways that the character of the French executive affects the organization of private interests and protest movements?

Interests, Social Movements, and Protest

Organized Interests

The executive has ample power and independence. It therefore has traditionally acted on its own, without consulting private interest groups. There are exceptions, including the farm lobby (the FNSEA) and the umbrella business

French Trade Unions

The French labor movement is quite weak. There are three reasons for this situation. First, the French state typically opposes consulting with interest groups, including unions. Second, the labor movement is quite divided. In many industrialized democracies, such as Britain, Germany, and Japan, a central trade union confederation groups most labor unions. As a result, organized labor speaks with relatively one voice. In France, there are four umbrella trade union confederations. Each confederation pursues its own economic and political agenda. The confederations compete with each other in recruiting members.

Third, relatively few workers belong to unions. The number of union members has declined from over 30 percent following World War II to considerably less than 10 percent today. This is the lowest figure of any industrialized democracy.

These factors explain why trade unions usually do not help to shape public policy over issues that affect their members.

Yet this picture is incomplete. Unions do have two significant resources that help them to play an important political role. First, they are on the governing boards of powerful public agencies, including the social security, health, pension, and unemployment insurance funds. Second, unions have the capacity to mobilize large numbers of members and nonmembers alike. Unions often take the lead in organizing popular protests, for example against plant closings or proposed cutbacks in social benefits. At these crisis points, employers and the state seek to persuade union leaders to restore calm. Feverish meetings are held between government administrators, business leaders, and union officials. Unions are often able to obtain wage gains and institutional reforms from these negotiations. When calm returns, unions again assume a marginal role—until the next explosion. ❖

association (whose name is Medef). These organizations participate in consultative commissions and have easy access to policy-makers. But most interest groups have little influence.

Social Movements and Protest

Fifth Republic institutions were designed to discourage citizens from acting autonomously. There are fewer organized interest groups and voluntary associations in France than in comparable countries. Those that exist, such as the trade union movement, are relatively weak. Perhaps partly as a result of this situation, France's centuries-old tradition of direct protest persists. France is second only to Italy in the proportion of European citizens who participate in demonstrations. Protests are the way that citizens press their demands in the absence of adequate institutional channels of representation. Groups that have engaged in strikes and demonstrations in recent years include farmers, postal workers, teachers, high school and university students, truckers, railway workers, health care workers, the unemployed, homeless, immigrants, actors, and research workers. This is a partial list!

To sum up, the Fifth Republic has proved better at strengthening the state than in developing mechanisms for representing citizens' interests. The political system has not achieved an adequate balance between executive leadership and popular participation and representation. This situation suggests a troubling question: Does the French political system have the capacity to address current challenges?

Summary

French society is composed of groups from a wide variety of religious, ethnic, and racial backgrounds. For generations, waves of immigrants arrived in France from southern and eastern Europe, northern and sub-Saharan Africa, and Southeast Asia. These groups contributed their intelligence, hard work, and vitality to making France a world cultural and economic leader. France has benefited immensely from the presence of immigrants. And it has granted immigrants, or at least their children, the right to citizenship. Further, in return for what they provided, immigrants were eligible to receive social benefits, including access to day care facilities and schools, public health programs, and public housing.

However, on an informal level, immigrants have often been regarded as second-class citizens. They are expected to abandon their own cultural practices and accept those of the dominant French society. They are given the least desirable jobs, or not offered jobs at all. The public housing projects and neighborhoods in which they live are often in shabby condition.

The position of immigrants illustrates the two faces of French political institutions. Public and private institutions can both set a high standard of quality but also inadequately represent the interests of many groups in French society. The result of the design flaws in public institutions and rigidity of political culture is that what often appears as a calm political situation may be the calm before the storm. The pattern of disruptive popular protests described in the next section is thus closely linked to the design of French political institutions described in Section 3 and cultural attitudes described in this section.

French Politics in Transition

In November 2005, France erupted in flames following a tragic accident at a rundown neighborhood outside Paris. Two adolescents of Algerian background, fleeing from the police, were accidentally electrocuted after entering an electrical power substation. Critics charged that the police had chased the youths in order to carry out an identity check—yet another one for second-generation immigrants of Algerian background. The police claimed that they did nothing to provoke the youths' flight.

News of the accident triggered riots in *cités* (impoverished neighborhoods) throughout France. For three weeks, bands of young men roamed nightly to torch cars, schools, and public buildings. (Ten thousand cars were burned.) The carnage ended when heavy police reinforcements were dispatched to the turbulent neighborhoods.

Why did the death of the two young men provoke such widespread destruction? One underlying cause of the widespread anger that erupted is France's persistently high rate of unemployment, described in Section 2. Moreover, young Muslim men were especially likely to be unemployed, both because many had little education and because they were victims of racial discrimination. Another factor is the tense relations between the police and youth of immigrant background in what the French call "sensitive neighborhoods." And it did not help that shortly before the incident, then-interior minister (and now president) Nicolas Sarkozy described juvenile delinquents as "scum." (For years after his remark, Sarkozy could not visit poor neighborhoods because his presence attracted angry crowds.)

Several months after the suburban riots, a government proposal triggered another massive wave of opposition. Although the issues and participants in the two uprisings are very different, the two disturbances share some common features.

In 2006, Prime Minister Dominique de Villepin sponsored a youth employment scheme designed to create jobs for young people, especially the less educated. The plan was called the First Employment Contract; its French initials are CPE. Villepin pointed to the 2005 urban riots described above to justify the CPE. The plan was designed to boost hiring young workers, especially those without advanced training. It did so by removing traditional restrictions on laying off workers. (Business groups often charged that these restrictions discouraged companies from hiring workers.) The CPE authorized employers to dismiss newly hired young workers without having to show cause.

Labor unions and student organizations fiercely opposed the plan. They charged that the reform allowed employers to arbitrarily dismiss workers. They warned that, once the CPE was implemented, it would be extended to make it easier for companies to dismiss workers of all ages.

When parliament passed the CPE, it produced an explosion. High school and university students throughout France voted to strike. Soon, half of all French universities were shut down. The conflict widened when unions joined the student movement. Demonstrations were held for weeks throughout France but the government refused to budge. When two million citizens in Paris, Lyon, Marseille, and other cities participated in a massive demonstration, the government admitted defeat and cancelled the CPE.

The two crises highlight political challenges in present-day France. Both call attention to the difficulties that young French people face in navigating the transition from school to work. The problem is most acute for school dropouts, many of whom participated in the wave of car burnings in 2005.

The two uprisings suggest the wide gulf between the state and many French citizens. Although Prime Minister de Villepin presented the CPE as a response to citizens' social and economic concerns, his government failed to consult with student organizations and labor unions when preparing the program. Although the two uprisings were very different, in both cases citizens engaged in direct action to challenge what they regarded as an unresponsive state.

FOCUS QUESTIONS

What are two features of France's political system, economy, and political culture that help explain the protest movements at the beginning of this section?

What are two major challenges facing the French political system?

What are two features of French political institutions and culture that might help and two features that make it difficult to meet these challenges?

Political Challenges and Changing Agendas

What a distance France has come since the 1980s! At that time, major political parties lined up quite neatly along a left-right continuum linked to social class and ideological divisions. In the early 1980s, the reform initiatives of the Socialist government dominated the news. When the center-right gained a parliamentary majority in 1986, it quickly rolled back many of the Socialist government's reforms.

Several years later, however, the governing parties on both sides of the ideological divide converged toward accepting France's mixed economy. They agreed on the desirability of combining a strong state with heavy reliance on private market forces. By the mid-1990s, it appeared that substantial ideological controversy among major political parties had ended.

In retrospect, the calm that prevailed was the prelude to the storm. We review here some political challenges in the past decade that highlight continuities and changes in France's political agenda. They raise troubling questions about the adequacy of the existing system to confront that agenda.

The Strikes of December 1995: May 1968 Redux?

In 1995, a series of strikes and demonstrations rocked France. They were the first act of a drama involving the government's attempt to reduce the size and cost of the French welfare state.

In the 1995 presidential election, Jacques Chirac lamented the "social fracture" that divided France into those enjoying economic prosperity and those excluded from its benefits. He promised that he would give first priority to repairing this situation. In his victory speech, he proclaimed, "Our battle has a name: the struggle against unemployment."

Only months after promising things could be different, however, he announced that France needed to comply with the strict fiscal requirements of the EU that limited budget deficits. This need collided with electoral promises, and the promises lost.

In order to reduce public spending, the government announced planned reforms that amounted to a declaration of war on labor unions and large sectors of the French population. Without consulting unions or interest groups, the government ordered a rise in payroll taxes and a cut in civil servants' pension benefits. The unions' role in governing the social security system would be reduced. University hiring would be frozen. The state-owned rail network would cut services.

Reaction to the proposed reforms was swift and massive. Strikes shut down Air France, railroads, buses, the Paris *métro* (subway), the postal system, and garbage collection. Mammoth demonstrations protested the government's plans. On one occasion, 2 million people turned out to oppose the reforms. In face of this massive opposition, the government abandoned many of the proposed changes.

Since 1995, strikes and demonstrations have occurred in the trucking industry in 2002, the health care sector in 2003 and 2004, the cultural sector in 2003, in opposition to pension benefits cutbacks in 2003 and 2005, the electrical power industry in 2004, and the youth employment reform in 2006 described above.

Oui to Roquefort Cheese, *Non* to Genetically Engineered Products

Several years after the 1995 strikes, an antiglobalization movement developed among far-leftists, intellectuals, farmers, and environmentalists. The movement's best-known leader is José Bové, a sheep farmer from southwestern France, where Roquefort cheese is produced. Small farmers like Bové oppose the standardized methods of farming that agribusiness corporations seek to impose. These methods often involve using genetically modified seed. Farmers also oppose the way that large corporations try to centralize food processing and distribution. When Bové ransacked a McDonald's construction site, for which he served a six-week prison sentence, he became a media hero. However, Bové was unable to translate his widespread popularity into political support. When he ran for president in 2007, he garnered a negligible 1.3 percent of the vote.

Globalization. This cartoon appeared when José Bové traveled to the Seattle meeting of the World Trade Organization in 1999. *(Source: Courtesy Plantu, Cartoonists and Writers Syndicate, Cartoon Arts International, Inc., from* Cassettes, Mensonges et Vidéo *(Paris: Le Seuil, 2000), p. 36.)*

The French antiglobalization movement includes participants from across the political spectrum. Opposition to globalization is a major theme in French political discourse. The French regard globalization as threatening cultural diversity. In particular, they fear that the "invasion" of American companies, products, and values will threaten France's cherished way of life. At the same time that France is in the forefront of opposition to globalization and U.S. domination, it is a major global competitor and the French flock to the latest American movies!

One of the organizations leading opposition to globalization is French-based ATTAC (Association in Support of the Tobin Tax). Yale economist and Nobel Prize winner James Tobin first proposed a tax on short-term capital movements to deter international financial speculation and pay for development projects in poor countries.

The Challenge of Le Pen and the FN

The antiglobalization movement is one response to France's position in a changing world. The growth of the Le Pen phenomenon and ethnic conflicts are others. The Front National (FN) has reaped a political harvest from the presence of Muslims in French society. Political sociologist Pierre Birnbaum observes, "What the National Front proposes to the French people . . . is a magical solution to their distress, to their loss of confidence in grand political visions of the nation."[13]

Le Pen became increasingly popular among native-born citizens on the margins of French society. In the 2002 presidential elections, the unemployed made up one-third of his electorate. More workers voted for Le Pen than for any other candidate.[14]

Muslim-Jewish Tensions

France has the largest number of both Muslims (5 million) and Jews (500,000) of any country in Europe. Israel's occupation of the West Bank in 2002 provoked hundreds of violent attacks on Jews and the defacing of dozens of synagogues, Jewish cemeteries, schools, kosher restaurants, and sports clubs. (In some cases, skinheads and neo-Nazis were behind the attacks. They have targeted Muslims as well as Jews.) French Jews are not responsible for Israel's actions. But they provide a convenient target for Muslim youth—often themselves victims of unemployment and racial discrimination.

France Falling?

France has been wracked by self-doubt in recent years, as illustrated by the publication of books with titles like *France Falling* and *France's Disarray*. One poll found that 63 percent of the French believe their country is in decline.

A balanced assessment would take note of France's recent achievements, along with its failings. Although the French economy has lagged recently in international economic competition, it remains among the world's leaders. The French government has enacted important reforms, including the parity law and decentralization. In 1999, parliament created the civil solidarity pact (*pacte civil de solidarité*, or PACS), a civil union between unmarried couples of the same or opposite sex. The PACS provides many of the legal rights formerly enjoyed only by married couples. The reform reflects a liberalization of French cultural attitudes, as well as a weakening of the institution of marriage. (The government statistical agency reported that in 2004, 47 percent of all French children were born out of wedlock; this compares with 6 percent in 1965.)[15]

Have recent economic and social changes produced a welcome pluralism or a disturbing fragmentation of French society? Many French regret that France's formerly highly stable and distinctive way of life has been destabilized. Can the positive features of the past be preserved while reforms are introduced to address pressing problems? What has to be sacrificed for the sake of what benefits?

France's Relation to Terrorism

France's relationship to terrorism is quite different from that of the United States. The United States has been the site of two terrorist attacks organized from outside the country—1993 and 2001. (Both targeted the World Trade Center in New York; the 2001 assault also attacked the Pentagon.) By contrast, for decades before 9/11 France was the target of domestic and international terrorist attacks, often linked to its brutal colonial war in Algeria.

Only a handful of France's 5 million Muslims are attracted to the radical variants of Islam that represent a prime source of recruits for terrorist activity. Further, France has been quite successful in containing terrorism. However, the threat of terrorist activity is real. In 2001, a plan was foiled to bomb the U.S. Embassy in Paris. In 2003, Richard Reid, a British citizen, was convicted of attempting to ignite explosives while on a plane flight from Paris to Miami. Also in 2003, French antiterrorist police detained eighteen Algerians and Pakistanis in the Paris area on charges that they were linked to Al Qaeda. In 2004, police arrested a dozen men near Paris on charges that they were seeking to wage a holy war in Iraq. In 2006, Zacarias Moussaoui, a French citizen, was sentenced to life imprisonment in the United States on charges that he helped plan the September 11 attack. In 2007, French antiterrorism police charged eleven people with participating in an Iraqi insurgency network linked to Al Qaeda.

France has developed extensive intelligence and counterterrorist services in the Defense and Interior Ministries. Although there is a need to counter the threat of terrorism, the government's antiterrorist activities have also caused concern. A shadow network of counterintelligence agencies operate in secret with little accountability. Critics have accused them of corruption, religious and ethnic discrimination, and abuses of human rights.

French Politics in Comparative Perspective

FOCUS QUESTIONS

What are two features of French politics that have surprised you after reading this chapter?

What are two features of French politics that are most useful and interesting to compare with those from another country or countries?

Is French politics becoming less exceptional? The case in favor rests on the fact that *dirigisme* and ideological conflict, two of the central features of the exceptionalist model, have declined in recent years. However, as described in Section 2, *dirigisme* has been transformed but not abandoned. Further, as this section analyzes, although left-right divisions have declined, new cleavages have developed. There is much to be learned, therefore, from including France in cross-national comparisons. One method is to compare France on the four core themes of this book. France lends itself to comparisons along all four dimensions. It can usefully be compared with countries where the state plays a less central role. Its statist style of economic management also offers interesting material to compare with countries in which market forces are less regulated. The French theory and practice of democracy also lend themselves to comparison with democracy elsewhere. And the ways that France deals with issues involving collective identity can be compared with regimes adopting a different approach.

A second kind of comparison involves historical comparisons within France. For example, the impact of institutions on political outcomes can be studied by comparing the Fourth and Fifth Republics. By studying the impact of the parity law, France provides a fine opportunity to analyze whether political institutions can be effective in reducing gender inequality.

Summary

France occupies an enviable position in the world. The majority of French citizens enjoy an excellent quality of life. In 2008, the Fifth Republic celebrated its fiftieth anniversary, a near-record for modern French regimes. Yet the French are divided and troubled about the future. Flaws in Fifth Republic political institutions make it harder to develop adequate responses. Yet the French political system and French society possess ample resources to meet the many challenges from within and outside the country. Forty years after youthful protesters chanted in May 1968, "The struggle continues," the words have lost none of their relevance.

Key Terms

conservative
socialist
ancien régime
revolution
republic
secularism
authoritarian
proportional representation
referendum
statism
dirigisme
indicative planning
nationalization
neoliberal
privatization
deregulation
decentralization
judicial review
cohabitation
grandes écoles
grands corps
prefects
fundamentalism
parity law

Suggested Readings

Bleich, Erik. *Race Politics in Britain and France: Ideas and Policymaking since the 1960s.* Cambridge: Cambridge University Press, 2003.

Brubaker, Rogers. *Citizenship and Nationhood in France and Germany.* Cambridge: Harvard University Press, 1992.

Elgie, Robert. *Political Institutions in Contemporary France.* New York: Oxford University Press, 2003.

Gopnik, Adam. *Paris to the Moon.* New York: Random House, 2000.

Gordon, Philip H., and Sophie Meunier. *The French Challenge: Adapting to Globalization.* Washington, D.C.: Brookings Institution, 2001.

Haus, Leah. *Unions, Immigration, and Internationalization: New Challenges and Changing Coalitions in the United States and France.* London: Palgrave, 2002.

Kastoryano, Riva. *Negotiating Identities: States and Immigrants in France and Germany.* Princeton: Princeton University Press, 2002.

Knapp, Andrew. *Parties and the Party System in France: A Disconnected Democracy?* Hampshire, Eng.: Macmillan, 2004.

Laurence, Jonathan, and Justin Vaisse. *Integrating Islam: Political and Religious Challenges in Contemporary France.* Washington, D.C.: Brookings Institution, 2006.

Levy, Jonah. *Tocqueville's Revenge: State, Society, and Economy in Contemporary France.* Cambridge: Harvard University Press, 1999.

Lewis-Beck, Michael S., ed. *The French Voter: Before and After the 2002 Elections.* London: Palgrave and Macmillan, 2004.

Robb, Graham. *The Discovery of France: A Historical Geography from the Revolution to the First World War.* New York: W. W. Norton, 2007.

Sa'adah, Anne. *Contemporary France: A Democratic Education*. Lanham, Md.: Rowman & Littlefield, 2003.

Schmidt, Vivien A. *From State to Market? The Transformation of French Business and Government*. Cambridge: Cambridge University Press, 1996.

Shields, James G. *The Extreme Right in France: From Pétain to Le Pen.* London: Routledge, 2007.

Tiersky, Ronald. *François Mitterrand: The Last French President.* New York: St. Martin's Press, 2000.

Notes

[1]Statistics derive from annual editions of INSEE, *Tableaux de l'Economie Française* (Paris: INSEE).

[2]*Le Monde*, March 20, 2007.

[3]Henri Mendras with Alistair Cole, *Social Change in Modern France: Towards a Cultural Anthropology of the Fifth Republic* (Cambridge: Cambridge University Press, 1991), p. 1.

[4]Peter A. Hall described the new economic orientation since the mid-1980s as a "neo-liberal modernization strategy." Hall, "From One Modernization Strategy to Another: The Character and Consequences of Recent Economic Policy in France" (paper presented to the Tenth International Conference of Europeanists, Chicago, March 15, 1996).

[5]Vivien A. Schmidt, *From State to Market? The Transformation of French Business and Government* (Cambridge: Cambridge University Press, 1996), p. 442.

[6]*Métro*, March 15, 2007.

[7]Sophie Meunier, "Free-Falling France or Free-Trading France?" *French Politics, Culture and Society* 22, no. 1 (Spring 2004): 98–107.

[8]Ezra Suleiman, "Les élites de l'administration et de la politique dans la France de la Ve République: Homogénéité, puissance, permanence," in Ezra Suleiman and Henri Mendras, eds., *Le recrutement des élites en Europe* (Paris: La Découverte, 1995), p. 33.

[9]John T. S. Keeler and Alec Stone, "Judicial-Political Confrontation in Mitterrand's France: The Emergence of the Constitutional Council as a Major Actor in the Policy-making Process," in Stanley Hoffmann, George Ross, and Sylvia Malzacher, eds., *The Mitterrand Experiment: Continuity and Change in Mitterrand's France* (New York: Oxford University Press, 1987), p. 176.

[10]*Le Monde*, March 26–27, 2006.

[11]Patrick Weil, *La France et ses étrangers* (Paris: Gallimard, 1991), p. 28.

[12]Charles Tilly's paraphrase (in the preface) of Gérard Noiriel's position, in Gérard Noiriel, *The French Melting Pot: Immigration, Citizenship, and National Identity* (Minneapolis: University of Minnesota Press, 1996), p. xii.

[13]Pierre Birnbaum, *The Idea of France* (New York: Hill & Wang, 2001), pp. 278–279.

[14]*Le Monde*, April 30, 2002.

[15]Reported in *Le Monde*, February 16, 2005.

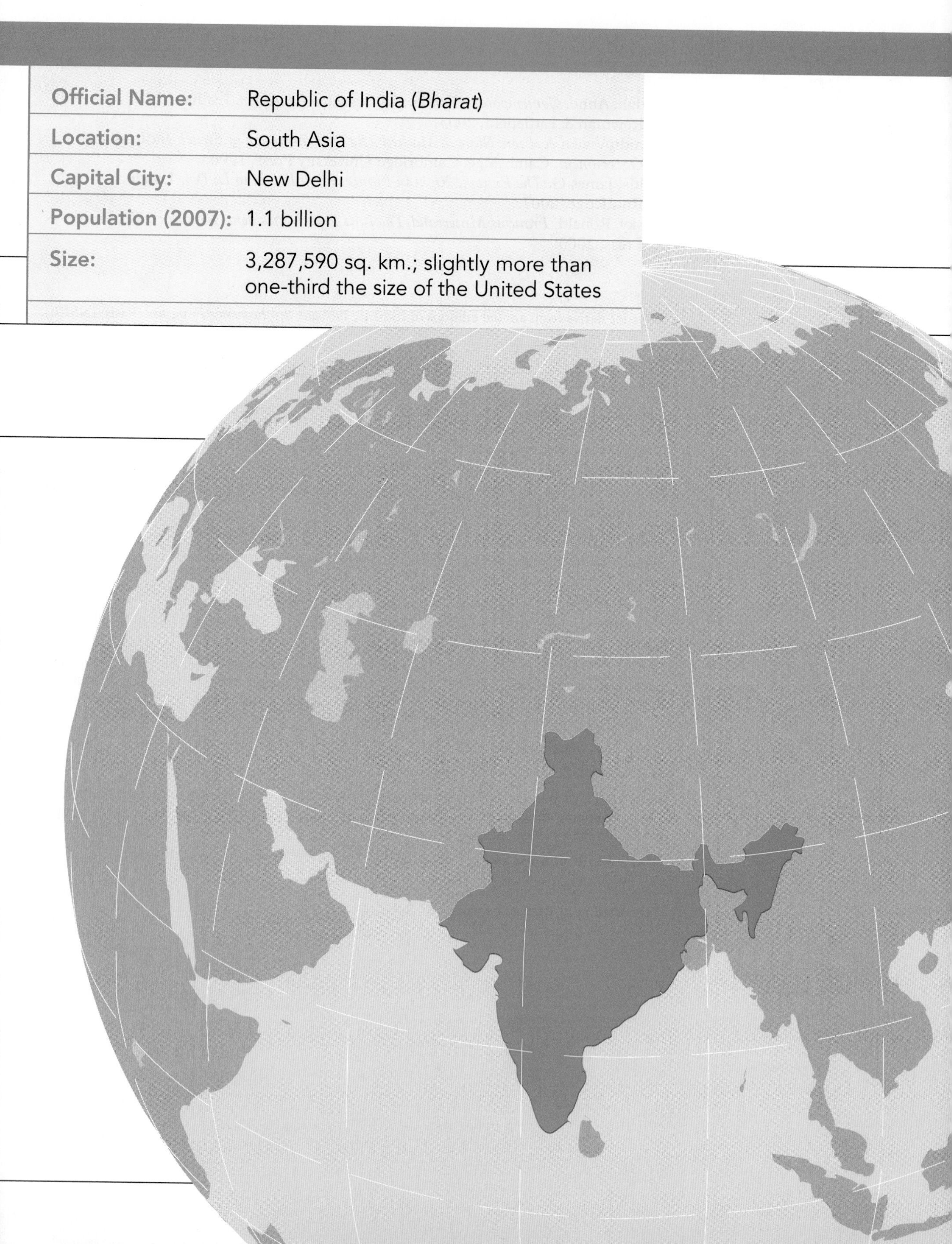

Official Name:	Republic of India (*Bharat*)
Location:	South Asia
Capital City:	New Delhi
Population (2007):	1.1 billion
Size:	3,287,590 sq. km.; slightly more than one-third the size of the United States

CHAPTER

4 India

Atul Kohli
Amrita Basu

Chronology of Modern India's Development

1526	1612–1690	1757	1857	1885
Mughal dynasty founded.	British East India Company establishes trading stations at Surat, Bombay, and Calcutta.	Britain establishes informal colonial rule.	Britain establishes formal colonial rule in response to Sepoy Rebellion.	Indian National Congress is created.

SECTION 1

The Making of the Modern Indian State

FOCUS QUESTION

How have political parties and insurgent movements responded to India's impressive economic growth amidst serious regional and class inequalities?

Politics in Action

India is experiencing two revolutions, alongside and in opposition to one another. The first is the revolution in technology, industry, and trade that is celebrated in special issues of *Time*, the *Economist*, and *Foreign Affairs*. Equally significant is the revolution of the rising expectations of the poor and the dispossessed. Those left out of the benefits of the technological revolution express their dissatisfaction in various arenas, anywhere from voting a party of the lowest strata into power, as in India's largest state, Uttar Pradesh, to waging violent insurgency, as in numerous districts in central India.

This political drama is unfolding in a growing but increasingly unequal national economy. For the last twenty-five years or so, the Indian economy grew between 5 to 6 percent annually. Today a growth rate of 9.2 percent has made India one of the world's fastest growing and potentially largest economies. Unfortunately, India's growing wealth has exacerbated inequalities along regional, rural-urban, and class lines. How India can ensure economic growth while moderating inequalities is the most pressing political challenge today. The rural poor have taken to armed rebellion in thirteen out of twenty-eight states. India's prime minister, Dr. Manmohan Singh has characterized the "Maoist rebels" as India's major "law and order problem." And yet, with over a billion people, many of them very poor, India has maintained democratic institutions since gaining independence after World War II.

Millions of Indians went to the polls in May 2004 and elected the Congress Party. But Congress was no longer a hegemonic ruling force. It could only rule with the support of various other parties, including India's main communist party, the Communist Party of India, Marxist (or CPM). (The CPM, a parliamentary party, is entirely distinct from the Communist Party Maoist, an underground party engaged in guerilla activity.) The departure from old patterns also introduced some novel developments for Indian democracy. Sonia Gandhi, heir to the Gandhi dynasty, stepped aside and passed the mantle of power to Manmohan Singh. For the first time ever, a man ruled India who was neither a leader of his own party nor that of the ruling alliance.

1947	1947–1964	1966–1984	1999–2004	2004
India achieves independence from Britain; India and Pakistan are partitioned; modern Indian state is founded.	Jawaharlal Nehru is prime minister.	Indira Gandhi is prime minister (except from 1977 to 1980).	Bharatiya Janata Party government in power.	Congress Party–dominated coalition government; the United Progressive Alliance comes to power.

From left to right: Sonia Gandhi, president of the Indian National Congress; Pratibha Patil, president of India; and Manmohan Singh, prime minister of India. *(Manish Swarup/AP Images)*

Instead, he was a scholar, a civil servant, and a member of the Sikh minority community.

None of India's ideologically diverse political parties enjoy unchallenged dominance. As a centrist party, the Congress presently stands for secularism, economic liberalization, and mild redistribution of wealth. The Bharatiya Janata Party (BJP), by contrast, in recent years has championed antiminority positions that undermine secularism in practice, if not in principle. Other major competitors include the all-India CPM and nearly thirty regional parties with a presence in parliament. The CPM, though communist in name and organization, has evolved into a social democratic party. It accepts a market economy and democracy. But it seeks greater benefits for India's poor. The most recent elections have been rightly interpreted as a victory, if temporarily, for secularism and limited redistribution.

TABLE 4.1

Political Organization

Political System	Parliamentary democracy and a federal republic.
Regime History	In 2004, the government was formed by the United Progressive Alliance; the Congress Party is the single largest party in the government, and Manmohan Singh is prime minister.
Administrative Structure	Federal, with 28 state governments.
Executive	Prime minister, leader of the party with the most seats in the parliament.
Legislature	Bicameral, upper house elected indirectly and without much substantial power; lower house, the main house, with members elected from single-member districts, winner-take-all.
Judiciary	Independent constitutional court with appointed judges.
Party System	Multiparty system. The Congress Party is the dominant party; the Bharatiya Janata Party (BJP) is the major opposition party.

FOCUS QUESTION

Although India is one of the most culturally diverse countries in the world, it has been a functioning democracy ever since Independence. In what ways has Indian geography contributed to Indian unity?

Geographic Setting

India is populous and geographically and culturally diverse. Its large size, approximately 2,000 miles in both length and width, is rivaled in Asia only by China. India includes three distinct topographic zones (the mountainous northern zone, the basin formed by the Ganges River, and the peninsula of southern India) and a variety of climates. Along with Pakistan and Bangladesh, the region is isolated from the rest of Asia by the Himalayas to the north and the Indian Ocean to the east, south, and west. The only permeable frontier is on the northwest. Successive invaders and migrants have followed this route into the region.

With over 1 billion people, India is second only to China in population. It is the world's largest democracy and the oldest democracy among the developing countries of Asia, Africa, and Latin America. India has functioned as a democracy with full adult suffrage since 1947, when it emerged as a sovereign nation-state, following the end of British colonial rule. The durability of Indian democracy is especially intriguing, considering the diversity of Indian society. Some fourteen major languages and numerous dialects are spoken. India contains many different ethnic groups and a host of regionally concentrated tribal groups, as well as adherents of the world's major religions. In addition to the majority Hindus, India includes Muslims, **Sikhs**, Jains, Buddhists, Christians, and even several tiny Jewish communities. Furthermore, Indian society, especially Hindu society, is divided into numerous occupationally based caste groupings. Most people are born into, marry, and die within their caste. India is still largely an agrarian society. Seventy percent of the population lives in far-flung rural villages. The major cities, Bombay (renamed Mumbai), Calcutta (renamed Kolkata), and New Delhi, the national capital, are densely populated.

Sikhs a minority religious community who practice Sikhism, constitute less than 2% of the Indian population and 76% of the state of Punjab.

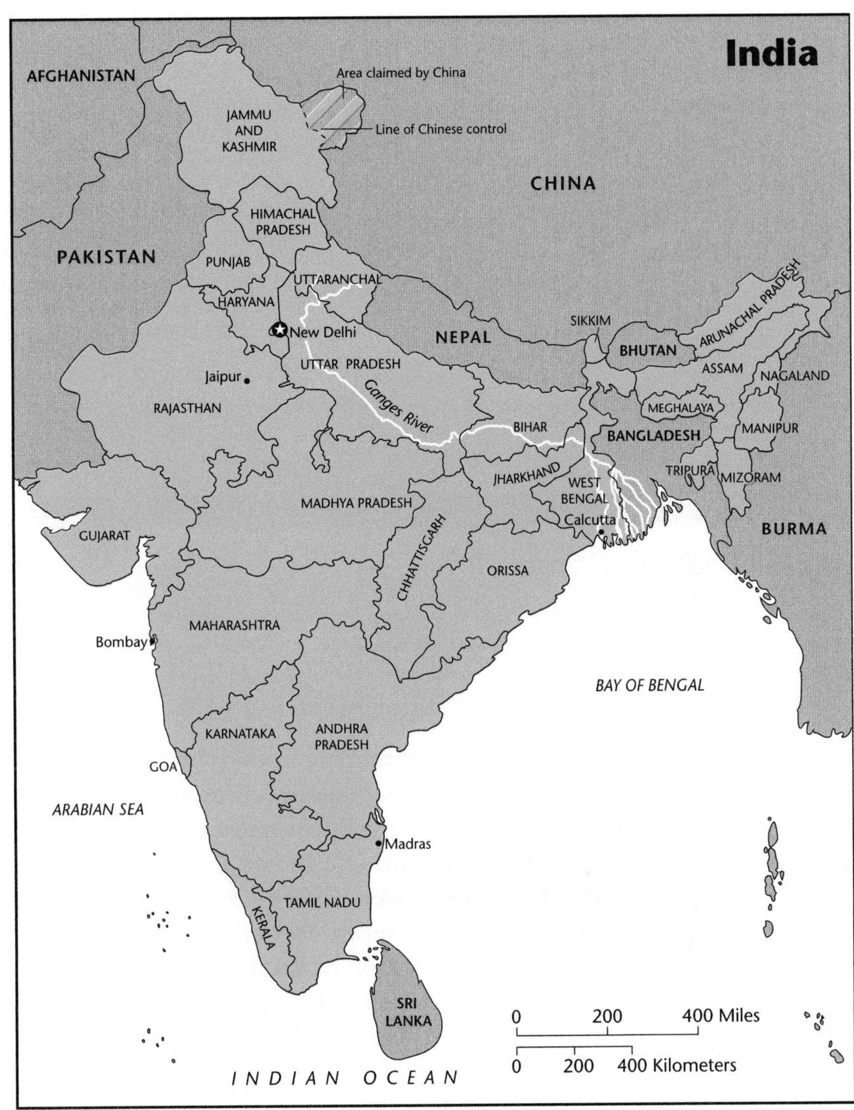

FOCUS QUESTION

Consider three critical junctures in Indian history. In what ways did each of them advance or delay progress toward Indian unity?

Critical Junctures

India's recorded history dates back to the Indus Valley Civilization of the third millennium BCE. The subcontinent, comprising Pakistan, India, and Bangladesh, has witnessed the rise and fall of many civilizations and empires. The invasion of northwestern India by Alexander the Great in 326 BCE introduced the development of trade and communication with western Asia. Shortly after Alexander left, the Maurya dynasty (322–185 BCE) under Emperor Ashoka united the kingdoms of Northern India into a single empire. The Mughal dynasty (early sixteenth century to mid-nineteenth century) further expanded its kingdom to include most of the Indian subcontinent and parts of what is now Afghanistan.

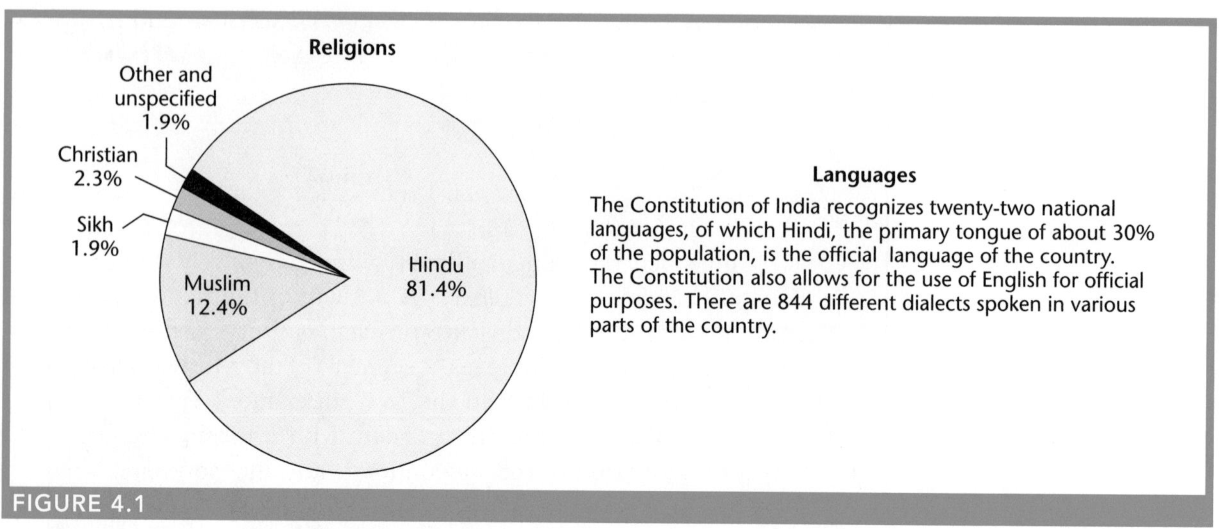

FIGURE 4.1

The Indian Nation at a Glance

The Colonial Legacy (1757–1947)

Sepoy Rebellion an armed uprising by Indian princes against expansion of British colonialism in India in 1857.

The British started making inroads into the Indian subcontinent in the late seventeenth and early eighteenth centuries. The East India Company, a large English trading organization with commercial interests in India and strong backing from the Crown played off one Indian prince against another, forming alliances with some, subduing others. Britain strengthened its control through a policy of divide and rule; after the **Sepoy Rebellion** or the Mutiny of 1857, the British Crown assumed direct control, retaining it until 1947.

The British sought to create a central government that controlled and led these various territories and indigenous authority structures. Important instruments included an all-India civil service, police force, and army. At first only British nationals could serve in these institutions, but with the introduction of modern educational institutions, some educated Indians were included in government services. Unlike many other colonies, particularly in Africa, the British helped create a relatively effective state structure in India. The civil administration, police, and armed services in contemporary India continue to be organized along the principles established by the British colonialists in the last century.

The Nationalist Movement (1885–1947)

After two centuries of British rule, India underwent intellectual and cultural ferment. The British rulers and traditional Indian elites had become allies, squeezing from the poor Indian peasantry resources that simultaneously maintained the colonial bureaucratic state and supported a landlord class. Indian nationalists opposed these arrangements through the Indian National Congress (INC), which was actually formed by an Englishman in 1885. In its early years, the INC was mainly a collection of Indian urban elites. They periodically met and petitioned India's British rulers, invoking liberal principles of political equality and requesting greater Indian participation in higher political offices. The British largely ignored these requests. Gradually, the requests became demands, pushing some nationalists into militancy and others into nonviolent mass mobilization.

Three characteristics of the nationalist movement greatly influenced state building and democracy in India. First, the INC's principle of unity within diversity served India well in creating and maintaining a relatively stable political system. Many conflicts could play themselves out within the INC. Second, the nationalist movement gave rise to divisions as well as unity. The most serious conflict was between Hindus and Muslims. A segment of the Muslim elite refused to accept the leadership of Gandhi and the INC, demanded separate political rights for Muslims, and called for an independent Muslim state when the INC refused. The resulting division of the subcontinent into two sovereign states in 1947—the Muslim state of Pakistan and the secular state of India, most of whose citizens were Hindu—was turbulent and bloody. At the time of partition, Pakistan consisted of two noncontiguous regions, East and West Pakistan. It was not until 1971 that East Pakistan, now Bangladesh, seceded.

Third, the nationalist movement laid the foundations for democracy in India. Mohandas Karamchand Gandhi pioneered the use of civil disobedience on the basis of profound ethical commitments and nonviolent means. Many of the INC's prominent leaders, like Jawaharlal Nehru, were committed democrats. Moreover, the INC participated in limited elections allowed by the British, ran democratic governments with limited powers in various British-controlled Indian provinces, and chose its own leaders through internal elections. These preindependence democratic tendencies were valuable assets.

During the 1920s and 1930s, Gandhi, Nehru, and other INC leaders were increasingly successful in mobilizing for India's independence. The more successful the INC became, the more the British either had to repress it or make concessions. They tried both. However, World War II consumed Britain's energies, and the political, economic, and symbolic costs of colonization became extremely onerous. To gain Indian support, the British promised independence. Soon after the war, India became a sovereign state in August 1947.

The Nehru Era (1947–1964)

After independence, India adopted a democratic constitution and established a British-style democracy with full adult suffrage. The INC had to transform itself from an opposition movement into a political party, the Congress Party. It succeeded in part by establishing a nationwide **patronage system** in which political supporters were given government-controlled posts or resources. Another important change in the decade following independence was the linguistic reorganization of states. The contentious political issue in the 1950s was the criterion by which regional groups could demand a state within the federal union. Concerned about domination by Hindi speakers, many non-Hindi groups demanded linguistic states. In 1956 the new Indian union formed around fourteen

patronage system
a political system in which government officials appoint loyal followers to positions rather than choosing people based on their qualifications.

Profile
Indian Political Leaders

Mahatma Gandhi

Born in 1869 in western India, Mohandas Gandhi studied law in London for two years and worked in Durban, South Africa, as a lawyer and an activist for twenty-one years before returning home to join the Indian nationalist movement. His work among the different communities in South Africa helped him to develop the political strategies of nonviolence, or *satyagraha* (grasp of truth). On his arrival in India in 1915, he set about transforming the Indian National Congress into a mass party by reaching out to the urban and rural poor, non-Hindu religious groups, and the scheduled castes, which he called *Harijans*, or Children of God. Following the British massacre of unarmed civilians in the Punjab (at Jallianwala Bagh, a location well-known in Indian history) in April 1919, Gandhi and Jawaharlal Nehru proposed a noncooperation movement. This required a boycott of British legal and educational institutions as well as British merchandise, for which were substituted indigenous, or *swadeshi*, varieties. Gandhi believed that mass civil disobedience could succeed only if people were truly committed. The involvement of some Congress workers in a violent incident in 1922 greatly disturbed him, causing him to call off the noncooperation movement. Gandhi was strongly opposed to the partition of India along religious lines in 1947, but because he had resigned from Congress in 1934, his protests were ignored. Nevertheless, he dominated India's nationalist movement for more than two decades until he was assassinated in January 1948, five months after India achieved its goal of self-rule, or *swaraj*, by a Hindu extremist who thought Gandhi was overly sympathetic to Muslim interests.

Jawaharlal Nehru

Jawaharlal Nehru was a staunch believer in liberal democratic principles. Along with Gandhi and others, he was at the forefront of India's nationalist movement against the British. When India became independent in 1947, Nehru became prime minister, as head of the Congress Party, and retained that position until his death in 1964. During this period, he established India as a socialist, democratic, and secular state in theory, if not always in practice. On the international front, he helped found the nonaligned movement, a forum for expressing the interests and aspirations of developing countries that did not want to ally with the United States or the Soviet Union during the cold war. Nehru attempted to set India on a rapid road to industrialization by establishing heavy industry. His efforts to effect redistribution of wealth through land reform were combined with an equally strong commitment to democratic and individual rights, such as the right to private property.

Indira Gandhi

Indira Gandhi (no relation to Mahatma Gandhi) became prime minister shortly after the death of her father, Jawaharlal Nehru, and dominated the Indian political scene until her assassination in 1984. Her years in power strengthened India's international position, but her domestic policies weakened the organizational structure of the Congress Party. Her tendencies toward centralization and the personalization of authority within the Congress and the concomitant use of demagogic rhetoric in electoral campaigns contributed to the erosion of the Congress Party. By defining the regional conflict in the Punjab and tensions with Pakistan as Hindu-Sikh and Hindu-Muslim problems respectively, she contributed to further erosion of the party's secular base and to rising religious factionalism. Her decision to send troops into the holiest of the holy Sikh temples in Amritsar, in order to root out Sikh militants using the temple as a sanctuary, deeply alienated Sikhs, a small but important religious group in India. The ensuing bloodshed culminated in her assassination by one of her Sikh bodyguards in 1984. Her death ushered in a new generation of the Nehru-Gandhi dynasty, as her son Rajiv Gandhi served as prime minister until 1989. ❖

linguistically defined states. Additional states were later carved out of existing ones. There are now twenty-eight major states.

Together with other postcolonial leaders of Asia and Africa, Nehru initiated the nonaligned movement, which united countries wishing to maintain a distance from the two superpowers. India and many other developing countries viewed both Western **capitalism** and Soviet communism with suspicion. Under Nehru, India played a leadership role among nonaligned developing countries. At home it pursued mixed economic policies—neither fully capitalist nor fully socialist (see Section 2).

capitalism an economic system, and the ideology behind it, that is based on private property, the profit motive, competition, and a free market in which the state plays a limited role.

Nehru put India on a stable, democratic road. However, powerful groups, including elite bureaucrats, wealthy landowners, entrepreneurs, and leaders of well-organized ethnic movements, enjoyed a favored position. While Nehru and the Congress Party maintained propoor, socialist rhetoric, they generally failed to deliver on their promises.

The Indira Gandhi Era (1966–1984)

When Nehru died in 1964, the Congress Party was divided over his successor. They hurriedly selected mild-mannered Lal Bahadur Shastri. When he died of a heart attack in 1966 and rivalry again broke out, party elites found a compromise candidate in Nehru's daughter, Indira Gandhi. They hoped that as Nehru's daughter, she would help the Congress Party garner the electoral support it needed to retain power. They also assumed that she would be a weak woman who could be manipulated by competing factions. They were right about the first point, but decisively wrong about the second.

As prime minister from 1966 to 1984, except for the brief period of 1977 to 1980, Indira Gandhi's rule had several legacies for contemporary Indian democracy. First, Indian politics became more personalized, populist, and nationalist. She soon consolidated her leadership over the Congress Party, and replaced critics with loyal allies. She created a new Congress Party in her own image. Subsequently, she portrayed the old Congress elite as conservative defenders of the status quo who prevented her from alleviating poverty. Gandhi's populist rhetoric won her immense popularity among India's poor. Second, Indira Gandhi further centralized the political system. Under Nehru, local elites had helped select higher political officeholders, but in the 1970s, Indira Gandhi directly appointed officeholders at both the national and regional levels. This strategy gave her a firm grip over the party. But it isolated her from broader political forces and eroded the legitimacy of local leaders.

Third, Indira Gandhi failed to translate populist rhetoric into real gains for India's poor. She was unable to redistribute agricultural land to those who worked the land or to generate employment, provide welfare, or improve access by the poor to education and medical services. Indian politics became increasingly turbulent under Indira Gandhi, a fourth legacy of her rule. The old Congress elite denounced her demagogic political style. Arguing that her government was corrupt, they began organizing mass demonstrations and strikes to press their case. In 1974, the political situation in India became unstable. With

Emergency (1975–1977) the period when Indian Prime Minister Indira Gandhi suspended many formal democratic rights and ruled in an authoritarian manner.

the opposition organizing general strikes, Indira Gandhi declared a national **Emergency**. She suspended many democratic rights and arrested most opposition leaders. The Emergency lasted nearly two years, the only period after 1947 when India was not a democracy.

In 1977, Indira Gandhi rescinded the Emergency and called for national elections. To her surprise, she was roundly defeated. Her authoritarian measures were so unpopular that the newly formed Janata Party was able to unite India's fragmented opposition groups and achieve electoral success. However, soon after the elections, Janata leaders became factionalized, and the Janata government collapsed.

Indira Gandhi regained power in 1980. Her tenure in power between 1980 and 1984 was marked by a continuity of personal and populist political style, an increasingly centralized political system, failure to implement antipoverty policies, and growing political turbulence. However, she departed from her previous approach in two ways. The first was economic. During the 1970s, India's industrial establishment grew relatively slowly because the government spent too much on buying political support and too little on investment. With few means to rechannel government spending or improve the spending capacity of the poor, Gandhi started changing the state-centered rules that had governed India's economy, especially embracing India's private sector as a means to improve economic performance.

The second important change concerns her strategy to achieve electoral support. Given her abandonment of appeals to socialism and secularism, she began religious appeals to the Hindu majority. By introducing religion into politics, the Congress Party sowed the seeds for the growth of the Hindu nationalist BJP. She also supported religious extremists in the Punjab to undermine moderate groups. This strategy backfired, and extremists groups became too strong for the government to control. She sent the army into the Golden Temple in the city of Amritsar, to attack Sikh militants besieged there. The anger among Sikhs was so intense that one of her Sikh bodyguards assassinated her in 1984.

Immediately after Gandhi's assassination, rampaging mobs of Hindus, some orchestrated by leading figures within the Congress Party, murdered 3,700 mostly poor Sikhs in New Delhi, Kanpur, and other north Indian cities.

Indira's son, Rajiv Gandhi, won a landslide victory in the subsequent national elections as a result of the sympathy wave that his mother's assassination generated. He promised clean government, a high-tech economy that would carry India into the next century, and reduced ethnic conflict. He was somewhat successful in ameliorating tensions in the state of Punjab. But he inflamed tensions between Hindus and Muslims by sponsoring a law that placed Muslim women under the purview of the family. His leadership was marred by allegations of corruption concerning an arms deal between the Indian government and the Swedish Bofors company.

With Indira Gandhi's death, the tradition of powerful, populist prime ministers came to an end. India has since faced governmental instability that began during the Indira Gandhi era. This was evident in increasing factionalism within the Congress Party. Since 1984, only three governments, the first two led by

Congress, have lasted their full terms: under Rajiv Gandhi (1984–1989), Narasimha Rao (1991–1996), and Atal Behari Vajpayee (1999–2004).

Coalition Governments (1989 to the Present)

No single party has won an absolute majority in any of the six parliamentary elections since 1989. The tendency for Indian elections to produce unstable or at best short-lived coalition governments at the national level has grown. No party has been able to fill the vacuum created by the old Congress Party's decline. Between 1998 and 2004, India was ruled by a BJP-led coalition government with Atal Behari Vajpayee as prime minister. The BJP was defeated in 2004 by a Congress Party government, with the support of a coalition of left-wing parties, headed by Manmohan Singh.

Coalition governments at the national level and in most states have generally been hurriedly arranged and poorly conceived. The cement that binds coalitions together has been more negative than positive. For example, opposition to Congress brought governments to power in 1977. By the early 1990s, opposition to the BJP provided the major incentive for coalitional arrangements among regional and lower-caste parties. The BJP-led government elected in 1998 lasted a full term but ruled as a coalition, as does the present Congress government (see Table 4.2).

TABLE 4.2

Prime Ministers of India, 1947–Present

	Years in Office	Party
Jawaharlal Nehru	1947–1964	Congress
Lal Bahadur Shastri	1964–1966	Congress
Indira Gandhi	1966–1977	Congress
Morarji Desai	1977–1979	Janata
Charan Singh	1979–1980	Janata
Indira Gandhi	1980–1984	Congress
Rajiv Gandhi	1984–1989	Congress
V. P. Singh	1989–1990	Janata
Chandra Shekhar	1990–1991	Janata (Socialist)
Narasimha Rao	1991–1996	Congress
Atal Bihari Vajpayee	1996 (13 days)	BJP & allies
H. D. Deve Gowda	1996–1997	United Front
I. K. Gujral	1997–1998	United Front
Atal Bihari Vajpayee	1998–1999, 1999–2004	BJP & allies
Manmohan Singh	2004–	Congress & allies

Regional political parties have also grown, as recent elections suggest. The Communist Party of India (M) performed well in the 2006 state elections, improving its electoral standing in both West Bengal and Kerala, and forming governments in the two states. The Communists' gains were of broader significance because the current Congress government in New Delhi is dependent on the Communists' support.

Themes and Implications

FOCUS QUESTIONS

Consider two of India's plans for social or economic development.
To what extent was each plan a success or failure?
How well did each plan lay the foundations for the next stage of development?

Historical Junctures and Political Themes

India in a World of States. India's attainment of nuclear weapons signaled the dawn of a new era. India now shares borders with two nuclear powers, China and Pakistan. It has engaged in wars and periodic border skirmishes with both. Politicians in India and Pakistan have exploited these tensions during domestic political crises. The challenge facing India is to prevent domestic pressures from escalating into international conflicts.

Governing the Economy. Indian policy-makers first sought economic self-sufficiency through state-led industrialization. They focused on meeting the needs of the large internal market. However, in recent years India, like many other developing nations, has begun to adjust its economic strategy to meet the demands of increasingly competitive and interdependent global markets. During the 1980s, these reforms consisted mainly of government incentives to India's established private sector to increase production. Since 1991, the reforms have opened the Indian economy to the outside world. The results include a growing economy but also growing inequalities. Indian leaders must ensure sustained growth while sponsoring measures to reduce economic inequalities.

The Democratic Idea. India can boast of a vibrant and vigilant civil society, periodic elections, unfettered media, and relatively autonomous courts and bureaucracy. Over the years India has become more democratic, though the reverse tendency is also noticeable in some areas. More groups, with more diverse identities, are participating in politics than ever before. The Indian political class can no longer be identified with a single region, caste, and class. However, India is less democratic than in the past with respect to protecting minority rights.

The Politics of Collective Identity. Democracy is supposed to provide a level playing field between different interests and identities. India faces the challenge of moderating the exercise of political power gained through electoral strategies of ethnic mobilization while sustaining economic growth.

Implications for Comparative Politics

Certain exceptional features of the Indian state have great significance for the study of comparative politics. First, despite widespread poverty and illiteracy, most Indians value their citizenship rights and exercise them vigorously. Second, unlike other multiethnic states such as Yugoslavia and the former Soviet Union, which disintegrated with the advent of democracy, the Indian state has managed to remain fairly cohesive and stable—although this must be qualified by severe turmoil at various times in the states of Assam, Punjab, Gujarat, and especially Kashmir. Indian politics offers a case study of how democracy can moderate ethnic cleavages. Contrast the BJP's exclusionary rhetoric when it was in opposition with its rhetorical shift toward moderation after becoming India's ruling party. A dilemma in comparative politics is how multiethnic democracies can develop a coherent institutional system that gives representation to diverse interests without degenerating into authoritarianism or total collapse.

Third, theorists dealing with recent transitions to democracy in Latin America and Eastern Europe have puzzled over two questions: What constitutes a consolidated democracy? How does one achieve such consolidation? Here, a comparison between India with Pakistan is instructive. At independence, both India and Pakistan started out as democracies but subsequently only India has continued to function as a democracy for all but two years since 1947, whereas Pakistan has functioned as an authoritarian state for most of the same period. Why this is so is complex but has to do with the fact that India's nationalist movement was mass-based and democratic whereas the movement that led to the creation of Pakistan was dominated by not-so-democratic landowning elites. Moreover, the Indian experience with authoritarianism during the Emergency era in the late 1970s and the resurgence of democratic norms when Indira Gandhi was voted out by an angry citizenry show the importance of elections. It also shows that democratic institutions and procedures can defuse democratic societal norms.

Fourth, comparativists have focused on whether poor countries can simultaneously achieve democracy and social equity. The case of Kerala, a state in southern India, suggests an affirmative answer. Although one of the poorest states in India, Kerala has achieved near-total literacy, long life expectancy, low infant mortality, and high access to medical care. Kerala's development indicators compare favorably with the rest of India, other low-income countries, and even wealthy countries like the United States.

Fifth, a lively debate concerns the impact of democracy on economic growth. Contrary to modernization theorists who posit that economic growth is a precondition for democracy, India became and remains a thriving democracy. While cross-national evidence remains inconclusive India's steady growth (approximately 6 percent annually for nearly 25 years) suggests the tantalizing possibility of successful economic management within a democratic framework.

This discussion of critical junctures in Indian history highlights the central challenge of contemporary Indian politics: how to establish a coherent, legitimate government that will facilitate both economic growth and equitable distribution. The former requires forming durable electoral coalitions without exacerbating political passions and ethnic conflicts. The latter requires careful implementation

The U.S. Connection

The American Presidential System and the Indian Parliamentary System Compared

In a presidential system, such as in the United States, the executive and the legislature are chosen separately. The two branches have independent powers. Neither one selects the other, is directly accountable to the other, or controls the other's agenda. Both institutions have fixed terms in office. Neither can force the other to resign and hold new elections. However the legislature can impeach and force the president to resign for treason or other grave misdeeds.

In India's parliamentary system, based on the British model, the executive and legislature do not have powers independent of each other. The government is accountable to parliament. Usually it must resign if parliament votes no confidence. The key official who heads the government and shapes policy is the prime minister, who leads the party coalition that has a majority in parliament. Although the president is the official head of the state, he or she is not independently powerful. The president is elected for a five-year term by an electoral college composed of elected representatives from the national and state governments.

The prime minister and other cabinet ministers are the most powerful political figures. Because they lead the majority party coalition in parliament, passing a bill is not as complicated as in a presidential system, especially one with a divided government. Nevertheless, as in most other parliamentary systems, such as those in Britain, Germany, and Japan, there is considerable overlap in India between the executive and the legislative branches of the government. ❖

of policies that help entrepreneurs produce goods and ensure a fair distribution of national income.

Summary

In part as a result of its geographic location, India represents a complex amalgam and coexistence of diverse religious, cultural, and societal influences. The old adage "unity in diversity" captures the common wisdom concerning a major source of Indian democracy. India's linguistic, regional, class, religious, and caste divisions have traditionally cross-cut one another and prevented any one set of cleavages from becoming polarized and any one identity from becoming dominant.

This discussion of critical junctures in Indian history highlights the central challenge of contemporary Indian politics: how to establish a coherent, legitimate government that will facilitate both economic growth and equitable distribution. The former requires forming durable electoral coalitions without exacerbating political passions and ethnic conflicts. The latter requires careful implementation of policies that help entrepreneurs produce goods and ensure a fair distribution of national income.

Political Economy and Development

At independence, India was largely a poor, agricultural economy. Although it still has a very large agricultural sector and considerable poverty, India today also has a substantial industrial base and a vibrant middle class. Since the introduction of economic liberalization policies under Narasimha Rao's Congress government in 1991, all Indian governments have supported economic reform.

FOCUS QUESTION

In what ways have social and economic development complemented or conflicted with one another?

State and Economy

The Economy after Independence

One of the central tasks facing Indian leaders after 1947 was to modernize the sluggish economy. Under Nehru, India adopted a development model based largely on private property, although there was extensive government ownership of firms and government guidance of private economic activity. Nehru created a powerful planning commission. Following the Soviet model, it made five-year plans for the Indian economy, outlining activities where government investment would be concentrated. Unlike plans in communist party states, however, Indian plans indicated priority areas for private entrepreneurs.

The Indian government levied high tariffs on imports, arguing that new Indian industries, so long disadvantaged under colonial rule, required protection from foreign competitors. The government tightly regulated the start-up and expansion of private industries. It presumed that the government was the best safeguard of public interests. This government-planned private economy achieved mixed results. It helped India create an impressive industrial base but did little to help the poor. Its protected industries were quite inefficient by global standards.

Congress leaders promised to redistribute land from landowners to tenants in order to weaken the former supporters of the colonial government and motivate farmers to increase production. Unlike the communist government in China, India's nationalist government had neither the will nor the capacity to undertake radical property redistribution. Although some of the largest landowners were indeed eliminated in the early 1950s, poor tenants and agricultural laborers received very little land. Most land remained in the hands of medium- to large-sized landowners. Many became part of the Congress political machine in the countryside. This weakened the Congress Party's capacity to assist the rural poor and undermined its socialist commitments.

green revolution a strategy for increasing agricultural (especially food) production, involving improved seeds, irrigation, and abundant use of fertilizers.

The failure of land reforms led to a new agricultural strategy in the late 1960s, known as the **green revolution**. Instead of addressing land redistribution, the state sought to provide landowners with improved seeds and access to subsidized fertilizer. The success of the green revolution was uneven. Production increased sharply in some areas, such as the Punjab. Other regions (especially the poorer farmers in these regions) lagged behind. Nevertheless, as a result of this strategy, India became self-sufficient in food (and even became a food exporter), avoiding the mass starvation and famines that had occurred in the past.

state-led economic development the process of promoting economic development using governmental machinery.

Between 1950 and 1980, the government facilitated **state-led economic development**. This development policy expanded the public sector, protected the domestic sector from foreign competition, and established rules and regulations to control private sector activity. Political leaders hoped to strengthen India's international position by promoting self-sufficient industrialization. To a great extent, the Indian government succeeded. By 1980, India could produce its own steel, airplanes, automobiles, chemicals, military hardware, and many consumer goods. In agriculture, although land reforms had failed, the revised agricultural strategy had improved food production.

State-led development insulated the Indian economy from global influences. The strategy resulted in modest economic growth—not as impressive as in Brazil, Mexico, or the Republic of Korea, but better than in many less developed countries. The main beneficiaries were business classes, medium and large landowning farmers, and political and bureaucratic elites. A substantial urban middle class also developed during this phase. However, state-led development created a number of problems. The elaborate rules and regulations controlling private economic activity encouraged corruption, as entrepreneurs bribed bureaucrats to get around the rules. And the focus on heavy industry directed a substantial portion of new investment into buying machinery rather than creating jobs. As a result, 40 percent of India's population, primarily poor tenant farmers and landless laborers, did not share in the fruits of this growth.

Economic Liberalization

economic liberalization the removal of government control and regulation over private enterprise.

A number of global and national changes moved India toward **economic liberalization** beginning in the 1980s and accelerating after 1991. Throughout the 1980s, socialist models of development came under attack. Within India, political and economic elites were increasingly dissatisfied with India's relatively sluggish economic performance, especially compared with dynamic East Asian economies. For example, during the 1970s, whereas India's economy grew at the rate of 3.4 percent per year, South Korea's grew at 9.6 percent. India's business and industrial classes increasingly found government intervention in the economy more of a hindrance than a help. Realizing that poverty limited the possibility for expanding domestic markets, they increasingly sought to export their products.

India's economy has done relatively well since the 1980s, especially when compared to the dismal performance of many debt-ridden Latin American and African economies, such as Brazil and Nigeria. Some of this improved performance resulted from domestic liberalization that, since the 1980s, has enabled Indian entrepreneurs to operate with fewer government restrictions. Since 1991, external liberalization has further integrated India into the global economy. Economic performance has also been improved by public loans to small factory owners and farmers and by public investments in their enterprises. However, a large part of economic growth in the 1980s was based on increased borrowing from abroad. This represented a shift from conservative fiscal policy. As a result, the need to repay foreign loans put enormous pressure on the government toward the end of the decade. India was forced in the early 1990s to borrow even more from such international agencies as the International Monetary Fund (IMF) and the World Bank. These organizations required the Indian government to reduce its deficit through such controversial measures as reducing subsidies to the poor and selling government shares in public enterprises to the private sector. Recent government policies have attempted to decrease the burden on the public sector and reduce restrictions on private enterprise. Alongside government reforms aimed at opening up and privatizing the economy have been policy moves to cut the work force in public enterprises in order to reduce public spending and deficits. The government has also sought to reduce workers' legal protections. Industrialists have demanded that the government raise the threshold in a law requiring government authorization before firms can lay off workers or close factories that employ from a hundred to a thousand workers. Industry also wants to ease restrictions on hiring temporary workers. Recent court decisions have also restricted workers' right to organize and strike, and have reduced traditional benefits.

Reforms in Agriculture

Agriculture, helped by good rains, made steady, modest progress during the 1990s. Weather patterns, especially the timeliness of monsoons, continue to have significant bearing on Indian agriculture. Drought hit large parts of the countryside and affected agricultural production and employment opportunities in 2002. Unable to find work or buy food, people faced starvation and suicide, and mass migration occurred in Rajasthan, Madhya Pradesh, and other states. The victims were invariably from the poorest, lowest-caste segments of the rural population.

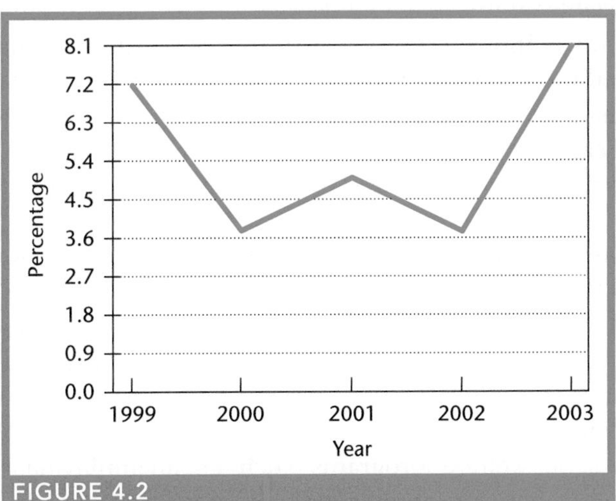

FIGURE 4.2

Recent GDP Growth, 1997–2003

Source: World Bank National Accounts data, and OECD National Accounts data files. http://devdata.worldbank.org/data-query/SMChartExp.asp.

With the goal of reducing subsidies, the central government excluded millions of impoverished families just above the poverty line from receiving publicly subsidized food supplies. Furthermore, the government sharply increased the price of food sold under the public distribution system.

The government's decision to remove restrictions on imports to conform to World Trade Organization (WTO) rules has important implications for the agriculture. Producers, such as coffee farmers in south India, are suffering from increased imports. Just when prices of primary commodities are falling worldwide, and the United States and other industrialized countries have maintained trade barriers on agricultural products and subsidized their domestic farmers, India's agriculture economy is being opened up to global forces without safety nets in place. To summarize, India's economy has grown at an impressive annual growth rate since 1980, averaging 6–7 percent per year, making it one of the world's fastest-growing economies. Although liberalizing economic policies may have contributed to this robust economic performance, especially in information technology and the growing service sector, their impact needs to be kept in perspective. Liberalization policies have failed to accelerate industrial growth. The significant growth of the Indian economy is most likely propelled by a number of other factors: the share of the slower-growing agricultural economy continues to decline steadily, both the knowledge and the stock of modern technology continues to grow, and the closer relationship between government and business has increased the share of private investment in overall investment, thereby increasing production.

Social Welfare Policy

India's poor, more than one-third of the population, are diverse, heterogeneous, and numerous. Since independence, the percentage of the poor has halved. However, because of India's rapid population growth, this advance has not been sufficient to reduce the absolute numbers of the poor, which increased from around 200 million in the 1950s to about 300 million in the new millennium. India has the largest number of poor people in the world. Nearly two-thirds of the Indian population and three-fourths of the poor live in rural areas. Urban poverty accounts for only one-fourth of the poor population, but the number of poor urban people, over 70 million, is staggering.

Although mostly unorganized, poor people exercise political influence in several ways. First, their sizable numbers and lower-caste status (especially within specific states) impel many Indian politicians to adopt populist or socialist electoral platforms and allow for a considerable impact on electoral outcomes. The poor in West Bengal and Kerala are well organized by communist or socialist parties and periodically help elect left-leaning governments. Second, the anger and frustration of the poor provide the raw material for many social movements.

Indian governments have undertaken various poverty alleviation programs, with relatively little success. Redistribution of agricultural land to the poor was mostly a failure compared to results in China. In some Indian states, such as West Bengal and Kerala, elected communist governments have been somewhat successful in land redistribution. Overall, land reforms have proved to be nearly impossible in India's democracy.

India has few Western-style welfare programs such as unemployment insurance, comprehensive public health programs, or guaranteed primary education. The size of the welfare problem would tax the resources of any government. No Indian government has ever attempted to provide universal primary education, although there has been considerable internal and external pressure to do so.

Public employment programs, however, have had some success. They enable the national and state governments to construct roads and bridges and maintain agricultural waterways. Because the rural poor are unemployed for nearly half the year when agricultural jobs are not available, public employment programs become a source of off-season employment. Many surveys have demonstrated that such programs help the poor, although mostly in the short run, and the programs rarely benefit the poorest citizens. However, many public employment programs were cut in the liberalization programs of the 1990s. The present government is undertaking a reform of the employment guarantee scheme to provide employment to India's rural poor.

FOCUS QUESTIONS

How is economic development changing India's class structure?

In what ways is this development easing or increasing social tensions?

Society and Economy

The fortunes that a small number of Indians have made in business and industry rival those of the richest corporate tycoons in the world. Below them, a much larger group, nearly 100 million Indians (approximately 10 percent) are relatively well off and enjoy a standard of living comparable to that of the middle classes in many developed countries. India has a sophisticated, technologically developed industrial sector that produces a variety of consumer products, military technologies, nuclear energy, computers, and computer software.

India's lower middle classes, about half of all Indians, are mainly small farmers or urban workers. Relatively poor by global standards, they barely eke out a living. Finally, at the bottom of the class structure, between a quarter and a third of the population is extremely poor. They are concentrated in villages as landless laborers or as the unemployed in city slums. Low levels of literacy, poverty, and primitive technology characterize a good part of India's rural society. Since India already has more labor than it can use productively, rapid population growth hinders economic growth.

India is one of the few countries in the world that has a lower percentage of females than men; the ratio is 1.06 males to females. Indian society favors boys over girls, as evidenced by all social indicators, from lower female literacy and nutrition rates to lower survival of female versus male infants. Prejudice against girls is reinforced through such traditions as the dowry system (the Hindu custom of giving the groom and his family assets, a dowry, at the time of a daughter's wedding). These traditions are deeply rooted and slow to change. They confine the majority of Indian women, particularly poor women, to a life of few opportunities.

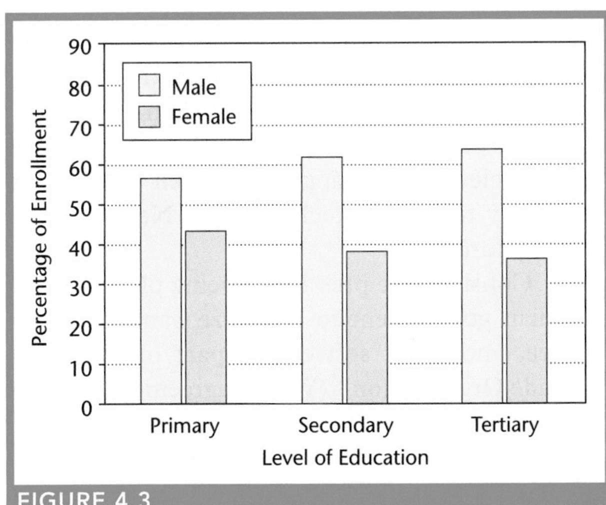

FIGURE 4.3

Educational Levels by Gender

Source: UNESCO Institute for Statistics, http://www.uis.unesco.org/en/stats/stats

FOCUS QUESTION

Why have some groups promoted economic liberalization in India, while others have opposed it?

nonaligned bloc countries that refused to ally with either the United States or the USSR during the Cold War years.

India in the Global Economy

Although India pursued an active foreign policy as a leader of the **nonaligned bloc**, it was defensive in its economic contacts with the global economy. During the decades when India's economy was relatively closed to outside influences, powerful groups emerged with vested interests in maintaining the old order. Many bureaucrats accepted bribes to issue government licenses to start private businesses. Indian industry was often relatively inefficient because neither cheaper foreign goods nor foreign investors could readily enter India. Moreover, organized labor, especially in government-controlled factories, had a stake in maintaining inefficient factories because they offered a greater number of jobs. These well-entrenched groups resisted liberalization and threatened to throw their political weight behind opposition parties, making the ruling government hesitant to undertake any decisive policy shift.

As the Indian government opened its economy in the 1980s, globalization quickly bore fruit. Foreign investment soared from $100 million a year between 1970 and 1991 to nearly $4 billion annually between 1992 and 1998, to $4.3 billion in 2003. However, the level of foreign direct investment in India remains relatively low. China and Brazil receive several times that volume each year. Because foreign investment focuses on the domestic market, it has not always facilitated export promotion, potentially a major benefit in poor countries.

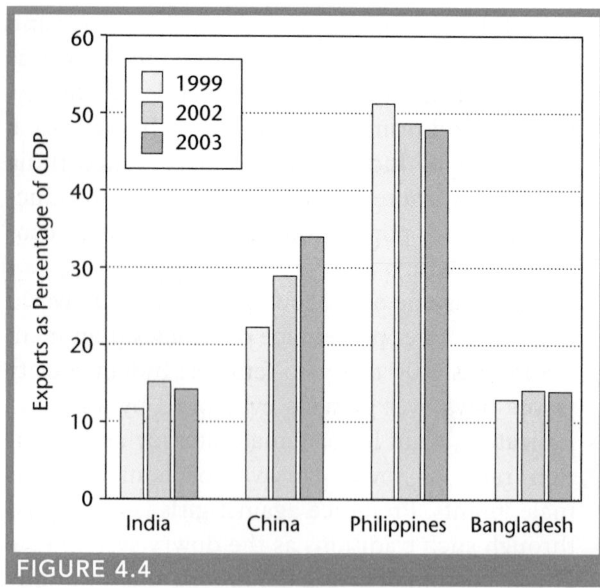

FIGURE 4.4

Exports of India and Its Trading Partners

Source: World Bank Country at a Glance, www.worldbank.org/data/countrydata/countrydata.html.

India is a world leader in the production of computer software. India can boast the equivalent of the Silicon Valley in the boom area around Bangalore in southern India, home to a large number of software firms. Within the past few years, transnational corporations have taken advantage of the fact that India's large numbers of scientifically trained graduates are fluent English speakers. When Americans have a problem in operating their computers, cable televisions, or appliances, their call for help is likely to go to a technician in New Delhi or Bangalore.

Considerable pressure is being placed on the Indian government to liberalize banking, insurance, and other services as part of the World Trade Organization's (WTO) agreement on trade in services. The result can be a mixed blessing. For example, foreign banks have focused on retail banking in profitable urban areas, ignoring less lucrative areas of lending. Small borrowers in agriculture and small-scale industrialists have found their access to banks curtailed. Loans to rural areas and poorer regions have fallen.

India's troubled relations with neighboring countries have created a low level of regional economic interactions. Figure 4.4 compares exports as a percentage of gross national product (GNP) for India and its major trading partners. India's export quantity and rate of growth are relatively low. As nations increasingly look to their neighbors for trade and investment, the pressure on India and its neighbors to increase economic contact is likely to grow. Some movement in this direction was already evident in the first half of the 1990s, especially toward China. But there is still a long way to go before South Asia develops an integrated zone of economic activity.

Summary

India has recently become a potential economic superpower. It may well reap the benefits of a large, well-trained, highly skilled population willing to work for low wages, and a growing number of world-class corporations. At the same time, however, globalization has increased economic inequality by generating more benefits for those in the middle and upper ranks than for the rural and urban poor. The challenge for the current Congress-dominated coalition is to devise ways for globalization to work for all.

Governance and Policy-Making

FOCUS QUESTION

In what ways has the Indian constitution promoted or hindered the flexibility that governments need to rule such a diverse country?

Organization of the State

The 1950 constitution created a democratic republic with a parliamentary and federal system of government. Although many profound changes have affected the distribution and use of power, the basic character of India's political system has remained unchanged. To simplify a complex reality, Indian democracy has proved so resilient because its political institutions have been able to accommodate many new power challenges and to repress the most difficult ones.

In contrast to the British constitution on which it is modeled, the Indian constitution is a written document that has been periodically amended by legislation. Unlike many constitutions, the Indian constitution goes beyond stipulating formal procedures of decision making and allocating powers among political institutions. It outlines policy goals that direct the government to promote social and economic equality and justice. The provisions ensure that issues of welfare and social justice are not entirely ignored. Second, the Indian constitution provides for freedom of religion and defines India as a secular state. (This was especially controversial during the late 1990s because the BJP was committed to establishing Hinduism as a state-sanctioned religion.) The constitution allows for the temporary suspension of many democratic rights under conditions of emergency. These provisions were used, somewhat understandably, during wars with Pakistan or China. But they have also been invoked, more disturbingly, to deal with internal political threats. During the national Emergency from 1975 to 1977, the politically vulnerable Indira Gandhi suspended many democratic rights and imprisoned her leading political opponents.

The central government controls the most essential government functions such as defense, foreign policy, taxation, public expenditures, and economic planning, especially industrial planning. State governments formally control such policy areas as agriculture, education, and law and order within the states. Because they depend heavily on the central government for funds in these areas, the power of states is limited.

Lok Sabha the lower house of parliament in India where all major legislation must pass before becoming law.

The Indian parliament, known as the ***Lok Sabha***, or House of the People, is the most significant political institution. The leader of the political party with the most seats in the *Lok Sabha* becomes the prime minister, who nominates a cabinet, mostly from the ranks of other members of parliament belonging to the ruling coalition. The prime minister and the cabinet, along with permanent civil servants, control much of the government's daily functioning. The system revolves around the prime minister, because all real decision-making authority is held by that office. Most of the country's important policies originate there. By contrast, the office of the president is largely ceremonial. In periodic national elections, 544 members of the *Lok Sabha*, the lower house of the bicameral parliament, are elected. The *Lok Sabha* is much more politically significant than the ***Rajya Sabha***, the upper house. The prime minister governs with the help of the cabinet, which periodically meets to discuss important issues, including any new legislation that is likely to be initiated. Individually, cabinet members are the heads of various ministries that direct the daily work of the government and make up the permanent bureaucracy.

Rayja Sabha India's upper house of parliament; considerably less significant politically than the *Lok Sabha*.

The Executive

FOCUS QUESTIONS

What factors allow the government and bureaucracy to work together in harmony? What factors hinder such cooperation?

The President and the Prime Minister

The president is the official head of the state and is elected indirectly every five years by an electoral college composed of elected representatives from the national and state governments. The president generally acts on the advice of the prime minister and is not very powerful. Occasionally, however, especially when selecting a prime minister becomes complex, the president plays an important role. In the recent past, the presidency has become more significant and more sharply contested, in part as a result of the failure of any political party to secure an absolute majority of votes in the parliamentary elections.

The prime minister and other cabinet ministers are the most powerful political figures. Because they represent the majority party coalition in parliament, passing a bill is not as complicated as in a presidential system, especially one with a divided government. The prime minister and the cabinet also head various ministries, so that after legislation is passed, they oversee its implementation.

In practice, the permanent bureaucracy, especially the senior and middle-level bureaucrats, are responsible for policy implementation. Nevertheless, as in most other parliamentary systems, such as those in Britain, Germany, and Japan, there is considerable overlap in India between the executive and the legislative branches of the government. This creates more centralization of power than is initially evident.

The prime minister's time in office has steadily shortened over time. Between 1947 and 1984, except for a few brief interludes, India had only two prime ministers: Nehru and Indira Gandhi (see Table 4.2). Since then, there has been a more rapid turnover. Rajiv Gandhi, Indira Gandhi's son, succeeded his mother after her assassination in 1984. When he lost power four years later, there were short-lived governments under the leadership of V. P. Singh and Chandra Shekhar. Narasimha Rao lasted his full term in office. Atal Behari Vajpayee (1999–2004) served an entire term in office, unlike his previous truncated terms.

The original choice of Nehru was natural, given his position in the nationalist movement and relationship to Mohandas Karamchand Gandhi. The choice of Indira Gandhi was less obvious. A group of prominent second-tier party leaders chose her to head the Congress Party because they calculated her national name would reap handsome electoral rewards. For similar reasons, party elites chose Rajiv Gandhi to succeed his mother. He benefited from the sympathy generated by her assassination and led the Congress Party back to power in 1984 with a handsome electoral majority.

Following Rajiv Gandhi's assassination, the Nehru-Gandhi family line appeared to have reached an end, since Rajiv Gandhi's wife, Sonia Gandhi, was of Italian background, and their children were too young to enter politics. In 1991, Narasimha Rao came back as an elder statesman who was nonthreatening and acceptable to competing factions within the Congress Party. Both subsequent United Front prime ministers were compromise candidates who lacked the personality and power to manage their disparate coalitions. In 1998, the Congress Party attempted to resurrect its fortunes by choosing Sonia Gandhi to head their party, creating the possibility that the political rule of the Nehru-Gandhi family would continue. The gamble paid off in 2004 when Congress, headed by Sonia Gandhi, narrowly edged the BJP out of power. Although she declined to be prime minister, mainly to avoid controversy about her Italian origins, as head of the Congress Party, she wields significant power over the government.

The Cabinet

When the prime minister chooses the cabinet, seniority, competence, and personal loyalty are the main criteria. Regional and caste representation are also important. Under Indira Gandhi, personal loyalty was critical. Rajiv Gandhi, however, put a premium on competence. Unfortunately he equated competence with youth and technical skills, at the expense of political experience. Since Vajpayee could form a government only with the help of many smaller parties in 1999, the heads of these parties had to be accommodated. This produced a vast, disparate cabinet.

The Bureaucracy

Each senior minister oversees a sprawling bureaucracy, staffed by some very competent, overworked, senior civil servants and by many not-so-competent, underlings.

Indian Administrative Service (IAS) India's civil service, a highly professional and talented group of administrators who run the Indian government on a day-to-day basis.

The **Indian Administrative Service** (IAS), constitutes a critical but relatively thin layer at the top of India's bureaucracy. Because political leaders come and go, but senior civil servants stay, many civil servants possess a storehouse of expertise that makes them very powerful. The attraction of the IAS has declined, however. Many talented young people now go into engineering or business, or leave the country. Government service has become tainted by corruption, and the level of professionalism within the IAS has eroded, mainly because politicians prefer loyalty over merit and seniority. Nevertheless, the IAS still recruits very talented young people.

Below the IAS, talent and professionalism drop sharply. Within national government and in many state governments, the bureaucracy is infamous for corruption and inefficiency. This leads to good policies made at the top and poor implementation at the local level.

FOCUS QUESTIONS

In what ways do state institutions such as the military, judiciary, and subnational governments provide checks and balances on the central government? How do these other institutions promote or retard democratic government?

Other State Institutions

The Military and the Police

The Indian military has never intervened directly in politics. With more than 1 million well-trained, well-equipped members, it is highly professional. The continuity of constitutional, electoral politics and a relatively apolitical military have reinforced and strengthened each other. Civilian politicians provide ample resources to the armed forces and, for the most part, let them function as a professional organization. The armed forces, in turn, obey the orders of democratically elected leaders. Although they lobby to preserve their own interests, they mostly stay out of democratic politics.

A large, sprawling, and relatively ineffective police service remains problematic. The Indian police organization was never as professionalized as the armed forces, and the police serve under the state, not the central government. State-level politicians regularly interfere in police personnel issues, and police officers regularly oblige politicians. The problem is especially serious at lower levels. The police are easily bribed and often allied with criminals or politicians. When the police take sides, they act in favor of dominant social groups such as landowners or upper castes or the majority Hindu religious community.

In addition to the regular armed forces and the state-level police forces, paramilitary forces, controlled by the national government, number nearly half a million men. As Indian politics became more turbulent in the 1980s, paramilitary forces steadily expanded. Because the national government calls on the regular armed forces only as a last resort in the management of internal conflicts and because state-level police forces are not very reliable, paramilitary forces are viewed as a way to maintain order.

The Executive Versus the Judiciary

Over the years, the Supreme Court has clashed head to head with the parliament as a result of the contradiction between principles of parliamentary sovereignty and judicial review that is embedded in India's constitution. For instance, during the early years of independence, the courts overturned state government laws to redistribute land from landlords (***zamindars***), saying that the laws violated the *zamindars'* fundamental rights. In retaliation, the parliament amended the constitution to ensure that the government could sponsor land redistribution. But matters did not end there. The Supreme Court responded by issuing a ruling that the parliament did not have the power to restrict what the court judged were fundamental rights. In 1970, the court also invalidated a law and a presidential order. Parliament responded by passing a series of amendments that undercut the Supreme Court's rulings. The duel continued when the Supreme Court responded that it retained the power to reject any constitutional amendments passed by parliament if they changed the constitution's basic structure. Since then, conflict between the Supreme Court, and the government and parliament has periodically erupted. Since the 1980s, the courts have increasingly tried to protect citizens' civil liberties from state coercion.

In recent years, the judiciary's performance has been greatly weakened by a phenomenal backlog of cases. The result is that cases drag on for years before they are decided. Because courts are a major arena where citizens seek to protect their rights, this has impaired citizens' ability to pursue social justice claims through democratic institutions. ❖

zamindars landlords who served as tax collectors in India under the British colonial government. The *zamindari* system was abolished after independence.

The Judiciary

A fundamental contradiction is embedded in the Indian constitution between parliamentary sovereignty and judicial review (see boxed feature: "The Executive Versus the Judiciary").

The supreme judicial authority is the Supreme Court, comprising a chief justice and seventeen other judges, appointed by the president—but only on the advice of the prime minister. Once appointed, judges cannot be removed from the bench until retirement at age sixty-five. The caseload on the Supreme Court is extremely heavy, with a significant backlog.

Because the Indian constitution is very detailed, the need for interpretation is not as great as in many other countries. Nevertheless, there are real conflicts to be adjudicated by the Supreme Court. For example, the constitution simultaneously protects private property and urges the government to pursue social justice. Indian leaders have often promulgated socialist legislation, for example, requiring the redistribution of agricultural land. Cases involving other politically significant issues, for instance, rights of religious minorities such as Muslims and the rights of women, also periodically reach the Supreme Court.

The Supreme Court often functions as a safeguard for citizens against state intervention. The Court introduced a system of public interest litigation that enabled bonded laborers, disenfranchised tribal people, the homeless, and indigent women to redress their claims. The Supreme Court has defended environmental causes. To protect the Taj Mahal from damage by air pollution, it ordered the closure of 212 nearby businesses that had chronically violated environmental regulations. The Court enforced clean water and air laws in New Delhi in 1996–1997 by ordering that polluting cars and buses be removed from the roads and by shutting down polluting enterprises. It required central and state governments to release food stocks and to promote education by providing school lunches and day care facilities.

Nevertheless, India's tradition of a strong, interventionist state has enabled the government to curtail civil liberties. After September 11, 2001, the BJP-led government used the war against terrorism to justify depicting proindependence groups in Kashmir, and Muslim groups throughout India, as terrorists. The government also banned the Students Islamic Movement of India (SIMI), the students' wing of the radical Islamic Jamaat-e-Islami political party in Pakistan. It however did not ban the Bajrang Dal, a militant organization with ties to the Visva Hindu Parisad, which has repeatedly organized anti-Muslim violence.

After September 11th, the Indian government issued the Prevention of Terrorism Ordinance (POTO), later enacted into law by parliament. Its definition of terrorism was extremely vague. Conspiring, attempting to commit, advocating, abetting, advising, or inciting such acts was punishable with penalties ranging from stiff prison sentences to death. Membership in a terrorist organization was punishable with life imprisonment. Confessions to police officers were admissible in courts, contrary to ordinary law, and confessions were brutally extracted in Indian police stations. The right to bail was severely restricted. The government primarily used POTO against Muslims and supporters of Marxist-Leninist groups. The largest number of arrests took place in Jharkhand. Shortly after Manmohan Singh became prime minister, the cabinet first approved the repeal of POTO. Instead it amended existing laws to tackle terrorism. Whereas POTO placed the burden of proof on the accused, the amended act shifts it back to the prosecutor.

Subnational Government

The more powerful and popular the central government, the less likely states are to pursue an independent course. But weak central governments enlarge the room for state governments to maneuver. When state governments are run by political parties other than the national ruling party—which often happens—there is considerable scope for center-state conflict.

In formal structure state governments parallel the national government. A chief minister heads the state government. The chief minister is the leader of the majority party (or the party with most seats) in the lower house of the state legislature. The chief minister appoints cabinet ministers who head various ministries staffed by a state-level, permanent bureaucracy. The quality of government below the national level is often poor, contributing to regional and ethnic conflicts.

Instead of a president, each state has a governor, appointed by the national president. The governors, like the president, are supposed to serve on the advice of the chief minister. But they often become independently powerful, especially when the national government is at odds with the state government or where state governments are unstable. Governors can dismiss elected state governments and proclaim temporary presidential rule if they deem state government ineffective. When this happens, the elected government is dissolved, and the state is governed from New Delhi until fresh elections are called and a new government is elected. Although intended to be a sensible constitutional option, intrusive national governments often use this procedure for partisan purposes.

Struggles between the central government and the states are ongoing. With many states inhabited by people with distinctive traditions, cultures, and languages, and with conflicting political parties in power at the national and state levels, substantial political and ethnic conflicts can disrupt central-state relations.

Indian politics has become increasingly regionalized. With economic liberalization, states can seek out investors independent of the national government. Some states have aggressively sought investments while some of the largest and poorest have fallen behind. As a result, regional inequalities have grown.

Since 1989, parties based in a single state have been a key to the success of coalition governments. In the five national elections between 1991 and 2004, the vote share of national parties (with bases in many states) dropped from 80.91 percent in 1991 to 67.98 percent in 1998 and the proportion of seats they controlled from 86 percent in 1991 to 72 percent in 1998. Parties based in single states increased their share of votes from 17 percent to 27 percent and their seats from 16 percent to 29 percent. Governing coalitions of disparate parties with little ideological or programmatic cohesion are often unstable. But national governments are less likely to dismiss state governments because national governments are likely to be composed of regional political parties.

panchayats elected bodies at the village, district, and state levels that have development and administrative responsibilities.

The ***panchayats***, at the local, district, and state levels, represent the most important mechanisms for the devolution of power. The *panchayats* are a precolonial institution that was responsible for adjudicating conflicts and presiding over community affairs in the rural areas. In 1959, the government introduced a three-tier model of *panchayats*, linked together by indirect elections. But the *panchayats* received meager resources, because national legislators saw them as potential rivals. By the mid-1960s, the *panchayats* were stagnating.

Some states revived the *panchayats* on their own initiative. Then, in 1992, a constitutional amendment enabled all states to strengthen the *panchayats*, although states were free to create their own models. It envisaged the *panchayats'* primary role as implementing development programs and encouraging greater local involvement in government. The amendment reserved 33 percent of the seats for women and allotted seats proportional to the population for scheduled castes and tribes. Most states met and several exceeded the 33 percent women's reservations at all three levels.

FOCUS QUESTION

Why do subnational governments often fail to implement central government policies, even when these policies are useful and well planned?

The Policy-Making Process

The government in New Delhi makes major policies. The prime minister and senior cabinet ministers generally initiate the process. Senior civil servants in each ministry, as well as in cross-ministry offices like the prime minister's secretariat and the planning commission, identify problems, synthesize data, and present to political leaders alternative solutions and their implications. After decisions have been made at the highest level, many require new legislation. Because the prime minister usually has a majority in parliament, most legislation passes.

Policy drama occurs early on, when major bills are under consideration, and during implementation. After adoption, implementation is far from assured. With liberalization, some aspects of the new policy have proven easier to implement than others. Changing the exchange rate was relatively easy because both the policy decision and its implementation require only a handful of politicians and bureaucrats to act. By contrast, simplifying procedures for Indian or foreign executives to create new enterprises proved far more complicated. Implementation of such policies involves layers of bureaucrats, most of whom benefit from the control they already exercise. Many dragged their feet and, where possible, sabotaged the newly simplified procedures.

Generating extra employment for the rural poor through public works projects has been somewhat more successful than land redistribution because such projects do not involve any direct confiscation of property. The main issues are the quality of projects chosen, whether they target the poor, and how honestly they are completed.

Because the quality of local governments is rarely high, many of the funds spent on poverty alleviation programs have been wasted. Public works policies have been most effectively implemented where there is considerable political pressure from caste or class politics, and in some southern states, where the local bureaucracy is more efficient.

Summary

The policy-making process, though relatively centralized, takes into account various interests and frequently produces well-developed policies. But implementation is quite decentralized and relatively ineffective. Sound policy ideas and positive intentions often fail from lackluster implementation at the state level.

Representation and Participation

Over the years, India has become a participatory democracy. Previously excluded social groups have entered the political arena and shaped the political process. At first the Congress Party mobilized most groups. But recently a proliferation of political parties has appealed to the Indian masses on ethnic grounds (particularly caste and religion). Simultaneously, in the institutional sphere the democratic idea led to an explosion of social movements in civil society. Poor women have marched to demand prohibition of the sale of liquor (because of the economic toll it inflicts and its association with domestic violence). Poor tribal peoples in Madhya Pradesh have protested their displacement by the construction of large dams. The democratic idea is so deeply rooted that today thousands of nongovernmental organizations function in the country. Some social movements have transformed themselves into political parties, while others militantly oppose the established political system. While Indian democracy has suffered from institutional decline and decay, it has flourished through the growth of popular participation within and outside the party system.

The Legislature

FOCUS QUESTIONS

To what extent can the Indian legislature create or guide national policies? How effectively can the legislature provide a check on government power?

A good place to begin the discussion of representation and participation in a democracy is with the legislature. The Indian parliament is bicameral, consisting of the *Rajya Sabha* and the *Lok Sabha*. Although the government dominates the parliament, election to the *Lok Sabha* is of vital importance. First, the outcome of parliamentary elections determines which party coalition will control the government. Second, although members of parliament are unable to influence policies directly, they enjoy considerable status, personal access to resources, and influence over allocations of government monies and contracts within their constituencies.

Elections to the *Lok Sabha* must be held at least every five years, but, as in other parliamentary systems, the prime minister may choose to call elections earlier. India is divided into 544 electoral districts of roughly equal population, each of which elects and sends one representative to the national parliament by a first-past-the-post electoral system. The major political parties nominate most candidates. Elections in India are won or lost mainly by parties, especially by party leaders, so most legislators are beholden to party leaders for securing a party ticket. Success in elections therefore does not depend on having an independent power base but on belonging to a party whose leader or whose programs are popular. Given the importance of the party label for nominations, members of parliament maintain strong voting discipline in the *Lok Sabha*.

The main business of the *Lok Sabha* is to pass new legislation as well as to debate government actions. Although members sometimes introduce bills, the government introduces most new legislation. After bills are introduced, they are assigned to parliamentary committees for detailed study and discussion. The committees report the bills back to the *Lok Sabha* for debate, possible amendment, and preliminary votes. They then go to the *Rajya Sabha*, the upper house, which is not a powerful chamber; it generally approves bills passed by the *Lok Sabha*. Most members of the *Rajya Sabha* are elected indirectly by state legislatures. After any final modifications by the *Rajya Sabha*, bills return to the *Lok Sabha* for a third reading, after which they are finally voted on in both houses and forwarded to the president for approval.

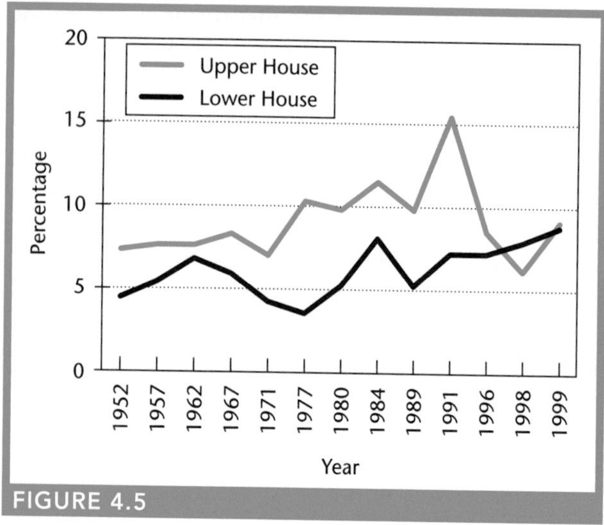

FIGURE 4.5

Women in Parliament

Source: India Together, http://indiatogether.org/manushi/issue116/Table-1.htm.

To understand why the *Lok Sabha* does not play a significant independent role in policymaking, keep in mind that (1) the government generally introduces new legislation; (2) most legislators, especially those belonging to the Congress Party, are politically beholden to party leaders; and (3) all parties use party whips to ensure voting along party lines. One implication of parliament's relative ineffectiveness is that routine changes in its social composition do not have significant policy consequences. Whether members of parliament are business executives or workers, men or women, members of upper or lower castes is not likely to lead to dramatic policy shifts. Nevertheless, groups in society derive satisfaction from having one of their own in the parliament, and dramatic shifts in social composition are bound to influence policy.

The typical Member of Parliament is a male university graduate between forty and sixty years old. Over the years, there have been some changes in the social composition of legislators. For example, legislators in the 1950s were likely to be urban men and were often lawyers and members of higher castes. Today, nearly half the members of parliament come from rural areas, and many have agricultural backgrounds. Members of the middle castes (the so-called backward castes) are also well represented today. These changes reflect some of the broad shifts in the distribution of power in Indian society. By contrast, the proportion of women and of poor, lower-caste individuals in the parliament remains low. The representation of women in parliament has not increased much from the 4.4 percent (or 22 women) in the first parliament (1952–1957) to 8.8 percent (48 women) in the 1998 elections, to 8.3 percent (45 women) in the lower house of parliament and 11.57 percent in the upper house of parliament in 2004 (see Figure 4.5).

FOCUS QUESTION

What explains the growing number and strength of Indian political parties in the past two decades in the face of the near-total domination of the Congress Party before that?

Political Parties and the Party System

Much of the real drama of Indian politics occurs in political parties and elections. Parties with a majority of seats in the national or state parliaments form the national or state governments and control government resources. Parties thus devote substantial energy to contesting and winning elections. Since independence, the party system has evolved into one in which Congress is among the major parties but far from dominant (see Table 4.3). Thus, what began as virtually a one-party system has evolved into a real multiparty system, with three main tendencies: centrist, center-left, and center-right. At least four potentially significant national parties and countless regional parties compete for power: the Congress, the Janata Party, the BJP, and the Communist Party of India (Marxist; CPM). Whereas the CPM is left-leaning and the BJP is religious and

TABLE 4.3

Major Party Election Results

	1991		1996		1998		1999		2004	
	%	**Seats**	**%**	**Seats**	**%**	**Seats**	**%**	**Seats**	**%**	**Seats**
Congress	37.3	225	29	143	25.4	140	28.4	112	26.69	145[a]
BJP & Allies	19.9	119	24	193	36.2	250	41.3	296	35.91	189
Janata	10.8	55	Joined with UF		Joined with UF		1	1	Joined with Congress	
United Front	—	—	31	180	20.9	98	—	—	—	—
Communists[b]	—	48	Joined with UF		Joined with UF		5.4	32	7.0	53
Others							23.9	107	19.9	78

[a]The more relevant figures in 2004 for Congress and allies were 35.82 and 219, respectively.
[b]Includes both the CPM and the CPI.

Source:
India Today, July 15, 1991, March 16, 1998; *Economic Times* website http://economictimes.indiatimes.com; and *The Hindu*, May 20, 2004.

right-leaning, both Congress and the Janata are more or less centrist. The major parties must stitch together coalitions that include many small, usually regionally based parties to form a government. Feverish negotiations among coalition parties take place over the allocation of cabinet positions and the policies of the governing coalition.

The Congress Party

Congress was originally the unquestioned ruling party. By the time Indira Gandhi assumed power in 1966, the old Congress Party had begun to lose its political sway, and anticolonial nationalism was fading. Democratic politics mobilized many poor, lower-caste citizens. Numerous regional parties challenged Congress's monopoly. Weather-related food shortages in the mid-1960s also hurt the Congress Party in the 1967 elections.

Indira Gandhi sought to reverse this decline. She mobilized India's vast majority, the poor. She promised poverty alleviation as her core program. Her personal success, however, came at a cost to the party. The old Congress split into two parties, with one branch, the Congress (O), becoming moribund, leaving the other, Congress (I) ("I" for Indira) to inherit the position of the old undivided Congress. Nevertheless, the Congress Party formed all governments from independence until 1989, except for 1977–1980 when the Janata Party formed the government. Congress headed governments from 1991 to 1996 and returned to power in 2004.

Before Indira Gandhi, the rank-and-file elected the lowest-level officers, who in turn elected officers at higher levels of the party organization, up to the position of the party leader, who was the prime minister during the long period when the Congress formed the government. Indira Gandhi created a top-down party in which leaders appointed party officers. With some modifications, including limited internal party elections, this is how the contemporary Congress Party is organized. The top-down structure enables the leaders to control the party. But it is a major liability when grassroots support is necessary.

During the 1970s Congress had a left-of-center, propoor political platform. It moved toward the center in 1984 under Rajiv Gandhi. For much of the 1980s and the 1990s, the party tilted right-of-center, elevating economic efficiency, business interests, and limited government spending over the rights of the poor and working people and over questions of health, education, and welfare. However, under Sonia Gandhi's leadership, Congress has moved somewhat to the left.

Congress has always attracted diverse social groups: rich and poor, upper and lower castes, Hindus and Muslims, northerners and southerners. Nevertheless, elections in the 1990s indicate that Congress has lost some of its traditional constituencies among the poor, lower castes, and Muslims.

The Janata Party

The Janata Party, India's other centrist party, formed short-lived national governments in 1977 and 1989 and participated in the United Front in 1996 and 1997. Janata, however, is not so much a political party as an umbrella for various parties and factions.

During the late 1980s, the Janata Party enjoyed a brief term as a national government under the leadership of breakaway Congress leader, V. P. Singh. The party won enough seats to form a minority government in 1989, but the government became factionalized. This second attempt at a non–Congress-led government collapsed after a little over two years. Since then, the Janata has survived only under the umbrella of the United Front, a collection of smaller parties, including the CPM. The Janata party has a weak organizational structure and lacks a distinctive, coherent political platform. Although most of its efforts at self-definition have been unsuccessful, V. P. Singh undertook one major policy initiative that distinguished it from other parties. His government accepted the **Mandal Commission**'s recommendation that India's **other backward classes**, generally, the middle, rural castes that constitute a near majority in the Indian countryside, be provided substantial **reservations** (or reserved access) to government jobs and educational institutions. When the government accepted this recommendation, the upper castes felt threatened and organized nationwide riots and violence. The uproar eventually contributed to the downfall of V. P. Singh's government.

Mandal Commission a government-appointed commission headed by J. P. Mandal to consider seat reservations and quotas to redress caste discrimination.

other backward classes the middle or intermediary castes in India that have been accorded reserved seats in public education and employment since the early 1990s.

reservations jobs or admissions to colleges reserved by the government of India for specific social groups, particularly underprivileged groups.

The Bharatiya Janata Party (BJP)

The BJP is a right-leaning, Hindu-nationalist party, the first major party to mobilize explicitly on the basis of religious identity and to often adopt an anti-Muslim stance. It is better organized than Congress and Janata.

The U.S. Connection

Indian and American Political Parties Compared

One of the most important dimensions along which the Indian and American party systems differ concerns the number of major parties that compete. In principle, the United States is a two-party system while India is a multiparty system but in fact the reality is more complex. There are a number of small parties in the United States but third-party candidates generally receive less than 5 percent of the vote. Most Americans vote for either the Republican or the Democratic parties. India, by contrast, has evolved from a one-party dominant system led by the Congress Party into a multiparty system. One of the reasons that India, unlike the United States, functioned for many years as a one-party dominant system was that Congress led the Nationalist movement that achieved independence from Britain. Although the United States was also colonized by Britain, no political party in the United States was identified as spearheading the anticolonial struggle.

Given India's vast size, extensive poverty, and high levels of illiteracy, it is impressive how many people turn out to vote. Nearly 500 million people are eligible to vote and close to 300 million do so. The turnout rate in the 1990s of over 60 percent was considerably higher than in the United States, although it declined slightly to 58 percent in 2004.

A larger range of ideological positions is represented by political parties in India than in the United States. The major parties in India are centrist, center-left, and right. Within this framework, there are at least four potentially significant national parties and countless regional parties. The four parties with significant national presence are Congress, the Janata Party, the Bharatiya Janata Party (BJP), and the Communist Party of India (Marxist), usually referred to as the CPM. Whereas the CPM is a left-leaning party and the BJP is a religious, right-leaning one, both Congress and the Janata are centrist parties. Although in the United States the Democratic party is usually considered center-leftist and the Republican party center-rightist, the differences between the two parties is much narrower than among Indian parties.

However, the ideological divide among Indian political parties has been reduced because no single party has been able to achieve power on its own since 1989. Parties have therefore been forced to ally within coalitions to form the government. Most of the coalition governments that have been formed have been unstable; only one, from 1991 to 1999, lasted a full term. Thus the more democratic India has become, with respect to increased party competition, the more unstable its governments have been. ❖

The party is closely affiliated with many related organizations, the most significant of which is the Rashtriya Swayam Sevak Sangh (RSS). Most BJP leaders were once members of the RSS, which recruits young people and involves them in a disciplined set of cultural activities, including the chauvinistic reinterpretation of India's "great Hindu past."

The BJP traditionally attracted urban, lower-middle-class groups, especially small business people. However it has widened its support appreciably by appealing to Hindu nationalism, especially in north-central India. The decline in the Congress Party's popularity created a vacuum that the BJP was well positioned to fill. Moreover, the BJP found in Indian Muslims a convenient scapegoat for the frustrations of various social groups.

In 1991, the BJP held the second-largest number of seats in parliament. To capitalize on the Hindu support, the BJP joined the RSS and its affiliated Vishva Hindu Parishad (VHP) in a campaign questioning the legitimacy of the Babri Masjid (a Muslim mosque) in Ayodhya. BJP leaders argued that the mosque was built on the birthplace of the Hindu god Rama. On December 6, 1992, thousands of Hindus, encouraged by the BJP, stormed and demolished the mosque. Seventeen hundred people were killed in the accompanying riots.

Six years later, as a result of the failures of other parties to lead effective governments, the BJP formed a governing coalition, the National Democratic Alliance, led by Prime Minister Atal Behari Vajpayee. It lasted only thirteen months. However, the BJP formed a new electoral coalition, again headed by Atal Behari Vajpayee; it was elected in 1999 and lasted a full term, until 2004. It was more broadly based than previous BJP-led coalition governments because it attracted the support of regionally based political parties in various states. The result strengthened the BJP's hold on power and also strengthened trends toward the regionalization of Indian politics.

In 1999, the BJP went to great lengths to project Atal Behari Vajpayee as a moderate, centrist leader. Moreover, the National Democratic Alliance platform shelved contentious issues that identified it with the interests of Hindus over and against those of religious minorities. In 2004, the BJP projected itself as the sponsor of "shining India," with a robust economy and nuclear might. Congress's commitment to secularism and the poor, along with its more deft approach to coalition building, won the day instead.

The BJP has never fully swung to the political center or abdicated its militancy. It was deeply implicated in mass violence in Gujarat in 2002. The catalyst for the violence was an attack on a trainload of Hindu pilgrims returning from Ayodhya, in which fifty-nine Hindus were killed. In the weeks that followed, Hindu groups engaged in a campaign of terror against the Muslim population of Gujarat in which over a thousand people were killed. The rampage was a particularly grave challenge to democratic principles because it was sanctioned by leading political officials of the BJP state government in Gujarat. The violence spread to the villages and gained the support of scheduled castes and tribals. It often included sexual assaults on women. However, with tacit support from the national government, the BJP government in Gujarat called for early elections in 2002 and won a landslide victory by capitalizing on the electoral support of Hindus that it had mobilized during the riots.

The BJP's commitment to privileging the interests of the Hindu majority has increased the vulnerability of the Muslim community. Although the BJP has consistently proclaimed its attachment to secularism, it has taken steps to undermine the conditions under which secularism flourishes. Its image of providing clean, honest governance has been damaged by charges of corruption by high-ranking officials, by the discriminatory distribution of relief after a massive earthquake in Gujarat in 2001, by evidence that the army engaged in corruption after a border clash with Pakistan in 1999, and by bribery in defense procurement in 2001.

The Communist Party of India (CPM)

Other than party cadres and a hierarchical authority structure, there is nothing communist about the CPM. Like the British Labour Party or the German Social Democratic Party, it accepts the framework of democracy and regularly participates in elections. It enjoys the support of the lower-middle and lower classes, factory workers, and poor peasants. Within the national parliament, CPM members often criticize policies that are likely to hurt the poor. On occasion, the CPM joins with other parties against the BJP, as it did in the 1996 elections by joining the United Front. At present, the CPM supports the Congress government in power but has not formally joined the government. Where the CPM runs state governments, in West Bengal and Kerala, it has provided a relatively honest and stable administration. It has also pursued a moderate but effective reform program, ensuring the rights of agricultural tenants, providing services to shantytowns, and encouraging public investments in rural areas.

Elections

FOCUS QUESTIONS

How can democracy function in a country where so many voters are illiterate? How do Indian political campaigns take account of illiteracy?

Like Britain, India has a first-past-the-post system. A number of candidates compete in an electoral district; the candidate with the most votes wins. This privileges the major political parties. It also generates considerable pressure for opposition parties to ally against the government.

Indian women hold up voting ID cards. *(Narinder Nanu/AFP/Getty Images.)*

Electoral tactics reflect the diverse voting population in India. Of the nearly 500 million people who are eligible to vote, approximately 300 million turn out. The rate in the 1990s exceeded 60 percent, but declined to 58 percent in 2004. Television plays an increasingly important role, but much campaigning still involves face-to-face contact between politicians and the electorate. Senior leaders tour the country, making speeches in tiny villages and district towns. Lesser politicians and thousands of party supporters travel the dusty streets, accompanied by blaring music and political messages from loudspeakers.

Given the high rate of illiteracy, party symbols are critical: a hand for the Congress (I); a lotus for the BJP; a hammer and sickle for the CPM. Illiterate voters vote for a candidate by putting thumb marks on one of these symbols. During the campaign, therefore, party representatives work hard to associate individuals and platforms with specific symbols. For instance, "Vote for the hammer and sickle because they stand for the rights of the working people."

One of the pillars of Indian democracy is its system of open, honest elections. Credit for this goes in part to the Election Commission, a constitutionally mandated central body that functions independently of the executive.

FOCUS QUESTIONS

In India political and public spheres are not clearly differentiated from personal and private spheres. How have these blurred boundaries hindered effective government? How have they promoted effective government?

Political Culture, Citizenship, and Identity

Several aspects of Indian political culture are noteworthy. First, political and public spheres are not sharply divided from personal and private spheres. Some Indians still consider that public office is a legitimate means for personal and familial enrichment. The positive aspect of this tendency is citizens' high level of political involvement in public life. Second, the Indian elite is extremely factionalized. Personal political ambitions prevent leaders from pursuing collective goals like forming cohesive parties, running stable governments, or focusing on national development. Unlike many East Asian countries, where consensus is powerful and political negotiation takes place behind closed doors, politics in India entails open conflicts.

Third, regions are differentiated by language and culture, villages are poorly connected with each other, and communities are stratified by caste. Politics is often fragmented along caste lines. Even caste grievances often remain local and do not become national or even regional. Some observers find this a blessing because it localizes problems, facilitating political stability. Others find it a curse because it obstructs national reforms to improve the lot of the poorest members of society.

Democratic politics fuels political conflicts. The most significant of these conflicts center on identity politics. Region, language, religion, and caste help Indians define themselves. Such differences generate political cleavages, underlining both the importance and the malleability of collective identities. A variety of ethnic conflicts were dormant when Nehru's secular nationalism and Indira Gandhi's poor-versus-rich cleavage defined the core political issues. In the 1980s and 1990s, however, with the relative decline of the Congress Party and with developments in telecommunications and transportation that have made

The Caste System

Originally derived from the Portuguese word *castas*, today the word *caste* inevitably evokes images of a rigid hierarchy that characterizes Indian society. In reality, however, castes are less immutable and timeless categories than suggested by the popular image.

Historically, the **caste system** compartmentalized and ranked the Hindu population of the Indian subcontinent through rules governing various aspects of daily life, such as eating, marriage, and prayer. Sanctioned by religion, the hierarchy of caste is based on a conception of the world as divided into realms of purity and impurity. Each hereditary and endogamous group (that is, a group into which one is born and within which one marries) constitutes a *jati*, which is itself organized by *varna*, or shades of color. The four main *varna* are the **Brahmin**, or priestly, caste; the Kshatriya, or warrior and royal, caste; the Vaishyas, or trading, caste; and the Shudra, or artisan, caste. Each of these *varna* is divided into many *jatis* that often approximate occupational groups (such as potters, barbers, and carpenters). Those who were not considered members of organized Hindu society because they lived in forests and on hills rather than in towns and villages, or were involved in "unclean" occupations such as sweepers and leather workers were labeled **untouchables**, outcastes, or **scheduled castes**. Because each *jati* is often concentrated in a particular region, it is sometimes possible to change one's *varna* when one moves to a different part of the country by changing one's name and adopting the social customs of higher castes, for example, giving up eating meat. Some flexibility within the rigidity of the system has contributed to its survival over the centuries. ❖

caste system India's Hindu society is divided into castes. According to the Hindu religion, membership in a caste is determined at birth. Castes form a rough social and economic hierarchy.

Brahmin the highest caste in the Hindu caste system of India.

untouchables the lowest caste in India's caste system, whose members are among the poorest and most disadvantaged Indians.

scheduled castes the lowest caste groups in India; also known as the untouchables.

people more aware of each other's differences, identity-based political conflicts have mushroomed.

For example, caste conflicts, formerly confined to local and regional politics, have acquired national dimensions. For example, backward castes had made a political mark in many states, but prior to Mandal, the backward castes were generally not a cohesive force in national politics. However when V. P. Singh sought to gain their support, the threatened upper castes reacted with demonstrations, riots, and violence. This disruption contributed to the Singh government's downfall and converted caste conflicts from local and regional issues to divisive national issues.

Another identity-based conflict pits Hindus and Muslims against each other. Political circumstances, especially political machinations by ambitious leaders, can inflame these tendencies and instigate overt conflict. This is what has happened, as the BJP has whipped up anti-Muslim sentiments to unite disparate Hindu groups into a political force.

FOCUS QUESTIONS

What are at least three characteristic forms of social protest in India? What is specifically Indian about such forms of protest?

Interests, Social Movements, and Protest

India has a vibrant tradition of political activism. Social movements, non-governmental organizations (NGOs), and trade unions have put pressure on the state to address the interests and needs of underprivileged groups and have checked its authoritarian tendencies. Among these groups, labor has played a significant but not leading role. Unions are politically fragmented, particularly at the national level. Instead of the familiar model of one factory/one union, several political parties often organize within a single factory. Above the factory level, several labor organizations compete for labor's support. Government generally stays out of labor-management conflicts. India's industrial relations are closer to the pluralist model of Anglo-American countries than to the corporatist model of Mexico. The political energies of unions are channeled into frequent local battles involving strikes, demonstrations, and a peculiarly Indian protest technique called *gherao*, which entails workers' encircling and holding executives of the firm hostage until their demands are met.

Social movements, the most important form of civil society activism, date back to the mid-1970s. During the national Emergency (1975–1977) when the government imprisoned members of the opposition, activists formed political parties and social movements, often with close ties to one another. In 1977, the Gandhian Socialist leader Jai Prakash Narayan organized the movement for total democracy. This ultimately brought about the downfall of Congress and the election of the Janata Party. A decade later, V. P. Singh resigned from Congress and formed the *Jan Morcha* (Peoples' Front), an avowedly nonpolitical movement that brought new groups into politics and helped bring the National Front to power in 1989.

Social movements continued to grow and assume new organizational forms in the 1980s. Some engaged in grassroots activism, while others worked more closely with the state. NGOs also grew. In the early 1980s under Indira Gandhi, the state sought to restrict what is commonly known in India as the voluntary sector. Rajiv Gandhi attempted to cultivate a closer relationship with NGOs, for he recognized their potential for taking over some of the development work that the state had traditionally performed. Over the years, financial support for NGOs from the national government has steadily increased. During the seventh five-year plan (1985–1990), the federal government spent about US$11 million each year through NGOs. By 2002 this had quadrupled. Today, the Ministry of Home Affairs conservatively lists 20,000. The most significant social movements organized around either distinctive themes or identities include the women's movement, the environmental movement, the farmers' movement, and the *dalit* (a term of pride used by untouchables) movement. Antinuclear and civil liberties activism have picked up. These numerous and extensive social movements make India quite distinctive among developing countries.

The environmental movement draws on educated urban activists and some of India's poorest and most marginal groups. India suffers from severe air pollution in large cities and contaminated lakes and rivers. The shortage of drinking water is worsened by salinization, water overuse, and groundwater depletion. Carbon dioxide emissions contribute to the greenhouse effect, raising

Placards protesting the construction of the Sardar Sarvodaya Dam. *(Tom Pietrasik/Corbis)*

the sea level, and destroying coastal croplands and fisheries. Commercial logging, fuel wood depletion, and urbanization cause serious deforestation, leading to droughts, floods, and cyclones.

The largest and most significant environmental movement in India is the Narmada Bachao Andolan (NBA) which has organized opposition to the construction of the Sardar Sarvodaya Dam on grounds that it will benefit already prosperous regions to the detriment of poor regions, lead to the large-scale displacement of people, and put in place vastly inadequate resettlement schemes. A large proportion of those who would be displaced are tribals who do not possess land titles. The movement has involved tens of thousands in nonviolent protest against the construction of the dam. The protest caused the World Bank to rescind promised loans, but the Indian government is still pursuing the project.

Since the 1980s a number of autonomous urban women's organizations have campaigned against rape in police custody, dowry murders, *sati* (the immolation of widows on their husbands' funeral pyres), female feticide (through the use of amniocentesis), media misrepresentation of women, harmful contraception dissemination, coercive population policies, and, most recently, the adverse impact of economic reforms.

The *dalit* movement looks back to Dr. Balasaheb Ambedkar, the *dalit* author of the Indian constitution, as the founding father of the movement. He was responsible for the creation of the Republican Party in the late 1960s. When the party disintegrated, a radical youth movement (the Dalit Panthers) emerged. The movement demanded that *dalits* be treated with dignity and given better educational opportunities.

Three important developments have influenced the character and trajectory of social movements in recent years. First, many social movements have increasingly engaged the state and electoral politics. Social movements used to be community-based and issue-specific. Although many social movements remain restricted in their focus, duration, and geographic reach, others seek to overcome these difficulties by engaging in electoral politics. The *dalit* movement and Hindu nationalism are two of the most important examples. Electoral politics has shaped and influenced their goals. Other movements have sought to work with particular branches of the state.

Second, the religious right poses a serious challenge to left-wing social movements. Unlike some regions of the world where the religious right and the secular left disagree on most issues, the situation in India is more complex. Segments of the religious right, like parts of the left, oppose economic liberalization and globalization. For example, both feminists and Hindu nationalists oppose the commodification of women's bodies in the media and in international beauty pageants. Similarly, the women's movement has put on the back burner its demand for a uniform civil code to provide equal treatment of men and women of all religious communities under the law because the BJP has made this very demand, albeit for very different reasons. Furthermore, several social movements have abandoned a commitment to poverty alleviation and have embraced the state-initiated shift toward the market.

Third, many social movements have developed extensive transnational connections. On the positive side, funding from foreign sources has been vital to the survival of NGOs and social movements. India lacks a tradition of donating to secular-philanthropic causes, and corporate funding is limited and tightly controlled. However, organizations receiving foreign funding are often viewed with suspicion and have difficulty establishing their legitimacy. Moreover, foreign funding has created a sharp division between activists with and without access to foreign donors.

There are greater opportunities than ever for social movements and NGO activists to take advantage of the resources that the state is making available. Some groups have already done this by putting candidates up for elections at the local level, as we have seen in the case of the *panchayats*. Furthermore, the BJP's defeat in the 2004 elections in part because its claims of "India shining" coupled with the relatively strong performance of left-of-center parties, may well revitalize underprivileged groups.

Summary

To summarize, India has a strong tradition of social movements that have directly influenced political life in two different ways. The first is by working with political parties to influence electoral outcomes as was most evident in the period 1975–1977 when social movements formed the Janata party that defeated the Congress Party for the first time ever. The second is by working with the state around development issues. With the growth of nongovernmental organizations (NGOs), the state's collaboration with civil society organizations has grown. Although social movements have faced a number of important challenges in recent years, they are likely to continue to play a vital role in Indian political life.

Indian Politics in Transition

FOCUS QUESTION

Consider the major challenges that India will confront in the coming years. How well are Indian institutions equipped to meet these challenges?

Political Challenges and Changing Agendas

On July 11, 2006, seven bombs struck a suburban train line in Mumbai, killing 207 people and injuring another 700. Mumbai is to India what New York City is to the United States, a commercial and cosmopolitan capital. Although it is not clear who was responsible, the Indian government blamed Pakistan-trained terrorists, while civil society groups made no assumptions about culpability and refrained from engaging in retaliatory violence. Clearly Mumbai's cosmopolitanism provides the city with the resources to cope with such crises. Meanwhile many questions about the violence remain unanswered. While most observers have assumed that the violence was a response to Hindu-Muslim tensions, they have devoted much less attention to the class dimensions, even though the perpetrators attacked only the first-class train compartments. India is simultaneously confronting heightened ethnic tensions and heightened class conflicts. Another set of conflicts result from the tensions between a centralized state and secessionist ambitions of subnational governments such as Kashmir.

Kashmir within a World of States

The roots of conflict within Kashmir have often been attributed to the ethnic and religious diversity of the state (roughly 65 percent Muslim and 35 percent Hindus and other minorities). The non-Muslim minorities—Hindus, Sikhs, and Buddhists, concentrated in the areas of the state called Jammu and Ladakh—largely wish to live under Indian sovereignty. The Kashmir Valley, predominantly Sunni Muslim, mostly want Kashmir to become an independent country or part of Pakistan. However, separatist sentiments cannot be explained primarily by ethnic differences. Rather, one must ask what led many Kashmiri Muslims to become progressively radicalized against India.

More than any other conflict, the Kashmir dispute is triggered and sustained by the international context. The timing of Indian independence and simultaneous partition of the subcontinent into India and Pakistan fueled tensions in Kashmir and created uncertainty over its status within the Indian union. Superpower rivalry in the Cold War deterred India and Pakistan from reaching an agreement on the status of Kashmir.

The Kashmir problem reveals the limits of Indian democracy, for the national government has ruled Kashmir more undemocratically than any other state in India. It has used repression, direct control, and manipulation to install unrepresentative governments. The constant rigging of elections has prevented free and autonomous competition among political parties. While elections were held in most parts of the country from 1952 onward, in Kashmir elections to the legislative assembly were held only in 1962 and to the parliament only in 1967. Most elections in Jammu and Kashmir were fraudulent, although 2002 and 2004 were partial exceptions. Although the police and army forced people to vote,

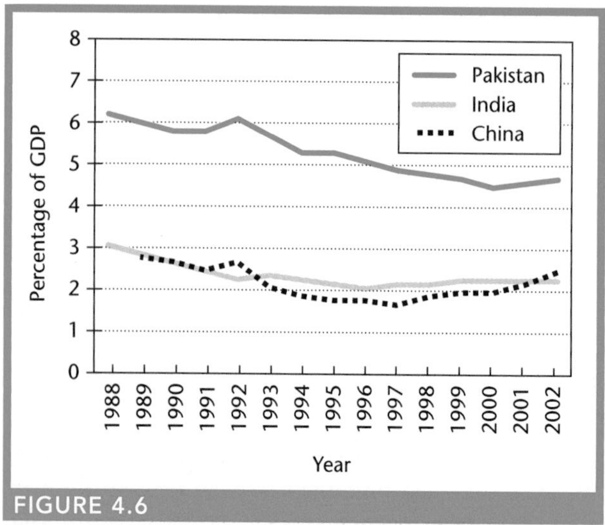

FIGURE 4.6

Military Expenditures as a Percentage of GDP

Source: Information from the Stockholm International Peace Research Institute (SIPRI), Military Expenditure Database, http://first.sipri.org/index.php?page=step3&compact=true.

in part in response to the separatists' call for an electoral boycott, the elections were more open and inclusive than they had previously been.

The other serious impediment to resolving the Kashmir dispute is continuing tension between India and Pakistan. This tension is one important reason for the two countries' high military expenditures (see Figure 4.6). Relations between the two countries have periodically swung from terrible to moderately good—only to decline again. After a military confrontation in 1999, followed by a thaw, relations again took a turn for the worse in 2001.

Soon after September 11, there was an exchange of fire on the border between the two countries. Relations plummeted further after October 1, 2001, with an attack by groups from Pakistan on the Jammu and Kashmir legislative assembly. An attack on the Indian parliament later that year was far more serious. India charged that the attacks on a key political institution were orchestrated by Pakistan and amassed over one million troops near the Pakistani border. Pakistan responded in kind. For several weeks, nuclear conflagration seemed a distinct possibility. Intense intervention by the United States helped to defuse the situation, and Pakistan and India withdrew most of their troops from the border. Since then the United States has worked behind the scenes to pressure Pakistan to restrain terrorists within its borders. The two countries subsequently restored full diplomatic ties, exchanged ambassadors, restored air travel links and, of great symbolic significance, resumed cricket matches.

Nuclear Power Status

Soon after the BJP first came to power in May 1998, it fulfilled an electoral promise by gate crashing the nuclear club. This triggered a nuclear arms race in South Asia. Although the Indian government cited regional threats from China and Pakistan, the decision to become a nuclear state has deeper roots. Electoral mobilization along ethnic lines (religious, language, or caste) in an atmosphere of economic turmoil and poverty prompted political parties to mobilize Indians' national pride, to deflect attention from domestic economic and political problems. Within a few weeks of India's nuclear test, Pakistan tested its own bomb. Many countries, including the United States, imposed economic and technology sanctions on both India and Pakistan.

Tensions between India and the global community on the nuclear testing issue have subsequently abated. In 1998, India announced its intention to sign the Comprehensive Test Ban Treaty if talks with the United States ended successfully. It also signaled its willingness to join other nuclear control groups. The following year India and Pakistan agreed to continue a moratorium on further nuclear tests. The Manmohan Singh government took a dramatic step toward defusing tensions around the nuclear issue. While emphasizing that decisions about India's nuclear programs must be made domestically—not in response to externally imposed sanctions—Singh emphasized India's nonproliferation record and commitment to preventing the proliferation of weapons of mass destruction. Parliament voted to propose a stricter regime of external transfers and tighter controls to prevent international leakages. In September 2004, Manmohan Singh and George W. Bush issued a joint statement emphasizing the commitment of the two countries to work together to stop the proliferation of weapons of mass destruction. In July 2005 they agreed that India could secure international help for its civilian nuclear reactors while retaining its nuclear arms. This agreement actually paved the way for removing a U.S. ban on nuclear technology sales to India. The Indo-U.S. nuclear treaty (which still needs to be ratified by both the countries) allows the two countries to cooperate on nuclear issues despite India's violation of nonproliferation norms and despite domestic opposition to the treaty both within India and in the United States. The United States would like to strengthen India as an alternate power to China in Asia; India in turn has been seeking to reorient its global position ever since the decline of its former ally, the Soviet Union.

How India confronts challenges on the nuclear front is closely tied to its success in several other areas, including resolution of the Kashmir dispute, the management of increasing ethnic tensions, and its economic performance.

The Challenge of Ethnic Diversity

Mobilized ethnic groups seeking access to state power and state-controlled economic resources are a basic component of the contemporary Indian political scene. Caste, language, and religion all provide identities around which to mobilize followers. Identification with a group grows in a democratic context, in which parties and leaders manipulate such symbols. India's political leaders will continue to experience pressures to expand their support base by promising economic improvements or manipulating nationalist symbols. Under what conditions will such political forces engage in constructive rather than destructive actions? Will democracy merely temper the effect of such forces, or will it channel identity politics positively? Answers to these questions partly hinges on India's economic performance.

Economic Performance

India's economic experience is neither a clear success nor a clear failure. Three conditions may explain this outcome. The first is the government's skill and commitment to promoting economic growth. In this, India has been fortunate to have enjoyed relatively good government since independence: its democratic system is mostly open and stable, its most powerful political leaders are public spirited, and its upper bureaucracy is well trained and competent.

The second condition concerns India's strategy for economic development. India in the 1950s chose to insulate its economy from global forces, limiting the role of trade and foreign investment and emphasizing the role of government in promoting self-sufficiency in heavy industry and agriculture. India now produces enough food to feed its large and growing population while it simultaneously produces a vast range of industrial goods. Most of India's manufactured goods, however, are produced rather inefficiently by global standards. India sacrificed the additional economic growth that might have come from competing effectively in global markets and by selling its products abroad. It also gave up another area of potential economic growth by discouraging foreign investment.

And last, during the phase of protective industrialization, India did little to alleviate its staggering poverty: land redistribution failed, job creation by heavy industries was minimal, and investment in the education and health of the poor was minuscule in relation to the magnitude of the problem. The poor also became a drag on economic growth because they were unable to buy goods and stimulate demand for increased production and because an uneducated and unhealthy labor force is not productive.

Despite this sluggish past, India's economy over the last quarter of a century has grown handsomely. The main forces propelling this change have been a closer relation between Indian governments and Indian business groups, liberalization of the economy, and integration in the global economy. However a variety of inequalities are growing. India's numerous poor are not benefiting as much from growth as they might. The reduction in public spending has hurt the poor by limiting their access to publicly funded education and health services.

FOCUS QUESTION

Consider at least three ways in which India provides a useful model of development for other countries. In what ways is India's model unique?

Indian Politics in Comparative Perspective

Some comparative scholars suggest that citizens' widespread desire to exercise some control over their government is a potent force encouraging democracy. Although democracy was introduced to India by its elites, it has established firm roots throughout society. A clear example is when Indira Gandhi declared Emergency rule (1975–1977) and curtailed democratic freedoms. In the next election, in 1977, Indian citizens decisively voted Indira Gandhi out of power, registering their preference for democratic rule.

Comparativists debate whether democracy or authoritarianism is better for economic growth. In the past, India did not compare well with the success stories of authoritarian East Asian countries. India's impressive economic growth in recent years reopens these old debates. Moreover, the collapse in the late 1990s of several East Asian economies and the subsequent rise of instability within those societies makes a study of Indian democracy more relevant to understanding the institutional and cultural factors underpinning long-run economic stability.

The rising tide of nationalism and the breakup of the Soviet Union and Yugoslavia, among others, have prompted closer examination of how and why India remains a cohesive entity. By studying India's history, particularly after 1947, comparativists could explore how cleavages of caste, religion, and language balance one another and curtail the most destructive elements. Comparativists have also puzzled about the conditions under which multiple and contradictory interests could be harnessed within a democratic setup to generate positive economic and distributional outcomes. For instance, two communist-ruled states, Kerala and West Bengal, have (to a certain extent) engaged in land redistribution policies. An examination of factors such as the role of the mobilizing parties and the interaction between the landless poor and the entrenched landed elite could provide answers. The main elements of the Kerala model are a land reform initiative that abolished tenancy and landlord exploitation, effective public food distribution that provides subsidized rice to low-income households, protective laws for agricultural workers, and pensions for retired agricultural laborers, and a high rate of government employment for low-caste communities.

Another question engaging comparativists is whether success in providing education and welfare inevitably leads to success in the economic sphere. Again, the case of Kerala provides pointers for further research. Kerala scores high on human development indicators such as literacy and health, and its economy has also grown in recent years.

What international and domestic challenges face India at the dawn of the twenty-first century? How will it cope with its new-found status as a nuclear power? How can it prevent further escalation of conflict in the region that could end in a nuclear conflagration? A worst-case scenario would be a conventional war with Pakistan that could escalate into a nuclear war. Domestically, both countries are wracked with ethnic tensions, one with a military dictatorship and the other with an elected coalition government. In an attempt to hold on to power, the leaders of each country could try to divert attention toward a national security threat from its neighbor, a ploy that politicians in both countries have used effectively. The challenge for India is to establish a stable relationship with its nuclear neighbors, Pakistan and China, that would eschew proliferation of their nuclear and ballistic missile arsenals and engage in constructive diplomatic and economic cooperation. India's history of wars with both countries is not an encouraging starting point, but the engagement of Western powers in generating a dialogue between these countries is a good omen. The recent initiation of people-to-people contacts and resumption of talks among leaders provides grounds for optimism. Whether such overtures will result in fruitful negotiations on Kashmir and on economic cooperation in the region remains to be seen. Answers to these questions depend at least in part on domestic political developments.

For nearly sixty years, democracy in India has been double-edged. Winning elections involves attracting votes. The practice of democracy, particularly electoral politics, has worsened ethnic relations between Hindus and Muslims, upper and lower castes, and north and south. Many dissatisfied groups are finding their voices and becoming politically mobilized. The challenge for Indian politics is to repair the divide within a democratic framework. Current voter emphasis on good governance and sound economic management rather than on religious or nationalist issues may transform electoral platforms.

Another challenge for India is to combine its global ambitions with its program for economic liberalization. The increasing interdependence of global economies should not be underestimated. While India was protected from the 1997 East Asian financial crisis because of the partially closed nature of its economy, the country nevertheless suffered some economic blows after becoming nuclear, when economic sanctions resulted in the loss of billions of dollars in foreign aid.

However, the Indian economy recovered relatively quickly. Even with modest liberalization, India is now attracting considerable foreign investment and growing at an impressive rate. The Indian case nevertheless embodies the tensions inherent in combining democracy with economic liberalization. Political parties in India face pressures to expand their support base by manipulating nationalist symbols, which sometimes clash with the task of economic liberalization.

Summary

How India reconciles its national political ambitions, domestic political demands for greater economic redistribution, and global pressures for an efficient economy will affect its influence on regional and global trends. Can India capitalize on its positive achievements, such as the longstanding democratic ethos framed by functioning institutions, a vibrant civil society and media, and a growing middle class imbued with the desire to succeed economically? Or will it be crippled by ethnic hostility resulting in inaction at best and total disintegration of the country at worst? The current trends indicate a scenario of two-party rule, with either a BJP-led or a Congress-led coalition ruling at the center. There also seems to be some room for optimism with regard to voter needs and interests on the international and domestic fronts. Public opinion polls show that an overwhelming number of people in India and Pakistan want improved relations. On the domestic side, the results of the 2004 elections demonstrate voters' commitments to secularism, equitable distribution, and economic management. Of course, balancing the demands of simultaneously achieving equity and efficiency generates its own problems. Understanding the ways in which India meets these challenges will be of enormous interest to students of comparative politics in the years to come.

Key Terms

Sikhs
Sepoy Rebellion
patronage system
capitalism
Emergency (1975–1977)
green revolution
state-led economic development
economic liberalization
nonaligned bloc
Lok Sabha
Rajya Sabha
Indian Administrative Service
zamindars
panchayats
Mandal Commission
other backward classes
reservations
caste system
Brahmin
untouchables
scheduled castes

Suggested Readings

Bardhan, Pranab. *The Political Economy of Development in India.* New Delhi: Oxford University Press, 1984.

Basu, Amrita. *Two Faces of Protest: Contrasting Modes of Women's Activism in India.* Berkeley: University of California Press, 1992.

———, and Atul Kohli, eds. *Community Conflicts and the State in India.* New Delhi: Oxford University Press, 1998.

Bayly, C. A. *The New Cambridge History of India: Indian Society and the Making of the British Empire*. Vol. 2, no. 1. Cambridge: Cambridge University Press, 1988.

Brass, Paul R. *The Production of Hindu-Muslim Violence in Contemporary India*. Madison: University of Wisconsin Press, 2005.

———. *The New Cambridge History of India: The Politics of India Since Independence*. Vol. 4, no. 1. Cambridge: Cambridge University Press, 1990.

Chatterjee, Partha, ed. *State Politics in India*. New Delhi: Oxford University Press, 1997.

Dreze, Jean, and Amartya Sen, eds. *Economic Development and Social Opportunity*. New Delhi: Oxford University Press, 1995.

Frankel, Francine. *India's Political Economy, 1947–2004: The Gradual Revolution*. New Delhi: Oxford University Press, 2005.

Gopal, Sarvepalli. *Jawaharlal Nehru: A Biography*. Vols. 2 and 3. New Delhi: Oxford University Press, 1984.

Graham, Bruce. *Hindu Nationalism and Indian Politics*. Cambridge: Cambridge University Press, 1990.

Hardgrave, Robert L., Jr., and Stanley A. Kochanek. *India: Government and Politics in a Developing Nation*. 4th ed. New York: Harcourt Brace Jovanovich, 1986.

Hasan, Zoya. *Quest for Power: Oppositional Movements and Post-Congress Politics in Uttar Pradesh*. Delhi: Oxford University Press, 1998.

Jaffrelot, Christophe. *The Hindu Nationalist Movement and Indian Politics, 1925 to the 1990s: Strategies on Identity Building, Implantation and Mobilization*. New York: Columbia University Press, 1996.

Jalal, Ayesha. *Democracy and Authoritarianism in South Asia*. Cambridge: Cambridge University Press, 1995.

Jenkins, Rob. *Regional Reflections: Contemporary Politics Across India's States*. New Delhi: Oxford University Press, 2004.

Kohli, Atul. *State Directed Development: Political Power and Industrialization in the Global Periphery*. Cambridge: Cambridge University Press, 2004.

———. ed. *The Success of India's Democracy*. Cambridge: Cambridge University Press, 2001.

———. *Democracy and Discontent: India's Growing Crisis of Governability*. Cambridge: Cambridge University Press, 1991.

———. *The State and Poverty in India: The Politics of Reform*. Cambridge: Cambridge University Press, 1987.

Misra, B. B. *Government and Bureaucracy in India: 1947–1976*. New Delhi: Oxford University Press, 1986.

Nayar, Baldev Raj. *India's Mixed Economy*. Bombay: Popular Prakashan, 1989.

Ray, Raka, and Mary Katzenstein, eds. *Social Movements in India: Poverty, Power and Politics*. Lanham, Md.: Rowman and Littlefield, 2005.

Rothermund, Dietmar. *An Economic History of India: From Pre-Colonial Times to 1986*. London: Croom Helm, 1988.

Rudolph, Lloyd, and Susanne Rudolph. *In Pursuit of Lakshmi: The Political Economy of the Indian State*. Chicago: University of Chicago Press, 1987.

Sarkar, Sumit. *Modern India: 1885 to 1947*. Madras: Macmillan, 1983.

Varshney, Ashutosh. *India and the Political Economy of Developing Countries: Essays in Honor of Myron Weiner*. New Delhi: Sage Publishers, 2004.

———, ed. *Ethnic Conflict and Civic Life: Hindus and Muslims in India*. New Haven, Conn.: Yale University Press, 2002.

Weiner, Myron. *The Indian Paradox: Essays in Indian Politics*. New Delhi: Sage, 1989.

Wilkinson, Steven. *Votes and Violence: Electoral Competition and Ethnic Riots in India*. Cambridge: Cambridge University Press, 2004.

Official Name:	Russian Federation (*Rossiyskaya Federatsiya*)
Location:	Eastern Europe/Northern Asia
Capital City:	Moscow
Population (2007):	141.4 million
Size:	17,075,200 sq. km.; approximately 1.8 times the size of the United States

CHAPTER

5 Russia

Joan DeBardeleben

Chronology of Soviet and Russian Political Development

1917	1918–1921	1921–1928	1929	1929–1953	1929–1938
The Bolshevik seizure of power	Civil War and war communism	New Economic Policy	Stalin consolidates power	Stalin in power	Collectivization and purges

1985–1991	1991	1992	1993	1995–1996
The Gorbachev era and *perestroika*	Popular election of Boris Yeltsin as president of Russia (July); collapse of the USSR and formation of fifteen independent states (December); establishment of the Russian Federation as an independent state	Market reforms launched in Russia (January)	Adoption of the new Russian constitution by referendum; first (multiparty) parliamentary elections in the Russian Federation (December)	Second parliamentary elections in the Russian Federation (December 1995) with the Communists winning the most seats; first presidential elections under the new Russian constitution (June–July 1996), with Yeltsin reelected in two rounds of voting.

SECTION 1 The Making of the Modern Russian State

FOCUS QUESTION

In what ways may terrorism present challenges to Russia's democratization processes?

Politics in Action

For children of Middle School No. 1 in Beslan (population about 34,000) in southern Russia, the first day of school in 2004 was marked by tragedy. As parents accompanied children to school, terrorist forces herded 1,000 children and family members into the gymnasium. Not permitting the victims food or water, the hostage takers made demands that were unacceptable to the Russian government: the removal of Russian troops from the neighboring secessionist region, the Republic of Chechnya, and the release of Chechen rebels held by the government. On Friday, September 3—fifty-two hours later—Russian special forces heard an explosion inside. They stormed the building in an effort to release the victims. Over 300 hostages, the majority children, were dead.

The Beslan massacre followed numerous other terrorist attacks since 1995. The previous month, two Russian passenger planes crashed simultaneously, killing at least eighty-nine passengers. In May 2004, a bomb killed Chechen president Akhmad Kadyrov. He had been installed by elections some claimed were unfairly controlled by Moscow. Two years earlier, bomb-laden terrorists took over 700 hostages in a Moscow theater; at least 120 died. Other attacks targeted theaters, apartment buildings, and public transport.

1941–1945	1953	1953–1955	1956–1964	1965–1982	1982–1985
Nazi Germany invades Soviet Union; "Great Patriotic War"	Death of Stalin	Leadership change after Stalin's death	The Khrushchev era and de-Stalinization 1962 Cuban Missile Crisis	The Brezhnev era and bureaucratic consolidation 1972 Initiation of détente (easing of tension between the USSR and the United States)	Leadership change after Brezhnev's death

1998	1999	2000	2003	2004	2007–2008
Financial crisis and devaluation of the ruble	Third parliamentary elections in the Russian Federation; Unity Party gains strong support, as does Communist Party; resignation of Yeltsin as president (December)	Election of Vladimir Putin as president of Russia	Third parliamentary elections in the Russian Federation; strong win for United Russia Party (December)	Reelection of Vladimir Putin as president of Russia (March); September hostage taking of school children and bloody conflict to free hostages in Beslan, southern Russia; Putin announces new centralizing measures	Most recent Russian election cycle, with parliamentary elections in December 2007 and presidential elections in March 2008, the latter marking the end of Vladimir Putin's two terms in office.

Although Chechen terrorists have links to international networks, including Al Qaeda, the context of the Russian problem is local. Terrorism responds to an extended war in the Russian republic of Chechnya resulting from Russia's efforts to control rebel secessionist forces. An increasingly prominent role for Chechen women among the suicide bombers suggests the depth of the social alienation that underlies the terrorist wave.

Following the Beslan tragedy, Russian president Putin announced reforms to increase central control over selection of regional governors. A counterterrorism law was proposed making it easier to restrict press freedom and civil liberties in the face of alleged terrorist threats. Just as economic revived beginning in 1999, worries about security increased. Russians wondered whether the state could ensure their well-being and security. While Western experts were debating whether Putin's centralizing reforms would undermine democratization, many Russians were just hoping that they would give the government the authority it needs to ensure a secure and stable way of life.

FOCUS QUESTION

In what ways does geography make Russia a difficult country to govern?

Geographic Setting

After the Soviet Union broke up in 1991, fifteen newly independent states emerged on its territory. This section focuses on the Russian Federation, the largest successor state and the largest European country in population (between

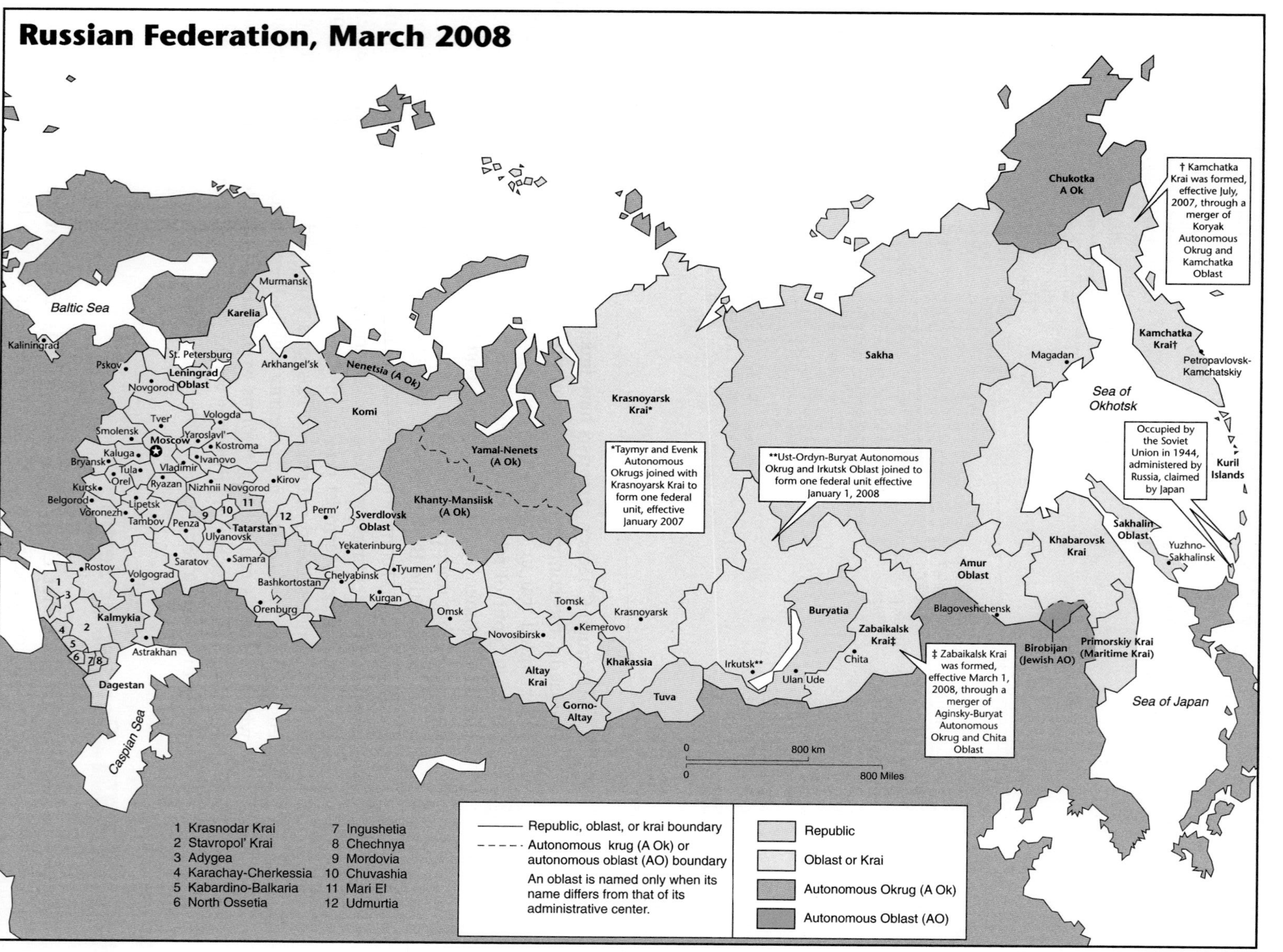
Russian Federation, March 2008
Baltic Sea
Kaliningrad
Pskov
St. Petersburg
Leningrad Oblast
Novgorod
Karelia
Murmansk
Arkhangel'sk
Nenetsia (A Ok)
Komi
Tver'
Vologda
Smolensk
Moscow
Yaroslavl'
Kostroma
Kaluga
Ivanovo
Bryansk
Tula
Vladimir
Orel
Ryazan
Nizhnii Novgorod
Kursk
Kirov
Belgorod
Lipetsk
Voronezh
Tambov
Penza
Ulyanovsk
Tatarstan
Perm'
Sverdlovsk Oblast
Yekaterinburg
Samara
Saratov
Bashkortostan
Chelyabinsk
Tyumen'
Kurgan
Orenburg
Rostov
Volgograd
Kalmykia
Astrakhan
Dagestan
Caspian Sea
Yamal-Nenets (A Ok)
Khanty-Mansiisk (A Ok)
Omsk
Novosibirsk
Tomsk
Kemerovo
Altay Krai
Gorno-Altay
Khakassia
Krasnoyarsk
Krasnoyarsk Krai*
Tuva
*Taymyr and Evenk Autonomous Okrugs joined with Krasnoyarsk Krai to form one federal unit, effective January 2007
**Ust-Ordyn-Buryat Autonomous Okrug and Irkutsk Oblast joined to form one federal unit effective January 1, 2008
Irkutsk**
Ulan Ude
Buryatia
Zabaikalsk Krai‡
Chita
‡ Zabaikalsk Krai was formed, effective March 1, 2008, through a merger of Aginsky-Buryat Autonomous Okrug and Chita Oblast
Sakha
Amur Oblast
Blagoveshchensk
Birobijan (Jewish AO)
Primorskiy Krai (Maritime Krai)
Khabarovsk Krai
Magadan
Chukotka A Ok
† Kamchatka Krai was formed, effective July, 2007, through a merger of Koryak Autonomous Okrug and Kamchatka Oblast
Kamchatka Krai†
Petropavlovsk-Kamchatskiy
Sea of Okhotsk
Occupied by the Soviet Union in 1944, administered by Russia, claimed by Japan
Kuril Islands
Sakhalin Oblast
Yuzhno-Sakhalinsk
Sea of Japan
0 800 km
0 800 Miles
1 Krasnodar Krai
2 Stavropol' Krai
3 Adygea
4 Karachay-Cherkessia
5 Kabardino-Balkaria
6 North Ossetia
7 Ingushetia
8 Chechnya
9 Mordovia
10 Chuvashia
11 Mari El
12 Udmurtia
Republic, oblast, or krai boundary
Autonomous krug (A Ok) or autonomous oblast (AO) boundary
An oblast is named only when its name differs from that of its administrative center.
Republic
Oblast or Krai
Autonomous Okrug (A Ok)
Autonomous Oblast (AO)

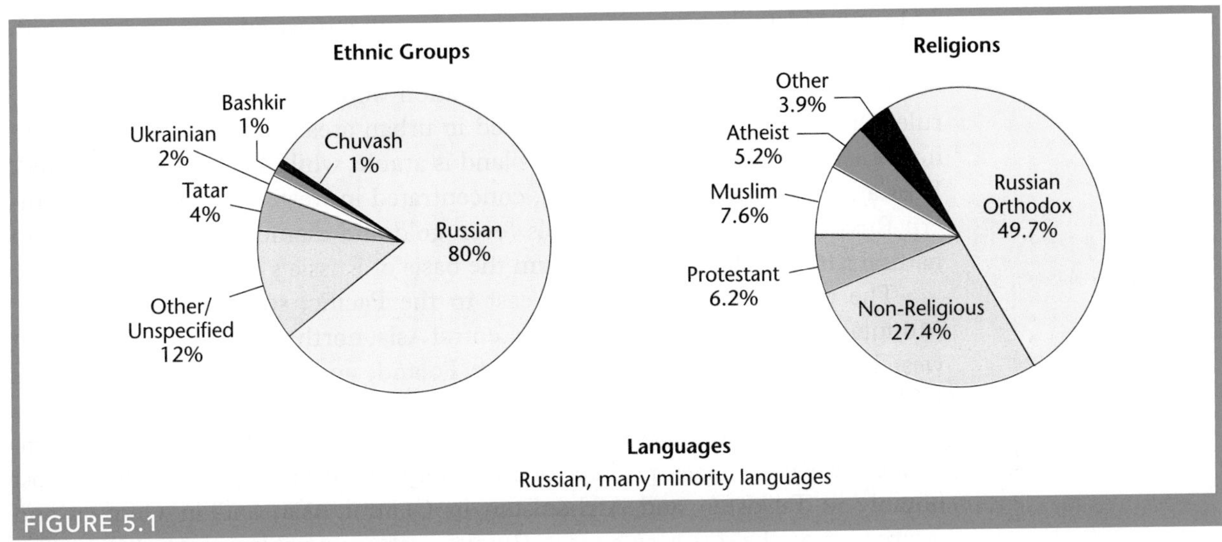

FIGURE 5.1

The Russian Nation at a Glance

TABLE 5.1

Political Organization

Political System	Constitutionally a federal state, semipresidential system.
Regime History	Re-formed as an independent state with the collapse of communist rule in December 1991; current constitution since December 1993.
Administrative Structure	Federal system, originally with eighty-nine subnational governments including twenty-one republics, fifty-five provinces (*oblast, krai*), eleven autonomous districts or regions (*okrugs* or autonomous *oblast*), and two cities of federal status. As of July 2007 the number of subnational governments was reduced to eighty-five, through a merger of regions.
Executive	Dual executive (president and prime minister). Direct election of president; prime minister appointed by the president with the approval of the lower house of the parliament (State *Duma*).
Legislature	Bicameral. Upper house (Federation Council) appointed by heads of regional executive and representative organs. Lower house (State *Duma*) chosen by direct election, with half of the 450 deputies chosen through a proportional representation system and half from single-member constituencies until 2007, when a full proportional representation system was introduced for all 450 deputies. Powers include proposal and approval of legislation, approval of presidential appointees.
Judiciary	Independent constitutional court with nineteen justices, nominated by the president and approved by the Federation Council, holding twelve-year terms with possible renewal.
Party System	Multiparty system with a dominant party (United Russia).

141 and 142 million in 2007) and, in area, the largest country in the world, spanning eleven time zones.

Russia underwent rapid industrialization and urbanization under Soviet rule. Only 18 percent of Russians lived in urban areas in 1917; 73 percent do now. Less than 8 percent of Russia's land is arable, while 45 percent is forested. Russia is rich in natural resources, concentrated in western Siberia and northern Russia. These include minerals (even gold and diamonds), timber, oil and natural gas exports, which now form the basis of Russia's economic wealth.

The czarist empire extended east to the Pacific, south to the Caucasus Mountains and the Muslim areas of Central Asia, north to the Arctic Circle, and west into present-day Ukraine, eastern Poland, and the Baltic states. In the USSR the Russian Republic formed the core of a multiethnic state. Russia's ethnic diversity and geographic scope have made it a hard country to govern. Currently Russia faces pockets of instability on several of its borders, most notably in Tajikistan and Afghanistan in Central Asia, and in Georgia and Azerbaijan on the southern border. Russia's western neighbors include Ukraine, Belarus, and several EU member states (Finland, Estonia, Latvia, Lithuania, and Poland). Located at a critical juncture between Europe, the Islamic world, and Asia, Russia's regional sphere of influence is now disputed.

FOCUS QUESTION

Consider three crucial junctures in Russian history. In what ways was each juncture a reaction to a recurring problem in Russian history?

Critical Junctures

The Decline of the Russian Tsarist State

Until 1917, an autocratic system headed by the tsar ruled Russia. Richard Pipes explains that before 1917, Russia had a **patrimonial state** that not only ruled the country but also owned the land.[1] The majority of the peasant population was tied to the nobles the state, or the church (through serfdom). The serfs were emancipated in 1861 as a part of the tsar's effort to modernize Russia and to make it militarily competitive with the West.

patrimonial state
A system of governance in which the ruler treats the state as personal property (patrimony).

The key impetus for industrialization came from the state and from foreign capital. Despite some reforms workers became increasingly discontented, as did liberal intellectuals, students, and, later, peasants, in the face of Russia's defeat in the Russo-Japanese war and continued tsarist repression. Revolution broke out in 1905. The regime, however maintained control through repression and economic reforms, until its collapse in 1917.

The Bolshevik Revolution and the Establishment of Soviet Power (1917–1929)

In March 1917, during the height of World War I, a revolution threw out Tsar Nicholas II and installed a moderate provisional government. In November, the Bolsheviks, led by Vladimir Lenin, overthrew that government. Instead of imitating Western European patterns, the Bolsheviks applied a dramatically different blueprint for economic, social, and political development.

The Bolsheviks were Marxists who believed their revolution reflected the political interests of a particular social class, the proletariat (working class). Most of the revolutionary leaders, however, were not themselves workers, but came from a more educated and privileged stratum, the intelligentsia. Nonetheless, their slogan, "Land, Peace, and Bread," appealed to both the working class and the discontented peasantry, which made up over 80 percent of Russia's population.

democratic centralism a system of political organization developed by V. I. Lenin and practiced, with modifications, by all communist party–states. Its principles include a hierarchical party structure.

vanguard party a political party that claims to operate in the "true" interests of the group or class it purports to represent, even if this understanding doesn't correspond to the expressed interests of the group itself.

The Bolsheviks formed a tightly organized political party. Their strategy was based on two key ideas: democratic centralism and vanguardism. **Democratic centralism** mandated a hierarchical party structure in which leaders were elected from below, but strict discipline was required in implementing party decisions once they were made. The centralizing elements of democratic centralism took precedence over the democratic elements, as the party tried to insulate itself first from informers of the tsarist forces and later from real and imagined threats to the new regime. The concept of a **vanguard party** governed the Bolsheviks' relations with broader social forces. Party leaders claimed that they understood the interests of the working people better than the people did themselves. Over time, this philosophy was used to justify virtually all actions of the party and the state it dominated. Neither democratic centralism nor vanguardism emphasized bottom-up democratic procedures or accountability of the leaders to the public. Rather, these concepts focused on achieving a "correct" political outcome that would reflect the "true" interests of the working class, as defined by the leaders of the party.

In 1922 the Bolsheviks formed the Union of Soviet Socialist Republics (USSR). The Bolsheviks took extraordinary measures to ensure the survival of the regime. The initial challenge was an extended civil war (1918–1921) for control of the countryside and outlying regions. The Bolsheviks introduced war communism to ensure materials necessary for the war effort. The state took control of key economic sectors and forcibly requisitioned grain from the peasants. The *Cheka*, the security arm of the regime, was strengthened, and restrictions were placed on other political groups, including other socialist parties. By 1921, the leadership had recognized the political costs of war communism. In an effort to accommodate the peasantry, the New Economic Policy (NEP) was introduced in 1921 and lasted until 1928. State control over the economy was loosened so that private enterprise and trade were revived. The state, however, retained control of large-scale industry.

Gradually, throughout the 1920s, the authoritarian strains of Bolshevik thinking eclipsed the democratic elements. Lacking a democratic tradition and bolstered by the vanguard ideology of the party, the Bolshevik leaders were plagued by internal struggles following Lenin's death in 1924. By 1929, however, all open opposition, even within the party itself, had been silenced.

The Bolshevik revolution also initiated a period of international isolation; to fulfill their promise of peace, the new rulers had had to cede important chunks of territory to Germany under the Brest-Litovsk Treaty (1918), which were returned to Russia's only after Germany was defeated by Russia's allies (the United States, France, and Britain). However these countries were hardly pleased with Russia's revolution, which led to expropriation of foreign holdings and which represented the first successful challenge to the capitalist order. The former allies sent material aid and troops to oppose the new Bolshevik government during the civil war.

The Stalin Revolution (1929–1953)

collectivization a process undertaken in the Soviet Union under Stalin from 1929 into the early 1930s and in China under Mao in the 1950s, by which agricultural land was removed from private ownership and organized into large state and collective farms.

From 1929 until his death in 1953, Stalin consolidated his power as Soviet leader. Stalin brought changes to virtually every aspect of Soviet life. The state became the engine for rapid economic development, with state ownership of virtually all economic assets. By 1935, over 90 percent of agricultural land had been taken from the peasants and made into state or collective farms. This **collectivization** campaign was justified as a means of preventing the emergence of a new capitalist class in the countryside. But it actually targeted the peasantry as a whole, leading to widespread famine and the death of millions. A program of rapid industrialization favored heavy industries, and consumer goods were neglected. Economic control operated through a complex but inefficient system of central economic planning, in which the state planning committee (Gosplan) set production targets for every enterprise in the country. Under the influence of rapid industrialization, people were uprooted from their traditional lives in the countryside and catapulted into the rhythm of urban industrial life. Media censorship and state control of the arts strangled creativity as well as political opposition. The party/state became the authoritative source of truth; anyone deviating from the authorized interpretation could be charged with treason.

Gradually, the party became subject to the personal whims of Stalin and his secret police. Overall, an estimated 5 percent of the Soviet population was arrested at one point or another under the Stalinist system, usually for no apparent cause. Only among trusted friends and family members did people dare to express their true views. Forms of resistance were evasive rather than active. Peasants killed livestock to avoid giving it over to collective farms. Laborers worked inefficiently. Absenteeism was high.

Isolation from the outside world was a key tool of Stalinist control. This policy did shield Soviet society from the Great Depression of the 1930s. But it also allowed an inefficient system of production to survive. Without foreign competition, the economy failed to keep up with the rapid economic and technological transformation in the West.

In 1941, Nazi Germany invaded the Soviet Union, and Stalin had little choice but to join the Allied powers. Casualties in the war were staggering, about 27 million people, including 19 million civilians. War sacrifices and heroism have remained powerful symbols of pride and unity for Russians up through the present day. After the war, the other Allied powers allowed the Soviet Union to absorb new territories into the USSR itself (these became the Soviet republics of Latvia, Lithuania, Estonia, Moldavia, and portions of western Ukraine). The allies implicitly granted the USSR free rein to shape the postwar governments and economies in East Germany, Poland, Hungary, Czechoslovakia, Yugoslavia, Bulgaria, and Romania. Western offers to include parts of the region in the Marshall Plan were rejected under pressure from the USSR. Local Communist parties gained control of all of these countries. Only in Yugoslavia were indigenous Communist forces sufficiently strong to hold power largely on their own and thus later to assert their independence from Moscow.

In the post-war period, the USSR emerged as a global superpower as the Soviet sphere of influence encompassed large parts of Central and Eastern Europe.

In 1947, in the face of crises in Greece and Turkey, the American president Harry Truman proclaimed a policy to contain further Soviet expansion (subsequently referred to as the Truman Doctrine). In 1949 a defensive military alliance, the North Atlantic Treaty Organization (NATO), was formed involving several West European countries, the United States, and Canada, to protect against potential Soviet aggression, and in 1955 the Soviet Union initiated the Warsaw Pact in response. These events marked the beginning of the Cold War, characterized by tension and military competition between the two superpowers (the United States and USSR), leading to an escalating arms race that was particularly costly to the Soviet Union. Tensions reached a high point during the Cuban Missile Crisis of 1962. In 1972, the initiation of détente brought some relaxation of relations between the two superpowers.

The Soviet Union isolated its satellite countries in Central and Eastern Europe from the West and tightened their economic and political integration with the USSR. Some countries within the Soviet bloc, however, had strong historic links to Western Europe (especially Czechoslovakia, Poland, and Hungary). Over time, these countries served not only as geographic buffers to direct Western influence but also as conduits for such influence.

Attempts at De-Stalinization (1953–1985)

Stalin's death in 1953 triggered another critical juncture in Soviet politics. Even the Soviet elite realized that Stalin's terror could be sustained only at great cost. The terror destroyed initiative and participation, and the unpredictability of Stalinist rule inhibited the rational formulation of policy. From Stalin's death until the mid-1980s Soviet politics became more regular and stable. Terror abated, but political controls remained in place, and efforts to isolate Soviet citizens from foreign influences continued.

Nikita Khrushchev, who eventually followed Stalin as party leader, embarked on a bold policy of de-Stalinization, rejecting terror as an instrument of political control. The secret police (KGB) was subordinated to party authority, and party meetings resumed on a regular basis. However, internal party structures remained highly centralized, and elections were uncontested. Khrushchev's successor, Leonid Brezhnev (party head 1964–1982) partially reversed Khrushchev's de-Stalinization efforts. Controls tightened again in the cultural sphere. Individuals who expressed dissenting views through underground publishing or publication abroad were harassed, arrested, or exiled. However, unlike in the Stalinist period, the political repression was predictable. People knew when they were transgressing permitted limits of criticism.

From the late 1970s onward, an aging political leadership was increasingly ineffective at addressing the mounting problems facing Soviet society. Economic growth rates declined, living standards improved only minimally, and opportunities for upward career mobility declined. To maintain the Soviet Union's superpower status, resources were diverted to the military sector, gutting the consumer and agricultural spheres. An inefficient economic structure meant that costs of exploiting new natural resource deposits soared. High pollution levels affected health through higher morbidity rates and declining life expectancy. At the same time, liberalization in some Eastern European states and the telecommunications revolution made it increasingly difficult to shield the population from exposure to Western lifestyles and ideas. Among a certain critical portion of the population, aspirations were rising just as the capacity of the system to fulfill them was declining.

Perestroika and *Glasnost* (1985–1991)

perestroika the policy of restructuring embarked on by Gorbachev when he became head of the Communist Party of the Soviet Union in 1985.

glasnost Gorbachev's policy of "openness" or "publicity," which involved an easing of controls on the media, arts, and public discussion.

demokratizatsiia the policy of democratization identified by former Soviet leader Mikhail Gorbachev in 1987 as an essential component of *perestroika*.

Mikhail Gorbachev took office as a Communist Party leader in March 1985. He endorsed a reform program that centered around four important concepts intended to spur economic growth and bring political renewal. These were *perestroika, glasnost, demokratizatsiia*, and "New Thinking." ***Perestroika*** (restructuring) involved decentralization and rationalization of economic structures to enable individual enterprises to increase efficiency and take initiative. ***Glasnost*** (openness) involved relaxing controls on public debate and allowing diverse viewpoints to be aired. ***Demokratizatsiia*** was an effort to increase the responsiveness of political organs to public sentiment. Finally, "New Thinking" referred to a foreign policy approach involving integration of the USSR into the global economy and emphasizing common challenges facing East and West, such as the cost and hazards of the arms race and environmental degradation.[2] Gorbachev's reform program was designed to adapt the communist system to new conditions rather than to usher in its demise.

The most divisive issues were economic policy and demands for republic autonomy. Only 50.8 percent of the Soviet population was ethnically Russian in 1989. Soon, demands for national autonomy arose in some of the USSR's union republics. This occurred first in the three Baltic republics (Latvia, Lithuania, and Estonia), then in Ukraine, Georgia, Armenia, and Moldova, and finally in the Russian Republic itself. Gorbachev's efforts failed to bring consensus on a new federal system.

Gorbachev's economic policies failed as well. Half-measures sent contradictory messages to enterprise directors, producing a drop in output and undermining established patterns that had kept the Soviet economy functioning, although inefficiently. To protect themselves, regions and union republics began to restrict exports to other regions, despite planning mandates. In "the war of laws," regional officials openly defied central directives.

Just as his domestic support was plummeting, Gorbachev was awarded the Nobel Peace Prize, in 1991. Under his New Thinking, the military buildup in the USSR was halted, important arms control agreements were ratified, and many controls on international contacts were lifted. In 1989, Gorbachev refused to prop up unpopular communist governments in the East European countries. First in Hungary and Poland, then in the German Democratic Republic (East Germany) and Czechoslovakia, pressure from below pushed the communist parties out of power. To Gorbachev's dismay, the liberation of Eastern Europe fed the process of disintegration in the Soviet Union itself.

Collapse of the USSR and the Emergence of the Russian Federation (1991 to the Present)

In 1985 Mikhail Gorbachev had drafted Boris Yeltsin into the leadership team as a nonvoting member of the USSR's top party organ, the Politburo. Little did he know the pivotal role that Yeltsin would play in bringing about the final demise of the Soviet Union. In December 1991, Yeltsin joined the leaders of Ukraine and Belorussia (later renamed Belarus) to declare the formation of a loosely structured entity, called the Commonwealth of Independent States, to replace the Soviet Union. The Russian Federation now stepped out as an independent country in the world of states.

As leader of the newly independent Russian Federation, Yeltsin took a more radical approach to reform than Gorbachev had done. He quickly proclaimed his commitment to Western-style democracy and market economic reform. However, that program was controversial and proved hard to implement. Russians faced an increasingly uncertain future, declining real wages, high inflation, and rising crime. A major financial crisis in August and September 1998 triggered a political one. Plagued by poor health and failed policies, Yeltsin could hope only to serve out his second presidential term and groom a successor.

In 1999, Yeltsin appointed Vladimir Putin to the post of prime minister of Russia. Putin, a little-known figure from St. Petersburg, was a former KGB operative in East Germany. His political advance was swift, and the rise in his popularity was equally meteoric. In December 1999, Yeltsin resigned as president of the Russian Federation. In the March 2000 elections Putin won a resounding

The White House, seat of the Russian parliament, burns while under assault from troops loyal to President Yeltsin during the confrontation in October 1993. *(Source: AP Images)*

Profile

Boris Nikolaevich Yeltsin

Like so many men of his generation who later rose to top Communist Party posts, Yeltsin's education was technical. His early jobs were as foreman, engineer, supervisor, and finally director of a large construction combine. Yeltsin joined the Communist Party of the Soviet Union (CPSU) in 1961. He made his career in the party, taking on full-time work in the regional party organization in 1968. In 1981, Yeltsin moved on to the national stage, as a member of the Central Committee of the CPSU, and was appointed to the top leadership group in 1985.

Yeltsin soon gained a reputation as an outspoken critic of party privilege. He became a popular figure in Moscow as he mingled with average Russians on city streets and public transport. In 1987, party conservatives launched an attack on Yeltsin for his outspoken positions. Yeltsin was removed from the Politburo and from his post as Moscow party leader in 1988. At the party conference in June 1988, Yeltsin defended his position in proceedings that were televised across the USSR; Russian citizens were mesmerized by this open display of elite conflict. Yeltsin's popular support soared as he single-handedly took on the party establishment.

Yeltsin articulated a radical reform path, in contrast to Gorbachev's gradualism. His political base was in the Russian Republic, one of the fifteen republics of the USSR. Under Yeltsin's leadership on June 8, 1990, the Russian Republic declared sovereignty (not a declaration of independence, but an assertion of the right of the Russian Republic to set its own policy). One month later, Yeltsin resigned his party membership. On June 12, 1991, Yeltsin became president of the Russian Republic through direct popular vote, establishing his democratic credentials. (Gorbachev never faced direct popular election.)

During an attempted coup d'état by party conservatives in August 1991, Yeltsin took a firm stand against the plotters while Gorbachev remained captive at his *dacha* in the Crimea. Yeltsin's defiance gave him a decisive advantage in the competition with Gorbachev and laid the groundwork for the December 1991 dissolution of the USSR engineered by Yeltsin (representing Russia) and the leaders of Ukraine and Belorussia.

In 1992, Yeltsin began implementing his radical reform policy in the newly independent Russian Federation. Unfortunately, economic crisis, rising corruption and crime, and a decline of state authority ensued. His reputation as a democratic reformer was marred by his use of force against the Russian parliament in 1993 and in the Chechnya war in 1994–1996. In December 1999, in the face of plummeting popularity, failing health, and an increasingly evident alcohol problem, Yeltsin resigned, appointing Vladimir Putin as acting president. However, by 2004 Yeltsin was expressing disillusionment with the direction of Putin's political reforms: "The stifling of freedoms and the rolling back of democratic rights will mean, among other things, that the terrorists will have won."* Mixed reviews of Yeltsin's achievements followed his death on April 23, 2007. Although some hailed his contribution to the development of Russian democracy, others decried his ineffectiveness in realizing those values. ❖

*"Yeltsin fears for Russia freedoms," *BBC News*, September 17, 2004, http://news.bbc.co.uk/2/hi/europe/3663788.stm (accessed May 12, 2005).

victory, with an even stronger show of support in elections that followed for the *Duma* in December 2003 and for the presidency in March 2004. Putin benefited from auspicious conditions, as high international gas and oil prices fed tax dollars into the state's coffers; in 1999, the economy began a period of sustained economic growth, the first in over a decade.

The relationship between President George W. Bush and Russian President Vladimir Putin reflects moments of tension in the light of Russian objections to the U.S.-led invasion of Iraq and U.S. criticism of Russian political developments. *(Source: AP Images)*

After September 11, 2001

After September 11, 2001, President Putin expressed solidarity with the American people in their struggle against terrorism. Terrorist attacks in Russia reinforced a sense of common purpose between the two world powers, but Russia withheld its support for the American incursion into Iraq, opening a period of renewed tension between the two countries. Still an outsider as more and more neighboring states joined NATO and the European Union (EU), Russia faced the issue of how to balance its global, European, and Eurasian roles.

Themes and Implications

Historical Junctures and Political Themes

FOCUS QUESTIONS

How has Russia had to redefine its place in the world since the breakup of the Soviet Union? What were its principal challenges in the earlier period? What are they now?

In the 1990s Russia's status as a world power waned, and the expansion of Western organizations (NATO, EU) to Russia's western border undermined its sphere of influence in Central and Eastern Europe. Russia's western neighbors, except Belarus, looked more to Europe than to Russia as a guidepost for the future. But Russia's economic recovery, the rise of energy prices and Europe's dependence on imports of Russian natural gas and oil provided an important basis for Russia's renewed international influence. No longer simply a supplicant in its relationship to the West, Russia reasserted itself as a major European power in 2005 under Putin's leadership. September 11, however, provided a new impetus for Russia's claim to be a key link in the antiterrorist chain, alongside the United States. Ironically, however, the war on terrorism expanded American influence into Russia's traditional sphere of influence as U.S. bases were established in post-Soviet Central Asia (as well as neighboring Afghanistan), creating the potential for new tensions between Russian and the United States.

By the late 1990s, the Russian public was disillusioned and distrustful of its leaders, and resentment remained over the disappointing results of the Western-inspired reform program. In recent years, however, the population has shown a marked increase in economic confidence and senses a return to some degree of normalcy in everyday life. Nonetheless problems remain. Wide disparities in wealth and income, as well as important regional inequalities, continue to plague the system. Reforms that weakened the social welfare system in 2005 fed fears that the state would not assure fulfillment of basic needs for those at the bottom of the social ladder.

On the positive side, the constitution adopted in 1993 has gained a surprising level of public acceptance, even as observers express intensifying concern about the democratic credentials of the Russian system. Key reforms after 2000 have seemed to undermine prospects for real political competition, accompanied by increased controls on the electronic media (especially TV). United Russia, favored by Putin, emerged as the dominant political party in the lead up to elections in December 2007 for the State *Duma* (the upper house of the legislature). Despite speculation, in 2008 Putin could not run for office again due to a constitutional provision prohibiting a third consecutive term as president. However, Putin identified a preferred successor, Dmitry Medvedev (since 2005 first deputy prime minister), who stood as the "establishment" candidate in the March 2008 presidential race. There was widespread speculation that Putin might be appointed prime minister after leaving the presidency.

The loss of superpower status, the dominance of Western economic and political models, and the absence of a widely accepted ideology have all contributed to uncertainty about what it means to be Russian and where Russia fits into the world as a whole. Meanwhile, Russia itself suffers from internal divisions. Overt separatism has been limited to the Republic of Chechnya, but differing visions of collective identity have emerged in some of Russia's ethnic republics, particularly in Muslim areas. Social class, a linchpin of Soviet ideology, may take on increasing importance in defining group solidarity, as working people seek new organizational forms to assert their rights. Changing gender roles have challenged both men and women to reconsider not only their relationships to one another, but also the impact of these changes on children and community values.

Summary

Russian history has been characterized by a series of upheavals and changes that have often made life unpredictable and difficult for the citizen. The revolutions of 1917 replaced tsarist rule with a political system dominated by the Communist Party. In the Stalinist period Communist rule involved a process of rapid industrialization, collectivization of agriculture, and purges of the party, followed by large losses of population associated with World War II. With the death of Stalin came another important transition, as politics was transformed into a more predictable system of bureaucratic authoritarianism, characterized by relative stability but without political competition or democratic control. The most recent transition, ushered in by the collapse of Communist Party rule in 1991, resulted in the emergence of the Russian Federation as an independent state. The new Russia experienced an almost immediate period of economic decline and halting efforts to democratize the system in the 1990s. However, since 1999, the economy has taken a turn for the better, at the same time that limits on political competition seem to be reversing some of the democratic gains of the 1990s. Throughout its entire history, Russian leaders have struggled to maintain control over a large expanse of territory with an ethnically diverse population, in part the legacy of Russia's imperial past.

Political Economy and Development

Market reforms introduced after 1991 brought a dramatic decline in economic performance and fundamental changes in social relationships. The Russian government struggled to create tools to regulate the new market forces. Since 1999, after an unprecedented period of economic depression, Russia experienced renewed economic growth (see Table 5.2). Rising energy prices and the 1998 ruble devaluations were important factors in this economic revival; experts disagreed about the role of the Russian government's economic policies. Developing a more balanced economic structure that could weather global shocks or falling oil or natural gas prices remains an important challenge.

State and Economy

FOCUS QUESTION

Describe Russia's principal problems in moving from a command economy toward a market economy. What are the principal advantages and disadvantages of each form of economy?

The Soviet Economy

In the Soviet period, land, factories, and all other important economic assets belonged to the state. Short- and long-term economic plans defined production goals, but these were frequently too ambitious to be fulfilled. Except in the illegal black market and peasant market, prices were controlled by the state. Firms and individuals were not permitted to develop direct links to foreign partners; these were all channeled through the central economic bureaucracy.

The Soviet economic model registered some remarkable achievements: rapid industrialization, provision of social welfare and mass education, relatively low levels of inequality, and advances in key economic sectors such as the military and space industries. Nonetheless, over time, the top-heavy nature of Soviet planning could no longer deliver increased prosperity at home and competitive products for export. Furthermore, the Soviet economy legacy complicated economic reform efforts due to a sagging infrastructure, outdated equipment, and inefficient production practices.

market reform a strategy of economic transformation that involves reducing the role of the state in managing the economy and increasing the role of market forces.

shock therapy a variant of market reform that involves the state simultaneously imposing a wide range of radical economic changes, with the purpose of "shocking" the economy into a new mode of operation.

State and Economy in the Russian Federation

In 1992, Boris Yeltsin endorsed radical **market reform**, sometimes referred to as **shock therapy**. The changes were to be rapid and thorough. Although shock therapy would inevitably throw large parts of the economy into an initial downward spin, reformers hoped that the initial jolt would be followed by a quick recovery.

Four main pillars of reform were (1) lifting price controls, (2) encouraging small private businesses and entrepreneurs, (3) privatizing most state-owned enterprises, and (4) opening the economy to international influences. The immediate impact of the reforms on the Russian public was dramatic. In January 1992, price controls on most goods were loosened or removed entirely. The consumer price index increased by about 2,500 percent between December 1991 and December 1992. Real wages declined by 50 percent.

TABLE 5.2

Economic Indicators for the Russian Federation (percent change from the previous year unless otherwise indicated)

	1991	1992	1993	1994	1995	1996	1997	1998	1999	2000	2001	2002	2003	2004	2005
Economic growth	−5.0	−14.5	−8.7	−12.6	−4.0	−3.5	0.9	−5.3	6.4	10.0	5.1	4.7	7.3	7.1	6.4
Industrial production	−8.0	−18.8	−16.2	−22.6	4.7	−6.5	0.3	−5.2	11.0	11.9	4.9	3.7	7.0	7.3	4.0
Consumer price inflation	93	1526	875	307	197	48	15	28	86	21	22	16	14	12	11
Unemployment rate	n.a.	4.8	5.5	7.5	8.8	9.3	10.7	12.3	12.6	9.8	8.9	8.6	8.4	8.0	7.6
Rubles per one USD[a]	169	415	1247	3550	4640	5560	5960	20.7	26.8	28.2	30.1	31.8	29.5	28.5	28.3
Population (in millions, Jan. 1)[b]	148.3	148.9	148.7	148.4	148.3	148.0	147.1	146.5	146.0	145.2	144.5	144.0	145.0	144.2	143.2

[a]At year end; figures for 1998 and after are in new redenominated rubles, where one new ruble = 1,000 old rubles. The redenomination occurred in January 1998.

[b]January 21, 2005—143.5.

Sources:

Data from 1991–2001 are reprinted from *Introduction to Comparative Politics* (Houghton Mifflin, 2004), 361; updates for 2002–2004 and some adjustments to previous data are from *EBRD Transition Report* 2004, and World Bank, *Russian Economic Report* (April 2005) (www.worldbank.org.ru); population figures are from State Statistical Agency of the Russian Federation, http://194.84.38.65/mdb/upload/RERIO.eng.pdf.

joint-stock company a business firm whose capital is divided into shares that can be held by individuals, groups of individuals, or governmental units.

insider privatization the transformation of formerly state-owned enterprises into joint-stock companies or private enterprises in which majority control is in the hands of employees and/or managers.

privatization voucher a certificate worth 10,000 rubles issued by the government to each Russian citizen in 1992 to be used to purchase shares in state enterprises undergoing privatization.

Privatization was rapid compared to other postcommunist countries. By early 1994, 80 percent of medium-sized and large state enterprises in designated sectors of the economy had been transformed into **joint-stock companies**. The most widely adopted method for privatizing state enterprises, called **insider privatization**, gave managers and workers of the enterprise (jointly) the right to acquire a controlling packet (51 percent) of enterprise shares at virtually symbolic prices. Each citizen of Russia was issued a **privatization voucher** with a nominal value of 10,000 rubles (about ten U.S. dollars).

Many analysts believe that insider privatization hampered reform of business operations and reduced the expected gains of privatization. Managers, many of whom did not have the skills needed to operate in a market environment, were reluctant to lay off excess labor or resisted overtures by outside investors who might gain control of the enterprise. Some managers extracted personal profit from enterprise operations rather than investing available funds to improve production. Productivity and efficiency did not increase significantly; unprofitable firms continued to operate; investment was weak; and the benefits of ownership were not widely or fairly distributed. The government continued to subsidize ineffective operations, leaving most Russian firms uncompetitive.

In 1995, a second stage of privatization was launched; firms could sell remaining shares for cash or investment guarantees. However, many firms were unattractive to potential Russian and foreign investors because their backward technology would require massive infusions of capital for restructuring. Some of the more attractive enterprises fell into the hands of developing financial-industrial conglomerates that had acquired their wealth through positions of power or connections in the government. At the same time, new ventures, which were generally more efficient than former state firms, faced obstacles: confusing regulations, high taxes, lack of capital, and poor infrastructure (transport, banking, communications).

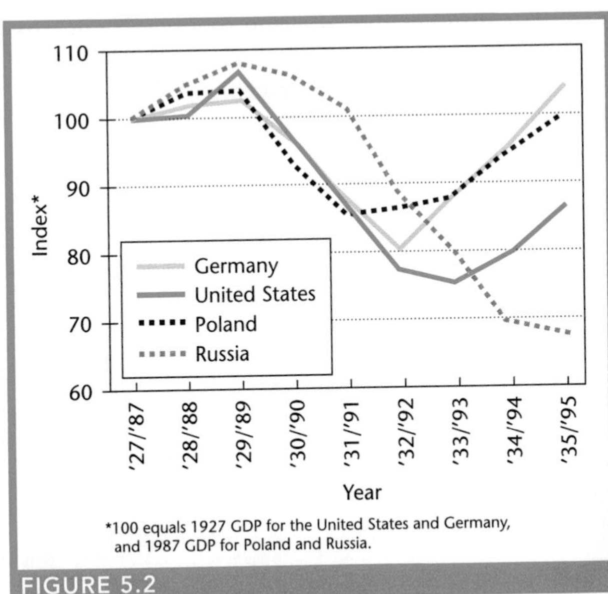

FIGURE 5.2

Downturn of the Russian Economy

Source: Copyright © 2002 by the National Bureau of Asian Research. Reprinted from Millar, James, R. "Normalization of the Russian Economy: Obstacles and Opportunities for Reform and Sustainable Growth," *NBR Analysis* 13, no. 2, April 2002, by permission of the National Bureau of Asian Research.

Reform of agriculture was even less satisfactory. Large joint-stock companies and associations of individual households were created on the basis of former state and collective farms. These privatized companies operated inefficiently, and agricultural output declined. Foreign food imports also undercut domestic producers, contributing to a downward spiral in agricultural investment and production.

By the late 1990s, it appeared that the government's reform program had failed (see Figure 5.2). Russia was in the grip of a severe depression. Industrial production was less than half the 1990 level. The depression fed on itself, as declining capacity in one sector deprived other sectors of buyers or suppliers. Even the state was behind in its wage, social benefit, and pension payments.

A key obstacle to the success of the market reform agenda was the weakness of state institutions. Without an effective tax collection system, for instance, the government cannot acquire revenues needed to pay its own bills on time, to provide essential services to the population, and to ensure a well-functioning economic infrastructure (such as transportation, energy, public utilities). State action is also needed to regulate the banking sector and to enforce, health, safety, and labor standards. If the state fails to carry out these functions, businesses may take matters into their own hands, for example, by hiring private security services, turning to the mafia for protection, or by paying bribes. Weak government feeds corruption and criminality, producing risks both to business and to the population at large.

oligarchs a small group of powerful and wealthy individuals who gained ownership and control of important sectors of Russia's economy in the context of the privatization of state assets in the 1990s.

mafia a term borrowed from Italy and widely used in Russia to describe networks of organized criminal activity.

The central state in Moscow also had difficulty exerting its authority in relation to regional authorities and in the face of increasing power of business **oligarchs**. These oligarchs, wealthy individuals who benefited from the privatization process, often held significant political influence as well.[3] Diverse methods of laundering money to avoid taxes became widespread. Corruption involving government officials, the police, and operators abroad fed a rising crime rate. Rich foreigners, Russian bankers, and outspoken journalists became targets of the Russian **mafia**. Policies of the Russian government itself had contributed to the creation of this new group of financial and business oligarchs.

pyramid debt a situation when a government or organization takes on debt obligations at progressively higher rates of interest in order to pay off existing debt.

A financial crisis in August 1998 brought the situation to a head. The government successively took on new loans at progressively higher rates of interest in order to pay off existing debts, creating a structure of **pyramid debt**. Following a sharp upturn in 1996–1997, in August 1998 the Russian stock market lost

Russian oil oligarch Mikhail Khodorkovsky, shown under arrest, displayed in a cage. *(Source: © Alexander Natruskin/ Reuters/Corbis)*

over 90 percent of its value. The government defaulted on its bonds. Many Russian banks, holders of the Russian government's short-term bonds, faced imminent bankruptcy. The government began to print more of the increasingly valueless rubles, threatening to undermine the ruble's value further and thus intensify the underlying financial crisis.

The government finally allowed a radical devaluation of the ruble. Within a two-week period, the ruble lost two-thirds of its value against the U.S. dollar, banks closed or allowed only limited withdrawals, supplies of imported goods decreased, and business accounts were frozen—forcing some firms to lay off employees and others to close their doors. Despite its immediate disastrous effects, the 1998 financial crisis ushered in positive changes. First, the devalued ruble made Russian products more competitive with foreign imports. Firms were able to improve their products, put underused labor back to work, and thus increase productivity. The state budget benefited from improved tax revenues. Barter declined, as did payment arrears.[4] Economic growth revived, beginning in 1999.[5] See Figure 5.3.

Experts have continued to debate the contribution of government policy to Russia's economic recovery. After a sluggish first year, an active legislative program emerged under President Putin. A 13 percent flat income tax, deemed easier to enforce, was one very visible aspect of the package. Other developments fueled optimism about Russia's economic future. A budget surplus replaced a deficit. The foreign debt load declined from 90 percent of GDP in 1998 to 28 percent in 2004.[6] By 2005 Russia had accumulated foreign reserves (including gold) of over $182 billion. Prospects for Russia's membership in the World Trade Organization also fueled optimism about Russia's trade growth.

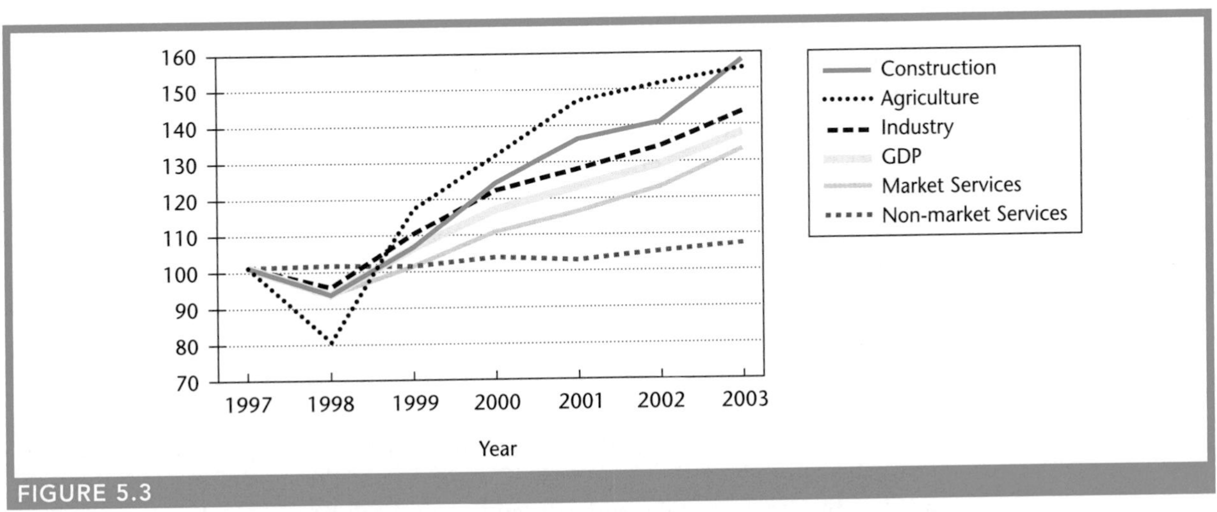

FIGURE 5.3

Economic Recovery Since 1998

Source: Data from the World Bank; http://194.84.38.65/mdb/upload/PAR_020805_eng.pdf.

Meanwhile, Putin made clear that economic oligarchs who used their financial positions to affect political outcomes would suffer sanctions. Charges of tax evasion and fraud were brought again media moguls, presented as part of the government's campaign to assure proper business practices. However, critics felt that enforcement efforts were selectively directed at critics of the government. One media magnate who had publicly criticized the Kremlin, Boris Berezovsky, fled to self-imposed exile in the United Kingdom. A particularly prominent case involved Mikhail Khodorkovsky, the chief executive officer and major shareholder of the giant Russian oil company Yukos. In October 2003 Khodorkovsky was placed under arrest for fraud and tax evasion, and in May 2005, he was sentenced by a Russian court to nine years in prison. Critics of the government charged that the process was motivated by political considerations because Khodorkovsky had provided financial support to opposition parties. The attack on Yukos undermined investor confidence with fears that political pretexts might justify future government economic takeovers.

Society and Economy

FOCUS QUESTIONS

In what ways did Soviet social policies accommodate or violate Russian social values?

Have recent Russian policies done a better or worse job of accommodating these values?

Soviet Social Policy

The Soviet leadership established priorities with little input from society. One was military production, but the regime's social goals also produced some of the most marked achievements of the Soviet system. Benefits to the population included free health care, low-cost access to essential goods and services, maternity leave (partially paid), child benefits, disability pensions, and mass education. Universal access to primary and secondary schooling led to nearly universal literacy in a short period of time. Postsecondary education was free of charge, with state stipends provided to university students.

Guaranteed employment and job security were other priorities. Almost all able-bodied adults worked outside the home. Citizens received many social benefits through the workplace, making it a social as well as an economic institution. The full-employment policy made unemployment compensation unnecessary. Modest pensions were guaranteed by the state, ensuring a stable but minimal standard of living for retirement.

Although basic social needs were met, the Soviet system was plagued by shortages and low-quality service. For example, advanced medical equipment was in limited supply; sometimes under-the-table payments were required to prompt better-quality service. Many goods and services, although economically in the reach of every citizen, were in short supply. Queues were a pervasive part of everyday life. Housing shortages restricted mobility and forced young families to share small apartments with parents. Labor in many sectors was in constant short supply, reflecting the inefficient use of the work force. Productivity was low by international standards, and work discipline weak; drunkenness, and absenteeism were not unusual. A Soviet saying illustrated the problem: "We pretend to work, they pretend to pay us."

As a matter of state policy, wage differentials between the best- and worst-paid were lower than in Western countries. Although reflecting cultural values, this approach reduced the incentive for outstanding achievements and innovation. Due to state ownership, individuals could not accumulate wealth in real estate, stocks, or businesses. Privileges that did exist were modest by Western standards. Although political elites had access to scarce goods, higher-quality health care, travel, and vacation homes, these privileges were hidden from public view.

Economic Reform and Russian Society

The Soviet experience led Russians to expect the state to assure a social welfare network, but in the 1990s, budget constraints necessitated cutbacks, just when social needs were greatest. In line with the new market ideology, tuition fees for postsecondary education were introduced in many cases. Although universal health care remained, higher-quality care and access to medicine depended more obviously on ability to pay. Benefits provided through the workplace were cut back, as businesses faced pressures to reduce costs.

Some groups have benefited from the reform process, for example, those with foreign language skills and highly skilled employees in the natural resource sectors (such as oil and gas), in banking and finance. At the top of the scale are the super-wealthy, including people who took advantage of privatization to gain positions in lucrative sectors like banking, finance, oil, and gas.

But losers have been more numerous. Poverty is highest among rural residents, the unemployed, children, the less educated, pensioners, and the disabled. As a result of low wage levels, the majority of those in poverty are the working poor. Other groups suffered dramatic declines in income, including unskilled laborers in low-priority sectors of the economy and people working in the public service such as education. Consumer price inflation gradually declined over the 1990s but still had an important impact on incomes.[7] Unemployment has been lower than expected because many enterprises kept underemployed staff on their rolls, at low wages or with temporary layoffs. Official estimates are about 9.8 percent in 2000 and between 7 and 9 percent in 2004 and 2005, but actual rates are probably higher.[8] Social impacts of economic stress have included higher rates of crime, suicide, and mortality; alcoholism has continued to be a significant problem, particularly for males. All of these factors have increased the likelihood of dysfunctional family structures, producing a particularly marked impact on children.

With the economic upturn following 1999, large differentials in income and wealth remain, but the portion of the population living below the subsistence level has declined noticeably (from 27.3 percent of the population in 2001 to 15.8 percent in 2005). In addition average real disposable income has increased. Since 2000, levels of personal consumption have grown following years of decline, but many individuals (particularly men) have two to three jobs just to make ends meet. Public opinion surveys indicate that between 2003 and 2006 most Russians expected little change in the economic situation of their families

Moscow protest against cuts in social benefits in 2005. *(Source: © Smolsky Sergei/ITAR-TASS/Corbis)*

in the near future.[9] Social indicators of economic stress have begun to decline only slowly.

A particularly contentious issue led to massive street demonstrations in several Russian cities in early 2005 over changes to social welfare policy. Called "monetarization of social benefits," the reforms involved replacing certain services (such as public transport) that were provided free to disadvantaged groups (pensioners, veterans, the disabled) with a modest monetary payment to the individual. Subsidies for public utilities and housing were also reduced. Many Russians viewed the measures as direct reductions in social welfare benefits for the neediest in society. After large-scale demonstrations, the government agreed to accompany the reforms by a modest increase in pensions and to restore subsidized transport. Although Putin's popularity suffered a temporary decline, it rebounded quickly.

In the post-Soviet period, women continue to carry the bulk of domestic responsibilities while still working outside the home to boost family income. Many women take advantage of the permitted three-year maternity leave, which is only partially paid. Fathers play a relatively small role in child rearing; many families rely on grandparents to help out. Some data suggest, however, that while women are more likely to register with unemployment offices, levels of actual unemployment are about equal for men and women.[10]

Russia has seen a steady decline in population since 1992, as the birthrate fell from 16.6 births per 1,000 people in 1985 to about 10 in 2004.[11] Life expectancy for Soviet men fell from sixty-six years in 1966–1967 to fifty-nine in 2007 (from seventy-four to seventy-three for women).[12] The decline in population has been tempered by the immigration of ethnic Russians from

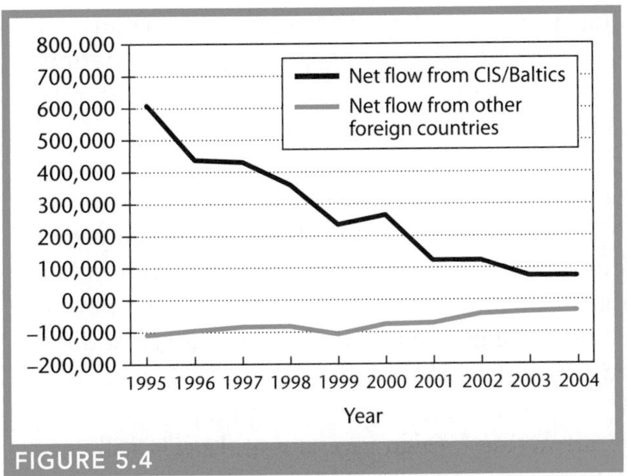

FIGURE 5.4

Immigration into Russia, 1995–2004

Source: Russian Annual Statistical Report 2003; Current Statistical Survey, no. 1 (48) 2004; and website of the Federal Statistical Agency of the Russian Federation, www.gks.ru.

other former Soviet republics (see Figure 5.4). Although declining birth rates often accompany economic modernization, in the 1990s many couples were especially reluctant to have children because of daily hardships, future uncertainty, a declining standard of living, and continuing housing shortages. To boost the birthrate, in May 2006 Putin announced a doubling of monthly child support payments and a large monetary bonus for women having a second child.

Russian Political Culture and Economic Change

Alongside more objective factors, culture affects economic change. Several aspects of Russian culture may have inhibited adaptation to a market economy: a weak tradition of individual entrepreneurship, widespread commitment to egalitarian values, and reliance on personal trust rather than written contracts. Profit is less important to many Russians than support for friends and coworkers; thus, firing redundant workers may be unpalatable. Business partners or personnel may be selected by personal contacts and relationships rather than by merit. Incentive structures of the Soviet period also have been internalized by older population groups, including features that encourage risk avoidance, low productivity, poor punctuality, absenteeism, lack of personal responsibility and initiative, and a preference for security over achievement.[13]

However, young people in Russia are adapting to a new work environment. Younger Russians are not only more flexible due to their age, but they also have different expectations from their elders. Consequently, they are more supportive of the market transition and are more oriented toward maximizing self-interest and demonstrating initiative. Nevertheless, many Russians of all age groups still question values underlying market reform, preferring an economy that is less profit driven and more oriented to equality and the collective good.

Russia in the Global Economy

FOCUS QUESTION

As Russia has become more closely tied to the world economy, what are the principal economic adjustments that Russia has had to make?

Right up to the end of the Soviet period, the economy remained relatively isolated from outside influences. Foreign trade was channeled through central state organs, so individual enterprises had neither the possibility nor the incentive to seek external markets. Over time, restrictions on foreign investment have been lifted, the ruble has been allowed to respond to market conditions, and firms are allowed to conclude agreements directly with foreign partners. In response, in the 1990s, Western governments (especially Germany) made fairly generous commitments of technical and humanitarian assistance. The World Bank, the IMF, and the EU also contributed substantial amounts of economic assistance, often in the form of repayable credits. In the past, release of IMF credit, issued to stabilize the ruble, was made contingent on Russia's pursuing a strict policy of fiscal and monetary control and lifting remaining price controls. The Russian government had difficulties in meeting these conditions, and thus the funds were released intermittently. After the August 1998 crisis, the Russian government defaulted first on the ruble-denominated short-term debt and then on the former Soviet debt. Since then, debt repayments have been made on time. In 2001, the government decided to forgo additional IMF credits. By 2004, it had paid off its IMF debt and, bit by bit, has cut its remaining debt obligation.[14]

Russia has had problems attracting foreign investment. Levels still remain low compared to other East European countries, despite some improvements since 2004. An upward trajectory was interrupted by the 1998 financial crisis. Major sources of foreign direct investment since 2000 have been Germany, the United States, and Cyprus (mainly recycled Russian capital, exported earlier for tax reasons). The focus of Russia's foreign trade activity has shifted significantly since the Soviet period. In 2004, Russia's foreign trade with countries of the expanded EU (more than 50 percent of the total) far exceeded combined exports to countries of the Commonwealth of Independent States (CIS).[15] In 2004, the EU confirmed its support for Russian membership in the World Trade Organization (WTO) and in November 2006 the United States and Russia agreed on a trade pact that overcame another obstacle to Russia's admission.

With a highly skilled work force and an advanced technological base in some sectors, Russia has many of the ingredients necessary to become a competitive and powerful force in the global economy. However, excessive reliance on natural resource exports will leave Russia vulnerable to global economic fluctuations in supply and demand. At the same time, these resources give Russia advantages compared to its neighbors, since these expensive materials do not need to be imported. Ultimately, Russia's position in the global economy will depend on the ability of the country's leadership to fashion a viable approach to domestic economic challenges and to facilitate differentiation of the country's export base.

Summary

If the heavy hand of state control contributed to the inefficiency of the Soviet economy, in the postcommunist period the new Russian state has often been ineffective in providing the legal framework and institutional structures necessary for the new market economy. In the early 1990s, the government lifted price controls, privatized state enterprises, and opened the economy to international influences. The result was rapid inflation, a fall in the standard of living, and dramatic economic decline even more extreme than the Great Depression of the 1930s in the West. In postcommunist Russia a wider range of goods has been available to the consumer, but many people have difficulty making ends meet and inequality increased dramatically compared to the Soviet period. Under Soviet rule, Russians came to expect the government to provide a certain level of social welfare, including guaranteed employment, subsidized prices on basic necessities, easy access to recreational facilities, and universally free higher education. Market economic reform undermined many of these policies, and some Russians felt that Western economic models were not well suited to Russia. With the revival of economic growth since 1999, the situation has improved, but the Russian economy is highly dependent on exports of oil, gas, and other natural resources, making it susceptible to global economic influences.

Governance and Policy-Making

When Russia became an independent country in December 1991, dramatic changes in state structure and governing processes followed. The new Russian leadership endorsed liberal democratic principles, and in April 2005 Putin declared, "[T]he development of Russia as a free and democratic state [is] the main political and ideological goal."[16] Over time, however, skeptics abound as Putin's measures to strengthen presidential power seem to many to have undermined some of the Russian Federation's founding democratic principles.

FOCUS QUESTION

How is the federal system of the Russian Federation different from the Soviet federal system or the American federal system?

Organization of the State

Ratification of a new Russian constitution in 1993 was a contested political process that followed a violent confrontation between the president and the parliament. Nonetheless, the new constitution has acquired broad-based popular legitimacy. The document affirms many established principles of liberal democratic governance—competitive multiparty elections, separation of powers, an independent judiciary, federalism, and protection of individual civil liberties. However, another key feature is the strength of the president's executive power. Nonetheless, in the 1990s the state demonstrated only a weak capacity to govern. During Putin's presidency (2000–2008), the power of the office was augmented in an effort to address the weakness of central state authority.

Between 1991 and 1993, negotiations between the central government and the various regions created a complicated federal structure with eighty-nine federal units (by mid-2008 reduced to eighty-three, through mergers). Some of these subnational governments demanded increased autonomy, even sovereignty, generating a process of negotiation and political conflict between the center and the regions that sometimes led to contradictions between regional and federal laws. The relationship between organs of the federal government itself also involved intense conflict. The constitution makes the executive dominant but still dependent on the agreement of the legislative branch to realize its programs. Tension between the two branches of government, which are selected in

The Chechnya Crisis

Despite its small size and population (estimated at 600,000 in 1994), the breakaway republic of Chechnya holds an important position on Russia's southern border. It is widely perceived as a safe haven for criminal elements that operate in Russia. In the early 1990s, the Russian leadership feared that Chechnya's attempted secession from the Russian Federation might embolden other republics to pursue a similar course and might lead to loss of control over Caspian Sea oil reserves. These concerns motivated Russia to send troops into Chechnya on December 11, 1994, fueling a regional civil war.

Before its incorporation into the Russian Empire in 1859 and again in 1917, local forces fought to maintain Chechnya's independence. In 1924, Chechnya was made part of the USSR, and in 1934 it was joined with an adjacent region, Ingushetia, to form a single autonomous republic within the Soviet Union.

In October 1991 the newly elected president of the republic, Dzhokar Dudaev, declared Chechnya's independence from Russia. In 1992, Checheno-Ingushetia was officially recognized by the Russian government as two separate republics. Intervention by Russian military forces in December 1994 evoked heated criticism within Russia. Some opposed the intervention completely, favoring a political solution; others were primarily critical of the ineffective manner in which the war effort was carried out. Civilians in Chechnya and the surrounding regions suffered at the hands of both sides, and the war imposed heavy economic costs on Russia and called into question the competence of the Russian military. The unpopular war became an important issue in the 1996 presidential campaign and threatened to undermine Yeltsin's already fragile support. In late May 1996, a cease-fire agreement was signed, and in June, Yeltsin decreed the beginning of troop withdrawals. In September 1996, an agreement with the rebels was again signed. The joint declaration put off a decision on Chechnya's status for five years, leaving the issue unresolved.

On January 27, 1997, an election was held for the president of the Republic of Chechnya. Observers generally considered the vote to be fair, with 79 percent of the eligible population participating. In a race involving thirteen candidates, Aslan Maskhadov received 59 percent of the vote. Relative to other leading candidates, Maskhadov was considered to be a moderate. However, he publicly supported Chechnya's independence, and later, after he was removed from power by Moscow, he became a rebel leader and was killed by Russian forces in March 2005.

In 1999, terrorist bombings, attributed to Chechen rebels, occurred in apartment buildings in Moscow and two other Russian cities, causing about 300 deaths. The second war in Chechnya was launched largely in response to these events. Allegations of human rights violations were made both against Russian troops and Chechen rebels; Western governments and international organizations such as Human Rights Watch demanded that the Russian government comply with international human rights standards. Russian authorities continue to resist external involvement in the situation, maintaining that the Chechnya crisis is a domestic political issue. President Putin has repeatedly emphasized links between Chechen rebels and international terrorist networks, including Al Qaeda, in an effort to gain Western acceptance for Russia's military actions.

The string of terrorist attacks by Chechen rebels since 1999, intensifying in 2004 with the Beslan tragedy, placed the problem clearly in the public mind. In March 2003, Russian authorities tried to set Chechnya on a track of normalization by holding a referendum on a new constitution in the republic that would confirm Chechnya's status within the Russian Federation. In October 2003, Akhmad Kadyrov was elected president of Chechnya with Russian support, only to be killed by Chechen rebels the next year. In July 2006 the radical insurgent Shamil Basayev, who claimed responsibility for the Beslan hostage taking, was killed, reportedly by Russian security forces. ❖

Source: Adapted from *Introduction to Comparative Politics*, 3rd ed. Copyright 2004 by Houghton Mifflin Company. Reprinted with permission.

nomenklatura a system of personnel selection in the Soviet period under which the Communist Party maintained control over the appointment of important officials in all spheres of social, economic, and political life.

republic one of 21 territorial units in the Russian federation defined by the constitution of 1993 to be among the 89 members of the federation and named after the indigenous non-Russian population group that inhabits the republic.

krai one of the six territorial units in the Russian Federation defined by the constitution of 1993 to be among the 89 members of the federation, with a status equal to that of the republics and oblasts.

oblast one of 49 territorial units in the Russian Federation defined by the constitution of 1993 to be among the 89 members of the federation, with a status equal to that of the republics and *krai*.

autonomous okrug one of originally 10 territorial units of the Russian Federation defined in the 1993 constitution to be among the 89 members of the federation, but reduced to 4 by 2008 as some of these ethnically-based units have been merged with the *oblast* or *krai* in which they are located.

separate electoral processes, was a persistent obstacle to effective governance under Yeltsin. The executive itself has two heads (the president and the prime minister), introducing another venue for intrastate tension. Establishing real judicial independence remained a significant political challenge. Finally, poor salaries and lack of professionalism in the civil service opened the door to corruption and political influence. Putin's centralizing measures tried to address all of these areas of contention, but, some would argue, in so doing may have undermined the very checks and balances that were supposed to offer protection against reestablishment of authoritarian control.

Many of the difficulties facing the new Russian state are, at least in part, legacies of the Soviet period. Following the collapse of the USSR, the new political leadership tried to wipe the slate clean and start anew. However, some observers see in Putin's reforms a reversion to practices and patterns reminiscent of the Soviet period, namely, centralization of power and obstacles to effective political competition. Other analysts interpret these measures as necessary to solidify rule of law and the state's capacity to govern.

The Soviet State

Before Gorbachev's reforms, top organs of the Communist Party of the Soviet Union (CPSU) dominated the state. The CPSU was hierarchical. Lower party bodies elected delegates to higher party organs, but elections were uncontested, and top organs determined candidates for lower party posts. The Politburo, the top party organ, was the real decision-making center. A larger body, the Central Committee, represented the broader political elite, including regional party leaders and representatives of various economic sectors. Alongside the CPSU were Soviet state structures that formally resembled Western parliamentary systems but had little decision-making authority. The state bureaucracy had day-to-day responsibility in both the economic and political spheres but followed the party's directives. People holding high state positions were appointed through a system (called the ***nomenklatura***) that allowed the CPSU to fill key posts with politically reliable individuals. The Supreme Soviet, the parliament, was a rubber-stamp body.

The Soviet constitution was of symbolic rather than operational importance since many of its principles were ignored. The constitution provided for legislative, executive, and judicial organs, but separation of powers was considered unnecessary because the CPSU claimed to represent the interests of society as a whole. When the constitution was violated (as it frequently was), the courts had no independent authority to protect its provisions.

The Soviet Union was also designated a federal system; but this was phony federalism, since all aspects of life were overseen by a highly centralized Communist Party. Nonetheless, the various subunits that existed within the Russian Republic (***autonomous republics***, ***krais***, ***oblasts***, and ***okrugs***) were carried over into the Russian Federation in an altered form.

Gorbachev introduced competitive elections, increased political pluralism, reduced Communist Party dominance, revitalized the legislative branch of

The U.S. Connection

Federalism in the United States and Russia

Like the United States, Russia is, according to its constitution, a federal system. This means that powers are divided between the central government (located in Moscow in Russia, or Washington, D.C., in the United States) and the constituent units. When the Russian constitution was adopted in 1993 there were eighty-nine federal units; due to mergers, in mid-2008 there were eighty-three compared to the fifty U.S. states.

Federalism operates quite differently in the two countries. In comparison to the American system, the Russian structure seems complicated. Russia's multiethnic population underlies this complexity because diverse ethnic groups in Russia are regionally concentrated, forming the basis for some of the federal units. Although the United States has racial and ethnic diversity, this does not affect the way the states were formed.

Some of Russia's federal units are called republics, while others are called *oblasts* (regions), *krais* (another type of region), autonomous *okrugs* (districts), or cities of federal status (Moscow and St. Petersburg). The twenty-one "republics" and the smaller autonomous *okrugs* are named after non-Russian ethnic groups that reside there. If you think this is complicated, some federal units are located within other federal units, leading to the term "*matrushka* federalism," a name inspired by the Russian wooden dolls that are nested one inside another.

As in the United States, Russia's federal units are represented in the upper house of the national legislature (in the United States in the Senate, in Russia called the Federation Council). In the United States, two senators from each state are directly elected by the people. In Russia, each region also has two representatives, but their method of selection has been a point of contest. In 1993 they were elected directly by the population. From the mid-1990s, the elected governor (or chief executive) of each region and the head of the regional legislature themselves sat in the Federation Council. Since 2000 the system has again shifted so that these representatives are appointed, one by the region's governor and the other by the region's legislature. All of these changes have occurred in less than fifteen years, making it hard for Russian citizens to keep up.

In the 1990s Russia's federal government had difficulty controlling what happened in the regions; regional laws sometime deviated or even violated federal law. Bilateral treaties between the federal government and some of the republics and regions granted special privileges, producing what some called "asymmetrical federalism." Since 2000, President Putin put measures in place to ensure a greater degree of legal and political uniformity throughout the country. Seven federal districts were created to monitor implementation of federal policy in the regions. Beginning in 1996 regional governors were directly elected, but in 2004 this was replaced by a quasi-appointment procedure. These centralizing measures have led some observers to question whether Russian is really a federal system at all. Like the United States, Russia does have a constitutional court to resolve disputes over the jurisdictions of the federal government and the states (regions), but in Russia the constitution does not provide a strong basis for regional power, whereas in the United States, both through court cases and through legislative acts, states' rights have often been effectively defended. ❖

government, and renegotiated the terms of Soviet federalism. He also tried to bring the constitution into harmony with political reality. Many constitutional amendments were adopted that altered existing political institutions. These changes moved the political system haltingly and unevenly closer to the liberal democratic systems of the West. However, ultimately they led to the collapse of the Soviet system itself.

The New Russian State

Even before the collapse of the USSR, political institutions began to change in the Russian Republic, a constituent unit of the Soviet Union. A new post of president was created, and on June 12, 1991, Boris Yeltsin was elected by direct popular vote as its first incumbent. Once the Russian Federation became independent, a crucial turning point was the adoption by referendum of a new Russian constitution in December 1993. This constitution provides the legal foundation for current state institutions (see Figure 5.5). But political practice goes far beyond constitutional provisions and sometimes alters their interpretation.

The Executive

FOCUS QUESTIONS

In what ways has the executive branch of government become less centralized than it was in Soviet times?
Are recent centralization measures changing this?

The constitution establishes a semipresidential system, formally resembling the French system but with stronger executive power. The president, who holds primary power, is the head of state, and the prime minister, appointed by the president but approved by the lower house of the parliament (the State *Duma*), is the head of government. This dual executive can introduce tensions within the executive branch, as well as between the president and the *Duma*. As a rule of thumb, the president has overseen foreign policy, relations with the regions, and the organs of state security, while the prime minister has focused his attention on the economy and related issues. However, with Yeltsin's continuing health problems in 1998 and 1999, operative power shifted in the direction of the prime minister. Following the election of Vladimir Putin in March 2000, however, the primary locus of power returned to the presidency.

In December 1999, Yeltsin resigned from office, making the prime minister, Vladimir Putin, acting president until the March 2000 elections, which he won handily. Putin's 2004 electoral victory was even more stunning (71 percent of the vote), but some international observers alleged that media bias raised questions about its genuine democratic character. Although the constitution excludes three consecutive terms as president, speculation is rife as to whether Putin might seek to return to the post after a break in his term of office beginning in 2008.

One of the president's most important powers is the authority to issue decrees, which Yeltsin used frequently to address contentious issues. Although presidential decrees may not violate the constitution or legislation passed by the bicameral legislature (the Federal Assembly), policy-making by decree can allow the president to ignore an uncooperative or divided parliament. Yeltsin's decision in 1994, and again in 1999, to launch the offensive in Chechnya was not approved by either house of parliament, despite strong objections from a broad range of political groups.

The president can also call a state of emergency, impose martial law, grant pardons, call referenda, and temporarily suspend actions of other state organs if he deems them to contradict the constitution or federal laws. Some of these actions must be confirmed by other state organs (such as the upper house of the

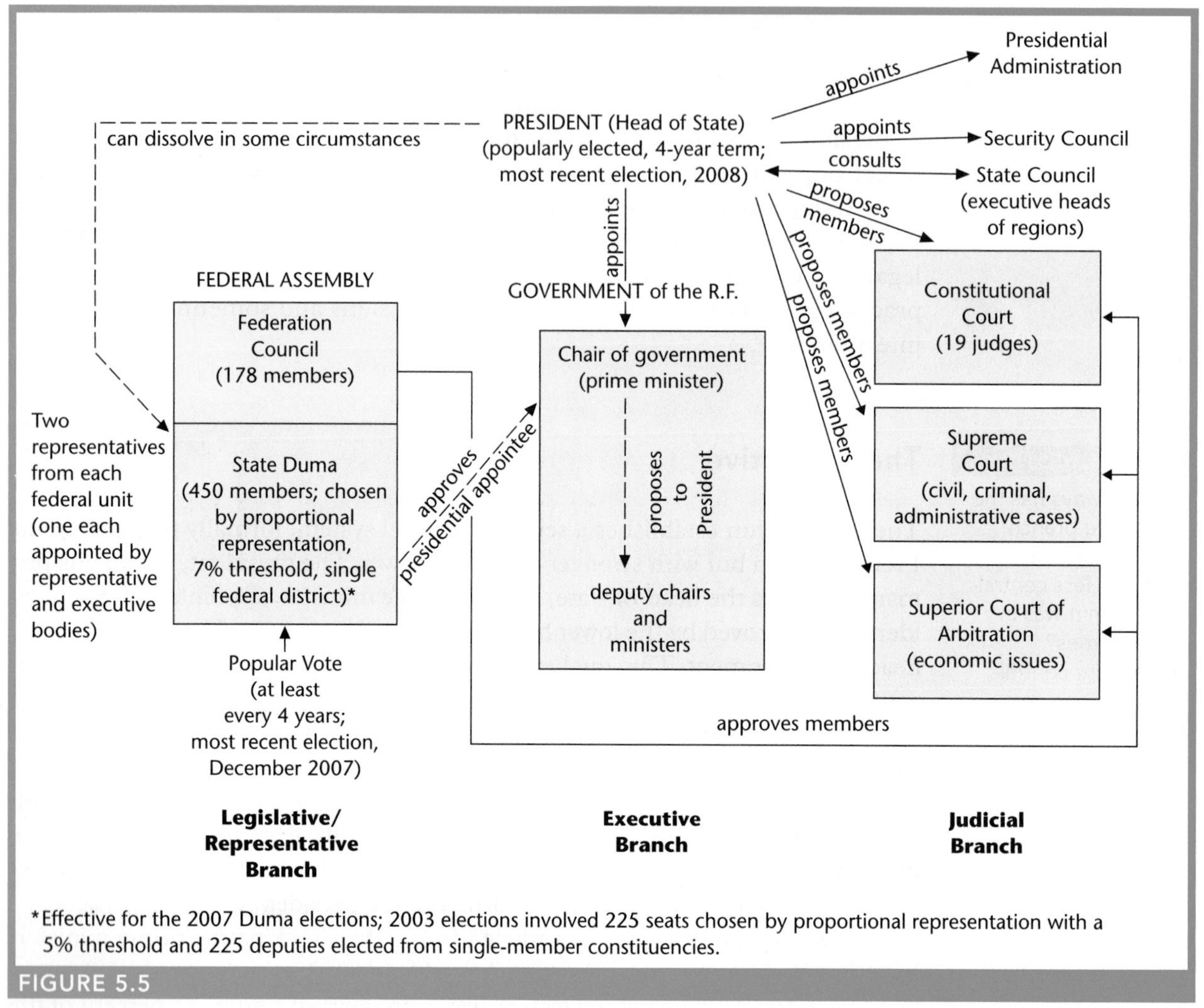

FIGURE 5.5

Political Institutions of the Russian Federation (R.F.), 2007

parliament, the Federation Council). The president is commander in chief of the armed forces and conducts affairs of state with other nations. Impeachment of the president involves the *Duma*, the Federation Council, the Supreme Court, and the Constitutional Court. If the president dies in office or becomes incapacitated, the prime minister fills the post until new presidential elections can be held.

The Russian government is headed by the prime minister, flanked by varying numbers of deputy prime ministers. The president's choice of prime minister must be approved by the *Duma*. During Yeltsin's presidency, six prime ministers held office. Between 2000 and 2008, Putin had three prime ministers, Mikhail Kosyanov (until February 2004, later turned opposition figure), Mikhail Fradkov (March 2004–September 2007, following a brief period with an interim prime minister), and Viktor Zubkov (from September 2007).

The prime minister can be removed by the *Duma* through two repeat votes of no confidence passed within a three-month period. The *Duma* has ultimately been reluctant to consistently defy the president because rejection of the candidate three times can lead to dissolution of the *Duma* itself. The prime minister has never been the leader of the dominant party or coalition in the *Duma*. Principles of party accountability that apply in most Western parliamentary systems are not operative in Russia. Without disciplined parties and with no formal links between parties and the executive branch, the process of gaining *Duma* acceptance of government proposals depends on the authority of the president and on the particular configuration of power at the moment.

The National Bureaucracy

Efforts to downsize the executive bureaucracy have been only partially successful. Alongside the state bureaucracy is the presidential administration, which serves the president directly. Some government ministries (such as the Foreign Affairs Ministry, the Federal Security Service, and the Defense Ministry) report directly to the president.[17] The president has created various advisory bodies that solicit input from important political and economic actors and also co-opt them into support for government policies. The most important are the Security Council and the State Council. Formed in 1992, the Security Council advises the president in areas related to foreign policy and security (broadly conceived) and includes heads of appropriate government bodies (the so-called power ministries such as Defense and the Federal Security Service), the prime minister, and in recent years the heads of seven newly created federal districts. The State Council was formed in September 2000 as part of Putin's attempt to redefine the role of regional leaders in federal decision making (see below). A smaller presidium, made up of seven of the regional heads selected by the president, meets monthly.

The bureaucratic agencies include ministries, state committees, and other agencies. Ministers other than the prime minister do not require parliamentary approval. The prime minister makes recommendations to the president, who appoints these officials. Ministers and other agency heads are generally career bureaucrats who have risen through an appropriate ministry, although sometimes more clearly political appointments are made. Many agencies have been reorganized, often more than once. Top leaders also use restructuring to place their clients and allies in key positions. For example, Putin has drawn heavily on colleagues with whom he worked earlier in St. Petersburg or in the security establishment, referred to as ***siloviki***, in staffing a variety of posts in his administration. In an effort to increase the role of merit and the professional character of the civil service, the president himself initiated a process of civil service reform in August 2002; legislation to begin the reform passed in 2004.

siloviki derived from the Russian word *sil*, meaning "force." Russian politicians and government officials drawn from security and intelligence agencies, special forces, or the military, many of whom were recruited to important political posts under Vladimir Putin.

In Putin's restructuring of government agencies, a new Ministry for Economic Development and Trade took over functions of several previously existing ministries, as did a new Ministry of Industry, Science, and Technology. Observers question whether such reorganizations produce substantive benefits, and some are particularly controversial. Functions of the State Committee on Northern Affairs were transferred to the Ministry for Economic Development and Trade, viewed by some as a downgrading of northern concerns on the government's agenda.

FOCUS QUESTIONS

How have the military, judiciary, and subnational governments evolved since the fall of the Soviet Union?

Have they gained or lost importance?

Other State Institutions

The Military and Security Organs

Because of Vladimir Putin's career background in the KGB, he drew many of his staff from this arena. Thus, while the formal rank of the Federal Security Service has not changed, the actual impact of the security establishment took on increasing importance in the Putin era. This development preceded 9/11, and the important role placed on security concerns reflects the orientation of the Russian state under Putin's leadership. Because many Russians are alarmed by the crime rate and terrorist bombings in the country, restrictions on civil liberties have not elicited strong popular concern. At the same time, there is widespread public cynicism about the honesty of the ordinary police (*militsiia*). Such suspicions are likely often correct.[18]

The Russian government attributes repeated bombings since 1999 to Chechen terrorists and has claimed that the terrorists have international links to the Al Qaeda network. The year 2004 was particularly traumatic with the downing of two airliners and a suicide-bomb attack in Moscow in August, followed by the Beslan incident in September. Attacks on civilians by Russian forces in Chechnya have elicited Western human rights protests. Since the September 11 attacks, cooperation between Russian and Western security agencies has increased, as Russia has shared security information. However, closer NATO and American ties in neighboring Georgia have been an irritant to Russia, which sees this region as part of its sphere of influence.

The Soviet military once ranked as one of the largest and most powerful forces in the world, second only to that of the United States and justifying the country's designation as a superpower. The Communist Party controlled military appointments, and the military never usurped political power. During the August 1991 coup attempt, troops remained loyal to Yeltsin and Gorbachev, even though the Minister of Defense was among the coup plotters. In October 1993, despite some apparent hesitancy in military circles, military units defended the government's position, this time firing on civilian protesters and shocking the country.

In the postcommunist period, the political power and prestige of the military have suffered. Both Gorbachev and Yeltsin oversaw a reduction in military expenditures, bringing a decline in facilities and a reduction in conventional and nuclear forces. The military's failure to implement a successful strategy in the Chechnya war led the government to increase the role of the Federal Security Service there instead of relying on the army alone.[19] Reports of deteriorating conditions in some Russian nuclear arsenals have raised international concerns about nuclear security. In addition, the situation of military personnel, from the highest officers to rank-and-file soldiers, has worsened dramatically, producing a potential source of political discontent.

As of 2007, the Russian Federation still maintains a system of universal male conscription, but noncompliance and draftees rejected for health reasons have been persistent problems. A law to permit alternative military service for conscientious objectors took effect in 2004. Although critics of the military service law welcome the concept, they are critical of the restrictive conditions that the law imposes on alternative service. Government proposals to supplement the conscript army by a smaller professional military corps are on the agenda, but there are no definite plans to abolish the military draft,[20] although by 2008 the term of military service had been reduced from two years to one year.

The Judiciary

Concepts such as judicial independence and the rule of law were poorly understood in both pre–Revolutionary Russia and the Soviet era. These concepts have, however, been embedded in the new Russian constitution and are, in principle, accepted both by the public and political elites. However, their implementation has been difficult and not wholly successful.

In Russia, a Constitutional Court was formed in 1991. Its decisions were binding, and in several cases even the president had to bow to its authority. After several controversial decisions, Yeltsin suspended the operations of the court in late 1993. However, the Russian constitution now provides for a Constitutional Court again, with the power to adjudicate disputes on the constitutionality of federal and regional laws, as well as jurisdictional disputes between various political institutions. Justices are nominated by the president and approved by the Federation Council, a procedure that produced a stalemate after the new constitution was adopted, so that the court became functional only in 1995. Since 1995, the court has established itself as a vehicle for resolving conflicts involving the protection of individual rights and conformity of regional laws with constitutional requirements. The court has been cautious in confronting the executive branch, on which it depends to enforce its decisions.

Alongside the Constitutional Court is an extensive system of lower and appellate courts, with the Supreme Court at the pinnacle. These courts hear ordinary civil and criminal cases. In 1995, a system of commercial courts was also formed to hear cases dealing with issues related to privatization, taxes, and other commercial activities. The Federation Council must approve nominees for Supreme Court judgeships, and the constitution also grants the president power to appoint judges at other levels. Measures to shield judges from political pressures include criminal prosecution for attempting to influence a judge, protections from arbitrary dismissal, and improved salaries for judges. The Russian judicial system operates on a civil code system, similar to most of continental Europe. One innovation in the legal system has included introduction of jury trials for some types of criminal offenses.

Subnational Government

The collapse of the Soviet Union was precipitated by the demands of some union republics for more autonomy and, then, independence. After the Russian Federation became an independent state, the problem of constructing a viable federal structure within Russia resurfaced. Between 1991 and 1993, negotiations between the central government and the various regions led to the establishment of a federal structure including eighty-nine units, which have different historical origins and designations (such as republics, territories, and cities with federal status, namely Moscow and St. Petersburg). Mergers of federal units, such as those that occurred recently, are subject to approval by popular referendum.

One of the first issues to arise in the development of Russia's federal system was whether all of the federal units should have equal status. The twenty-one republics viewed themselves as a special category because of their different status in the Soviet period and the presence of significant minority groups within their borders. They have also been the most assertive in putting forth claims for autonomy or even sovereignty. The most extreme example is Chechnya, whose demand for independence has led to a protracted civil war. The ethnic dimension complicates political relations with some of the republics. The titular nationalities of several of the republics, including Tatarstan and Bashkortostan, which occupy relatively large territories in the center of the country, are of Islamic cultural background. Islamic fundamentalism has not, however, been a significant problem in Russia, since decades of Soviet socialization seems to have acculturated most parts of the Muslim population to secular, scientific values.

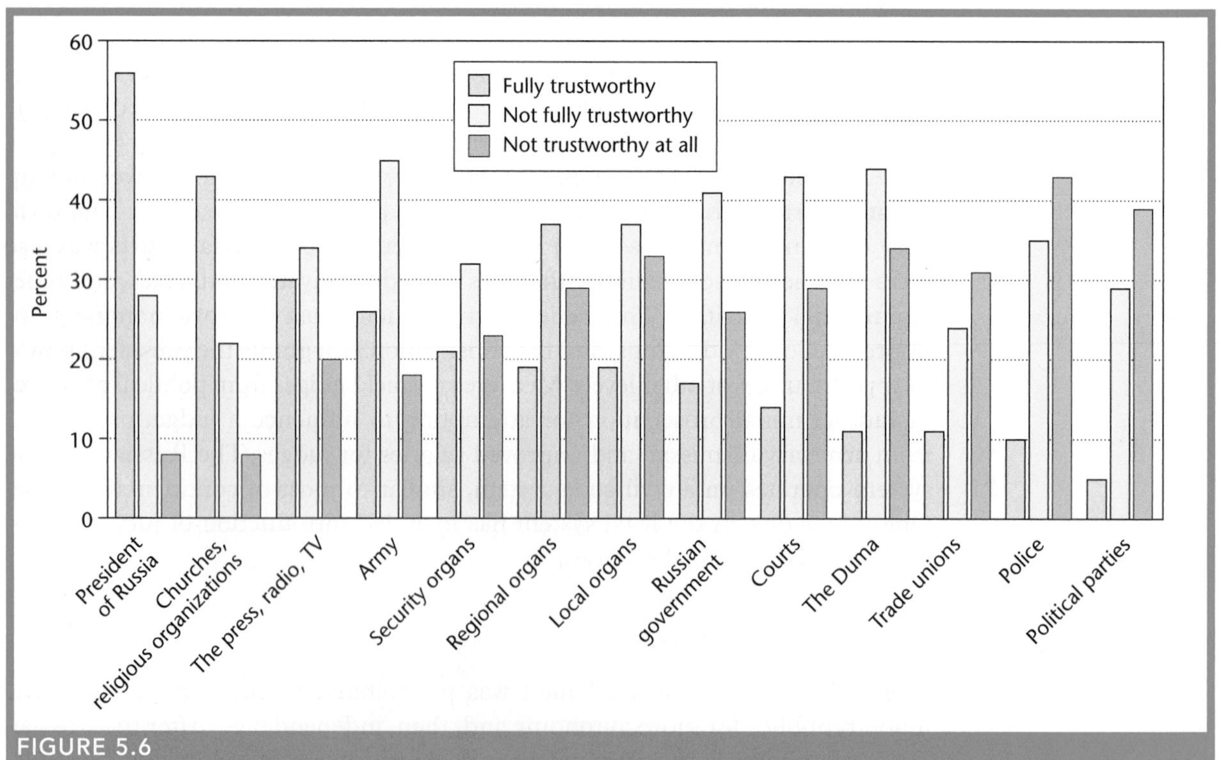

FIGURE 5.6

Level of Trust in Various Institutions in Russia

Source: Levada Center, http://www.levada.ru/press/2004092702.html (accessed April 28, 2005).

Following the March 2000 election Putin identified the establishment of a uniform system of federal-regional relations, governed by uniform legal principles, as an important priority. Steps to realize this objective included harmonization of regional laws and republic constitutions with federal legislation and constitutional provisions. Another measure gave the president the power, pending approval by a court, to remove a governor and disband a regional legislature if they engaged in anticonstitutional activity. In 2002, the Constitutional Court upheld the measure, but with many restrictions.[21]

power vertical a term used by Russian president Vladimir Putin to describe a unified and hierarchical structure of executive power ranging from the federal level to the local level.

Other reforms to the federal system introduced by Putin were even stronger measures to strengthen what Putin has called the "**power vertical**." This concept involves the strengthening of an integrated structure of executive power from the presidential level down through to the local level. Critics have questioned whether the idea is consistent with federal principles, and others see it as undermining Russia's fledgling democratic system. A first step in creating the power vertical was the creation of seven federal districts on top of the existing federal units. Although not designed to replace regional governments, the districts were intended to oversee the work of federal offices operating in these regions and to ensure compliance with federal laws and the constitution. Putin's appointees to head these new federal districts included several individuals (all male) with backgrounds in the security or military services, reinforcing concerns that the districts could become a powerful instrument of central control. In practice, the federal districts have been less intrusive in the affairs of the regions than many feared.

A second set of changes to create the power vertical has involved a weakening of the independence of governors (and republic presidents). Yeltsin agreed to their popular election, which gave them greater legitimacy and independence from Moscow. Beginning in 1996, the governors, along with the heads of each regional legislative body, also sat as members of the upper house of the Russian parliament, the Federation Council. This arrangement gave the regional executives a direct voice in national legislative discussions and a presence in Moscow. In 2001, Putin gained approval for a revision to the composition of the Federation Council. Regional executives were, as of January 2002, no longer members of the Federation Council. Rather, one regional representative is appointed by the regional executive and the other by the regional legislature. Some governors resisted this change, seeing it as an assault on their power (they also lost the legal immunity that goes along with being a member of parliament). Putin made concessions to make the change more palatable, for example, giving governors the right to recall their representatives. The State Council was formed to try to assure the regional executives that they would retain some role in the federal policy-making arena, although losing their seats in the Federation Council.

Following the Beslan massacre, Putin identified corruption and ineffective leadership at the regional level as culprits in allowing terrorists to carry out the devastating school hostage taking. Accordingly, he proposed an additional reform that created a decisive element of central control over regional politics. Approved by the State *Duma* in December 2004, the change eliminated popular election of governors. Governors are now nominated by the president and approved by the regional legislature. As in the system for approving the prime minister, if the regional legislature refuses the nomination three times, the president may disband the body and call for new elections. With governors and republic presidents dependent on the goodwill of the president for appointment and reappointment, a self-perpetuating political process has taken on a formal character, leading some observers to declare the death of Russian federalism and the weakening of Russian democracy.

The Policy-Making Process

FOCUS QUESTIONS

What are the principal policy-making bodies in modern Russian?

To what extent do these bodies really formulate policy, and to what extent do they simply rubberstamp policies that have really been made elsewhere?

Policy-making occurs both formally and informally. The federal government, the president and his administration, regional legislatures individual deputies, and some judicial bodies may, according to the constitution, propose legislation. In the Yeltsin era, conflict between the president and *Duma* made policy-making a contentious and fractious process; under Putin, the *Duma* generally went along with proposals made by the president and the government, and the proportion of legislation initiated by the executive branch increased significantly.

Sometimes, the government, deputies, or parliamentary factions offer competing drafts of laws, leading to protracted and complicated bargaining. In order for a bill to become law, it must be approved by both houses of the parliament in three readings and signed by the president. If the president vetoes the bill, it must be passed again in the same wording by a two-thirds majority of both houses of parliament in order to override the veto. Budgetary proposals can be put forth only by the government, and they have, in the past, elicited sharp controversy in the parliament since proposed budget reductions affect key interests and groups, such as regional and local governments, other state agencies, the military, trade unions, enterprise directors, state employees, and pensioners. Many policy proclamations are made through presidential or governmental decrees, without formal consultation with the legislative branch. This decision-making process is much less visible and may involve closed-door bargaining rather than an open process of debate and consultation.

Informal groupings also have an important indirect impact on policy-making. During the Yeltsin period, business magnates were able to exert behind-the-scenes influence to gain benefits in the privatization of lucrative firms in sectors such as oil, media, and transport. Putin has attempted to reduce the direct political influence of these powerful economic figures and to formalize business input through bodies such as the Entrepreneurship Council. Some observers see this development as an example of corporatism, a system in which the government identifies (or sometimes helps create) organizations that are consulted to represent designated societal interests (in this case, business interests) in the policy-making process. The emerging Russian corporatism seems to be a state corporatist variant, a top-down variety in which the government itself plays an active role in defining these vehicles of societal input.[22] One problem is that some interests, particularly those that are less powerful or well organized, may be excluded from the process. Another less formal linkage between the government and business is through continued government ownership of enterprise shares. This allows the government to influence leadership positions in key firms such as Gasprom, the main exporter of natural gas. Through such personal links, the president can maintain some leverage in the economic sphere, even without a clear policy or legislative basis. In almost all cases, participation in policy-making does not extend to representatives of more broadly based citizens' groups.

A continuing problem is the inefficacy of policy implementation. Under Communist rule, the party's control over political appointments enforced at least some degree of conformity to central mandates. Under Yeltsin, fragmented and decentralized political power gave the executive branch few resources to ensure compliance. Pervasive corruption, including bribery and selective enforcement, hindered enforcement of policy decisions. Although Putin stated his commitment to restrict these types of irregularities, they no doubt continue. However, his commitment to reestablishing order and a rule of law has been an important foundation of his public support and his justification for the centralization of power we have discussed in this chapter.

Summary

When the Russian Federation was formed in 1991, new political structures needed to be constructed. A constitution was adopted in 1993, which involved a directly elected president who had strong political powers. In addition, a federal system was established with the result that the central government had difficulty controlling actions of regional governments in the 1990s. Since 1999, the political system saw increased centralization under Vladimir Putin's leadership, including a harmonization of central and regional laws, quasi-appointment of regional governors, and a more unified executive structure in the country. Under Putin the role of the security forces increased; the military lost its previous stature; and the judiciary took on increased, although not complete, independence. Policy-making is largely under the guidance of the executive organs of the state with little real input or influence from society or political parties. Whereas in the 1990s the relationship between the executive and legislative branches (Federal Assembly) was characterized by conflict that often produced political deadlock, under Putin's leadership the legislative branch was relatively compliant, reinforcing the president's dominant role.

SECTION 4 Representation and Participation

Gorbachev's policies in the 1980s brought a dramatic change in the relationship between state and society, as *glasnost* sparked new public and private initiatives. Most restrictions on the formation of social organizations were lifted, and a large number of independent groups appeared. Hopes rose that these trends might

civil society refers to the space occupied by voluntary associations outside the state, for example, professional associations, trade unions, and student groups.

indicate the emergence of **civil society**, an autonomous sphere of social life that could act on the state without being dependent on it. However, just a few years later, only a small stratum of Russian society was actively engaged; the demands of everyday life as well as cynicism about politics has led many people to withdraw into private life. With minor fluctuations, Putin's approval rating stabilized at 65 to 70 percent after his election in 2000, while trust in public institutions remained low and the public's ability to affect policy seemed questionable.

FOCUS QUESTIONS

What are the functions of the chambers in the Russian legislature?

Can the Russian legislature act as an effective check on the executive branch or in representing the population?

The Legislature

The Russian legislature, the Federal Assembly, came into being after the parliamentary elections of December 12, 1993, when the referendum ratifying the new Russian constitution was also approved. The upper house, the Federation Council, represents Russia's constituent federal units. The lower house, the *Duma*, has 450 members and involves direct popular election of candidates and parties. The first Federal Assembly served only a two-year term. Subsequent elections to the *Duma* have occurred every four years, in 1995, 1999, 2003, and 2007.

Within the *Duma*, factions unite deputies from the same or allied parties. The *Duma* also has a number of standing committees; in 2005 all twenty-nine heads came from the dominant United Russia faction, with just six committees having first deputy chairs from other party factions.[23] The *Duma* elects its own speaker (or chair); since July 2003 this has been Boris Gryzlov, head of the United Russia Party, who, in Putin's circles, enjoys the highest level of support next to the president.[24] After the 1995 and 1999 elections, the speaker of the *Duma* came from the Communist Party, which had the highest electoral showing in those votes.

Compared to the Communist period, deputies reflect less fully the demographic characteristics of the population at large. For example, in 1984, 33 percent of the members of the Supreme Soviet were women;[25] in 2005 they constituted less than 10 percent. In 2000, manual workers made up less than 1 percent of *Duma* deputies, in contrast to 35 percent in the 1985 Supreme Soviet.[26]

The upper house of the Federal Assembly, the Federation Council, has two members from each of Russia's federal regions and republics, but the method of selection has varied over time. A new procedure, phased in between 2000 and 2002, involves appointment of one representative by the regional executive and the other by the regional legislature, whereas from 1995 until that time, the elected governor/president of each region and the regional legislative head were themselves members. Many prominent businessmen are among the appointees, and in some cases the posts may be granted in exchange for political loyalty, raising doubts about the likelihood that the body adequately represents interests of the regions.

The constitution grants parliament powers in the legislative and budgetary areas, but if there is conflict with the president or government, these powers can be exercised effectively only if parliament operates with a high degree of unity. In practice, the president can often override the parliament through mechanisms such as the veto of legislation. Each house of parliament has the authority to confirm certain presidential appointees, in addition to the prime minister. The Federation Council must also approve presidential decrees relating to martial law and state emergency, as well as deploying troops abroad.[27]

Following electoral rebuffs in the 1993 and 1995 parliamentary elections, Yeltsin confronted a parliament that obstructed many of his proposed policies, but the parliament did not have the power or unity to offer a constructive alternative. Since the 2003 election, however, the *Duma* has cooperated with the president; in 2006 over two-thirds of the deputies were tied to the dominant United Russia faction, closest to the president, even though this party won only 49 percent of the seats in 2003 Duma election (2003).[28]

Society's ability to affect particular policy decisions through the legislative process is minimal. Parties in the parliament are isolated from the public at large, suffer low levels of popular respect, and the internal decision-making structures of parties are generally elite-dominated. Interest associations to lobby the parliament are weak, and public hearings on controversial issues are rare.

Political Parties and the Party System

FOCUS QUESTIONS

What are the bases of support of the most important Russian political parties?

How has the United Russia Party been able to gain a dominant position in such a short period of time?

One of the most important political changes following the collapse of communism was the shift from a single-party to a multiparty system. In the USSR, the CPSU not only dominated state organs but also oversaw all social institutions, such as the mass media, trade unions, youth groups, educational institutions, and professional associations. It defined the official ideology for the country, set the parameters for state censorship, and ensured that loyal supporters occupied all important offices. Approximately 10 percent of adults in the Soviet Union were party members, but there were no effective mechanisms to ensure accountability of the party leadership to its members.

National competitive elections were held for the first time in the USSR in 1989, but new political parties were not formal participants in Russia until 1993. Since then, a confusing array of political organizations has run candidates in elections (see Table 5.3). Until 2003, these included not only political parties but also political and socioeconomic movements. A new law on political parties went into effect in July 2001; the law tightened the conditions for party formation and registration, which were further strengthened in 2006. Although critics have portrayed these changes as artificially reducing voter choice, defenders argue that they will help to bring order to a chaotic and fragmented party system.

In the 1990s, many parties formed around prominent individuals, making politics very personalistic. Most Russian parties do not have a firm social base or stable constituency. Furthermore, other than the Communist Party, Russian parties are young, so deeply rooted political identifications have not had time to develop. Finally, many citizens do not have a clear conception of their own interests or of how parties might represent them. In this context, image making is as important as programmatic positions, so parties appeal to transient voter sentiments.

TABLE 5.3

Top Parties in the State Duma Elections[a]

Party or Bloc[b]	Percent of 1995 Party List Vote[c]	Percent of 1999 Party List Vote[c]	Percent of 2003 Party List Vote[c]	Percent of Duma Seats 2003[d]	Percent of 2007 Party List Vote[e]	Percent of Duma Seats Based on 2007 Vote	Comments	Party Leader
Centrist/Establishment								
United Russia	—	(23.3)	37.6	49.3	64.1	70.0	Formed as Unity Party in 1999, then merged with Fatherland, All-Russia to form United Russia	Boris Gryzlov, party chair, but Vladimir Putin to head the party list on the ballot (2007)
A Just Russia	—	—	—	—	7.8	8.4	Formed in 2006 from three political parties: Life, Rodina, and the Russian Party of Pensioners	Sergey Mironov
Fatherland, All-Russia	—	13.3	—	—	—	—	Merged into United Russia in 2001	Yuri Lyzhkov, Evgenii Primakov (1999)
Our Home Is Russia	10.1	1.2	—	—	—	—	Chernomyrdin was prime minister, 1992–1998	Viktor Chernomyrdin (1995, 1999)
Liberal/Reform								
Union of Rightist Forces	(3.9)	8.5	4.0	0.7			Russia's Choice (1993), Russia's Democratic Choice/ United Russia (1995)	Nikita Belykh
Yabloko	6.9	5.9	4.3	0.9			Opposition liberal/reform party	Grigoriy Yavlinsky

Communist/Socialist								
Communist Party of the Russian Federation	22.3	24.3	12.6	11.6	11.6	12.7		Gennady Zyuganov
Nationalist/Patriotic								
Liberal Democratic Party of Russia	11.2	6.0	11.5	8.0	8.2	8.9	In 1999 participated in elections as Bloc Zhirinovsky	Vladimir Zhirinovsky
Rodina (Motherland Bloc)	—	—	9.0	8.2	—	—	Left/center nationalist party; merged into A Just Russia	Dmitry Rogozin, Sergey Glaziev (2003)

[a]As of 2008, blocs of parties were not permitted to stand in elections.

[b]Figures may not add to 100 percent or to the total number of deputies in the State Duma because smaller parties and independents are excluded. Table includes only parties winning at least 4.0 percent of the national party list vote in one of the three elections (but not all such parties).

[c]Percentage of the total popular vote the party or bloc received on the proportional representation portion of the ballot in the year indicated. A dash indicates that the party or bloc was not included on that ballot or did not win a significant portion of the vote. Numbers in parentheses are votes for predecessor parties, similar to the one running in 2003.

[d]The sum of seats won in the proportional representation (party list) vote and the single-member district vote. Number of deputies in the faction changed over time following the elections.

[e]In 2007 all of the seats were allocated according to the party list (proportional representation) ballot for parties receiving at least 7% of that vote; the single-member district vote was discontinued. The final distribution of seats in the Duma is an estimate at the time of printing, based on results reported by the Russian Electoral Commission, December 3, 2007.

Source:

Revised from DeBardeleben, Joan, "Russia" in *Introduction to Comparative Politics*. Copyright 2004 by Houghton Mifflin Company. Reprinted with permission; and for the 2003 figures, *The Economist. Country Briefings: Russia*. http://www.economist.com, April 25, 2005.

Since 2003, one political party, United Russia, has taken on political dominance at both the national and regional levels. Although Putin is neither a leader nor member of this party, United Russia serves as a major source of political support for the system of power that has been erected under his leadership.

While individual leaders play an important role in political life in Russia, some key issues have divided opinions in the post-1991 period. One such issue is economic policy. Nearly all political parties have mouthed support for creation of a market economy to replace the centralized Soviet economy. However communist/socialist groupings have been more muted in their support and have argued for a continued state role in providing social protection and benefits for vulnerable parts of the population. The liberal/reform groupings, on the other hand, have advocated more rapid market reform, including privatization, free prices, and limited government spending. The now dominant United Russia party charts a middle ground, appealing to voters from a wide ideological spectrum.

Another dividing line relates to national identity. The nationalist/patriotic parties emphasize the defense of Russian interests over Westernization. They strongly criticize the westward expansion of NATO into regions neighboring Russia; they favor a strong military establishment, protection from foreign economic influence, and reconstitution of some former Soviet republics into a larger federation. Liberal/reform parties, on the other hand, advocate integration of Russia into the global market and the adoption of Western economic and political principles. Again, the United Russia party has articulated an intriguing combination of these viewpoints, identifying Europe as the primary identity point for Russia, but at the same time insisting on Russia's role as a regional power, pursuing its own unique path of political and economic development.

Ethnic and regional parties have not had a significant impact on the national scene. Amendments to the party law make it even more difficult than previously for regional parties to form. Similarly, religion, although an important source of personal meaning, has not emerged as a significant source of political identity for ethnic Russians, who are primarily Russian Orthodox Christians. Nonetheless, in recent years, rising expressions of Russian nationalism and ethnic intolerance, have erupted, particularly in relation to the primarily Muslim Chechens.

Russian political parties do not fit neatly on a left-right spectrum. Nationalist sentiments crosscut economic ideologies, producing the following party tendencies:

- The traditional left, critical of market reform and often mildly nationalistic
- Liberal/reform forces, supporting assertive Western-type market reform and political norms
- Centrist "parties of power," representing the political elite
- Nationalist/patriotic forces, primarily concerned with identity issues and national self-assertion

The most important parties in all four groupings have not challenged the structure of the political system but have chosen to work within it.

The Dominant Centrist Party: United Russia

United Russia's predecessor, the Unity Party, rose to prominence together with Vladimir Putin in the elections of 1999 and 2000. Although Putin is neither head nor member of the party, United Russia is clearly a vehicle for cementing his political power. Following its formation in the late 1990s, the party made a meteoric rise, finishing a close second runner to the CPRF in the 1999 *Duma* elections and winning nearly 50 percent of seats in the *Duma* in 2003. By 2005, through party mergers and individual shifts, 67 percent of *Duma* deputies joined the United Russia faction. In the 2007 Duma elections the party won 64 percent of the vote.

What explains United Russia's success? An important factor is the association with Putin, but the party has also built an effective political machine that could generate persuasive incentives for regional elites. A bandwagon effect and desire to be on the winning side have bolstered the party's fortunes. The party has a rather poorly defined program, which emphasizes the uniqueness of the Russian approach (as distinct from Western models), an appeal to values of order and law, and a continued commitment to moderate reform. The party is truly a party of power, focused on winning to its side prominent and powerful people, who will then use their influence to further bolster the party's support. By 2005, United Russia had, through a combination of carrots and sticks, brought sixty-four regional executives into the fold, along with increased influence in regional legislatures.[29] Combined with increasingly centralized control within the party, the result is a powerful political machine reinforced by the president's power over gubernatorial appointments. At the same time, United Russia's voters represent a broad spectrum of the population and the party has drawn support from every other part of the political spectrum, making the party a catchall electoral organization. A major question in the run-up to the 2007–2008 election cycle in Russia was whether an opposition party would be able pose a real and viable challenge to United Russia's dominance. Some observers speculated that the formation of a second centrist party, A Just Russia, had the blessing of the Kremlin in order to impart the impression that real competition existed in a situation where various informal mechanisms of power were increasingly marginalizing opposition political parties, though, for example, selective enforcement of complex electoral and party legislation. In the 2007 Duma elections the party A Just Russia won just under 8 percent of the vote, reducing its credibility as a viable competitor to United Russia.

The Russian Left: The Communist Party of the Russian Federation

The CPRF was by far the strongest parliamentary party after the 1995 elections, winning over one-third of the seats in the *Duma*. Since then its strength has steadily declined. In May 2005, only 10.4 percent of deputies were in the CPRF faction.[30] The CPRF, the clearest successor of the old CPSU, appears to be a party in decline. With the second strongest showing after United Russia in the 2007 Duma elections, the party nonetheless got only 11.7 percent of the vote.

In addition to its socialist economic approach, the CPRF espouses its own brand of Russian patriotism. The party defines its goals as being democracy, justice, equality, patriotism and internationalism, a combination of civic rights and duties, and socialist renewal. Primary among the party's concerns are the social costs of the reform process. Thus, it has supported state subsidies for industry to ensure timely payment of wages and to prevent enterprise bankruptcies. Support for the party is especially strong among older Russians, the economically disadvantaged, and rural residents. It appears to represent those who have adapted less successfully to the radical and uncertain changes of recent years, as well as some individuals who remain committed to socialist ideals. Its principal failures have been an inability to adapt its public position to attract significant numbers of new adherents, particularly among the young, as well as the absence of a charismatic and attractive political leader. Although one might expect Russia to offer fertile ground for social democratic sentiments like those that have been successful in the Scandinavian countries of Western Europe, the CPRF has not capitalized on these sentiments, nor has it made room for a new social democratic party that could be more successful.

Liberal/Reform Parties

The liberal/reform parties have found it hard to build a stable and unified electoral base. Many Russians held aspects of the liberal program, such as privatization and shock therapy, responsible for Russia's economic decline. Since the first competitive elections in 1993, various liberal/reform parties have split the vote among themselves. On November 21, 1998, the brutal murder by contract killers of the liberal/reform politician and *Duma* member Galina Starovoitova (one of Russia's most prominent female politicians) resulted in renewed efforts to form a united political bloc in the form of the Union of Rightist Forces (URF).[31] In 1999, the URF received only 8.5 percent of the party-list vote, while another liberal reform party, Yabloko, with its more critical stance toward the government, ran separately, polling just 5.9 percent. In 2003, for the first time, neither Yabloko nor the URF reached the 5 percent cutoff; thus, this tendency is currently not represented in the *Duma* at all, following further electoral declines in 2007.

These groups espouse a commitment to traditional liberal values, such as a limited economic role for the state, support for free-market principles, and the protection of individual rights and liberties. The unpopularity of Yeltsin's reform approach undermined their support. Although liberal/reform figures are often referred to as the "democrats" many Russians associate them with Russia's economic and national decline, thus giving the word *democrat* a negative connotation in some circles. Support for liberal/reform parties generally is stronger among the young, the more highly educated, urban dwellers, and the well-off.

Nationalist/Patriotic Parties

The Liberal Democratic Party of Russia (LDPR), headed by Vladimir Zhirinovsky, got the strongest support on the party ballot in 1993, winning almost 23 percent of the vote; this declined to 11 percent in 1995 and 6 percent in 1999, but rebounded to 11.5 percent in 2003, and 8.2 percent in 2007, placing a close third behind the Communist Party. Neither liberal nor particularly democratic in its platform, the party might more properly be characterized as nationalist and populist. Zhirinovsky openly appeals to the anti-Western sentiments that grew in the wake of Russia's decline from superpower status and the government's perceived groveling for Western economic aid. Concern with the breakdown of law and order seems to rank high among its priorities. Zhirinovsky's support has been especially strong among working-class men and military personnel. Continuing support for the LDPR and the increasingly nationalist tone in the programs of other parties suggest that nationalist sentiment in Russia is increasing, not declining.

FOCUS QUESTIONS

In what ways have Russian elections come to resemble elections in the United States or Western Europe? In what ways are they different?

Elections

The initial euphoria with the competitive electoral structure has been replaced by voter fatigue, although turnout in federal elections remains respectable, generally between 60 and 70 percent, but somewhat lower (56 percent) in the 2003 *Duma* election. In 2006 national legislation removed the requirement of a minimum 50 percent turnout to make an election valid. National elections receive extensive media coverage, and campaign activities begin as long as a year in advance. Elections are now big business, involving extensive use of polling firms and public relations experts. Up until 2003, national elections were generally considered to be reasonably fair and free, but international observers expressed serious concerns about the conduct of the 2003 and 2007 votes and the campaigns that preceded them.[32]

proportional representation (PR) a system of political representation in which seats are allocated to parties within multi-member constituencies, roughly in proportion to the votes each party receives.

single-member plurality district an electoral system in which candidates run for a single seat from a specific geographic district.

Up through 2003, the electoral system for selecting the *Duma* resembled the German system, combining **proportional representation** with winner-take-all districts. Half of the 450 deputies were selected on the basis of nationwide party lists, with any party gaining 5 percent of the national vote entitled to a proportional share of these 225 seats. The remaining 225 deputies were elected in **single-member plurality districts**; these races usually involved local notables. The final balance of forces in the parliament was determined by the combined result of the party-list vote and the single-member district votes. Some independent candidates joined party factions once they are in the *Duma*. Until 1999, despite the electoral rebuffs in 1993 and 1995, Yeltsin did not install a prime minister reflecting party strength in the *Duma*. In 1999 and 2003, parliamentary elections offered qualified support for the government.

In 2005, changes to the electoral law were approved, to take effect with the 2007 *Duma* elections. These involved abolition of the single-member districts, subsuming selection of all 450 deputies on the party-list ballot into one national proportional representation district, with a minimum threshold for representation raised to 7 percent. Parties are required to include regional representatives on their lists from across the country. Although this aspect of the legislation appears to prevent dominance by Moscow-based or other regional cliques, it is not clear whether this will be the actual effect, given strong central control within some party structures. In addition, the overall reform has a strongly centralizing character. Over time, the number of successful parties is likely to decline, and these parties will probably be more dependent on national party machines. Higher hurdles for competing parties to gain representation may mean reduced opportunities for public input. These changes, plus allegations of interference with nomination and party registration processes, may reduce the effectiveness of elections as vehicles of popular control.

Since 1999, opposition parties have experienced a sharp decline in electoral success, with the rapid ascent of the United Russia party. One reason is genuine popular support for Putin, as well as the failure of the opposition parties to develop appealing programs or field attractive candidates. Media coverage has also favored the "party of power" and the president. Administrative control measures and selective enforcement have delimited the scope of acceptable political opposition, particularly when this has involved potential elite support for challengers. In addition, the carrot-and-stick method has wooed regional elites, producing a bandwagon effect, reinforced by the abolition of gubernatorial elections. Dependent on the president's nomination for reappointment, regional leaders have a further incentive to support the president's political position. Finally, potential opposition forces have been co-opted through party mergers and through formation of fellow-traveler parties (such as the Rodina Party before the 2003 election and A Just Russia before the 2007 election).

Results of presidential elections have not mirrored parliamentary election outcomes, and Russia has yet to experience a real transfer of power from one political grouping to another, which some scholars consider a first step in consolidating democratic governance. Under the Russian constitution, presidential elections are held every four years. If no candidate receives a majority of the votes in the first round, a runoff election is held between the two top contenders. In the 2000 and 2004 elections, runoff election was not required because Putin gained over 50 percent of the popular vote in the first round of voting.

Political Culture, Citizenship, and Identity

FOCUS QUESTIONS

How has Russian political culture evolved since the Soviet era?

Has Russian political culture become closer to Western patterns, or is it evolving in unique directions?

Political culture can be a source of great continuity in the face of radical upheavals in the social and political spheres. Attitudes toward government that prevailed in the tsarist period seem to have endured with remarkable tenacity. These include a tradition of personalistic authority, highly centralized leadership, and a desire for an authoritative source of truth. The Soviet regime embodied these and other traditional Russian values, such as egalitarianism and collectivism. At the same time, the Soviet development model glorified science, technology, industrialization, and urbanization—values superimposed on the traditional way of life of the largely rural population. When communism collapsed, Soviet ideology was discredited, and the government embraced Western political and economic values. Many citizens and intellectuals are skeptical of this "imported" culture, partly because it conflicts with other traditional civic values such as egalitarianism, collectivism, and a broad scope for state activity.

Public opinion surveys suggest considerable support for liberal democratic values such as an independent judiciary, a free press, basic civil liberties, and competitive elections. Colton and McFaul conclude from survey results that "a significant portion of the Russian population acquiesces in the abstract idea of democracy without necessarily looking to the West for guidance."[33] The authors find that Russians are divided on the proper balance between defense of individual rights and the maintenance of order. Other experts conclude that Russians' desire for a strong state and strong leaders does not imply support for authoritarian government.[34] On the other hand, democratic values may not be deeply enough entrenched to provide a safeguard against authoritarian rule.

In the USSR, just over 50 percent of the population was ethnically Russian. Since most of the major ethnic minorities now reside in other Soviet successor states, Russians now make up just under 80 percent of the population. The largest minority group is the Tatars, a traditionally Muslim group residing primarily in Tatarstan, a republic of Russia. Other significant minorities are the neighboring Bashkirs, various indigenous peoples of the Russian north, the many Muslim groups in the northern Caucasus region, and ethnic groups (such as Ukrainians and Armenians) of other former Soviet republics. Some 25 million ethnic Russians reside outside the Russian Federation in other former Soviet republics.

The Russian language itself has two distinct words for *Russian: russkii,* which refers to an ethnicity, and *Rossiiskii,* a broader concept referring to people of various ethnic backgrounds included in Russia as a political entity. Although the civic definition forms the basis of citizenship, both anti-Semitic and anti-Muslim sentiments surface in everyday life. Muslim groups from Russia's southern regions have been the target of ethnic stereotyping. In addition, refugee flows from some of the war-torn regions of the Tran-Caucasus (Georgia, Azerbaijan, and neighboring regions of southern Russia such as Chechnya and Ingushetia) have heightened national tensions.

Today, the Russian Orthodox Church appeals to many citizens who are looking for a replacement for the discredited values of the Communist system. A controversial law, directed primarily at Western proselytizers, passed in 1997, made it harder for new religious groups to organize. Human rights advocates and foreign observers protested strongly, again raising questions about the depth of Russia's commitment to liberal democratic values.

In the Soviet period, the mass media, the educational system, and a variety of other social institutions played a key role in propagating the party's political values. Now, students are presented with a wider range of views, and the print media represent a broad spectrum of political opinion. But the electronic media increasingly reflects the government position. The electronic media are particularly susceptible to political pressure, given the costs and limited availability of the technology needed to run television stations. Unequal media access, in favor of the pro-presidential forces, was criticized by international observers in relation to recent elections. Financial interests and mafia attacks on investigative journalists have inhibited press freedom, and journalists have been frequent targets of political killings.

FOCUS QUESTIONS

What kinds of social movements have become prominent since the fall of the Soviet Union?

Do these movements reflect longstanding Russian values, or are they reactions to changing social conditions?

Interests, Social Movements, and Protest

Since the collapse of the USSR, numerous political and social organizations have sprung up in every region of Russia, representing the interests of groups such as children, veterans, women, environmental advocates, pensioners, and the disabled. Many observers saw such blossoming activism as the foundation for a fledgling civil society that would nurture the new democratic institutions established since 1991. Despite limited resources and small staffs, these non-government organizations (NGOs) provided a potential source of independent political activity. However, there have been many obstacles to realizing this potential. In the past, many groups relied on Western aid to support their activities, potentially diverting them from concerns of their constituents to priorities of their foreign sponsors. Others depend on support from local governments or commercial activities.

In January 2006 Putin signed legislation amending laws on public associations and noncommercial organizations. These controversial changes, protested widely by Western governments, placed new grounds for denying registration to such organizations, established new reporting requirements (particularly for organizations receiving funds from foreign sources), and increased government supervisory functions. Particular requirements are placed on foreign noncommercial nongovernmental organizations operating in Russia; accordingly, several foreign organizations, such as Amnesty International and Human Rights Watch, were forced to temporarily suspend activities while seeking to comply with the new requirements. The new measures were justified as necessary to respond to external terrorist threats, but many commentators saw them as an effort to reduce the likelihood that civil society activists with external contacts might foment a colored revolution in Russian similar to what happened in Ukraine in 2004 or in Georgia in 2005.

The government has also attempted to channel public activism through official forums, such as the Civic Forum, an unprecedented all-Russian congress of nongovernmental organization activists held in November 2001 in Moscow. A new initiative is the Public Chamber, created in 2005 by legislation proposed by the president. Based on voluntary participation by presidential appointees and representatives recommended by national and regional societal organizations, the organization is presented as a mechanism for public consultation and input, as well as a vehicle for creating public support for government policy. It appears to reflect a corporatist approach that might serve to co-opt public activists from more disruptive forms of self-expression. Putin supporters have encouraged the formation of public associations, such as the youth group Nashi ('Our') that support the president's approach.

The year 2005 commenced with an outburst of public protests, mainly associated with cutbacks in social benefits, as noted in Section 2. Despite such sporadic outbursts, at present, one cannot say that civil society has really formed in Russia. Social forces still do not easily find avenues to exert constructive and organized influence on state activity. Russian citizens seem to sway between

The U.S. Connection

Journalism and Freedom of the Press in the United States and Russia

Freedom of the press is considered a fundamental safeguard of democracy in the United States, protected by the constitution itself. The Russian constitution also states that "freedom of the mass media shall be guaranteed. Censorship shall be prohibited." This is an important statement, since censorship was a key element of the system of political control in the Soviet Union.

In the United States, the media not only provide up-to-date information about current issues, but journalists often perform an important watchdog function, helping to keep public figures accountable to the public. Investigative journalists can have a big impact; investigative work on the Watergate break-in, carried out by *Washington Post* reporters Carl Bernstein and Bob Woodward, laid the groundwork for the eventual resignation of Richard M. Nixon.

Most Americans wouldn't consider journalism a particularly dangerous profession unless posted abroad to a war zone. However in Russia journalists investigating sensitive topics are often at risk. A high profile victim, Anna Politkovskaia, was shot on October 7, 2006, at her apartment building in Moscow. Politkovskaia, a reporter for the independent newspaper *Novaia gazeta*, was an outspoken critic of the government, focusing on violations of human rights in Chechnya. Another prominent victim, Dmitriy Kholodov (1994), died when a bomb exploded in the editorial office of the popular Russian newspaper *Moskovskii Komsomolets*. Khodolov had highlighted corruption in the Russian army.

According to the Committee to Protect Journalists, an international NGO devoted to protecting press freedom, these cases are among forty-three journalists murdered in Russia since 1993, making Russia one of the most dangerous countries for journalists in the world.* Although many of the deaths are related to reporting in war-torn Chechnya, others could be classified as contract murders or assassinations. Why are journalists at risk in Russia? A fundamental cause is the incapacity of the state to protect the security of its citizens. Businessmen, politicians, and even scholars have also been targets of contract murders.

Freedom of the press faces other threats in Russia too. Although Russians have access to a wide range of independent newspapers, readership has declined radically since the Soviet period, and news coverage in particular outlets is often openly biased. The lack of a vibrant civil society may also partly explain the inadequate public base to generate newspapers in Russia with high professional standards comparable to the *New York Times* or the *Washington Post*.

An independent international organization, Reporters Without Borders, placed Russia 147th out of 168 countries surveyed, based on a press freedom index. The organization cited increasing control of major media outlets by industrial groups close to Putin. While powerful economics interests own major media outlets in the United States as well, their direct impact on media operations is limited by public expectations about journalistic standards and media objectivity.

Although ranking substantially better than Russia, the United States placed fifty-third on the index, along with Botswana, Tonga, and Croatia. In commenting on this evaluation, the organization's website notes the failure of federal courts to protect journalists' right not to reveal sources, as well as President Bush's suspicion of journalists questioning the war on terrorism. ❖

*Committee to Protect Journalists, "Journalists Killed: Statistics and Background," http://www.cpj.org/killed/killed_archives/stats.html (accessed Dec. 31, 2006).

activism and apathy, and the political system wavers along a path between fledgling democratic innovations and renewed authoritarianism.

Summary

The bicameral legislature of the Russian parliament has played a relatively ineffective role in policy-making throughout the postcommunist period, despite its legal power to approve legislation. In the 1990s the legislature lacked the necessary unity to act decisively. Despite the introduction of competitive elections, political parties have had a hard time establishing themselves as credible vehicles of popular influence; most political parties have weak linkages to society, are strongly marked by the image of their leaders, and have not played a significant role in forming the government. High levels of political party fragmentation characterized Russian politics until 2003, when United Russia, a party of the political establishment, established itself as the dominant political force in the country, enjoying a rapid rise in electoral success and popular support. This was in part due to its close association with Vladimir Putin and partly due to a "bandwagon" effect in which regional politicians and other important political figures have rushed to join the "party of power." While elections in the 1990s were considered by most international observers to be relatively fair, observers now have greater doubts about whether there is a level playing field, as opposition forces have been subject to various types of political controls that limit their ability to gain support or even compete in elections.

SECTION 5 Russian Politics in Transition

In April 2005, Putin made a dramatic admission: "Above all, we should acknowledge that the collapse of the Soviet Union was a major geopolitical disaster of the century. As for the Russian nation, it became a genuine drama."[35] About the same time, in several cities throughout Russia, local officials decided to erect new monuments to Joseph Stalin to commemorate the sixtieth anniversary of the end of World War II, a move Putin neither approved nor obstructed. President George Bush, in visiting Latvia before arrival in Moscow to celebrate the events, also evoked images of the past, referring to the Soviet Union's unlawful annexation and occupation of the Baltic states.[36] A Kremlin spokesperson vehemently denied this depiction of the postwar events. The verbal sparring was followed by two apparently congenial leaders in Moscow, honoring the veterans who brought the defeat of Germany. These events show how the Soviet past continues to haunt and obscure not only Russia's path forward, but also relations with neighbors and potential allies.

FOCUS QUESTION

Describe three of the most important political challenges now facing the Russian state. For each one, outline how you think Russia will meet these challenges.

Political Challenges and Changing Agendas

When the first edition of this book was published in 1996, five possible scenarios for Russia's future were presented:

- A stable progression toward marketization and democratization
- The gradual introduction of "soft authoritarianism"
- A return to a more extreme authoritarianism of a quasi-fascist or communist variety
- The disintegration of Russia into regional fiefdoms or de facto individual states
- Economic decline, civil war, and military expansionism[37]

Just before Putin's appearance as a major political figure, it appeared that the more pessimistic scenarios were the more likely. Under Putin, optimism grew that a strong leader might move Russia toward its own self-defined version of democracy. At the time of this writing, the "soft authoritarian" scenario seems to the most likely.

Russia in the World of States

In the international sphere, Russia's flirtation with Westernization in the early 1990s produced ambiguous results, including severe recession, social dislocation, and dependence on the West for economic aid. Russia's protests against international developments such as NATO expansion, the Desert Fox operation against Iraq in December 1998, and NATO's bombing of Yugoslavia in 1999 revealed Moscow's underlying resentment against Western dominance, as well as the country's relative powerlessness in affecting global developments. Russia could do little more than issue verbal protests. The West's recognition that Russia's involvement was crucial to finding a diplomatic solution to the Kosovo crisis in 1999 marked a turning point, heralding a new period of increased cooperation between Russia and the Western world. The events of September 11 reinforced these cooperative ventures. Evidence of warmer relations included the formation of a NATO-Russia Council in May 2002, marking an era of closer cooperation in areas such as control of international terrorism, arms control, nonproliferation, and crisis management.[38]

New tensions have emerged, however, in the face of American withdrawal from the Anti-Ballistic Missile Treaty, Russian objections to the American incursion into Iraq, and the American proposal to place a missile defense system in Central Europe. Russian leaders have expressed particular irritation at the possibility of NATO membership for former Soviet republics on the border of Russia, particularly Georgia and Ukraine. At the same time, Russian actions toward Ukraine and Belarus have added to the tension. For example when Russian increased prices for energy exports to these countries, conflicts ensued that temporarily jeopardized the flow of energy resources to Western Europe.

Although criticism of Russia's Chechnya policies by Western governments was tempered after the events of September 11, organizations such as Human Rights Watch have continued to charge Russia with acts of violence against the Chechen civilian population, as well as instances of arbitrary arrests and sexual attacks on women in Chechnya.[39] Since 2004 American officials have more generally criticized Putin's centralizing moves as antidemocratic. Figures in American business circles viewed attacks on prominent Russian businessmen as interference in business operations, producing inhibitions to investments in the crucial energy sector.

A critical element of Russia's relations with both the United States and its West European neighbors rests with Russia's rich endowment of oil and natural gas. It is the source of about 10 percent of the world's oil production and the country most richly endowed with natural gas (about a third of the world's total reserves). (See Figure 5.7) The United States began an "energy dialogue" with Russia in 2002, hoping to increase energy imports from Russia to diversify its international energy dependence. An energy dialogue had been initiated between the EU and Russia even earlier, in 2000, with a goal of increased integration of EU-Russian energy markets and assurances of energy security for the EU.[40] Russian imports support almost 20 percent of EU gas consumption and 16 percent of oil consumption. In 2004, the EU agreed to support Russia's bid to join the WTO in an implicit quid pro quo involving Russian ratification of the Kyoto climate change protocol, but also Russian agreement to bring a gradual adjustment of its domestic gas prices to bring them closer to world market levels. Will Russia be able to leverage energy and other resources to reestablish itself as a regional and potentially a global power? This may depend on whether the leadership can build a stable economic and political structure within the country.

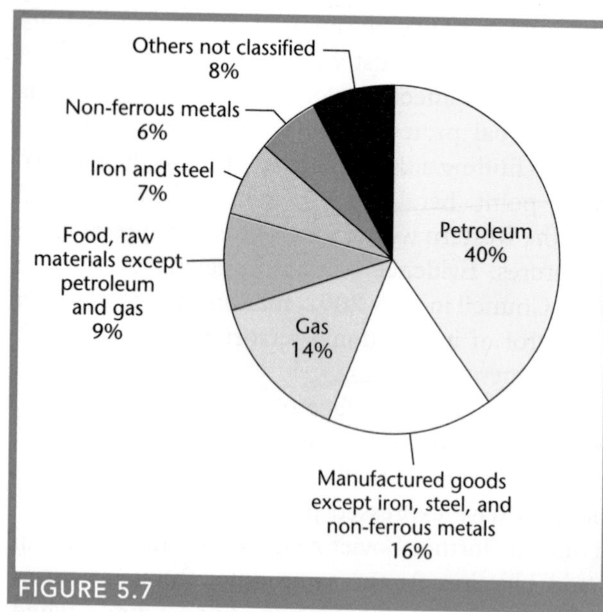

FIGURE 5.7

Exports from Russia, 2003

Source: OECD Economic Survey of the Russian Federation 2004: The Sources of Economic Growth, p. 15, 2004.

Governing the Economy

The upturn in the Russian economy that began in 1999 may have been a watershed in the struggle to overcome the transitional recession that plagued Russia from the late 1980s onward. Nevertheless, severe disparities in income and wealth remain. A restoration of economic growth has raised consumption levels and disposable income for large parts of the population, but vulnerable population groups still fall below the poverty line. Questions also remain about whether income from oil and gas exports will feed the investment needs of other sectors of the economy, or whether they will be appropriated by a privileged elite. Making the economy attractive to foreign investors will require a continued development of the banking sector, legal institutions to ensure enforcement of contracts, and controls on crime and corruption. Although the 1998 devaluation of the ruble brought decreased reliance on Western imports (as they become too expensive), the so-called Dutch disease, in which heavy reliance on export income pushes the value of the currency up, now threatens again to undermine prospects for domestic producers. Reverberations in international markets and foreign economies can now have a direct impact on the Russian economy as well. Perhaps the greatest economic challenge facing the Putin administration is to establish policies to ensure a greater diversity of Russia's economic base.

The Democratic Idea

Russia's attempted democratization has been formally successful, but it is marred by corruption, the power of big money, and the limited accountability of its leaders. The political structures put in place by the 1993 constitution have not produced the strong and effective government most Russians desire. The continuing disjuncture between high personal support for Vladimir Putin and a continuing lack of confidence in the ability of political central institutions to address the country's problems suggests that the legitimacy of the system is still on thin ice. The more positive working relationship between the executive and legislative branches that emerged under Putin's leadership, as well as efforts to regularize relations between the center and regions, provides prospects for improved institutional performance. But the reduction of vehicles for popular input already shows signs of producing poor policy choices.

Although it is difficult to conceive that the freedoms that have been exercised since 1986 could be easily withdrawn, a reversion to a more centralized and predictable set of political practices may, on a conscious or unconscious level, seem familiar and therefore comfortable for many Russians. If the security and stability can be combined with rising prosperity, then many Russians may be willing to sacrifice democratic rights in exchange for economic improvement and political stability.

The Politics of Collective Identities

The formation of new political identities remains unfinished business. Most people are preoccupied by the struggle to make ends meet or to increase personal welfare. They have little time or energy to forge new forms of collective action to address underlying problems. Under such circumstances, the appeal to nationalism and other basic sentiments can be powerful. Indications of this are already evident in the fact that political parties with nationalist messages seem to be doing better than liberal forces. The weakness of Russian intermediary organizations (interest groups, political parties, or associations) means that politicians can more easily appeal directly to emotions because people are not members of groups that help them evaluate the politicians' claims. These conditions are fertile ground for authoritarian outcomes, which the government itself might use to keep the public compliant. Still, the high level of education and increasing exposure to international media may work in the opposite direction. Also, many Russians identify their country as part of Europe and its culture, an attitude echoed by the government. (See Table 5.4.) Exposure to alternative political systems and cultures may make people more critical of their own political system and seek opportunities to change it.

TABLE 5.4

Attitudes toward Foreign Countries

In general, what is your attitude toward the following foreign countries?

	USA	The European Union	Ukraine
Very positive	6%	6%	7%
Basically positive	57	67	60
Basically negative	22	12	19
Very negative	7	3	4
Hard to say	8	12	10

Note:

Based on a survey carried out April 15–18, 2005, among 1,600 residents of Russia (128 sampling points in 46 regions).

Source:

Levada Center, http://www.levada.ru/press/2005050401.html.

Russia remains in what seems to be an extended period of transition. In the early 1990s, Russians frequently hoped for "normal conditions," that is, an escape from the shortages, insecurity, and political controls of the past. As the new situation becomes familiar, *normality* has been redefined in less glowing terms than those conceived in the late 1980s.

FOCUS QUESTIONS

In what ways is Russia's transition to a market economy similar to or different from such transitions in other countries? How has Russia's previous industrialization complicated this transition?

Russian Politics in Comparative Perspective

The ways in which politics, economics, and ideology were intertwined in the Soviet period has profoundly affected the nature of political change in all of the former Soviet republics and generally made the democratization process more difficult. Unlike developing countries currently experiencing democratization and economic transformation, Russia is a highly industrialized country with a skilled and educated work force. Although this offers advantages, the high level of development is associated with a host of problems: a heavily damaged natural environment, obsolescent industries, entrenched bureaucratic structures, a nuclear arsenal that must be monitored and controlled, and a public that expects the state to provide a stable system of social welfare. These problems make it more difficult for the state to manage the domestic and international challenges it confronts.

How is Russia faring compared to some of the other postcommunist systems that faced many of these same challenges? The nations of Eastern Europe and the former Soviet Union were all subjected to a similar system of economic, political, and ideological power during the period of communist rule. Some were under communist rule for a shorter period of time, but most parts of the Soviet Union shared with Russia more than seven decades of the communist party state. Despite the efforts of the Soviet leadership to establish conformity throughout the region, national differences did emerge. The countries of Eastern Europe had a history of closer ties and greater cultural exposure to Western Europe; ideas of liberalism,

Joining the West or Aid Recipient?

The Russian Federation is now open to global influences, in contrast to the isolation imposed by the Soviet government. The Russian government has sought equal membership in some international organizations from which it was previously excluded, and it has forged partnerships with others. In the 1990s, Western governments and international agencies were welcomed by Russian authorities as they provided aid to Russia's developing market economy and fledgling democratic political structures, but now Russia's leaders are more resistant to Western influence with Russia.

An important aspect of these processes in the 1990s was the notion of **conditionality**, namely, the requirement that Russia meet certain conditions to be eligible to receive international assistance or to join certain international clubs. Conditionality is a controversial foreign policy tool because it grants foreign governments and agencies a certain leverage in domestic political and economic policy of recipient countries. It has been a particularly powerful tool used by the European Union in relation to candidate countries since strict conditions are set for membership. These requirements speeded transition processes in Central Europe (Czech Republic, Slovakia, Poland, Hungary, Slovenia) and the Baltic States before they were admitted as members in May 2004. Russia, viewing itself as a regional power that should have an equal partnership role, has been resistant to conditionality. This may be one reason that Russia has not adopted the goal of EU accession.

Following are some of the most important international agencies that Russia has become involved with in one way or another over the past fifteen years.

The International Monetary Fund (IMF). The IMF was founded in 1944, and during most of the 1990s it was the most influential international agency in Russia. Its general mandate is to oversee the international monetary system and help maintain stability in exchanges between its 184 member countries, which can draw on the fund's resources. The Soviet Union applied for membership in 1991 but was dissolved before acceptance. Russia was admitted to the IMF in 1992, and funds were issued to Russia as short- and medium-term credits to help stabilize the ruble and Russia's internal and external monetary balance. The disbursement of these funds was made contingent on the fulfillment of certain conditions by the Russian government, particularly the maintenance of noninflationary fiscal and monetary policies. These policies, in turn, necessitated cutbacks in social services and subsidies to troubled economic sectors. In 1999, a final loan was granted, and since then Russia has forgone further credits, choosing to manage its own macroeconomic fiscal policy. By 2004, Russia had paid off its IMF debt (www.imf.org).

The World Bank. Also founded in 1944, the World Bank has as its purpose to promote and finance economic development in the world's poorer countries. After World War II, this involved assistance in financing reconstruction in war-torn Europe. The agency is an investment bank with 184 member countries. As with the IMF, the Russian Federation was admitted in 1992. Through its International Bank for Reconstruction and Development (IBRD), the World Bank has provided loans to support development programs in Russia in sectors such as agriculture, the environment, energy, and social welfare. From 1991 to 2002, Russia borrowed US$12.5 billion from the IBRD, and in January 2005 its outstanding debt stood at $5.7 billion* (www.worldbank.org).

conditionality the requirement that certain commitments be made by receiving governments in exchange for credits or other types of assistance provided by international or foreign agencies, to ensure that the goals of the donor agency are respected.

*Central Bank of the Russian Federation website, at http://www.cbr.ru/statistics/credit_statistics/print.asp?file=debt.htm (accessed May 10, 2005).

continued

continued

The European Bank for Reconstruction and Development (EBRD). EBRD, formed in 1991, promotes the development of market economies in postcommunist countries. Specific current priorities include measures to "advance technological modernization and efficiency improvements in key sectors of the economy"† and helping economic diversification as well as supporting small business development. The EBRD provides loans and guarantees, and supports equity investments (www.ebrd.com).

The European Union (EU). The EU initiated the Tacis program in 1991 as a vehicle for providing grants to finance the transfer of knowledge to Russia and other countries in the former Soviet Union. Now the largest source of aid to Russia, annual contributions ran at about 90 million euros in 2002 and 2003. In addition to such assistance efforts, the EU's Partnership and Cooperation Agreement with Russia sets out a strategy for development of four "Common Spaces": Common Economic Space (to create an integrated market), Common Space for Freedom, Security, and Justice (relating to media, travel, human contact); Common Space for External Security (multilateralism, crisis management, antiterrorism); and Common Space for Research, Education, and Culture (http://europa.eu.int/comm/external_relations/russia/summit_05_05/index.htm).

North Atlantic Treaty Organization (NATO). NATO was formed in 1949 by ten European countries, the United States, and Canada to safeguard the security of its members in response to the perceived Soviet threat. Following the collapse of the communist system in Eastern Europe, NATO has had to rethink its mandate and the nature of potential threats. Among its duties are crisis management, peacekeeping, opposing international terrorism, and prevention of nuclear proliferation. In 2004, Bulgaria, Estonia, Latvia, Lithuania, Romania, Slovakia, and Slovenia became NATO members, following Hungary, the Czech Republic, and Poland in 1999. Albania, Croatia, and Macedonia (FYROM) are preparing for possible future membership. While raising strong objections to NATO expansion into its former sphere of influence, Russia has, over time, also developed a stronger working relationship with the organization. The Partnership for Peace program was the first important step in the process in 1994, and in 1997, the NATO-Russia Founding Act on Mutual Relations, Cooperation and Security was concluded. A further step was taken in 2002 with the establishment of the NATO-Russia Council, in which Russia holds an equal seat with the twenty-six NATO member states. Working groups deal with issues such as peacekeeping actions, international terrorism, and nuclear proliferation (http://www.nato.int/issues/nrc/index.html).

The G-8 and Russia. In 1998, Russia was accepted as a full member into the G-8 (Group of Eight), an expanded G-7. The G-8 is an informal international body consisting of the leading industrial nations; G-8 countries hold regular summits dealing with such issues as the international economy, trade relations, and foreign exchange markets. Although Russia is still too weak to exert much influence on G-8 issues, its membership in the organization is valuable, allowing Russia to maintain a presence on the world stage. In July 2006, Russia hosted the G-8 for the 2006 summit.

The World Trade Organization (WTO). The WTO is a powerful international organization, responsible for regulating international trade, settling trade disputes, and designing trade policy through meetings of its 148 member countries. Because of the increasingly global nature of trade, membership in the WTO is an essential prerequisite for increasing economic prosperity and for avoiding international economic isolation. Russia's membership is supported by powerful actors such as the European Union, but Russia still must conclude bilateral agreements with some member countries before accession can proceed. An agreement with the United States was reached in November 2006. The World Bank estimates that membership will bring Russian annual benefits of $19 billion through increased exports, opening the country to multilateral services and increased foreign direct investment†† (www.wto.org). ❖

†European Bank for Reconstruction and Development website, at http://www.ebrd.com/about/strategy/country/russia/main.htm (accessed May 10, 2005).

††"Russian Economic Report #10: April 2005," *The World Bank Group*, http://194.84.38.65/mdb/upload/RER10_eng.pdf (accessed May 10, 2005).

private property, and individualism were less foreign to citizens in countries such as Czechoslovakia, East Germany, and Hungary than in regions farther east, including Russia. Within the Soviet Union, too, there was also considerable variation among the union republics. The Baltic republics of Latvia, Lithuania, and Estonia took a more experimental approach in many spheres of activity and had a more Western European atmosphere. At the other extreme, the Central Asian republics retained aspects of traditional Muslim culture, preserved the extended family structure, and maintained within the structure of the communist party a greater prominence for links rooted in the clan system indigenous to the region.

All fifteen countries that gained independence after the collapse of the Soviet Union, as well as several countries of Central and Eastern Europe, have experienced the collapse of the communist system of power since 1989. Given the diversity characterizing these countries, it is not surprising that their postcommunist experiences also varied. A rule of thumb, simple as it seems, is that the further east one goes in the postcommunist world, the more difficult and prolonged the transition period has been. This is partly because the more westerly countries of Central Europe that were outside the USSR (Poland, Hungary, Czech Republic, Slovakia), as well as the Baltic states, faced the realistic prospect of joining the EU and thus had a strong motivation to embark on fundamental reform to meet the EU's conditions. Also, these countries were under communist rule for a shorter period of time. Although political and economic liberalization generally follows this West-East axis, an exception is Belarus, which has liberalized less than Russia.

In terms of economic performance, postcommunist countries that liberalized the least, such as Uzbekistan and Belarus, suffered lesser recessions in the 1990s because state institutions remained more fully intact. However, these less-reformed economies may face painful adjustments in the future. Russia has had the advantage of possessing rich deposits of natural resources (including energy resources), giving it better possibilities than most other postcommunist states for coping with the ruptured economic ties resulting from the collapse of the Soviet. Ukraine and particularly Belarus are still suffering from the severe economic and health effects of the accident at the 1986 Chernobyl nuclear power plant. The Central Asian states confront the disastrous effects of Soviet-imposed emphasis on cotton production and associated environmental degradation (the Aral Sea crisis). On the other hand, Russia (along with Ukraine) has been the focal point of international economic assistance because of its large nuclear arsenal, its size, and its geopolitical importance (see "Joining the West or Aid Recipient?").

Progression along the various dimensions of the postcommunist transition are uneven across postcommunist countries, and Russia seems now to be progressing economically, while regressing politically, with nationalism on the rise and aspirations to status of a regional superpower resurfacing. In the political sphere, virtually all of the postcommunist states claim to be pursuing some form of democratization, but in some cases, this is more in name than in practice, particularly in Central Asia. Belarus has a distinctively authoritarian government. In all of the postcommunist states, the attempt to construct democratic political institutions has been characterized by repeated political crises, weak representation of popular interests, executive-legislative conflict, faltering efforts at constitutional revision, and corruption. In Russia, there is considerable skepticism about adopting the Western model of political development. Although the concept of democracy has a distinct appeal in the region, to much of the population it means, above all, personal freedom rather than support for notions of political accountability, rule of law, or the civic role of the citizen.

Although Russian politics has been highly contentious and the government has operated at very low levels of efficacy and legitimacy for most of the past decade, with the exception of the Chechnya conflict, Russia has escaped major domestic violence and civil war, unlike Yugoslavia, Armenia, Azerbaijan, Georgia, Moldova, and the Central Asian state of Tajikistan. For all their problems, Russian politicians have conducted themselves in a relatively civil manner. Citizenship rights for all ethnic groups have been maintained. State-sponsored racism is largely absent. The Russian government can be credited with avoiding marginalization of major social groups.

Russia will undoubtedly continue to be a key regional force in Europe and Asia. Its vast geographic expanse, rich resource base, large and highly skilled population, and the legacy of Soviet rule will ensure this. Yet its former allies in Central Europe, as well as the Baltic states, are gradually drifting into the orbit of Western Europe economically and politically. Following the 2004 EU enlargement, Russia's most important Western neighbor, Ukraine, aspires to EU membership, a goal the Russian leadership has not articulated. Although Ukraine is divided internally over its future course, the European dream is an increasingly important reference point. Russian leaders seem to appreciate the isolation this could imply, but seem unwilling to adopt certain crucial aspects of Western political practice. Thus, over the past few years, while Russia has resisted a monopolar world order dominated by the United States and its leaders have shown a desire and willingness to identify as a European country, Russia has an ambivalent relationship to accepting crucial norms that would underlie an effective and enduring partnership with the EU.

Will Russia be able to find a place for itself in the world of states that meets the expectations of its educated and sophisticated population? If Russia's experiment produces a stable outcome that benefits the majority of the population, then it may offer a path of quasi-democratic development that could serve as a model for countries further east. If instability and popular discontent rise, then incipient democracies elsewhere in the region may also take a further backward step.

Summary

Russia's political course since 1991 has been profoundly influenced by the fact that the country underwent simultaneous and radical transformations in three spheres: politics, economics, and ideology. Managing so much change in a short time has been difficult and has produced mixed results. Efforts to democratize the political system have been only partially successful, and experts disagree about whether Putin's efforts to strengthen the central state have contributed to rising authoritarian tendencies or whether they are needed to provide the stability that is necessary for democratic development. In the economic sphere, after recovering from a period of deep economic decline, Russia's renewed growth depends largely on exports of energy and natural resources. The country faces the challenge of effectively using its natural resource wealth to rebuild other sectors of the economy. In terms of ideology, nationalism threatens to reinforce intolerance and undermine social unity. Continuing high levels of corruption also undermine popular confidence in state institutions. Whereas those postcommunist countries that have joined the European Union seem, for the most part, to have successfully established viable democratic systems with functioning market economies, other post-Soviet states in Eastern Europe and Central Asia face similar challenges to Russia's in consolidating democracy and market reform. With its increased economic power, Russia has sought to reassert its role as a regional and global force, but increasing tensions have come to characterize Russia's relationship with the West as Russia sees its influence under challenge in neighboring countries.

Key Terms

patrimonial state
democratic centralism
vanguard party
collectivization
perestroika
glasnost
demokratizatsiia
market reform
shock therapy
joint-stock companies
insider privatization
privatization voucher
oligarchs
mafia
pyramid debt
nomenklatura
autonomous republics
krai
oblast
okrug
siloviki
power vertical
civil society
proportional representation
single-member plurality district
conditionality

Suggested Readings

Aslund, Anders. *Building Capitalism: The Transformation of the Former Soviet Bloc.* Cambridge, UK, and New York: Cambridge University Press, 2002.

Black, J. L. *Vladimir Putin and the New World Order: Looking East, Looking West?* Lanham, Md.: Rowman and Littlefield, 2004.

Blasi, R. Joseph, Maya Kroumova, and Douglas Kruse. *Kremlin Capitalism: The Privatization of the Russian Economy.* Ithaca, N.Y.: Cornell University Press, 1997.

Colton, Timothy J. *Transitional Citizens: Voters and What Influences Them in the New Russia.* Cambridge: Harvard University Press, 2000.

DeBardeleben, Joan, ed. *Soft or Hard Borders: Managing the Divide in an Enlarged Europe.* Aldershot, UK: Ashgate, 2005.

Eckstein, Harry, Frederic J. Fleron, Jr., Erik P. Hoffman, and William M. Reisinger. *Can Democracy Take Root in Russia? Explorations in State-Society Relations.* Lanham, Md.: Rowman & Littlefield, 1998.

Fish, M. Steven. *Democracy Derailed in Russia: The Failure of Open Politics.* Cambridge University Press, 2005.

Freeland, Chrystia. *Sale of the Century: Russia's Wild Ride from Communism to Capitalism.* New York: Doubleday, 2000.

Getty, J. Arch. *Origins of the Great Purges: The Soviet Communist Party Reconsidered.* Cambridge: Cambridge University Press, 1985.

Hoffman, David E. *The Oligarchs: Wealth and Power in the New Russia.* New York: Public Affairs Press, 2002.

Hough, Jerry, and Merle Fainsod. *How the Soviet Union Is Governed.* Cambridge: Harvard University Press, 1979.

Humphrey, Caroline. *The Unmaking of Soviet Life: Everyday Economies after Socialism.* Ithaca, N.Y.; London: Cornell University Press, 2002.

Karlkins, Rasma. *The System Made Me Do It: Corruption in Postcommunist Societies.* M.E. Sharpe, 2005.

Ledeneva, Alena V., *How Russia Really Works.* Cornell University Press, 2006.

Lewin, Moshe. *The Gorbachev Phenomenon: A Historical Interpretation.* Berkeley: University of California Press, 1991.

Motyl, Alexander J., Blair A. Ruble, and Lilia Shevtsova, eds. *Russia's Engagement with the West: Transformation and Integration in the Twenty-First Century.* Armonk, New York: M. E. Sharpe, 2005.

Pål, Kolsto, and Helge Blakkisrud, eds. *Nation-Building and Common Values in Russia.* Lanham, Md.: Rowman and Littlefield Publishers, 2004.

Pipes, Richard. *Russia Under the Old Regime.* New York: Scribner, 1974.

Reddaway, Robert, and Robert Orttung, eds. *The Dynamics of Russian Politics: Putin's Reform of Federal-Regional Relations.* 2 vols. Rowman & Littlefield, 2004 (volume 1); 2005 (volume 2).

Remington, Thomas F. *Politics in Russia.* 3rd ed. Boston: Pearson Education, 2004.

Sakwa, Richard. *Putin: Russia's Choice.* London and New York: Routledge, 2004.

Shevstsova, Lilia, *Putin's Russia.* rev. ed. Moscow: Carnegie Institute, 2004.

Solomon, Peter H., Jr., and Todd S. Fogelson. *Courts and Transition in Russia: The Challenge of Judicial Reform.* Boulder, Colo.: Westview Press, 2000.

Tolz, Vera. *Russia.* London: Arnold; New York: Oxford University Press, 2001.

Wilson, Andrew. *Virtual Politics: Faking Democracy in the Post-Soviet World.* Yale University Press, 2005.

Notes

[1]Richard Pipes, *Russia Under the Old Regime* (London: Widenfeld & Nicolson, 1974, pp. 22–24.

[2]Mikhail Gorbachev, *Perestroika: New Thinking for Our Country and the World* (New York: Harper, 1987).

[3]Sergei Peregudov, "The Oligarchic Model of Russian Corporatism," in Archie Brown (ed.), *Contemporary Russian Politics: A Reader* (New York: Oxford University Press, 2001), p. 259.

[4]Jacques Sapir, "Russia's Economic Rebound: Lessons and Future Directions," *Post-Soviet Affairs* 18, no. 1 (January–March 2002): 6.

[5]Economist Intelligence Unit (EIU), *Country Report: Russia* (London: EIU, March 8, 2005).

[6]Central Intelligence Agency, CIA Factbook, 2004, Russia https://www.cia.gov/cia/publications/factbook/geos/rs.html.

[7]EIU, Country Report: Russia (March 2005).

[8]EIU, *Country Report: Russia* (March 2002), 13; *Rossiiskii statisticheskii ezhegodnik* (Russian Statistical Yearbook), Moscow: Goskomstat, 2004.

[9]Levada Centre, *Vestnik obshchestvennogo mnenia* (November–December 2004), p. 104; and Levada Center data, http://www.levada.ru/economic.htmlonlinel (January 2, 2007).

[10]Sarah Ashwin and Elaine Bowers, "Do Russian Women Want to Work?" in Mary Buckley (ed.), *Post-Soviet Women: From the Baltics to Central Asia* (Cambridge: Cambridge University Press, 1997), p. 23. Also *Rossiiskii statisticheskii ezhegodnik* (2004).

[11]Goskomstat (Russian Statistical Agency), http://www.gks.ru/bgd/free/b05_00/IswPrx.dll/Stg/d010/i010180r.htm (accessed January 2, 2007).

[12]*Rossiiskii statisticheskii ezhegodnik* (Russia Statistics Annual). Moscow: Federal Service of State Statistics, 2004.

[13]Victor Zaslavsky, "From Redistribution to Marketization: Social and Attitudinal Change in Post-Soviet Russia," in Gail W. Lapidus (ed.), *The New Russia: Troubled Transformation* (Boulder, Colo.: Westview Press, 1994), 125.

[14]"*Putin Urges Early Repayment of Russia's Whole External Debt*," Moscow News Online, Feb. 11, 2005, http://www.mosnews.com/money/2005/02/11/putindebt.shtml (accessed April 14, 2005).

[15]Economist Intelligence Unit, Russia: Country Profile 2004, pp. 53, 63.

[16]Vladimir Putin, Address to the Federal Assembly, April 25, 2005, http://www.kremlin.ru/eng/speeches/2005/04/25/2031_type70029type82912_87086.shtml (accessed January 2, 2007).

[17]Thomas Remington, *Politics in Russia*, 2nd ed. (New York: Longman, 2001), 53–54.

[18]Ibid.

[19]Fred Weir, "Putin's Endgame for Chechen Bear Trap," *Christian Science Monitor*, January 25, 2001.

[20]"Society Is Afraid of Our Army," interview with Defense Minister Sergei Ivanov, April 13, 2005, http://mosnews.com/interview/2005/04/13/ivanov.shtml (accessed April 20, 2005). Interview conducted by Natalia Kalashnikova.

[21]Svetlana Mikhailova, "Constitutional Court Confirms Federal Authorities' Ability to Fire Governors, Disband Legislatures," *Russian Regional Report*, April 10, 2002, http://se2.isn.ch/serviceengine/FileContent?serviceID=RESSpecNet&fileid=219CFDBC-C014-1DC1-C198-FFF9F76C3522&lng=en (accessed January 2, 2007).

[22]On corporatism, see Philippe C. Schmitter and Gerhard Lehmbruch, *Trends Towards Corporatist Intermediation* (Thousand Oaks, Calif.: Sage, 1979).

[23]Compiled by the author from the website of the State Duma, http://www.duma.gov.ru/ (accessed December 12, 2006).

[24]Levada Center, public opinion poll, March 18, 2005, http://www.levada.ru/press/2005041801.html (accessed May 2, 2005).

[25]David Lane, *State and Politics in the USSR* (Oxford: Blackwell, 1985), 184–185.

[26]Thomas Remington, *Politics in Russia* (New York: Longman, 2001), 102.

[27]See the Constitution of the Russian Federation, Article 102.

[28]http://www.duma.gov.ru (May 2, 2005).

[29]Darrell Slider, "'United Russia' and Russia's Governors: The Path to a One-Party System," paper presented the American Assocation for the Advancement of Slavic Studies National Convention, Washington, D.C., November 17, 2006.

[30]These numbers also include seats won in single-member districts, as discussed below.

[31]See the official website at http://www.sps.ru/ (accessed January 2, 2007).

[32]Office for Democratic Institutions and Human Rights, "Russian Federation: Election to the State Duma 7 December 2003, OSCE/ODHIR Election Observation Mission Report" (Warsaw, January 27, 2004), http://unpan1.un.org/intradoc/groups/public/documents/UNTC/UNPAN016105.pdf (accessed January 2, 2007).

[33]Timothy J. Colton and Michael McFaul, "Are Russians Undemocratic," *Post-Soviet Affairs* 18 (April–June 2002): 102.

[34]William M. Reisinger, Arthur H. Miller, Vicki L. Hesli, and Kristen Hill Maher, "Political Values in Russia, Ukraine, and Lithuania: Sources and Implications," *British Journal of Political Science* 24 (1994): 183–223.

[35]http://www.kremlin.ru/eng/speeches/2005/04/25/2031_type70029type82912_87086.shtml (accessed January 2, 2007).

[36]Elisabeth Bumille, "Bush, Arriving in Baltics, Steps Into Argument With Russia," *New York Times*, May 7, 2005.

[37]Joan DeBardeleben, "Russia," in Mark Kesselman, Joel Kreiger, and William A. Joseph (eds.), *Comparative Politics at the Crossroads* (Lexington, Mass.: Heath, 1996): 355–357.

[38]For the official statement, see the NATO website, "NATO-Russia Relations: A New Quality," Declaration by Heads of State and Government of NATO Member States and the Russian Federation, http://www.nato.int/docu/basictxt/b020528e.htm (accessed January 2, 2007).

[39]Human Rights Watch webpage, http://hrw.org/english/docs/2005/05/07/russia10586.htm (accessed January 2, 2007).

[40]EU-Russia Energy Dialogue, Fifth Progress Report, November 2004, Moscow-Brussels http://europa.eu.int/comm/energy/russia/joint_progress/doc/progress5_en.pdf (accessed January 2, 2007).

Official Name:	United Mexican States (*Estados Unidos Mexicanos*)
Location:	Southern North America
Capital City:	Mexico City
Population (2007):	108.7 million
Size:	1,972,550 sq. km.; slightly less than three times the size of Texas

CHAPTER

6 Mexico

Merilee S. Grindle

Chronology of Mexico's Political Development

1521 Spaniards led by Hernán Cortés capture the Aztec capital, initiating three centuries of colonial rule.

1810–1821 War of independence from Spain

1876–1911 Dictatorship of Porfirio Díaz

1910–1920 Mexican Revolution

1917 Mexican Constitution

1929 Plutarco Elías Calles founds PRI.

1934–1940 Presidency of Lázaro Cárdenas; incorporation of workers and peasants in political system

1968 Massacre of Tlaltelolco; hundreds of protesting students killed

1978–1982 State-led development reaches peak with petroleum boom and bust.

1982 Market reformers come to power in PRI.

SECTION 1 The Making of the Modern Mexican State

FOCUS QUESTION

In what ways have recent presidential elections reflected changing social conditions and political realignments in Mexico?

Politics in Action

On July 2, 2006, Mexicans went to the polls to elect a new president. Public opinion polls had indicated a dead heat between two candidates. Felipe Calderón, representing the party of the incumbent administration, promised a right-of-center approach to public problems, encouraging private sector development, foreign investment, and job creation as a way to deal with the county's development challenges. Andrés Manuel Lopez Obrador represented a left-of-center party, and promised more government action to deal with problems of poverty and inequality in the country.

Calderón garnered a bare 0.6 percent lead over Lopez Obrador, election results were contested, and the Federal Election Institute, responsible for monitoring elections and declaring official results, delayed the official announcement for two months and ordered a recount of 9 percent of the polling places in the country. Meanwhile, partisans of Lopez Obrador blocked major avenues in Mexico City, causing millions of dollars in lost revenues per day. Eventually, Felipe Calderón was officially declared the winner on September 6, 2006. The new administration would begin, however, in a context of distrust and without a clear mandate to carry out its electoral promises. The congress was similarly divided, with no party having a clear majority.

The election of 2006 followed the historic 2000 election, in which for the first time in seven decades, the president of Mexico did not represent the Institutional Revolutionary Party (PRI, pronounced "pree"), which had governed the country without interruption since 1929. A different party won the election largely because the old civil-authoritarian system could no longer ensure political stability, economic progress, and responsiveness to the demands of a society that was increasingly characterized by inequality.

The elections of 2000 and 2006 signaled a new stage in Mexico's quest for democracy. People who questioned the PRI's monopoly of power had usually

1988	1989	1994	1996	1997	2000	2006
Carlos Salinas is elected amid charges of fraud.	First governorship is won by an opposition party.	NAFTA goes into effect; uprising in Chiapas; Colosio assassinated.	Political parties agree on electoral reform.	Opposition parties advance nationwide; PRI loses absolute majority in congress for first time in its history.	PRI loses presidency; Vicente Fox of PAN becomes president, but without majority support in congress.	Election of Felipe Calderón fiercely contested by PRD, causing serious public disruption; the winning party, the PAN, lacks a clear majority in congress.

been co-opted with promises and benefits, or they were quietly but effectively repressed. For several decades, this system produced political stability and economic growth. But during the 1980s and 1990s, Mexicans began to press for fairer elections and more responsive public officials.

Today, despite these two elections, political and economic dissatisfaction continues to plague the country. For elites, the opportunities of globalization have provided unprecedented wealth and cosmopolitan lifestyles. Yet indicators of increased poverty are everywhere. The two most democratic elections in Mexico's modern history drew attention to ongoing and interrelated challenges:

- Would a country with a long tradition of authoritarian government be able to sustain a democratic political system in the face of increasing demands and high expectations?
- Would a country that had long sought economic development through government activism and the domestic market be able to compete effectively in a competitive, market-driven global economy?
- Would a country long noted for severe inequalities between the rich and the poor be capable of providing better living standards for its growing population?

FOCUS QUESTION

What are the most important geographical features that have created challenges or opportunities for social and economic development in Mexico?

Geographic Setting

Mexico encompasses snow-capped volcanoes, coastal plains, high plateaus, fertile valleys, rain forests, and deserts within an area slightly less than three times the size of Texas. To the north, it shares a 2,000-mile-long border with the United States, to the south, a 600-mile-long border with Guatemala and a 160-mile-long border with Belize. Two imposing mountain ranges run the length of Mexico: the Sierra Madre Occidental to the west and the Sierra Madre Oriental to the east. Mexico is noted for peaks, plateaus, and valleys with an astonishing number of microclimates and a rich diversity of plants and animals. The country is rich in oil, silver, and other natural resources.

Profile

Felipe Calderón

Felipe de Jesús Calderón Hinojosa became President of Mexico on December 1, 2006, after a hotly contested election. His six-year period in office follows that of another president from the Partido Acción Nacional (PAN), Vicente Fox. Unlike Fox, however, Calderón is a long-time party activist and politician, with a long history of elected positions and party leadership.

Felipe Calderón was born in Morelia, the capital of the state of Michoacán, in 1962, one of four children in his family. He studied law as an undergraduate at the Escuela Libre de Derecho and then obtained a master's degree in economics from the Instituto Tecnológico Autónomo de México (ITAM). Later in his life, he attended the mid-career Master in Public Administration program at Harvard's John F. Kennedy School of Government.

His political career began early. He became president of the youth movement of the PAN in the 1980s and then won election as a state representative in Michaocán. From there, he won election for two terms as a deputy (representative) in the national congress. He became president of the PAN in 1996. When Vicente Fox became president in late 2000, Calderón was his choice to become director of a government development bank, Banobras. Subsequently, he became secretary of energy in the Fox cabinet.

President Calderón is known for his strong Roman Catholic beliefs and his commitment to free market principles. In his first year in office, he moved strongly against drug trafficking and the violence associated with it. He is committed to encouraging immigration reform in the United States and has sought to expand trade within NAFTA and with others countries in Latin America and the world. Although not without critics, he has shown himself to be an astute politician by building coalitions with other parties and by working closely with a newly powerful legislature. ❖

mestizo a person of mixed white, indigenous (Amerindian), and sometimes African descent.

Amerindian original peoples of North and South America; indigenous people.

indigenous groups population of Amerindian heritage in Mexico.

maquiladora factories that produce goods for export, often located along the U.S.-Mexican border.

With 100 million inhabitants, Mexico is the largest Spanish-speaking nation in the world. Sixty percent of the population is ***mestizo***, or people of mixed **Amerindian** and Spanish descent. About 30 percent of the population claims indigenous (Amerindian) descent, although only about 6 percent of the population speaks an indigenous language rather than Spanish. The rest of the population is made up of Caucasians and people with other backgrounds. The largest **indigenous groups** are the Maya in the south and the Náhuatl in the central regions, with well over 1 million members each.

Over 75 percent of the population now lives in urban areas. Mexico City has become one of the world's largest cities, with about 20 million inhabitants.[1] Annual population growth has slowed to about 1.4 percent, but society continues to adjust to the baby boom of the 1970s and early 1980s as those born at that time seek jobs and form families. Migration both within and beyond Mexico's borders has become a major issue. Greater economic opportunities in the industrial cities of the north lead many men and women to seek work there in the ***maquiladoras***, or assembly industries. Many job seekers continue on to the United States, lured by a larger job market and higher wages.

TABLE 6.1

Political Organization

Political System	Federal republic.
Regime History	Current form of government since 1917.
Administrative Structure	Federal with thirty-one states and a federal district.
Executive	President, elected by direct election with a six-year term of office; reelection not permitted.
Legislature	Bicameral Congress. Senate (upper house) and Chamber of Deputies (lower house); elections held every three years. There are 128 senators, 3 from each of the 31 states, 3 from the federal (capital) district, and 32 elected nationally by proportional representation for six-year terms. The 500 members of the Chamber of Deputies are elected for three-year terms from 300 electoral districts, 300 by simple majority vote and 200 by proportional representation.
Judiciary	Independent federal and state court system headed by a Supreme Court with eleven justices appointed by the president and approved by the Senate.
Party System	Multiparty system. One-party dominant (Institutional Revolutionary Party) system from 1929 until 2000. Major parties: National Action Party, Institutional Revolutionary Party, and the Democratic Revolutionary Party.

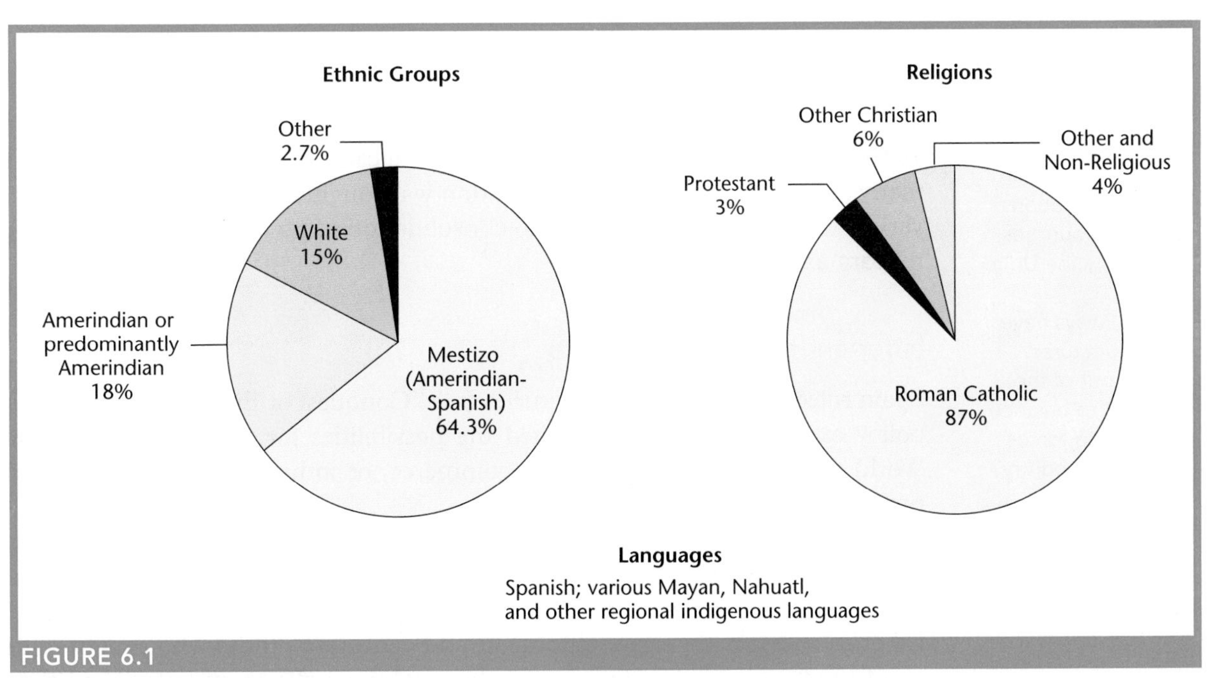

FIGURE 6.1

The Mexican Nation at a Glance

Critical Junctures

> **FOCUS QUESTIONS**
> In what ways have the critical junctures of Mexican history grown out of the country's relations to other countries, especially the United States?
> In what ways have these junctures grown out of the attempt to balance competing forces within the country?

The most formative event in Mexico's modern history was the Revolution of 1910. The conflict lasted for more than a decade and claimed the lives of as many as 1 million people. The revolution was fought by a variety of forces for a variety of reasons, which made the consolidation of power that followed as significant as the revolution itself.

Independence and Instability (1810–1876)

Spain ruled Mexico for three centuries (see "Conquest or Encounter?"). Colonial policy extracted wealth and limited the possibilities for Spaniards in the New World to benefit from agriculture, commerce, or industry without at the same time benefiting the mother country.

In 1810, a parish priest in central Mexico named Miguel Hidalgo called for an end to Spanish misrule. Although independence came in 1821, Mexico struggled to create a stable and legitimate government for decades after. Liberals and conservatives, federalists and centralists, those who sought to expand the power of the church and those who sought to curtail it, and those

Conquest or Encounter?

In 1519 the Spanish did not come to an uninhabited land waiting to be excavated for gold and silver. The land that was to become New Spain and then Mexico was home to extensive and complex indigenous civilizations that were advanced in agriculture, architecture, and political and economic organization—civilizations that were already over a thousand years old. The Mayans of the Yucatán and the Toltecs of the central highlands had reached high levels of development long before the arrival of the Europeans. By 1519, diverse groups had fallen under the power of the militaristic Aztec Empire, which extended throughout what is today central and southern Mexico.

The great Aztec city of Tenochtitlán—the site of Mexico City today—was captured and largely destroyed by the Spanish conquerors in 1521. Cortés and the colonial masters who came after him subjected indigenous groups to forced labor; robbed them of gold, silver, and land; and introduced flora and fauna from Europe that destroyed long-existing aqueducts and irrigation systems. They also brought alien forms of property rights and authority relationships, a religion that viewed indigenous practices as the devil's work, and an economy based on mining and cattle. Within a century, wars, savage exploitation, and European diseases had reduced the indigenous population from an estimated 25 million to 1 million or fewer.

The Spanish never constituted more than a small percentage of the total population. Massive racial mixing among the Indians, Europeans, and to a lesser extent Africans produced a new *raza*, or *mestizo* race. While celebrating Amerindian achievements in food, culture, the arts, and ancient civilization, middle-class Mexico has the contradictory sense that to be "Indian" nowadays is to be backward. But perhaps the situation is changing, with the upsurge of indigenous movements from both the grass roots and the international level striving to promote ethnic pride, defend rights, and foster the teaching of Indian languages.

The collision of two worlds resonates in current national philosophical and political debates. Many Mexicans at once welcome and fear full integration into the global economy, asking themselves: Is globalization the new conquest? ❖

who wanted a republic and those who wanted a monarchy were all engaged in the battle for Mexico's soul.

During this disorganized period, Mexico lost half its territory to the United States. Its northern territory of Texas won independence in a war ending in 1836. The Lone Star Republic was then annexed by the United States in 1845. Then, after the Mexican-American War an 1848 treaty gave the United States title to what later became the states of Texas, New Mexico, Utah, Nevada, Arizona, California, and part of Colorado for about $18 million. The war left a legacy of deep resentment toward the United States.

Liberals and conservatives continued their struggle over issues of political and economic order and, in particular, the power of the Catholic Church. The Constitution of 1857 incorporated many of the goals of the liberals, such as a somewhat democratic government, a bill of rights, and limitations on the power of the church. In 1861, Spain, Great Britain, and France occupied Veracruz to collect debts owed by Mexico. The French army then continued on to Mexico City, where it established the rule of Emperor Maximilian (1864–1867). Conservatives welcomed this respite from the liberal rule. Benito Juárez returned to the presidency in 1867 after defeating and executing Maximilian. Juárez, a

Zapotec Indian from Oaxaca who came to be a liberal hero, is still hailed in Mexico today as an early proponent of more democratic government.

The Porfiriato (1876–1911)

A popular retired general named Porfirio Díaz became increasingly dissatisfied with what he thought was a "lot of politics" and "little action" in Mexico's government. After several failed attempts to win and then take the presidency, he finally succeeded in 1876. His dictatorship lasted thirty-four years and was at first welcomed by many because it brought sustained stability to the country.

Díaz imposed a highly centralized authoritarian system to create political order and economic progress. Deeply disdainful of the vast majority of the country's population, Díaz and his technocrat advisors, the *científicos* (scientists) encouraged foreign investment and amassed huge fortunes for themselves. But economic and political opportunities were closed off for new generations of middle- and upper-class Mexicans.

The Revolution of 1910 and the Sonoran Dynasty (1910–1934)

In 1910, Díaz had pledged himself to an open election for president, and Francisco I. Madero, a landowner from the northern state of Coahuila, presented himself as a candidate. When opposition swelled, Díaz jailed Madero and tried to repress growing dissent. The clamor for change, however, forced Díaz into exile. Madero was elected in 1911, but he was soon using the military to put down revolts from reformers and reactionaries alike. When Madero was assassinated during a **coup d'état** in 1913, political order in the country virtually collapsed.

coup d'état a forceful, extra-constitutional action resulting in the removal of an existing government, usually carried out by the military.

While middle-class reformers struggled to displace Díaz, a peasant revolt that focused on land claims erupted in the central and southern states. Encouraged by the weakening of the old regime and driven to desperation by increasing landlessness, villagers armed themselves and joined forces under a variety of local leaders. The most famous was Emiliano Zapata. His manifesto, the Plan de Ayala, became the cornerstone of the radical agrarian reform that would be incorporated into the Constitution of 1917.

In the north, Francisco "Pancho" Villa rallied his own army of workers, small farmers, and ranch hands. In 1916, troops from the United States entered Mexico to punish Villa for an attack on U.S. territory. Although this badly planned, poorly executed military operation failed to locate Villa, the presence of U.S. troops on Mexican soil resulted in increased public hostility toward the United States.

The Mexican Constitution of 1917 was forged out of the diverse and often conflicting set of interests represented by the various revolutionary factions. The document established a formal set of political institutions and guaranteed citizens a range of progressive social and economic rights: agrarian reform, social security, the right to organize in unions, a minimum wage, an eight-hour workday, profit sharing for workers, universal secular education, and adult male suffrage. But the constitution did not provide suffrage for women, who had to wait until 1953 to vote in local elections and 1958 to vote in national elections. The constitution declared that only Mexican citizens or the government could own land or rights to water and other natural resources. It also contained numerous articles that severely limited the power of the Roman Catholic Church. The constitution signaled the formal end of the revolution. But violence continued as competing leaders asserted power and displaced their rivals. By 1920, a modicum of stability had emerged, but not before many of the revolutionary leaders—including Zapata and President Carranza—had been assassinated.

Power was gradually consolidated in the hands of a group of revolutionary leaders from the north of the country. Known as the Sonoran Dynasty, after their home state of Sonora, they were committed to a capitalist model of economic development. Eventually, one of the Sonorans, Plutarco Elías Calles, emerged as the *jefe máximo*, or supreme leader. After his presidential term (1924–1928), Calles selected and dominated his successors from 1929 to 1934. The consolidation of power under his control was accompanied by extreme **anticlericalism**, which eventually resulted in warfare between the government and the conservative leaders of the Catholic Church and their followers.

anticlericalism opposition to the power of churches or clergy in politics. In some countries, for example, France and Mexico, this opposition has focused on the role of the Catholic Church in politics.

In 1929, Calles brought together many of the most powerful contenders for leadership, including many regional warlords, to create a political party. He offered a simple bargain: contenders for power would accommodate each other's interests in the expectation that without political violence, the country would prosper and they could reap the benefits of even greater power and economic spoils. For the next seven decades, Calles's bargain ensured nonviolent conflict resolution among elites and the uninterrupted rule of the Institutional Revolutionary Party (PRI) in national politics.

There were five clear results of this protracted conflict. First, the power of traditional rural landowners was undercut. Second, the influence of the Catholic Church was strongly curtailed. Third, the power of foreign investors was severely limited; prior to the revolution, foreign investors had owned much of the country's land as well as many of its railroads, mines, and factories. Fourth, a new political elite consolidated power and agreed to resolve conflicts through accommodation and bargaining rather than through violence. And fifth, the new constitution and the new party laid the basis for a strong central government that could assert its power over the agricultural, industrial, and social development of the country.

In 1914, Pancho Villa (right) met with Emiliano Zapata in Mexico City to discuss the revolution and their separate goals for its outcome. *(Source: Robert Freck/Odyssey/Chicago.)*

Lázaro Cárdenas, Agrarian Reform, and the Workers (1934–1940)

In 1934, Calles handpicked Lázaro Cárdenas for the presidency. Calles anticipated that Cárdenas would go along with his behind-the-scenes management of the country and that the new president would continue the economic policies of the postrevolutionary coalition. But Cárdenas executed a virtual coup that established his own supremacy and sent Calles packing to the United States for an "extended vacation."[2] Even more unexpectedly, Cárdenas mobilized peasants and workers in pursuit of the more radical goals of the 1910 revolution. He encouraged peasant associations to petition for land and claim rights promised in the Constitution of 1917. During his administration, more than 49 million acres of land were distributed, nearly twice as much as had been parceled out by all the previous postrevolutionary governments combined.[3] Most of these lands were distributed in the form of ***ejidos*** (collective land grants) to peasant groups. ***Ejidatarios*** (those who acquired *ejido* lands) became one of the most enduring bases of support for the government. Cárdenas also encouraged workers to form unions and demand higher wages and better working conditions. He established his nationalist credentials in 1938 when he wrested the petroleum industry from foreign investors and placed it under government control.

ejido land granted by Mexican government to an organized group of peasants.

ejidatario recipient of an *ejido* land grant in Mexico.

Under Cárdenas (1934–1940), the bulk of the Mexican population was incorporated into the political system. Organizations of peasants and workers, middle-class groups, and the military were added to the official party, and the voices of the poor majority were heard within the councils of government, reducing the risk that they would become radicalized outside them. The Cárdenas government encouraged investment in industrialization, provided credit to agriculture, and created infrastructure.

Lázaro Cárdenas continues to be a national hero to Mexicans. His other legacy was to institutionalize patterns of political succession and presidential behavior that continue to set standards for Mexico's leaders. He campaigned extensively, and his travels took him to remote villages and regions, where he listened to the demands and complaints of humble people. Cárdenas served a single six-year term, called a ***sexenio***, and then relinquished full power to his successor—a pattern of presidential succession that still holds in Mexican politics.

sexenio the six-year administration of Mexican presidents.

The Politics of Rapid Development (1940–1982)

Cárdenas' successors used the institutions he created to counteract his reforms. Local and regional party leaders and leaders of peasants' and workers' groups used their organizations as pawns in exchange for political favors. Gradually, the PRI developed a huge patronage machine, providing union and *ejido* leaders with jobs, opportunities for corruption, land, and other benefits in return for delivering their followers' political support. Extensive chains of personal relationships based on the exchange of favors allowed the party to amass far-reaching political control and limit opportunities for organizing independent of the PRI. These exchange relationships, known as **clientelism**, became the cement that built loyalty to the PRI and the political system.

clientelism an informal relationship in which a powerful patron offers resources in return for the support and services of lower-status and less powerful clients.

Presidents after Cárdenas reoriented the country away from egalitarian social goals toward a development strategy in which the state actively encouraged industrialization and the accumulation of wealth. Initially, industrialization created jobs and made available a wide range of basic consumer goods to Mexico's burgeoning population. Economic growth rates were high during the 1940s, 1950s, and 1960s. Mexicans flocked to the cities to take advantage of the jobs created in the manufacturing and construction industries. By the 1970s, however, industrial development policies were no longer generating rapid growth and could not keep pace with the rapidly rising demand for jobs.

By the mid-1970s, the economy was in deep crisis. Just as policy-makers began to take corrective actions, vast new amounts of oil were discovered in the Gulf of Mexico. Soon, rapid economic growth in virtually every sector of the economy was refueled by extensive public investment programs paid for with oil revenues. Based on the promise of petroleum wealth, the government and private businesses borrowed huge amounts of capital from foreign lenders, who were eager to do business with a country that had so much oil. Unfortunately for Mexico, international petroleum prices plunged sharply in the early 1980s. Almost overnight, there was no more credit and much less money from petroleum to pay for economic expansion or the interest on the debts incurred in preceding years. Mexico plunged into a deep economic crisis that affected many other countries around the world.

Crisis and Reform (1982–2001)

This economic crisis led two presidents, Miguel de la Madrid (1982–1988) and Carlos Salinas (1988–1994), to introduce the first major reversal of the country's development strategy since the 1940s. New policies limited the government's role in the economy and made it easier for Mexican producers to export their goods. In 1993, by signing the **North American Free Trade Agreement (NAFTA)**, which committed Mexico, the United States, and Canada to the elimination of trade barriers among them, Mexico's policy-makers signaled the extent to which they envisioned that the future prosperity of their country would be linked to that of its two neighbors to the north.

North American Free Trade Agreement (NAFTA) a treaty among the U.S., Mexico, and Canada implemented on Jan. 1, 1994, that largely eliminates trade barriers among the three nations and establishes procedures to resolve trade disputes.

In 1994, billions of dollars of foreign investment fled the country. This revealed a new international vulnerability. The peso lost half of its value against the dollar within a few days, and the government lacked the funds to pay its debt obligations. Suddenly, Mexico's status among nations seemed dubious once more. The Mexican economy shrank by 6.2 percent in 1995, inflation soared, taxes rose while wages were frozen, and the bank system collapsed. The United States orchestrated a $50 billion bailout, $20 billion of which came directly from the U.S. Treasury. Faced with limited options, the administration of Ernesto Zedillo (1994–2000) implemented a severe and unpopular economic austerity program, which restored financial stability over the next two years.

On January 1, 1994, a guerrilla movement, the Zapatista Army of National Liberation (EZLN), seized four towns in the southern state of Chiapas. The group demanded land, democracy, indigenous rights, and an immediate repeal of NAFTA. Many citizens throughout the country openly supported the aims of the rebels, pointing out that the movement brought to light the reality of two different Mexicos: one in which the privileged enjoyed the fruits of wealth and

Mexican presidential candidates are expected to campaign hard, traveling to remote locations, making rousing campaign speeches, and meeting with citizens of humble origins. Here, presidential candidate Felipe Calderón is on the campaign trail. (*Source:* © *Erich Schlegel*/Dallas Morning News/*Corbis*)

influence and another in which citizens were getting left behind because of poverty and repression. The government and the military were also criticized for inaction and human rights abuses in Chiapas.

Following close on the heels of rebellion came the assassination of the PRI's presidential candidate, Luis Donaldo Colosio. The assassination shocked all citizens and shook the political elite deeply. The murder opened wide rifts within the PRI and unleashed a flood of speculation and distrust among the citizenry. Many Mexicans were convinced that the assassination was part of a conspiracy of party "dinosaurs," political hardliners who opposed any kind of democratic transformation.[4] Nevertheless, fear of violence provided the PRI with strong support in the August 1994 elections.

Even though the PRI remained in power, these shocks provoked widespread disillusionment and frustration with the political system. Many citizens, especially in urban areas, decided that there was no longer any reason to support the PRI. Buoyed by a 1996 electoral reform, the opposition made important gains in the legislative elections the following year. For the first time in modern Mexican history, the PRI had lost its absolute majority in the Chamber of

Deputies, the lower house of the national legislature. Since then, the congress has shown increasing dynamism as a counterbalance to the presidency, blocking executive decisions, demanding unrestricted information, and initiating new legislation. In addition, opposition parties have won important governorships and mayorships. The 2000 election of Vicente Fox as the first non-PRI president in seven decades was the culmination of this electoral revolution.

The Fox Presidency and Post–9/11 Mexico (2001 to the Present)

When Vicente Fox became president, Mexicans hoped his administration would consolidate the progress toward democracy that had been made, while improving public services and reducing poverty. However, Fox found it difficult to bring about the changes that he had promised. His difficulties arose in part because he and his team lacked experience in governing on a national scale. He also lacked the compliant congressional majority and the close relationship with his party that his PRI predecessors had enjoyed. Proposals to reform the tax code and restructure the government-controlled electricity corporation went down to defeat.

Fox hoped achievements in international policy would enhance his prestige at home. He particularly hoped a close personal connection with the new U.S. president, George W. Bush, would facilitate an agreement under which a greater number of Mexicans could migrate to the United States to work. After 9/11, however, top U.S. officials immediately turned attention away from Mexico and Latin America and toward Afghanistan and the Middle East. It did not help that some in Washington felt Mexico had been slow to express its solidarity with the United States. The possibility of an agreement on migration disappeared as Washington moved to assert control over its borders and to restrict access to the United States. In 2002, Mexico began a two-year term as a member of the United Nations Security Council. As deliberations at the UN headquarters focused increasingly on U.S. proposals for the use of force against Iraq, the Bush administration believed that Mexico could be convinced to support its position on the issue. Public opinion in Mexico was so deeply opposed to an invasion of Iraq, however, that Fox's government decided to reject U.S.-sponsored resolutions on the subject. Indeed, memories of past U.S. invasions and occupations still made questions involving national sovereignty very sensitive. Any Mexican government that effectively sponsored a U.S. attack on a smaller, weaker country would have to confront a tremendous backlash.

Themes and Implications

FOCUS QUESTION

In what ways has civil society shaped Mexican politics?

Historical Junctures and Political Themes

The modern Mexican state emerged out of a popular revolution that proclaimed goals of democratic government, social justice, and national control of the country's resources. In the chaotic years after the revolution, the state created conditions for political and social peace. By incorporating peasants and workers into party and government institutions and by providing benefits to low-income groups during the 1930s, it became widely accepted as legitimate. In encouraging considerable economic growth in the years after 1940, it also created a belief in its ability to provide material improvements in the quality of life for large portions of the population. These factors worked together to create a strong state capable of guiding economic and political life in the country. Only in the 1980s did this system begin to crumble.

In its external relations, Mexico has always prided itself on ideological independence from the world's great powers. For many decades, its large population, cultural richness, political stability, and front-line position regarding the United States led Mexico to consider itself a natural leader of Latin America and the developing world in general. After the early 1980s, however, the government rejected this position in favor of rapid integration into a global economy. Although the reforms of the 1980s and 1990s, and especially NAFTA, have advanced this goal, many fear that the government has accepted a position of political, cultural, and economic subordination to the United States.

Mexico enjoyed considerable economic advancement after the 1940s, but economic and political crises after 1980 shook confidence in its ability to achieve its economic goals and highlighted the conflict between a market-oriented development strategy and the country's philosophical tradition of a strong and protective state. Larger questions continue to challenge the country: whether a new development strategy can generate growth, whether Mexican products can find profitable markets overseas, whether investors can create extensive job opportunities for millions of unemployed and part-time workers, and whether the country can maintain the confidence of those investors over the longer term.

After the Revolution of 1910, the country opted not for true democracy but for representation through government-mediated organizations within a **corporatist state**. Interest groups became part of state structure rather than independent sources of advocacy. This increased state power in relation to **civil society**. The state took the lead in defining goals for the country's development. Through the school system, the party, and the media, it inculcated in the population a broad sense of its legitimate right to set such goals. The state also had extensive resources at its disposal to control or co-opt dissent and purchase political loyalty. The PRI was an essential channel through which material goods, jobs, the distribution of land, and the allocation of development projects flowed to increase popular support for the system or to buy off opposition to it.

corporatist state a system in which important interests, such as unions and business associations, are formally included in government decision-making processes.

civil society refers to the space occupied by voluntary associations outside the state, for example, professional associations, trade unions, and student groups.

This does not mean that Mexican society was unorganized or passive. Indeed, many Mexicans were actively involved in local community organizations, religious activities, unions, and public interest groups. But traditionally, the scope for challenging the government was very limited. Even so, Mexico's strong state did not become openly repressive except when directly challenged. On the contrary, officials in the government and the party generally worked hard to find ways to resolve conflicts peacefully and to use behind-the-scenes accommodation to bring conflicting interests into accord.

By the 1980s, cracks began to appear in the traditional ways in which Mexican citizens interacted with the government. The PRI began to lose its capacity to control political activities, and civic groups increasingly insisted on their right to remain independent from the PRI and the government. The terms of the state-society relationship were clearly in need of redefinition. The administration of President Zedillo signaled its willingness to cede political power to successful opposition parties in fair elections, and electoral reform in 1996 and competitive elections in 1997 were significant steps that led to the defeat of the PRI in 2000. Mexico's future stability depends on how well a more democratic government can accommodate conflicting interests while at the same time providing economic opportunities to a largely poor population.

Summary

The Mexican political system is unique among developing countries in the extent to which it has managed to institutionalize and maintain civilian political authority for a very long time. The country's development has been significantly shaped by its proximity to the United States and its contemporary economic development is linked to the expansion of globalization. Nevertheless, the critical junctures in the country's history also show the importance of domestic political and economic conflicts. Although the Revolution of 1910 happened a century ago, its legacies continue to mark development in Mexico, as does its earlier history of industrialization and urbanization. And the impact of particular leaders and their presidential administrations also mark the emergence of the country. In a world of developing nations wracked by political turmoil, military coups, and regime changes, the PRI regime established important conditions for political stability, even though it stifled democratic freedoms.

Currently, Mexico is undergoing significant political change without widespread violence, transforming itself from a corporatist state to a democratic one. Its industrial and petroleum-based economy gives the country a per capita income higher than those of most other developing nations. But Mexico suffers from great inequalities in how wealth is distributed, and poverty continues to be a grim reality for millions. The way the country promoted economic growth and industrialization is important in explaining why widespread poverty has persisted and why political power is not more equitably distributed.

Political Economy and Development

FOCUS QUESTIONS

In what ways have various theories of economic development affected

State and Economy

During the years of the Porfiriato (1876–1911), policy-makers were convinced that Mexico could grow rich by exporting its raw materials to more economically advanced countries. Soon, the country had become so attractive to foreign government policies? Which policies have been the most successful? The least successful?

state capitalism a strategy of economic development in which the state guides industrial, agricultural, and financial policy and aims to create the political conditions for its success.

import substituting industrialization (ISI) a strategy for industrialization based on domestic manufacture of previously imported goods to satisfy domestic market demands.

investors that large amounts of land, the country's petroleum, its railroad network, and its mining wealth were largely controlled by foreigners.

After the revolution, Mexicans generally believed the state had the responsibility to generate wealth for all its citizens. As a result, the country adopted a strategy in which the government guided the process of industrial and agricultural development. Often called **state capitalism**, this strategy relied heavily on government actions to encourage private investment and reduce risks for private entrepreneurs. After the revolution, many became convinced that economic growth would not occur unless Mexico could industrialize more fully.

Import Substitution and Its Consequences

Between 1940 and 1982, Mexico pursued a form of state capitalism and a model of industrialization known as import substitution, or **import substituting industrialization (ISI)**. It promoted the development of industries to supply the domestic market by encouraging domestic and international investment; providing credit and tax incentives to industrialists; maintaining low rates of inflation; and keeping wage demands low through subsidized food, transportation, housing, and health care for workers. It established state-owned steel mills, electric power generators, ports, and petroleum production. It used tariffs and import licenses to protect Mexican industries from foreign competition. These policies had considerable success until the 1970s.

With the massive agrarian reform of the 1930s (see Section 1), the *ejido* had become an important structure in the rural economy. After Cárdenas left office, however, government policy-makers moved away from the economic development of the *ejidos*. They became committed instead to developing a strong, entrepreneurial private sector in agriculture. To encourage these goals, the government invested in transportation networks, irrigation projects, and agricultural storage facilities. It provided extension services and invested in research. It encouraged imports of technology to improve output and mechanize production. Believing modern commercial farmers would respond better to these investments and services than peasants on small plots of land, the government provided most of its assistance to large landowners.

Between 1940 and 1950, GDP grew at an annual average of 6.7 percent, while manufacturing increased at an average of 8.1 percent. In the following two decades, GDP growth rates remained impressive, and manufacturing growth continued to outpace overall growth in the economy. In the 1950s, manufacturing achieved an average of 7.3 percent growth annually and in the 1960s, 10.1 percent annually. Agricultural production grew rapidly as new areas were brought under cultivation and the technology of the green revolution (scientifically improved seeds, fertilizers, and pesticides) was extensively adopted on large farms. Even the poorest Mexicans believed that their lives were improving.

Business elites in Mexico received subsidized credit to invest in equipment and plants; they benefited from cheap, subsidized energy; and they rarely had to pay taxes. These protected businesses emerged as powerful players in national politics. The government remained the source of most policy initiatives, but

TABLE 6.2

Mexican Development, 1940–2005

	1940	1950	1960	1970	1980	1990	2005
Population (thousands)	19,815	26,282	38,020	52,771	70,416	88,598	103,100
Life expectancy (years)[a]	—	51.6	58.6	62.6	67.4	68.9	75.4
Infant mortality (per 1,000 live births)	—	—	86.3	70.9	49.9	42.6	22.0
Illiteracy (% of population age 15 and over)	—	42.5	34.5	25.0	16.0	12.7	9.0
Urban population (% of total)	—	—	50.7	59.0	66.4	72.6	76.0
Economically active population in agriculture (% of total)	—	58.3	55.1	44.0	36.6	22.0	18.0[b]

	1940–1950	1950–1960	1960–1970	1970–1980	1980–1990	1990–2003
GDP growth rate (average annual percent)	6.7	5.8	7.6	6.7	1.6	1.3
Per capita GDP growth rate	—	—	3.7	3.7	–0.7	–0.2

[a]Five-year average.

[b]2001.

Sources:

Statistical Abstract for Latin America (New York: United Nations, Economic Commission for Latin America, various years); Roger Hansen, *The Politics of Mexican Development* (Baltimore, Md.: Johns Hopkins University Press, 1971); *Statistical Bulletin of the OAS*. World Bank Country Data for Mexico, http://www.worldbank.org/data/countrydata/countrydata.html; World Bank, World Development Indicators.

generally it was not able to move far in the face of opposition from those who benefited most from its policies.

At the same time, unions became more dependent on the government for benefits and protection. The government also limited the right to strike. Although unions were closely controlled, organized workers continued to be an elite within the country's working classes. Union membership meant job security and important benefits such as housing subsidies and health care. These factors helped compensate for the lack of democracy within the labor movement. Moreover, labor leaders had privileged access to the country's political leadership and benefited personally from their control over jobs, contracts, and working conditions. In return, they guaranteed labor peace.[5]

By the 1950s, a group of large, commercially oriented farmers had emerged to dominate the agricultural economy.[6] Like their urban counterparts in business, they became rich and powerful. But government policies eventually limited the potential for further growth.[7] Industrialists who received extensive subsidies and benefits from government had few incentives to produce efficiently. High tariffs kept out foreign competition, further reducing reasons for efficiency or quality in production. Importing technology to support industrialization eventually became a drain on the country's foreign exchange. In addition, the costs of providing benefits to workers increased beyond the capacity of the government to generate revenue. Providing benefits to large farmers meant significant limitations on what could be provided for poor peasants.

The ranks of the urban poor grew steadily, particularly from the 1960s on. Mexico developed a sizable **informal sector**—workers who produced and sold goods and services at the margin of the economic system and faced extreme insecurity.

informal sector (economy) economic activities outside the formal economy that are unregulated by economic or legal institutions.

Also left behind in the country's development after 1940 were peasant farmers. Their lands were often the least fertile, plot sizes were minuscule, and access to markets was impeded by poor transportation and exploitive middlemen who trucked products to markets for exorbitant fees. Government banks provided some credit, but usually only to those who had political connections.

By the early 1970s, it was becoming evident that the size of the population, growing at a rate of some 3.5 percent a year, and the structure of income distribution were impeding further industrial development. The government had hoped industrialization would free the economy from excessive dependence on the industrialized world, particularly on the United States. By the late 1960s, the country was no longer able to meet domestic demand for basic foodstuffs and was forced to import increasingly large quantities of food, which cost the government foreign exchange that it could have used for better purposes. By the 1970s, some policy-makers had become convinced that industrialization had actually increased the country's dependence on advanced industrial countries and particularly on the United States.

Sowing the Oil and Reaping a Crisis

In the early 1970s, Mexico faced the threat of social crisis brought on by rural poverty, chaotic urbanization, high population growth, and the questioning of political legitimacy. The government responded by increasing investment in infrastructure and public industries, regulating the flow of foreign capital, and increasing social spending. Between 1971 and 1976, inflation rose from an annual average of 5.3 percent to almost 16 percent. The foreign debt more than tripled. In response, the government devalued the peso in 1976 to encourage exports and discourage imports. It also signed a stabilization agreement with the International Monetary Fund (IMF) to reduce government spending, increase tax collection, and control inflation. Just as the seriousness of the economic situation was being recognized, however, vast new finds of oil came to the rescue.

The administration of President José López Portillo (1976–1982) embarked on vast investment projects and major new initiatives to reduce poverty and deal with declining agricultural productivity. Oil revenues paid for much of this expansion. But foreign debt also mounted as both public and private sectors borrowed heavily to finance investments and lavish consumer spending.

Among those who have benefited least from the government's development policies are the rural poor. *(Source: Marco Ugarte/AP Images)*

By 1982, Mexico's foreign debt was $86 billion, and the peso was seriously overvalued, making Mexican products more expensive on the world market. Oil accounted for 77.2 percent of the country's exports, making the economy extremely vulnerable to changes in oil prices. Global overproduction brought the international price for Mexican petroleum down to $26.30 a barrel in 1982 and to even lower levels in the years that followed. The United States tightened its monetary policy by raising interest rates. Access to foreign credit dried up. Wealthy Mexicans sent vast amounts of capital abroad, and at the same time the country's international creditors were demanding repayment on their loans. In August 1982, the government announced that the country could not pay the interest on its foreign debt. This triggered a crisis throughout the world. Mexican GDP growth in 1982 was –0.6 percent and fell to –4.2 percent the following year.

In this severe economic crisis, unions lost much of their bargaining power with government over issues of wages and protection. A shift in employment from the formal to the informal economy further fragmented what had once been the most powerful sector of the party. Cuts in government subsidies for public transportation, food, electricity, and gasoline created new hardships for workers.

A wide variety of interests began to organize outside the PRI to demand that government do something about the situation. Massive earthquakes in Mexico City in September 1985 proved to be a watershed for Mexican society. Hundreds of communities organized rescue efforts, soup kitchens, shelters, and rehabilitation initiatives. A surging sense of political empowerment developed.[8]

Moreover, the PRI was challenged by the increased popularity of opposition political parties. The elections of 1988 became a focus for protest against economic dislocation and political powerlessness. Carlos Salinas, the PRI candidate, received a bare majority of 50.7 percent and opposition parties claimed widespread electoral fraud.

New Strategies: Structural Reforms and NAFTA

Between 1988 and 1994, the mutually dependent relationship between industry and government was weakened. New free-market policies were put in place. Deregulation gave the private sector more freedom to pursue economic activities and less reason to seek special favors from government. A number of large government industries were reorganized and sold to private investors. A constitutional revision allowed *ejidatarios* to become owners of individual plots of land. In addition, reforms in the financial sector changed banking laws and established a stock exchange. This encouraged the emergence of new banks, brokerage firms, and insurance companies.

The New Federalism attempted to give greater power and budgetary responsibilities to state and local governments, which had been historically very weak. Additionally, the central bank, which made national monetary policy, became independent in 1994, although exchange rates are still determined by the finance ministry.

NAFTA, an agreement with Canada and the United States, created the basis for gradual introduction of free trade among the three countries. However, the liberalization of the Mexican economy and opening of its markets to foreign competition increased Mexico's vulnerability to changes in international economic conditions. These factors, as well as mismanaged economic policies, led to a major economic crisis at the end of 1994 and profound recession in 1995. NAFTA has meant that the fate of the Mexican economy is increasingly linked to the health of the American economy.

Society and Economy

FOCUS QUESTIONS

Which economic developments in Mexico have most greatly affected social progress, for better or worse?

To what degree has government policy affected these developments?

To what degree are they shaped by outside forces?

Mexico's economic development has had a significant impact on social conditions in the country. Overall, the standard of living rose markedly after the 1940s. Rates of infant mortality, literacy, and life expectancy have steadily improved. Provision of health and education services expanded until the government cutbacks on social expenditures in the early 1980s. Among the most important consequences of economic growth was the development of a large middle class, most of which lives in Mexico's numerous large cities. By the 1980s, a third or more of Mexican households could claim a middle-class lifestyle: a steady income, secure food and shelter, access to decent education and health services, a car, some disposable income and savings, and some security that their children would be able to experience happy and healthy lives.

These achievements reflect well on the ability of the economy to increase social well-being in the country. However, the impressive economic growth through the early 1970s and between 1978 and 1982 could have produced greater social progress. In terms of standard indicators of social development—infant mortality, literacy, and life expectancy—Mexico fell behind a number of Latin American countries that grew less rapidly but provided more effectively for their populations. Mexico's economic development also resulted in a widening gap between the wealthy and the poor and among different regions in the country. Although the poor are better off than they were in the early days of the country's drive toward industrialization, they are worse off when compared to middle- and upper-income groups. In 1950, the bottom 40 percent of the country's households accounted for about 14 percent of total personal income, while the top 30 percent had 60 percent of total income.[9] In 2004, it is estimated, the bottom 40 percent accounted for about 13.7 percent of income, while the top 40 percent shared 72.2 percent.[10] As the rich grew richer, the gap between the rich and the poor increased.

Among the poorest are people in rural areas who have little or no access to productive land. Harsh conditions in the countryside have fueled a half-century of migration to the cities. Nevertheless, some 25 million Mexicans continue to live in rural areas, many of them in deep poverty. Many work for substandard wages and migrate seasonally to search for jobs in order to sustain their families. Among rural inhabitants with access to land, almost half have five hectares or less. This land is usually not irrigated and depends on erratic rainfall. It is often leached of nutrients as a result of centuries of cultivation, population pressure, and erosion. The incidence of disease, malnutrition, and illiteracy is much higher in Mexico's rural areas than in urban areas.

Poverty has a regional dimension in Mexico. The northern areas of the country are significantly better off than the southern and central areas. In the north, large commercial farms using modern technologies grow fruits, vegetables, and grains for export. The U.S. border, the principal destination of agricultural products, is close at hand, and transportation networks are extensive and generally in good condition. Moreover, industrial cities such as Monterrey and Tijuana provide steady jobs for skilled and unskilled labor. Along the border, a band of manufacturing and assembly plants, called *maquiladoras*, provides many jobs, particularly for young women who are seeking some escape from the burdens of rural life or the constraints of traditional family life.

In the southern and central regions of the country, the population is denser, the land poorer, and the number of *ejidatarios* eking out subsistence greater. Transportation is often difficult, and during parts of the year, some areas may be inaccessible because of heavy rains and flooding. Most of Mexico's remaining indigenous groups live in the southern regions, often in remote areas where they have been forgotten by government programs and exploited by regional bosses for generations. The conditions that spurred the Chiapas rebellion are found throughout the southern states.

The economic crisis of the 1980s had an impact on social conditions in the country as well. Wages declined by about half, and unemployment soared as businesses collapsed and the government laid off workers in public offices and privatized industries. The informal sector expanded rapidly. Here, people eked out a living by hawking chewing gum, umbrellas, sponges, candy, shoelaces, mirrors, and a variety of other items in the street; jumping in front of cars at stoplights to wash windshields and sell newspapers; producing and repairing cheap consumer goods such as shoes and clothing; and selling services on a daily or hourly basis. Although the informal sector provides important goods and services, conditions of work are often dangerous, and uncertainty as to where the next peso will come from is endemic.

The economic crisis of the 1980s also reduced the quality and availability of social services. Expenditures on education and health declined after 1982 as the government imposed austerity measures. Salaries of primary school teachers declined by 34 percent between 1983 and 1988, and many teachers worked second and even third jobs in order to make ends meet. Per capita health expenditures declined from a high of about $19 in 1980 to about $11 in 1990. Although indicators of mortality did not rise during this troubled decade, the incidence of diseases associated with poverty—malnutrition, cholera, anemia, and dysentery—increased. The crisis began to ease in the early 1990s, however, and many came to believe that conditions would improve for the poor. The government began investing in social services. When a new economic crisis occurred, however, unemployment surged, and austerity measures severely limited investments. Despite considerable recovery in the late 1990s and again in the 2000s, wages remain low for the majority of workers while taxes and the cost of living have increased.

FOCUS QUESTIONS

How well have Mexican development strategies linked Mexico to the global economy?

In what ways have global linkages helped or harmed the lives of various social groups?

Mexico in the Global Economy

The crisis that began in 1982 altered Mexico's international policies. In response to that crisis, the government relaxed restrictions on the ability of foreigners to own property, reduced and eliminated tariffs, and did away with most import licenses. Foreign investment was courted in the hope of increasing the manufacture of goods for export. The government also introduced a series of incentives to encourage the private sector to produce goods for export. In 1986, Mexico joined the General Agreement on Tariffs and Trade (GATT), a multilateral agreement that seeks to promote freer trade among countries that later became the basis for the World Trade Organization (WTO), and in the 1990s and early 2000s Mexico signed trade pacts with many countries in Latin America, Europe, and elsewhere.

The government's effort to pursue a more outward-oriented development strategy culminated in the ratification of NAFTA in 1993, with gradual implementation beginning on January 1, 1994. This agreement is important to Mexico. In 2000, 89 percent of the country's exports were sent to the United States, and 74 percent of its imports came from that country.[11] Access to the U.S. market is essential to Mexico and to domestic and foreign investors. NAFTA signaled a new period in U.S.-Mexican relations by making closer integration of the two economies a certainty.

NAFTA also entails risks for Mexico. Domestic producers worry about competition from U.S. firms. Farmers worry that Mexican crops cannot compete effectively with those grown in the United States; for example, peasant producers of corn and beans have been hard hit by the availability of lower-priced U.S.-grown grains. In addition, many believe that embracing free trade with Canada and the United States indicates a loss of sovereignty. Certainly, Mexico's economic situation is now more vulnerable to the ebb and flow of economic conditions in the U.S. economy. Some are also concerned with increasing evidence of "cultural imperialism" as U.S. movies, music, fashions, and lifestyles increasingly influence consumers. Indeed, for Mexico, which has traditionally feared the power of the United States in its domestic affairs, internationalization of political and economic relationships poses particularly difficult problems of adjustment.

On the other hand, the United States, newly aware of the importance of the Mexican economy to its own economic growth and concerned about instability on its southern border, hammered together a $50 billion economic assistance program composed of U.S., European, and IMF commitments to support its neighbor when crisis struck in 1994. The Mexican government imposed a new stabilization package that contained austerity measures, higher interest rates, and limits on wages. Remarkably, by 1998, Mexico had paid off all of its obligations to the United States.

Globalization is also stripping Mexico of some of the secrecy that traditionally surrounded government decision making, electoral processes, and efforts to deal with political dissent. International attention increasingly focuses on the country, and investors want clear and up-to-date information on what is occurring in the economy. The Internet and e-mail, along with lower international telephone rates, are increasing information flows across borders. The government can no longer hope to suppress news about events such as the peasant rebellion in Chiapas, alleged electoral fraud, or the management of exchange rates. It now must consider how such actions will look in Tokyo, Frankfurt, Ottawa, London, or Washington.

Summary

Mexico's development from the 1930s to the 1980s was marked by extensive government engagement in the economy. During this period, the country industrialized and became primarily urban. At the same time, the life conditions of most Mexicans improved, and standards of health, longevity, and education grew. Yet, along with these achievements, development strategies led to industrial and agricultural sectors that were often inefficient and overly protected by government. Inequalities in the distribution of income and opportunities increased, and growth was threatened by a combination of domestic policies and international economic conditions. In the 1980s, the earlier model of development collapsed in crisis, and more market-oriented policies have significantly reduced the role of government in the economy and have opened the country up to global economic forces. But growth has been slow under the new policies, and inequalities have increased. Economic growth, social inequality, and the legacies of an authoritarian past continue to affect the development of the country.

SECTION 3 Governance and Policy-Making

Mexico is a federal republic, although until the 1990s, state and local governments had few resources and a limited sphere of action when compared with the national level. Under the PRI, the executive branch held almost all power, while the legislative and judicial branches followed the executive's lead and were considered rubber-stamp bodies. During the years of PRI hegemony, the government was civilian, authoritarian, and corporatist. Currently, Mexico has multiparty competitive elections, and power is less concentrated in the executive branch and the national government. Since the mid-1980s, great efforts have been made to reinvigorate the nation's laws and institutions and to make the country more democratic.

Organization of the State

FOCUS QUESTIONS

In what ways does the actual exercise of state power differ from the model outlined in the Constitution? What are the main reasons for these discrepancies?

According to the supreme law of the land, the Constitution of 1917, Mexico's political institutions resemble those of the United States. There are three branches of government, and a set of checks and balances limits the power of each. The congress consists of the Senate and the Chamber of Deputies. One hundred twenty-eight senators are elected, three from each of the country's thirty-one states; three from the Federal District, which contains the capital, Mexico City; and another thirty-two elected nationally by **proportional representation**. The 500 members of the Chamber of Deputies are elected from 300 electoral districts—300 by simple majority vote and 200 by proportional representation. State and local governments are also elected. The president, governors, and senators are elected for six years, and deputies (representatives in the lower house) and municipal officials are elected for three.

proportional representation (PR) a system of political representation in which seats are allocated to parties within multi-member constituencies, roughly in proportion to the votes each party receives.

In practice, the Mexican system is very different from that of the United States. The constitution is a very long document that is easily amended, especially when compared to that of the United States. It lays out the structure of government and guarantees a wide range of human rights, including familiar ones such as freedom of speech and protection of the law, but also economic and social rights such as the right to a job and the right to health care. Economic and social rights are acknowledged but in practice do not reach all of the population. Although there has been some decentralization of power, the political system is still much more centralized than that of the United States. Congress is now more active as a decision-making arena and as a check on presidential power, but the executive remains central to initiating policy and managing political conflict. Similarly, the judiciary has increased its capacity to rule against powerful political actors and institutions, but it is not fully independent of the executive.

FOCUS QUESTION

In what ways do Mexican officeholders exercise power in addition to the powers formally granted to them by law?

The Executive

The President and the Cabinet

The presidency is the central institution of governance and policy-making in Mexico. Until the 1990s, the incumbent president always selected who would run as the PRI's next presidential candidate, appointed officials to all positions of power in the government and the party, and often named the candidates who almost automatically won elections as governors, senators, deputies, and local officials. Even with a non-PRI incumbent, the president continues to set the broad outlines of policy for the administration and has numerous resources to ensure that those policy preferences are adopted. Until the mid-1970s, Mexican presidents were considered above criticism in national politics and revered as symbols of national progress and well-being. Although economic and political events from the 1980s to the 2000s diminished presidential prestige and politicians are showing an increasing willingness to stand up to the chief executive in today's multiparty system, the extent of presidential power remains a legacy of the long period of PRI ascendance.

Mexican presidents have a set of formal powers that allows them to initiate legislation, lead in foreign policy, create government agencies, make policy by decree or through administrative regulations and procedures, and appoint a wide range of public officials. More important, informal powers provide them with the capacity to exert considerable control. The president manages a vast patronage machine for filling positions in government and initiates legislation and policies that were, until recently, routinely approved by the congress.

Under the PRI, presidents were always male and almost always members of the outgoing president's cabinet. Four of the five presidents who served between 1946 and 1976 had previously been ministers of the interior, with responsibility for the maintenance of law and order in the country. With the expansion of the government's role in economic development, candidates in the 1970s and 1980s were selected from the ministries that managed the economy. José López Portillo (1976–1982) had been minister of finance, and Miguel de la Madrid (1982–1988) and Carlos Salinas (1988–1994) had served as ministers of planning and budgeting. The selection of Luis Donaldo Colosio, who had been minister of social development and welfare, was thought by political observers to signal renewed concern with social problems. When Colosio was assassinated in 1994, the selection of Ernesto Zedillo, who had first been minister of planning and budgeting and then minister of education, was interpreted as reflecting an ongoing concern with social issues and as an effort to maintain the policies of economic liberalization that Salinas had introduced. With the victory of the PAN in 2000, this long tradition came to an end. Before running for president, Vicente Fox had been in business and had served as the governor of the state of Guanajuato. In 2006, Felipe Calderón became president; in his previous work, he served in congress and in the cabinet and was president of his political party.

Mexican presidential candidates since the mid-1970s have had impressive educational credentials and have tended to be trained in economics and management rather than in the traditional field of law. Presidents since López

technocrats career-minded bureaucrats who administer public policy according to a technical rather than a political rationale.

Portillo have had postgraduate training at elite institutions in the United States. By the 1980s, a topic of great debate in political circles was the extent to which a divide between *políticos* (politicians) and *técnicos* (**technocrats**) had emerged within the national political elite. Among the old guard of the PRI, there was open skepticism about the ability of young technocrats like Carlos Salinas and Ernesto Zedillo to manage political conditions in the country. During the presidential campaign of 1994, considerable efforts were made to stress the more humble origins of Colosio and Zedillo and the fact that they had had to work hard to get an education. Under Fox, the ties of the president to business elites raised similar fears that the government would not respond to the concerns of everyday citizens, a concern that was echoed in 2006 when Felipe Calderón was elected.

Once elected, the president moves quickly to name a cabinet. Under the PRI, he usually selected those with whom he had worked over the years as he rose to political prominence. He also used cabinet posts to ensure a broad coalition of support; he might, for example, appoint people with close ties to the labor movement, business interests, or some of the regional strongholds of the party. Only in rare exceptions were cabinet officials not active members of the PRI. When the PAN assumed the presidency, the selection of a cabinet and close advisers was more difficult. Until then, the party had elected officials only to state and local governments and to congress. As a consequence, the range of people with executive experience to whom Fox could turn was limited. He appointed U.S.-trained economists for his economic team and business executives for many other important posts. Few of these appointees had close ties to the PAN, and few had prior experience in government. Felipe Calderón's cabinet was more closely identified with those who had long histories as PAN party members. Over the years, few women have been selected for ministry-level posts—there are a handful of examples in recent administrations—and thus far they have only presided over agencies with limited influence over decision making, such as the ministries of tourism, ecology, and foreign relations.

The president has the authority to fill numerous other high-level positions, which allows him to provide policy direction and keep tabs on what is occurring throughout the government. The range of appointments that a chief executive can make means that each administration begins with extensive turnover of positions. Progress on the president's policy agenda can be slow during his first year in office as newly appointed officials learn the ropes and assemble their staffs. The president's power to make appointments provides him with the capacity to build a team of like-minded officials in government and ensure their loyalty. This system traditionally served the interests of presidents and the PRI well; under the PAN, given the limited number of its partisans who have experience at national levels, the system has not guaranteed the president as much power over the workings of the executive branch. In addition, with pressure mounting for a less politicized civil service in a more democratic Mexico, Fox committed himself to retaining qualified people in their positions and making many fewer changes than was customary. Under his administration, a civil service system was introduced, and was given added impetus under the administration of Felipe Calderón. The number of government officials who are incorporated into this system, however, remains limited.

Mexican presidents, though powerful, are not omnipotent. They must, for example, abide by a deeply held constitutional norm, fully adhered to since 1940, by stepping down at the end of their term, and they must adhere to tradition by removing themselves from the political limelight to allow their successors to assume full presidential leadership. All presidents, regardless of party, must demonstrate their loyalty to the myths and symbols of Mexican nationalism, such as the indigenous roots of much of its culture and the agrarian origins of the revolution, and they must make a rhetorical commitment to social justice and sovereignty in international affairs. Moreover, in the 1990s, President Zedillo relinquished a number of the traditional powers of the presidency. He announced, for example, that he would not select his PRI successor but would leave it up to the party to determine its candidate. In doing so, however, he created considerable conflict and tension since the PRI had to take on unaccustomed roles and politicians sought to fill the void left by the "abandonment" of presidential power. Fox inherited a system in which he was expected to set the policies and determine the priorities for a very wide range of government activity. Without a strong party in congress to back him or many experienced people in his government, he was often unable to deliver. Without strong presidential leadership, Mexico's government often seemed to flounder. On assuming office in December 2006, President Calderón initiated a major military and police campaign against drug lords and drug trafficking, in part as an effort to demonstrate his capacity to take decisive action and to be the kind of presidential leader that many Mexicans had hoped for under the previous administration.

The Bureaucracy

Mexico's executive branch is large and powerful. Almost 1.5 million people work in the federal bureaucracy, most of them in Mexico City. An additional 1 million work for the large number of state-owned industries and semiautonomous agencies of the government. State and local governments employ over 1.5 million people.

Officials at lower levels in the bureaucracy are unionized and protected by legislation that gives them job security and a range of benefits. At middle and upper levels, most officials are called "confidence employees"; they serve as long as their bosses have confidence in them. These officials have been personally appointed by their superiors. Their modest salaries are compensated for by the significant power that they can have over public affairs. For aspiring young professionals, a career in government is often attractive because of the challenge of dealing with important problems on a daily basis. Some employees also benefit from opportunities to take bribes or use other means to promote their personal interests. A new civil service system was introduced under President Fox, but, as yet, those who are part of the new system are a very small proportion of those who work in the public service.

The Para-Statal Sector

para-statals state-owned, or at least state-controlled, corporations, created to undertake a broad range of activities.

The **para-statal** sector—composed of semiautonomous or autonomous government agencies, many of which produce goods and services—was extremely large and powerful in Mexico. Because the government provided significant support for the development of the economy as part of its post-1940 development strategy, it engaged in numerous activities that in other countries are carried out by the private sector. Thus, until the Salinas administration, the country's largest steel mill was state-owned, as were the largest fertilizer producer, sugar mills, and airlines. In addition, the national electricity board still produces energy and supplies it at subsidized prices to industries. The state-owned petroleum company, PEMEX, grew to enormous proportions in the 1970s and 1980s under the impact of the oil boom. NAFIN, a state investment corporation, provides a considerable amount of investment capital for the country. At one point, a state marketing board called CONASUPO was responsible for the importation and purchase of the country's basic food supplies. In the 1970s, it played a major role in distributing food, credit, and farm implements in rural areas.

This large para-statal sector was significantly trimmed by the economic policy reforms that began in the 1980s. In 1970, there were 391 para-statal organizations in Mexico. By 1982, their number had grown to 1,155, in part because of the expansion of government activities under presidents Echeverría and López Portillo and in part because of the nationalization of private banks in 1982. Shortly afterward, concerted efforts were made to privatize many of these industries, including the telephone company, the national airlines, and the nationalized banks. By 1994, only 215 state-owned industries remained, and efforts continued to sell or liquidate many of them. However, some core components of the para-statal sector will likely remain in government hands for the foreseeable future because an influential bloc of nationalist political actors insist on the symbolic importance of public ownership of key industries. The Fox government, a partisan of the private sector, raised the possibility of privatizing PEMEX and the electricity board, but quickly retreated to very partial measures in the face of extensive opposition to private ownership of the "national patrimony."

Other State Institutions

FOCUS QUESTIONS

To what extent are state institutions like the military and the judiciary truly independent of the executive branch of government?

In what ways have these institutions promoted or hindered the growth of democracy in recent years?

The Military

Mexico is one of only a few countries in the developing world, particularly in Latin America, to have successfully marginalized the military from centers of political power. Although former military leaders dominated Mexican politics during the decades immediately after the Revolution of 1910, Calles, Cárdenas, and subsequent presidents laid the groundwork for civilian rule by introducing the practice of rotating regional military commands so that generals could not build up geographic bases of power. In addition, postrevolutionary leaders made an implicit bargain with the military leaders by providing them with opportunities to engage in business so that they did not look to political power as a way of gaining economic power. After 1946, the military no longer had institutional representation within the PRI and became clearly subordinate to civilian control. No military officer has held the presidency since that time.

This does not mean that the military has functioned outside politics. It has been called in from time to time to deal with domestic unrest: in rural areas in the 1960s, in Mexico City and other cities to repress student protest movements in 1968, in 1988 in the arrest of a powerful labor leader, in 1989 to break a labor strike, in 1990 to deal with protest over electoral fraud, in Chiapas beginning in late 1994, to manage the Mexico City police in 1997, and to move against drug lords in 2007. The military was also called in to deal with the aftermath of the earthquake in Mexico City in 1985, but its inadequate response to the emergency did little to enhance its reputation in the eyes of the public. In recent years, the military has been heavily involved in efforts to combat drug trafficking, and rumors abound about deals struck between military officials and drug barons. Such fears were confirmed when General Jesús Gutierrez Rebollo, the head of the antidrug task force, was arrested in 1997 on accusations of protecting a drug lord. When the PAN government made it possible for citizens to gain greater access to government information, it was discovered that the military had been involved in political repression, torture, and killing in the 1970s and 1980s. The scandal created by such revelations further lowered its reputation.

Whenever the military is called in to resolve domestic conflicts, some Mexicans become concerned that the institution is becoming politicized and may come to play a larger role in political decision making. Thus far, such fears have not been realized, and many believe that as long as civilian administrations are able to maintain the country's tradition of stability, the military will not intervene directly in politics. The fact that the country successfully observed the transfer of power from the PRI to the PAN also has increased a sense that the military will remain subordinate to civilian control.

The Judiciary

Unlike Anglo-American legal systems, Mexico's law derives from the Roman and Napoleonic tradition and is highly formalized and explicit. The Constitution of 1917 is a lengthy document that has been amended many times and contains references to a wide range of civil rights, including items as broad as the right to a healthy environment. Because Mexican law tends to be very explicit and because there are no punitive damages allowed in court cases, there are fewer lawsuits than in the United States. One important exception to this is the *amparo*, whereby individual citizens may ask for a writ of protection claiming that their constitutional rights have been violated by specific government actions or laws.

There are federal and state courts in Mexico. The federal system is composed of the Supreme Court, which decides the most important cases in the country; circuit courts, which take cases on appeal; and district courts, where all cases enter the system. As in the United States, Supreme Court justices are nominated by the president and approved by the Senate. Since most of the important laws in Mexico are federal, state courts have played a subordinate role.

However, this is changing. As Mexican states become more independent from the federal government, state law has been experiencing tremendous growth. In addition, there are many important specialized federal courts, such as labor courts, military courts, and electoral courts.

Like other political institutions in Mexico, the judiciary was for many decades politically, though not constitutionally, subordinate to the executive. The courts occasionally slowed the actions of government by issuing *amparos*; however, in almost every case in which the power of government or the president was at stake, the courts ruled on the side of the government. The Zedillo administration tried to change this by emphasizing the rule of law over that of powerful individuals. Increasing interest in human rights issues by citizens' groups and the media has added pressure to the courts to play a stronger role in protecting basic freedoms. Zedillo's refusal to interfere with the courts' judgments also strengthened the judiciary. This tendency continued under Fox and Calderón, with increasing evidence of judicial independence. Nevertheless, the judicial system remains the weakest branch of government.

Subnational Government

As with many other aspects of the Mexican political system, regional and local government in Mexico is quite different from what is described in the constitution. Mexico has a federal system, and each state has its own constitution, executive, unicameral legislature, and judiciary. Municipalities (equivalent to U.S. counties) are governed by popularly elected mayors and councils. But most state and municipal governments are poor. Most of the funds they command come to them from the central government, and they have little legal or administrative capacity to raise their own revenue. States and localities also suffer greatly from the lack of well-trained and well-paid public officials. As at the national level, many jobs are distributed as political patronage, but even officials who are motivated to be responsive to local needs are often ill equipped to do so. Since the early 1990s, the government has made several serious efforts to decentralize and devolve more power to state and local governments. At times, governors and mayors have resisted such initiatives because they meant that regional and local governments would have to manage much more complex activities and be the focus of demands from public sector workers and their unions. Local governments were also worried that they would be unable to acquire the budgetary resources necessary to carry out their new responsibilities.

There are exceptions to this picture of regional and local government impoverishment and lack of capacity. The governments of some northern states, such as Nuevo León, have been more responsive to local needs and better able to administer public services. In such states, local municipalities have become famous for the extent to which they differ from the norm in most of Mexico. The city of Monterrey, for example, has a reputation for efficient and forward-looking municipal government. Much of this local capacity can be credited to a regional political tradition that has stressed independence from—and even hostility to—Mexico City and the PRI. In addition, states and localities that have stronger governments and a tradition of better service tend to be areas of greater wealth, largely in the north of the country. In these cases, entrepreneurial groups and private citizens have often invested time and resources in state and local government.

Until 1988, all governors were from the PRI, although many believe that only electoral fraud kept two governorships out of the hands of an opposition party in 1986. Finally, in 1989, a non-PRI governor assumed power in Baja California, an important first. By late 2005, thirteen states and the Federal District were governed by parties other than the PRI. Also, municipalities have increasingly been the focus of authentic party competition. As opposition parties came to control these levels of government, they were challenged to improve services such as police protection, garbage collection, sanitation, and education. PRI-dominated governments have also tried to improve their performance because they are now more threatened by the possibility of losing elections.

The Policy-Making Process

FOCUS QUESTIONS

In what ways does the six-year presidency vary the rhythm of policy change in Mexico? In what ways does this rhythm accompany the expansion or decline of democracy?

The Mexican system is very dependent on the quality of its leadership and on presidential understanding of how economic and social policies can affect the development of the country. As indicated throughout this chapter, the six-year term of office, the *sexenio*, is an extremely important fact of political life in Mexico. New presidents can introduce extensive change in positions within the government. They are able to bring in their own people, who in turn build teams of *their* people within ministries, agencies, and party networks. This generally provides the president with a group of high- and middle-level officials who share a general orientation toward public policy and are motivated to carry out his goals. When the PRI was the dominant party, these officials believed that in following presidential leadership, they enhanced their chances for upward political mobility. In such a context, even under a single party, it was likely that changes in public policies could be introduced every six years, creating innovation or discontinuity, or both. As indicated, the limited experience of the PAN in executive office and the increasing role of congress in policy-making meant that the influence of the president on government became less strong after 2000. Nevertheless, Mexicans continue to look to the president and the executive branch for policy leadership.

Together with the bureaucracy, the president is the focal point of policy formulation and political management. Until 1997, the legislature always had a PRI majority and acted as a rubber stamp for presidentially sponsored legislation. Since then, the congress has proven to be a more active policy-maker, blocking and forcing the negotiation of legislation, and even introducing its own bills. The president's skills in negotiating, managing the opposition, using the media to acquire public support, and maneuvering within the bureaucracy can be important to ensure that his program is fully endorsed.

Significant limits on presidential power occur when policy is being implemented. In fact, in areas as diverse as the regulation of working conditions, antipollution laws, tax collection, election monitoring, and health care in remote rural areas, Mexico has extremely advanced legislation on the books. Yet the persistence of unsafe factory conditions, pollution in Mexico City, tax evasion, electoral fraud, and poor health care suggests that legislation is not always translated into practice. At times, policies are not implemented because public officials at the lower levels disagree with them or make deals with affected interests in order to benefit personally. This is the case, for example, with taxes that remain uncollected because individuals or corporations bribe officials to overlook them. In other cases, lower-level officials may lack the capacity or skills to implement some policies, such as those directed toward improving education or rural development services. For various reasons, Mexican presidents cannot always deliver on their intentions. Traditionally, Mexican citizens have blamed lower-level officials for such slippage, but exempting the president from responsibility for what does or does not occur during his watch has become much less common since the 1970s.

Summary

On paper, Mexico's government is modeled on that of the United States, with three branches of government, checks and balances among them, and federalism defining the relationship between national, state, and local governments. In practice, however, the country developed a political system that concentrated most power in the hands of the president and the executive branch and managed political conflict through a dominant party. Much of the power of the president and the PRI was based on their capacity to use patronage to respond to political conflicts. This system is undergoing rapid change, as the legislature and court systems develop more independent roles, state and local governments acquire more independence, and the PRI no longer dominates the party system.

Representation and Participation

Mexico has had a relatively peaceful history since the revolution. Throughout this long history, the political system has emphasized compromise among contending elites, behind-the-scenes conflict resolution, and distribution of political rewards to those willing to play by the formal and informal rules of the game. It has also responded, if reluctantly and defensively, to demands for change.

Often, citizens are best able to interact with the government through a variety of informal means rather than through the formal processes of elections, campaigns, and interest group lobbying.

FOCUS QUESTIONS

Since the early 1980s, how has the balance of power shifted between the

The Legislature

Under the old reign of the PRI in Mexico, opposition to presidential initiatives by Mexico's two-chamber legislature, the Senate and the Chamber of Deputies, was rarely heard. If representatives did not agree with policies, they counted on legislative and executive branches of government? How do these shifts correspond to changes in the overall political landscape?

the fact that policy implementation was flexible and allowed for after-the-fact bending of the rules or disregard of measures that were harmful to important interests.

Members of the Mexican congress are elected through a dual system of "first past the post" (that is, the candidate with the most votes wins) and proportional representation. Each state elects three senators. Two of them are determined by majority vote, and the third is determined by whichever party receives the second-highest number of votes. In addition, thirty-two senators are determined nationally through a system of proportional representation that awards seats based on the number of votes cast for each party. Senators serve six-year terms. The same type of electoral system works in the Chamber of Deputies, with 300 selected on the basis of majority vote and 200 additional representatives chosen by proportional representation. Deputies are elected for three-year terms.

The PRI's grip on the legislature was broken in 1988. The growing strength of opposition parties, combined with legislation that provided for greater representation of minority parties in the congress, led to the election of 240 opposition deputies (out of 500) that year, depriving the PRI of the two-thirds majority it needed for major pieces of legislation or constitutional amendments. The two-thirds PRI majority was returned in 1991 and presidentialism was reasserted. Nevertheless, the strong presence of opposition parties continued to encourage debate as PRI delegates were challenged to defend proposed legislation. In 1997, the PRI lost its majority when 261 deputies were elected from opposition parties.

Since the late 1990s, the role of congress in the policy process has been strengthened considerably.[12] The cost of greater power sharing between the executive and the legislature, however, has been to stall the policy process. Under the Fox administration, the president had a difficult time promoting his investment plan, labor code reform, and the liberalization of the energy sector. As a consequence of muscle flexing, congressional committees that once were important only for their control over patronage have acquired new relevance, and committee members and chairs are becoming somewhat more like their U.S. counterparts. Party caucuses have also emerged as centers of power in the legislature. Calderón, elected president in 2006, faced a significant challenge in building a coalition across parties to support his policies, because no party had a clear majority in the congress.

FOCUS QUESTIONS

What are the power bases of the main political parties in Mexican politics? As these power bases have grown stronger or weaker, what has happened to the political parties they support?

Political Parties and the Party System

Even under the long reign of the PRI, a number of political parties existed in Mexico. By the mid-1980s, some of them were attracting more political support, a trend that continued into the 1990s and 2000s. Electoral reforms made it easier for opposition parties to contest elections and win seats in the legislature. In 1990, an electoral commission was created to regulate campaigns and elections. In 1996 it became fully independent of the government. Now all parties receive funding from the government and have access to the media.

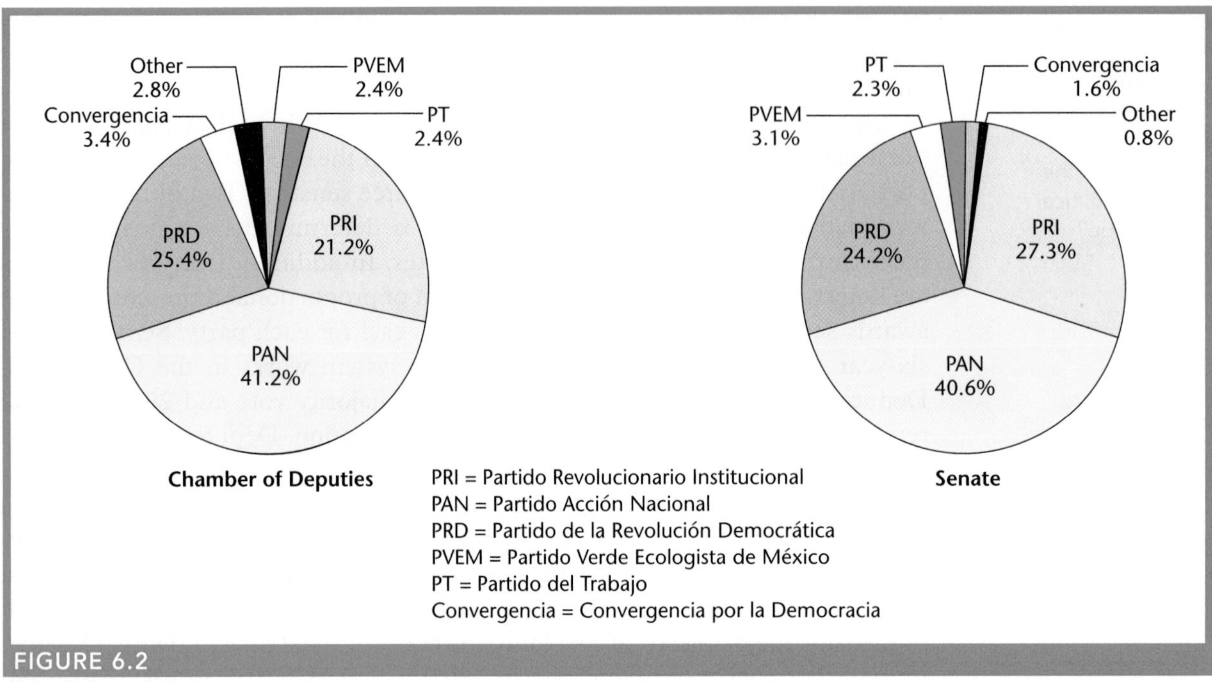

FIGURE 6.2

Congressional Representation by Party

Source: CIA World Factbook, http://www.cia.gov/cia/publications.factbook/geos/mx.html; see also http://www.senado.gob.mx and http://camaradediputados.gob.mx.

The PRI

In the 1930s, the forerunner of the PRI incorporated a wide array of interests, becoming a mass-based party that drew support from all classes in the population. Over seven decades, its principal activities were to generate support for the government, organize the electorate to vote for its candidates, and distribute jobs and resources in return for loyalty to the system.

Until the 1990s, party organization was based largely on the corporate representation of class interests. Labor was represented within party councils by the Confederation of Mexican Workers (CTM). Peasants were represented by the National Peasant Confederation (CNC). The so-called popular sector, comprising small businesses, community-based groups, and public employees, had less internal cohesion but was represented by the National Confederation of Popular Organizations (CNOP). Of the three, the CTM was consistently the best organized and most powerful. Traditionally, the PRI's strongest support came from the countryside, where *ejidatarios* and independent small farmers were grateful for and dependent on rewards of land or jobs. As the country became more urbanized, the support base provided by rural communities remained important to the PRI. But it produced many fewer votes than were necessary to keep the party in power.

Within its corporate structures, the PRI functioned through extended networks that distributed public resources—particularly jobs, land, development projects, and access to public services—to lower-level activists who controlled

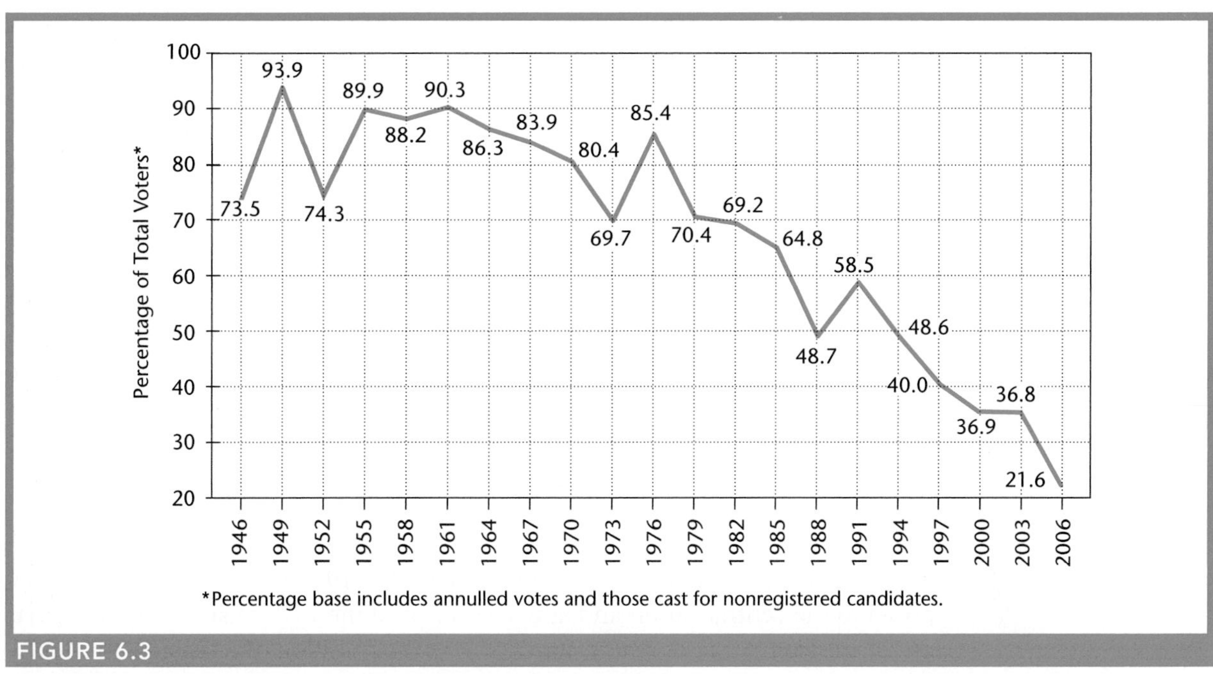

FIGURE 6.3

PRI Support in Congressional Elections, 1946–2003

Sources: For 1946–1988: Juan Molinar Horcasitas, *El Tiempo de la legtimidad: Elecciones, autoritarismo y democracia en México* (México, D.F.: Cal y Arena, 1991). For 1991: Secretaría Nacional de Estudios, Partido Acción Nacional, *Análisis del Proceso Federal Electoral 1994, 1995.* For 1994: Instituto Federal Electoral, *Estadística de las Elecciones Federales de 1994, Compendio de Resultados* (Mexico, D.F., 1995). For 1997: http://www.ife.org.mx/ww-worge/tablas/mrent.htm. For 2000 and 2003: Instituto Federal Electoral, http://www.ife.org.mx. Figures for 2003 include votes received by the Alianza para Todos (Alliance for Everyone), which brought the PRI and the much smaller PVEM together on a single ticket in some states.

votes at the local level. In this system, those with ambitions to public office or to positions within the PRI put together networks of supporters from above (patrons), to whom they delivered votes, and supporters from below (clients), who traded allegiance for access to public resources. For well over half a century, this system worked extremely well (see Figure 6.3). Although the PRI became much weaker in the 1980s and 1990s, it was still the only political party that could boast a network of constituency organizations in virtually every village and urban community in the country.

Within the PRI, power was centralized, and the sector organizations (the CTM, the CNC, and the CNOP) responded primarily to elites at the top of the political pyramid rather than to member interests. Over time, the corporate interest group organizations, particularly the CTM and the CNC, became widely identified with corruption, bossism, centralized control, and lack of effective participation. When the administrations of de la Madrid, Salinas, and Zedillo imposed harsh austerity measures, the PRI was held responsible for the resulting losses in incomes and benefits. Simultaneously, as the government cut back sharply on public sector jobs and services, the PRI had far fewer resources to distribute to maintain its traditional bases of support.

As the PRI faced greater competition from other parties and continued to suffer from declining popularity, efforts were made to restructure and reform it. Party conventions were introduced in an effort to democratize the internal workings of the party, and some states and localities began to hold primaries to select PRI candidates, a significant departure from the old system of selection by party bosses.

The PRI continues to face a difficult future. Voters are younger, better educated, more middle class, and more likely to live in urban areas than they were in the days of the PRI's greatest success. With the vast majority of the country's population now living in cities, the PRI will have to win the support of more urban voters in order to remain a relevant political force. That task looks all the more difficult after the historic election of 2000. Not only did opposition campaigns tap into a deep well of resentment against evidence of corruption and mismanagement in the PRI, but Fox's victory stripped the party of the aura of invincibility that had helped to cement its dominance of Mexican politics for decades. In 2006, the PRI's candidate for president won only 22 percent of the vote.

The PAN

The National Action Party (PAN) was founded in 1939 to represent interests opposed to the centralization and anticlericalism of the PRI. Historically, this party has been strongest in northern states, where the tradition of resistance to Mexico City is also strongest. It has also been primarily an urban party of the middle class and is closely identified with the private sector. The PAN has traditionally campaigned on a platform endorsing greater regional autonomy, less government intervention in the economy, reduced regulation of business, clean and fair elections, rapprochement with the Catholic Church, and support for private and religious education. When PRI governments of the 1980s and 1990s moved toward market-friendly and export-oriented policies, policy differences were significantly reduced. Nevertheless, a major difference of perspectives about religion continued to characterize the two parties. The PAN has always favored a closer relationship with the Catholic Church.

In the early 1980s, and especially after President López Portillo nationalized the banks, opposition to centralism and state control of the economy grew more popular. The PAN began to develop greater capacity to contest elections at higher levels of government. In particular, the party gained popularity among urban middle-class voters, won elections in several provincial cities, and came close to winning governorships in two states. By late 2005, the PAN controlled the governorships in nine states, and in one more the governor had been elected as the candidate of an alliance between the PAN and another political party (see below). And, of course, the PAN won the presidency in 2000 with 42.7 percent of the total vote.

The PAN has traditionally set relatively high standards for activism among its party members; as a consequence, the membership of the party has remained small, even as its capacity to attract votes has grown.

President Fox hoped that mid-term congressional elections in 2003 would return a PAN majority. Instead, many voters expressed their frustration with the administration's lack of effectiveness by casting their ballots for non-PAN candidates. In 2006, the party won 35.9 percent of the vote, only 0.6 percent ahead of his main rival, the candidate of the PRD.

TABLE 6.3

Voting in Presidential Elections, 1934–2006

Year	Votes for PRI Candidate[a]	Votes for PAN Candidate	Votes for All Others[b]	Turnout (% Voters Among Eligible Adults)[c]
1934	98.2%	—	1.8%	53.6%
1940	93.9	—	6.1	57.5
1946	77.9	—	22.1	42.6
1952	74.3	7.8%	17.9	57.9
1958	90.4	9.4	0.2	49.4
1964	88.8	11.1	0.1	54.1
1970	83.3	13.9	1.4	63.9
1976[d]	93.6	—	1.2	29.6
1982	71.0	15.7	9.4	66.1
1988	50.7	16.8	32.5[e]	49.4[f]
1994	50.1	26.7	23.2	77.16
2000	36.1	42.5[g]	19.2[h]	64.0
2006	22.2	35.9	35.3 for the PRD, 6.6 percent for all others	58.1

[a]From 1958 through 1982, includes votes cast for the Partido Popular Socialista (PPS) and the Partido Auténtico de la Revolución Mexicana (PARM), both of which regularly endorsed the PRI's presidential candidate. In 1988, they supported opposition candidate Cuauhtémoc Cárdenas.

[b]Excludes annulled votes; includes votes for candidates of nonregistered parties.

[c]Eligible population base for 1934 through 1952 includes all males ages 20 and over (legal voting age: 21 years). Both men and women ages 20 and over are included in the base for 1958 and 1964 (women received the franchise in 1958). The base for 1970–1988 includes all males and females ages 18 and over (the legal voting age was lowered to 18, effective 1970).

[d]The PRI candidate, José Lopez Portillo, ran virtually unopposed because the PAN failed to nominate a candidate. The only other significant candidate was Valentín Campa, representing the Communist Party, which was not legally registered to participate in the 1976 election. More than 5 percent of the votes were annulled.

[e]Includes 31.1 percent officially tabulated for Cuauhtémoc Cárdenas.

[f]Estimated using data from the Federal Electoral Commission. However, the commission itself has released two different figures for the number of eligible voters in 1988. Using the commission's larger estimate of eligible population, the turnout would be 44.9 percent.

[g]Votes cast for Alianza por el Cambio, formed by the Partido Acción Nacional (PAN) and the Partido Verde Ecologista de Mexico (PVEM).

[h]Includes votes cast for Alianza por México, formed by the Partido de la Revolución Democrática (PRD), the Partido del Trabajo (PT), Convergencia por la Democracia, the Partido Alianza Social (PAS), and the Partido de la Sociedad Nacionalista (PSN).

Sources:

From *Comparative Politics Today: A World View*, 4th ed. by Gabriel Almond and G. Bingham Powell, Jr. Copyright ©1988. Reprinted by permission of Addison-Wesley Educational Publishers, Inc. For 1994: Instituto Federal Electoral, *Estadística de las Elecciones Federales de 1994, Compendio de Resultados* (Mexico, D.F., 1995). For 2000 and 2006: Instituto Federal Electoral, www.ife.org.mx.

The PRD

Another significant challenge to the PRI has come from the Democratic Revolutionary Party (PRD), a populist and nationalist alternative to the PRI whose policies are left of center. Its candidate in the 1988 and 1994 elections was Cuauhtémoc Cárdenas, the son of Mexico's most famous and revered president. He was a PRI insider until party leaders virtually ejected him for demanding internal reform of the party and a platform emphasizing social justice. In the 1988 elections, Cárdenas was officially credited with winning 31.1 percent of the vote, and his party captured 139 seats in the Chamber of Deputies. He benefited from massive political defection from the PRI and garnered support from workers disaffected with the boss-dominated unions as well as from peasants who remembered his father's concern for agrarian reform and the welfare of the poor.

Even while the votes were being counted, the party began to denounce widespread electoral fraud and to claim that Cárdenas would have won if the election had been honest. Considerable public opinion supported the party's challenge. In the aftermath of the 1988 elections, then, it seemed that the PRD was a strong contender to become Mexico's second most powerful party.

However, in the aftermath of these elections, the party was plagued by internal divisions. By 1994, it still lagged far behind the PRI and the PAN in establishing and maintaining the local constituency organizations needed to mobilize votes and monitor the election process. In addition, the PRD found it difficult to define an appropriate left-of-center alternative to the market-oriented policies carried out by the government. Although the claims that such policies ignored the need for social justice were popular, policies to respond to poverty that did not imply a return to unpopular government intervention were difficult to devise. In the aftermath of the Colosio assassination, citizens also became more alarmed about violence, and some were concerned that the level of political rivalry represented by the PRD threatened the country's long-term political stability.

Thanks to the government's continued unpopular economic policies and the leadership of a successful grass-roots mobilizer named Andrés Manuel López Obrador, who was elected to head the party in 1996, the PRD began to stage a remarkable turnaround. Factional bickering was controlled, and organizational discipline increased. In addition, the PRD proved successful in moving beyond its regional strongholds and established itself as a truly national party. In 2000, López Obrador was elected mayor of Mexico City with 39.5 percent of the vote, signaling again the political importance of the capital city. The PRD retained 16 seats in the Senate, but lost 58 in the Chamber of Deputies, holding only 67 seats.

Thanks largely to its control over the capital city and the existence of PRD administrations on the municipal level in parts of the country, the party was able to boast that about a quarter of the country's population lived under a PRD government. Although it continues to occupy fewer offices than the other two major parties, the party garnered 35.3 percent of the vote for its candidate in the 2006 presidential elections, former Mexico City mayor Andrés Manuel López

Obrador, who challenged the Federal Electoral Institute to recount the vote because it was so close.

Other Parties

A number of smaller parties contest elections in Mexico. In 2003, the Green Ecologist Party of Mexico (PVEM), the Labor Party (PT), and Convergence for Democracy (Convergencia) each won between 2.3 and 4.0 percent of the vote for congressional seats. Small parties usually do win a few of the seats in the Chamber of Deputies and the Senate that are filled by proportional representation. Also, these groups sometimes wield influence on national politics by forming alliances with the larger parties, either endorsing their candidates for president or governor in national and state elections or backing a single slate of candidates for congress.

FOCUS QUESTIONS

Why have Mexican elections, at all levels, generally become fairer and more contentious? What does this imply about the ability of Mexican political institutions to adapt to changing social conditions?

Elections

Each of the three main political parties draws voters from a wide and overlapping spectrum of the electorate. Nevertheless, a typical voter for the PRI is likely to be from a rural area or small town, to have less education, and to be older and poorer than voters for the other parties. A typical voter for the PAN is likely to be from a northern state, to live in an urban area, to be a middle-class professional, to have a comfortable lifestyle, and to have a high school or even a university education. A typical voter for the PRD is likely to be young, to be a political activist, to have an elementary or high school education, to live in one of the central states, and to live in a small town or an urban area. The support base for the PRI is the most vulnerable to economic and demographic changes in the country. Voting for opposition parties is an urban phenomenon, and Mexico continues to urbanize at the rate of 3 percent per year.

Elections are becoming more competitive and fairer in Mexico. Now all parties receive government funding and have guaranteed access to the media. These and other laws that limit campaign spending and campaign contributions were a response to demands that the government level the playing field between the PRI and the other parties. Voter registration was reformed to ensure that fraud would be more detectable. Election monitoring was also strengthened, and another reform increased the chances for opposition parties to win representation in the Senate. Some state and local elections continue to be questioned, however, especially in rural areas in the south, where local PRI bosses remain powerful.

FOCUS QUESTIONS

What are the essential rules of the game in Mexican political life?

Political Culture, Citizenship, and Identity

Most citizens in Mexico demonstrate overall commitment to the political system while expressing considerable criticism about how it works. Many criticize corruption in government, but remain proud that their country has become more democratic.

Campaigning with Comic Books

Political leaders have found they must find new and imaginative ways to communicate with voters and to seek their backing. As clientelist networks decline, candidates for public office and government officials are increasingly turning to strategies used in other democratic systems to win support for themselves and their programs. For example, public opinion polling and elaborate marketing plans are now becoming important tools for Mexican politicians who previously relied on patronage and strategies of co-optation and accommodation.

Some politicians are also reaching out to their constituents in a distinctly Mexican way: through comic books. Although the comic books published by officials and aspirants to higher office tend to be less lurid and suggestive than the enormously popular pocket-sized publications sold throughout the country, they reach a wide audience since they are generally distributed free of charge.

Mexico City Mayor Andrés Manuel López Obrador of the left-of-center Democratic Revolutionary Party (PRD) was among the first to use comic books. In a series entitled *Stories of the City*, the popular head of the government of the Federal District is depicted as a defender of the poor and downtrodden residents of the capital. Later, when allegations of corruption in his administration threatened to derail the mayor's bid for the presidency in 2006, the municipal government issued another edition of *Stories of the City* to expose what it called "the dark forces against López Obrador." President Vicente Fox also recognized the usefulness of comic books. In 2002, faced with the widespread perception that his administration had failed to bring about substantial change, the president's office commissioned a comic book called *July 2nd: Now Nobody Will Stop Change in Mexico!* in which a group of university students convince skeptical classmates that the date of Fox's election—July 2, 2000—was a historic milestone. After discussing the various achievements of the Fox administration, the students conclude that the president "always speaks openly, is honest, and works every day for the good of all Mexicans." Mexican political comic books have even had an impact in the realm of international affairs. When the Mexican foreign ministry issued a comic book–style *Guide for the Mexican Migrant* late in 2004, a number of U.S. legislators complained that the Mexican government appeared to be offering its citizens tips on how to flout American immigration laws. Although the publication noted that the safest way to travel abroad was with a passport and a visa, it also explained how to avoid dehydration when passing through remote desert regions and how to reduce the danger of drowning when crossing rivers. The Mexican Foreign Ministry insisted that the guide had been prepared for humanitarian reasons.

Politicians and government agencies alike have recognized that comic books can be an effective way to reach a large number of Mexican citizens. The speed with which publications of this sort have proliferated shows the resourcefulness of Mexican political actors as they seek to adapt to a new political landscape that is more competitive and open and that places more of a premium on successful communication with the citizenry. ❖

To what extent do they promote or hinder political participation by a broad range of the population?

Most Mexicans understand the informal rules of the game in Mexican politics, which have helped maintain political stability despite extensive inequalities in economic and political power. Clientelism has long been a form of participation in the sense that through their connections, many people, even the poorest, are able to interact with public officials and get something out of the political system. This informal system is a fundamental reason that many Mexicans continued to vote for the PRI for so long.

However, new ways of interacting with government are emerging. They coexist along with the old clientelistic style. An increasing number of citizens are seeking to negotiate with the government on the basis of citizenship rights, not personal patron-client relationships. The movements that emerged in the 1980s sought to form broad but loose coalitions with other organizations and attempted to identify and work with reform-oriented public officials. Their suspicion of traditional political organizations such as the PRI and its affiliates also led them to avoid close alliances with other parties, such as the PAN and the PRD.

In the past, public opinion polling was often contaminated by the dominance of the PRI. Some polling organizations were even subsidized by the party or the government. Increasingly, however, even the PRI and the government are interested in objective analysis of public opinion. These data have influenced the content and timing of government decisions and the development of strategies in election campaigns. In the past, it was not easy for newspapers, magazines, or radio and television stations to be openly opposed to the government. For many years, the government used access to newsprint, which it controlled, to reward sympathetic news coverage and penalize coverage it considered hostile. In addition, the government and ambitious officials paid stipends to reporters who covered their activities favorably. A considerable amount of the revenue of newspapers and other media organizations came from advertising placed by the government.

As with other aspects of Mexican politics, the media became more independent in the 1980s.[13] There are currently several major television networks in the country, and many citizens have access to CNN and other global networks. The number of newspapers is expanding, as is their circulation, and several news magazines play the same role in Mexico that *Time* and *Newsweek* do in the United States.

FOCUS QUESTIONS

Why has the notion of accommodation played such an important role in Mexican political life?

In what ways has it hindered or promoted the development of stable political institutions?

Interests, Social Movements, and Protest

The Mexican system has long responded to groups of citizens through pragmatic **accommodation** to their interests. Even when open conflict has occurred, it has generally been met with efforts to find some kind of compromise solution. Accommodation has been particularly apparent in response to the interests of business. Although elites were the primary beneficiaries of the country's development, they were never directly incorporated into the PRI. Instead, elites represent themselves through business-focused interest groups and personal relationships with influential officials.

accommodation an informal agreement or settlement between the government and important interest groups that is responsive to the interest groups' concerns for policy or program benefits.

Wage levels for unionized workers grew fairly consistently between 1940 and 1982, when the economic crisis caused a significant drop in wages. At the same time, labor interests received concrete benefits and limitations on the rights of employers to discipline or dismiss workers. Union leaders controlled their rank and file to strengthen their own power to negotiate with government. At the same time, they sought benefits for workers who continued to provide support for the PRI. The power of the union bosses has declined, in part because the unions are weaker than in the past, in part because union members are demanding greater democratization, and in part because the PRI no longer monopolizes political power.

co-optation incorporating activists into the system while accommodating some of their concerns.

Under the PRI, accommodation was often coupled with **co-optation** as a means of incorporating dissidents into the system so that they did not threaten its continuity. In 1968, for example, students protesting against authoritarianism, poverty, and inequity challenged the government just before the opening of the Olympic games. The government responded with force—in one instance killing several hundred students in Mexico City—sparking even greater animosity. When Luis Echeverría became president in 1970, he recruited large numbers of the student activists into his administration. He also dramatically increased spending on social services, putting many of the young people to work in expanding antipoverty programs in the countryside and in urban slums. Through these actions, a generation of political and social activists was incorporated into the system, and there was some accommodation to their concerns. We also know now, however, that his government allowed the military to kidnap, arrest, torture, and kill some political dissidents.

The country also has a tradition of civic organizations that operate at community and local levels with considerable independence from politics. Many of their activities are not explicitly political, although they may have political implications in that they encourage individuals to work together to find solutions to problems or to organize around common interests. Other organizational experiences are more clearly political. The student movement of 1968 provided evidence that civil society in Mexico had the potential to challenge the power of the state. The emergence of independent unionism in the 1970s was another indication of renewed willingness to question the right of the state to stifle dissenting voices.

In October 1983, as many as 2 million people participated in a civic strike to call attention to the economic crisis and demand a forceful government response. In urban areas, citizen groups demanded land rights in squatter settlements, as well as housing, infrastructure, and urban services. They made these claims as rights of citizenship, not as a reward for loyalty to the PRI.[14]

Women, with a strong cultural role as caretakers of the home, have begun to mobilize in many cities to demand community services, equal pay, legal equality, and opportunities in business traditionally denied them.[15] Religious groups, both Catholic and Protestant, have begun to demand greater government attention to problems of poverty and inequity, as well as more government tolerance of religious education and religious practices. In the early 1990s, the government's social development program, which many critics claim was an initiative by President Salinas to win back respect for his government after the flawed elections of 1988, helped organize thousands of grass-roots organizations and may have contributed to a trend toward broader mobilization independent of PRI clientelist networks.[16]

In the countryside, too, rural organizations in the 1980s demanded greater independence from government and the leaders of the PRI and the CNC (the national peasant association).[17] Since 1994, the rebels in Chiapas have become a focal point for broad alliances of those concerned about the rights of indigenous groups (ethnic minorities) and rural poverty. Indigenous groups have also emerged to demand that government respond to their needs and respect their traditions.

The U.S. Connection

Civic Engagement in Mexico and the United States

The United States has long been noted as a country with active citizen engagement in public life. This is particularly true at the local level, where citizens regularly become involved in local school and environmental committees, community development and beautification initiatives, clean-up and health drives, and other public activities. In Mexico, civic life tends to be more limited. Mexicans vote regularly and are often actively engaged in election campaigns. Beyond this, however, they have had fewer opportunities than their U.S. counterparts to contribute to public discussion and decision making, or to work together to achieve public benefits.

Of course, on some occasions, Mexican citizens have become powerful actors in political life. The Revolution of 1910 is one such occasion, as was the mobilization of peasants and workers in the 1930s, the student rebellion of the late 1960s, and the organization of urban residents around issues of public services, security, and the environment that began in the 1980s. In general, however, for most of the time, most Mexicans were not joiners or activists in public life.

Most recently, however, civic life in Mexico has become much more active. Throughout the country, in small towns as well as big cities, in rural areas as well as in industrial zones, Mexicans are joining a multitude of civic organizations concerned about issues such as effective participation in government decision making, accountability in government, human rights violations, citizen rights, local improvement, and the costs of public services.

This trend has been spurred in part by the emergence, since the early 1990s, of more competitive electoral campaigns. Increasingly, citizens believe that they can communicate their concerns to those running for office and that they have the capacity to hold elected officials accountable for their actions. At the same time, the country is experimenting with a greater degree of government decentralization, and local governments are taking on much responsibility to provide public goods and services. In this regard, government is now closer to citizens and they are beginning to realize that they can have important input into policies and practices that directly affect their lives: the quality of their local environment, security, economic opportunities, the use of public spaces, and the allocation of resources for municipal improvements. Also, a wide network of nongovernmental organizations concerned about public affairs has become much more evident in recent years and is drawing members from across the country.

Mexico is developing more democratic institutions. As it does so, its citizens are learning new ways of organizing and affecting the decisions that their governments make. From a heritage of a relatively low level of citizen engagement, Mexicans are looking more like their North American neighbors when it comes to organizing and attempting to influence the performance and policies of government. ❖

Summary

Democratic politics is growing stronger in Mexico. The elections of 2000 and 2006 demonstrated that a transition of power from a civilian authoritarian regime to a more democratic one could take place relatively peacefully. The causes of this important change emerged gradually, as Mexican citizens developed the capacity to question the dominance of the PRI regime and as the government introduced important changes that opened up opportunities for opposition parties to develop and for people to vote more easily for these parties.

Mexican Migration to the United States

The contrast between the poverty of much of the developing world and the prosperity of industrialized nations is nowhere more vividly displayed than along the 2,000-mile-long border between Mexico and the United States. Because of the economic disparities between the two neighboring countries, Mexicans with limited opportunities at home have long been venturing north of the border. The money that these migrants send back to Mexico helps to sustain not just their own families but entire regions that have been left behind by the country's uneven pattern of growth and development.

Mexicans began moving to the United States in substantial numbers late in the nineteenth century. Although some of these early migrants found work in northern industrial centers such as Chicago, most settled in California and Texas, where they joined Mexican communities that had been there since the days when the American southwest had been part of Mexico. Even greater numbers of migrants began to arrive during World War II, when the U.S. government allowed Mexican workers, known as *braceros*, to enter the country to provide much-needed manpower for strategic production efforts. The *bracero* program remained in place after the war, and under it, a predominantly male Mexican work force provided seasonal labor to U.S. employers, mostly in agriculture.

After the *bracero* program ended in 1964, Mexicans continued to seek work in the United States, despite the fact that most then had to enter the country illegally. To a large extent, the U.S. government informally tolerated the employment of undocumented migrants until the 1980s. The 1986 Immigration Reform and Control Act (IRCA) allowed migrants who had been in the United States for a long period of time to gain legal residency rights. but it called for tighter controls on immigration in the future.

However, IRCA and subsequent efforts to deter illegal immigration simply turned a pattern of seasonal migration into a flow of migrants that settled permanently north of the border. Before 1986, most Mexican migrant workers left their families at home and worked in the United States for only a few months at a time before returning home. But many of the seasonal migrants who gained amnesty under IRCA then sent for their families to join them, creating a more permanent immigrant community. Also, with increased vigilance and new barriers making the crossing of the border more difficult, more of the migrants who arrived in the United States decided to remain there rather than risk apprehension by traveling back and forth between the two countries. High-profile efforts to patrol the border led migrants to use more remote crossing points. Although the number of Mexicans who died trying to reach the United States increased, the overall rate of illegal immigration was not affected by the government's crackdown. The U.S. government has also responded to illegal immigration with an initiative to build a wall along the border separating the two countries.

In the 1990s, growing Mexican communities in the United States spread into areas such as North Carolina, Georgia, Arkansas, and Iowa, where few Mexicans had lived before. These communities also mobilized politically to resist anti-immigrant legislative initiatives.

Their political importance in Mexico has reached unprecedented heights as officials recognize the critical importance to the Mexican economy of the $16.6 billion that the country receives each year in remittances from migrants working in other countries. Mexican governors, mayors, and federal officials now regularly visit representatives of migrant groups in the United States, often seeking their support and funding for projects at home. Moreover, a 1996 law allowing Mexicans to hold dual citizenship could allow many Mexican migrants to have a voice in the governance of both countries. In 2005, Mexican legislators finally approved a system under which registered Mexican voters living abroad could participate in federal elections using mail-in ballots. It is easy to imagine that this huge group could play a decisive role in future electoral contests. For the United States, Mexican immigration continues to be a hotly debated and divisive issue. ❖

Parties such as the PAN and the PRD are developing greater capacity to campaign effectively for office, and civil society groups are becoming better organized and more capable of having an impact on government policies. Citizens are also enjoying greater access to a variety of sources of information about government. Challenges remain in terms of how citizens in Mexico relate to the political system and the government, but trends toward the consolidation of an effective democratic political system are positive.

SECTION 5

Mexican Politics in Transition

FOCUS QUESTIONS

In what ways is economic integration with the rest of the world affecting political and social changes in Mexico? Which groups of people is it hurting most? Helping most?

Political Challenges and Changing Agendas

Mexico confronts a world of increasing interdependence among countries. For all countries, economic integration raises issues of national sovereignty and identity. Mexicans define themselves in part through a set of historical events, symbols, and myths that focus on the country's troubled relationship with the United States. Among numerous national heroes and martyrs are those who distinguished themselves in confrontations with the United States.

The country's sense of national identity is affected by international migration. Of particular importance in the Mexican case is labor migration. Every year, large numbers of Mexicans enter the United States as workers. Many return to their towns and villages with new values and new views of the world. Many stay in the United States, where Hispanics have become the largest ethnic population in the country. Most continue to believe that Mexican culture is preferable to American culture, which they see as excessively materialistic and violent. Although they believe that Mexico is a better place to nurture strong family life and values, they are nevertheless strongly influenced by U.S. mass culture, including popular music, movies, television programs, fast food, and consumer goods (see "Mexican Migration to the United States").

The inability of the Mexican economy to create enough jobs pushes additional Mexicans to seek work in the United States, and the cash remittances that migrants abroad send home to their families and communities are now almost as important a source of income for Mexico as PEMEX's oil sales. There is disagreement about how to respond to the economic challenges that Mexico faces. Much of the debate surrounds the question of what integration into a competitive international economy really means. For some, it represents the final abandonment of Mexico's sovereignty. For others, it is the basis of future prosperity. Those who are critical of the market-based, outward-oriented development strategy are concerned about its impact on workers, peasants, and national identities. They argue that the state has abandoned its responsibilities to protect the poor from shortcomings of the market and to provide for their basic needs. They believe that U.S. and Canadian investors have come to Mexico only to find low-wage labor for industrial empires located elsewhere, and they argue that those investors will not hesitate to abandon Mexico for even lower-wage countries such as China when the opportunity arises. They see little benefit in further industrial development based on importation of foreign-made parts, their assembly in Mexico, and their export to other markets. This kind of development, they argue, has been prevalent in the *maquiladoras*, or assembly industries, many of which are located along the U.S.-Mexico border. Those who favor closer integration with Canada and the United States acknowledge that some foreign investment does not promote technological advances or move the work force into higher-paying, more skilled jobs. They emphasize, however, that most investment will occur because Mexico has a relatively well-educated population, the capacity to absorb modern technology, and a large internal market for industrial goods.

In addition to economic challenges, Mexico provides a testing ground for the democratic idea in a state with a long history of authoritarian institutions. The democratic ideas of citizen rights to free speech and assembly, free and fair elections, and responsive government are major reasons that the power of the PRI came under so much attack beginning in the 1980s. Currently, Mexico is struggling with opening up its political institutions to become more democratic. Efforts to bring about greater transparency in the Mexican political system have sometimes run up against obstacles as government ministries have resisted pressures to release sensitive documents and as investigations into the repressive activities of the PRI regime in decades past have been stymied. These setbacks leave some Mexicans skeptical of claims that a truly open, democratic political culture is being forged. Meanwhile, when Fox demonstrated little capacity to set priorities and communicate a vision for his government, many government agencies found it difficult to act, given their long history of dependence on presidential leadership. This has left many citizens with questions about the effectiveness of democratic institutions, but the Calderón administration showed itself capable of more sustained activity.

Mexico is also trying to revise its legacy of centralized power and decision making. Countries around the globe increasingly recognize that the solutions to many policy problems lie at regional and local levels. Although the government has introduced the decentralization of a number of activities and services, state and municipal governments are struggling to meet the demands of citizens who want competence, responsiveness, and accountability from their local and regional public officials.

Improving social conditions is an important challenge for Mexico. Although elites enjoy the benefits of sumptuous lifestyles, education at the best U.S. universities for their children, and luxury travel throughout the world, large numbers of Mexicans remain ill educated, poorly served with health care, and distant from the security of knowing that their basic needs for food, shelter, and employment can be met. The Chiapas rebellion of 1994 made the social agenda a topic of everyday conversation by reminding Mexicans that some people lived in appalling conditions with little hope for the future.

Finally, Mexico is confronting major challenges of adapting newly democratic institutions to reflect ethnic and religious diversity and provide equity for women in economic and political affairs. The past decade has witnessed the emergence of more organized and politically independent ethnic groups demanding justice and equality from government. These groups claim that they have suffered for nearly 500 years and that they are no longer willing to accept poverty and marginality as their lot. The Roman Catholic Church, still the largest organized religion in the country, is losing members to Protestant sects that appeal particularly to the everyday concerns of poor Mexicans. Women, who make up 32 percent of the formal labor force but 40 percent of professional and technical workers, are becoming more organized, but they still have a long way to go before their wages equal those of men or they have equal voice in political and economic decisions.

Summary

Mexico faces many of the same challenges that beset other countries: creating equitable and effective democratic government, becoming integrated into a global economy, responding to complex social problems, and supporting increasing diversity without losing national identity.

What will the future bring? How much will pressures for change and potential loss of national identity affect the nature of the political system? In 1980, few people could have foreseen the extensive economic policy reforms and pressures for democracy that Mexico would experience in the next quarter century. Few would have predicted the defeat of the PRI in the elections of 2000. In considering the future of the country, it is important to remember that Mexico has a long tradition of relatively strong institutions. It is not a country that will easily slip into sustained political instability. A tradition of constitutional government, a strong presidency, a political system that has incorporated a wide range of interests, little military involvement in politics, and a deep sense of national identity—these are among the factors that need to be considered in predicting the political consequences of democratization, economic integration, and greater social equality in Mexico.

Key Terms

mestizo
Amerindian
indigenous groups
maquiladoras
coup d'état
anticlericalism
ejidos
ejidatarios
sexenio
clientelism
North American Free Trade Agreement (NAFTA)
corporatist state
civil society
state capitalism
import substituting industrialization (ISI)
informal sector
proportional representation
technocrats
para-statal
accommodation
co-optation

Suggested Readings

Babb, Sarah L. *Managing Mexico: Economists from Nationalism to Neoliberalism.* Princeton, N.J.: Princeton University Press, 2001.

Bethell, Leslie, ed. *Mexico Since Independence.* Cambridge: Cambridge University Press, 1991.

Castañeda, Jorge G. *Perpetuating Power: How Mexican Presidents Were Chosen.* New York: New Press, 2000.

Chand, Vickram K. *Mexico's Political Awakening.* Notre Dame, Ind.: University of Notre Dame Press, 2001.

Collier, Ruth Berins. *The Contradictory Alliance: State-Labor Relations and Regime Change in Mexico.* Berkeley: University of California Press, 1992.

Cook, Maria Lorena, Kevin J. Middlebrook, and Juan Molinar (eds.). *The Politics of Economic Restructuring in Mexico.* San Diego: Center for U.S.-Mexican Studies, University of California, 1994.

Cornelius, Wayne A. "Nation-Building, Participation, and Distribution: The Politics of Social Reform Under Cárdenas," in Gabriel A. Almond, Scott Flanagan, and Robert J. Mundt (eds.), *Crisis, Choice, and Change: Historical Studies of Political Development.* Boston: Little, Brown, 1973.

Cornelius, Wayne A., Todd A. Eisenstadt, and Jane Hindley (eds.). *Subnational Politics and Democratization in Mexico.* San Diego: Center for U.S.-Mexican Studies, University of California, 1999.

Davidow, Jeffrey. *The U.S. and Mexico: The Bear and the Porcupine.* Princeton, N.J.: Markus Wiener Publishers, 2004.

Dominguez, Jorge I., and Chappell H. Lawson (eds.). *Mexico's Pivotal Democratic Election: Candidates, Voters, and the Presidential Campaign of 2000.* Stanford, Calif.: Stanford University Press, 2004.

Durand, Jorge, Douglas S. Massey, and Emilio A. Parrado. "The New Era of Mexican Migration to the United States," *The Journal of American History* 86 (September 1999): 2.

Foweraker, Joe, and Ann L. Craig (eds.). *Popular Movements and Political Change in Mexico.* Boulder, Colo.: Lynne Rienner, 1990.

Grindle, Merilee S. *Going Local: Decentralization, Democratization, and the Promise of Good Governance.* Princeton, N.J.: Princeton University Press, 2007.

———. *Challenging the State: Crisis and Innovation in Latin America and Africa.* Cambridge: Cambridge University Press, 1995.

Harvey, Neil. *The Chiapas Rebellion: The Struggle for Land and Democracy.* Durham, N.C.: Duke University Press, 1998.

Krauze, Enrique. *Mexico, Biography of Power: A History of Modern Mexico, 1810–1996.* Trans. by Hank Heifetz. New York: HarperCollins, 1997.

Lawson, Chappell H. *Building the Fourth Estate: Democratization and the Rise of a Free Press in Mexico.* Berkeley: University of California, 2002.

Levy, Daniel C., and Kathleen Bruhn. *Mexico: The Struggle for Democratic Development.* Berkeley: University of California Press, 2001.

Lustig, Nora. *Mexico: The Remaking of an Economy*, 2nd ed. Washington, D.C.: Brookings Institution, 1998.

Meyer, Michael C., William L. Sherman, and Susan M. Deeds. *The Course of Mexican History.* 7th ed. New York: Oxford University Press, 2002.

Paz, Octavio. *The Labyrinth of Solitude: Life and Thought in Mexico.* New York: Grove Press, 1961.

Preston, Julia, and Samuel Dillon. *Opening Mexico: The Making of a Democracy.* New York: Farrar, Straus and Giroux, 2004.

Salinas de Gortari, Carlos. *México: The Policy and Politics of Modernization.* Trans. by Peter Hearn and Patricia Rosas. Barcelona: Plaza & Janés Editores, 2002.

Suárez-Orozco, Marcelo, ed. *Crossings: Mexican Immigration in Interdisciplinary Perspective.* Cambridge: Harvard University Press, 1998.

Ugalde, Luis Carlos. *The Mexican Congress: Old Player, New Power.* Washington, D.C.: Center for Strategic and International Studies, 2000.

Womack, John, Jr. *Zapata and the Mexican Revolution.* New York: Vintage Books, 1968.

Notes

[1]This figure represents an estimate of the metropolitan area of Mexico City, which extends beyond the official boundaries of the city.

[2]An excellent history of this event is presented in Wayne A. Cornelius, "Nation-Building, Participation, and Distribution: The Politics of Social Reform Under Cárdenas," in Gabriel A. Almond, Scott Flanagan, and Robert J. Mundt (eds.), *Crisis, Choice and Change: Historical Studies of Political Development* (Boston: Little, Brown, 1973).

[3]Michael C. Meyer and William K. Sherman, *The Course of Mexican History*, 5th ed. (New York: Oxford UP, 1995), 598–599.

[4]Although the self-confessed "lone gunman" was jailed, the ensuing investigation raised concerns about a possible conspiracy involving party and law enforcement officials as well as drug cartels. Rumors circulated about a cover-up scandal. Eventually, skepticism about the integrity of the inquiry was so great that President Salinas called for a new investigation. At this point, little remains known about what exactly happened in Tijuana and why.

[5]Kevin J. Middlebrook (ed.), *Unions, Workers, and the State in Mexico* (San Diego: Center for U.S.-Mexican Studies, University of California Press, 1991).

[6]Merilee S. Grindle, *State and Countryside: Development Policy and Agrarian Politics in Latin America.* (Baltimore, Md.: The Johns Hopkins University Press, 1986), 79–111.

[7]For a description of this process, see Carlos Bazdresch and Santiago Levy, "Populism and Economic Policy in Mexico," in Rudiger Dornbusch and Sebastian Edwards (eds.), *The Macroeconomics of Populism in Latin America* (Chicago: University of Chicago Press, 1991), 72.

[8]Joe Foweraker and Ann L. Craig (eds.), *Popular Movements and Political Change in Mexico* (Boulder, Colo.: Lynne Rienner, 1989).

[9]Roger Hansen, *The Politics of Mexican Development* (Baltimore: Johns Hopkins University Press, 1971), 75.

[10]World Bank, *World Development Indicators, 2007, Povcal Net, Mexico.*

[11]Economist Intelligence Unit, *Country Commerce, Mexico* (London: EIU, September 2001), 43.

[12]See Luis Carlos Ugalde, *The Mexican Congress: Old Player, New Power* (Washington, D.C.: Center for International and Strategic Studies, 2000).

[13]See Chapell H. Lawson, *Building the Fourth Estate: Democratization and the Rise of a Free Press in Mexico* (Berkeley: University of California Press, 2002).

[14]Susan Eckstein (ed.), *Power and Popular Protest: Latin American Social Movements* (Berkeley: University of California Press, 1989).

[15]Foweraker and Craig, *Popular Movements and Political Change in Mexico.*

[16]Jonathan Fox and Gustavo Gordillo, "Between State and Market: The Campesinos' Quest for Autonomy," in Wayne A. Cornelius, Judith Gentleman, and Peter H. Smith (eds.), *Mexico's Alternative Political Futures* (San Diego: Center for U.S.-Mexican Studies, University of California Press, 1989).

[17]Wayne A. Cornelius, Ann L. Craig, and Jonathan Fox (eds.), *Transforming State-Society Relations in Mexico: The National Solidarity Strategy* (San Diego: Center for U.S.-Mexican Studies, University of California Press, 1994).

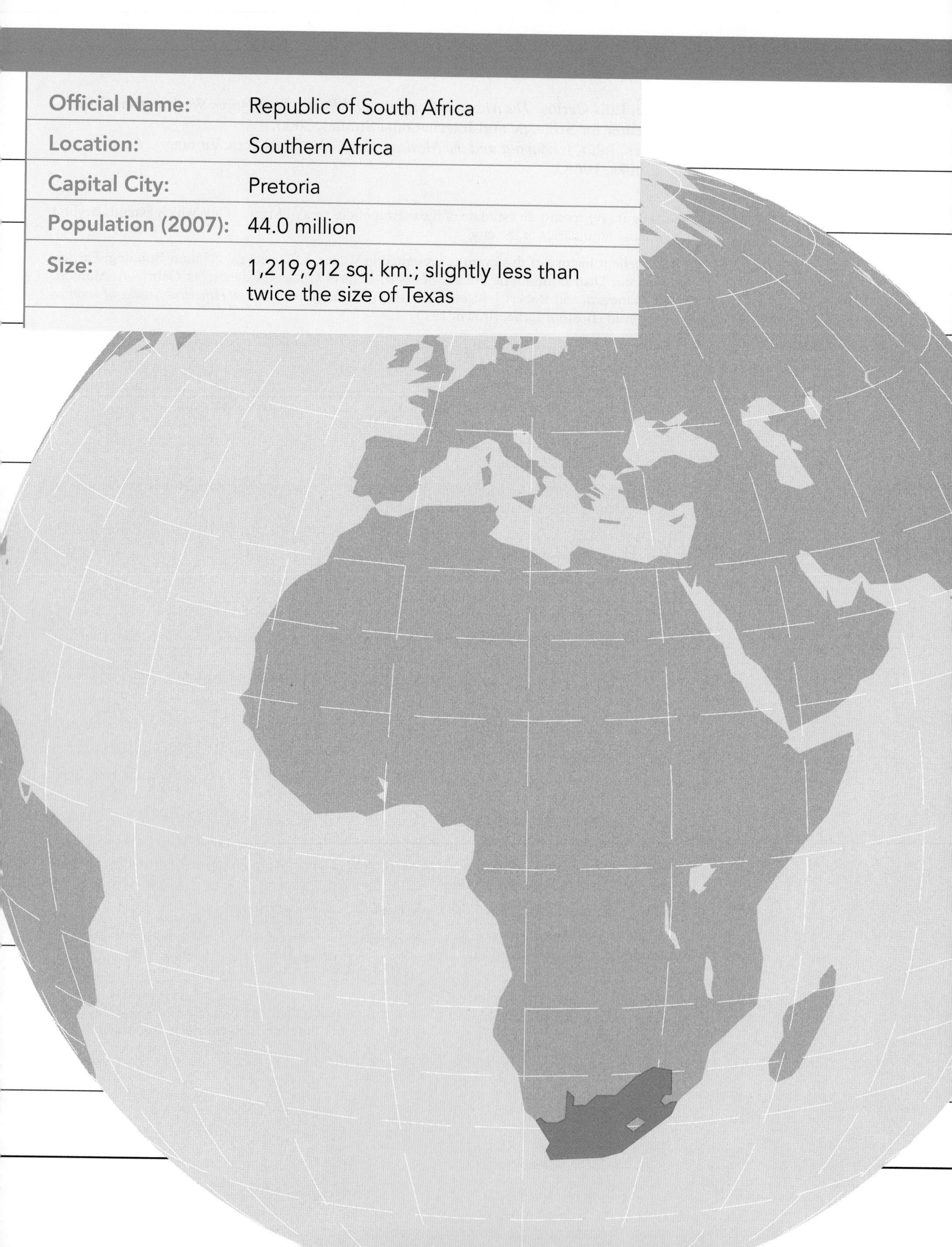

Official Name:	Republic of South Africa
Location:	Southern Africa
Capital City:	Pretoria
Population (2007):	44.0 million
Size:	1,219,912 sq. km.; slightly less than twice the size of Texas

CHAPTER

7 South Africa

Tom Lodge

Chronology of South Africa's Political Development

1688
Establishment of settlement at Cape Town by Dutch East India Company.

1779
First Frontier War in the Eastern Cape between settlers and Xhosa kingdoms.

1806
Incorporation of Cape Colony in British Empire.

1820
Arrival of British settlers in Eastern Cape.

1833
Abolition of slavery.

1836
Great Trek and subsequent establishment of Afrikaner republics of the Orange Free State and the Transvaal (South African Republic).

1860
Arrival of first Indian indentured laborers in Natal.

1899–1902
Anglo-Boer War and British occupation of Afrikaner republics.

1910
Act of Union.

1912
Formation of the African National Congress.

1913
Land Act.

1922
Rand Rebellion by white mineworkers.

SECTION 1

The Making of the Modern South African State

FOCUS QUESTION

Why might Jacob Zuma's ascendancy to presidential office represent a threat to South African democracy?

Politics in Action

On 10 May 2006, when a judge acquitted him of rape, the African National Congress's (ANC's) Deputy President, Jacob Zuma, expressed remorse. He did this even though the judge had found Zuma not guilty, after accepting his argument that his accuser had consented to sex. Zuma had argued that the woman, his house guest, had showed that she was available by wearing a short skirt and failing to cross her legs, wanton behavior from the standpoint of decorous Zulu convention. Zuma had known she was HIV positive, but this did not dissuade him. He did not use a condom, because he thought it was difficult for the AIDS virus to pass from a woman to a man.

Now, after emerging from his court victory, Zuma "apologized to the nation." He had "erred" in having unprotected sex with a woman who was HIV positive. He hoped his trial would not set back the struggle against HIV and AIDS. He would now return to his duties as the ANC's deputy leader. If he was called upon for an even higher office, he said, he would not refuse.

Jacob Zuma still faces another political obstacle. In 2005, his former financial advisor Shabir Schaik was convicted for corruption. The evidence in Schaik's trial suggested that Zuma had accepted bribes in return for various favors that he had done for Shaik himself and for contractors in a massive government arms purchase. In 2005, Zuma himself was charged with corruption. He resigned as President Thabo Mbeki's deputy in government although he remained vice-president of the party. During Shaik's trial Zuma projected himself as a victim of political enemies in the courts who wanted to keep him from becoming Mbeki's heir. In particular trade union officials endorsed this view. A "Friends of Jacob Zuma" committee began raising funds.

In mid-2006, the court proceedings against Zuma collapsed. Though he was technically innocent, Zuma has still not cleared his name, for the evidence against

1923
Native Urban Areas Act codifies urban racial segregation.

1926
Institution of job reservation for white workers in the Mines and Works Amendment Act.

1948
Election into power of National Party and the inception of Apartheid program.

1960
Sharpeville massacre and prohibition of the two main African nationalist organizations, the ANC and the PAC.

1976
Soweto uprising.

1986
Repeal of the pass laws.

1990
Unbanning of the ANC and the PAC and release of political prisoners.

1992
Opening of constitutional negotiations.

1994
First universal suffrage election under a transitional constitution.

1996
Adoption of final constitution.

1999
Thabo Mbeki succeeds Nelson Mandela as president.

2004
ANC wins third victory in national elections.

him that emerged in Shabir Shaik's trial has not been refuted. Zuma may still believe that his opponents represent only a minority within the ANC. Outside the ruling party's support base, however, his political advancement will certainly cause controversy. Within the ANC there are deep divisions over who should succeed Thabo Mbeki as president—of the party and the country. To external observers, Zuma's continuing popularity indicates a significant shift away from

TABLE 7.1

Political Organization

Political System	Parliamentary democracy and federal republic.
Regime History	Governed by an African National Congress–led coalition from 1994. Between 1910 and 1994 governments were formed by parties representing a white minority and were elected through racially restricted franchises. A British dominion until 1961 and then a republic.
Administrative Structure	Nine regional governments sharing authority with a national administration. Regional governments have few exclusive legislative powers and can be overridden on most significant issues by national legislatures.
Executive	President elected by parliament. President selects cabinet.
Legislature	National assembly and regional legislatures elected on the basis of party list proportional representation. National Council of Provinces made up by delegations from each regional government serves as a second chamber of parliament.
Judiciary	Independent constitutional court with appointed judges.
Party System	Multiparty system. African National Congress predominates. Other important parties: Democratic Alliance, Inkatha Freedom Party, United Democratic Movement, African Christian Democratic Party.

the high moral ground that seemed to characterize South African politics during the Mandela era. In replacing its leaders, South African democracy confronts its most severe test to date.

FOCUS QUESTION

In which ways does racial segregation persist in South Africa?

African South African usage refers to Bantu language speakers, the demographic majority of South African citizens.

Geographic Setting

South Africa is about twice the size of Texas. In 2001 the population was around 44 million, suggesting an annual increase of 2 percent, the lowest growth rate in Africa; 55 percent of this population lives in towns and cities. Government statistics divide the population into four main race groups: 35 million Bantu-language-speaking **Africans**, descend from successive waves of migrants who originally came from Central Africa. They began to inhabit the territory at least 2,000 years ago. The first European settlers arrived in the seventeenth century. Their descendants make up 4 million whites. The 4 million Coloureds (the term used universally in South Africa) represent a group whose ancestry includes the earliest indigenous Khoi-San hunter-gatherers, as well as slaves from Indonesia and the offspring from unions between white settlers and these groups. Just over 1 million Indians are mostly descendents of indentured laborers who were recruited from India during the nineteenth century. Each group used to have different legal status. Today, racial segregation is no longer the law, but social life is still influenced by the communal identities created by official racial classification. Most blacks still live in historically segregated ghetto-like neighborhoods, and most whites live in the more comfortable suburbs.

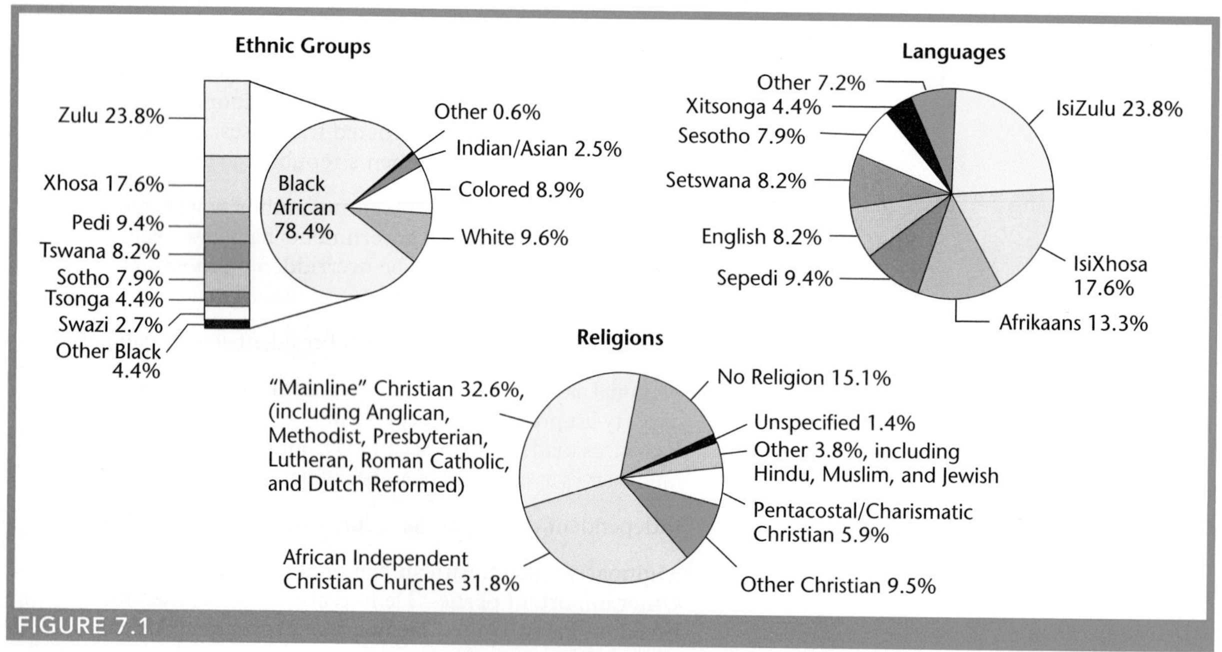

FIGURE 7.1

The South African Nation at a Glance

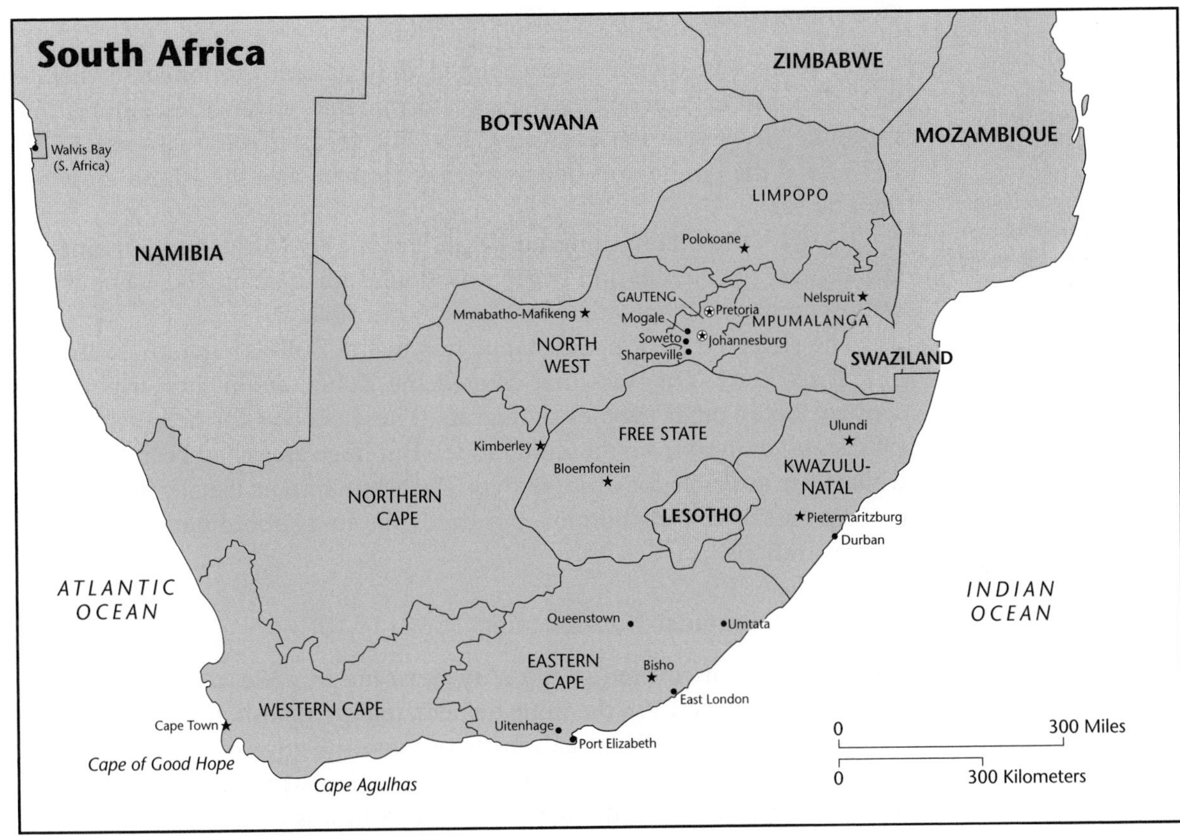

In general, those provinces that have incorporated the governments of the former ethnic homelands are those that experience the most administrative problems. They tend also to be poorer than the other provinces.

Source: From Tom Lodge, *South African Politics Since 1994*, pp. vi–vii. Reprinted with permission.

FOCUS QUESTION

Why did institutionalized racism become such a central characteristic of South African social life in the twentieth century?

Critical Junctures

Settlement, 1688–1911

In 1652 the Dutch East India Company established a reprovisioning station for its merchant ships. The Dutch settlers did not arrive first. Bantu-language-speaking Africans had arrived in South Africa at least 2,000 years ago. By 1250, well-organized societies lived in the northern regions, who could build extensive stone fortifications. Bantu-language speakers drove away or merged with the San and the Khoi-Khoi—earlier hunter-gatherer and pastoral communities.

Afrikaner descendants of Dutch, French, German, and Scots settlers speaking a language (Afrikaans) derived heavily from Dutch and politically mobilized as an ethnic group through the twentieth century.

By the eighteenth century Dutch settlers were identifying themselves as **Afrikaners**. In 1806, the British annexed the company's territory. Because they resented British policies (including the abolition of slavery in 1833), about one-tenth of the Afrikaner population—the ***voortrekkers***—migrated northwards between 1836 and 1840. The voortrekkers established the Orange Free State in 1852 and the Transvaal in 1854.

voortrekkers pastoralist descendants of Dutch-speaking settlers in South Africa who moved north from the British-controlled Cape in 1836 to establish independent republics; later regarded as the founders of the **Afrikaner** nation.

Dynamics of the Frontier, 1779–1906

White settlement quickly overwhelmed the pastoral economies of the Khoi-San. The settlers encountered more formidable adversaries among Xhosa-speaking Africans in the Eastern Cape. The frontier wars between 1779 and 1878 fixed the boundaries between white farmers and the Xhosa kingdoms of the Transkei.

In 1843, the British annexed Natal. From 1860, British immigrants established sugar plantations and began recruiting Indian labor. Today about 80 percent of the Indian population lives in KwaZulu-Natal.

The strongest African resistance was in the Zulu Kingdom, an impressive militarized state. The wars that created the Zulu state in the early nineteenth century forced other peoples to migrate. These peoples formed their own powerful states derived from the Zulu model. But huge areas had been depopulated, which were available for white settlers. The white settlers usually preserved some precolonial African institutions, but these played a subordinate role in colonial administrations.

Imperialists against Republicans, 1867–1910

After gold was discovered in the Witwatersrand in 1886, a massive mining industry grew up. By 1898 the mine owners, mainly British, increasingly objected to the government in Pretoria, mostly because the government tended to favor landholders over mine owners in official programs to enlist African labor. By the late 1890s, however, the British government was more receptive to the concerns of the mine owners, or "Randlords," since global competition from Germany and the United States, increased the strategic value of the Transvaal gold reserves. Before the British could invade, the republics declared war on October 11, 1899. The savage Anglo-Boer War (1899–1902) confirmed British ascendancy in the region and helped set up an industrial capitalist society in South Africa.

Boer Literally "farmer"; modern usage is a derogatory reference to Afrikaners.

The **Boers** (farmers) launched guerrilla campaigns that prolonged the war. Casualties included 28,000 Afrikaner civilians who died in concentration camps. One hundred thousand Africans served in the armies on both sides, and 14,000 Africans died in internment camps that were separate from the ones for white people. Voting was already color-blind in the Cape, and Africans hoped that after the war they would be able to vote throughout the country. But during the 1902 peace negotiations at *Vereeniging* (union), the British considered good relations between the Afrikaners and the English more important. In the Cape, a small African elite retained the vote, but in the other provinces the agreement denied Africans any enfranchisement.

Under the new British administration, imperial officials constructed an efficient bureaucracy. A customs union between the four South African territories eliminated tariffs. A new Native Affairs Department reorganized labor recruitment. In May 1910, negotiations with the former guerrilla generals resulted in the Act of Union. The four territories became provinces. Africans outside the Cape would be excluded from voting.

The Origins of Modern Institutionalized Racism, 1910–1945

These arrangements confirmed the essential features of South Africa's racist social order. The need to recruit and coerce cheap African labor guided public policy. In gold mining, profits depended on very cheap labor. Like the diamond mines, the gold mines used a closed compound system, which was originally developed to stop smuggling, but on the Witwatersrand it became a system of controlling African workers. The compounds were enclosed dormitories, constructed around a courtyard, with a single guarded entrance and barred external windows. Recruiting workers demanded an extremely repressive political order.[1] Beginning with the 1913 Land Act, laws were passed after the union to enforce racial discrimination. These laws were supposed to meet the needs of a mining economy, which needed cheap labor that could not rebel.[2] The Land Act allowed Africans to own land only inside a patchwork of native reserves. Outside these areas, Africans could not own land.

In the 1880s Afrikaner nationalism constructed an "imagined community" based on language standardization and literary culture. This "imagined community" attracted white people who had been forced off the land during the Anglo-Boer War.[3] During the white miners' armed insurrection in 1922 Afrikaner workers resurrected a Boer commando system. This underlined the emotional appeal of Afrikaner republicanism among impoverished white migrants from the countryside.

The miners protested because their employers were giving certain semiskilled work to Africans, jobs that only white people had been allowed to do. In putting down the rebellion, 153 people were killed. Two years later, a coalition or Pact government of the Labour Party and the (Afrikaner) National Party set up a "civilized labor" policy. All whites, even ones without any skills, should earn enough to maintain "civilized" standards of living. Semiskilled and certain unskilled jobs were reserved for whites. The Pact government also invested in public industries. The pace of industrialization accelerated after 1933. During an economic recession, a fusion between the National Party led by General Herzog and Jan Smuts's pro-imperial South African Party created a new United Party administration. After the currency was devalued, fresh waves of investment flowed in from overseas, beginning a decade of manufacturing expansion.

Apartheid and African Resistance, 1945–1960

Social tensions prompted two different sets of political challenges to Smuts's United Party administration. After Hertzog decided to join Jan Smuts in the United Party, a Purified National Party established itself in 1934. Meanwhile, Afrikaner nationalism became a mass movement under the direction of a secret *Broederbond* that sponsored savings banks, trade unions, and voluntary organizations. During the early 1940s, Afrikaner nationalism developed a program around the idea of **apartheid** (apartness). This emphasized even more rigid racial separation. Apartheid policies restricted Indians and Coloureds and halted permanent African urbanization. This appealed to white workers who feared African competition for their jobs. The National Party also drew support from

apartheid in Afrikaans, "separateness." First used in 1929 to describe Afrikaner nationalist proposals for strict racial separation and "to ensure the safety of the white race."

farmers, who found it more and more difficult to recruit labor during rapid industrialization. The National Party won a narrow electoral victory in 1948, and it remained in power for the next forty-six years. More racist legislation followed the Nationalist victory, extending **pass laws** to African women and banning interracial sex. To travel to towns and live and work in urban centers blacks needed permits.

pass laws laws in apartheid South Africa that required Africans to carry identity books in which were stamped the permits required for them to travel between the countryside and the cities.

African politics became a mass movement in the 1940s. Middle-class notables in the ANC first competed with Communists and then collaborated with them. In 1945 the Natal Indian Congress, a body first formed by Mohandas Gandhi, led an Indian passive resistance movement that inspired ANC leaders to embrace civil disobedience.

The Sharpeville Massacre and Grand Apartheid, 1960–1976

In the Sharpeville massacre, March 21, 1960, police killed approximately eighty people who had assembled outside a police station to protest the pass laws. This was the first critical juncture during the apartheid era. In the 1950s, African politicians had reacted to fresh restrictions and new segregation laws with civil disobedience campaigns, general strikes, and consumer boycotts. After the government prohibited the Communist Party in 1950, the ANC and allied Indian and Coloured organizations became more radical, as Communists began to play a more assertive role in their leadership. White Communists remained active in a secret underground party and played a prominent role in black trade unions. After the Sharpeville shootings, the authorities banned the ANC and a more militant offshoot, the Pan-Africanist Congress, which had organized the antipass protests.

While the African liberation movements reorganized in exile and prepared for guerrilla warfare, National Party governments under Hendrik Verwoerd and John Vorster began an increasingly ambitious program of racial separation.[4] Ethnically constituted administrations were set up in all the native reserves. All Africans would be assigned as citizens to these native reserves, which were to become supposedly sovereign states. The ten **homelands**, as they became known in official terminology, became increasingly overcrowded as 1.4 million farm workers were forcibly resettled within them. In addition, several hundred thousand city dwellers were deported to the homelands. Apartheid planners forecast that African urban workers would become permanent **migrant laborers**, renewing their contracts every year and leaving their families in the homelands.

homelands areas reserved for exclusive African occupation, established through the provisions of the 1913 and 1936 land legislation and later developed as semi-autonomous ethnic states during the apartheid era.

migrant laborer refers to laborers who move to another location to take a job, often a low-paying, temporary one.

Anticipating this outcome, the central government took control of African **township** administration. In 1970 it completely halted the construction of family housing in the major cities, building instead huge dormitory-like hostels for "bachelor" workers. A program of Bantu education, stressing menial vocational training, had already been introduced into primary schools in 1954. It was extended to African secondary schooling through the 1960s. Restrictions were placed on African, Indian, and Coloured enrollment in the major universities. Special segregated colleges were established. Fierce antiterrorist laws allowed detention without trial and made it easier to torture prisoners. Through an

township South African usage refers to a segregated residential area reserved for Africans, during apartheid tightly controlled and constituted mainly by public housing.

A policeman stands over a corpse after the Sharpeville massacre. Survivors today claim that some of the wounded were killed as they lay on the ground by black police constables brought in from Johannesburg. *(Source: Central Press/Getty Images)*

extensive network of informers, the police located most of the networks responsible for brief campaigns of sabotage and insurgency that had been mounted by the ANC and the Pan-Africanist Congress. By 1965, most significant African leaders who had not left the country were beginning life sentences on Robben Island, a former leper colony offshore from Cape Town where authorities established a maximum security prison. These leaders included Nelson Mandela, ANC deputy president and commander in chief of its armed wing, ***Umkhonto-we-Sizwe*** (Spear of the Nation).

Umkhonto-we-Sizwe Zulu and Xhosa for "Spear of the Nation," the armed wing of the African National Congress, established in 1961 and integrated into the South African National Defence Force in 1994.

During this era foreign capital and public investment built up strategic industries such as armaments and synthetic petrol. Annual gross national product (GNP) growth rates peaked at 8 percent. The government invested in these strategic industries after the 1965 United Nations resolution recommended oil and arms embargoes on South Africa.

Generational Revolt and Political Reform, 1976–1990

In 1976, riots by schoolchildren put rulers on the defensive. Many Africans had gained jobs in semiskilled manufacturing work. This gave black workers new leverage against employers. Wildcat strikes broke out in 1973 as a combative trade union movement gained strength. Daily tabloid newspapers aimed at township readers had appeared in the mid-1960s. These papers took advantage of mass literacy and helped form a new generation of political organizations that were inspired by the U.S. black power movement and were led by the expanding numbers of graduates from the segregated universities.

Starting in 1974 the collapse of Portuguese colonial power in Angola and Mozambique supplied a fresh source of militant inspiration. The ideas of the racially assertive black consciousness movement percolated down to secondary schools. They found ready adherents in an educational system under increasing strain. The Education Ministry rashly decided to enforce a decades-old requirement that half the curriculum should be taught in Afrikaans. This provoked demonstrations on June 16, 1976, in the townships that bordered Johannesburg. The police fired into a crowd of 15,000 children, killing two. In the following days, the revolt spread to fifty Transvaal centers. The subsequent year saw insurrectionary street battles, strikes, and classroom boycotts. At least 575 protesters died. Several thousand more crossed South Africa's borders to join the exiled liberation organizations.

By the mid-1970s, Afrikaner nationalism had altered. Two-thirds of Afrikaners were now white-collar workers. Afrikaner firms were now among the most advanced manufacturers. Their directors were increasingly bothered by apartheid restrictions on black labor mobility.[5] African workers gained collective bargaining rights. Black trade unions won legal recognition. Another series of reforms followed, which attempted to solicit support from the most urbanized Africans. By 1986 these reforms included the repeal of the system of pass laws and **influx control**. In 1983 a new set of organizations, based around student movements, trade unions, and township-based civic associations formed a United Democratic Front (UDF). They proclaimed their loyalty to the "nonracial" ideology of the ANC. The UDF first focused on the boycotts it led in reaction to elections for a "tricameral" parliament, which had been set up by the government in 1984 with the addition of Coloured and Indian chambers alongside the all-white legislature. UDF affiliates were conspicuous in the insurrectionary climate that developed in the townships in late 1984 in response to rent hikes. Township rioting, military repression, guerilla warfare, and conflict between supporters of liberation movements and the adherents of homeland regimes each contributed to the bloodiest phase of South Africa's political history since the Anglo-Boer war. Between 1984 and 1994, politically motivated killings claimed 25,000 lives.

influx control a system of controls that regulated African movement between cities and between towns and the countryside, enforcing residence in the homelands and restricting African choice of employment.

The South African Miracle, 1990–1999

On February 12, 1990, a new president, Frederick De Klerk created a bombshell when he announced the repeal of prohibitions on the ANC and other proscribed organizations. His government was ready to begin negotiating a democratic political system. De Klerk was a conservative, but he was dismayed by the prospect of tightening economic **sanctions** and was encouraged by the collapse of the Communist governments that had previously been such important supporters of the ANC. He hoped that through abandoning apartheid and beginning negotiations for a power-sharing dispensation, the National Party could build black support. The existence of a powerful political

sanctions international embargos on economic and cultural contracts with a particular country; applied selectively to South Africa by various governments and the United Nations from 1948 until 1994.

movement organized around the KwaZulu homeland authority, the Inkatha Freedom Party, led by a Zulu prince, Chief Mangosuthu Buthelezi, represented another reason to believe that an anti-ANC coalition could prevail. ANC leaders, in turn, were willing to make concessions, acknowledging the impossibility of a revolutionary seizure of power. They too were alarmed at the prospect of national economic degeneration. Opinion polls assured them of their growing public support.

At the time, it seemed miraculous that such bitter adversaries could be ready to collaborate so closely in designing a fresh political dispensation. Their success was all the more remarkable, given the continuing political hostilities between their supporters. Between 1990 and 1994, 14,000 people died in warfare between the ANC, Inkatha, and various state-sponsored vigilante groups. In 1993 two years of bargaining produced a transitional constitution in which the main parties would hold cabinet positions in accordance with their shares of the vote in **proportional representation** elections. Anybody who had participated since 1960 in politically motivated violence, including torture of prisoners and terrorist attacks, would be able to obtain immunity from prosecution. All public servants would keep their jobs. Power would be divided between a national assembly and nine provincial legislatures, the latter absorbing the homeland bureaucracies. Parliament would sit as a constitutional assembly to draw up a final constitution, which would have to follow the fundamental principles agreed to in the 1993 document.

proportional representation (PR) a system of political representation in which seats are allocated to parties within multi-member constituencies, roughly in proportion to the votes each party receives. In South Africa the entire country serves as a single 400-seat parliamentary constituency.

In May 1994, the Government of National Unity (GNU) took office, presided over by Nelson Mandela and including representatives of the ANC, the National Party, and the Inkatha Freedom Party (see "Nelson Mandela"). With just over 62 percent of the ballot, the ANC achieved an overwhelming

An Afrikaner leader protests the freeing of Nelson Mandela
(© Patrick Durand/Corbis Sygma)

Profile
Nelson Mandela

Born in a tiny Transkei village in 1918, Nelson Mandela could claim Thembu royal lineage. After he rebelled against an arranged marriage and was suspended from Fort Hare University for his role in a student strike, he traveled to Johannesburg to begin work as a legal clerk. Joining the ANC in 1942, Mandela helped to establish the Youth League. This group wanted to radicalize the ANC's temperate philosophy in favor of a militant, racially exclusive nationalism. By 1951, however, Mandela had become friends with Indian activists and white Communists. This led him to revise his belief that African nationalists should not cooperate across race lines. That year, Mandela helped plan a "defiance campaign" against "unjust laws." Thereafter, as the ANC's deputy president, Mandela, played a major role as an ANC strategist. In 1952, he founded a law firm with his comrade Oliver Tambo. He married twice, the second time in 1958 to Nomzamo Winifred Madkizela.

Following the Sharpeville massacre, Mandela was detained for five months, and the ANC was outlawed. In 1961, he led a nationwide general strike on May 29–31. In October, he helped form a sabotage organization, *Umkhonto we Sizwe* (Spear of the Nation). Mandela left South Africa in January 1962 to seek financial and military support. He returned in July and was arrested. Imprisoned for incitement, he was convicted again after the capture of other *Umkhonto* leaders.

During nearly three decades of imprisonment, Mandela maintained his authority over successive generations of convicted activists. Beginning in 1985, a series of meetings with government leaders initiated by Mandela helped to persuade the authorities to initiate constitutional negotiations with the ANC.

On February 11, 1990, Mandela was unconditionally released. As ANC president from 1991, his leadership was crucial in curbing the expectations of his organization's often unruly following. He shared the Nobel Peace Prize in 1993 with President F. W. de Klerk. After the ANC's electoral victory in 1994, he served as South African president until 1999. His personal achievements during this period included symbolic acts of reconciliation with the Afrikaner minority and vigorous defense of constitutional undertakings. Divorcing in 1995, he married Graca Machel in 1998. Remaining active after his retirement from public office, he became chair of the Burundi peace talks in 2000.

Nelson Mandela contributed significantly to the ANC's ideological formation in the 1950s. He was a powerful proponent of the multiracial Congress Alliance. Although influenced by Marxism, he maintained an admiration for British parliamentary democracy. Although he advocated working-class mobilization, Mandela rook advantage of his social connections with the rural aristocracy, and he skillfully balanced his pronouncements to the various constituencies within the ANC's popular following. After 1960, his personal courage and theatrical style were vital in keeping the rank-and-file militants loyal to the ANC. He pioneered the ANC's transformation to a clandestine insurgent body and led its second metamorphosis into an electorally oriented political party. His speech at his trial in 1964 increased his stature making him, in the words of the *London Times*, "a colossus of African nationalism." Four decades later, he remains Africa's most internationally influential statesman. ❖

majority among black voters except in KwaZulu-Natal, where Inkatha obtained a narrow victory. With 20 percent of the national vote, De Klerk's New National Party drew substantial support among Coloureds and Indians, as well as taking most white votes. Eight more parties achieved parliamentary representation. For many observers South Africans had achieved an astonishing historical turnaround.

A South African cartoon published during Nelson Mandela's first official visit as head of state to the United Kingdom in 1996. *(© Zapiro, Cartoonists and Writers Syndicate, Cartoon Arts International, Inc., from* The Mail and Guardian*, Johannesburg, South Africa)*

In office, the GNU began the Reconstruction and Development Programme (RDP), a plan drawn up originally by the ANC's labor ally, the Congress of South African Trade Unions (COSATU). The RDP emphasized people-driven development, which would include a more egalitarian allocation of public goods and industrial reorganization to promote local employment. ANC leaders in power still used the Marxist-Leninist phraseology of what they called a national democratic revolution. But their economic policies were surprisingly orthodox. Under both Mandela and his successor, Thabo Mbeki, ANC-led administrations have attempted to address the basic needs of poor people. Social expenditure has been limited, however, by tight budgetary discipline. With the adoption in 1996 of the Growth, Employment, and Redistribution policy (GEAR), the ANC leadership's embrace of liberal free-market reforms, including **privatization** and tariff reduction, became uncomfortably obvious to its trade union allies. Much of the present-day support for Jacob Zuma is attributable to working-class objections to government economic policy. Zuma has been careful to retain his membership of the Communist Party and remains on good terms with trade union leaders who see him as an ally.

privatization the sale of state-owned enterprises to private companies or investors.

South Africa after 9/11

International terrorist networks have only a very limited presence in South Africa. Several suspected Al Qaeda operatives were deported in May 2004, and police subsequently supplied information leading to further arrests in Jordan, Syria, and Britain. Five months later, however, the U.S. Central Intelligence Agency (CIA) suggested that South Africa might still be accommodating "second tier" Al Qaeda leaders.

By 2001, however, police had immobilized the main local terrorist agency, a clandestine Islamist network that had operated within the Cape Town–based vigilante group, People Against Drugs and Gangsterism (PAGAD). This group undertook a series of attacks targeting tourist facilities, a gay bar, and a synagogue. The government drafted additional antiterrorism legislation. This gave the police new powers of search and allowed detention without charge for up to fourteen days. By the end of 2001 officials were defending the draft bill against criticism from human rights groups. Officials claimed it was a necessary measure in the global fight against terrorism. Such reasoning is disputed by most local specialists given the absence of a significant local constituency that might support terrorist activity. South African Muslims are relatively affluent and are increasingly middle class, and they are more likely to live outside traditional Muslim neighborhoods. Local Islamist political parties perform poorly in elections.

Diplomatically, South Africa has taken a relatively independent tack. The government withheld any endorsement of the American-led invasion of Iraq in 2003. The ANC itself maintained quite friendly relations with Saddam Hussein's administration, and the party benefited from illicit donations that accompanied South African purchases of Iraqi oil. One month after the fall of Baghdad, however, Thabo Mbeki hosted a visit by President Bush during which the two leaders discussed a program of American assistance to strengthen South African border security.

FOCUS QUESTION

Why has South Africa attracted so much international attention?

Themes and Implications

Historical Junctures and Political Themes

South Africa in a World of States. South Africa's political economy has been shaped decisively by inflows of capital and population. Throughout the twentieth century the economy remained dependent on imported technology and hence vulnerable to international pressure. Although the major powers implemented sanctions only reluctantly, the country's institutionalized racial segregation attracted unanimous censure within the post–World War II world of states. Ever since the Anglo-Boer War, South Africa, for a small, semicolonial territory, has attracted an unusual degree of international political attention. This attention is partly the effect of successive inflows of European immigration.

settler state colonial or former colonial administrations controlled by the descendants of immigrants who settled in the territory.

These external influences have complicated South Africa's relationship with the rest of Africa. As a **settler state**, South Africa was perceived by pan-African politicians as a residual element of the colonial world, a perception that was reinforced by South Africa's alignment with Western powers during the Cold War. Even with the advent of democracy and the accession of an African government, South Africa's economic preponderance in Africa excites resentment as much as admiration.

Governing the Economy. State-induced industrialization was encouraged with the establishment in 1928 of the public Iron and Steel Corporation. Such expansion of public enterprise accelerated during the apartheid era. The threat of foreign trade embargoes prompted an intensification of the regime of protective trade tariffs to encourage import substitution during the 1960s.

Between 1993 and 2001 South Africa removed about two-thirds of these tariffs. Tariff reform affected some industries harshly but was gentler on others in which South Africa might expect to become competitive internationally. The extent to which South African policy-makers could decide the details of trade reform reflected the degree of autonomy that the South African government enjoyed as a consequence of its relatively low foreign debt, which was itself an effect of financial sanctions and disinvestments during the 1980s.

The Democratic Idea. South African democracy is the product of an array of traditions. Immigrants reinforced key features of South African political culture. In the twentieth century, this included a tradition of militant socialism that accompanied the influxes from Cornish tin mines and Australian gold fields before World War I. Baltic Jewish refugees included in their numbers veterans of Russian revolutionary movements. Communists, through their interaction with African nationalists, helped to ensure that black opposition to apartheid was led by advocates of a racially inclusive South African nation. Nonracial themes in South African politics were also shaped by the heritage of liberal institutions that had accompanied earlier arrivals from Europe, for example, the influential network of Methodist-sponsored secondary schools and colleges attended by ANC leaders. Modern South African democratic thought reflects each of these different legacies, as well as the social ethics derived from indigenous African statecraft, with its premiums on consensual decision making and the etiquette of kinship.[6]

Modern democracy in South Africa is also to a considerable extent influenced by the ideas of an African trade union movement that was built in the late 1970s and which emphasized accountable leadership. South Africa's adoption of a constitutionally entrenched bill of rights was colored by important new sources of inspiration from other countries. A succession of recent transitions from authoritarian regimes in Latin America inspired negotiators across the political spectrum of the merits of a consensual political order that would initially develop through a fixed period of coalition **power sharing**.

power sharing constitutional arrangements to ensure that the major political parties share executive authority. These can include mandatory coalitions and allocation of senior official positions between parties.

Collective Identity. In six sets of elections since 1994, parliamentary and municipal, South African voters for the most part appear to have been influenced by their feelings of racial identity. Africans overwhelmingly support African nationalist parties. Despite the conspicuous presence of whites in its leadership, only minuscule numbers of white South Africans support the ANC. Among all groups, notions of racial community may be reinforced by material interests. Virtually all very poor people are African; for them it can be very difficult to feel any sense of shared social identity with generally affluent white South Africans. The prospects for democratic progress are limited in a South African politics in which racial solidarities are so decisive.

Implications for Comparative Politics

democratization transition from authoritarian rule to a democractic political order.

The most recent comparative analysis of South African politics emphasizes its significance as a relatively successful example of third wave **democratization**. Post-apartheid politics in South Africa offers to comparativists useful insights into the factors that sustain and consolidate democratic life: these certainly include a developmental sequence in which the construction of a modern economy preceded universal enfranchisement; the role played in making democracy work by a vigorous civil society; as well as the effects of a carefully assembled set of state institutions designed to promote social inclusion and reward consensus. South Africa may yet offer an encouraging model of a racially segmented society that has succeeded in nurturing stable and democratic political institutions.

Summary

A unified South Africa was established in the aftermath of the Anglo-Boer War, a conflict that made the British Empire the dominant force in the subcontinent. A modern administration, geared to providing cheap labor to the gold mining industry, restricted African access to land. In the decades following Union, white workers succeeded in securing rights and privileges as citizens, while the legal status of black South Africans deteriorated. Afrikaner nationalists held office from 1948 and established a strict regime of racial apartheid. Popular African resistance was suppressed in 1960. In exile, the main African movements embraced guerrilla warfare. From 1976 onwards, urbanization, industrialization, and mass literacy prompted powerful challenges to white minority rule. In 1990, in response to insurgency and international pressure, the South African political leadership lifted the ban on the main African political organizations and began negotiating a political settlement. In 1994 a democratically elected government began its attempts to reduce poverty and inequality while at the same time encouraging economic regeneration.

Political Economy and Development

FOCUS QUESTION

In which ways has the state's role in the economy changed since 1970?

State and Economy

Apartheid Economics

Apartheid policies were reinforced through extensive economic intervention by the state. From 1952, laws prohibited Africans from living in any town unless they had been born there or had worked for the same employer for ten years. Migrant workers without urban residential rights had to live in tightly controlled hostels. By the mid-1960s, political repression had virtually eliminated most of the more militant African trade unions. In 1968 the Armaments Development and Manufacturing Corporation (Armscor) was created. This greatly expanded the scope of public industrial enterprise. By 1981, Armscor was at the center of a defense industry employing 100,000 people.

A Racially Segmented Welfare State

Apartheid economics was buttressed by a welfare state, even though it functioned in a racially discriminatory fashion. Public construction of African housing began on a significant scale in Orlando, outside Johannesburg, during the 1930s. This was the first of a series of projects of a vast township—later named Soweto (the administrative acronym from southwestern townships). Wartime industrialization prompted the government to suspend pass laws. During the 1940s, as Africans rapidly moved to the cities, illegal shanty settlements mushroomed on the fringes of most major cities. Although they restricted further African urbanization, governments after 1948 funded a rapid expansion of public housing to accommodate those Africans who were permitted to live in towns. In 1971, African public housing totaled more than 500,000 family dwellings. During the 1960s, official policy increasingly favored single workers' hostel construction instead of family housing. Most townships included bleak barrack-like hostels in which African migrant workers slept in bunks and used communal bathrooms and kitchens. In the 1960s, the state extended its control over African educational institutions. But it also increased school enrollment massively. By the end of the decade, most children of school-going age were attending public schools, although there were huge inequalities in the amount of

Meadowlands, a district in Soweto in which people were forcibly resettled from their previous homes in Sophiatown, an inner-city suburb in which Africans had owned land. *(Source: Bettmann/Corbis.)*

public money spent per capita on white and black children. Pension payments between the races were equalized only in 1993. South Africa's universal public pension, together with disability grants and other kinds of welfare payments, remain unusual in sub-Saharan African states today.

Liberalization and Deregulation

economic deregulation the lifting or relaxation of government controls over the economy, including the reduction of import taxes (tariffs) and the phasing out of subsidized prices for producers and consumers.

From 1970 the dismantling of apartheid was accompanied by wider kinds of **economic deregulation**. Effectively by 1984, most official employment discrimination had been removed except in gold mining. In the mid-1980s, the government began to dismantle the protections and subsidies that had supported white agriculture. Parallel to these developments, the Iron and Steel Corporation and the public road freight company were privatized. In the 1990s rising defense expenditure and expanding public debt introduced fresh reasons to deregulate and privatize. When the government abolished influx control in 1986, this should have opened up the labor market, at least in theory, but by this time, the main labor shortages were in skilled sectors. These shortages resulted because generations of Africans had not been able to receive industrial training and technical education. Once Africans were allowed to move to the cities, urban growth quickly picked up. In the last two decades of the twentieth century, most South African towns at least doubled in population.

Since 1994, ANC governments have maintained and expanded the liberal economic policies of the late apartheid era. Redistributive policies have attempted to expand the scope of private ownership rather than broaden the breadth of the public sector. For instance, since 1994 the government has helped to finance the construction of more than 2 million low-cost houses, but this is through one-time grants to impoverished families. The grants enable them to buy their own houses, built by private contractors on cheap former public land. For many residents in the townships, home ownership was more expensive than public rented housing or the site payments they had made to shacklords in squatter camps: R16,000 housing subsidies usually did not cover construction costs, and poor families who moved into RDP houses often spent a greater share of their income on bond repayments at commercial interest rates than they had paid on rents.

In 1994, the government agreed to reduce industrial tariffs by two-thirds by 2001 and agricultural tariffs by 36 percent within a decade. In 1997, industries stopped receiving export incentive subsidies. Exchange controls were substantially relaxed as well. Since 1994, privatization policies have had their most profound effect on municipal administration. Heavily indebted local authorities now contract out basic services such as water supply and garbage collection. Trade union opposition, however, delayed privatization of major public corporations such as Telkom, the telephone utility. To put the railroad network on a commercial footing, a majority of smaller rural stations were closed. Effectively, the state abandoned a major share of its former duty to provide cheap, subsidized public transport. To offset the social effects of withdrawing from many of its traditional areas of activity, the state has invested considerable effort to address basic needs and alleviate poverty. The government is also beginning to expand its authority over environmental issues.

Environmental Politics

African trade unions had long opposed unsafe working conditions. By the beginning of the 1990s, this opposition expanded into a broader concern with the effects of industrial pollution. The environmental movement acquired a popular base, and its causes broadened to embrace "brown" issues of the industrial landscape as well as the more tradition interests of "green" conservationism. A series of trade union campaigns moved environmentalist issues into the mainstream of national liberation politics. These campaigns opposed establishing toxic landfills and dumping poisonous waste chemicals. The campaigns began with a successful lawsuit against Thor Chemicals in 1992. In 1993, ANC negotiators insisted that clauses on environmental health and ecological sustainability should go into the constitution.

Since 1994, government policies have attempted to integrate ecological concerns with the requirements of social justice. A series of land restitution court cases have produced settlements in which historically dispossessed communities have signed "co-management" agreements with the National Parks Board. The 1998 Marine Living Resources Act has opened up fishing grounds to impoverished village communities who had previously been excluded by antipoaching legislation. In return, villagers are expected to keep the size of their catches within sustainable limits. New mining laws have introduced tighter regulations against pollution. Meanwhile, environmental protests have become increasingly likely to draw mass participation. In 2002, for example, environmental activists in Durban mobilized community protests against plans to expand a local oil refinery. Activists are not always successful, however. When nongovernmental organizations (NGOs) oppose industrial development, they sometimes stir up strong hostility from local people suffering from unemployment. This happened in Saldanha Bay in 1998 when environmentalists opposed building a new steelworks and were accused of elevating the welfare of penguins over the livelihoods of people. Environmental groups are likely to oppose the government's plans to build a pebble bed reactor at the existing nuclear facility at Koeberg. In 2005, activists from Earthlife Africa succeeded in obtaining a High Court ruling that ordered the authorities to make an environmental impact assessment.

FOCUS QUESTION

Why is South Africa so socially unequal today?

Society and Economy

Social Inequality

South Africa remains one of the most unequal societies in the world despite the government's efforts to alleviate poverty. Measured through the Gini-coefficient statistical measure of income inequality, in 2001 South Africa inequality was calculated at 0.72, a disturbingly high degree of inequality. Moreover, inequality was far higher than in 1991 when it was estimated at 0.62.[7] Today, however,

Africans in middle-class occupations outnumber whites. However, among Africans, income equality has increased dramatically. Rising unemployment has increased the numbers of very poor people, almost exclusively African; 28.1 percent of the African population were identified as unemployed by the 2001 Census, up from 23.4 percent in 1996. The main reason was that people entering the labor market for the first time could not find jobs. In 2000, researchers concluded that 45 percent of South Africans were living in poverty, on incomes of less than R1,500 a month (US$200).[8] The proportions of poor people were probably about the same as in 1996, but within this group the share of the really desperately poor is probably larger. South African social inequality is, to a large extent, the historic product of government policies. Whites moved ahead economically at the expense of Africans.

Although government programs may have alleviated poverty, social inequality has increased. Table 7.2 shows the expanding difference between the earnings of top managers and blue collar workers in an average South African company from 1992 through 2002.

Racial inequities in government expenditure were especially obvious in education. In the 1950s, more whites than Africans were trained as teachers; even though the number of African children of school-going age was five times greater than the figure for whites. The 1960s witnessed a swift expansion of

TABLE 7.2

Earnings Gap

Differential between earnings of a chief executive and manual worker in a medium-to-large South African company employing 2500 staff

Year	Differential
1992	33
1993	33
1994	35
1995	38
1996	42
1997	46
1998	49
1999	50
2000	52
2001	53
2002	55

Source:

Sunday Times, Johannesburg, 8 September 2002. Reprinted with permission.

African enrollment, but as late as 1984, the number of Africans completing the final grade of high school was only 60 percent of the total of white pupils in grade 12. In 1985, the government was still spending half its educational budget on white schools.

After 1994, government policies attempted to equalize entitlements and allocations as well as broaden access to public goods, though without dramatic expansion in public spending. Today, public expenditure on education is roughly uniform. Africans now outnumber other racial groups attending universities. Welfare grants to low-income families have fallen in value, but more people receive them. Measures to alleviate poverty have included housing subsidies and setting up running water for about a third of the rural population. In 1999, municipalities began to implement free water and electricity allowances. During the 1990s, the electricity supply commission substantially expanded the electricity network to embrace poorer rural communities. In addition, 1,300 new clinics have given free public health care to millions of pregnant women and small children. However, hospitals in the main urban centers have deteriorated because health funding has gone to the countryside.

Poverty

Have such efforts resulted in less poverty? Probably not, though more people use public facilities. Since 1994, poor people may have benefited more from government services and public support, but their numbers did not decrease. Indeed they may have expanded. Unemployment and HIV/AIDS have offset the government's efforts to address poverty. The manufacturing work force shrank by 400,000 in

New houses constructed with the aid of government low-cost housing subsidies. *(Source: © Silva Joao/Corbis)*

ten years after 1988, a 25 percent fall. In the same period 500,000 workers left farms. More recently, however, the number of manufacturing jobs has stabilized, and the numbers employed on commercial farms have increased. Public sector employment contracted only slightly, a reflection of the leverage exercised by public sector trade unions. In the late 1990s they were the major players in the still powerful union movement. Despite unemployment, union membership grew rapidly. In 2003 overall union membership was 2.7 million. Unemployment is concentrated among school dropouts and rural people. Africans continue to be much more likely to be unemployed than other groups.

Between 1996 and 2000, despite wider access to public health facilities, infant mortality rose from 51 per 1,000 to 59 per 1,000, and life expectancy fell from 64 to 53. UN statistics suggest that in 2005 life expectancy had fallen to 42 years, lower than in 1950.[9] These statistics reflected the devastating impact of the HIV/AIDS pandemic, which, according to South Africa's Medical Research Council, was responsible for 25 percent of deaths in 2000. Between 1990 and 2010 six million South Africans will have died of AIDS.[10] South Africa's rate of HIV/AIDS infection is among the highest in the world. In the late 1980s and early 1990s, accelerating urbanization combined with structural unemployment, political violence, and labor migration to loosen social cohesion in poor communities, creating an especially severe version of the high-risk situation identified by HIV/AIDS epidemiologists.[11]

Black women experience poverty especially acutely. Significantly higher percentages of women live in poverty than men, and the growing number of households headed by women are especially likely to be very poor. Women are at higher risk of HIV/AIDS infection. Dramatic rises in economic growth are needed to alleviate poverty significantly. Such rises are unlikely in the short term, without sharp increases in levels of investment in economic activity.

FOCUS QUESTION

How did sanctions affect the South African economy?

South Africa and the International Political Economy

Throughout the twentieth century, South Africa's economy depended heavily on foreign trade, with imports and exports representing between 50 and 65 percent of GDP and primary commodities, especially gold, predominating in exports. From the mid-1940s, protectionist policies promoted manufacturing for the domestic market. These policies, together with the restrictions on the use of black labor, caused growing inefficiencies, which economists believe constrained growth by the early 1970s.[12] Protectionist policies favored the manufacture of consumption rather than capital goods. This helps explain why, in contrast to other middle-income developing countries, South Africa lagged behind in producing machines and equipment. In comparison to most primary commodity producers, high gold prices and well-diversified markets for exports helped to keep terms of trade in South Africa's favor throughout most of the apartheid era, despite the rising cost of oil imports.

One important consequence of the international sanctions campaign was that the South African government began to invest in local branches of production, fearing a time when sanctions might become more effective. For example, one oil embargo imposed extra costs on the South African economy, but it also stimulated a petrochemical industry that remains one of South Africa's more competitive export sectors.

More significant in its political effect than trade sanctions on South African policy-makers was the impact of divestment and credit denial by companies and banks, principally American, in reaction to the state of emergency that was imposed in 1985. Divestment was a direct response to threats by colleges as well as state and local governments to withdraw their holdings in companies with South African interests. This was the expression of a movement that began on U.S. college campuses in the mid-1960s but gathered force in the early 1980s. The divestment campaign culminated in the passage in the U.S. Congress of the Comprehensive Anti-Apartheid Act in October 1986. Divestment did not directly contract South African economic activity, for South African domestic capital formation was the major source of investment in the economy. To an increasingly indebted administration, however, the prospect of future limitations in its ability to secure foreign loans was extremely alarming. By 1987, South African industrialists were dismayed about the difficulties they expected to encounter in obtaining access to advanced technology.[13]

South Africa's changing economic relationship with the countries of the region also had political implications. Traditionally, South Africa dominated the regional economy through such institutional arrangements as the South African Customs Union (which linked South Africa, Namibia, Lesotho, Swaziland, and Botswana in a free-trade and revenue-sharing zone). During the 1980s, however, the region's economic significance as a trading partner with South Africa substantially increased at the same time that labor migration from the region into South Africa slackened. In the early 1980s, at a time of balance-of-payments difficulties (the government in 1982 had to seek an IMF standby loan), regional annual trade surpluses in South Africa's favor reached $1.8 billion. South Africa's regional trading partners bought 40 percent of its manufacturing exports. By the end of the decade, however, regional trade was contracting because of the warfare that stepped up when South Africa sponsored insurgencies in Angola and Mozambique. Such destabilization created growing unease within industrial concerns, as well as disagreements within government itself.

South Africa's post-1994 reintegration into the international economy has been generally disheartening. On the positive side, a revival of foreign direct investment—much of it by companies that had divested earlier—helped revive growth to modest rates (between 2 and 3 percent), significantly better than the 1.8 percent growth that prevailed in the 1980s before the recession of the early 1990s. Much of the fresh foreign investment was concentrated in the service sector rather than, as the government hoped, in export-oriented manufacturing, the sector that was the most likely to generate local employment in the long term. The lifting of sanctions was accompanied by an expansion of trade with African and other Third World countries, but it also facilitated an outflow of South African capital to countries with cheaper labor costs and more efficient work forces. Local investment levels after 1994 remained at around 15 percent of GDP, up from 12 percent in 1983, but comparatively a very low rate of domestic saving. Foreign direct investment has therefore become increasingly important in South Africa's future growth prospects.

Tariff reductions embarked on in 1994 helped to close down historically protected sectors. Certain export-oriented industries, however (automobile components, for example), benefited from the currency devaluations that resulted from the gradual lifting of exchange controls that started in 1995. Even so, after the abandonment of protection industrial restructuring resulted in a substantial decline of factory employment between 1994 and 2000—particularly in textiles and clothing.

Given the harsh consequences of South Africa's economic liberalization and its consequent exposure to foreign competition, macroeconomic policy has become a profoundly contested issue in South Africa's political life for the first time in its history.

Summary

Racial segregation required considerable state intervention in the economy. In particular until 1986 the state restricted Africans' mobility, in order to ensure adequate supplies of cheap black labor for mining and agriculture. State-owned enterprises, however, helped to develop a substantial manufacturing sector from the late 1920s onward. During the 1960s and 1970s public investments in strategic synthetic fuel and armaments diversified the industrial base further. Increasingly comprehensive social welfare programs accompanied these developments. From the 1970s, external anti-apartheid pressures as well as shortages of crucial skills began to prompt liberalization. Even before the advent of universal suffrage in 1994, most apartheid restrictions had been dismantled. Since then, democratic governments have continued to expand economic liberalization, reducing tariffs and selling public enterprises. Rising unemployment, partly a consequence of market reform, as well as the effects of the HIV-AIDS pandemic, have frustrated the government's efforts to reduce poverty and inequality.

Governance and Policy-Making

FOCUS QUESTION

How did South Africa's constitutional drafters try to ensure that racial minorities would be protected?

Organization of the State

Modern state organization in South Africa emerged from four years of bargaining between 1992 and 1996. A transitional constitution settled the details of how South African would be governed after the first democratic elections, which were held in 1994. Parliament, acting as a constitutional assembly, then debated a final document that had to incorporate key principles adopted at the earlier multi-party talks. This was a way of ensuring that racial and other minority concerns would receive enduring protection. In the end, 243 clauses embody a very detailed constitution. A bill of rights supplies safeguards that range from traditional civil liberties to environmental protections and sexual choice. Most clauses of the constitution can be changed through a two-thirds vote in the National Assembly. However, an opening section of the Constitution lists a set of key values for which a 75 percent majority is needed.

To date, there have been fourteen amendments to the 1996 Constitution, a considerable number. This is the result of the Constitution's detail, and most of the amendments have been relatively minor.

Since 1994, the South African state has been quasi-federal. The national government has the power to override laws passed by nine provincial regional legislatures. The provincial administrations depend on funds allocated by the central government.

Between 1994 and 1999, the transitional constitution compelled the executive to be composed of a coalition of party representatives, with posts being distributed roughly proportionately to parties that achieved more than 5 percent of the vote. The National Party withdrew from the GNU in 1996, partly because of its failure to impose its will on the drafting of the 1996 constitution. The requirement for power sharing did not feature in the 1996 constitution.

FOCUS QUESTION

Why is the executive branch of government so powerful in South Africa?

The Executive

The Presidency

South African governments are formed by the president, who must be a member of the National Assembly. When elected by the Assembly, the president vacates his or her parliamentary seat and appoints and subsequently chairs a cabinet of ministers as well. He also chooses a deputy president, a post with no constitutionally designated special powers. Since 1994, the president can serve only two five-year terms. South Africa's first president after universal suffrage elections in 1994 was Nelson Mandela, who served one term, declining to serve another on grounds of age. His single term was decisive in establishing the prestige of the new government both abroad, and more importantly, at home, among all sections of the ANC, including supporters of the previous regime, winning them over through informal warmth and imaginative gestures of public empathy. His successor was Thabo Mbeki who followed Mandela's example in taking care to cultivate strong personal relationships with members of the Afrikaner elite. Before their appointments, both were elected (though secret ballots) as the presidents of the ANC at delegate conferences. The president can be impeached or removed from office by a two-thirds vote of the National Assembly, but only on grounds of disability or serious misconduct. The president must choose a deputy from members of the National Assembly. The president can dismiss the deputy president at any time. After Thabo Mbeki became president, the office accumulated functions and resources. Even as Mandela's deputy, Mbeki was largely responsible for the day-to-day management of the administration as well as managing the cabinet.

Although the South African system of government has inherited many features of the Westminster model, the South African president is considerably more powerful than the British prime minister, both constitutionally and through the accumulation of functions in his office that has developed under Mbeki. In certain respects, although the South African president is not elected through a separate public ballot, the South African political system has presidential characteristics.

Cabinet

Unlike the president, ministers remain members of parliament and are accountable to it through question-time sessions. These are regularly scheduled occasions, in which ministers have to reply to queries from backbenchers. Ministers are also accountable to various parliamentary standing committees. The president may also appoint deputy ministers. Parliamentarians lose office if they are expelled from membership by their parties. In the South African political system this gives the executive great power. Elected by a parliamentary majority, the president will normally be a political party leader, enjoying a controlling influence over the makeup of parliamentary representation. Given the president-as-party-leader's de facto power over parliamentary office holding, a revolt by ruling party backbenchers is extremely unlikely. In 1999, Thabo Mbeki could appoint his cabinet without any restrictions. He chose, however, to maintain the coalition with Inkatha, which he inherited from the power-sharing provisions of the Mandela administration. In 2004, Mbeki made room in his cabinet for Marthinus van Schalwyk, then the leader of the National Party, who became Minister for the Environment and Tourism. Although there is no formal requirement for socially representative cabinets, ANC governments embody a racial cross-section. Twenty-two ministers and deputy ministers are women, a reflection of the ANC's commitment to gender equity, which has also ensured that at least one-third of ANC parliamentarians are female.

In summary, South African government is characterized by powerful executive authority. There are very few checks other than constitutional restraints on the leadership of the ruling party. The enlargement of the president's office at the inception of the Mbeki era encouraged observers to believe that in comparison to the relaxed and conciliatory manner of the Mandela administration, "under Mbeki there [would] be tighter control on management and delivery."[14]

Implications of Centralized Authority

Certainly, Mbeki has attempted to impose his personal authority more frequently than his predecessor. For example, he dictated the choice of premiers to

The U.S. Connection

Organization of the State: South Africa Compared to the United States

In South Africa, as in the United States, the Constitution lays down the essential features of state organization. In the United States the Supreme Court has the final say on constitutional interpretation. In South Africa the Constitutional Court performs this function. In both countries politicians appoint the judges, but in South Africa Constitutional Court judges hold office for fixed terms whereas in the United States Supreme Court judges are appointed for life. In South Africa, it is easier for politicians to amend the constitution. Most changes require only a two-thirds vote in parliament. In the United States, however, three-fourths of the fifty state governments need to approve constitutional amendments, which also need two-thirds votes in Congress and the president's approval.

South Africa follows the Westminster system of government in which the party winning parliamentary elections sets up an executive. This is different from the American separation of presidential and legislature elections. American presidents have formidable powers, but Congress can check these powers to some degree, especially when it comes to budgets and treaties. In South Africa the parliament tends to defer to the presidency. South African executive authority has grown through the use of national list proportional representation, which centralizes party organization and empowers party leaders. South African parliamentarians hold their seats at the will of the party leadership, not because the voters chose them individually. Unlike in the United States parliamentarians do not represent particular districts.

In both countries presidents may serve only two terms and in both presidents can be removed from office through impeachment (and, in the case of the United States, trial by the Senate). In South Africa, political parties can use any method they want to choose presidential candidates and all other candidates for elected public offices. The relative weakness of American political parties in contrast to those of South Africa is partly a result of the primary elections that give ordinary citizens such an important role in deciding who runs for office. Unlike in the United States, South African presidents must appoint their cabinets from serving parliamentarians. Cabinet ministers remain subject to the normal rules of parliamentary accountability because one party (the ANC) dominates the political system, however, the executive enjoys considerable autonomy. In both countries executive power derives partly from a spoils system in which politicians appoint senior officials in the civil service.

Both countries are federations, but in South Africa, the nine regions depend almost entirely upon the central government for their budgets. Provincial governments can pass legislation, but the National Assembly can override all their laws. This is very different from the great powers that American states, cities, and towns exercise in areas such as welfare and education. The United States possesses a relatively accessible political system with a great many places where citizens and lobbies can affect policy-making. This openness is the result of several factors: federalism, a decentralized party system, separation of powers, and the fact that office holders are personally accountable to the voters. In comparison, the South African political system is less open and more centralized. This is the result of its constitutional structure and a tradition of hierarchical party organization. ❖

the ANC regional organization. In 1998 an ANC "deployment committee" was set up. This decides on key appointments in para-statal organizations, as well having the final decision in the makeup of the party's electoral lists. This arrangement has extended and systemized a patronage system with its center in Thabo Mbeki's office.

State Capacity

Centralization of political authority does not necessarily imply more effective government. Certainly, since 1994, ANC-led administrations have attracted praise for their restraints on public expenditure, their efforts to reduce public employment, and their success in reducing the deficit. Spending government money effectively, however, is much more difficult than saving it, and public welfare and public investment are much less tightly administered. Generally, Mbeki's centralizing and technocratic predispositions are subverted by a weak bureaucracy, especially in several of the nine provinces that together employ the vast majority of the country's public servants (750,000 of 1.1 million) as well as spending two-thirds of the budget.

This bureaucracy is partly controlled by the central government and partly by the regions. Certain departments—defense, security, justice, finance, trade and industry, and home affairs—are administered in a centralized fashion by national government ministries. For other departments—education, social services and health—regional administrations headed by elected regional governments enjoy considerable discretion over official appointments, allocating resources, and deciding the more detailed aspects of policy. Certain central governments are extremely efficient—finance, for example, especially with respect to tax collection; others still suffer from reputations for corruption and incompetence carried over from the apartheid era.

Under Mbeki, patronage has proliferated, impeding the development of competent public administration. This began at the top of the state. Unlike Mandela's charismatic authority, Mbeki's accession to the ANC's leadership was contested. As leader, he places a high premium on personal loyalty. Since his accession, he has tended to use his powers of appointment to reward his closest and oldest associates, and rivals have been displaced. Mbeki's use of patronage has resulted in a proliferation of factionalism within both the ANC and the administrations it controls. ANC "deployments" (the term the organization uses for politically motivated public appointments) ensure that high offices (in both the public and the private sectors) become enmeshed in personalized networks of power, influence, and cronyism. Estimates of the annual cost of public corruption—one result of such managerial tendencies—suggest that as much as R4 billion a year is lost through corruption and waste. This is a substantial sum, though less than 1 percent of the government's budgeted expenditure of R419 billion for 2006–2007.

Other State Institutions

FOCUS QUESTION

Why is public confidence in the legal system so limited?

The Judiciary

To the government's credit, the senior levels of the judiciary are freer of executive influence than they were before 1994. All judges are appointed through a constitutional process that limits executive discretion. Court judgments demonstrate robust judicial independence, despite complaints by cabinet ministers that the courts are trying to make themselves policy-makers.

This independence has been especially obvious with respect to the Constitutional Court. In two key judgments, in 2001 and in 2002, the court ruled on how the government should allocate public resources, to meet its constitutional duty to supply shelter for a group of forcibly evicted squatters in Grootboom near Cape Town and to provide antiretroviral medication for HIV/AIDS patients. In the fifty-eight cases addressed by the Court between 1994 and 2004 that tested judicial readiness to challenge the executive, the court ruled against the government 40 percent of the time. Judgments against the government became even more frequent after 1999.[15]

Public respect for legal institutions needs more than the autonomy and integrity represented by the Constitutional Court and the other senior levels of judicial decision making. For most citizens, courts are inaccessible and inefficient. Huge caseloads make legal proceedings extremely slow. Nearly half of South Africa's prisoners are awaiting trial. Several thousand cases a year do not reach trial because criminal syndicates bribe court officials to destroy dockets.

South Africa has one of the highest crime rates in the world. In 2003 it had seven and a half times as many homicides as the United States. This is a consequence of gross social inequalities, a violent political history, and a general disrespect for the law that apartheid engendered, although rising rates of youth unemployment supply a more contemporary explanation for crime.

Police

One way of measuring the efficacy of a justice system is through arrests and convictions for reported crimes. Overall, conviction rates in South Africa, at 8 percent in 2002, represent one of the lowest levels in the world. This is a reflection of poor police work and courtroom shortcomings. Police weaknesses are historic. They partly result from neglecting criminal investigation in favor of the counterinsurgency role assigned to the police force after 1960. Up to the 1990s judges tolerated routine use of torture to extract confessions even in petty criminal cases. This undermined the ability of the police to investigate crimes.

Since 1994, police competence has weakened even further. The unification of the national police force with a number of separate homeland forces has resulted in an organization that is top heavy in its rank structure. Only a third of South Africa's 17,000 police officers work in the field. Police training is poor. One reason that conviction rates are low is that semiliterate constables ignore basic rules of evidence. Bottom-ranking pay scales are the lowest in the public sector, which makes the force exceptionally vulnerable to corruption. Between 2000 and 2003 police corruption was said to have doubled. In 2004 researchers discovered that at any one time 4,000 policemen were likely to be suspended for misconduct.[16]

South African National Defence Force and Other National Security Agencies

The South African soldiery is not in much better shape than the police forces. The South African National Defence Force (SANDF), an amalgamation of the old South African Defence Force, homeland militias, and the guerrilla armies, employed 75,000 soldiers, sailors, and airmen in 2005, about half the size of the full-time army during the apartheid era. The small size of the army is appropriate enough, given the absence of any external military threat to South Africa. Its quality is another matter. One reason that has made South Africa reluctant to play a major role in continental peacekeeping operations is the poor quality of its forces, which ceased active recruitment between 1994 and 2000. Like the police the army is top-heavy in rank structure, and spends most of its budget on salaries and gratuities and only 0.5 percent of its funding on new equipment. In 2005, up to 23 percent of Force members were thought to be HIV positive. UN regulations prohibit deploying HIV-positive soldiers in peacekeeping, which is now a major SANDF commitment. The transformation of apartheid's aggressive war machine into what opposition politicians deride as "an armed welfare department" may not be permanent, however. In 1998, the government committed itself to an ambitious program of expenditure on military aircraft, submarines, and light destroyers for the navy, while recruitment was to be stepped up to an annual rate of 10,000. The first of these purchases arrived in 2003, a warship for the navy. It will be the SANDF's investment in its human capital that will be the critical factor in its future effectiveness, however.

South African Intelligence agencies supply an additional dimension to the national security system. In 1999 a separate ministry was created for intelligence, and since the Al Qaeda attack on the World Trade Center the budgets of the externally oriented Secret Service and the larger domestically focused National Intelligence Agency have both expanded.

Subnational Government

A more serious limitation on state powers than its military weakness is shortcomings of the subnational governments, both in regional administrations and in local authorities.

The nine regional governments are led by premiers, who are limited to two terms in office. In principle, premiers are elected by their legislatures, but in the seven provinces in which the ANC predominates, such elections are formalities. Premiers are in reality appointed and dismissed by the president.

Each premier appoints a mini-cabinet, called an executive council. Regional revenues derive mainly from central government. The Financial and Fiscal Commission distributes what are referred to as "equitable shares" of national revenues between the regions, calculated on the basis of developmental needs in each province. In addition, provinces receive conditional grants for particular

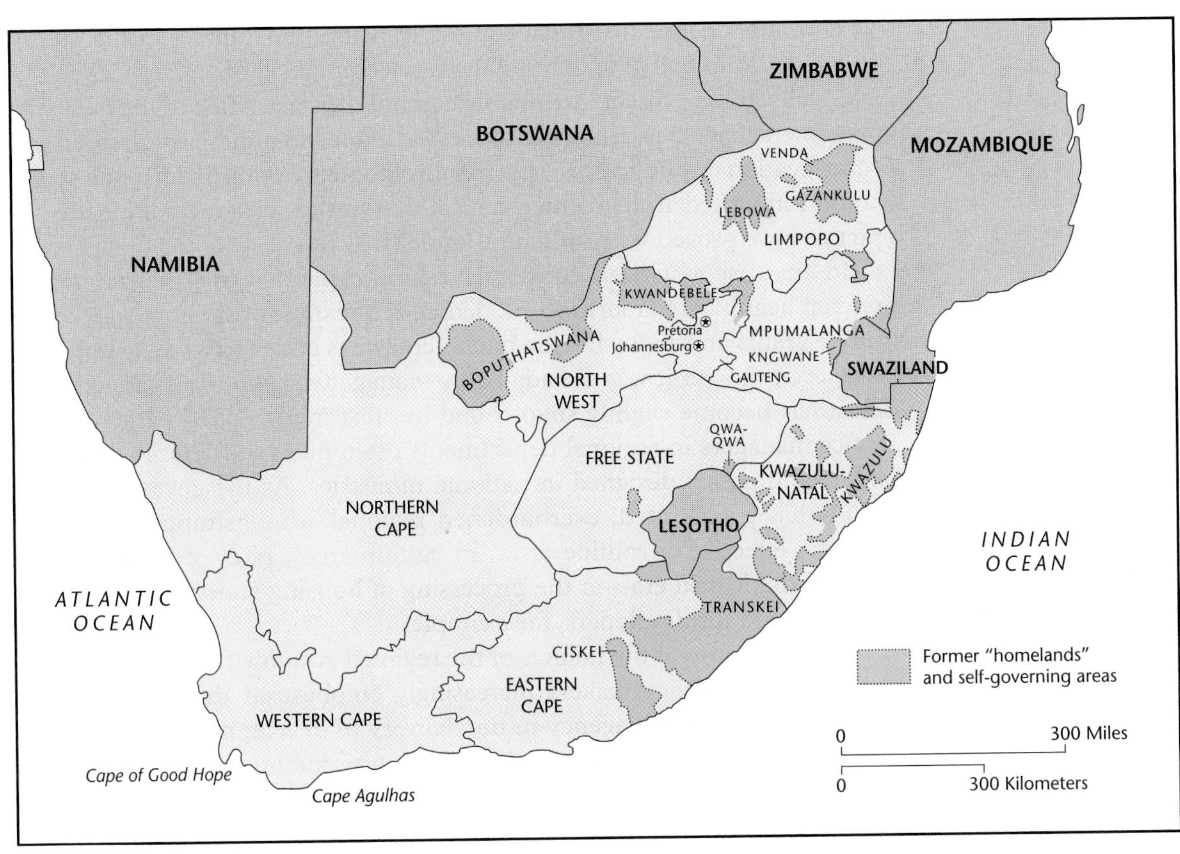

projects from the national ministries. Regional administrations must allocate their expenditure between departments in accordance with national budgetary prescriptions. However, within these structures they enjoy a measure of financial discretion in deciding how to spend their equitable shares, in contracting for services and equipment, for example.

At their inception, most of the regions had to amalgamate several different civil services from different homelands or from the separate establishments that existed for white, Coloured, and Indian people, each of which had developed its own managerial styles. The new regional boundaries brought together rival elites who sometimes remained jealous of each other's influence. For example, bureaucrats in the former Transkei resented deeply the decision to locate the Eastern Cape's capital in Bisho, the former capital of the Ciskeien homeland, and they resisted its authority. In many of the former homelands, bureaucratic systems had undergone considerable degeneration. Because governments did not have strong accountability mechanisms, administrations were often short of key skills such as financial record keeping, and civil servants were as a consequence often very corrupt.

Reforming such administrations was extremely difficult, particularly because it was impossible to dismiss public servants during the Mandela era. This was an unfortunate consequence of the transition guarantees in the 1993 constitution. Additionally, militant public service unions affiliated to COSATU, the ANC's ally, often protect identifiably corrupt officials. Most of the new regional governments lack basic information, even about the number of their employees or the location of public property. Finally, the new South African public administration inherited from its hierarchical and authoritarian traditions, which in practice have proved very difficult to modify.

In any case as citizen entitlements have expanded in social reforms—free prenatal health care, abortions on demand, housing subsidies, a wider range of welfare grants and so forth—the bureaucracy has acquired a whole range of new tasks, even though it was already badly managed and poorly qualified. In addition it has become slightly smaller and has lost many skilled personnel. Public service managers in regional departments often find it difficult to interpret and understand policy designed in national ministries. As the government's policy agenda has proliferated, overburdened regional administrations have become even less effective at routine tasks. In certain areas, rates of "delivery" slowed down in the Mbeki era—in the processing of housing subsidies and the release of public land for developers, for example.

Partly because of the failings of the regional administrations, from 1999 onwards national policy-makers increasingly emphasized the role of municipal government as the key agency in the delivery of development projects. An ambitious reform strategy launched in 2000 was intended to rationalize South African local authority, by combining 843 councils in 299 municipalities, and combining bankrupt rural governments with richer urban authorities in the hope of making them financially self-sufficient. Because of their taxation powers, local governments in many respects have greater discretionary power than regional administrations, especially in the case of the six metropolitan councils in South Africa's main cities. Although the big cities draw most of their revenues from local taxes, the smaller authorities remain heavily dependent on government grants. Politically motivated embargoes on taxes and service charges in the 1980s bankrupted township councils. When they were combined with white municipalities in 1993, they brought their debts with them. Only a minority of councils could persuade their poorer citizens to resume payments for services, and the councils accumulated huge debts with the Electricity Supply Commission. In the 2006 local authority elections, the ANC retained control of most of the councils that it had won five and ten years earlier in the first and second democratic polls. Today about 75 percent of South Africa's cities are governed by ANC-dominated administrations. However, there was very low voter turnout, and at public meetings there was heavy criticism of the way local councils were performing. The public was clearly disappointed with the first decade of democratic local government. After 2000, the Ministry of Provincial and Local Government invested considerable effort to train councilors as well as to set up a system of ward committees to improve accountability and public participation in planning. Reforms do not seem to have improved the quality of representation in local government. In the 2006 local elections, 60 percent of the candidates the ANC fielded were new, because the party itself was worried about the poor quality of its elected officials in local authorities.

The Policy-Making Process

Since 1999, South African government policy-making has become increasingly centralized. Before 1994 the ANC appeared to be committed to participatory ways of making policy. This appeared to be the implication of the way the Reconstruction and Development Programme (RDP) was adopted. The RDP was originally prepared by in-house economists at the Congress of South African Trade Unions (COSATU). Five drafts of the RDP were debated and subsequently modified at meetings held by the ANC with its allies. The RDP's original emphasis on "stakeholder" consultation in development planning and institutional accountability was reflected in the new government's early rhetoric. For example, the 1995 White Paper on the RDP advocated setting up "structured consultations" at all levels.

The early Mandela administration seemed to take its cue from such injunctions when it came to making policy. Assertive parliamentary portfolio committees and ministers who were prepared to work closely with them broadened the social scope of policy, making it more open to the influence of an infant lobbying industry. For example, key labor relations legislation was adopted only after lengthy efforts to obtain business and trade union agreement. Departments conscientiously circulated Green Papers and White Papers (successive drafts of policy proposals) to all conceivably interested parties, and they received public feedback at policy presentations up and down the country.

The minister of finance's announcement on June 14, 1996, of the essential tenets of an official Growth, Employment, and Redistribution policy (GEAR) policy represented an abrupt turnaround from this relatively open and receptive kind of decision making. From now on, the minister warned, macroeconomic management would stress deficit reduction, the removal of tariff protection, government right-sizing, privatization, exchange control relaxation, and the setting of wage increases below rates of productivity growth. The ANC's trade union allies clearly could not endorse these objectives. June 1996 certainly represented a policy switch even though GEAR's exponents could claim with a degree of justification that the RDP itself contained language in accord with the measures the minister for finance, Trevor Manuel, was proposing. Essentially, the RDP, and earlier official pronouncements on economics, suggested that redistributive measures would supply the main stimulation for growth. A currency crisis in late 1995 checked such equitable thinking. From now on, creating jobs in the private sector was to be the main engine for ensuring social progress. The government itself was not in the business of creating jobs. Between 1994 and 1999, the civil service contracted by 100,000.

A technical team of experts from the Reserve Bank, the Development Bank, and the World Bank prepared the GEAR document. The team worked under Alec Erwin, then the deputy minister of finance. The team presented its draft recommendations to Thabo Mbeki in March, and shortly before its public release a revised version went to members of the ANC's national working committee as well as Communist Party and trade union leaders. In contrast to earlier broad policy statements, GEAR's scripting was secretive and highly technocratic. Trevor Manuel's statement, immediately after GEAR's publication, that its content was nonnegotiable, also made it different from any other official policy announcements released in the form of Green or White papers. GEAR's adoption set the tone for the new style of policy-making. Since 1996, policy shifts have occurred in a characteristically sudden fashion. ANC backbenchers have become much less likely to challenge ministers, and the references to "people-driven development" have almost all disappeared from official phraseology. The "policy communities" that were beginning to develop around ministries and portfolio committees before 1996 have stagnated. Instead, the surest way to influence policy from outside government is through obtaining direct access to the president's office and the informal networks that surround it. The internal party rebellion that is represented by support within the ANC for Jacob Zuma is mainly a consequence of this authoritarian trend.

The government is determined to maintain its commitment to fiscally conservative policies. This has put economic issues at the center of modern political conflict. COSATU opposed GEAR from its inception, though COSATU leaders cannily maintained their loyalty to the ANC alliance. COSATU hostility to the program has been expressed in several demonstrative national strikes. Other kinds of dissent, both by unions and the broader public, have shown hostility to official financial policies. Trade unions joined civic associations to mobilize popular protest against contracting out municipal services as well and to challenge the moral right of municipalities to evict delinquent tenants and to withdraw services from payment defaulters. The austerity measures implicit in GEAR's economies have had an especially severe effect on municipalities, which have received less and less funding from the central government. Support among trade unionists and communists for Jacob Zuma expresses discontent within the ANC's left wing at the government's economic policies ("Succession Politics"). In May 2006, COSATU's secretary general accused Thabo Mbeki of leading South Africa to a dictatorship, citing the intimidation of journalists and the removal from within the ANC of pro-Zuma officials. This kind of attack from an allied organization was unprecedented in its hostility. At the beginning of the Mandela government, ANC leaders hoped to maintain their activist traditions in the ways in which they made decisions and exercised power. More than ten years after the coming of democracy, the worlds of policy decision making and popular political activism, have become increasingly insulated from each other.

Summary

Today an extensive constitution includes an entrenched bill of rights. For a transition period, between 1994 and 1999, a power-sharing coalition helped to reassure racial minorities. Nine regional governments give South African

Profile
Jacob Zuma

Jacob Zuma used to be regarded as a stalwart party loyalist. After he was elected deputy-president of the ANC in 1997 and then appointed deputy head of state in 1999, the ANC thought that it could delay deciding who would eventually replace Thabo Mbeki. Zuma himself had no higher ambitions, party insiders believed. Polygamous marriages and very limited formal education also seemed to make it unlikely that Zuma would ever become president.

Among ANC leaders, however, Jacob Zuma was unusual in his command of personal support within the organization and its allies. Zuma's enthusiastic maintenance of his Communist Party affiliations encouraged trade unionists to think he was a champion of their concerns. There are other reasons for his popularity within the ANC, however. He stands out among the ANC's present leadership for the depth of his political experience. His "struggle history" includes ten years in prison for his role in an early sabotage campaign. Also, his reputation as a "traditionalist" man of the people makes him especially popular in the countryside. With his warm manner and down-to-earth style, he is also well liked among ordinary ANC members. His efforts in the early 1990s to broker peace in Kwa-Zulu Natal earned him respect and trust outside the ANC. Because there were no other obvious replacements for Thabo Mbeki after the president had completed his constitutionally limited two terms, Jacob Zuma's political stock began to rise.

In 2005, on the day of his arraignment on rape charges, several thousand Zuma supporters surrounded the Supreme Court building, singing his personal anthem, "Bring Me My Machine Gun," and wearing T-shirts printed with the slogan, "Zuma: 100 percent Zulu Boy." The reference to Zuma's ethnicity reflected a popular belief that Xhosa personalities (who supposedly predominate within the ANC's senior ranks) were blocking his rise to the presidency. Ethnic sensitivities are not unusual within the ANC's internal politics but it is very unusual for such feelings to be voiced so publicly.

Zuma's trial on corruption charges will resume shortly. Here the evidence against the ANC's deputy leader is formidable. In the trial of Shabir Shaik, Zuma's former financial adviser, prosecutors were able to demonstrate that Shaik had negotiated a bribe from a French arms contractor on Zuma's behalf. Tested again before a different judge the same evidence and the same witnesses may be less convincing. But in the version of things accepted by the court in Shaik's trial, Jacob Zuma was an active and knowing accomplice in corrupt business practices.

Jacob Zuma's substantial support within the ANC was overwhelmingly evident at the party's congress held in December 2007. He easily defeated Mbeki in the contest for the party presidency. He still faces corruption charges; the charges were reinstated with new evidence just after the conference. The trial will begin in August 2008 and may not be over by the time of the next election. At this stage, though, the party seems to have no obvious alternative candidates who might have comparable support, within or outside the ANC. ❖

politics a quasi-federal character and offer smaller political parties the possibility of executive office. Despite such safeguards, the ruling party and its leaders are very powerful, a consequence of ANC majorities in the National Assembly. Presidential authority gains strength from an electoral system that makes members of parliament very dependent on the party leadership. Continuing shortcomings in the police, the judicial system, and the regional administrations effectively limit executive power. Meanwhile policy-making has become increasingly centralized.

Representation and Participation

FOCUS QUESTION

Why has the South African National Assembly been so ineffectual in checking executive power?

The Legislature

Lawmaking

The legislature consists of a 400-member National Assembly located in Cape Town as well as the National Council of Provinces. In general elections, parties compete for parliamentary seats by offering single lists of candidates. If a ruling party's leadership predominates within the executive branch, as is the case with the ANC, then the executive branch's power over parliament is much greater than in most other systems in which the executive branch is accountable to parliament. This is because MPs hold their seats at the will of leadership, not through being personally elected. In practice, most of legislation since 1994 has been drafted by ministers and their departments. Draft laws must be read in the National Assembly before portfolio committees review their content. These committees usually call for public submissions on the bill before recommending revision, acceptance, or rejection of the law. Once a bill has received its second reading in the House of Assembly, it can be enacted. Portfolio committees review the work of different government departments. Standing Committees on Public Accounts and Public Finance monitor general public spending, and they can summon ministers and public servants to appear before them.

In 1999, a second chamber of the parliament in Cape Town was set up, the National Council of the Provinces. Its ninety members are made up of nine equal delegations drawn from the regional legislatures. To encourage consensus within each provincial delegation, each province can cast only one vote within the Council. The National Council for the Provinces reviews all legislation. But for most laws its functions are only advisory.

Parliamentary Assertiveness

Much depends on the feelings of the ANC caucus, which represents well over two-thirds of the votes in the National Assembly. The ANC's record is a mixed one. Some of its early shortcomings in parliament were the result of inexperience. For example, between 1994 and 1999, ANC MPs asked only 15 percent of the questions put to ministers even though they held nearly two-thirds of the seats in the National Assembly.

South Africa uses a national list system of proportional representation. In national and provincial elections (held simultaneously every five years), parties nominate lists of candidates—one list for the National Assembly and nine lists for the provinces. Voters use two ballot papers, one for the Assembly and one for their provincial legislature, on which they indicate their preferred party. In this way, voters can divide their support between two parties. Names of candidates do not appear on the ballot papers. Seats are allocated in proportion to each party's share of the votes.

The list system through which MPs hold their seats at the discretion of party leaders means that MPs can defy party policy or leadership directives only if they are willing to risk heavy penalties.

During constitutional negotiations, both the National Party and the ANC leadership agreed to discourage MPs from changing their party affiliations. In 2003 legislation was enacted to authorize "floor-crossing" during brief "window periods." In this way MPs can change their party affiliation or even leave an existing party and establish a new group. The law required a constitutional amendment, a change that was opposed without success in the Constitutional Court by lawyers acting for some of the smaller and more vulnerable political parties. As its critics predicted, floor crossing has strengthened the ruling party. In the latest round in September 2005, the ANC enlarged its caucus with fourteen new adherents, including all seven MPs from the National Party. The ANC is protected against floor crossing by the 10 percent clause in the legislation: MPs can only cross in groups that make up at least 10 percent of their party's parliamentary representation. This proviso makes it much more difficult for members of a large party to change their affiliation because of the planning that is needed to make sure that enough MPs made the switch. Such planning would have to be done before the window period, and if party leaders discovered the identities of any would-be defectors they could be expelled.

ANC MPs have occasionally been willing to confront the executive branch. During the Mandela government, this was evident at the hearings on child welfare grants. It was also a feature of how the portfolio committee on defense did business. After the 1999 election, during the Mbeki administration, committee assertiveness became much rarer, and ministers treat committees scornfully.

In 2001, the ANC established a political committee to monitor the hearings of the Select Committee on Public Accounts (SCOPA), which was investigating allegations of corrupt arms contracting. SCOPA's inquiry followed allegations that a former defense minister had accepted an R11 million bribe. SCOPA, chaired according to convention by an opposition MP but containing a majority of ANC members, recommended in November 2000 that the Special Investigations Unit should participate in the official investigation. President Mbeki rejected this recommendation. The leader of the ANC group within SCOPA, Andrew Feinstein, was demoted and resigned subsequently, complaining of ministerial efforts to "rein me in."[17] In January 2001, the ANC chief whip, Tony Yengeni, established a special political committee of twenty-two senior ANC MPs "to provide greater political direction to the ANC's parliamentary caucus." Yengeni announced that he would attend ANC study group meetings of SCOPA members to supply "political authority and guidance."[18] Two years later, however, Yengeni was compelled to leave parliament after being convicted for accepting a vehicle from one of the arms contractors under investigation. In February 2001, the official joint investigation published its report. This did not implicate senior politicians, but it did accuse top civil servants of nepotism and lying. After 2002, SCOPA, ceased to play any further role in the arms contracting saga, despite later courtroom revelations about much more serious wrongdoings than those identified in the joint report. For its critics, SCOPA's inability to investigate the arms purchases adequately demonstrated the ANC leadership's tight control of parliament.

FOCUS QUESTION

Why have opposition parties remained so weak in South African politics?

Political Parties and the Party System

The most significant political parties were founded well before South Africa achieved universal suffrage: the African National Congress in 1912, the (Afrikaner) National Party in 1914, the Democratic Party in its original incarnation as the Progressive Party in 1959, Inkatha in 1975, and the Pan-Africanist Congress in 1959. With stable organizations and enduring support bases, these groups embody a resilient party system. Since several of the organizations began as racially or ethnically defined movements, each party draws support mainly from a different ethnic or racial group, although less so today than formerly.

The African National Congress

The ANC began in a conference of African notables that assembled in 1912 to protest the impending South African Land Act. Years later, during World War II, the ANC began to build a mass membership. By this time, several of its leaders were also members of the Communist Party. Within the ANC, both Communists and Africanists (racially assertive African nationalists) who formed the Youth League influenced the ANC to embrace more aggressive tactics. The Communist Party was banned in 1950; its members then worked within the ANC and allied organizations. Communist influence and older liberal traditions instilled by Methodist schools, which trained most African political leaders, ensured that although the ANC itself remained an exclusively African body, it defined its program on a broader basis. In 1956, the ANC's Freedom Charter proposed a democratic future in which all races would enjoy equal rights. A "Defiance Campaign" of civil disobedience against new apartheid laws swelled membership. A breakaway movement, the Pan-Africanist Congress, formed in 1959 as a more radical alternative to the ANC. In response to PAC calls to action, the new organization's supporters assembled outside police stations on March 21, 1960, demanding to be arrested for not carrying their passes. In Sharpeville police fired into a crowd of 5,000, killing 80. In the following uproar, the government banned both the ANC and the PAC. Moving underground and into exile, they began planning armed insurgencies.

During its thirty years in exile, the ANC strengthened its alliance with the Communist Party. Partly because of this alliance, it opened its ranks to whites, Indians, and Coloureds. Because survival in exile required discipline and authority, the ANC patterned its internal organization on the centralized model of communist parties.

After 1976, ANC guerrillas attracted public attention with attacks on symbolic targets. A charismatic cult developed around the imprisoned leaders on Robben Island, especially Nelson Mandela. Mandela's stature helped the ANC to achieve recognition and acceptance internationally. By the late 1980s, meetings between its leaders and Western statesmen underlined its status as a government in waiting. The ANC began to establish secret preliminary contacts with South African officials in the mid-1980s. After the return home in 1990, the international recognition the ANC had obtained in exile brought the financial resources needed to build a sophisticated mass organization in South Africa. This organization would absorb not just the exiled bureaucrats and the returning soldiers; it would also bring together a variety of movements that had developed inside South Africa. These included some of the homeland-based political parties as well as the vast federation of civic bodies led by the United Democratic Front.

Today the ANC's overwhelming predominance remains partly a result of its legitimacy as a national liberation movement in the struggle against apartheid. Its political authority also results from an extensive political organization, represented through local branches throughout the country. To reinvigorate its internal life, ANC leaders declared 2002 to be a Year of the Volunteer. The party sponsored local volunteer activities. Surveys later confirmed widespread and enthusiastic participation in projects like tree planting, hospital visiting, and school cleaning.

Smaller Parties

After Sharpeville, the National Party maintained its commitment to racial segregation and white privilege, but it defined its vision and programs in more universal language to win supporters among conservative groups in western countries. Portraying Southern Africa as a strategic area in the conflict between the West and the Soviets was a key ingredient in this project. A narrow majority of English-speaking South Africans supported the National Party during the 1980s. Meanwhile, the Progressives, represented in parliament by the lone voice of Helen Suzman between 1961 and 1974, won twenty-six seats and 20 percent of the white vote in 1981. Traditionally, their support derived from affluent urban English-speaking neighborhoods. During the 1960s, Suzman ensured that the party's appeal rested on advocating civil liberties. Popularity brought increased sensitivity to mainstream white political preoccupations: Progressive constitutional proposals emphasized decentralization and minority protection. Such proposals appealed to the leadership of Inkatha, the ruling party in the Zulu homeland, which had its own reasons for favoring federal constitutional arrangements. Control of state machinery as well as its association with the Zulu royal house enabled Inkatha to build a formidable organization. This became increasingly militarized throughout the 1980s during the ferocious struggle for territorial dominance in the shanty communities on the outskirts of Natal's urban centers.

In negotiating the new constitutional settlement, most parties attempted to broaden their support bases. The ANC built branches outside African neighborhoods. The "New" National Party enlisted a Coloured following. Although working-class Coloureds suffered racial oppression to some extent, they had benefited from apartheid, which had protected their jobs from African competition. In 1990, the Progressives combined with a group of breakaway parliamentarians from the National Party to form a Democratic Party (DP). The Democrats recruited fresh support from the Indian and Coloured chambers in the tricameral parliament while positioning itself as the party of meritocracy, business, and free enterprise. Meanwhile, the Inkatha Freedom Party (IFP) gave conspicuous positions to a number of white sympathizers. Of the older parties, only the PAC remained within its traditional boundaries. It believed that its continuing sponsorship of guerrilla warfare, and its racial assertiveness, would win majority support.

Seven parties won seats in the National Assembly in 1994. They included the ANC, NNP, DP, IFP, and PAC, as well as two new parties. The Freedom Front hoped to secure future arrangements for Afrikaner self-determination. More realistically, they believed their presence in parliament would protect the status of existing Afrikaner institutions, especially in education. The African Christian Democratic Party was a product of an evangelical Protestant revival movement, especially influential within middle-class Coloured areas in the Western Cape.

Electoral Trends

Between 1994 and 2004, support for the ruling party has remained fairly stable and has somewhat increased (see Table 7.3). Most of the ANC's support in these elections was African, although it also succeeded in winning substantial minorities of the votes in Indian and Coloured communities.

The use of a proportional representation system encourages the inclusion of small parties in parliament, an underlying intention of South African constitutional architects. As Table 7.3 indicates, the number of parties enjoying representation nearly doubled in 1999, despite the ANC winning a slightly larger majority.

Voters no longer identify quite so emotionally with parties: people are less likely to believe that they "belong" to a party or that it is "theirs."[19] Party membership remains extensive, however. Despite its electoral successes, however, the ANC may have to struggle to maintain a vigorous internal life.

Meanwhile the authoritarian tendencies of the party may have strengthened. Its 1997 constitutional amendments endorsed democratic centralism and prohibited factionalism. This makes it difficult for caucuses to emerge around a policy position that disagrees with the leadership. Party officials are also promoting authoritarian patterns of party discipline by reinforcing a new Africanist advocacy of deference and respect for elders in society. This is a risky posture in a country where the electorate will grow progressively younger for at least the next ten years. Shortly before the 2002 elections, the National Working Committee had circulated a "discussion document" emphasizing the risks of any competition for leadership positions and proposing that candidates for party office should avoid campaigning and that delegates who elected party leaders should be guided by the existing leadership.[20]

TABLE 7.3

National Assembly Election Results, 1994–2004

	1994			1999			2004		
Party	**Votes**	**Percentage**	**Seats**	**Votes**	**Percentage**	**Seats**	**Votes**	**Percentage**	**Seats**
ACDP	88,104	0.45	2	228,975	1.43	6	250,272	1.60	7
AEB				46,403	0.29	1	Did not contest		
ANC	12,237,655	62.65	252	10,601,330	66.35	266	10,889,915	69.69	279
AZAPO				27,257	0.17	1	39,116	0.27	1
DP/DA	338,426	1.73	7	1,527,337	9.56	38	1,931,201	12.37	50
FA				86,704	0.54	2	Did not contest		
ID							269,765	1.73	7
IFP	2,058,294	10.54	43	1,371,477	8.58	34	1,088,664	6.97	28
MF	13,433	0.07	0	48,277	0.30	1	55,267	0.35	2
NNP	3,983,690	20.39	82	1,098,215	6.87	28	257,824	1.65	7
PAC	243,478	1.25	5	113,125	0.71	3	113,512	0.73	3
GPDP				9,193	0.06	0	Did not contest		
SOPA				9,062	0.06	0	14,853	0.1	0
UCDP				125,280	0.78	3	117,792	0.76	3
UDM				546,790	3.42	14	355,717	2.28	9
FF	424,555	2.17	9	127,217	0.80	3	139,465	0.89	4
AITUP				10,611	0.07	0	Did not contest		
Other	145,863*	.75					98,308		
Total	19,533,498		400	15,977,253	100	400	15,612,671		
Spoiled ballots	193,112	1.02		251,320	1.55		250,887	1.58	
Voter turnout		**			86.7			57.8	

*This number reflects votes for 11 small parties that did not contest the national poll in 1999.

**No accurate turnout percentage exists for 1994. There was no electoral register and noncitizens were allowed to vote.

Source:

Government Gazette, June 11, 1999.

The Democratic Party and Opposition Politics

Among the historically white-led parties, the Democrats claim to have built 150 township-based branches since 1994. In the 2006 local elections, where it contested black township wards the Democrats collected around 5 percent of the vote in each township, better than before but hardly a decisive advance. It did well among Coloured municipal voters in 2006, however, winning over about 40 percent of the Coloured vote in Cape Town The party remains in public perceptions a predominantly white party, however.

Meanwhile, the National Party's fortunes plummeted. The party's ineffectual role as a junior coalition partner in the Government of National Unity between 1994 and 1996 undermined confidence among its white supporters who would have preferred combative opposition to the ANC. A brief alliance with the Democratic Party, the Democratic Alliance (DA), between 1999 and 2002 introduced new sources of ideological tension. The subsequent history of the Democratic Alliance was unedifying. Democrats disliked the patronage machine through which Coloured former Labour Party bosses built National Party support in the Western Cape, whereas National Party organizers perceived Democrats as effete and finicky amateurs, ill prepared for the rough dynamics of winning power in poor communities.

By the beginning of 2002, the Democratic Alliance had sprung apart, though the Democrats retained their new name contesting subsequent elections as the Democratic Alliance. The ostensible cause of the breakup was disagreement between the Alliance leaders over the dismissal of Peter Marais as Cape Town mayor. Marais had displeased old Democratic Party leadership by faking the results of an opinion poll as well as awarding jobs and houses to his relatives. His dismissal was succeeded by a rebellion in the leadership of the DA by former National Party officeholders. Shortly after, a joint statement from the ANC and the NNP announced that the parties would cooperate in government at all levels and that a policy forum would be established to seek consensus on policy issues.

In withdrawing from the alliance, NNP leaders emphasized that their differences with the Democrats involved issues of political substance, not just personal conflicts. They were more predisposed than the DP to the ANC's vision of cooperative participatory government, and they maintained that they too, like the ruling party, had a historical affinity with poor people. The DA's assault on Peter Marais was forcing "our white, black and coloured communities apart."[21] The NNP favored a constructive opposition, not one that had been "reduced to an angry white voice, mudslinging and character assassination."[22] It is probably true that the tensions within the alliance were attributable not only to personality conflicts. Despite DP/NPP agreement about policy issues, the two parties were still influenced by quite different philosophies—the one rooted in a liberal conception of individual citizenship and the other still based on community-centered notions of rights and obligations. However self-serving their rationalizations may have been, it is probably true that many NNP politicians have fewer principled objections to the ANC's performance in government than the liberal free marketers who lead the Democratic Party. Opinion poll evidence indicated that NNP supporters tended to be more concerned by the kinds of issues that animated the ANC's social base (job creation, for example) and less inclined than Democrats to assign the first government priority to fighting crime.

In 2002, the National Party announced that in the future it would cooperate with the government, another turnaround that diminished its credibility further. In the 2004 elections the support for NNP contracted to a quarter of its level in 1999. However, the National Party's leader, Marthinus van Schalkwyk received a cabinet position, and he and the six other NNP parliamentarians joined the ANC in 2005. The NNP announced its dissolution in 2006, ninety-two years after its foundation.

Neither white-led Democrats nor ethnic regionalists appear very likely groups to create a popularly credible opposition to the ANC. The ANC's monopoly on black electoral support will probably break only when tensions between Right and Left within the ANC reach the point of rupture. To date, the ANC's alliance with organized labor and the Communist Party has held up, despite deep and frequently voiced disagreements about the government's commitment to privatization, liberalization, deficit reduction, and most recently, the prosecution of Jacob Zuma. Generally, workers have been among the beneficiaries of ANC rule: between 1994 and 2001, wages rose faster than inflation, and legal reforms enhanced the collective bargaining capacity of trade unions as well as instituting new rights and entitlements for workers. Relations between trade unions and the government are likely to become more brittle. COSATU committed itself to supporting the ANC in the 2004 elections, but today there are increasing calls within its affiliates for an independent labor-based party. Even Thabo Mbeki has suggested that sooner or later the ANC's traditional alliance with the Left will end.

FOCUS QUESTION

Which factors encourage parties to take up centrist or moderate positions during elections?

Elections

Despite generally predictable outcomes, the main parties still campaign in ways that suggest that victory is almost certainly within their grasp. They use opinion polling, market research, image consultants, advertising agencies, and many other techniques of modern electioneering. Political advertising is prohibited on television, but party events are calculated to project compelling visual images to news cameras.

In 1994, organizations that were still influenced by their experience as military formations continued to defend their territory. They assaulted any rival party's workers who were bold enough to visit their home locations. By 2004, however, such "no-go zones", where one party could keep out its opponents, had virtually disappeared. In black townships workers from both the DA and the ANC could visit the same streets on the same days.

Arguably, the electoral system promotes the formation of socially inclusive political parties and civil electioneering. In South Africa, the double-ballot, list-proportional representation electoral system contains strong incentives for moderation because the electorate is so spread out. All parties are encouraged to seek votes outside their core support or base areas. The system is less likely to promote ethnic bloc voting than one that is geographically defined. Party leaders put people on their lists who might not win popular support in electoral contests that were focused around individual candidates: members of racial minorities or women, for example. The drawback is that parliamentarians hold their seats at the will of party leaders, and this has produced a parliament that tends to be deferential toward the executive.

South African voting is generally well organized, and voters mostly respect the electoral process. Parties do not question electoral outcomes. In national elections, voter participation is high.

FOCUS QUESTION

Why may racial identity continue to influence political behavior?

Political Culture, Citizenship, and Identity

Relatively high turnout rates in national elections are encouraging signs of good citizenship. So were rising levels of approval and satisfaction with democracy during the Mandela administration. Evidence from polls is mixed about levels of trust in government in the Mbeki era. However, all pollsters agree that people are more likely to trust national government than provincial or local authorities.

Opinion polls indicate that South Africans tend to believe that race relations have improved since 1994. But racial divisions continue to affect patterns of political support, though analysts disagree how much people are consciously influenced by racial considerations when they vote. Although public schools and middle-class neighborhoods have become desegregated, most black people still live in ghetto-like townships or in the historical homeland areas; racial distinctions still remain very conspicuous in South African social geography. However, since 1994, new patterns of public behavior seem to have created more conciliatory attitudes among South Africans. A national survey in May 2004 found that 60 percent of South Africans believed that race relations were improving and 30 percent thought they had remained the same. Blacks were more likely than other groups to think that race relations were better. In general among all groups perceptions about the future are becoming more optimistic.[23]

Even so, there remain sources of racial tension. Government is critical of what it takes to be the slow progress of black business, and ANC leaders routinely blame the absence of quicker social change on "white economic selfishness" (Thabo Mbeki's phrase). In any case, class-based political organization was generally quite comfortably accommodated within the ANC's fold during this struggle, for most of its active followers were workers and their families, and the war against apartheid could just as easily be considered an offensive against capitalism. Even today, union leaders hold back from organizing a workers' party separately from the ANC, recognizing that many workers are likely to retain the loyalties fostered by decades of nationalist politics.

In the 1950s, a powerful women's movement developed within the ANC to resist extending the pass laws to African women. More and more women were heading single-parent households, and many women were moving into industrial occupations and higher education, which led to feminist movements. One of the first major social reforms enacted by Mandela's government was authorizing abortion on demand. In general, its female members have forced the ANC to pay at least some attention to women's rights and entitlements.

FOCUS QUESTION

Why do social movements and social organizations remain racially separate in South Africa?

Interests, Social Movements, and Protests

Social movements continue to be unusually well organized for a developing country. Surveys confirm that about half the population does voluntary work for charitable organizations. The proportion increases among younger people.[24] Though participation at union meetings may have dwindled, the unions have extensive financial resources, since dues are automatically deducted from workers' wages, and unions often organize entire economic sectors. The ranks of organized labor include 2.8 million members.

In townships, residents' associations have created an impressive associational network. Surveys suggest that people are more likely to participate in civic associations than in political parties. In 2002, a new generation of local single-issue movements addressed the problems of landlessness, electricity cut-offs, and evictions of bond or municipal tax defaulters.

With the exception of COSATU, which invites white participation, associational life remains racially segregated. Business organizations, for example, continue to represent white and black firms separately. The larger corporations are still perceived to represent white privilege. Churches may have racially integrated hierarchies (Anglicans, Methodists, and Catholics have black leaders), but most South Africans worship in racially exclusive congregations. Only black South Africans attend football grounds in significant numbers to watch the multiracial teams in the Premier Soccer League. Rugby and cricket fans remain predominantly white despite efforts within the sporting administrations to make the teams more diverse. South African democracy is still weakened by divisions between ethnic groups that prevent people from recognizing common interests and shared enthusiasms.

Summary

On the whole, since 1994 members of parliament within the ruling party have failed to exercise formal oversight. This failure was especially clear in a parliamentary investigation of corrupt arms contracting. Party caucuses within parliament are generally tightly disciplined, a reflection of a strong party system. The African National Congress inherited from an eighty-year liberation struggle a tightly centralized organization structure and a mass following that was grouped into an extensive network of local branches. It remains the predominant organization among black South Africans. Any effective challenge to its authority will require smaller parties, mainly based among racial or ethnic minorities, to draw away significant numbers of the ANC's core support. Electoral trends since 1994 confirm that the ANC has successfully maintained its political base. The more likely scenario may be a future split among ANC voters as a consequence of union opposition to free-market policies. South Africa may represent a racially divided dominant-party democracy, but elections are fair, and strong social movements increase the prospects for democratic consolidation.

SECTION 5

South African Politics in Transition

FOCUS QUESTION

What are likely to be the long-term effects of HIV-AIDS in South Africa?

Political Challenges and Changing Agendas

HIV/AIDS, unemployment, inequality, and maintaining democracy are the chief challenges confronting South African leaders.

The impact of AIDS on South African society is hard to overestimate. AIDS is likely to kill between 5 and 7 million South Africans in the next ten years. 20 percent of the population is currently HIV-positive. A million South Africans have already died of HIV/AIDS. Its victims tend to be young, between the ages of fifteen and fifty—the most economically active members of the population. Because of these deaths, the dependency ratios between income earners and those they support may double. Poor households that support AIDS patients can spend up to two-thirds of their income on the cost of care.[25] This holocaust is removing a whole generation of parents.

In contrast to other African governments that have attempted to cope with the epidemic, South Africa's initial efforts to combat its spread and deal with its effects were tentative and confused. Belatedly, a public education program, including the free distribution of condoms began, toward the end of the Mandela presidency, to promote awareness of the disease. Surveys suggest that AIDS awareness is not enough. It does not seem to reduce the sexual behavior that spreads the disease. At the beginning of the program, however, education was presented as an alternative to medical treatment. In October 1998, the minister of health announced that the government would cease supplying antiretroviral drugs to hospitals that up to then had prescribed them to pregnant women to prevent mother-to-child transmission of AIDS. The R80 million saving would be used instead for distributing 140 million contraceptives and training 10,000 teachers in life skills. One month later, Thabo Mbeki, as chairman of a ministerial committee on AIDS, defended the minister's decision by claiming that the drug concerned, azidothymidine (AZT), was "dangerously toxic."

Thabo Mbeki and his minister of health, Manto Tshabala-Msimang, fiddle while Rome burns in this caustic comment on the president's refusal to sanction the public prescription of antiretrovitral drugs. (*Source: Zapiro, Cartoonists and Writers Syndicate, Cartoon Arts International, Inc. from* The Mail and Guardian, *Johannesburg, South Africa.*)

Hostility to the public prescription of drugs stemmed from more complicated considerations, however. President Mbeki began publicly expressing doubts about the scientific status of the disease in late 1999 and in particular questioned the generally accepted link between HIV and AIDS. He believed that conventional scientific explanations about the disease's causes stem from racial prejudice. In 2001, Mbeki referred to the "insulting"

Black Empowerment

Enlarging the share of black ownership in the economy has become a major policy priority for Thabo Mbeki's administration. In Mbeki's words, "the struggle against racism in our country must include the objective of creating a black bourgeoisie." Drawing its inspiration from both U.S. and, more importantly, Malaysian experience, the government has enacted a series of laws since 1999 to promote black business. The Preferential Procurement Act of 2000 established a set of criteria in awarding government contracts that require companies that win them to allocate shares to "previously disadvantaged" people. The Promotion of Equality Act of 2001 set up a monitoring system to record how well companies were "deracializing" their managements. The National Empowerment Fund Act reserves 2 percent of the proceeds from the sale of public corporations to finance black shareholding in these concerns. Mining and energy are economic sectors that traditionally have benefited from government protection and subsidies. Here the government has used its leverage to extract commitments to black empowerment. In November 2000, the six major oil companies signed a Charter committing themselves to achieving (and financing) black ownership of 25 percent of the oil and petroleum industry by 2014. In 2002, a similar mining industry charter was proclaimed. It promised to transfer 15 percent of mining assets to black companies within five years. Meanwhile the government has been providing black entrepreneurs about R2.5 billion a year of start-up capital.

How successful has this program been in "deracializing" South African capitalism? Measured by the proportion of black-owned companies on the Johannesburg stock exchange, the share of the economy owned by a "black bourgeoisie" remains modest: between 2 and 5 percent since 2000. In certain sectors, black companies are more significant, in oil for example (14 percent). However black participation in the economy is not limited to predominantly black-owned companies. Political pressure has prompted all major companies to appoint black people to their boards: in 2002 for example, more than 11 percent of company directors were black, a proportion which has probably increased since then. Shareholding has spread swiftly among black South Africans. For example, nearly a million black people registered for the sale of shares in 2002 in the previously state-owned telecommunications company. Black participation in the real estate business, almost nonexistent in 1990, now matches the numbers of white realtors, a fairly telling instance of the proliferation of property ownership in black communities.

Whether black empowerment has made South Africa more socially stable is another question. With the rising black share of economic ownership the government certainly has an incentive to maintain business-friendly policies. The people who have benefited most from these empowerment measures have often been politically well-connected, many of them former activists. However black empowerment has not reduced black poverty. Indeed it may have promoted economic inefficiencies that have curbed growth and job creation. Also despite the achievements of Black Economic Empowerment, to most poor black South Africans, wealth still appears predominantly white. ❖

theory that AIDS originated in Africa. In reality, Mbeki contended, South Africans who were dying of the illnesses that immune deficiency exposed them to (tuberculosis for example) were not victims of a virus; they were instead the casualties of poverty. Mbeki was aligning himself with a small minority of dissident scientists and doctors who have either denied AIDS' existence altogether or have disputed the causal link between HIV and AIDS. In 2000, the president established a panel to investigate the scientific evidence about the causes of AIDS and appointed several dissidents to join this body; the panel has yet to report.

The president's skepticism about AIDS certainly undermined attempts to combat the pandemic. Between 1998 and 2001, public hospitals were prevented from using antiretroviral drugs, including nevirapine, a much cheaper alternative to AZT—even for treating rape victims. In fact, several provinces, including two ANC administrations in the Eastern Cape and Gauteng, resumed using nevirapine quite widely during 2001 but elsewhere provincial health ministers loyally maintained the ban for several years more, firing doctors who questioned such policy. Taking their cue from the president, cabinet ministers began questioning AIDS statistics and projections, suggesting these were derived from faulty sampling procedures. After the Treatment Action Campaign successfully obtained a Constitutional Court judgment (see "Treatment Action Campaign and ACT-UP") compelling the government to use nevirapine in hospitals, government nominees on the Medical Control Council began warning that the drug might need to be deregistered on grounds of toxicity.

As well as aggravating the death rates attributable to HIV/AIDS, the most serious consequences of government support for "dissident" positions is the absence of any serious planning to cope with the consequences of the pandemic. At the very least, increased numbers of child-care facilities, the introduction of public hospices, and a comprehensive overhaul of social security and medical insurance would be reasonable things to expect from government; no such measures have yet been adopted. Although in August 2002, after a Constitutional Court judgment, and in response to internal pressures within the ANC, the Cabinet appeared to commit itself to provision of antiretroviral treatment, the health ministry resisted. The Treatment Action Campaign organized a civil disobedience campaign during 2003 to protest against the delay. Although treatment is now available from nearly 200 government health facilities, official figures in December 2005 suggest that only a fraction of HIV-positive South Africans are receiving antiretroviral medication (around 200,000 out of five million or so).

Despite increasing death rates among the economically active, high-level unemployment is likely to persist: HIV/AIDS will cut already low saving rates and deepen the shortages of skilled workers.

Modern governments are not in the business of creating jobs, Mbeki's ministers insist. The removal of subsidies and tariffs has encouraged more competitive industries, they maintain. South Africa has adopted the "correct macro financial policy fundamentals," they insist. Critics of government argue that one factor that deters investors, high crime rates, is partly the result of the government's failure to undertake thorough police reform. Fairly modest levels of public debt compared to that of most other developing countries prompt left-wing economists to suggest that heavier foreign borrowing might finance higher levels of public investment in services and fighting poverty and stimulate the kinds of growth rates needed to reduce unemployment significantly. Since 1994, growth rates have improved but not enough to cause a major fall in unemployment (see Figure 7.2).

The U.S. Connection

Treatment Action Campaign and ACT-UP

In both the United States and in South Africa direct-action protest movements have addressed the AIDS crisis. Their experiences demonstrate how much activists can challenge authority in both countries.

Growing out of local networks of gay activism in the United States, the AIDS Coalition to Unleash Power has pioneered a range of nonviolent confrontational tactics since 1987. In campaigns directed chiefly at bringing down drug prices and expanding government support for HIV/AIDS patients, ACT-UP supporters occupied offices, blocked traffic, organized mass "phone-zaps," and mounted a variety of other kinds of protest.

Initially, ACT-UP emphasized changes in local government policies, AIDS wards, or clean needle programs. As better medication became more available, the ACT-UP's constituency changed from its original base amongst white gay men to include people in poorer communities. Its leadership became increasingly female. Meanwhile, ACT-UP broadened its concerns to embrace more general issues of access to health care within the United States and the plight of HIV-AIDS patients internationally.

In contrast to the United States, citizen action based on a single issue is still comparatively unusual in South Africa. The Treatment Action Campaign (TAC) is one of the most successful of South Africa's new social movements. It was formed in 1998 in Cape Town by a group of HIV-positive activists, several of them members of the ANC, to persuade or compel the government to provide wider access to treatment for HIV-positive patients. The TAC draws on the tactical methods of the 1980s civil disobedience movements, to which many of its leading participants belonged. It also uses litigation to challenge government policy. The TAC has good relations with COSATU, the ANC's trade union ally, with which it drafted a national AIDS plan.

The TAC is effective partly because of lessons that its leading officials learned from their anti-apartheid activist experience, but also because today these people are often well connected politically. The TAC prides itself on being media friendly in packaging its message. It is able to ensure the visibility of "a nicely photogenic crowd" clad in T-shirts proclaiming "HIV-positive" at every stage in its protests.

Not all TAC activities target the government. In 2000, a TAC Defiance Campaign organized pickets and demonstrations against high prices charged by the drug companies that hold patents on the main antiretroviral medicines. The TAC began recruiting a network of doctors and pharmacists who were willing to prescribe generic substitutes for such drugs, and the TAC officials traveled to Brazil and Thailand to buy initial supplies of these medicines. The organization subsequently, with some justification, claimed credit for price reductions announced by the pharmaceutical companies Pfizer and Glaxo Wellcome.

TAC protests have also won sympathetic responses from ANC notables. Nelson Mandela lent his personal support to the campaign when in July 2001 he visited Zackie Achmat, the TAC's president. Achmat had announced that he would refuse antiretroviral medication until the government was willing to make such drugs readily and freely available. TAC litigation to compel the government to do this ended up in the Constitutional Court after the authorities appealed earlier high court judgments in favor of the TAC.

How do the two movements compare? Successes notwithstanding, ACT-UP remains a movement representing minority preoccupations and outside the political mainstream. This is partly a consequence of the demographics of the HIV-AIDS pandemic in the United States. It is also a legacy of ACT-UP's origins in a tradition of radical activism. Its successes are all the more impressive, and they do suggest a political system susceptible to leverage by quite small but well-organized groups of citizens. In South Africa, the TAC's direct constituency is much larger, and its needs are a much more central concern among policy-makers. From its beginnings the TAC has directed its efforts at shaping national policy, and the leadership has exploited its connections within the ruling party. For these reasons the TAC has tended to rely more than ACT-UP upon formal channels of political access, although it has also used litigation and lobbying on the one hand and civil disobedience on the other, in undertakings directly inspired by its American counterpart. ❖

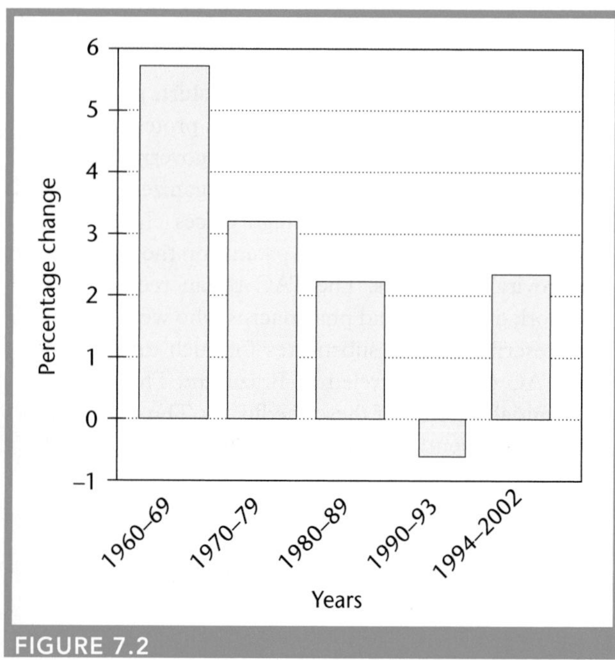

FIGURE 7.2

Economic Performance, Annual Change in GDP

Growth slackened continuously after the high rates of the 1960s. During the uncertainties of political transition, between 1990 and 1993, the South African economy contracted. Since 1994 growth statistics have revised modestly. Growth in the last three years (2005, 2006, and 2007) has been at 5 percent. Economists estimate that a 6 percent growth rate is needed to eliminate unemployment.

Source: www.economist.com.

Government social expenditure has helped to soften the effects of poverty but social inequality remains as strong as ever before. Absolute poverty has probably receded a little given the construction of more than one million houses now inhabited by poor people and a wider distribution of welfare grants. Since 1994, the rise of black people into leadership positions in the public sector, social organizations, and certain sectors of business may have helped to soften popular perceptions of social injustice. Agricultural landownership is one domain, however, in which white privileges remain especially visible, and so far the government has made only very gradual progress to change racial patterns of landholding. Since 2000, a succession of illegal land occupations, both urban and rural, by homeless people outside towns, has underlined how volatile landlessness can be as a political issue, especially when many South Africans bitterly remember being forced off the land. South African land reform is based on a principle of paying market-level prices to landowners. Even when historically dispossessed communities win back their original land rights, the process of restitution is subject to protracted negotiations over compensation. In a signal of its increasing impatience, the government announced at the beginning of 2006 that in future if such bargaining became too protracted the government would itself decide the price and expropriate the land. Landowners would certainly challenge such a move in the Constitutional Court.

Democracy's prospects will be fragile if its institutions are too frequently invoked to protect property rights. On the other hand, it is also possible in modern South Africa that constitutional arguments help the poor and helpless, most notably HIV patients. Defending and extending democracy may become much more challenging, however, if resources available for public services become scarcer and it becomes more difficult to decide who should receive them. Such conditions are likely in a stagnant South African economy decimated by AIDS. Pollsters confirm that South African public ideas of democracy emphasize improvements in living conditions. In other words, people associate democracy with the provision of livelihoods and basic necessities; they attach less importance to its political and procedural dimensions, particularly since many people still distrust institutions. Democracy in general will lose ground if people lose hope that their life will become easier materially.

Summary

The four main challenges to South Africa's political leadership are HIV-AIDS, unemployment, social inequality, and maintaining democracy. Even with the mass-provision of medication, HIV-AIDS will kill millions of citizens. Every year half a million students leave high school without graduating. When they enter the labor market without skills, they ensure that unemployment will remain at high levels for a long time. Extreme social inequality may reduce public support for democracy and open up opportunities for populist authoritarian politics. Compared to other new democracies, however, the South African political future appears hopeful. South Africans began their democracy with a relatively diversified economy and quite strong political institutions. Government has observably tried to reduce hardship, and support for the political system is widespread.

South African Politics in Comparative Perspective

FOCUS QUESTION

In certain respects it has been easier to institute and consolidate democracy in South Africa than in many other developing countries that underwent democratic transitions in the 1980s and 1990s. Why?

Unlike many of the countries that moved from authoritarian administrations to democratic governments in the late 1980s and early 1990s, South Africa's political economy was developed through a settler minority that became a permanent part of its population. This made the transition to democracy both easier and more challenging.

Between two world wars, a politically independent settler state could invest the revenues from the local production of primary commodities to develop a relatively diversified industrial economy. It expropriated land from its African subjects and recruited a modern working class from them. Later, unlike many former colonial countries in Africa, powerful and well-organized social forces could mobilize to support democratization in South Africa, in particular the African trade unions, which had evolved around industrial assembly lines. Democratic politics within the settler minority prompted wider kinds of political organization across the population almost from the beginning of South Africa's Act of Union. Today the organizations that are represented in the South African parliament are among the oldest political parties in the developing world. Ironically, in spite of its efforts during the apartheid era to promote ethnic division, the effective authority of the South African state through most of the twentieth century was probably a more decisive influence in stimulating a national consciousness than many more benign governments elsewhere in the colonial and postcolonial world.

However, South African society was deeply divided in the 1990s at the beginning of democratization. With the exception of the churches, most institutions and organizations were segmented, separated, or stratified by race. In addition, material inequalities between rich and poor were among the most polarized in the world, and their injustice was reinforced because they ran along racial lines.

In certain respects, South African democratization represents a success story. National government created trust among citizens. Its political procedures were recognized to be fair, and political leaders have generally observed its rules. A constitution that was designed to be socially inclusive has fostered widely representative institutions. Popular support of government is partly a result of its efforts to extend services to poor people, distribute resources fairly, and expand and improve infrastructure and education. Disciplined public finance has encouraged a modest revival of economic growth.

One reason that democratization has brought about more effective government is that it was preceded by a much longer process of political and economic reform. The dismantling of the tariffs and subsidies that nurtured and protected industry and commercial agriculture began more than a decade before the universal right to vote. Unlike in the countries of the postcommunist world, the coming of democracy did not bring a sudden exposure to the harsh shocks of international competition. Economic liberalization has continued at a relatively measured pace compared to the experience of many Third World countries, which have been compelled to undergo very rapid structural adjustment of their economies. The welfare state created under apartheid has maintained many of its provisions and extended certain of them, in sharp contrast to the shrinking scope of social services offered by most governments in the developing world.

Similarly, political liberalization preceded universal enfranchisement over a relatively long period. Industrial relations reform enabled black trade unions to participate in institutionalized collective bargaining through the 1980s. This encouraged the growth of well-structured associational life, both inside and outside the workplace, that reinvigorated older political organizations. Elsewhere, new democracies have been fragile because they have not had strong representative movements. In South Africa, constitutional negotiations did not take place in a political vacuum or in a situation of near state collapse. Until the 1994 elections, the apartheid state retained effective authority, and because the negotiations could be so protracted, the settlement reached a high degree of consensus.

Will South Africa manage to maintain a developmental administration under democratic conditions? To redress poverty and reduce inequality significantly, the state will have to make much more serious inroads into minority privileges. Although the constitution makes meeting basic needs of citizens a government obligation, it was also designed to reassure economically dominant groups that their interests would be safeguarded under democracy. It is likely that the constitution's meaning will become increasingly contested if the government attempts to address inequality through expanding the scope of administrative regulation—through compulsory purchase orders to accelerate land reform, for example.

Today, South Africa's political leaders sometimes blame the constitutional compromises for their slow progress in creating a fairer society, even though these compromises were necessary ten years ago. But as we have seen, shortcomings in their performance may be more attributable to administrative incapacity (as in policing and justice) or deference to presidential eccentricity (as with AIDS policy). Even so, South Africa provides grounds for hope that democracy and development can be combined in the Third World.

South Africa's relatively restrained response to the security issues posed by the Anglo-American war on terror supplies a final set of comparative insights. As we have noted, a fairly secularized and relatively affluent Muslim minority provides quite limited local hospitality and rhetorical support for the more radical strands of Islamic activism. The ANC's historical experience of seeking and balancing its support from governments across international geostrategic divisions, has led the South African government to withhold formal public support for America's offensive against fundamentalist Islamic movements while offering discreet cooperation with both American and British intelligence. More generally, however, South Africans do not view their political world as significantly altered by Al Qaeda's attack of 9/11. Distance from the main theatres of the global war on terror and still recent memories of a brutal civil war help to explain why South African politicians identify their chief strategic priorities differently from their counterparts in Washington and London.

Key Terms

African
voortrekkers
Afrikaner
Boer
apartheid
pass laws
homelands
migrant laborer
township
Umkhonto-we-Sizwe
influx control
sanctions
proportional representation
privatization
settler state
power sharing
democratization
economic deregulation

Suggested Readings

Davenport, Rodney, and Christopher Saunders. *South Africa: A Modern History*, 5th ed. New York: St. Martin's Press, 2000.

Frankel, Philip. *An Ordinary Atrocity: Sharpeville and Its Massacre.* New Haven, Conn.: Yale University Press, 2001.

Gevisser, Mark. *Thabo Mbeki: The Dream Deferred.* Johannesburg: Jonathan Ball, 2007.

Gibson, James L. *Overcoming Apartheid: Can Truth Reconcile a Divided Nation?* New York: Russell Sage Foundation, 2004.

Glaser, Darryl. *Politics and Society in South Africa.* Thousand Oaks, Calif.: Sage, 2001.

Gumede, William Mervin. *Thabo Mbeki and the Battle for the Soul of the ANC.* Cape Town: Zebra Press, 2005.

Lipton, Merle. *Capitalism and Apartheid: South Africa, 1910–1986.* Aldershot, England: Wildwood House, 1986.

Lodge, Tom. *South African Politics from Mandela to Mbeki.* Bloomington: Indiana University Press, 2002.

Mandela, Nelson. *Long Walk to Freedom.* New York: Little, Brown, 1994.

Marais, Hein. *South Africa: Limits to Change: The Political Economy of Transition.* New York: Zed Books, 2001.

Marx, Anthony. *Making Race and Nation: A Comparison of the United States, South Africa and Brazil.* Cambridge: Cambridge University Press, 1998.

Nattrass, Nicoli. *The Moral Economy of AIDS in South Africa.* Cambridge: Cambridge University Press, 2004.

O'Meara, Dan, *Forty Lost Years: The Apartheid State and the Politics of the National Party.* Athens: Ohio University Press, 1996.

Picard, Louis. *The State of the State: Institutional Transformation, Capacity and Political Change in South Africa.* Johannesburg: Witwatersrand University Press, 2005.

Piombo, Jessica, and Lia Nijzink. *Electoral Politics in South Africa: Assessing the First Democratic Decade.* New York: Palgrave Macmillan, 2005.

Robins, Steven L. *Limits to Liberation after Apartheid: Citizenship, Governance and Culture.* Athens: Ohio University Press, 2005.

Seekings, Jeremy. *The UDF: A History of the United Democratic Front in South Africa, 1983–1991.* Athens: Ohio University Press, 2000.

Sparks, Allister. *Tomorrow Is Another Country: The Inside Story of South Africa's Negotiated Revolution.* Sandton: Struik Book Distributors, 1994.

Spitz, Richard, and Matthew Chaskelson. *The Politics of Transition: A Hidden History of South Africa's Negotiated Settlement.* Oxford: Hart Publishing and Johannesburg: Witwatersrand University Press, 2000.

Wilson, Richard. *The Politics of Truth and Reconciliation in South Africa: Legitimizing the Post-Apartheid State.* Cambridge: Cambridge University Press, 2001.

Notes

[1]Shula Marks and Stanley Trapido, "Lord Milner and the South African State," *History Workshop* 8 (1979): 50–80; David Yudelman, *The Making of Modern South Africa: State, Capital, and the Incorporation of Organized Labour on the South African Gold Fields* (Westport, Conn.: Greenwood Press, 1983).

[2]Stanley Trapido, "South Africa in a Comparative Study of Industrialization," *Journal of Development Studies* 3 (1971): 311–320; Frederick A. Johnston, *Class, Race and Gold: A Study of Class Relations and Racial Discrimination in South Africa* (London: Routledge, 1976).

[3]Hermann Giliomee, "Constructing Afrikaner Nationalism," *Journal of Asian and African Studies* 18 (1983): 83–98; Isabel Hofmeyr, "Building a Nation from Words: Afrikaans Language, Literature and Ethnic Identity, 1902–1924," in Shula Marks and Stanley Trapido, eds., *The Politics of Race, Class and Nationalism in Twentieth Century Nationalism* (London and New York: Longman, 1987).

[4]Deborah Posel, *The Making of Apartheid, 1948–1961: Conflict and Compromise* (Oxford: Clarendon Press, 1997), chap. 9.

[5]Heribert Adam and Hermann Giliomee, *The Rise and Crisis of Afrikaner Power* (Cape Town: David Philip, 1979), 169–185.

[6]Andrew Nash, "Mandela's Democracy," *Monthly Review* (April 1999): 18–28.

[7]Craig Schwabe, "Fact Sheet: Poverty in South Africa." *GIS Centre, Human Sciences Research Council* (July 26, 2004), http://www.sarpn.org.za/documents/d0000990/index.php.

[8]J. P. Landman, Haroon Bhorat, Servaas van der Berg, and Carl van Aardt, "Breaking the Grip of Poverty and Inequality in South Africa 2004–2014." *Ecumenical Foundation of South Africa* (December 2003), http://www.sarpn.org.za/documents/d0000649/P661-Povertyreport3b.pdf.

[9]Jeffrey Lewis, "Assessing the Demographic and Economic Impact of HIV/AIDS," in Kyle Dean Kauffman and David L. Lindauer, eds. *AIDS and South Africa: The Social Expression of a Pandemic* (Basingstoke: Palgrave Macmillian, 2004), 103.

[10]Lewis, 99.

[11]Shula Marks, "An Epidemic Waiting to Happen," *African Studies* 61, no. 1 (2002): 13–26.

[12]Terence Moll, "Did the Apartheid Economy Fail?" *Journal of Southern African Studies* 17, no. 2 (1991): 289–291.

[13]Neta Crawford and Audie Klotz, *How Sanctions Work: Lessons from South Africa* (New York: St. Martin's Press, 1999).

[14]Frederick Van Zyl Slabbert, "South Africa Under Thabo Mbeki: The Challenge of Democratic Stability," in Andrew Reynolds, ed., *Election '99: From Mandela to Mbeki* (New York: St. Martin's Press, 1999), 212.

[15]Rod Alence, "South Africa after Apartheid: The First Decade," *Journal of Democracy* 15, no. 3 (July 2004), 87.

[16]Roy Jankielsohn, "Political Will Needed to Root Out in the Police," *The Star* (November 23, 2004), http://www.thestar.co.za/index.php?fSectionId=327&fArticleId=2309404.

[17]*Sunday Independent* (September 2, 2001).

[18]*Mail and Guardian* (February 2, 2001).

[19]Robert Mattes, "Public Opinion since 1994," in Jessica Piombo and Lia Nijzink, eds., *Electoral Politics in South Africa: Assessing the First Democratic Decade* (New York: Palgrave Macmillian, 2005), 55.

[20]Anthony Butler, "How Democratic is the African National Congress?" *Journal of Southern African Studies* 31, no. 4 (December 2005), 733.

[21]*Cape Times* (December 8, 2001).

[22]*The Star* (December 12, 2001).

[23]Markinor, "SABC/Markinor Opinion 2004—Racial Relations in South Africa," (November 18, 2004), http://www.biz-community.com/Article.aspx?c=11&l=196&ai=5200.

[24]"Volunteer Statistics in South Africa," *The Star* (December 11, 2004).

[25]Lewis, 111.

Official Name:	Islamic Republic of Iran (*Jomhuri-ye Eslami-ye Iran*)
Location:	Middle East (West Asia)
Capital City:	Tehran
Population (2007):	65.4 million
Size:	approximately 1,648,000 sq. km.; slightly larger than Alaska

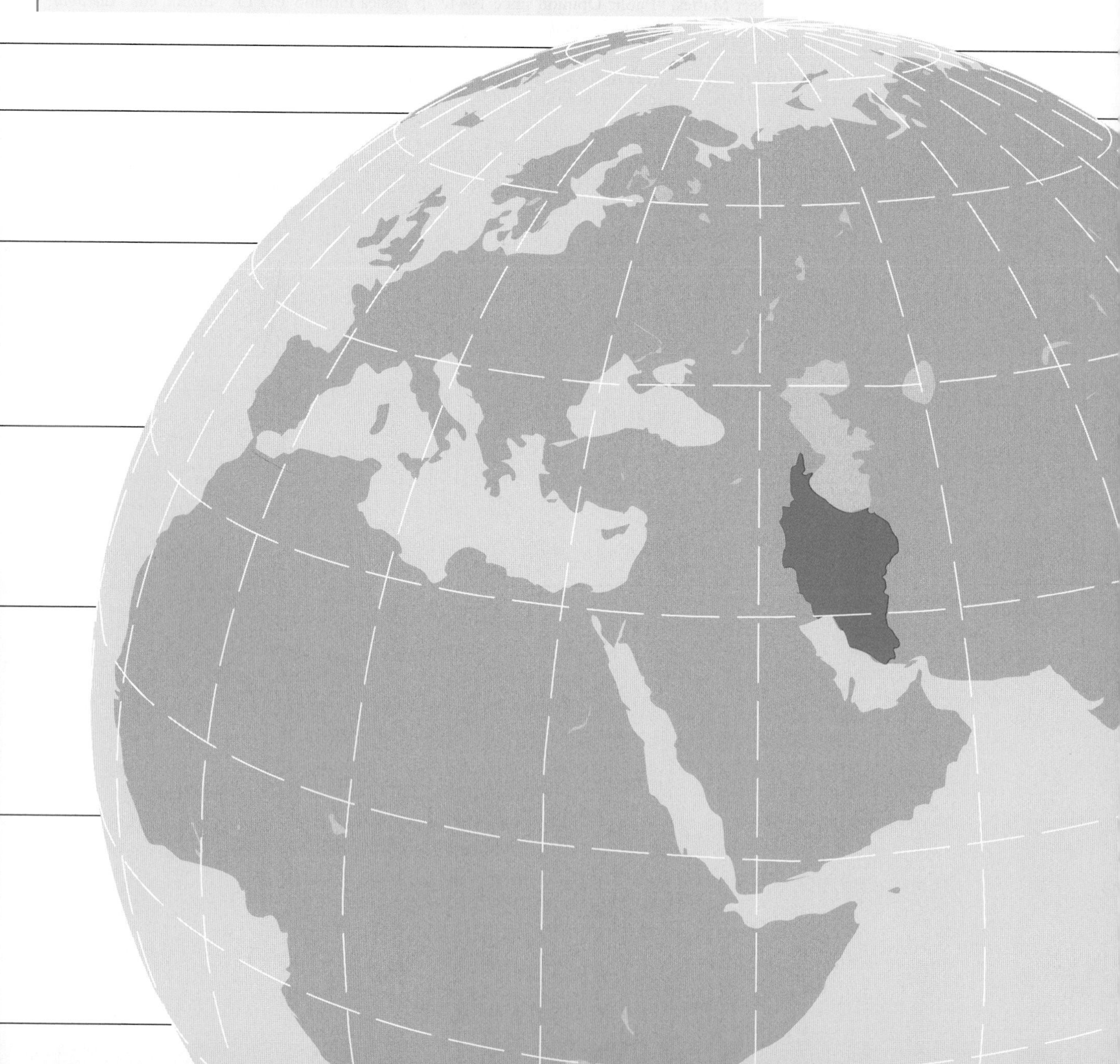

CHAPTER

8 Iran

Ervand Abrahamian

Chronology of Modern Iran's Political Development

1905–1911	1921	1925	1941–1945	1941
Constitutional Revolution.	Colonel Reza Khan's military coup.	Reza Khan establishes the Pahlavi dynasty.	Allied occupation of Iran during World War II.	Muhammad Reza Pahlavi becomes Shah of Iran.

1979–1981	December 1979	January 1980	March 1980	1980–1988
Hostage crisis—52 U.S. embassy employees held by radical students.	Referendum on the Islamic constitution.	Abol-hassan Bani-sadr elected president.	Elections for the First Islamic *Majles* (parliament). Subsequent Majles elections every four years.	War with Iraq.

SECTION 1 The Making of the Modern Iranian State

FOCUS QUESTION

To what extent is Iran a democracy or a theocracy?

Politics in Action

In 1997, Iran elected Muhammad Khatami president of the Islamic Republic. He was reelected in 2001 by an increased majority. Khatami a middle-ranking cleric was not a high-ranking **ayatollah**. He had promised to create a more open **civil society** and improve the country's "sick economy." He stressed the importance of protecting individual liberties, freedom of expression, women's rights, political pluralism, and the rule of law. He even promoted better relations with the United States and other Western nations.

ayatollah literally, "sign of God." High-ranking clerics in Iran.

civil society refers to the space occupied by voluntary associations outside the state, for example, professional associations, trade unions, and student groups.

Commentators, inside and outside the country, had considered the election a shoo-in for Khatami's conservative rival. But Khatami won 70 percent of the vote. Once in office, President Khatami liberalized the press, established new political parties, and initiated a "dialogue of civilizations" with the West.

In 2005, Iranian voters again voted for change—in the opposite direction. Mahmoud Ahmadinejad, the ultraconservative mayor of Teheran, won over 60 percent of the vote. He had promised to reduce poverty, promote social justice, and end corruption. He also promised to reverse many of the liberal changes implemented under Khatami. He denounced the West as "decadent" and took a hard line on relations with the United States and on Israel, which he said should be "wiped off the map." He particularly defended Iran's right to develop nuclear energy, which he claimed would be used only for peaceful purposes. He insisted the United States had no right to tell other nations what types of technology they could develop.

These very different electoral outcomes illustrate the contradictory political forces at work in the Islamic Republic of Iran. Iran is a mixture of **theocracy** and democracy. Its political system is based on both clerical authority and popular sovereignty, on the divine right of the clergy and the rights of the

theocracy a state dominated by the clergy, who rule on the grounds that they are the only interpreters of God's will and law.

1951	1953	1963	1975	1979
Nationalization of the oil industry by government of Prime Minister Mossadeq.	CIA-supported coup overthrows Mossadeq.	Shah launches "White Revolution."	Shah establishes the Resurgence Party.	Islamic Revolution; Shah forced into exile; Iran becomes an Islamic Republic; Ayatollah Khomeini becomes Leader.
June 1981	**October 1981**	**1989**	**1997**	**2005**
President Bani-Sadr ousted by Khomeini, replaced by Mohammad Ali Rajai.	Ayatollah Ali Khamenei elected president.	Khomeini dies; Khamenei appointed Leader; Rafsanjani elected president (reelected in 1993).	Muhammad Khatami elected president on reform platform (reelected in 2001).	Ultra-conservative Mahmoud Ahmadinejad elected president.

Majles The Iranian parliament, from the Arabic term for "assembly."

Guardian Council a committee created in the Iranian constitution to oversee the *Majles* (the parliament).

Leader/Supreme Leader cleric elected to be the head of the Islamic Republic of Iran.

people, on concepts derived from early Islam and from modern democratic principles. Iran has regular elections for the presidency and the ***Majles*** (Parliament), but the clerically dominated **Guardian Council** determines who can run. The president is the formal head of the executive branch. But he can be overruled, even dismissed, by the chief cleric, the **Leader** known in the West as the **Supreme Leader**. The president appoints the minister of justice, but the whole judiciary is under the supervision of the chief judge, who is appointed directly by the Leader. The *Majles* is the legislature, but bills do not become law unless the Guardian Council deems them compatible with Islam and the Islamic constitution.

FOCUS QUESTION

To what extend does geography give Iran a distinct identity?

Geographic Setting

Iran is three times the size of France, slightly larger than Alaska, and much larger than its immediate neighbors. Most of its territory is inhospitable to agriculture. Rain-fed agriculture is confined mostly to the northwest and the provinces along the Caspian Sea. Only pastoral nomads can survive in the semiarid zones and in the high mountain valleys. Thus, 67 percent of the total population of 65 million is concentrated on 27 percent of the land—mostly in the Caspian region, in the northwest provinces, and in the cities of Tehran, Mashed, Isfahan, Tabriz, Shiraz, and Qom.

Iran is the second-largest oil producer in the Middle East and the fourth-largest in the world, and oil revenues have made Iran an urbanized and partly industrialized country. Nearly 67 percent of the population lives in urban centers; 70 percent of the labor force is employed in industry and services; 77 percent of adults are literate; life expectancy has reached seventy years; and the majority of Iranians enjoy a standard of living well above that found in most of Asia and Africa.

TABLE 8.1

Political Organization

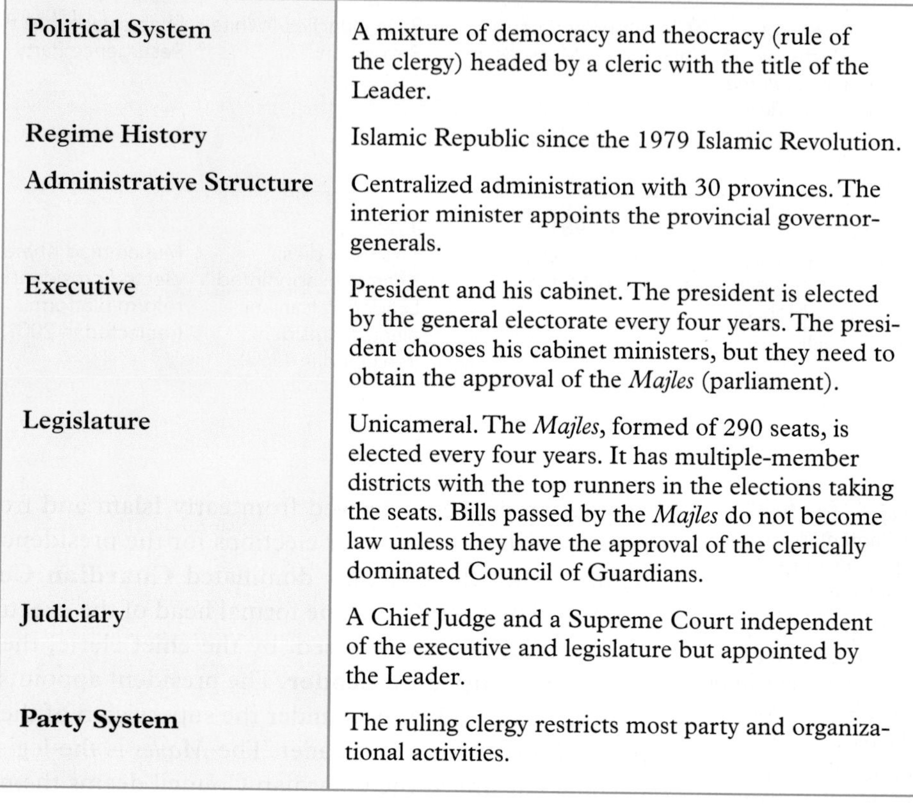

Political System	A mixture of democracy and theocracy (rule of the clergy) headed by a cleric with the title of the Leader.
Regime History	Islamic Republic since the 1979 Islamic Revolution.
Administrative Structure	Centralized administration with 30 provinces. The interior minister appoints the provincial governor-generals.
Executive	President and his cabinet. The president is elected by the general electorate every four years. The president chooses his cabinet ministers, but they need to obtain the approval of the *Majles* (parliament).
Legislature	Unicameral. The *Majles*, formed of 290 seats, is elected every four years. It has multiple-member districts with the top runners in the elections taking the seats. Bills passed by the *Majles* do not become law unless they have the approval of the clerically dominated Council of Guardians.
Judiciary	A Chief Judge and a Supreme Court independent of the executive and legislature but appointed by the Leader.
Party System	The ruling clergy restricts most party and organizational activities.

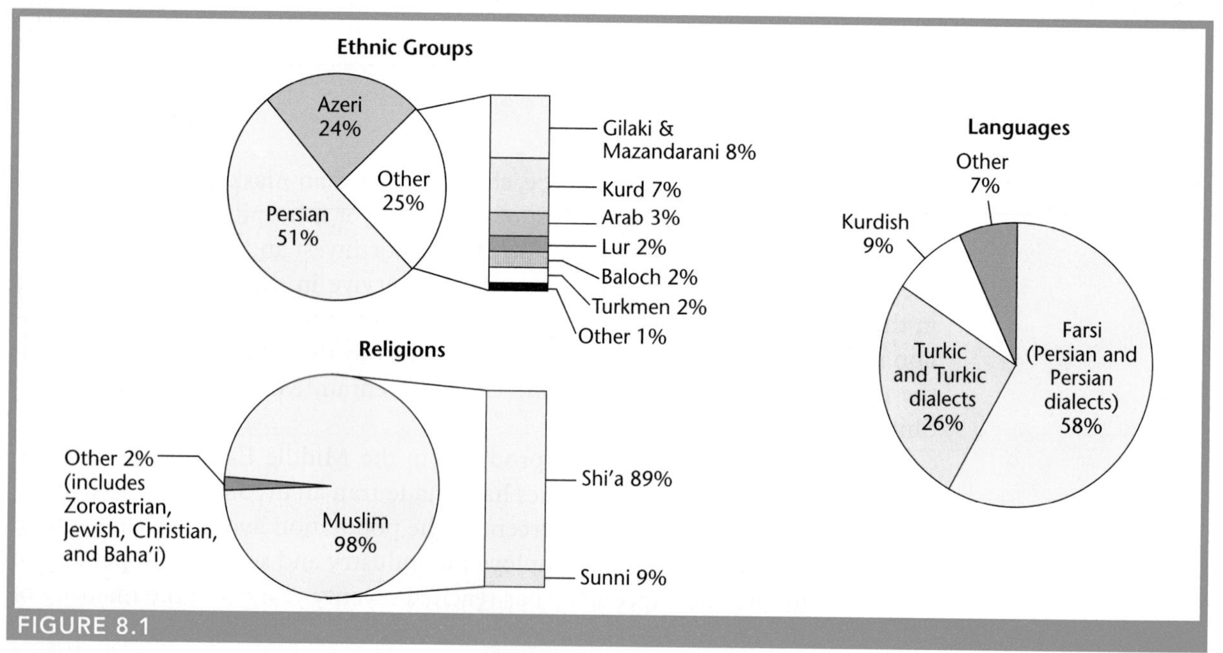

FIGURE 8.1

The Iranian Nation at a Glance

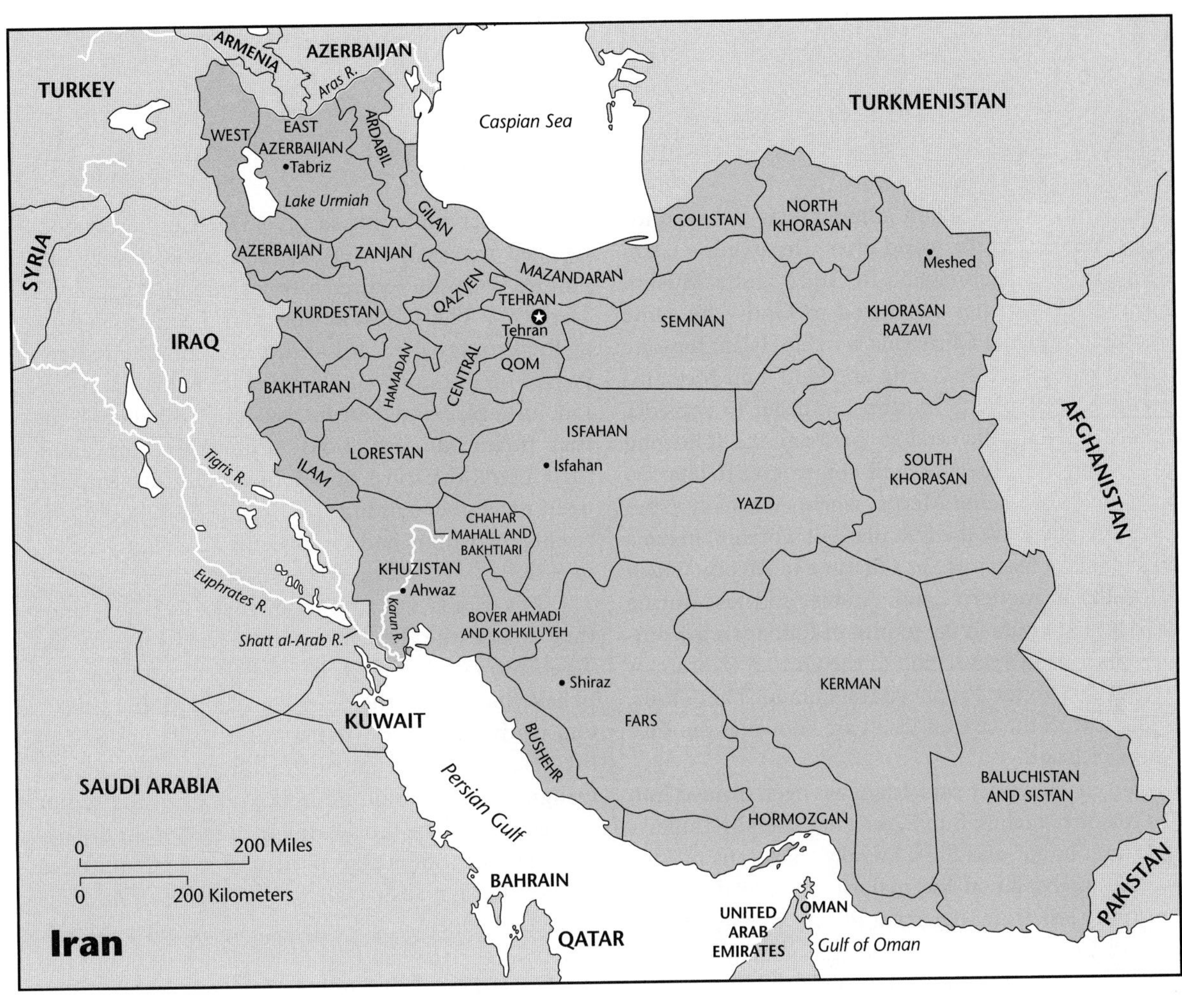

Iran lies on the strategic crossroads between Central Asia and Turkey, between the Indian subcontinent and the Middle East, and between the Arabian Peninsula and the Caucasus Mountains, which are often considered a boundary between Europe and Asia. This has made the region vulnerable to invaders.

Farsi Persian word for the Persian language. Fars is a province in Central Iran.

The population today reflects these historic invasions. Some 51 percent speak Persian (**Farsi**), an Indo-European language, as their first language; 26 percent speak dialects of Turkic, mainly Azeri and Turkman; 8 percent speak Gilaki or Mazandarani, distant Persian dialects; 7 percent speak Kurdish, another Indo-European language; and 3 percent speak Arabic. Use of Persian, however, has dramatically increased in recent years because of successful literacy campaigns. Over 86 percent of the population can now communicate in Persian, the national language. This gives Iran a national identity distinct from its neighbors—especially from Arabs and Turkic-speakers. Although Iran shares many religious and cultural features in common with the rest of the Middle East, its Persian heritage gives it a national identity distinct from that of the Arab and Turkish world. Iranians by no means consider themselves part of the Arab world.

Islam and Shi'ism

Islam, with over 1 billion adherents, is the second-largest religion in the world after Christianity. Islam means literally "submission to God," and a Muslim is someone who has submitted to God—the same God that Jews and Christians worship. Islam has one central tenet: "There is only one God, and Muhammad is His Prophet." Muslims, in order to consider themselves faithful, need to perform the following four duties to the best of their ability: give to charity; pray every day facing Mecca, where Abraham is believed to have built the first place of worship; make a pilgrimage at least once in a lifetime to Mecca, which is located in modern Saudi Arabia; and fast during the daytime hours in the month of Ramadan to commemorate God's revelation of the Qur'an (Koran, or Holy Book) to the Prophet Muhammad. These four, together with the central tenet, are known as the Five Pillars of Islam.

From its earliest days, Islam has been divided into two major branches: Sunni, meaning literally "followers of tradition," and Shi'i, literally "partisans of Ali." Sunnis are by far in the majority worldwide. Shi'is constitute less than 10 percent of Muslims worldwide and are concentrated in Iran, southern Iraq, Bahrain, eastern Turkey, Azerbaijan, and southern Lebanon.

Although both branches accept the Five Pillars, they differ mostly over who should have succeeded the Prophet Muhammad (d. 632). The Sunnis recognized the early dynasties that ruled the Islamic empire with the exalted title of caliph ("Prophet's Deputy"). The Shi'is, however, argued that as soon as the Prophet died, his authority should have been passed on to Imam Ali, the Prophet's close companion, disciple, and son-in-law. They further argue that Imam Ali passed his authority to his direct male heirs, the third of whom, Imam Husayn, had been martyred fighting the Sunnis in 680, and the twelfth of whom had supposedly gone into hiding in 941.

The Shi'is are also known as Twelvers since they follow the Twelve Imams. They refer to the Twelfth Imam as the *Mahdi*, the Hidden Imam, and believe him to be the Messiah who will herald the end of the world. Furthermore, they argue that in his absence, the authority to interpret the *shari'a* (religious law) should be in the hands of the senior clerical scholars—the ayatollahs. Thus, from the beginning, the Shi'is harbored ambivalent attitudes toward the state, especially if the rulers were Sunnis or lacked genealogical links to the Twelve Imams. For Sunnis, the *shari'a* is based mostly on the Qur'an and the teachings of the Prophet. For Shi'is, it is based also on the teachings of the Twelve Imams. ❖

FOCUS QUESTION

To what extent does history give Iran a distinct identity?

Critical Junctures

The Safavids (1501–1722)

The Safavids conquered the territory in the sixteenth century and forcibly converted their subjects to Shi'ism, even though the vast majority had been Sunnis (see "Islam and Shi'ism"). By the mid-seventeenth century, Sunnism survived only among the tribal groups at the periphery.

Safavid Iran also contained small communities of Jews, Zoroastrians, and Christians. The Safavids tolerated religious minorities as long as they paid special taxes and accepted royal authority. According to Islam, Christians, Jews, and Zoroastrians were to be tolerated as legitimate **People of the Book**, because they were mentioned in the Holy **Qur'an** and possessed their own sacred texts: the Bible, the Torah, and the Avesta.

People of the Book the Muslim term for recognized religious minorities, such as Christians, Jews, and Zoroastrians.

Qur'an the Muslim Bible.

The Safavids governed through Persian scribes and Shi'i clerics as well as through tribal chiefs, large landowners, religious notables, city merchants, guild elders, and urban ward leaders.

The Safavid army was formed mostly of tribal cavalry led by tribal chieftains. Their revenues came mostly from land taxes levied on the peasantry. The Safavids claimed absolute power; but they lacked a central state and had to cooperate with many semi-independent local leaders.

The Qajars (1794–1925)

In 1722 Afghan tribesmen invaded the capital. After a half-century of civil war the Qajars reconquered much of Iran. They moved the capital to Tehran and recreated the Safavid system of central manipulation and court administration. They also declared Shi'ism to be the state religion even though they, unlike the Safavids, did not boast of genealogical links to the Twelve Imams. Since these new shahs did not pretend to wear the Imam's mantle, Shi'i clerical leaders could claim to be the main interpreters of Islam.

Qajar rule coincided with the peak of European imperialism in the nineteenth century. The Russians seized parts of Central Asia and the Caucasus region from Iran and extracted major economic concessions. The British Imperial Bank won the monopoly to issue paper money. The Indo-European Telegraph Company got a contract to extend communication lines through the country. Exclusive rights to drill for oil in the southwest were sold to a British citizen. Iranians increasingly felt their whole country had been auctioned off.

These resentments culminated in the constitutional revolution of 1905–1909. The 1906 constitution introduced elections, separation of powers, laws made by a legislative assembly, and the concepts of popular sovereignty and the nation (*mellat*). It retained the monarchy, but centered political power in a national assembly called the *Majles.*

The constitution gave the *Majles* extensive authority over all laws, budgets, treaties, loans, concessions, and the make-up of the cabinet. The ministers were accountable to the *Majles*, not to the shah. The constitution also included a bill of rights guaranteeing equality before the law, protection of life and property, safeguards from arbitrary arrest, and freedom of expression and association.

Shi'ism was declared Iran's official religion. Clerical courts continued to implement the ***shari'a*** (religious law based on the Qur'an). A Guardian Council of senior clerics elected by the *Majles* had veto power over parliamentary bills it deemed un-Islamic.

shari'a Islamic law derived mostly from the Qur'an and the examples set by the Prophet Muhammad.

The initial euphoria gave way to deep disillusionment in the next decade. Pressures from the European powers continued, and a devastating famine after World War I took some 1 million lives, almost 10 percent of the total population. Internal conflicts polarized the *Majles* into warring liberal and conservative factions. Liberals, mostly members of the intelligentsia, championed social reforms, especially the replacement of the *shari'a* with a modern legal code. Conservatives, led by landlords, tribal chiefs, and senior clerics, vehemently opposed such reforms, particularly land reform, women's rights, and the granting of full equality to religious minorities.

The central government, without any real army, bureaucracy, or tax-collecting machinery, could not administer the provinces. During World War I, Russia and Britain formally carved up Iran into three zones. Russia occupied the north, Britain the south. Iran was left with a small middle "neutral zone."

By 1921, Iran was in complete disarray. According to a British diplomat, the propertied classes, fearful of communism, were anxiously seeking "a savior on horseback."[1]

The Pahlavis (1925–1979)

coup d'état a forceful, extra-constitutional action resulting in the removal of an existing government, usually carried out by the military.

In February 1921 Colonel Reza Khan carried out a **coup d'état**. He replaced the cabinet and consolidated power in his own hands. Four years later, he deposed the Qajars and crowned himself shah-in-shah and established the Pahlavi dynasty. This was the first nontribal dynasty to rule the whole of Iran.

Reza Shah ruled with an iron fist until 1941, when the British and the Soviets invaded Iran to stop Nazi Germany from establishing a foothold there. Reza Shah promptly abdicated in favor of his son, Muhammad Reza Shah, and went into exile, where he soon died. In the first twelve years of his reign, the young shah retained control over the armed forces but had to tolerate a free press, an independent judiciary, competitive elections, assertive cabinet ministers, and boisterous parliaments. He also had to confront two vigorous political movements: the communist Tudeh (Masses) Party and the National Front, led by the charismatic Dr. Muhammad Mossadeq (1882–1967).

The Tudeh drew its support mostly from working-class trade unions. The National Front drew its support mainly from the salaried middle classes and campaigned to nationalize the British company that controlled the petroleum industry. Mossadeq also wanted to sever the shah's links with the armed forces. In 1951, Mossadeq was elected prime minister and promptly nationalized the oil industry. The period of relative freedom, however, ended abruptly in 1953, when royalist army officers overthrew Mossadeq and installed the shah with absolute power. The coup was financed by the U.S. Central Intelligence Agency (CIA) and the British. This intensified anti-British sentiment and created a deep distrust of the United States. It also made the shah appear to be a puppet of foreign powers.

The Pahlavi dynasty built Iran's first highly centralized state. The armed forces grew from fewer than 40,000 in 1925 to 124,000 in 1941, and to over 410,000 in 1979. The armed forces were supplemented by a pervasive secret police known as SAVAK.

Iran's bureaucracy expanded to twenty-one ministries employing over 300,000 civil servants in 1979. The Education Ministry grew twentyfold. The powerful Interior Ministry appointed provincial governors, town mayors, district superintendents, and village headmen; it could even rig *Majles* elections and create rubber-stamp parliaments.

The Justice Ministry supplanted the *shari'a* with a European-style civil code and the clerical courts with a modern judicial system culminating in a Supreme Court. The Transport Ministry built an impressive array of bridges, ports, highways, and railroads known as the Trans-Iranian Railway. The

Ministry of Industries financed numerous factories specializing in consumer goods. The Agricultural Ministry became prominent in 1962 when the shah made land reform the centerpiece of his "White Revolution." This White Revolution was an effort to promote economic development and such social reform as extending the vote to women. It also created a Literacy Corps for the countryside. Thus, by the late 1970s, the state had set up a modern system of communications, initiated a minor industrial revolution, and extended its reach into even the most outlying villages.

The state also controlled the National and the Central Banks; the Industrial and Mining Development Bank; the Plan Organization in charge of economic policy; the national radio-television network; and most important, the National Iranian Oil Company.

The dynasty's founder, Reza Shah, used coercion, confiscations, and diversion of irrigation water to make himself one of the largest landowners in the Middle East. This wealth transformed the shah's court into a large military-landed complex, providing work for thousands in its numerous palaces, hotels, casinos, charities, companies, and beach resorts. This patronage system grew under his son, Muhammad Reza Shah, particularly after he established his tax-exempt Pahlavi Foundation, which eventually controlled 207 large companies.

The Pahlavi drive for secularization, centralization, industrialization, and social development won some favor from the urban propertied classes. But arbitrary rule, the 1953 coup that overthrew a popular prime minister, the disregard for constitutional liberties, and the stifling of independent newspapers, political parties, and professional associations produced widespread resentment. The Pahlavi state, like the Safavids and the Qajars, hovered over, rather than embedded itself into, Iranian society.

In 1975, the shah formed the Resurgence Party. He declared Iran a one-party state and threatened imprisonment and exile to those refusing to join the party. The Resurgence Party was designed to create yet another organizational link with the population, especially with the **bazaars** (traditional marketplaces), which, unlike the rest of society, had managed to retain their guilds and thus escape direct government control. The Resurgence Party promptly established its own bazaar guilds as well as newspapers, women's organizations, professional associations, and labor unions. It also prepared to create a Religious Corps to teach the peasants "true Islam."

bazaar an urban marketplace where shops, workshops, small businesses, and export-importers are located.

The Islamic Revolution (1979)

These grievances were best summed up by an exile newspaper in Paris on the very eve of the 1979 revolution. In an article entitled "Fifty Years of Treason," it charged the shah and his family with establishing a military dictatorship; collaborating with the CIA; trampling on the constitution; creating SAVAK—the secret police; rigging parliamentary elections; organizing a fascistic one-party state; taking over the religious establishment; and undermining national identity by disseminating Western culture. It also accused the regime of inducing millions of landless peasants to migrate into urban shantytowns; widening the gap between rich and poor; funneling money away from the small bourgeoisie into the pockets of the wealthy comprador bourgeoisie (the entrepreneurs linked to foreign companies and multinational corporations); wasting resources on bloated military budgets; and granting new capitulations to the West.

These grievances took sharper edge when the leading opposition cleric, Ayatollah Ruhollah Khomeini—exiled in Iraq—formulated a new version of Shi'ism (see "Ayatollah Ruhollah Khomeini"). His version has often been labeled Islamic **fundamentalism**. It would better to call it political Islam or even more accurately as Shi'i populism. The term *fundamentalism*, derived from American Protestantism, implies religious dogmatism, intellectual inflexibility and purity, political traditionalism, social conservatism, rejection of the modern world, and the literal interpretation of scriptural texts. Khomeini, however, was more of a political revolutionary and a blatant populist than a social conservative.

fundamentalism a term recently popularized to describe radical religious movements throughout the world.

Khomeini denounced monarchies in general as part of the corrupt elite exploiting the oppressed masses. Oppressors were courtiers, large landowners, high-ranking military officers, wealthy foreign-connected capitalists, and millionaire palace dwellers. The oppressed were the masses, especially landless peasants, wage earners, bazaar shopkeepers, and shantytown dwellers.

Khomeini gave a radically new meaning to the old Shi'i term *velayat-e faqih* (**jurist's guardianship**). He argued that jurist's guardianship gave the senior clergy all-encompassing authority over the whole community, not just over widows, minors, and the mentally disabled (the previous interpretation). Only the senior clerics could understand the *shari'a;* the divine authority given to the Prophet and the Imams had been passed on to their spiritual heirs, the clergy. He further insisted the clergy were the people's true representatives, since they lived among them, listened to their problems, and shared their everyday joys and pains. He claimed that the shah secretly planned to confiscate all religious endowment funds and replace Islamic values with "cultural imperialism."

jurist's guardianship Khomeini's concept that the Iranian clergy should rule on the grounds that they are the divinely appointed guardians of both the law and the people.

In 1977–1978, the shah tried to deal with a 20 percent rise in consumer prices and a 10 percent decline in oil revenues by cutting construction projects and declaring war against "profiteers," "hoarders," and "price gougers." Shopkeepers believed the shah was diverting attention from court corruption and planning to replace them with government-run department stores. They also thought he intended to destroy the bazaar.

The shah was also subjected to international pressure on the sensitive issue of human rights—from Amnesty International, the United Nations, and the Western press, as well as from the recently elected Carter administration in the United States. In 1977, the shah gave the International Red Cross access to Iranian prisons and permitted political prisoners to have defense attorneys. This international pressure allowed the opposition to breathe again after decades of suffocation.[2]

This slight loosening of the reins sealed the fate of the shah. Political parties, labor organizations, and professional associations—especially lawyers, writers, and university professors—regrouped after years of being banned. Bazaar guilds regained their independence. College, high school, and seminary students took

Profile
Ayatollah Ruhollah Khomeini

Ruhollah Khomeini was born in 1902 into a landed clerical family in central Iran. During the 1920s, he studied in the famous Fayzieh Seminary in Qom with the leading theologians of the day, most of whom were scrupulously apolitical. He taught at the seminary from the 1930s through the 1950s, avoiding politics even during the mass campaign to nationalize the British-owned oil company. His entry into politics did not come until 1962, when he, along with most other clerical leaders, denounced Muhammad Reza Shah's White Revolution. Forced into exile, Khomeini taught at the Shi'i center of Najaf in Iraq from 1964 until 1978.

During these years, Khomeini developed his own version of Shi'i populism by incorporating socioeconomic grievances into his sermons and denouncing not just the shah but also the whole ruling class. Returning home triumphant in the midst of the Iranian Revolution after the shah was forced from power in 1979, he was declared the Imam and Leader of the new Islamic Republic. In the past, Iranian Shi'is, unlike the Arab Sunnis, had reserved the special term *Imam* only for Imam Ali and his twelve direct heirs, whom they deemed to be semidivine and thereby infallible. For many Iranians in 1979, Khomeini was charismatic in the true sense of the word: a man with a special gift from God. Khomeini ruled as Imam and Leader of the Islamic Republic until his death in 1989. ❖

to the streets—with each demonstration growing in size and vociferousness. On September 8, 1978, remembered in Iran as Black Friday, troops shot and killed a large but unknown number of unarmed civilians in central Tehran. This dramatically intensified popular hatred for the regime. By late 1978, general strikes throughout the country were bringing the whole economy to a halt. Oil workers vowed that they would not produce any petroleum for the outside world until they had exported the "shah and his forty thieves."[3]

pasdaran Persian term for guards, used to refer to the army of Revolutionary Guards formed during Iran's Islamic Revolution.

In urban centers, local committees attached to the mosques and financed by the bazaars were distributing food to the needy, supplanting the police with militias known as ***pasdaran*** (Revolutionary Guards). They replaced the judicial system with ad hoc courts applying the *shari'a.* Equally significant, antiregime rallies were now attracting as many as 2 million protesters. Protesters demanded the abolition of the monarchy, the return of Khomeini, and the establishment of a republic that would preserve national independence and provide the downtrodden masses with decent wages, land, and a proper standard of living.

Although led by pro-Khomeini clerics, these rallies drew support from a broad variety of organizations: the National Front; the Lawyer's, Doctor's, and Women's associations; the communist Tudeh Party; the Fedayin, a Marxist guerrilla group; and the Mojahedin, a Muslim guerrilla group formed of nonclerical intellectuals. The rallies also attracted students, from high schools and colleges, as well as shopkeepers and craftsmen from the bazaars. A secret Revolutionary Committee in Tehran coordinated protests throughout the country. This was also one of the first revolutions to be televised worldwide. Many would later feel that these demonstrations had inspired the revolutions that swept through Eastern Europe in the 1980s.

Confronted by this opposition and by increasing numbers of soldiers who were deserting to the opposition, the shah decided to leave Iran. A year later, when he was in exile and dying of cancer, many speculated that he might have mastered the upheavals if he had been healthier, possessed a stronger personality, and received full support from the United States. But even a man with an iron will and full foreign backing would not have been able to deal with millions of angry demonstrators, massive general strikes, and debilitating desertions from his own pampered armed forces.

On February 11, 1979, a few hours of street fighting put the final touch to the fifty-four-year-old dynasty that claimed a 2,500-year-old heritage. The monarchy had been replaced by a republic.

The Islamic Republic (1979–present)

Seven weeks after the February revolution, a nationwide referendum replaced the monarchy with an Islamic Republic. Liberal and lay supporters of Khomeini, including Mehdi Bazargan, his first prime minister, had hoped to offer the electorate a third choice: a democratic Islamic Republic. But Khomeini overruled them. He declared the term *democratic* was redundant because Islam itself was democratic. Khomeini was now hailed as the Leader of the Revolution, Founder of the Islamic Republic, Guide of the Oppressed Masses, Commander of the Armed Forces, and most potent of all, Imam of the Muslim World.

Assembly of Experts group that nominates and can remove the Supreme Leader in Iran. The assembly is elected by the general electorate but almost all its members are clerics.

Hezbollahis literally "partisans of God." In Iran, the term is used to describe religious vigilantes. In Lebanon, it is used to describe the Shi'i militia.

hojjat al-Islam literally, "the proof of Islam." In Iran, it means a medium-ranking cleric.

A new constitution was drawn up in late 1979 by the **Assembly of Experts** (*Majles-e Khebregan*). Although this seventy-three-man assembly—later increased to eighty-six—was elected by the general public, almost all secular organizations as well as clerics opposed to Khomeini boycotted the elections because the state media were controlled, independent papers had been banned, and voters were being intimidated by club-wielding vigilantes known as the **Hezbollahis** ("Partisans of God"). The vast majority of those elected, including forty ***hojjat al-Islams*** and fifteen ayatollahs, were pro-Khomeini clerics. They drafted a highly theocratic constitution vesting much authority in the hands of Khomeini in particular and the clergy in general—all this over the strong objections of Prime Minister Bazargan, who wanted a French-style presidential republic that would be Islamic in name but democratic in structure.

When Bazargan threatened to submit his own constitution to the public, the state television network, controlled by the clerics, showed him shaking hands with U.S. policy-makers. Meanwhile, Khomeini denounced the U.S embassy as a "den of spies" plotting a repeat performance of the 1953 coup. This led to mass demonstrations, a break-in at the embassy, the seizure of dozens of American hostages, and eventually the resignation of Bazargan. Some suspect that the hostage crisis had been engineered to undercut Bazargan.

A month after the embassy break-in, Khomeini submitted the theocratic constitution to the public and declared that all citizens had a divine duty to vote; 99 percent of those voting endorsed it.

In the first decade after the revolution, a number of factors helped the clerics consolidate power. First, few people could challenge Khomeini's overwhelming

The shah's statue on the ground, February 1979. *(Source: © Abbas/Magnum Photos)*

charisma and popularity. Second, the Iraqi invasion of Iran in 1980 rallied the Iranian population behind their endangered homeland. Third, international petroleum prices shot up, sustaining Iran's oil revenues. The price of a barrel of oil, which had hovered around $30 in 1979, jumped to over $50 by 1981, which enabled the new regime, despite war and revolution, to continue to finance existing development programs.

The second decade after the revolution brought the clerics serious problems. Khomeini's death in June 1989 removed his decisive presence. His successor, Ali Khamenei, lacked not only his charisma but also his scholastic credentials and seminary disciples. The 1988 UN-brokered cease-fire in the Iran-Iraq War ended the foreign danger. A drastic fall in world oil prices, which plunged to less than $10 a barrel by 1998, placed a sharp brake on economic development. Even more serious, by the late 1990s, the regime was facing a major ideological crisis, with many of Khomeini's followers, including some of his closest disciples, now stressing the importance of public participation over clerical hegemony, of political pluralism over theological conformity, of populism over fundamentalism, and of civil society over state authority—in other words, of democracy over theocracy.

Iran after 9/11

The terrorist attacks of September 11, 2001, and the subsequent American invasions of Afghanistan in October 2001 and Iraq in March 2002, had profound consequences on Iran—probably more profound than on any other country with the exception of these three directly involved in the so-called War on Terror. At first, the American war on terror brought Iran and the United States closer together since Iran for years had seen both the Taliban and Saddam Hussein as its own mortal enemies. Saddam Hussein was hated for the obvious reason that he had waged an eight-year war on Iran. The Taliban was hated in part because it had been created by Pakistan—Iran's main rival to the east; in part because it had massacred large number of Shi'i Afghans; and in part because being Sunni fundamentalists financed by the Wahhabis, the main Sunni fundamentalists in Saudi Arabia, the Taliban considered Shi'ism as well as all innovations since the very beginnings of Islam to be unacceptable heresies. In fact, these Sunni fundamentalists consider Shi'is to be as bad if not worse than non-Muslim infidels. Not surprisingly, Iran helped the United States replace the Taliban in 2001. It used its considerable influence among the Iraqi Shi'is to install a pro-American government in Baghdad in 2003. It offered the United States in 2003 a "grand bargain" to settle all major differences, including those over nuclear research, Israel, Lebanon, and the Persian Gulf. Iran also offered to give a greater hand in helping the United States stabilize Iraq.

These hopes, however, were soon dashed—first by President Bush's famous Axis of Evil, which named Iran as part of the "evil enemy" and then by his refusal to enter serious negotiations until Iran unconditionally stopped nuclear research. This cold-shouldering played a major role in both undermining the liberal President Khatemi and paving the way for the electoral victory of the bellicose and ultraconservative Ahmadinejad. Reformers did not want to be associated with an American administration that not only insisted Iran should not have a nuclear program but also aggressively advocated regime change in Tehran. For most Iranians, this resurrected the specter of the 1953 CIA coup. These issues increased tensions and brought Iran and the United States closer to a diplomatic, if not military confrontation, in 2007–2008. The United States insists that it will not begin serious negotiations with Iran unless the latter stops its nuclear enrichment program. Iran insists that its nuclear program has no military intentions and that it conforms to international guidelines set by international treaties. On one hand, the United States would like "behavioral" change if not "regime change" in Iran. On the other hand, the United States needs Iran's cooperation in Iraq to prevent the situation there from going completely out of control, and, at the same time, does not have the military capacity at present to coerce Tehran to give up its nuclear program. Only time will show how the crisis will work itself out.

FOCUS QUESTION

What are some of the basic problems confronting the Islamic Republic?

Themes and Implications

Historical Junctures and Political Themes

Khomeini argued that Islam and democracy were compatible since the vast majority respected the clerics as the true interpreters of the *shari'a*, and wanted them to oversee state officials. Islam and democracy, however, appear less reconcilable now that the public has lost its enthusiasm for clerical rule. Khomeinism has divided into two divergent branches in Iran: political liberalism and clerical conservatism.

Democracy is based on the principles that all individuals are equal, especially before the law, and that all people have inalienable natural rights. The *shari'a* is based on inequalities—between men and women, between Muslims and non-Muslims, between legitimate minorities, known as the People of the Book, and illegitimate ones, known as unbelievers. Moderate clerics, however, advocate reforming the *shari'a* to make it compatible with individual freedoms and human rights.

The Islamic Republic is determined to remain dominant in the Persian Gulf. By denouncing the United States as an "arrogant imperialist," canceling military agreements with the West, and condoning the taking of United States diplomats as hostages, Khomeini asserted Iranian power but also inadvertently prompted Saddam Hussein to launch the Iraq-Iran War in 1980.

Khomeini's policies made it difficult for his successors to improve relations with the West. He called for revolutions throughout the Muslim world, denouncing Arab rulers in the region, particularly in Saudi Arabia, as the "corrupt puppets of American imperialism." He strengthened Iran's navy, and bought nuclear submarines from Russia. He launched a research program to build medium-range missiles and nuclear power—possibly even nuclear weapons. He denounced the proposals for Arab-Israeli negotiations over Palestine. He sent money as well as arms to Muslim dissidents abroad, particularly Shi'i groups in Lebanon, Iraq, and Afghanistan. He permitted the intelligence services to assassinate some one hundred exiled opposition leaders living in Western Europe. These policies isolated Iran not only from the United States but also from the European Community, human rights organizations, and the United Nations.

In the 1980s, peasants continued to migrate to the cities because of the lack of both agricultural land and irrigation. Industry suffered from lack of investment capital. Inflation and unemployment were high. The population steadily increased, and real per capita income fell due to forces outside state control. Some leaders favored conventional state-interventionist strategies. Others advocated equally conventional **laissez-faire** strategies.

laissez-faire a term taken from the French, which means "to let be," in other words, to allow to act freely.

The stress on Shi'ism has alienated the 10 percent of Iranians who are Sunnis. In addition, the regime's insistence on a theocratic constitution antagonized other top clerics as well as lay secular Muslims, who lead most of the political parties. Similarly, the association of Shi'ism with the central, Persian-speaking regions of Iran may possibly in the future alienate the important Turkic minority in Azerbaijan province.

Implications for Comparative Politics

Many Americans believe a new specter is haunting the West: Islamic fundamentalism. Islam was seen as a major threat not only because of its size but also because it was deemed "inherently bellicose," "militant," and antagonistic to the West.

Such dire predictions have turned out to be gross exaggerations. It is true that the early Islamic Republic began denouncing the United States, arming

The U.S. Connection

The Nuclear Power Issue

At the heart of U.S.-Iran tensions lies the nuclear issue. For Iran, nuclear technology—always defined as a "civilian program"—is a non-negotiable right of an independent nation essential not only for its long-term energy needs but also to attain the hallmark of a developed country. It sees nuclear power as a matter of both sovereignty and modernity.

For the United States, any nuclear technology—even one developed for peaceful means—in the hands of Iran is too risky to be acceptable. The United States argues that such technology could be expanded into a weapons program, and nuclear weapons could then be used on Israel or passed on to "terrorist organizations." It seems that the only way to resolve the issue is for the United States to accept Iran's civilian program, and Iran, in return, to provide verifiable guarantees that its program would not trespass into the military realm. ❖

jihad literally "struggle." Often used to mean armed struggle against unbelievers; can also mean spiritual struggle for self-improvement.

militants in other parts of the Middle East, and calling for a struggle, sometimes termed a ***jihad*** (crusade), against the West. But such rhetoric became quieter in the late 1990s with the election of the reformist Khatami as president. The call for Muslim unity has largely fallen on deaf ears, especially in Sunni countries. In Afghanistan, Iran pressured its Shi'i allies to help the United States overthrow the Taliban after 9/11. It also urged Iraq's Shi'i population not to resist the American invasion and to channel their activities into the electoral arena. Anti-American rhetoric from Teheran has certainly increased, however, since President Ahmadinejad took office in 2005.

Iran has one of the region's biggest armies and the largest navy in the Persian Gulf, a large land mass, considerable human resources, a respectable gross domestic product (GDP), and vast oil production. Iran also has plans to become a nuclear power, the major issue of tension in U.S.-Iranian relations.

But Iran's GDP is only about that of New Jersey, and its armed forces are a mere shadow of their former selves. Its military hardware has been exhausted by war, age, and lack of spare parts. In the last years of the shah, military purchases accounted for 17 percent of the GDP; they now account for 2 percent. In 2005, Iran spent only $4.1 billion on arms whereas Turkey spent as much as $10 billion, Saudi Arabia $21 billion, and even tiny Kuwait and United Arab Emirates together more than $6.6 billion. What is more, Iran's plans to build nuclear plants have been delayed largely because the United States has persuaded Europe not to transfer such technology to Iran. Iran is unlikely to obtain nuclear weapons in the immediate future. Moreover, the United States, after 9/11 and the occupation of Iraq in March 2003, surrounded Iran with military bases in the Gulf, Turkey, Azerbaijan, Georgia, Afghanistan, and Central Asia. The United States, which spends more than a trillion dollars a year on defense, can now be considered Iran's neighbor.

Summary

The Iranian state—unlike many others in the Middle East—is viable and well established. It has a long history. Its official religion—Shi'ism—binds the elite with the masses, the government with the governed, the rulers with the ruled. Its ministries are embedded deep into society providing multiple social services. It has substantial oil revenues, which, although fluctuating, provide the government the means to finance the ever-growing ministries. What is more, the recent past—especially the Islamic Revolution and the eight-year war with Iraq—have helped create a strong sense of national solidarity against the outside world—not just against the West but also much of the rest of the Sunni Muslim World.

Political Economy and Development

FOCUS QUESTION

What are some of the ways in which the oil industry has advanced or distorted development in Iran?

State and Economy

The radical followers of Ayatollah Khomeini, the founder of the Islamic Republic, once denounced foreign investors as imperialist exploiters and waxed eloquent about economic self-sufficiency. But in 2002, Iran contemplated a dramatically new law permitting foreigners to own as much as 100 percent of any firm in the country, to repatriate profits, to be free of state meddling, and to have assurances against both arbitrary confiscations and high taxation. The regime as a whole now is eager to attract foreign investment and to rejoin the world economy.

The Economy in the Nineteenth Century

The integration of Iran into the world system began in the latter half of the nineteenth century. Several factors account for this nineteenth-century integration: concessions granted to the European powers; the Suez Canal and the Trans-Caspian and the Batum-Baku railways; telegraph lines across Iran linking India with Britain; the outflow of capital from Europe after 1870; and, most important, the Industrial Revolution in Europe and the subsequent export of European manufactured goods to the rest of the world. In the nineteenth century, Iran's foreign trade increased tenfold.

Economic dependency resulted, a situation common in much of the Third World. Less-developed countries become too reliant on developed countries; poorer nations are vulnerable to sudden fluctuations in richer economies and dependent on the export of raw materials, whose prices often stagnate or decline, while prices for the manufactured products they import invariably increase.

Cash crops, especially cotton, tobacco, and opium, reduced the acreage for wheat and other edible grains. Many landowners stopped growing food and turned to commercial export crops. This led to disastrous famines in 1860, 1869–1872, 1880, and 1918–1920.

Furthermore, many local merchants, shopkeepers, and workshop owners in the bazaars now formed a national propertied middle class aware of their common interests against both the central government and the foreign powers. This new class awareness played an important role in Iran's constitutional revolution of 1905.

The Oil Economy

British prospectors struck oil in Khuzistan province in 1908, and the British government in 1912 decided to fuel its navy with petroleum rather than coal. It also decided to buy most of its fuel from the Anglo-Iranian Oil Company. Iran's oil revenues increased modestly in the next four decades, reaching $16 million in 1951. After the nationalization of the oil industry in 1951 and the agreement with a consortium of U.S. and British companies in 1955, oil revenues rose steadily, from $34 million in 1955 to $5 billion in 1973 and, after the quadrupling of oil prices in 1974, to over $23 billion in 1976. Between 1953 and 1978, Iran's cumulative oil income came to over $100 billion.

rentier state a country that obtains much of its revenue from the export of oil or other natural resources.

Oil financed over 90 percent of imports and 80 percent of the annual budget and far surpassed total tax revenues. Oil also enabled Iran not to worry about feeding its population. Instead, it could undertake ambitious development programs that other states could carry out only if they could squeeze scarce resources from their populations. In fact, oil revenues created a **rentier state,** a country that obtains a lucrative income by exporting raw materials or leasing out natural resources to foreign companies. Iran as well as Iraq, Algeria, and the Gulf states received enough money from their oil wells to be able to disregard their internal tax bases. The Iranian state thus became relatively independent of society. Society, in turn, had few inputs into the state. Little taxation meant little representation.

Muhammad Reza Shah tried to encourage other exports and attract foreign investment into non-oil ventures. Despite some increase in carpet and pistachio exports, oil continued to dominate. In 1979 oil still provided 97 percent of the country's foreign exchange. Foreign firms invested no more than $1 billion in Iran—and much of this was not in industry but in banking, trade, and insurance. In Iran, as in the rest of the Middle East, foreign investors were put off by government corruption, labor costs, small internal markets, potential instability, and fear of confiscations.

FOCUS QUESTION

In what ways did Iran change in the twentieth century?

Society and Economy

Despite waste and corruption significant sums went into socioeconomic development during the shah's reign. There was significant growth in many modern sectors of the economy. (See Table 8.2.) GNP grew at an average rate of 9.6 percent

TABLE 8.2

Industrial Production

Product	1953	1977
Coal (tons)	200,000	900,000
Iron ore (tons)	5,000	930,000
Steel (tons)	—	275,000
Cement (tons)	53,000	4,300,000
Sugar (tons)	70,000	527,000
Tractors (no.)	—	7,700
Motor vehicles (no.)	—	109,000

Source:
E. Abrahamian, "Structural Causes of the Iranian Revolution," *Middle East Research and Information Project*, no. 87 (May 1980), 22.

per year from 1960 to 1977. This made Iran one of the fastest-growing economies in the world. Land reform created over 644,000 moderately prosperous farms. The number of modern factories tripled. Enrollment in primary schools grew from fewer than 750,000 to over 4 million; in secondary schools from 121,000 to nearly 740,000; in vocational schools from 2,500 to nearly 230,000; and in universities from under 14,000 to more than 154,000. The Trans-Iranian Railway was completed. Roads were built connecting most villages with the provincial cities.

Between 1963 and 1977, the number of hospital beds increased from 24,126 to 48,000; medical clinics from 700 to 2,800; nurses from 1,969 to 4,105; and doctors from 4,500 to 12,750. These improvements, together with the elimination of epidemics and famines, lowered infant mortality and led to a population explosion.

The shah's approach to development, however, increased his unpopularity with many sectors of Iranian society. The shah believed that if economic growth benefited those who were already better off, some of the wealth would gradually trickle down to the lower levels of society. But these benefits got stuck at the top and never trickled down. By the mid-1970s, Iran had some of most unequal incomes in the world.[4] Similarly, land reform created a small layer of prosperous farmers but left the vast majority of peasants landless or nearly landless (see Table 8.3).

The new factories drew criticism that they were mere assembly plants that used cheap labor and were poor substitutes for real industrial development that would benefit the nation. The shah's medical programs still left Iran with one of the worst doctor-patient ratios and child mortality rates in the Middle East. The per capita income in the richest provinces was ten times more than in the poorest ones. The ratio of urban to rural incomes was 5 to 1, one of the worst in the world.[5]

TABLE 8.3

Land Ownership in 1977

Size (Hectares)	Number of Owners
200+	1,300
51–200	44,000
11–50	600,000
3–10	1,200,000
Landless	700,000

Note:

One hectare is equal to approximately 2.47 acres.

Source:

E. Abrahamian, "Structural Causes of the Iranian Revolution," *Middle East Research and Information Project*, no. 87 (May 1980).

dual society a society and economy that are sharply divided into a traditional, usually poorer, and a modern, usually richer, sector.

These inequalities created a **dual society**—on one side the modern sector, headed by elites with close ties to the oil state, on the other side the traditional sector, the clergy, the bazaar middle class, and the rural masses. Each sector, in turn, was sharply stratified into unequal classes (see Figure 8.2).

The upper class—the Pahlavi family, the court-connected entrepreneurs, the military officers, and the senior civil servants—made up less than 0.01 percent of the population. In the modern sector, the middle class—professionals, civil servants, salaried personnel, and college students—formed about 10 percent of the population. The bottom of the modern sector—the urban working class, factory workers, construction laborers, peddlers, and unemployed—constituted over 32 percent. In the traditional sector, the middle class—bazaar merchants, small retailers, shopkeepers, workshop owners, and well-to-do family farmers—made up 13 percent; the rural masses 45 percent.

In 1972, the richest 20 percent of urban households accounted for 47.1 percent of total urban family expenditures; by 1977, it accounted for 55.5 percent. In 1972, the poorest 40 percent accounted for 16.7 percent of urban family expenditures; by 1977, this had dropped to 11.7 percent. In other words, in Iran's cities, the rich were getting richer, and the poor were getting poorer.

These inequalities fueled resentments, which were expressed more in cultural and religious terms than in economic and class terms. Among the fiercest critics was Jalal Al-e Ahmad (1923–1969). He argued that the ruling class was destroying Iran by mindlessly imitating the West; neglecting the peasantry; showing contempt for popular religion; worshipping mechanization, regimentation, and industrialization; and flooding the country with foreign ideas, tastes, luxury items, and mass-consumption goods. He stressed that developing countries such as Iran could survive this "plague" of Western imperialism only by returning to their cultural roots and developing a self-reliant society, especially a fully independent economy. Al-e Ahmad is deemed to be not only the main intellectual critic of the old order but also the launcher of the "back to roots" movement in Iran.

FIGURE 8.2

Iran's Class Structure in the Mid-1970s

Iranian society was divided sharply not only into horizontal classes, but also into vertical sectors—the modern and the transitional, the urban and the rural. This is known as a dual society.

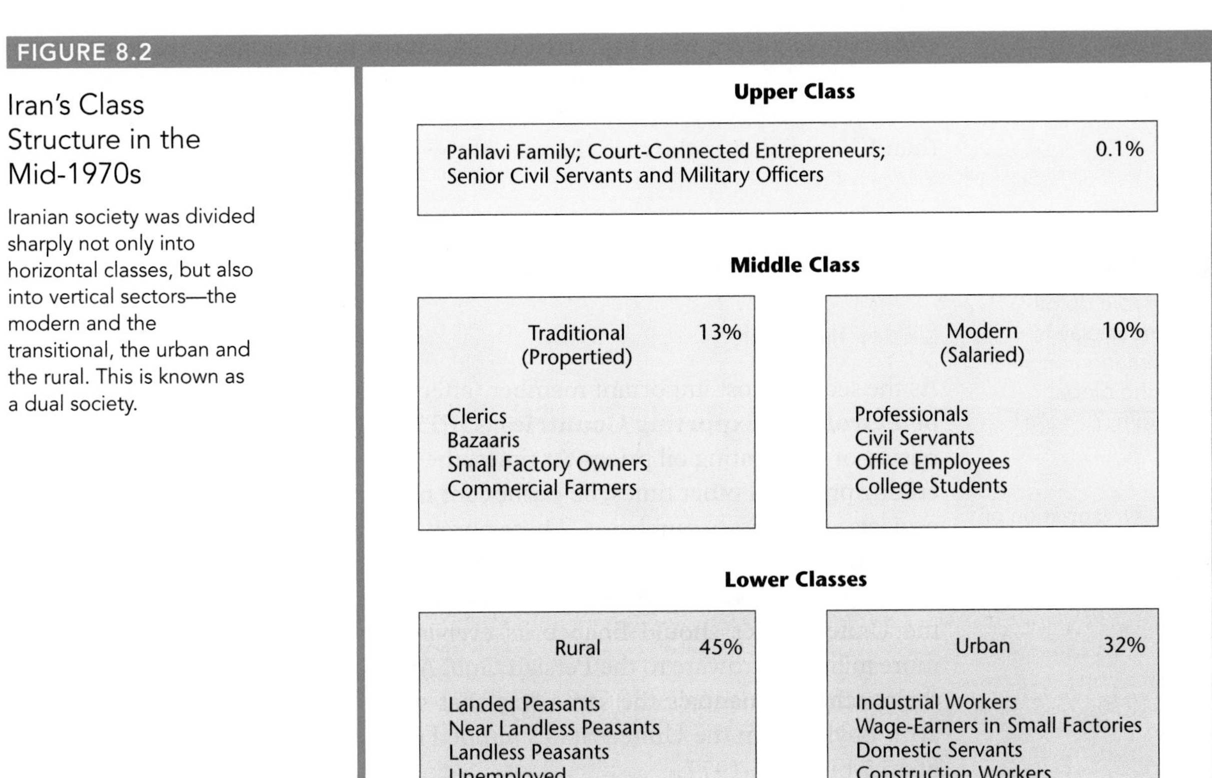

These themes were developed further by another young intellectual, Ali Shariati (1933–1977). Studying in Paris during the 1960s, Shariati was influenced by Marxist sociology, Catholic liberation theology, the Algerian revolution, and, most important, Frantz Fanon's theory of violent Third World revolutions against colonial oppression as laid out in *The Wretched of the Earth.*

Shariati argued that history was a continuous struggle between oppressors and oppressed. Each class had its own interests, its own interpretations of religion, and its own sense of right and wrong. God periodically sent down prophets, such as Abraham, Moses, Jesus, and Muhammad. Muhammad had been sent to launch a dynamic community in "permanent revolution" toward the ultimate utopia: a perfectly classless society.

Although Muhammad's goal had been betrayed by his illegitimate successors, his radical message had been preserved by the Shi'i Imams, especially by Imam Husayn, who had been martyred to show future generations that human beings had the moral duty to fight oppression in all places at all times. According to Shariati, the contemporary oppressors were the imperialists, the modern-day feudalists, the corrupt capitalists, and their hangers-on. He criticized the conservative clerics who had tried to transform revolutionary religion into an apolitical public opiate. Shariati died on the eve of the revolution, but his prolific works were so widely read and so influential that many felt that he, rather than Khomeini, was the true theorist of the Islamic Revolution.

FOCUS QUESTION

What role do oil revenues play in integrating Iran into the global economy?

Iran in the Global Economy

Under the Shah

OPEC Organization of Petroleum Exporting Countries.

As the second most important member (after Saudi Arabia) of the **Organization of Petroleum Exporting Countries (OPEC)**, Iran could cast decisive votes for raising or moderating oil prices. At times, the shah curried Western favor by moderating prices. At other times, he pushed for higher prices to finance his ambitious projects and military purchases. These purchases rapidly escalated once President Richard Nixon began to encourage U.S. allies to take a greater role in policing their regions. Moreover, Nixon's secretary of state, Henry Kissinger, argued that the United States should finance its ever-increasing oil imports, by exporting more military hardware to the Persian Gulf. Arms dealers joked that the shah read their technical manuals the same way that some men read *Playboy.* The shah's arms buying from the United States jumped from $135 million in 1970 to a peak of $5.7 billion in 1977.

This military might gave the shah a reach well beyond his immediate boundaries. He occupied three small but strategically located Arab islands in the Strait of Hormuz, thus controlling the oil lifeline through the Persian Gulf but also creating distrust among his Arab neighbors. He talked of establishing a presence well beyond the Gulf on the grounds that Iran's national interests reached into the Indian Ocean.

In the mid-1970s, the shah dispatched troops to Oman to help the local sultan fight rebels. He offered Afghanistan $2 billion to break its ties with the Soviet Union, a move that probably prompted the Soviets to intervene militarily in that country. A U.S. congressional report summed up: "Iran in the 1970s was widely regarded as a significant regional, if not global, power. The United States relied on it, implicitly if not explicitly, to ensure the security and stability of the Persian Gulf sector and the flow of oil from the region to the industrialized Western world of Japan, Europe, and the United States, as well as to lesser powers elsewhere."[6]

These vast military expenditures, as well as the oil exports, tied Iran closely to the industrial countries of the West and to Japan. Iran was now importing millions of dollars' worth of rice, wheat, industrial tools, construction equipment, pharmaceuticals, tractors, pumps, and spare parts, the bulk of which came from the United States. Trade with neighboring and other developing countries was insignificant.

The oil revenues thus had major consequences for Iran's political economy, all of which paved the way for the Islamic Revolution. They allowed the shah to pursue ambitious programs that inadvertently widened class and regional divisions within the dual society. They drastically raised public expectations without necessarily meeting them. They made the rentier state independent of society. Economic slowdowns in the industrial countries, however, could lead to a decline in their oil demands, which could diminish Iran's ability to buy such essential goods as food, medicine, and industrial spare parts. One of the major promises made by the Islamic Revolution was to end this economic dependency on oil and the West.

Iran's Economy under the Islamic Republic

Iran's main economic problem has been instability in the world oil market. Oil revenues, which continued to provide the state with 80 percent of its hard currency and 75 percent of its total revenues, fell from $20 billion in 1978 to less than $10 billion in 1998. They did not improve until the early 2000s.

To raise oil production, Iran needs an influx of capital and new deep-drilling technology, both of which can be found only in the West. This explains why the Islamic Republic has tried so dramatically to change policy toward foreign investment.

Iran's economic problems have been compounded by the population explosion, the Iran-Iraqi war, and the emigration of some 3 million Iranians. The annual population growth rate, which had hit 2.5 percent in the late 1970s, jumped to nearly 4 percent by the late 1980s, the highest rate in the world. The Iraqi war wrought as much as $600 billion in property damage and half a million Iranian casualties. The Islamic Revolution itself frightened many professionals and highly skilled technicians, as well as wealthy entrepreneurs, and industrialists into fleeing to the West.

The overall result was a twenty-year economic crisis lasting well into the late 1990s. The value of real incomes, including salaries and pensions, dropped by as much as 60 percent. Unemployment hit 20 percent; over two-thirds of entrants into the labor force could not find jobs. Peasants continued to flock to urban shantytowns. Tehran grew from 4.5 million to 12 million people. The total number of families living below the poverty level increased. By the late 1990s, over 9 million urban dwellers lived below the official poverty line.[7] Shortages in foreign exchange curtailed vital imports, even of essential manufactured goods. What is more, the regime that came to power advocating self-sufficiency now owed foreign banks and governments over $30 billion, forcing it to renegotiate foreign loans constantly. In the 2005 presidential elections, these problems help explain the strong victory of Ahmadinejad, the conservative populist candidate.

Nevertheless, the Islamic Republic has scored some notable successes. The Reconstruction Ministry, built 30,000 miles of paved roads, 40,000 schools, and 7,000 libraries. It brought electricity and running water to more than half of the country's 50,000 villages. The number of registered vehicles on the roads increased from 27,000 in 1990 to over 2.9 million in 1996. More dams and irrigation canals were built, and the Agricultural Ministry distributed some 630,000 hectares of confiscated arable land to peasants and gave farmers more favorable prices. By the late 1990s, most independent farmers owned radios, televisions, refrigerators, and pickup trucks. The extension of social services narrowed the gap between town and country and between the urban poor and the middle classes. The adult literacy rate grew from 50 percent to 76 percent, and by 2000 the literacy rate among those in the six to twenty-nine age range hit 97 percent. The infant mortality rate fell from 104 per 1,000 in the mid-1970s to 33 per 1,000 in 2003. Life expectancy climbed from fifty-five years in 1979 to sixty-eight in 1993 and further to seventy in 2004—one of the best in the Middle East. The UN estimates that by 2000, 94 percent of the population had access to health services and 95 percent to safe water. On the whole, the poor in Iran are better off now than their parents had been before the Islamic Revolution. Moreover, the country, despite initial setbacks, was able to become more self-sufficient in food production. Ironically, the impressive growth in private cars and public transport strained the refineries and forced Iran to become more dependent on imported gasoline.

The Islamic Republic also made major strides toward population control. At first, it closed down birth control clinics. But it reversed direction once the ministries responsible for social services felt the full impact of this growth. In 1989, the government declared that Islam favored healthy rather than large families and that one literate citizen was better than ten illiterate ones. It reopened birth control clinics, cut subsidies to large families, and announced that the ideal family should consist of no more than two children. It even took away social benefits from those having more than two children. By 2003, population growth had fallen to 1.2 percent a year; and by 2005 to 0.66 percent.

The government has exercised control over most of Iran's economy for the entire history of the Islamic Republic. Reformist president Khatami took steps to reduce the role of the state in governing the economy by allowing the privatization in some sectors of the economy (including banking) and relaunching a stock market to sell shares of government businesses to private investors. Even Ayatollah Khameni, the chief religious leader, and current conservative president Ahmadinejad have endorsed limited privatization. Ahmadinejad has initiated a program to give "justice shares" of state-owned industries to low-income citizens. Nevertheless, about 70 percent of the Iranian economy continued to be under state control.

The 2000–2005 rise in petroleum prices—from $19 per barrel in 1999 to $53 per barrel in 2005—further helped the situation. Oil revenues jumped from less than $10 billion in 1998 to over $28 billion in 2001 and nearly $47 billion in 2006. Foreign reserves increased to $4.8 billion, stabilizing the currency and improving the country's creditworthiness. Iran became one of the few developing countries to be free of foreign debt. It was even able set aside some oil revenues as a hedge against leaner times. The GDP now grows at over 5 percent a year. Both the official unemployment and inflation rates, while still high, have fallen, and the currency has stabilized. The government has floated its first international bond, and foreign investments have been contracted to flow into oil and gas ventures, petrochemicals, minerals, and car factories. The World Bank lent Iran $232 million for medical services and sewage lines. Oil revenues have allowed the government to channel additional funds into the infrastructure. President Ahmadinejad has promised to steer more of the oil wealth to projects and programs that directly help the poor.

Summary

It has often been said that oil is the "curse" of the producing countries. It has been blamed for creating "rentier states," "dual societies," autocratic governments, unpredictable budgets, and retardation of other economic activities. Although this may be true in some parts of the world, in Iran oil has been the main engine driving state development and social modernization. It is mainly due to oil that Iran enters the twenty-first century with a strong state and a fairly modernized society in which almost all citizens have access to schools, medical clinics, modern sanitation, piped water, electricity, radios, televisions, and basic consumer goods.

Governance and Policy-Making

FOCUS QUESTION

In what ways do the clergy have extraordinary powers in Iran?

Organization of the State

The political system of the Islamic Republic of Iran is unique. It is a theocracy with important democratic features. It is a theocracy (from the Greek, "God rules") because the religious clerics control the most powerful political positions. But the system also contains elements of democracy with some high officials, including the president, elected directly by the general public.

The state rests on the Islamic constitution implemented immediately after the 1979 revolution and amended between April and June 1989 during the last months of Khomeini's life by the Council for the Revision of the Constitution, which was handpicked by Khomeini himself. The final document is a highly complex mixture of theocracy and democracy.

The preamble affirms faith in God, Divine Justice, the Qur'an, the Day of Judgment, the Prophet Muhammad, the Twelve Imams, the eventual return of the Hidden Imam (the Mahdi), and, of course, Khomeini's doctrine of jurist's guardianship that gives supreme power to senior clergy. All laws, institutions, and state organizations must conform to these "divine principles."

The Leader and Major Organizations of Clerical Power

The constitution named Khomeini to be the Leader for life on the grounds that the public overwhelmingly recognized him as the "most just, pious, informed, brave, and enterprising" of the senior clerics—the grand ayatollahs. It further described him as the Leader of the Revolution, the Founder of the Islamic

FIGURE 8.3

The Islamic Constitution

The general public elects the *Majles*, the president, and the Assembly of Experts. But the Leader and the Guardian Council decide who can compete in these elections.

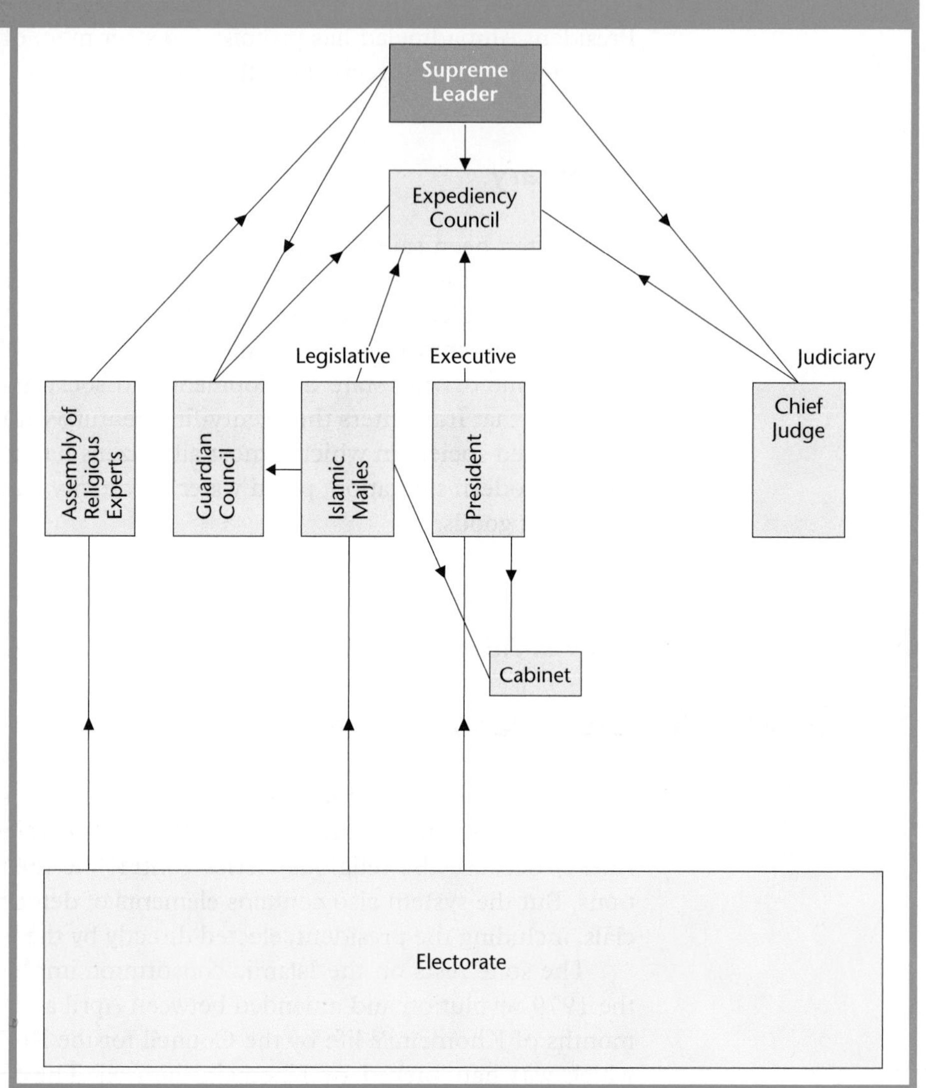

Republic, and, most important, the Imam of the Muslim Community. It stipulated that if no single Leader emerged after his death, then all his authority would be passed on to a leadership council of senior clerics.

After Khomeini's death, however, his followers distrusted the other senior clerics so much that they did not set up such a council. Instead, they elected one of their own, Ali Khamenei, a middle-ranking cleric, to be the new Leader. The Islamic Republic has often been described as a regime of the ayatollahs (high-ranking clerics). It could be more aptly called a regime of the *hojjat al-Islams* (middle-ranking clerics), since few senior clerics want to be associated with it. None of the grand ayatollahs and few of the ordinary ayatollahs subscribed to Khomeini's notion of jurist's guardianship. In fact, most disliked his radical populism and political activism.

Profile
Ayatollah Ali Khamenei

Ali Khamenei succeeded Khomeini as Leader in 1989. He was born in 1939 in Mashed into a minor clerical family originally from Azerbaijan. He studied theology with Khomeini in Qom and was briefly imprisoned in 1962. Active in the antishah opposition movement in 1978, he was given a series of influential positions immediately after the revolution, even though he held only the middle-level clerical rank of *hojjat al-Islam*. He became Friday prayer leader of Tehran, head of the Revolutionary Guards, and, in the last years of Khomeini's life, president of the republic. After Khomeini's death, he was elevated to the rank of Leader even though he was neither a grand ayatollah nor a recognized senior expert on Islamic law. He had not even published a theological treatise. The government-controlled media, however, began to refer to him as an ayatollah. Some ardent followers even referred to him as a grand ayatollah qualified to guide the world's whole Shi'i community. After his elevation, he built a constituency among the regime's more diehard elements: traditionalist judges, conservative war veterans, and antiliberal ideologues. Before 1989, he often sported a pipe in public, a mark of an intellectual, but gave up the habit upon becoming Leader. ❖

The Leader is elected by the eighty-six-member Assembly of Experts. The constitution gives wide-ranging powers to the Leader. As the vital link between the three branches of government, he can mediate between the legislature, the executive, and the judiciary. He can "determine the interests of Islam," "supervise the implementation of general policy," and "set political guidelines for the Islamic Republic." He can eliminate presidential candidates and dismiss the duly elected president. He can grant amnesty. As commander-in-chief, he can mobilize the armed forces, declare war and peace, and convene the Supreme Military Council. He can appoint and dismiss the commanders of Revolutionary Guards as well as those of the regular army, navy, and air force.

The Leader has extensive power over the judicial system. He can nominate and remove the chief judge, the chief prosecutor, and the revolutionary tribunals. He can dismiss lower court judges. He also nominates six clerics to the powerful twelve-man Guardian Council, which can veto parliamentary bills. It has also obtained (through separate legislation) the right to review all candidates for elected office, including the presidency and the national legislature, the *Majles*. The other six members of the Guardian Council are jurists nominated by the chief judge and approved by the *Majles*. Furthermore, the Leader appoints the powerful **Expediency Council**, which has the authority to resolve differences between the Guardian Council and the *Majles* (the legislature) and to initiate laws on its own.

Expediency Council a committee set up in Iran to resolve differences between the *Majles* (parliament) and the Guardian Council.

The Leader also fills a number of important nongovernment posts: the preachers **(Imam Jum'ehs)** at the main city mosques, the director of the national radio-television network, and the heads of the main religious endowments, especially the **Foundation of the Oppressed** (see below). By 2001, the Office of the Leader employed over six hundred in Tehran and had representatives in most sensitive institutions throughout the country. The Leader has obtained more constitutional powers than the shah ever dreamed of.

Imam Jum'ehs prayer leaders in Iran's main urban mosques.

Foundation of the Oppressed a clerically controlled foundation set up after the revolution in Iran.

The Assembly of Experts is elected for an eight-year term every four years by the general public. Its members must have an advanced seminary degree, so it is packed with clerics. The Assembly has the right to oversee the work of the Leader and to dismiss him if he is found to be "mentally incapable of fulfilling his arduous duties." In effect, the Assembly of Experts has become an even-more powerful upper chamber to the *Majles*.

FOCUS QUESTION

What role does the democratically elected president play within the Islamic Republic?

The Executive Branch

The President and the Cabinet

The constitution of the Islamic Republic reserves some power for the president. He is described as the chief executive and the highest state official after the Leader. He is chosen every four years through a national election. If a candidate does not win a majority of the vote in the first round of the election, a run-off chooses between the two top vote-getters. The president cannot serve more than two terms.

The constitution says the president must be a pious Shi'i faithful to the principles of the Islamic Republic, of Iranian origin, and between the ages of 25 and 75. The president must also demonstrate "administrative capacity and resourcefulness" and have "a good past record." There has been some dispute about whether the language used in the constitution restricts the presidency to males.

The president has the power to

- conduct the country's internal and external policies, including signing all international treaties, laws, and agreements;
- chair the National Security Council, which is responsible for defense matters;
- draw up the annual budget, supervise economic matters, and chair the state planning and budget organization;
- propose legislation to the *Majles*;
- appoint cabinet ministers, with a parliamentary stipulation that the minister of intelligence must be from the ranks of the clergy;
- appoint most other senior officials, including provincial governors, ambassadors, and the directors of some of the large public organizations, such as the National Iranian Oil Company, the National Electricity Board, and the National Bank.

Iran has no single vice president. Instead the president may select "presidential deputies" to help with "constitutional duties." There are currently ten such vice presidents. One is designated as the "first vice president." The others have specific responsibilities, such as presiding over the national atomic energy organization or veterans' affairs. One is a woman. She has a Ph.D. in geology and is in charge of environmental policy.

Profile

President Mahmoud Ahmadinejad

Mahmoud Ahmadinejad was elected president of Iran in 2005. He was born in 1956 into a working class family in a small town in central Iran. He grew up mostly in Tehran where his father worked as a blacksmith. At the outbreak of the Islamic revolution in the late 1970s, he was studying engineering in Tehran and was active in the Islamic student movement. He volunteered to fight in the Iraqi war, and, after the cease-fire, returned to Tehran to complete a Ph.D. in urban planning.

Ahmadinejad served as governor of Ardabil province and then as mayor of Tehran (2003–2005) before running for president. As mayor of Iran's capital city, he rolled back some of the reforms that had been implemented before he took office. For example, he ordered that men and women use separate elevators in city office buildings. This earned him a reputation as a hard-line conservative and a political following among those who believed that the government of president Mohammad Khatami was too liberal. His presidential campaign was based on a combination of a pledge to restore the values of the Islamic Revolution and to attend to the needs of the poor.

After becoming president, Ahmadinejad continued to promote conservative policies. But in April 2006, he announced the removal of the ban on women attending events in which male athletes participated. This displeased some of his supporters, and the Leader overruled the president and ordered the ban upheld.

Ahmadinejad has reversed steps taken by the previous government to improve relations with the United States. He insists on Iran's right to develop nuclear power, including weapons, although he asserts that country has only peaceful intentions. He has been very critical of U.S. policy in the Middle East and of Israel, which he claims "was created to establish dominion of arrogant states over the region and to enable the enemy to penetrate the heart Muslim land."* He has made statements and hosted international conferences that question the historical context of the Holocaust.

There are signs that Ahmadinejad's popularity is weakening—especially since his economic promises to the poor have failed to bear fruit. On the contrary, some of his policies have further inflamed inflation and unemployment. In December 2006, there was a fairly large student demonstration denouncing the Holocaust conference as bringing shame to Iran. In the same month, conservative candidates allied with the president did not do well in elections for the Assembly of Experts and local councils. The results of this election, for which there was a 60 percent turnout, suggest that the mood of Iran's voters may be shifting again. The next presidential election in 2009 will be an important indicator of the ideological balance of power in Iran. Iran has truly entered the age of electoral politics however flawed and restricted. ❖

*Islamic Republic News Agency (IRNA), "President Ahmadinejad, Palestinian PM meet in Doha," December 2, 2006.

Khomeini often promised that trained officials would run the executive branch in the Islamic Republic, but clerics—also called mullahs have, in fact, dominated the presidency. Of the five presidents since the revolution, three have been clerics: Khamenei, Rafsanjani, and Khatami. The first president, Abol-Hasan Bani-Sadr, a lay intellectual was ousted in 1981 precisely because he denounced the regime as "a dictatorship of the mullahtariat," comparing it to a communist-led "dictatorship of the proletariat." Bani-Sadr's successor, who also was not a mullah, was assassinated shortly after taking office. The current president, Ahmadinejad, is not a cleric, but has strong support within the clerical establishment.

The Bureaucracy

As chief of the executive branch the president, heads a huge bureaucracy. In fact, this bureaucracy continued to proliferate after the revolution even though Khomeini had often criticized the shah for having a bloated government. It expanded, for the most part, to provide jobs for the many college and high school graduates. On the eve of the revolution, the ministries had 300,000 civil servants and 1 million employees. By the early 1990s, they had over 600,000 civil servants and 1.5 million employees.

Among the most important ministries of the Islamic Republic are Culture and Islamic Guidance, which has responsibility for controlling the media and enforcing "proper conduct" in public life; Intelligence, which has replaced the shah's dreaded SAVAK as the main security organization; Heavy Industries, which manages the nationalized factories; and Reconstruction, which has the dual task of expanding social services and taking "true Islam" into the countryside. Its mission is to build bridges, roads, schools, libraries, and mosques in the villages so that the peasantry will learn the basic principles of Islam. "The peasants," declared one cleric, "are so ignorant of true Islam that they even sleep next to their unclean sheep."[8]

The clergy dominate the bureaucracy as well as the presidency. They have monopolized the most sensitive ministries—Intelligence, Interior, Justice, and Culture and Islamic Guidance—and have given posts in other ministries to relatives and protégés. These ministers appear to be highly trained technocrats, sometimes with advanced degrees from the West. In fact, they are often fairly powerless individuals dependent on the powerful clergy—chosen by them, trusted by them, and invariably related to them.

Semipublic Institutions

The Islamic Republic has set up a number of semipublic institutions. They include the Foundation of the Oppressed, the Alavi Foundation (named after Imam Ali), the Martyrs Foundation, the Pilgrimage Foundation, the Housing Foundation, the Foundation for the Publication of Imam Khomeini's Works, and the Fifteenth of Khordad Foundation, which commemorates the date (according to the Islamic calendar) of Khomeini's 1963 denunciation of the shah's White Revolution. Although supposedly autonomous, these foundations are directed by clerics appointed personally by the Leader. According to some estimates, their annual income may be as much as half that of the government.[9] They are exempt from state taxes and are allocated foreign currencies, especially U.S. dollars, at highly favorable exchange rates subsidized by the oil revenues. Most of their assets are property confiscated from the old elite.

The largest of these institutions, the Foundation for the Oppressed, administers over 140 factories, 120 mines, 470 agribusinesses, and 100 construction companies. It also owns the country's two leading newspapers, *Ettela'at* and *Kayhan*. The Martyrs Foundation, in charge of helping war veterans, controls confiscated property that was not handed over to the Foundation for the

Oppressed. It also receives an annual subsidy from the government. These foundations together control $12 billion in assets and employ over 400,000 people. They are clerical domains favored by the Leader.

FOCUS QUESTION

What are some of the ways by which the clergy, especially the Leader, limit the powers of the president?

Other State Institutions

The Military

The clergy have taken special measures to control Iran's armed forces—both the regular army of 370,000, including 220,000 conscripts, and the new forces formed of 120,000 Revolutionary Guards established immediately after 1979, and 200,000 volunteers in the Mobilization of the Oppressed (*Basej-e Mostazafin*) created during the Iraqi war. The Leader, as commander-in-chief, appoints the chiefs of staff as well as the top commanders and the defense minister. He also places chaplains in military units to watch over regular officers.

After the revolution, the new regime purged the top ranks of the military, placed officers promoted from the ranks of the Revolutionary Guards in command positions over the regular divisions, and built up the Revolutionary Guards as a parallel force with its own uniforms, budgets, munitions factories, recruitment centers, and even small air force and navy. According to the constitution, the regular army defends the external borders, whereas the Revolutionary Guards protect the republic from internal enemies. Political sentiments within the regular military remain unknown, if not ambivalent.

The Judiciary

The constitution makes the judicial system the central pillar of the state, overshadowing the executive and the legislature. But it also gives wide-ranging judicial powers to the Leader in particular and to the clerical strata in general. Laws are supposed to conform to the religious law, and the clergy are regarded as the ultimate interpreters of the *shari'a* (Islamic law). Bills passed by the *Majles* are reviewed by the Guardian Council to ensure that they conform to the *shari'a.* The minister of justice is chosen by the president but needs the approval of both the *Majles* and the chief judge.

The judicial system itself has been Islamized down to the district-court level, with seminary-trained jurists replacing university-educated judges. The Pahlavis purged the clergy from the judicial system; the Islamic Republic purged the university educated. The penal code, the Retribution Law, is based on a reading of the *shari'a* that was so narrow that it prompted many modern-educated lawyers to resign in disgust, charging that it contradicted the United Nations Charter on Human Rights. It permitted injured families to demand blood money on the biblical and Qur'anic principle of "an eye for an eye, a tooth for a tooth, a life for a life." It mandated the death penalty for a long list of "moral transgressions," including adultery, homosexuality, apostasy, drug trafficking, and habitual drinking. It sanctioned stoning, live burials, and finger amputations. It divided the population into male and female and Muslims and non-Muslims and treated them unequally. For example, in court, the evidence of one male Muslim is equal to that of two female Muslims. The regime also passed a "law on banking without usury" to implement the *shari'a* ban on all forms of interest taking and interest giving.

Although the law was Islamized, the modern centralized judicial system established under the shah was not dismantled. For years, Khomeini argued that in a truly Islamic society, the local *shari'a* judges would pronounce final verdicts without the intervention of the central authorities. Their verdicts would be swift and decisive. This, he insisted, was the true spirit of the *shari'a.* After the revolution, however, he discovered that the central state needed to retain ultimate control over the justice system, especially over life and death issues. Thus, the revolutionary regime retained the appeals system, the hierarchy of state courts, and the power to appoint and dismiss all judges. State interests took priority over the spirit of the *shari'a.*

Practical experience led the regime to gradually broaden the narrow interpretation of the *shari'a.* To permit the giving and taking of interest, without which modern economies would not function, the regime allowed banks to offer attractive rates as long as they avoided the taboo term *usury.* To meet public sensitivities as well as international objections, the courts rarely implemented the harsh penalties stipulated by the *shari'a.* They adopted the modern method of punishment, imprisonment, rather than the traditional one of corporal public punishment. By the early 1990s, those found guilty of breaking the law were treated much as they would be in the West: fined or imprisoned rather than flogged in the public square.

Subnational Government

Although Iran is a highly centralized state, it is divided administratively into provinces, districts, subdistricts, townships, and villages. Provinces are headed by governors-general, districts by governors, subdistricts by lieutenant governors, towns by mayors, and villages by headmen.

The constitution declares that the management of local affairs in every village, town, subdistrict, district, and province will be under the supervision of councils whose members would be elected directly by the local population. It also declares that governors-general, governors, and other regional officials appointed by the Interior Ministry have to consult local councils.

Because of conservative opposition, no steps were actually taken to hold council elections until 1999 when Khatami, the new reform-minded president, insisted on holding the country's very first nationwide local elections. Over 300,000 candidates, including 5,000 women, competed for 11,000 council seats—3,900 in towns and 34,000 in villages. Khatami's supporters won a landslide victory taking 75 percent of the seats, including twelve of the fifteen in Tehran. The top vote getter in Tehran was Khatami's former interior minister, who had been impeached by the conservative *Majles* for issuing too many publishing licenses to reform-minded journals and newspapers. Conservatives did well in the 2003 local elections, due largely to widespread voter abstention, but moderates and reformers made a comeback in 2006 when the turnout was about 60 percent of voters.

FOCUS QUESTION

What are the hurdles in transforming bills into laws in the Islamic Republic?

The Policy-Making Process

Policy-making in Iran is highly complex in part because of the cumbersome constitution and in part because factionalism within the ruling clergy have resulted in more amendments, which have made the original constitution even more complicated. Laws can originate in diverse places, and they can be modified by pressures from numerous directions. They can also be blocked by a wide variety of state institutions. In short, the policy-making process is highly fluid and diffuse, often reflecting the regime's factional divisions.

The clerics who destroyed Iran's old order remained united while building the new one. They were convinced that they alone had the divine mandate to govern. They followed the same leader, admired the same texts, cited the same potent symbols, remembered the same real and imaginary indignations under the shah, and, most important, shared the same vested interest in preserving the Islamic Republic. Moreover, most had studied at the same seminaries and came from the same lower-middle-class backgrounds. Some were even related to each other through marriage and blood ties.

But once the constitution was in place, the same clerics drifted into two loose but identifiable blocs: the Society (*Majmu'eh*) of the Militant Clergy, and the Association (*Jam'eh*) of the Militant Clergy. The former can be described as statist reformers or populists, and the latter as laissez-faire (free-market) conservatives. The radicals hoped to consolidate lower-class support by using state power for redistributing wealth, eradicating unemployment, nationalizing enterprises, confiscating large estates, financing social programs, rationing and subsidizing essential goods, and placing price ceilings on essential consumer goods. In short, they espoused the creation of a comprehensive welfare state. The conservatives hoped to retain middle-class support, especially in the bazaars, by removing price controls, lowering business taxes, cutting red tape, encouraging private entrepreneurs, and balancing the budget, even at the cost of sacrificing subsidies and social programs. In recent years, the statist reformers have begun to emphasize the democratic over the theocratic features of the constitution, stressing the importance of individual rights, the rule of law, and government accountability to the electorate. In many ways, they have become like social democrats the world over.

The conservatives were originally labeled middle-roaders and traditionalists. The statists were labeled progressives, seekers of new ideas, and Followers of the Imam's Line. The former liked to denounce the latter as extremists, leftists, and pro-Soviet Muslims. The latter denounced the free-marketers as medievalists, rightists, capitalists, mafia bazaaris, and pro-American Muslims. Both could bolster their arguments with apt quotes from Khomeini.

This polarization created a major constitutional gridlock, since the early Islamic *Majles* was dominated by the reformers, whereas the Guardian

Council was controlled by the conservatives appointed by Khomeini. Between 1981 and 1987, over one hundred bills passed by the reformer-dominated *Majles* were vetoed by the Guardian Council on the grounds that they violated the *shari'a*, especially the sanctity of private property. The vetoed legislation included a labor law, land reform, nationalization of foreign trade, a progressive income tax, control over urban real estate transactions, and confiscation of the property of émigrés whom the courts had not yet found guilty of counterrevolutionary activities. Introduced by individual deputies or cabinet ministers, these bills had received quick passage because radicals controlled the crucial *Majles* committees and held a comfortable majority on the *Majles* floor. Some ultraconservatives had countered by encouraging the faithful not to pay taxes and instead to contribute to the grand ayatollahs of their choice. After all, they argued, one could find no mention of income tax anywhere in the *shari'a*.

Both sides cited the Islamic constitution to support their positions. The conservative free-marketers referred to the long list of clauses protecting private property, promising balanced budgets, and placing agriculture, small industry, and retail trade in the private sector. The reformers referred to an even longer list promising education, medicine, jobs, low-income housing, unemployment benefits, disability pay, interest-free loans, and the predominance of the public sector in the economy.

maslahat Arabic term for "expediency," "prudence," or "advisability," now used in Iran to refer to reasons of state or what is best for the Islamic Republic.

To break the constitutional gridlock, Khomeini boldly introduced into Shi'ism the Sunni Islamic concept of ***maslahat***—that is, "public interest" and "reasons of state." Over the centuries, Shi'i clerics had denounced this as a Sunni notion designed to bolster illegitimate rulers. Khomeini now claimed that a truly Islamic state could safeguard the public interest by suspending important religious rulings, even over prayer, fasting, and the pilgrimage to Mecca. He declared public interest to be a primary ruling and the others mere secondary rulings. In other words, the state could overrule the views of the highest-ranking clerics. In the name of public interest, it could destroy mosques, confiscate private property, and cancel religious obligations. Khomeini added that the Islamic state had absolute authority, since the Prophet Muhammad had exercised absolute (*motalaq*) power, which he had passed on to the Imams and thus eventually to the Islamic Republic. Never before had a Shi'i religious leader claimed such powers for the state, especially at the expense of fellow clerics.

As a follow-up, Khomeini set up a new institution named the Expediency Council for Determining the Public Interest of the Islamic Order—known for short as the Expediency Council. He entrusted it with the task of resolving conflicts between the Islamic *Majles* and the Guardian Council. He packed it with thirteen clerics, including the president, the chief judge, the Speaker of the *Majles*, and six jurists from the Guardian Council. The Expediency Council eventually passed some of the more moderate bills favored by the reformers. These included a new income tax, banking legislation, and a much-disputed labor law providing workers in large factories with a minimum wage and some semblance of job security.

The constitutional amendments introduced after Khomeini's death institutionalized the Expediency Council. The new Leader could now not only name its members but also determine its tenure and jurisdiction. Not surprisingly, Khamenei packed it with his supporters—none of them prominent grand ayatollahs. He also made its meetings secret and allowed it to promulgate new laws rather than restrict itself to resolving legislative differences between the Guardian Council and the *Majles.* The Expediency Council is now a secretive body that is accountable only to the Leader. It stands above the constitution. In this sense, it has become a powerful body rivaling the Islamic *Majles*, even though it did not exist in the original constitution.

There are thirty-four members of the Expediency Council. These included the president; chief judge; Speaker of the *Majles*; ministers of intelligence, oil, culture, and foreign affairs; chief of the General Staff; commander of the Revolutionary Guards; jurists from the Guardian Council; directors of radio and television as well as of the Central Bank, Atomic Energy Organization, and National Oil Company; heads of the main religious foundations; chairman of the Chamber of Commerce; and editors of the main conservative newspapers. Seventeen were clerics. These thirty-four can be considered the inner circle of Iran's ruling elite.

Summary

The clergy exercise authority over elected officials in three separate ways: the Leader, a cleric, supervises the three branches of government; the Guardian Council can veto legislation passed by parliament; and the same Council can vet all candidates running for high office. Despite these restrictions, the constitution has the possibility of moving away from theocracy toward democracy. After all, the constitution enshrines the public's right to elect parliament, president, and even the Leader. The main obstacle to democracy is the vetting process, not the constitution itself.

Representation and Participation

Although the Islamic Republic is mainly a theocracy, some claim that it is also has some features of a democracy. According to the constitution, the voters directly choose the president and the Assembly of Experts, which in turn chooses the Leader. What is more, the elected legislature, the *Majles*, exercises considerable power. According to one of the founders of the regime, it is the centerpiece of the Islamic constitution.[10] Another architect of the constitution has argued that the people, by carrying out the Islamic Revolution, implicitly favored a type of democracy confined within the boundaries of Islam and the guardianship of the jurist.[11] But another declared that if he had to choose between the democracy and power of the clergy as specified in the concept of jurist's guardianship, he would not hesitate to choose the latter, since it came directly from God.[12] On the eve of the initial referendum, Khomeini himself declared: "This constitution, which the people will ratify, in no way contradicts democracy. Since the people love the clergy, have faith in the clergy, want to be guided by the clergy, it is only right that the supreme religious authority oversee the work of the [government] ministers to ensure that they don't make mistakes or go against the Qur'an."[13]

FOCUS QUESTION

What are the powers and limitations of parliament?

The Legislature

According to Iran's constitution, the *Majles* "represents the nation" and possesses many powers, including making or changing ordinary laws (with the approval of the Guardian Council), investigating and supervising all affairs of state, and approving or ousting the cabinet ministers. In describing this branch of government, the constitution uses the term *qanun* (statutes) rather than *shari'a* (divine law) so as to gloss over the fundamental question of whether legislation passed by the *Majles* is derived from God or the people. It accepts the reasoning that God creates divine law (*shari'a*) but elected representatives can draw up worldly statutes (*qanuns*).

The *Majles* has 290 members and is elected by citizens over the age of sixteen. It can pass *qanuns* as long as the Guardian Council deems them compatible with the *shari'a* and the constitution. It can choose, from a list drawn up by the chief judge, six of the twelve-man Guardian Council. It can investigate at will cabinet ministers, affairs of state, and public complaints against the executive and the judiciary. It can remove cabinet members—with the exception of the president—through a parliamentary vote of no confidence. It can withhold approval for government budgets, foreign loans, international treaties, and cabinet appointments. It can hold closed debates, provide members with immunity from arrest, and regulate its own internal workings, especially the committee system.

The *Majles* plays an important role in everyday politics. Sometimes, it has changed government budgets, criticized cabinet policies, modified development plans, and forced the president to replace some of his ministers. In 1992, 217 deputies circulated an open letter that explicitly emphasized the powers of the *Majles* and thereby implicitly downplayed those of the Leader. Likewise, the Speaker of the House in 2002 threatened to close down the whole *Majles* if the judiciary violated parliamentary immunity and arrested one of the liberal deputies.

FOCUS QUESTION

What role do political parties play?

Political Parties and the Party System

Iran's constitution guarantees citizens the right to organize, and a 1980 law permits the Interior Ministry to issue licenses to political parties. But political parties were not encouraged until Khatami was elected president in 1997. Since then, three parties have been active: the Islamic Iran Participation Front and the Islamic Labor Party, both formed by Khatami reformist supporters, and the more conservative Servants of Reconstruction created by *Hojjat al-Islam*

Ali-Akbar Hashemi Rafsanjani, the former president and now chairman of the Expediency Council. In general, formal parties are less important in Iranian politics than reformist and conservative coalitions and groups that form along ideological and policy lines. For example, the current president, Ahmadinejad, has his power base in the Alliance of Builders of Islamic Iran, a coalition of several conservative political parties and organizations that delivered votes very effectively in recent local (2003), parliamentary (2004), and presidential (2005) elections. According to the Interior Ministry, licenses have been granted to some seven hundred political, social, and cultural organizations, but all are led by people considered politically acceptable by the regime.

Real political opposition has been forced into exile, mostly in Europe. The most important opposition groups are:

- **The Liberation Movement.** Established in 1961 by Mehdi Bazargan, the Islamic Republic's first prime minister. Bazargan had been appointed premier in February 1979 by Khomeini himself, but had resigned in disgust ten months later when the Revolutionary Guards had permitted students to take over the U.S. embassy. The Liberation Movement is a moderate Islamic party. Despite its religious orientation, it is secular and favors the strict separation of mosque from state.

- **The National Front.** Originating in the campaign to nationalize the country's oil resources in the early 1950s, the National Front remains committed to Mossadeq's twin political ideals of nationalism and secularism. Because the conservative clergy feel threatened by the National Front's potential appeal, they have banned it.

- **The Mojahedin.** Formed in 1971 as a guerrilla organization to fight the shah's regime, the Mojahedin tried to synthesize Marxism and Islam. It interpreted Shi'i Islam as a radical religion favoring equality, social justice, martyrdom, and redistribution of wealth. Immediately after the revolution, the Mojahedin opposed the clerical regime and attracted a large following among students. The regime retaliated with mass executions forcing the Mojahedin to move their base of operations to Iraq. Not unexpectedly, the Mojahedin became associated with a national enemy and thereby lost much of its appeal.

- **The Fedayin.** Also formed in 1971, the Fedayin modeled itself after the Marxist guerrilla movements of the 1960s in Latin America, especially those inspired by Che Guevara and the Cuban revolution. Losing more fighters than any other organization in the struggle against the shah, the Fedayin came out of the revolution with great mystique and popular urban support. But it soon lost much of its strength because of massive government repression and a series of internal splits.

- **The Tudeh (Party of the Masses).** Established in 1941, the Tudeh is a mainstream, formerly pro-Soviet communist party. Although the Tudeh initially supported the Islamic Republic as a "popular anti-imperialist state," it was banned, and most of its organizers were executed during the 1980s.

FOCUS QUESTION

What role do elections play in the Islamic Republic?

Elections

All citizens over the age of sixteen are eligible to vote in Iran. The constitution promises free elections. In practice, however, *Majles* elections, which are held every four years, have varied from relatively free but disorderly in the early days of the Islamic Republic, to controlled and highly unfair in the middle years, and back again to relatively free, but orderly in the late 1990s. At present the actual voting process is generally free of intimidation, but voter choice is highly constrained.

In the 1980s, ballot boxes were placed in mosques with Revolutionary Guards supervising the voting. Neighborhood clerics were on hand to help illiterates complete their ballots. Club-wielding gangs assaulted regime opponents. Now electoral freedom is restricted by the government-controlled radio-television network, the main source of information for the vast majority of citizens. The Interior Ministry can ban dissident organizations, especially their newspapers on the grounds they are anti-Islamic. Moreover, the electoral law, based on a winner-take-all majority system rather than on proportional representation, is designed to minimize the voice of the opposition.

But the main obstacle to fair elections has been the Guardian Council with its powers to approve all candidates. For example, the Council excluded some 3500 candidates (nearly half of the total) from running in the parliamentary elections of 2004 by questioning their loyalty to the concept of jurist's guardianship. The purge of reformers was facilitated both by President Bush's labeling of Iran as a member of the global "Axis of Evil" in 2002 and by the American military occupation of Afghanistan and Iraq. Reluctant to rock the boat at a time of

Electoral campaigners. *(Source: © Lynsey Adderio/Corbis)*

apparent and imminent "national danger," most reformers restrained themselves and withdrew from active politics. Not surprisingly, the conservatives won a hollow victory in the 2004 *Majles* elections. They received a clear majority of the seats, but the voter turnout was less than 51 percent, and in Tehran only 28 percent. This was the worst showing since 1979. For a regime that liked to boast about mass participation, this was seen as a major setback—even as a crisis of legitimacy. There was a bit of an upturn, to about 60 percent, in the turnout in both rounds of the presidential election of 2005. Still this was still a sharp downturn from the more than 80 percent that had voted in the 1997 presidential contest that brought the reformist Khatami to power.

Political Culture, Citizenship, and Identity

FOCUS QUESTIONS

What social groups are most likely to support the Islamic Republic?
What groups are least likely to do so?

In theory, the Islamic Republic of Iran should be a highly viable state. After all, Shi'ism is the religion of both the state and the vast majority of the population. Shi'ism is the central component of Iranian popular culture. Also, the constitution guarantees basic rights to religious minorities as well as to individual citizens. All citizens, regardless of race, color, language, or religion, are promised the rights of free expression, worship, and organization. They are guaranteed freedom from arbitrary arrest, torture, and police surveillance.

The constitution extends additional rights to the recognized religious minorities: Christians, Jews, and Zoroastrians. Although Christians (Armenians and Assyrians), Jews, and Zoroastrians form just 1 percent of the total population, they are allocated five *Majles* seats. They are permitted their own community organizations, including schools, their own places of worship, and their family laws. The constitution, however, is ominously silent about Sunnis and Baha'is. The former are treated in theory as full citizens, but their actual status is not spelled out. The latter are considered heretics because their nineteenth-century founder had proclaimed his own teachings to supersede that of not only the Old and New Testaments but also of the Qur'an and the Shi'i Imams. Moreover, some ultraconservative Shi'is deem Baha'is to be part of the "international Zionist conspiracy" on the grounds their main shrine is located in modern-day Israel.

The constitution also gives guarantees to non-Persian speakers. Although 83 percent of the population understands Persian, thanks to the educational system, over 50 percent continue to speak non-Persian languages at home—languages such as Azeri, Kurdish, Turkic, Gilaki, Mazandarani, Arabic, and Baluchi. The constitution promises them rights unprecedented in Iranian history. It states that "local and native languages can be used in the press, media, and schools." It also states that local populations have the right to elect provincial, town, and village councils. These councils can watch over the governors-general and the town mayors, as well as their educational, cultural, and social programs.

These generous promises have often been honored more in theory than in reality. The local councils—the chief institution that protected the provincial minorities—were not held until twenty years after the revolution. Subsidies to non-Persian publications and radio stations remain meager. Jews have been so harassed as "pro-Israeli Zionists" that more than half—40,000 out of 80,000—have left the country since the revolution. Armenian Christians have had to end coeducational classes, adopt the government curriculum, abide by Muslim dress codes, including the veil. The Christian population has declined from over 300,000 to fewer than 200,000.

The Baha'is, however, have borne the brunt of religious persecution. Their leaders have been executed as "heretics" and "imperialist spies." Adherents have been fired from their jobs, had their property confiscated, and been imprisoned and tortured to pressure them to convert to Islam. Their schools have been closed, their community property expropriated, and their shrines and cemeteries bulldozed. It is estimated that since the revolution, one-third of the 300,000 Baha'is have left Iran. The Baha'is, like the Jews and Armenians, have migrated mostly to Canada and the United States. This persecution did not ease until the 1997 election of President Khatami.

The Sunni population, which forms as much as 10 percent of the total, has its own reasons for being alienated. The state religion is Shi'ism, and high officials have to be Shi'i. Citizens must abide by Khomeini's concept of jurists' guardianship, a notion derived from Shi'ism. Few institutions cater to Sunni needs. There is not a single Sunni mosque in the whole of Tehran. Iran's Kurds, Turkmans, Arabs, and Baluchis are also Sunnis, and it is no accident that immediately after the 1979 revolution, the new regime faced its most serious challenges in precisely the areas of the country where these linguistic minorities lived. It crushed these revolts by rushing in Revolutionary Guards from the Persian Shi'i heartland of Isfahan, Shiraz, and Qom.

The regime's base among the Azeris, who are Shi'i but not Persian speakers, remains to be tested. In the past, the Azeris, who form 24 percent of the population and dwarf the other minorities, have not posed a serious problem to the state. They are part of the Shi'i community, and have prominent figures in the Shi'i hierarchy—most notably the current Leader, Khamenei. What is more, many Azeri merchants, professionals, and workers live and work throughout Iran. In short, Azeris can be considered well integrated into Iran.

But the 1991 creation of the Republic of Azerbaijan on Iran's northeastern border following the disintegration of the Soviet Union has raised new concerns, since some Azeris on both sides of the border have begun to talk of establishing a larger unified Azerbaijan. It is no accident that in the war between Azerbaijan and Armenia in the early 1990s, Iran favored the latter. So far, the concept of a unified Azerbaijan appears to have limited appeal among Iranian Azeris.

FOCUS QUESTION

Does discontent necessarily have to take a revolutionary rather than a reform course in the Islamic Republic?

Interests, Social Movements, and Protest

In the first two decades after its founding, the government of the Islamic Republic often violated its own constitution. It closed down newspapers, professional

Executions in Kurdestan, 1979. *(Source: Jahangir Razmi, © Bettmann/Corbis)*

associations, labor unions, and political parties. It banned demonstrations and public meetings. It imprisoned tens of thousands without due process. It systematically tortured prisoners to extract false confessions and public recantations. And it executed some 25,000 political prisoners, most of them without due process of law. The United Nations, Amnesty International, and Human Rights Watch all took Iran to task for violating the UN Human Rights Charter as well its own Islamic constitution. Most victims were Kurds, military officers from the old regime, and leftists, especially members of the Mojahedin and Fedayin.

Although the violation of individual liberties affected the whole population, it aroused special resentment among three social groups: the modern middle class, educated women, and organized labor. The modern middle class, especially the intelligentsia, has been secular and even anticlerical ever since the 1905 revolution. Little love is lost between it and the Islamic Republic. Not surprisingly, the vast majority of those executed in the 1980s were teachers, engineers, professionals, and college students. Youth, especially college students, are a force to be reckoned with: over half the current population was born after 1979 and as many as 1.15 million are enrolled in higher education. In 1999, eighteen different campuses, including Tehran University, erupted into mass demonstrations against the chief judge, who had closed down a reformist newspaper. Revolutionary Guards promptly occupied the campuses, killing or seriously injuring an unknown number of students. Again in late 2002, thousands of students protested the death sentence handed down to a reformist academic accused of insulting Islam. But in 2004, when the Guardian Council barred thousands of reformers from the parliamentary elections, the campuses remained quiet, partly out of fear, partly out of disenchantment with the reformers for failing to deliver on their promises, and partly because of the concern about the looming danger from United States military presence in Iraq.

Educated women in Iran also harbor numerous grievances against the conservative clerics in the regime, especially in the judiciary. Although the Western press often dwells on the veil, Iranian women consider the veil one of their less important problems. Given a choice, most would probably continue to wear it out of personal habit and national tradition. More important are work-related grievances: job security, pay scales, promotions, maternity leave, and access to prestigious professions. Despite patriarchal attitudes held by the conservative clergy, educated women have become a major factor in Iranian society. They now form 54 percent of college students, 45 percent of doctors, 25 percent of government employees, and 13 percent of the general labor force, up from 8 percent in the 1980s. They have established their own organizations and journals reinterpreting Islam to conform to modern notions of gender equality. Women do serve in the *Majles* (there are twelve in the current parliament, 4 percent of the total) and on local councils. One grand ayatollah has even argued that they should be able to hold any job, including president, court judge, and even Leader.

Factory workers in Iran are another significant social group with serious grievances. Their concerns deal mostly with high unemployment, low wages, declining incomes, lack of decent housing, and an unsatisfactory labor law, which, while giving them mandatory holidays and some semblance of job security, denies them the right to call strikes and organize independent unions. Since 1979, wage earners have had a Workers' House—a government-influenced organization—and its affiliated newspaper, *Kar va Kargar (Work and Worker)*, and since 1999 the Islamic Labor Party has represented their interests. In most years, the Workers' House flexes its political muscle by holding a May Day rally. In 1999, the rally began peacefully with a greeting from a woman reform deputy who had received the second-most votes in the 1996 Tehran municipal elections. But the rally turned into a protest when workers began to march to parliament denouncing conservatives who had spoken in favor of further watering down of the Labor Law. On May Day 2006, an estimated 10,000 workers marched to demand that the labor minister resign. Bus drivers in Teheran, who had been active in earlier protests, went on strike in January 2006 to protest the arrest and maltreatment of one of their leaders.

Summary

The Bush administration likes to denounce Iran as a "totalitarian state" tyrannized by unelected unpopular leaders. While Iran is no liberal democracy, it hardly fits the "totalitarian" category. The clergy, despite opposition from the intelligentsia, continue to rule in part because they still enjoy much legitimacy—especially among the bazaars, rural population, and urban poor; in part because they have brought economic benefits to the wider population; and in part because they have left some room for civil society and have permitted interest groups to function so long as they do not violate red lines and directly question the clergy's legitimacy. They have also been greatly helped by the perceived notion that the nation is under siege—even under imminent threat—from the United States.

Iranian Politics in Transition

FOCUS QUESTION

What are the most important challenges that now face Iran?

Political Challenges and Changing Agendas

Contemporary Iran faces two major challenges—one internal, the other external. Internally, the Islamic Republic continues to struggle with the troubling question of how to combine theocracy with democracy, and clerical authority with mass participation. After several years when Iran's reformers seemed to be on the political rise, the conservative clerics and their supporters, who already controlled the judiciary, took over the *Majles* in 2004. In June 2005 they took over the executive as well with the election of Ahmadinejad as president. In 2009, they may well lose again to the reformers.

Many observers think that even though the conservatives appear to have gained the upper hand politically, they have lost touch with the grassroots of Iranian society since their political base is less than 20–25 percent of the electorate. It is estimated that over 70 percent of the public favors the reformers, and, much of this majority, if not offered real choices, will, at a minimum, protest by staying home on election days. In fact, conservatives do best when the turnout is low, reformers benefit when it is high. The results of the December 2006 elections for local council and the Assembly of Experts, which had a turnout of around 60 percent, were widely seen as a rebuke to Ahmadinejad and the conservatives. The ruling conservatives now face the challenge of how to maintain some pretence of popular political legitimacy while not actually sharing power with the reformers.

This challenge is troubling to the clerical leadership since the country has in recent decades gone through a profound revolution in political values, with much of the population embracing key aspects of the democratic idea including political pluralism, mass participation, civil society, human rights, and individual liberties. Even conservatives have begun to use such terms, openly describing themselves as "neoconservatives," "constructivists," and "pragmatic."

Meanwhile, those in the general public who feel excluded from national politics remain active in forceful nongovernmental organizations that make up an important part of Iranian civil society. The most visible of these is a human rights group headed by Shirin Ebadi, the winner of the Nobel Peace Prize in 2003. Ms. Ebadi has been a lawyer, judge (until the Islamic Republic barred

The U.S. Connection

Conservatives Versus Liberals

Iran and the United States have more in common than either would admit. In both, the conservatives—calling themselves "compassionate conservatives" in the United States and "principalists" in Iran—have a core base limited to less than 30 percent of the electorate. To win national elections, they have to reach out to others while continuing to energize their supporters to vote. To reach out, they both resort to patriotic and populist language—stressing "national security," accusing "weak-kneed liberals" for not standing up to foreign enemies, claiming to represent the "ordinary folks" and appealing to cultural values. In 2005, Ahmadinejad won the presidential elections in part because he presented himself as a "man of the people." He also won partly because his liberal opposition was badly divided. But the biggest reason for the conservative victory was probably because he projected himself as a tough patriot who could better defend the nation from foreign threats—especially after President Bush named Iran as a member of the "Axis of Evil" in his 2002 State of the Union address. ❖

women from holding such positions), writer, teacher, and activist, and has been most prominent in the struggle to protect the rights of women and children. Even if they are completely excluded from the political arena by the conservative religious establishment, so far concerned citizens such as Ebadi remain committed to using legal, nonviolent means to promote change. They do not want to be associated with American projects for "regime change."

The Islamic Republic's first attempt to enter the international arena as a militant force to spread its theocratic version of Islam proved counterproductive. This effort diverted scarce resources to the military and contributed to the disastrous war with Iraq. It drove Saudi Arabia and the Gulf sheikdoms into a closer relationship with the United States. It prompted the United States to isolate Iran, discouraged foreign investment, and prevented international organizations from extending economic assistance. Iran's militancy has also alarmed nearby secular Islamic states such as Turkey, Tadzhikistan, and Azerbaijan. In recent years, the regime has managed to repair some of this damage. It has won over many Arab states and has established cordial relations with its neighbors. It has managed to repair bridges to the European Community.

The major external challenge to the Islamic Republic comes from the United States. The Bush administration, by naming Iran as a member of the "Axis of Evil" in 2002 (along with Iraq under Saddam Hussein and North Korea) and openly calling for "regime change," (and promoting such change by military means in neighboring Afghanistan and Iraq) has dramatically increased pressures on Iran beyond those that already existed because of American economic sanctions, lack of diplomatic relations, and successful barring of Iran from the World Trade Organization. The United States has accused Iran of sabotaging the Arab-Israeli peace process, helping terrorist organizations,

Two men in search of their future. *(Source: Courtesy LePelley © 1979 The Christian Science Monitor (www.csmonitor.com). All Rights Reserved).*

especially Hamas in Palestine and Hezbollah in Lebanon, and "grossly violating" democratic and human rights of its own citizens. More recently the United States has highlighted the danger of "weapons of mass destruction" in Iran and accused the country of intending to transform its nuclear energy program into a nuclear weapons program. Even more recently, it has accused Iran of arming and training insurgents in Iraq. Some analysts remain skeptical of such accusations.

The conservative clerics who now dominate Iranian politics have been able to transform this external threat into a political asset. They have intimidated many reformers into toning down their demands for domestic change, even silencing them, by declaring that the country was in danger, that the enemy was at the gates, and that any opposition to the government in such times would play into the hands of those who wanted to do harm to Iran. Even in the United States people have speculated about whether the Bush administration was seriously considering taking some type of military action against Iran—perhaps a preemptive air strike against its nuclear reactors. These speculations have fed the perception of threat. Few Iranians are willing to appear unpatriotic by openly criticizing their government at a time of external danger.

Iranian Politics in Comparative Perspective

FOCUS QUESTION

What are some of the ways Iran is different from other Third World countries?

Unlike most developing countries, Iran was never formally colonized by the European imperial powers and has always been independent. It is, in many ways, an old state with many institutions that date back to ancient times. Furthermore, while many other Third World states have weak connections with their societies, Iran has a religion that links the elite with the masses, the cities with the villages, the government with the citizenry. Shi'ism, as well as Iranian national identity, serves as social and cultural cement, that gives the population a strong collective identity. Iran also has the advantage of abundant oil resources that can be the basis for economic growth that would be the envy of most developing countries.

Nevertheless, Iran also has much in common with other Third World countries. Despite some modern aspects, its economy remains largely underdeveloped, highly dependent on one commodity, and unable to meet the rising expectations of its population. Iran's collective identity, although strong in religious terms, is strained by other internal fault lines, especially those of class, ethnicity, gender, and political differences. It wants to enter the world of states as an important player, but international, domestic, and regional problems have combined to keep the country pretty much on the global sidelines.

The development of the democratic idea in Iran has been constricted by theocracy. Some argue that Islam has made this inevitable. But Islam, like the other major religions, can be interpreted in ways that either promote or hinder democracy. Some interpretations of Islam stress the importance of justice, equality, and consultation as political principles. Islam also has a tradition of tolerating other religions, and the *shari'a* explicitly protects life, property, and honor. In practice, Islam has often separated politics from religion, government legal statutes from holy laws, spiritual affairs from worldly matters, and the state from the clerical establishment.

Moreover, theocracy in Iran originates not in Islam itself but in the very specific concept of the jurist's guardianship as developed by Khomeini. On the whole, Sunni Islam considers clerics to be theological scholars, not a special political class. This helps explain why the Iranian regime has found it difficult to export its revolution to other parts of the Muslim world. The failure of democracy in Iran should be attributed less to anything intrinsic in Islam than to the combination of crises between 1979 and 1981 that allowed a particular group of clerics to come to power. Whether they remain in power depends not so much on Islamic values but on how they handle socioeconomic problems, especially the demands for public participation.

Politics in the Islamic Republic of Iran is sharply divided over the question of how to govern an economy beset by rising demands, wildly fluctuating petroleum revenues, and the nightmarish prospect that in the next two generations, the oil wells will run dry. Most clerics favor a rather conventional capitalist road to development, hoping to liberalize the market, privatize industry, attract foreign capital, and encourage the propertied classes to invest. Others envisage an equally conventional statist road to development, favoring central planning, government industries, price controls, high taxes, state subsidies, national self-reliance, and ambitious programs to eliminate poverty, illiteracy, slums, and unemployment. Some are hoping to find a third way, combining elements of state intervention with free enterprise that is similar to the social democracy favored, for example, by the Labour Party in Britain.

Economic problems like those that undermined the monarchy could well undermine the Islamic Republic, particularly if there was another sharp drop in oil prices. The country's collective identity has also come under great strain in recent years. The emphasis on Shi'ism has antagonized Iran's Sunnis as well as its non-Muslim citizens. The emphasis on clerical Shi'ism has further alienated all secularists, including lay liberals and moderate nationalists, to say nothing of a large majority of Iranians who live abroad. Furthermore, the official emphasis on Khomeini's brand of Shi'ism has alienated those Shi'is who reject the whole notion of jurist's guardianship. The elevation of Khamenei as the Leader has also antagonized many early proponents of jurist's guardianship on the grounds that he lacks the scholarly qualifications to hold the position that embodies the sacred and secular power of the Islamic Republic.

Iran's ruling clerical regime has gradually eroded the broad social base that brought it to power in the Islamic Revolution nearly three decade ago. Growing discontent may be expressed through apolitical channels, such as apathy, emigration, inward-looking religion, or even drug addiction. There is also a possibility that those seeking change may turn to radical action if they cannot attain their goals through legal reformist movement. Those who want to understand the possibilities for political change in Iran would do well to remember that the country produced two popular upheavals in the twentieth century that fundamentally transformed the political system: the constitutional (1905) and the Islamic (1979) revolutions.

Summary

To predict the future is a hazardous task. Iran could meet its internal challenge by becoming more flexible, liberalizing, giving greater scope to civil society, and allowing more public participation and competitive elections—in short, strengthening the democratic as opposed to the theocratic features of the constitution. If it did so, it would transform itself closer to democracy. If it does not, it could freeze up, alienate the public, lose legitimacy, and thereby make itself vulnerable to destruction. Iran could also meet its external challenge by following a cautious foreign policy, going slow on its nuclear program, providing verifiable guarantees that it was not building nuclear weapons, toning down its rhetoric, and assuring its neighbors as well as the United States that it was a "normal state" uninterested in the export of revolution. If it does not, it could well end up with a confrontation with the United States—a confrontation that would be disastrous for both countries.

Key Terms

ayatollah
civil society
theocracy
Majles
Guardian Council
Supreme Leader
Farsi
People of the Book
Qur'an
shari'a
coup d'état
bazaars
fundamentalism
jurist's guardianship
pasdaran
Assembly of Experts
Hezbollahis
hojjat al-Islam
laissez-faire
jihad
rentier state
dual society
Organization of Petroleum Exporting Countries (OPEC)
Expediency Council
Imam Jum'ehs
Foundation of the Oppressed
maslahat

Suggested Readings

Abrahamian, Ervand. *Khomeinism.* Berkeley: University of California Press, 1993.

———. *Tortured Confessions: Prisons and Public Recantations in Modern Iran*. Berkeley: University of California Press, 1999.

Ansari, Ali M. *Confronting Iran: The Failure of American Foreign Policy and the Next Great Crisis in the Middle East.* New York: Perseus, 2006.

Beeman, William O. *The "Great Satan" vs. the "Mad Mullahs": How the United States and Iran Demonize Each Other*. New York: Praeger, 2005.

Clawson, Patrick, and Michael Rubin. *Eternal Iran: Continuity and Chaos*. New York: Palgrave Macmillan, 2005.

Cook, Michael. *The Koran: A Very Short Introduction*. New York: Oxford University Press, 2000.

Ebadi, Shirin, and Azadeh Moaveni. *Iran Awakening: A Memoir of Revolution and Hope*. New York: Random House, 2006.

Garthwaite, Gene R. *The Persians.* Malden, Mass.: Blackwell, 2005.

Gheissari Ali, and Vali Nasr. *Democracy in Iran: History and the Quest for Liberty*. New York: Oxford University Press, 2006.

Keddie, Nikki. *Modern Iran: Roots and Results of Revolution*, updated edition. New Haven, Conn.: Yale University Press, 2006.

Kinzer, Stephen. *All the Shah's Men: An American Coup and the Roots of Middle East Terror.* New York: John Wiley & Sons, 2004.

Moin, Baqer. *Khomeini: Life of the Ayatollah.* New York: Thomas Dunne Books, 2000.

Nafisi, Azar. *Reading Lolita in Tehran: A Memoir in Books.* New York: Random House, 2003.

Pollack, Kenneth. *The Persian Puzzle: The Conflict Between Iran and America.* New York: Random House, 2005.

Ruthven, Malise. *Islam: A Very Short Introduction.* New York: Oxford University Press, 2000.

Takeyh, Ray. *Hidden Iran: Paradox and Power in the Islamic Republic.* New York: Times Books, 2006.

Notes

[1]British Financial Adviser to the Foreign Office in Tehran, *Documents on British Foreign Policy, 1919–39* (London: Her Majesty's Stationery Office, 1963), First Series, XIII, 720, 735.

[2]M. Bazargan, "Letter to the Editor," *Ettela'at*, February 7, 1980.

[3]*Iran Times*, January 12, 1979.

[4]International Labor Organization, "Employment and Income Policies for Iran" (unpublished report, Geneva, 1972), Appendix C, 6.

[5]*Wall Street Journal*, November 4, 1977.

[6]U.S. Congress, *Economic Consequences of the Revolution in Iran, 5.*

[7]Cited in H. Amirahmadi, *Revolution and Economic Transition* (Albany: State University of New York Press, 1960), p. 201.

[8]Cited in *Iran Times*, July 9, 1993.

[9]J. Amuzegar, *Iran's Economy Under the Islamic Republic* (London: Taurus Press, 1994), 100.

[10]A. Rafsanjani, "The Islamic Consultative Assembly," *Kayhan*, May 23, 1987.

[11]S. Saffari, "The Legitimation of the Clergy's Right to Rule in the Iranian Constitution of 1979," *British Journal of Middle Eastern Studies* 20, no. 1 (1993): 64–81.

[12]Ayatollah Montazeri, *Ettela'at*, October 8, 1979.

[13]O. Fallaci, "Interview with Khomeini," *New York Times Magazine*, October 7, 1979.

Official Name:	People's Republic of China (*Zhonghua Remin Gongheguo*)
Location:	East Asia
Capital City:	Beijing
Population (2007):	1.3 billion
Size:	9,596,960 sq. km.; slightly smaller than the United States

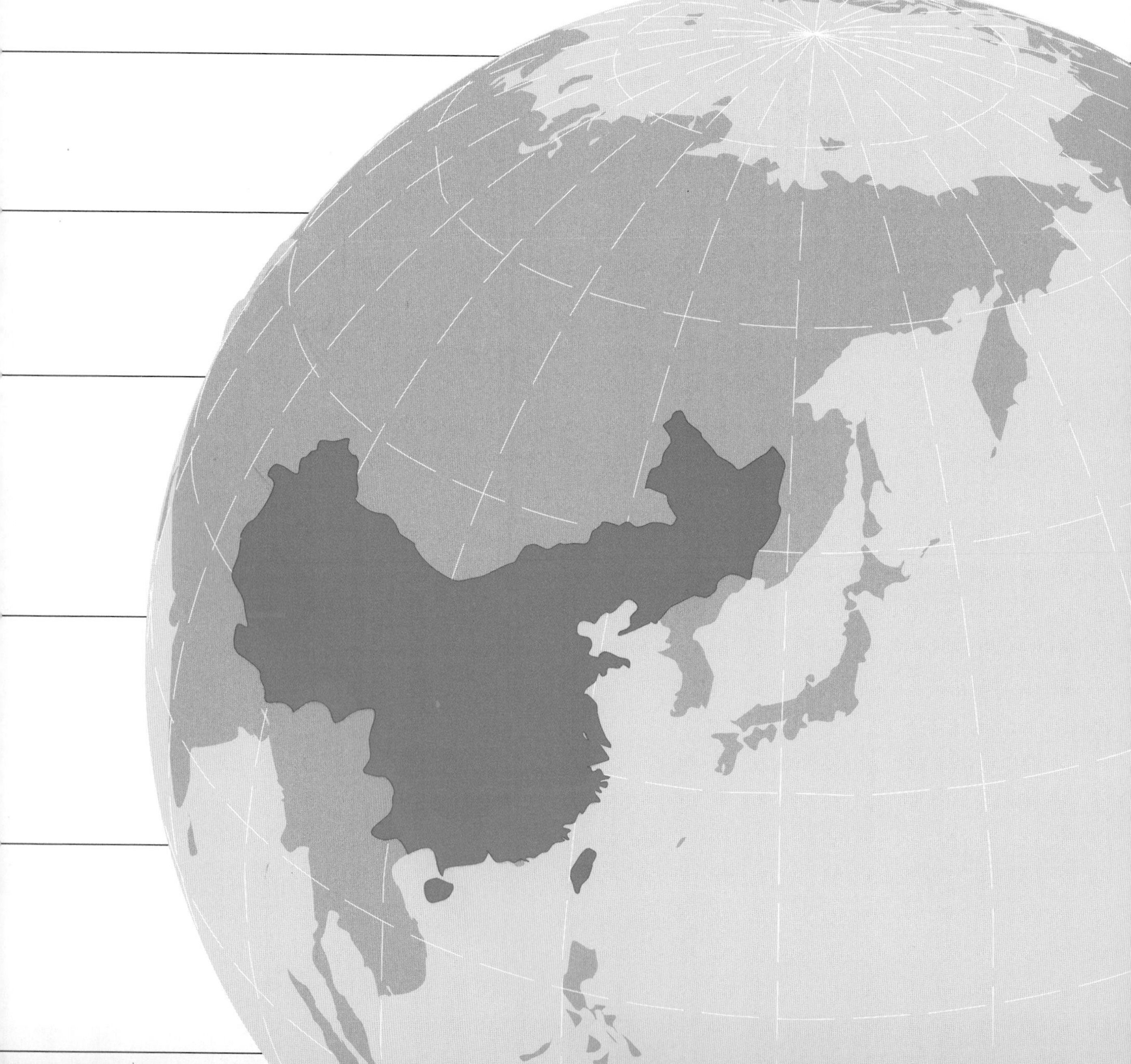

CHAPTER

9 China

William A. Joseph

Chronology of Modern China's Political Development

1911	1912	1921	1927	1934	1937	1949
Revolution led by Sun Yat-sen overthrows 2,000-year-old imperial system and establishes the Republic of China.	Sun Yat-sen founds the Nationalist Party (*Guomindang/ Kuomintang*) to oppose warlords who have seized power in the new republic.	Chinese Communist Party (CCP) is founded.	Civil war between Nationalists (now led by Chiang Kai-shek) and Communists begins.	Mao Zedong becomes leader of the CCP.	Japan invades China, marking the start of World War II in Asia.	Chinese Communists win the civil war and establish the People's Republic of China.

SECTION 1 The Making of the Modern Chinese State

FOCUS QUESTION

What is the major contradiction, or tension, in contemporary Chinese politics?

Politics in Action

In the center of Beijing, China's capital, is one of the world's largest and most magnificent public spaces, Tiananmen ("Gate of Heavenly Peace") Square. It is about a square mile in size—vast enough to hold ninety football fields. It is named after the entrance to a palace ten times bigger than the square, the Forbidden City, which housed China's emperors for nearly 500 years, that frames its northern border.

Over the last century Tiananmen has been the site of some of the most momentous events in Chinese history.[1] In 1919, large protests by intellectuals and students against the country's weak government set in motion the revolutionary process that led to the founding of the Chinese Communist Party (CCP). In 1949, the leader of the communist party, Chairman Mao Zedong, stood atop Tiananmen gate to proclaim the establishment of the People's Republic of China (PRC) after his forces had triumphed in the Chinese civil war. In 1966, Chairman Mao stood on the same spot, this time to greet and give his political blessing to more than a million Red Guards, high school and college students—the shock troops in his bloody crusade to rid China of those he believed were betraying his vision of Chinese communism. In 1989, more than ten years after Mao's death, Tiananmen again witnessed huge student protests, this time calling for greater democracy, that were brutally crushed when China's communist leaders sent in the army to clear the square.

More recently, in July 2001, over 200,000 Chinese citizens joyfully poured into Tiananmen Square to celebrate the announcement of the International Olympic Committee (IOC) that Beijing would be the site of 2008 summer games. They saw the awarding of the Olympics as long overdue recognition of the remarkable modernization of the Chinese economy, the stunning successes of Chinese athletes in international sports competitions, and the emergence of the PRC as a major global power.

1958–1960	1966–1976	1976	1978	1989	1997	2002–2003
Great Leap Forward.	Great Proletarian Cultural Revolution.	Mao Zedong dies.	Deng Xiaoping becomes China's most powerful leader.	Tiananmen massacre.	Deng Xiaoping dies; Jiang Zemin becomes China's top leader.	Hu Jintao succeeds Jiang as head of the CCP and president of the People's Republic of China.

But many voices around the world were extremely critical of the IOC's decision to give the games to Beijing. Human rights organizations such as Amnesty International argued that the decision rewarded one of the world's most oppressive governments. Some compared the Beijing Games to the ones in Berlin, in 1936, shortly after Hitler had come to power—games that the Nazis used to gain international legitimacy. Others argued that China has become much more open economically and that further involvement with the international community, including hosting the 2008 Olympics, could be a force for positive political change. They cite as a parallel, not the 1936 Berlin games, but the 1988 Olympics in Seoul, which helped bring about South Korea's transition from military dictatorship to democracy.

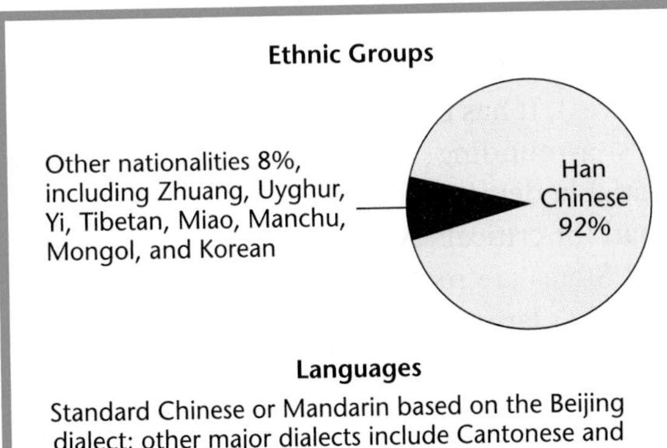

Languages

Standard Chinese or Mandarin based on the Beijing dialect; other major dialects include Cantonese and Shanghaiese. Also various minority languages, such as Tibetan and Mongolian.

Religions

Officially atheist;
Daoist (Taoist), Buddhist, Christian 3–4%
Muslim 1–2%

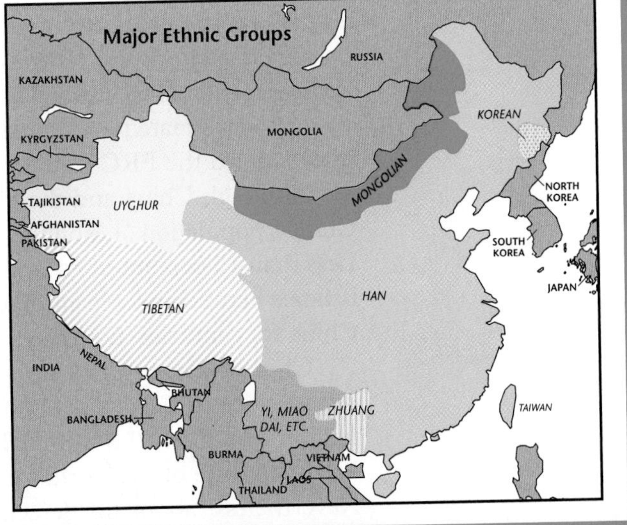

FIGURE 9.1

The Chinese Nation at a Glance

communist party-state a type of nation-state in which the Communist Party attempts to exercise a complete monopoly on political power and controls all important state institutions.

Marxism-Leninism the theoretical foundation of communism based on the ideas of the German philosopher, Karl Marx (1818–1883), and the leader of the Russian Revolution, V. I. Lenin (1870–1924).

The controversy over the Beijing Olympics reflects the fundamental contradiction of Chinese politics today. The People's Republic of China is one of only a few countries in the world that is still a **communist party-state** where the ruling party claims an exclusive monopoly on political power and proclaims allegiance (at least officially) to the ideology of **Marxism-Leninism**. But the country has experienced dramatic economic and social reform—and even considerable political relaxation since the Tiananmen bloodshed in 1989. It is more fully integrated into the world than at any other time in its history. But the Chinese Communist Party rejects any meaningful movement toward democracy. The rift between China's dictatorial political system and its increasingly open economy and globalized society remains deep and ominous.

Geographic Setting

FOCUS QUESTION

How does China compare with the United States in terms of area and population?

autonomous region in the People's Republic of China, a territorial unit equivalent to a province that contains a large concentration of ethnic minorities.

China is located in the eastern part of mainland Asia. It is at the heart of one of the world's most strategically important regions. It is slightly smaller than the United States in land area, and is the fourth-largest country in the world, after Russia, Canada, and the United States.

The PRC is made up of twenty-two provinces, five **autonomous regions**, four centrally administered cities (including the capital, Beijing), and two Special Administrative Regions (Hong Kong and Macau), former European colonies that are only indirectly ruled by China. The vast, sparsely populated western part of the country is mostly mountains, deserts, and high plateaus. The northeast is much like the U.S. plains states in terms of weather and topography. This wheat-growing area is also China's industrial heartland. Southern China has a much warmer climate. In places it is even semitropical, which allows year-round agriculture and intensive rice cultivation. The country is very rich in natural resources, particularly coal and petroleum (including significant, but untapped onshore and offshore reserves). It has the world's greatest potential for hydroelectric power. Still, China's astounding economic growth in recent decades has created an almost insatiable demand for energy resources. This, in turn, has led the PRC to look abroad for critical raw materials.

Although China and the United States are roughly equal in geographic size, China's population (1.3 billion, the world's largest) is more than four times greater. Less than 15 percent of its land, however, is usable for agriculture. The precarious balance between people and the land needed to feed them has been a dilemma for China for centuries. It remains one of the government's major concerns.

China has nearly 150 cities with a population of a million or more. The three largest cities are Shanghai (17.8 million), Beijing (15.4 million), and Tianjin (10.4 million). In 1997, the former British colony of Hong Kong became part of the PRC. It is one of the world's great commercial centers (population 6.9 million). Nevertheless, about 60 percent of China's people still live in rural areas. The countryside has played—and continues to play—a very important role in China's political development.

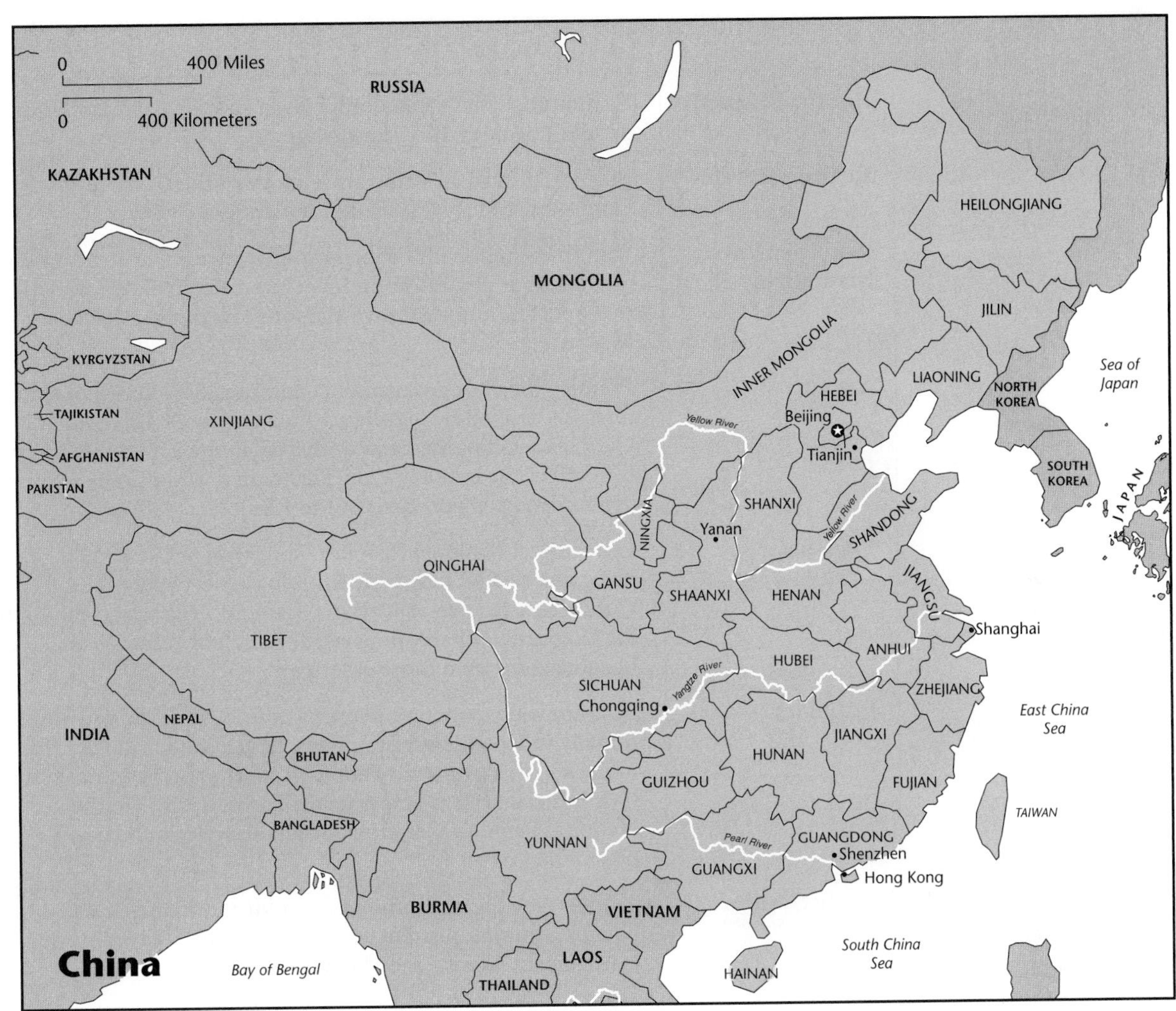

FOCUS QUESTIONS

How and why did the Chinese Communist Party come to power in China?

What impact did Mao Zedong and Deng Xiaoping have on China's political and economic development?

Critical Junctures

Chinese history falls into three broad periods. In the imperial period (221 BCE–1911 CE), a series of dynasties and emperors ruled China. During the relatively brief republican period (1912–1949), civil war and foreign invasion plagued the country. The communist period began in 1949.

From Empire to Republic (221 BCE–1911 CE)

Traditional Chinese culture was based on the teachings of the ancient philosopher, Confucius (551–479 BCE). Confucianism emphasizes obedience to authority, respect for your superiors and elders, as well as the responsibility of rulers to govern benevolently, and the importance of education. The Chinese empire took political shape in 221 BCE, when China's first emperor unified a

TABLE 9.1

Political Organization

Political System	Communist party-state; officially, a socialist state under the people's democratic dictatorship.
Regime History	Established in 1949 after the victory of the Chinese Communist Party (CCP) in the Chinese civil war.
Administrative Structure	Unitary system with twenty-two provinces, five autonomous regions, four centrally administered municipalities, and two Special Administrative Regions (Hong Kong and Macau).
Executive	Premier (head of government) and president (head of state) formally elected by legislature, but only with approval of CCP leadership; the head of the CCP, the general secretary, is in effect the country's chief executive, and usually serves concurrently as president of the PRC.
Legislature	Unicameral National People's Congress; about 3000 delegates elected indirectly from lower-level people's Congresses for five-year terms. Largely a rubber-stamp body for Communist Party policies, although in recent years it has become somewhat more assertive.
Judiciary	A nationwide system of people's courts, which is constitutionally independent but, in fact, largely under the control of the CCP; a Supreme People's Court supervises the country's judicial system and is formally responsible to the National People's Congress, which also elects the court's president.
Party System	A one-party system, although in addition to the ruling Chinese Communist Party, there are eight politically insignificant "democratic" parties.

number of small kingdoms. He laid the foundation of an imperial system that lasted for more than twenty centuries until it was overthrown by a revolution in 1911. During those many centuries, about a dozen different family-based dynasties ruled China. The country went through extensive geographic expansion and far-reaching changes. But the basic political and social institutions remained remarkably consistent. One of the most distinctive aspects of imperial China was its national bureaucracy, which developed much earlier than similar government institutions in Europe. Imperial bureaucrats were appointed by the emperor only after they had passed a series of very difficult examinations that tested their mastery of the classic books of Confucianism.

Imperial China experienced many internal rebellions, often quite large in scale. Some led to the downfall of the ruling dynasty. But new dynasties always kept the Confucian-based imperial political system. However, in the late eighteenth and nineteenth centuries, the Chinese empire faced an unprecedented combination of internal crises and external challenges. A population explosion (resulting from a long spell of peace and prosperity) led to economic stagnation and growing poverty. Official corruption in the bureaucracy and exploitation of the peasants by both landlords and the government increased. This caused widespread social unrest. One massive revolt, the Taiping Rebellion (1850–1864), took 20 million lives and nearly overthrew the imperial government.

By the early nineteenth century, the European powers had surged far ahead of China in industrial and military development and were pressing the country to open its markets to foreign trade. China tried to limit the activities of Westerners. But Europe, most notably Britain, was in the midst of its era of great commercial and colonial expansion. Britain was importing huge amounts of tea from China, and in order to balance the trade, used its superior military power to compel China to buy opium from the British colony of India. After a humiliating defeat by the British in the so-called Opium War (1839–1842), China was forced to sign a series of unequal treaties. These opened its borders to foreign merchants, missionaries, and diplomats on terms dictated by Britain and other Western powers. China also lost significant pieces of its territory to foreigners (including Hong Kong, which remained a British colony until 1997). Important sectors of the Chinese economy fell under foreign control.

There were many efforts to revive or reform the imperial government in the late nineteenth and early twentieth centuries. But political power in China remained in the hands of staunch conservatives who resisted change. When change came in 1911, it was a revolution that toppled the ruling dynasty and ended the 2,000-year-old empire.

Warlords, Nationalists, and Communists (1912–1949)

The Republic of China was established in 1912. Dr. Sun Yat-sen,* then China's best-known revolutionary, became president. However, the American-educated Sun could not hold on to power. China soon fell into a lengthy period of conflict and disintegration. Rival military leaders known as warlords ruled large parts of the country. Sun organized another revolution to try to reunify the country under his Nationalist Party (the *Guomindang* or *Kuomintang*).

In 1921, a few intellectuals, inspired by the Russian revolution in 1917 founded the Chinese Communist Party. They were looking for more radical solutions to China's problems than that offered by Sun Yat-sen and his Nationalist Party. But, encouraged by the Soviet Union, the small Chinese Communist Party joined with the Nationalists to fight the warlords. After initial successes, this alliance came to a tragic end in 1927. Chiang Kai-shek, a military leader who had become the head of the Nationalist Party after Sun's death in 1925, turned against his communist partners. He ordered a bloody suppression that nearly wiped out the CCP. Chiang proceeded to unify the Republic of China under his personal rule. He did this largely by striking deals with some of the country's most powerful remaining warlords who supported him in suppressing the communists.

---

*In China, family names come first. For example, Sun Yat-sen's family name was "Sun," and his given name was Yat-sen, and he is referred to as Dr. Sun.

The Republic of China on Taiwan

Despite being defeated by Mao Zedong and the communists on the mainland in October 1949, Chiang Kai-shek's Nationalist Party and the Republic of China (ROC) continued to function on the island of Taiwan, just 90 miles off the coast. The Chinese communists would probably have taken over Taiwan if the United States had not intervened to prevent an invasion. Taiwan remains politically separate from the People's Republic of China and still formally calls itself the Republic of China.

The Nationalist Party imposed a harsh dictatorship on Taiwan after its forced exile from the mainland in 1949. This deepened the sharp divide between the mainlanders who had arrived in large numbers with Chiang in 1949 and the native Taiwanese majority, whose ancestors had settled there centuries before and who spoke a distinctive Chinese dialect.

But with large amounts of U.S. aid and advice, the Nationalist government under Chiang Kai-shek sponsored a successful, peaceful program of land reform and rural development. It attracted extensive foreign investment and promoted economic growth by producing very competitive exports. This made Taiwan a model **newly industrializing country (NIC)**. The government also modernized Taiwan's roads and ports. It implemented policies that have given the island health and education levels that are among the best in the world. Its standard of living is one of the highest in Asia.

After Chiang Kai-shek died in 1975, his son, Chiang Ching-kuo, became president of the Republic of China and head of the Nationalist Party. Most people expected him to continue **authoritarian** rule. Instead, he permitted some opposition and dissent. He gave important government and party positions, previously dominated by mainlanders, to Taiwanese. When he died in 1988, the Taiwanese vice president, Lee Teng-hui, became president and party leader.

Under President Lee, Taiwan made great strides toward democratization. Laws used to imprison dissidents were revoked, the media were freed of all censorship, and open multiparty elections were held for all local and island-wide positions. In the 1996 presidential elections, Lee won 54 percent of the vote in a hotly contested four-way race. Lee's relatively small margin of victory reflected the new openness of the political system, but his victory reflected the credit that voters gave the Nationalist Party for the island's progress.

In 2000, an opposition party candidate, Chen Shui-bian of the Democratic Progressive Party (DPP), won the presidency. Chen's victory was partly due to a combination of the desire for change, especially in light of a serious downturn in the island's economic growth and a split within the Nationalist Party. It was also evidence of the further maturing of Taiwan's democracy.

The most contentious political issue in Taiwan is whether the island should continue to work, however slowly, toward reunification with the mainland. This was the Nationalists' policy under Lee Teng-hui. Or should it declare formal independence from China? A big factor in Chen's election in 2000 was the growing popularity of the DPP's position that Taiwan should seriously consider independence. Public opinion is sharply divided on this issue. But most people seem to prefer the status quo in which Taiwan is, for all intents and purposes (including its own strong military), a separate political entity from China, but not an internationally recognized independent country.

Chen was re-elected in 2004 in a close and contentious election. He and the DPP have toned down their independence rhetoric. The United States is committed to a "peaceful solution" of the Taiwan issue. It continues to sell military technology to Taiwan so it can defend itself. China regards Taiwan as a part of China, and Beijing has refused to renounce the use of force if the island moves toward formal separation. The PRC government often criticizes American policy toward Taiwan as interference in China's internal affairs, even though

newly industrializing countries (NICs) a group of countries that achieved rapid economic development beginning in the 1960s, stimulated by robust international trade and guided by government policies.

authoritarianism a system of rule in which power depends not on popular legitimacy but on the coercive force of the political authorities.

the United States only has informal diplomatic relations with Taiwan. Taiwan actually has formal diplomatic relations with very few other countries because doing so would anger the PRC.

Taiwan and China have developed extensive economic relations. Millions of people from Taiwan go to the mainland to do business, visit relatives, or just sightsee. The PRC and ROC have engaged in negotiations about further reconciliation and possible reunification. In 2005 the current head of the Nationalist Party went to the mainland and held talks with CCP leader (and PRC president) Hu Jintao. This was the first direct contact between the two political parties since the end of the civil war. In 2008, the Nationalists were returned to power and promised to seek closer ties with the PRC. ❖

Taiwan

Land area	13,895 sq mi/35,980 sq km (slightly smaller than Maryland and Delaware combined)
Population	23 million
Ethnic composition	Taiwanese 84%, mainland Chinese 14%, aborigine 2%
GDP at purchasing power parity (US$)	$690 billion, which ranks it 18th in the world behind Australia and ahead of Turkey
GDP per capita at purchasing power parity (US$)	$29,800, about the same as Greece or New Zealand

To survive, the Communist Party relocated its headquarters deep into the Chinese countryside. Ironically, this retreat created the conditions for the eventual rise to power of the man who would lead the CCP to nationwide victory, Mao Zedong. Mao had been one of the junior founders of the Communist Party. He had strongly advocated paying more attention to China's suffering peasants as a potential source of support. "In a very short time," he wrote in 1927, "several hundred million peasants will rise like a mighty storm, like a hurricane, a force so swift and violent that no power, however great, will be able to hold it back."[2] While the CCP was based in the rural areas Mao began his climb to the top of the party leadership.

In late 1934, the CCP was surrounded by Chiang Kai-shek's army and forced to begin a year-long, 6000-mile journey called the Long March, which took them across some of the most remote parts of China. In October 1935, the communists established a base in an impoverished area of northwestern China. It was there that Mao consolidated his political and ideological control of the CCP, sometimes through ruthless means. He was elected party chairman in 1943. He held this position until his death in 1976.

In 1937 Japan invaded China, which started World War II in Asia. The Japanese army pushed Chiang Kai-shek's Nationalist government to the far southwestern part of the country. This effectively eliminated the Nationalists as an active combatant against Japanese aggression. In contrast, the CCP base in the northwest was on the front line against Japan's troops. Mao and the Communists successfully mobilized the peasants to use **guerrilla warfare** to fight the invaders. This gained them a lot of support among the Chinese people.

guerrilla warfare a military strategy based on small bands of soldiers (guerrillas) who use hit-and-run tactics to attack a numerically superior and better-armed enemy.

By the end of World War II in 1945, the CCP had vastly expanded its membership. It controlled much of the countryside in north China. The Nationalists were isolated and unpopular with many Chinese because of corruption, political repression, and economic mismanagement.

After the Japanese surrender, the Chinese civil war quickly resumed. The communists won a decisive victory over the U.S.-backed Nationalists. Chiang Kai-shek and his supporters had to retreat to the island of Taiwan, 90 miles off the Chinese coast. On October 1, 1949, Mao Zedong declared the founding of the People's Republic of China.

Mao in Power (1949–1976)

The CCP came to power on a wave of popular support because of its reputation as a party of social reformers and patriotic fighters. Chairman Mao and the CCP quickly turned their attention to some of the country's most glaring problems. A nationwide land reform campaign redistributed property from the rich to the poor and increased agricultural production in the countryside. Highly successful drives eliminated opium addiction and prostitution from the cities. A national law greatly improved the legal status of women in the family. It allowed many women to free themselves from unhappy arranged marriages. The CCP did not hesitate to use violence to achieve its objectives and silence opponents. Nevertheless the party gained considerable legitimacy among many parts of the population because of its successful policies during the first period of its rule.

collectivization a process undertaken in the Soviet Union under Stalin in the late 1920s and early 1930s and in China under Mao in the 1950s, by which agricultural land was removed from private ownership and organized into large state and collective farms.

socialism an economic system in which the state plays a leading role in organizing the economy, and most business firms are publicly owned.

Between 1953 and 1957, the PRC implemented a Soviet-style five-year economic plan. The complete takeover of industry by the government and the **collectivization** of agriculture in these years were decisive steps toward **socialism**. The plan achieved good economic results for the country. But Mao disliked the growth of the government bureaucracy and the persistence of inequalities, especially those caused by the emphasis on industrial and urban development and the relative neglect of the countryside.

This discontent led Mao to launch the **Great Leap Forward** (1958–1960). The Leap was a utopian effort to speed up the country's development so rapidly that China would catch up economically with Britain and the United States in just a few years. It relied on the labor power and revolutionary enthusiasm of the masses while at the same time aiming to propel China into an era of true **communism** in which there would be almost complete economic and social equality.

Great Leap Forward a movement launched by Mao Zedong in 1958 to industrialize China very rapidly and propel it toward communism.

communism a system of social organization based on the common ownership and coordination of production.

The Great Leap Forward turned into "one of the most extreme, bizarre, and eventually catastrophic episodes in twentieth-century political history."[3] In the rural areas, bad weather, irrational policies, wasted resources, poor management, and Mao's willful refusal to slow down the Great Leap combined to produce a famine. Between 20 and 30 million people died. An industrial depression soon followed the collapse of agriculture. China suffered a terrible setback in economic development.

In the early 1960s, Mao took a less active role in day-to-day decision making. Two of China's other top leaders at the time, Liu Shaoqi and Deng Xiaoping, were put in charge of reviving the economy. They used a combination of careful government planning and market-oriented policies to stimulate production, particularly in agriculture.

This strategy did help the Chinese economy. Once again, however, Mao became profoundly unhappy with the consequences of China's development. By the mid-1960s, the chairman had concluded that the policies of Liu and Deng had led to a resurgence of elitism and inequality. He thought they were threatening his revolutionary goals by setting the country on the road to capitalism. China also broke relations with the Soviet Union, which Mao had concluded was no longer a revolutionary country. The two communist countries nearly went to war in the late 1960s.

Great Proletarian Cultural Revolution the political campaign launched in 1966 by Chairman Mao Zedong to stop what he saw as China's drift away from socialism and toward capitalism.

The **Great Proletarian Cultural Revolution** (1966–1976) was an ideological crusade designed to jolt China back toward Mao's radical vision of communism. Like the Great Leap Forward, the Cultural Revolution was a campaign of mass mobilization and utopian idealism. Its methods, however, were much more violent. Its main objective was not accelerated economic development, but the political purification of the party and the nation through struggle against so-called class enemies. Using his unmatched political clout and charisma, Mao put together a potent coalition of radical party leaders, loyal military officers, and student rebels (called Red Guards) to support him and attack anyone thought to be guilty of betraying his version of communist ideology known as Mao Zedong Thought.

In the Cultural Revolution's first phase (1966–1969), 20 million or so Red Guards rampaged across the country. They harassed, tortured, and killed people accused of being class enemies, particularly intellectuals and discredited party officials. During the next phase (1969–1971), Mao used the People's Liberation Army (PLA) to restore political order. Many Red Guards were sent to live and work in the countryside. The final phase of the Cultural Revolution (1972–1976) involved intense power struggle over who would succeed the old and frail Mao as the leader of the Chinese Communist Party.

Mao died in September 1976 at age eighty-two. A month later, a group of relatively moderate leaders settled the power struggle. They arrested their radical rivals, the so-called Gang of Four, led by Mao's wife, Jiang Qing. This marked the end of the Cultural Revolution. It had claimed at least a million lives and brought the nation close to civil war.

Deng Xiaoping and the Transformation of Chinese Communism (1977–1997)

To repair the damage caused by the Cultural Revolution, China's new leaders restored to power many veteran officials who had been purged by Mao and the radicals. These included Deng Xiaoping. By 1978, Deng had clearly become the country's most powerful leader, although he never took for himself the formal positions of head of either the Communist Party or the Chinese government. Instead he appointed younger, loyal men to those positions.

Deng's policies were a profound break with the Maoist past. He had long believed that Mao put too much emphasis on politics and not enough on the economy. That was why he had been purged by Mao during the Cultural Revolution. Under Deng, state control of the economy was significantly reduced.

Market forces were allowed to play an increasingly important role. Private enterprise was encouraged. The government allowed unprecedented levels of foreign investment. Chinese artists and writers saw the shackles of party control that had bound them for decades greatly loosened. Deng took major steps to revitalize China's government by bringing in younger, better-educated officials. After decades of stagnation, the Chinese economy experienced spectacular growth throughout the 1980s. (See Section 2.)

Then came June 1989 and the Tiananmen Square massacre. For more than a year, discontent had been growing over inflation and official corruption. Many people, especially students and intellectuals, desired more political freedom. Large-scale demonstrations began in Beijing and several other Chinese cities that spring. At one point more than a million people from all walks of life gathered in and around Tiananmen. For several months, CCP leaders disagreed about how to handle the protests. They did little other than engage in threatening rhetoric in the hope that the demonstrators would leave. But they stayed, and China's leaders ran out of patience. The army received orders to clear the Square during the very early morning hours of June 4. By the time dawn broke in Beijing, the army had indeed cleared Tiananmen Square. The Chinese government has never revealed the exact death toll which very likely numbered in the hundreds. Indeed, the government still insists that it did the right thing in the interests of national stability.

This cartoon captures the contradiction between economic reform and political repression that characterized China under the leadership of Deng Xiaoping. *(© Tribune Media Services, Inc. All Rights Reserved. Reprinted with permission.)*

Following the Tiananmen crisis, China went through a few years of intense political repression and a slowdown in the pace of economic change. Then in early 1992, Deng Xiaoping took some bold steps to accelerate reform of the economy. He hoped reform would help the PRC avoid a collapse of China's communist system such as had happened in the Soviet Union in 1991.

From Revolutionaries to Technocrats (1997 to the Present)

In mid-1989, Deng Xiaoping had promoted the former mayor and communist party leader of Shanghai, Jiang Zemin, to become the head of the CCP. Although Deng remained the power behind the throne, he gradually turned over greater authority to Jiang, who, in addition to his positions as head (general secretary) of the CCP and chair of the powerful Central Military Commission, became president of the PRC in 1993. When Deng Xiaoping died in February 1997, Jiang was secure in his position as China's top leader.

Under Jiang's leadership, China continued its economic reforms and remarkable economic growth. The PRC became an even more integral part of the global economy. It enhanced its regional and international stature. But the country also faced serious problems, including mounting unemployment, pervasive corruption, and widening gaps between the rich and the poor. Overall, China was politically stable during the Jiang era. But the CCP still repressed any individual or group it perceived as challenging its authority.

Upon Jiang's retirement, Hu Jintao, China's vice president, became CCP general secretary in November 2002 and PRC president in March 2003. Hu was sixty years old when he took over the highest party and government offices, which was considerably younger than most of China's recent leaders. But both Jiang and Hu represented a new kind of leader for the PRC. Mao Zedong and Deng Xiaoping were career revolutionaries. They had participated in the CCP's long struggle for power dating back to the 1920s. They were among the founders of the Communist regime in 1949. In contrast, Jiang and Hu were **technocrats**. They were officials with academic training (in their cases, as engineers) who had worked their way up the party ladder by professional competence and political loyalty.

technocrats career-minded bureaucrats who administer public policy according to a technical rather than a political rationale.

The transfer of power from Jiang to Hu was remarkably predictable and orderly. Some observed that it was the first relatively tranquil top-level political succession in China in more than 200 years. Jiang had retired after two terms in office, as required by both party rules and the state constitution, and Hu had, for several years, been expected to succeed Jiang.

Hu Jintao has tried to project himself as a leader who not only wants to promote economic growth, but who is also more concerned than his predecessor about some of the country's serious problems, such as the enormous inequalities between regions, rural poverty, and the environment. But Hu has also taken a hard line on political dissent. There is little reason to expect he will deviate significantly from the combination of economic reform and political repression that has been the CCP's formula for retaining power since the days of Deng Xiaoping.

Themes and Implications

FOCUS QUESTIONS

In what ways might China be compared to other countries? In what ways is it unique?

Historical Junctures and Political Themes

The World of States. At the time the People's Republic was established in 1949, China occupied a weak position in the international system. For more than a century, its destiny had been shaped by incursions and influences from abroad that it could do little to control. Mao made many tragic and terrible blunders. But one of his great achievements was to build a strong state able to affirm and defend its sovereignty. China's international stature has increased as its economic and military strength have grown. Although still a relatively poor country by many per capita measures, the sheer size of its economy makes the PRC an economic powerhouse. Its import and export policies have an important impact on many other countries. China is a nuclear power with the world's largest conventional military force. It is an active and influential member of nearly all international organizations, including the United Nations, where it sits as one of the five permanent members of the Security Council. China has become a major player in the world of states.

Governing the Economy. Since coming to power in 1949, the Chinese Communist Party has experimented with a series of very different economic systems for China: a Soviet-style bureaucratic planning system in the early 1950s, the radical egalitarianism and mass mobilization of the Maoist model, and market-oriented policies implemented by Deng Xiaoping and his successors. Ideological disputes over these development strategies were the main cause of ferocious political struggles within the CCP. Deng began his bold reforms in the hope that improved living standards would restore the legitimacy of the CCP, which had been badly tarnished by the economic failings and political chaos of the Maoist era. The remarkable successes of those reforms have sustained the CCP at a time when most of the world's other Communist regimes have disappeared.

The Democratic Idea. Any hope that democracy might take root in the early years of Communist rule in China quickly vanished by the mid-1950s with the building of a one-party Communist state and Mao's unrelenting campaigns against alleged enemies of his revolution. The Deng Xiaoping era brought much greater economic, social, and cultural freedom. But time and again the CCP strangled the stirrings of the democratic idea, most brutally in Tiananmen Square in 1989. Jiang Zemin and Hu Jintao have been faithful disciples of Deng. They have vigorously championed economic reform in China. They have also made sure that the CCP retains its firm grip on power.

The Politics of Collective Identity. Because of its long history and ancient culture, China has a very strong sense of national identity. China's cultural and ethnic homogeneity has also spared it the kind of widespread communal

In an act of outrage and protest, an unarmed civilian stood in front of a column of tanks leaving Tiananmen Square the day after the Chinese army had crushed the pro-democracy demonstration in June 1989. This "unknown hero" disappeared into the watching crowd. Neither his identity nor his fate are known. *(Source: Jeff Widener/AP Images)*

violence that has plagued so many other countries in the modern world. The exception has been in the border regions of the country where there is a large concentration of minority peoples, including Tibet and the Muslim areas of China's northwest (see Section 4).

Implications for Comparative Politics

The PRC can be compared with other countries that have been or are ruled by a communist party. From this perspective, China raises intriguing questions: Why has China's communist party–state so far proved more durable than that of the Soviet Union and nearly all other such regimes? By what combination of reform and repression has the CCP held onto power? What signs are there that it is likely to continue to be able to do so for the foreseeable future? What signs suggest that Communist rule in China may be weakening?

China can also be compared with other developing nations that face similar economic and political challenges. Although the PRC is part of the Third World as measured by the average standard of living of its population, its record of growth in the past several decades has far exceeded almost all other developing countries. Furthermore, the educational and health levels of the Chinese people are quite good when compared with many other countries at a similar or somewhat higher level of development, for example, India and Mexico. How has China achieved such relative success in its quest for economic and social development? By contrast, much of the Third World has become democratic in recent decades. How and why has China resisted this wave of democracy? What does the experience of other developing countries say about how economic modernization might influence the prospects for democracy in China?

Napoleon Bonaparte, emperor of France in the early nineteenth century, is said to have remarked, "Let China sleep. For when China wakes, it will shake the world."[4] It has taken awhile, but China certainly has awakened. Will it shake the world?

Summary

China has experienced more dramatic changes over the last century than almost any other country. Until 1912, it was an imperial system headed by an emperor. From then until 1949 it was known as the Republic of China, but the government was never in full control. Warlords ruled various parts of the country. China suffered terribly from a brutal invasion by Japan during World War II. In 1949, a civil war that had been waged for two decades ended when the Chinese Communist Party under Chairman Mao Zedong came to power and established the People's Republic of China. From then until his death in 1976, Mao imposed a kind of radical communism on China. This had a mostly disastrous political and economic impact. Deng Xiaoping became China's most powerful leader in 1978. He implemented major reforms that helped make China the fastest growing economy in the world. But he and his successors have suppressed all challenges to the authority of the Communist Party.

Political Economy and Development

FOCUS QUESTION

What are the major differences between Mao Zedong's approach to governing the economy and Deng Xiaoping's?

State and Economy

The Maoist Economy

When the Chinese Communist Party came to power in 1949, China's economy was suffering from more than a hundred years of rebellion, invasion, civil war, and bad government. The country's new communist rulers seized much property from wealthy landowners, rich industrialists, and foreign companies. Nevertheless, it allowed some private ownership and many aspects of capitalism to continue in order to gain support for the government and revive the economy.

command economy a form of socialist economy in which government decisions ("commands") rather than market mechanisms (such as supply and demand) are the major influences in determining the nation's economic direction.

In early 1950s, the CCP followed the socialist model of a **command economy** as practiced in the Soviet Union. The state owned or controlled most economic resources. Government planning and commands, not market forces, drove economic activity.

At first, China's command economy yielded impressive results. But it also created huge bureaucracies and new inequalities, especially between the heavily favored industrial cities and the investment-starved rural areas. Both the Great Leap Forward (1958–1961) and the Cultural Revolution (1966–1976) embodied the unique and radical Maoist approach to economic development. This was intended to be less bureaucratic and more egalitarian than the Soviet model.

Under Mao, the PRC built a strong industrial base. The people of China became much healthier and better educated. But the Maoist economy was plagued by political interference, poor management, and ill-conceived projects. This led to wasted resources of truly staggering proportions. Overall, China's economic growth rates, especially in agriculture, barely kept pace with population increases. The average standard of living changed little between the 1950s and Mao's death in 1976.

China Goes to Market

After Deng Xiaoping consolidated power in 1978, he took China in an economic direction far different from Mao's or that of any other communist party-state. In 1962 Deng had remarked in a speech, "It doesn't matter whether a cat is white or black, as long as it catches mice."[5] He meant that the CCP should not be overly concerned about whether a particular policy was socialist or capitalist if it helped the economy. Such sentiments got Deng in trouble with Mao. They made Deng one of the principal victims of the Cultural Revolution.

Once in charge, Deng spearheaded sweeping reforms that transformed the Chinese economy. They also touched nearly every aspect of life in the PRC. They redefined the role of the communist party and the meaning of socialism in China. These reforms greatly reduced the role of government control and increased that of the market economy. Authority for making economic decisions passed from government bureaucrats to families, factory managers, and even the owners of private businesses. Individuals were encouraged to work harder and more efficiently to make money rather than to "serve the people" as had been the slogan during the Maoist era.

In most sectors of the economy the state no longer dictates what to produce and how to produce it. Almost all prices are now set according to supply and demand, as in a capitalist economy, rather than by administrative decree. Many government monopolies have given way to fierce competition between state-owned and non–state-owned firms. A decade ago there were over 100,000 state-owned enterprises (SOEs) in China; now there are about a quarter of that number. In 1978, SOEs generated about 80 percent of China's gross domestic product; by 2004 that number had dropped to about 25 percent. But state-owned enterprises still employ nearly 70 millions workers. They also dominate critical parts of the economy such as steel and petroleum.

But even SOEs must now respond to market forces. If they cannot turn a profit, they have to restructure or even go into bankruptcy. Some have been semiprivatized. But many are vastly overstaffed. Many are economic dinosaurs with outdated facilities and machinery that make them unattractive to potential foreign or domestic investors. The state-owned sector remains a huge drain on the country's banks (mostly government-controlled), which are still required to bail out many failing SOEs. These large loans are rarely, if ever, paid back. Many economists think that even more drastic SOE reform is needed. The country's leaders understandably fear the political and social consequences that would result from a massive layoff of industrial workers.

Although it is somewhat ironic, the Chinese Communist Party now strongly encourages and supports private businesses. The private sector is the fastest growing part of China's economy. It now accounts for more than two-thirds of the PRC's industrial output and employs nearly 200 million workers.

The results of China's move from a command toward a market economy have been phenomenal (see Figure 9.2). The PRC has been the fastest-growing major economy in the world for more than two decades. China's GDP per capita (that is, the total output of the economy divided by the total population) grew at an average rate of nearly 9 percent per year from 1990 to 2006. During the same period, the per capita GDP of the United States grew at a little under 2 percent per year during the same period, Japan's at about 1 percent, and India's at around 4 percent.

There has also been a consumer revolution in China. In the late 1970s, people in the cities could only shop for most consumer goods at state-run stores. These carried a very limited range of products, many of which were of shoddy quality. Today most of China's urban areas are becoming shopping paradises. They have domestic and foreign stores of every kind, huge malls, fast-food outlets, and a great variety of entertainment options. A few decades ago, hardly anyone owned a television. Now nearly every urban household and 75 percent of rural households have a color TV. Cell phones are everywhere. In the cities, the new middle class is starting to buy houses, condominiums, and cars.

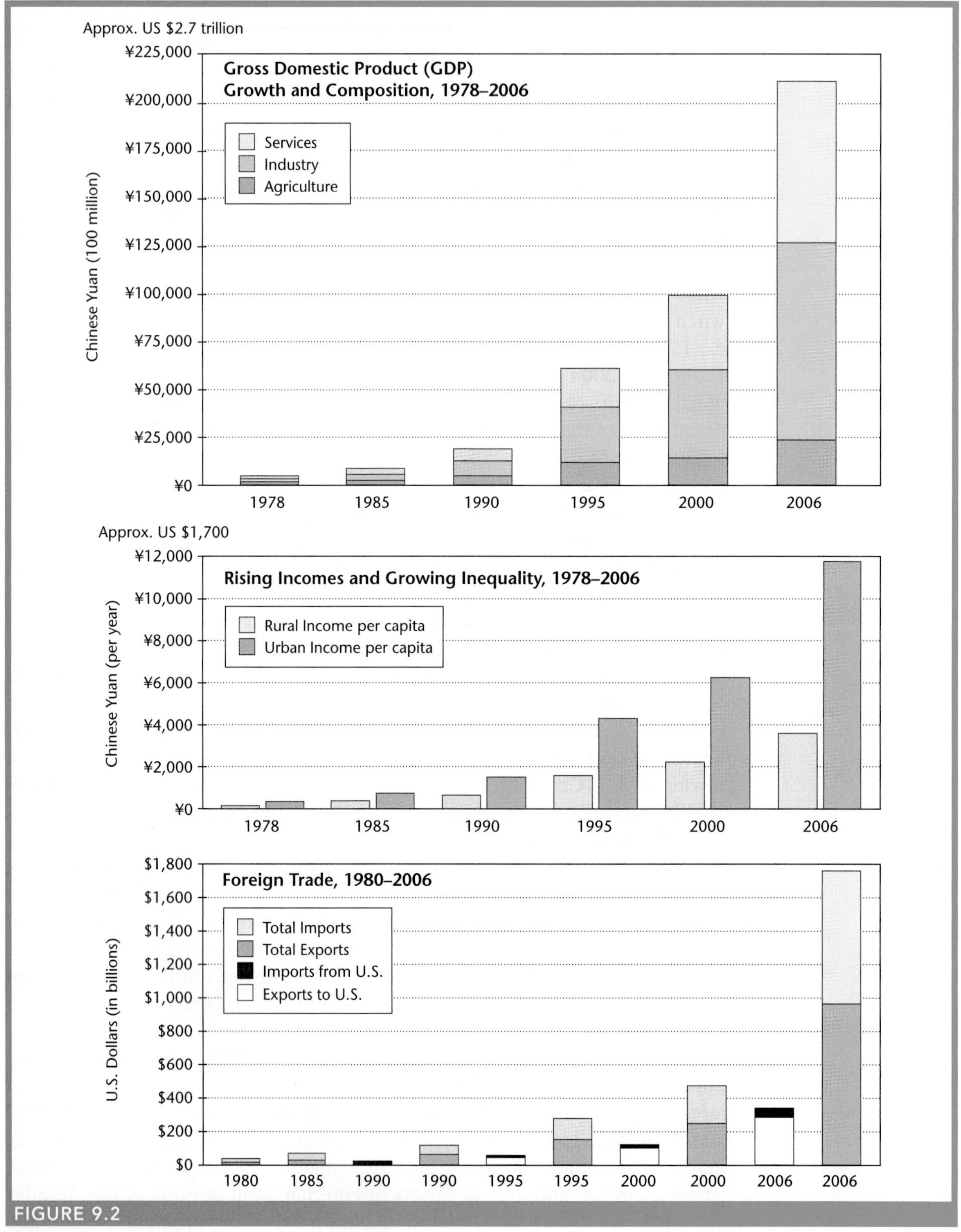

FIGURE 9.2

The Economic Transformation of China

These charts show how dramatically the Chinese economy has been transformed since the market reforms were introduced by Deng Xiaoping in 1978.

Source: *China Statistical Yearbooks*, United States-China Business Council.

Despite these changes, government commands and central planning, although greatly refined and reduced, have not disappeared altogether. China is still not fully a free market economy. National and local bureaucrats continue to exercise a great deal of control over the production and distribution of goods, resources, and services. The extent of private property is still restricted. Market reforms have gained substantial momentum that would be nearly impossible to reverse. But the CCP still wields the power to decide the direction of China's economy.

Remaking the Chinese Countryside

One of the first revolutionary programs launched by the Chinese Communist Party when it came to power in 1949 was land reform that confiscated the property of landlords and redistributed it as private holdings to the poorer peasants. But in the mid- to late 1950s peasants were reorganized by the state into collective farms and communes in which the village, not individuals, owned the land and government officials directed all production and labor. Individuals were paid according to how much they worked on the collective land. Most crops and other farm products had to be sold to the state at low fixed prices. The system of collectivized agriculture was one of the weakest links in China's command economy because it was very inefficient and people had little incentive to work hard. Per capita agricultural production and rural living standards were stagnant from 1957 to 1977.

Deng Xiaoping made the revival of the rural economy one of his top priorities when he became China's most powerful leader in the late 1970s. He abolished collective farming and established a **household responsibility system**, which remains in effect today. Farmland is now contracted out by the villages (which still technically own the land) to individual families, who take full charge of the production and marketing of crops. Agricultural productivity and income have sharply increased for most farm families. It is estimated that more than 200 million rural residents have been lifted out of extreme poverty in the last two decades.

household responsibility system the system put into practice in China beginning in the early 1980s in which the major decisions about agricultural production are made by individual farm families based on the profit motive rather than by a people's commune or the government.

Economic life in the Chinese countryside has also been transformed by the remarkable growth of rural industry and commerce. Rural factories and businesses range in size from a handful of employees to thousands; some are privately owned, but many are run by local governments. They even attract considerable foreign investment.

Certainly life is much better for the vast majority of the more than 600 million people who still live in China's rural areas. But there are also serious problems in the countryside. Health care, education, disability pay, and retirement funds for people in the countryside receive little government support. They now depend almost entirely on the relative wealth of families and villages. Rural protests, sometimes violent, have increased significantly in recent years. The protests have been about high taxes, corrupt local officials, pollution, illegal land seizures by developers, and delays in payments for agricultural products purchased by the government.

A view of Shanghai's ultramodern skyline. The city is China's financial and commercial center and one of the world's busiest ports. *(Source: © Xiaoyang Liu/Corbis)*

Society and Economy

FOCUS QUESTION

What have been some of the major downsides to China's spectacular economic growth over the last two or three decades?

Market reform and globalization have made Chinese society much more diverse and open. People are vastly freer to choose jobs, travel about the country and internationally, practice their religious beliefs, buy private homes, join nonpolitical associations, and engage in a wide range of other activities that were prohibited or severely restricted during the Maoist era. But economic change has also caused serious social problems. Crime, prostitution, and drug use have sharply increased. Although such problems are still far less prevalent in China than in many other countries, they are severe enough to worry national and local authorities.

Economic reform has also brought significant changes in China's basic system of social welfare. The Maoist economy was characterized by what was called the **iron rice bowl**. As in other communist party-state economies such as the Soviet Union, the government guaranteed employment, a certain standard of living (although, a low one), and basic cradle-to-grave benefits to most of the urban and rural labor force. In the cities, the workplace was more than just a place to work and earn a salary. It also provided housing, health care, day care, and other services.

iron rice bowl a feature of China's socialist economy during the Maoist era (1949–76) that provided guarantees of lifetime employment, income, and basic cradle-to-grave benefits to most urban and rural workers.

China's economic reformers believed that such guarantees led to poor work motivation and excessive costs for the government and businesses. They implemented policies designed to break the iron rice bowl. Income and employment are no longer guaranteed. They are now directly tied to individual effort. An estimated 45 to 60 million workers have been laid off from state-owned

Despite China's spectacular economic progress in recent decades, tens of millions of people still live in dire poverty in rural areas such as that shown in this photograph. Inequality between city and countryside is one of the biggest challenges facing China's government. *(Source: © Keren Su/Corbis)*

enterprises in recent years. Many are too old or too unskilled to find good jobs. The official unemployment rate is about 4 percent of the urban labor force. But it is generally believed to be at least twice that and to be as high as 40 percent in some parts of the country. China has very little in the way of unemployment insurance or social security for its displaced workers. Work slowdowns, strikes, and large-scale demonstrations are becoming more frequent, particularly in China's northeastern rust belt, where state-owned industries have been particularly hard hit. If unemployment continues to surge, labor unrest could be a political time bomb for China's communist party-state.

Welfare subsidies have been greatly reduced or eliminated entirely. China's health care system is in shambles. Less than a quarter of the urban population, and only 10 percent of those who live in the rural areas, have health insurance.

Market reforms have also opened China's cities to a flood of rural migrants. After the agricultural communes broke up in the early 1980s, many peasants headed to the urban areas to look for jobs. The more than 150 million people in this so-called floating population reflect the biggest population movement in human history. They are mostly employed in low-paying jobs, but fill an important niche in China's changing labor market, particularly in boom areas like construction. But they also put increased pressure on urban housing and social services. Their presence in Chinese cities could become politically destabilizing if they find their economic aspirations thwarted by a stalled economy or if they are treated too roughly or unfairly by local governments, which often see them as intruders.

China's economic boom has also created enormous opportunities for corruption. Officials still control numerous resources and retain power over many economic transactions from which large personal profits can be made. The government recognizes the threat corruption poses to its legitimacy. It has repeatedly launched well-publicized campaigns against official graft, with severe punishment, including execution, for some serious offenders. In the fall of 2006, even the head of the communist party in Shanghai was kicked out of office and charged with misuse of nearly $400 million in pension funds.

The benefits of economic growth have reached most of China. But the market reforms and economic boom have created sharp class differences, and inequalities between people and parts of the country have risen significantly.

A huge gap separates the average incomes of urban residents and those in the countryside (see Fig. 2.1). Farmers in China's poorer areas have faced years of stagnating or even declining incomes. The gap is also widening between the prosperous coastal regions and the inland areas of the country.

Such inequalities are an embarrassing contradiction for a party that still claims to believe in communist ideals. The current administration of Hu Jintao has begun to promote the development of what it calls a "harmonious society." This emphasizes not only achieving a higher average standard of living, but a more equitable distribution of income and basic social welfare, including health and education. There is more attention being paid to the rural economy, and new poverty alleviation programs and increased investment have brought some progress to the less developed western regions. In early 2006, the government announced that it was abolishing all taxes on agriculture.

Gender inequalities also appear to have grown in some ways since the introduction of the economic reforms. There is no doubt that the social status, legal rights, employment opportunities, and education of women in China have improved enormously since 1949. Women have also benefited from rising living standards and economic modernization of recent decades. But the trend toward a market economy has not benefited men and women equally. In the countryside, it is almost always the case that only male heads of households sign contracts for land and other production resources. And so men dominate rural economic life. This is true even though farm labor has become increasingly feminized as many men move to jobs in rural industry or migrate to the cities.

Economic and cultural pressures have also led to an alarming suicide rate (the world's highest) among rural women. Over 70 percent (about 120 million) of illiterate adults in China are female. Although China has one of the world's highest rates of female urban labor participation, the market reforms have "strengthened and in some cases reconstructed the sexual division of labor, keeping urban women in a transient, lower-paid, and subordinate position in the workforce."[6] Women workers are the first to be laid off or are forced to retire early when a collective or state-owned enterprise downsizes.

Finally, the momentous economic changes have had serious environmental consequences. Industrial expansion has been fueled primarily by highly polluting coal. The air in China's cities and even many rural areas is among the dirtiest in the world. Soil erosion, the loss of arable land, and deforestation are serious. The dumping of garbage and toxic wastes goes virtually unregulated. It is estimated that 80 percent of China's rivers are badly polluted. One of the most serious problems is a critical water shortage in north China due to urbanization and industrialization. Private automobile use is just starting to take off. This will greatly add to the country's pollution concerns (and demand for more oil) in the very near future. **Sustainable development**, which balances economic growth and environmental concerns, is a key part of the party-state's current emphasis on building a "harmonious society."

sustainable development an approach to promoting economic growth that seeks to minimize environmental degradation and depletion of natural resources.

Dealing with some of the negative consequences of fast growth and market reforms is one of the main challenges facing China's government. The ability of citizen associations—including labor, women's, and environmental organizations—to place their concerns about these problems on the nation's political agenda remains limited by the party's tight control of political life and by restrictions on the formation of autonomous interest groups (see Section 4).

FOCUS QUESTION

In what ways has China's economy become globalized?

China in the Global Economy

China was not a major trading nation when Deng Xiaoping took power in 1978. Total foreign trade was around $20 billion (approximately 10 percent of GDP). Foreign investment in China was minuscule. The stagnant economy, political instability, and heavy-handed bureaucracy did not attract potential investors from abroad.

In the early 1980s, China embarked on a strategy of using trade as a central component of its drive for economic development. In some ways it followed the model of export-led growth pioneered by Japan and newly industrializing countries (NICs) such as the Republic of Korea (South Korea). This model takes advantage of low-wage domestic labor to produce goods that are in demand internationally. It then uses the earnings from those goods to modernize the economy.

In terms of goods and services, China is now the world's second-largest trading nation behind the United States. China's main exports are office machines, data-processing and telecommunications equipment, clothing and footwear, toys, and sporting goods. It mostly imports industrial machinery, technology and scientific equipment, iron and steel, and raw materials (including oil) needed to support economic development. In 2007, a large number of Chinese goods, including pet food, seafood, toys, and tires were recalled from the American market because of health and safety concerns. This reflected both the enormous growth of China as a key part of the global factory of the twenty-first century and the lack of effective regulation in many sectors of China part-command, part-market economy.

The U.S. Connection

Sino*–American Relations

China and the United States were allies during World War II. At that time, the Chinese government was controlled by the pro-American Nationalist Party of Chiang Kai-shek. The United States supported Chiang and the Nationalists in the civil war against the Chinese Communist Party. When the CCP took power and established the People's Republic of China in 1949, Sino-American relations plunged into a period of Cold War hostility that lasted for more than two decades.

The United States continued to support Chiang and the Nationalists after they fled to Taiwan and protected Taiwan from an attack by the PRC. China and the United States also fought against each other in the Korean War (1950–1953). That war ended in a stalemate. That is why the Korean peninsula is still divided between a communist North Korea and a democratic, capitalist South Korea.

Furthermore, the PRC was closely allied with its communist big brother, the Soviet Union, America's archenemy, for much of the 1950s. Relations between Moscow and Beijing soured in the early 1960s, and the two communist powers became ideological rivals. But China and the United States still saw each other as enemies, and, for example, backed different sides in the Vietnam War.

In the early 1970s, Sino-American relations began to warm up. Each country saw the Soviets as its main enemy and decided to cooperate with each other in order to weaken their common foe. In 1972, Richard Nixon became the first U.S. president to visit the People's Republic (in fact, he was the first U.S. president ever to visit China). Formal diplomatic relations between Washington and Beijing were established in 1978. Since then, economic, cultural, and even military ties have deepened, despite some disruptions, such as following the Tiananmen massacre in 1989, and recurring tensions over Taiwan, Tibet, trade, human rights, and other issues. Many scholars and diplomats believe that U.S.-China relations are the most important bilateral relationship in the post–Cold War world.

Economic relations between China and the United States are particularly important and complex. China now trades with the United States more than it does with any other country, while China is America's third-largest trading partner (after Canada and Mexico). The United States imports far more from China than it exports (over $200 billion dollars more). Wal-Mart alone buys about $20 billion of goods from China. Wal-Mart also runs over sixty stores in China and recently bought a chain that will add another hundred.

There are many people in the United States who think that importing such a huge quantity of "cheap" products from China means lost jobs and lower wages for Americans. They argue that American firms can't compete with Chinese companies because labor costs in China are so much lower. They also say that China engages in unfair trade practices, exploits sweat-shop labor, and suppresses independent union activity. Since exports are so vital to the PRC's economic growth, they conclude that America's huge trade deficit with China indirectly helps keep the Chinese Communist Party in power. They want the United States government to put more restrictions on trade with China, particularly on imports.

On the other side, there are those who say that the benefits of U.S. trade with China far outweigh the negative impacts. First of all, consumers benefit greatly by the availability of a large variety of less-expensive products. Furthermore, in their view, the United States should focus on developing more high-tech businesses to create jobs rather than trying to compete with China and other countries in "old-fashioned" labor-intensive industries. They point out that many American firms have huge investments in China, which will grow—as will demand for American products—as that country becomes more modern and prosperous. Chinese investments in the United States and the PRC's purchase of several hundred billion dollars worth of U.S. government bonds has helped keep inflation low and the economy growing in the United States. Finally, the pro-China trade side argues that Sino-American economic engagement is one important way to promote not only the free market in China but also a more open society and democracy. ❖

**Sino* is a term derived from Latin that is often used to refer to China. For example, scholars who specialize in the study of China are "sinologists." Sino-American relations is another way of saying United States–China relations.

Foreign investment in the PRC has also skyrocketed. China is now one of the world's largest targets of foreign direct investment. Each year tens of billions of dollars are invested in tens of thousands of businesses and projects. More than 400 of the world's 500 top corporations have operations in the PRC. Foreign firms operating in China generally pay their workers considerably more than the average wage of about 60 cents per hour in Chinese-owned factories. But the low cost of labor in China is still a major attraction to investors from abroad.

Another lure to foreign investment is the huge Chinese domestic market. As incomes rise, corporations like Coca-Cola, General Motors, Starbucks, and Wal-Mart have poured vast amounts of money into China. American tobacco companies are hoping that China's 350 million smokers can make up for sharply declining cigarette sales in the United States. In 2005, Philip Morris signed an agreement with a Chinese company to jointly produce Marlboros (2 billion in the first year!) to be sold in China.

China is itself becoming a major investor in other countries. In a sign of how far the PRC has come as a world economic power, the Chinese company, the Lenovo Group, bought IBM's personal computer business in late 2004 and is now actively marketing its machines in the United States and elsewhere.

China occupies an important, but somewhat contradictory, position in the global economy. On the one hand, the PRC's relatively low level of economic and technological development makes it very much a part of the Third World. On the other hand, the total output and rapid growth of its economy, expanding trade, and vast resource base (including its population) make it a rising economic superpower among nations.

Summary

During the Maoist era (1949–1976), the communist party-state thoroughly dominated the economy. It did this both through a system of central planning in which government bureaucrats determined economic policies and by radical politics that suppressed any kind of private economic activity as counterrevolutionary. This approach achieved some success in promoting industrialization and raising the educational and health standards of the Chinese people. But, overall, it left China as a very poor country with little involvement in the global economy. Under Deng Xiaoping and his successors, the party-state has given up much of its control of the economy and encouraged free market forces, private ownership, international trade, and foreign investment. Living standards, modernization, and globalization have all increased dramatically. But serious problems challenge China's current leaders. For example, there is enormous inequality between city and countryside. More than 150 million people have moved from the rural to urban areas. Health care and other social services have collapsed in many parts of the country. The environment has been badly damaged. The government is now showing concern about these downsides to China's economic miracle. It remains to be seen how this concern will be translated into action.

SECTION 3 Governance and Policy-Making

FOCUS QUESTIONS

What are the most important features of a communist party-state as a type of political system?

What is the relationship between the government of the People's Republic of China and the CCP?

How does the CCP justify its continuing rule?

Organization of the State

The People's Republic of China, Cuba, Vietnam, North Korea, and Laos are the only remaining communist party-states in the world. Like the Soviet Union before its collapse in 1991, the political systems of these countries are characterized by Communist Party domination of all state (or government) institutions; that is why they are called "party-states"). Such political systems also have an official state ideology based on Marxism-Leninism, and, to varying and changing degrees, government control of key aspects of the economy. Ruling communist parties assert that only they can govern in the best interests of the entire nation. Therefore they claim the right to exercise what is called the "leading role" throughout society. Political opposition is not permitted in communist party-states.

The government of communist party-states like China is organizationally and functionally distinct from the Communist Party. But the government essentially acts as the administrative agency for carrying out and enforcing policies made by the party. The Communist Party exercises direct or indirect control over all government organizations and personnel. High-ranking government officials with any substantive authority are also members of the Communist Party.

Ideology is an important feature of a communist party-state. Despite China's sharp move toward a market economy, the CCP still asserts that it is building socialism in China with the ultimate objective of creating an egalitarian and classless communist society. It claims to be guided by the fundamental principles of Marxism-Leninism. Marxism refers to the part of communist ideology based on the writing of Karl Marx (1818–1883) that is centrally concerned with economic exploitation of the poor working classes (the "proletariat") by the rich property owners (the "capitalists"). Leninism refers to the theories developed by the Russian revolutionary, Vladimir Lenin (1870–1924) who founded the Soviet Union. It emphasizes how the proletariat should be organized and led by a communist party to seize political power from the capitalists.

The CCP says that Mao Zedong made a highly original and significant contribution to communist ideology. He adapted Marxism-Leninism, which had evolved in Europe and Russia, to China's special circumstances. In particular he emphasized the peasant-based revolution that brought the communist party to power in China. The party continues to praise Mao and what they call "Mao Zedong Thought." But they acknowledge that Mao made serious mistakes, such as in his views about class struggle that led to the Cultural Revolution.

Chinese communist ideology has continued to develop in ways that reflect the priorities of the leadership. In 1997, the CCP added "Deng Xiaoping Theory" to its official ideology. This reflected Deng's use of market forces to promote the economy in a socialist country led by a communist party. In 2002, when Jiang Zemin retired as general secretary, his ideas (called the "Three Represents") about expanding the CCP to incorporate all sectors of Chinese society, including owners of private businesses, became part of the party's core ideology. And, in 2007, party leader Hu Jintao's goals for creating a "harmonious society" were added to the CCP constitution and referred to as "the Scientific Outlook on Development."

The focus of Chinese communism, in both theory and practice, has shifted from revolutionary change to economic development. But most people in China have lost faith in communist ideology because of the CCP's erratic and repressive leadership. Or else they simply consider it largely irrelevant to their daily lives. Many of those who join the party now do so mainly for career advancement. But the latest Chinese communist variant of Marxism-Leninism still provides the framework for governance and policy-making. And it sets the boundaries for what is permissible in politics.

The underlying organizing principles of China's party-state appear in the constitution of the People's Republic (which is a separate document from the party constitution). The preamble of the PRC constitution repeatedly declares that the country is under "the leadership of the Communist Party of China." Article 1 defines the PRC as "a socialist state under the people's democratic dictatorship." It declares that "disruption of the socialist system by any organization or individual is prohibited." Such provisions imply that the Chinese "people" (implicitly, supporters of socialism and the leadership of the party) enjoy democratic rights and privileges. But the constitution also gives the CCP authority to exercise dictatorship over any person or organization that, it believes, opposes socialism and the party.

China's constitution is less a governing document of enduring principles than a political statement. Constitutional change (from minor amendments to total replacement) during the last fifty years has reflected the shifting political winds in China. The character and content of the state constitution in force at any given time bear the ideological stamp of the prevailing party leadership. The constitution of the Mao era stressed the importance of continuing the revolution and class struggle while the current one emphasizes national unity in the pursuit of economic development and modernization.

The Executive

FOCUS QUESTIONS

What are the most powerful executive positions and organizations in the PRC and the CCP?

What is the relationship between government and party executives?

The government of the People's Republic of China and the Chinese Communist Party have separate, but connected executive offices and organizations. The party executive is clearly the more powerful.

The Party Executive

According to the constitution of the Chinese Communist Party, the "highest leading bodies" of the party are the National Party Congress and the Central Committee (see Figure 9.3). But the National Party Congress meets for only one week every five years, and it has more than 2,200 delegates. This means that the role of the Congress is more symbolic than substantive. The essential function of the National Party Congress is to approve decisions already made by the top leaders and to provide a showcase for the party's current policies. There is little debate about policy and no contested voting of any consequence. The party congress

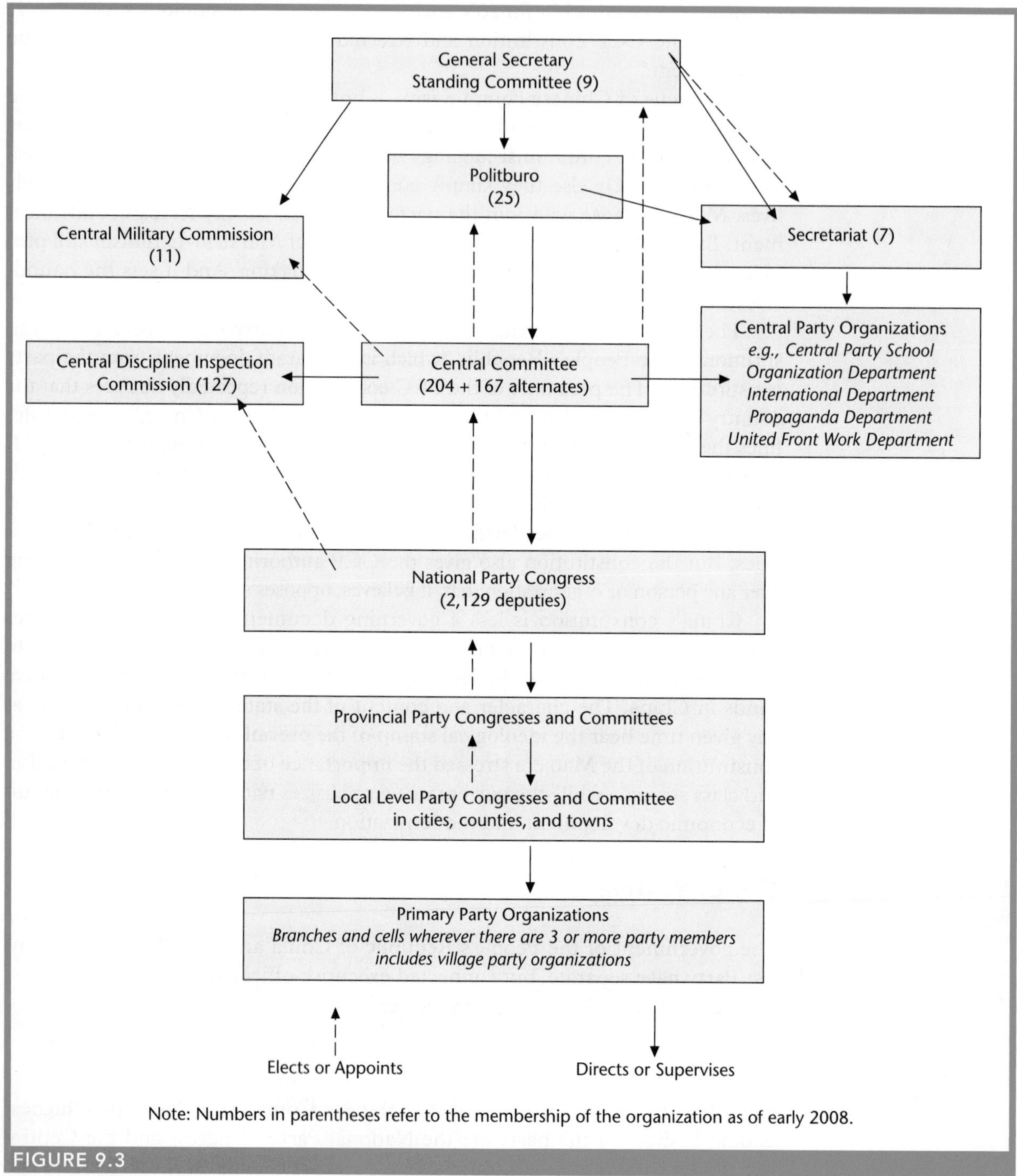

FIGURE 9.3

Organization of the Chinese Communist Party (73 million)

does not function as a legislative check or balance of the power of the party's executive leadership.

The Central Committee (currently 204 full members and 167 alternates) is the next level up in the pyramid of party power. It consists of CCP leaders from around the country who meet annually for about a week. Members are elected for a five-year term by the National Party Congress by secret ballot, with a limited choice of candidates. Contending party factions may jockey to win seats, but the overall composition of the Central Committee is closely controlled by the top leaders to ensure compliance with their policies.

In theory, the Central Committee directs party affairs when the National Party Congress is not in session. But its size and short, infrequent meetings (called plenums) also greatly limit its effectiveness. However, Central Committee plenums and occasional informal work conferences do represent significant gatherings of the party elite. They can be a very important arena of political maneuvering and decision making.

The most powerful political organizations in China's communist party-state are the two small executive bodies at the very top of the CCP's structure: the Politburo (or Political Bureau) and its even more exclusive Standing Committee. These bodies are elected by the Central Committee from among its own members under carefully controlled and secretive conditions. The current Politburo has twenty-five members. Nine of them also belong to the Standing Committee, the formal apex of power in the CCP.

People who study Chinese politics scrutinize the membership of the Politburo and Standing Committee for clues about leadership priorities, the balance of power among party factions, and the relative influence of different groups in policy-making. Seven of the nine members of the Standing Committee elected in 2007 and about half of the members of the Politburo were trained as engineers before beginning political careers. Almost all the other members of the top leadership have university degrees in business, law, the social sciences, or the humanities. This is dramatic evidence of the shift in China's ruling circles from the revolutionary leaders of Mao's and Deng's generations to college-educated technocrats who place the highest priority on science and technology as the keys to the country's development. No wonder China's government is sometimes called a "technocracy": Time.com once even referred to the rise to power of the engineers and other well-educated leaders in China as "The Revenge of the Nerds" since intellectuals and technical specialists were persecuted during the Maoist era.[7]

The Politburo and Standing Committee are not responsible to the Central Committee or any other institution in any meaningful sense. The operations of these organizations are generally shrouded in secrecy. Key leaders work and often live in a huge walled compound called Zhongnanhai ("Middle Southern Sea") on a lake in the center of Beijing quite near the Forbidden City that once housed China's emperors. Zhongnanhai is not only heavily guarded as any government executive headquarters would be, but it also has no identifying signs on its exterior, nor does it appear on any public maps.

Profile
Hu Jintao

China's current president and Communist Party leader, Hu Jintao, is, in many ways, typical of the kind of people who now lead the country. For a Chinese leader, he was relatively young (60) when he assumed power in 2002–2003. He is also well-educated and had a more-or-less smooth rise to the top up the party career ladder. He fits the definition of a "technocrat," a term often used to describe China's current generation of leaders who have backgrounds in technical fields and spent most of their working lives as bureaucrats within the Chinese Communist Party.

Hu was born into a family of tea merchants in 1942, and grew up in a small city in the central coastal province of Jiangsu, not far from Shanghai. He was just six years old when the Chinese Communist Party came to power. Hu did very well in school and attended Qinghua University, China's best school of science and technology, where he studied hydroelectric engineering. He joined the Communist Party while at Qinghua. He graduated in 1965. This was right before the start of Chairman Mao's Great Proletarian Cultural Revolution, a period of political and social chaos when China's universities were shut down as part of the campaign to destroy those who were seen as enemies of Chinese Communist Party.

Hu Jintao did not participate as a Red Guard in the Cultural Revolution. But he did witness a lot of violence, and his father was persecuted for being a "capitalist" and imprisoned. This experience is one influence that made Hu turn against the kind of radical communism preached by Chairman Mao.

In the late 1960s, Hu was among the millions of young people sent to the rural areas and the frontier as part of their revolutionary education. He spent about a decade living and working in the poor, remote desert province of Gansu in China's far west. At first he did manual labor in housing construction, but he was transferred to work in the provincial ministry of water resources and electric power because of his high level of specialized training. It was then that he also became actively involved in Communist Party politics.

In Gansu, Hu formed a close relationship with the top party official in the province—also a Qinghua University graduate—who became a member of the CCP's powerful Standing Committee after Deng Xiaoping had consolidated his power as China's dominant leader in the early 1980s. Hu's political career rose with that of his mentor—a good example of the importance of *guanxi* ("connections") in Chinese politics. He was given the critical opportunity to study at the Central Party School in Beijing, which is a training ground for the CCP's future elite. He became a specialist in youth affairs and rose to the position of head of the Communist Youth League.

Hu was then appointed to be Communist Party leader in Guizhou province and Tibet. These appointments gave him an unusual amount of experience in areas of the country inhabited by large numbers of China's minorities (see Section 4). When he was the party leader in Tibet, he imposed **martial law** to suppress demonstrations in favor of Tibetan independence. In 1992, he joined the CCP Secretariat, a key group that manages the party leadership's day-to-day work. In the late 1990s, he became a member of the powerful Standing Committee and China's vice-president. He also emerged as Deng Xiaoping's choice to succeed Jiang Zemin as head of the Communist Party and country. The fact that Deng could anoint not only his successor, but also his successor's successor reflected both the extent of Deng's personal power and the informal means by which such important decisions are made in China.

Hu Jintao became general secretary of the Chinese Communist Party in 2002 (re-elected in 2007) and president of the People's Republic of China in 2003 (re-elected in 2008). Like Deng and Jiang, he has been committed both to promoting rapid economic growth and free market reforms and to maintaining the rule of the Communist Party. He has also proclaimed that his goal for China is to create a "harmonious society" that pays more attention to problems like growing inequality, rural poverty, and pollution that have accompanied the PRC's rapid development. In late 2007, the meeting of the National Congress of the Chinese Communist Party (held every five years) was a showcase for Hu's power and policies, and his "Scientific Outlook on Development" was added to the party's constitution as the CCP's current guiding version of Marxism-Leninism. ❖

martial law a period of time during which the normal procedures of government are suspended and the executive branch enforces the law with military power.

The party's top leader is the general secretary, who presides over the Politburo and the Standing Committee. Jiang Zemin (1989–2002) and Hu Jintao (2002–present) have held this position most recently. Neither Jiang nor Hu have had the personal clout or charisma of either Deng or Mao. They have governed as part of a collective leadership that included their fellow members on the Standing Committee and Politburo. Nevertheless, both have tried to put their own stamp on the party's major policy direction.

Below the national level, the CCP has a hierarchy of local party organizations in provinces, cities, and counties, each headed by a party secretary and party committee. There are also more than 3.5 million primary party organizations, called branches. These are found throughout the country in workplaces, government offices, schools, urban neighborhoods, rural towns, villages, and army units where there are three or more party members. Local and primary organizations extend the CCP's reach throughout Chinese society. They are also designed to ensure coordination within the vast and complex party structure and subordination to the central party authorities in Beijing.

The Government Executive

Government authority in China is formally vested in a system of people's congresses that begins at the top with the National People's Congress (NPC), which is a completely different organization than the National *Party* Congress. The NPC is China's national legislature and is discussed in more detail in Section 4. There are also people's congresses at the subnational levels of government, including provincial people's congresses, city people's congresses, and rural township people's congresses (see Figure 9.4). In theory, these congresses (the legislative branch) are empowered to supervise the work of the "people's governments" (the executive branch) at the various levels of the system. But in reality, government executives (such as cabinet ministers, provincial governors, and mayors) are more accountable to party authority than to the people's congresses. For example, the city of Shanghai has both a mayor and a party secretary, each with distinct and important powers. But the party secretary's power is more consequential.

The National People's Congress formally elects the president and vice president of China. But there is only one candidate, chosen by the Communist Party, for each office. The president's term is concurrent with that of the congress (five years). There is a two-term limit. The position is largely ceremonial, although a senior Communist Party leader has always held it. As China's head of state, the president meets and negotiates with other world leaders. Both Jiang Zemin and Hu Jintao served concurrently as CCP general secretary and PRC president.

The premier (prime minister) has authority over the government bureaucracy and policy implementation. The premier is formally appointed by the president with the approval of the National People's Congress. But in reality,

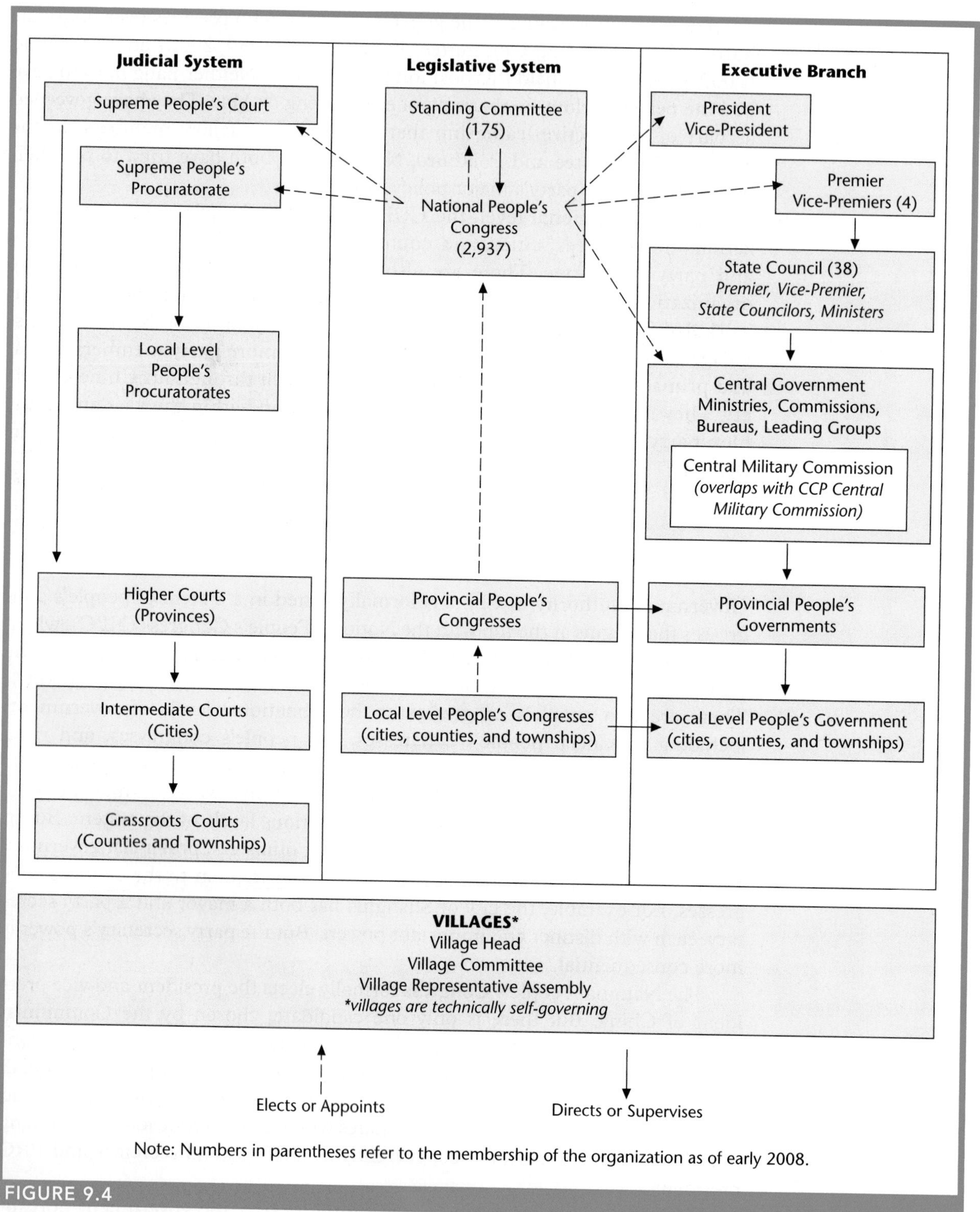

FIGURE 9.4

Organization of the Government of the People's Republic of China (PRC)

The Chinese Communist Party Standing Committee. *(Source: Ng Han Guan/AP Images)*

the Communist Party decides who will serve as premier. A very high-ranking member of the CCP Standing Committee has always held that post. Like the president, the premier may serve only two five-year terms. The current premier, Wen Jiabao, was trained as a geological engineer and is another good example of the technocrats who now run China.

The premier directs the State Council, which is constitutionally "the highest organ of state administration" (Article 85) in the PRC. It functions much like the cabinet in a parliamentary system. It includes the premier, a few vice premiers, the heads of government ministries and commissions, and several other senior officials. The National People's Congress appoints the State Council, although its membership is determined by the party leadership.

State Council ministers run either functionally specific departments, such as the Ministry of Health, or organizations with more comprehensive responsibilities, such as the State Commission of Science, Technology and Industry for National Defense. Beneath the State Council is an array of support staffs, research offices, and bureaucratic agencies charged with policy implementation.

cadre a person who occupies a position of authority in a communist party–state; cadres may or may not be Communist Party members.

China's bureaucracy is immense in size and in the scope of its reach throughout the country. The total number of **cadres**—people in positions of authority paid by the government or party—in the PRC is around 40 million. A minority of these cadres work directly for the government or the CCP. The remainder occupy key posts in economic enterprises (such as factory directors); schools (such as principals); and scientific, cultural, and other state-run institutions. There have been important moves toward professionalizing the bureaucracy, particularly at the city level of government. More official positions are now subject to competition through civil service exams rather than the still-prevalent method of appointment from above.

One of the most significant administrative reforms of the post-Mao era—quite unprecedented in a communist party-state—has been to take measures to limit how long officials can stay in their jobs. Depending on their position, both government and party cadres must now retire between the ages of sixty and seventy. A two-term limit has been set for all top cadres.

FOCUS QUESTIONS

What are the most important features of China's military, police, legal system, and local government?

How and why does the CCP closely supervise these state institutions?

Other State Institutions

The Military, the Police, and the Judiciary

The China's People's Liberation Army (PLA) encompasses all the country's ground, air, and naval armed services. It is the world's largest military force, with about 2.3 million active personnel. The PLA also has a formal reserve of another 1 million or so and a backup people's militia of 12 to 15 million, which could be mobilized in the event of war. The level of training and weaponry available to the militia are generally minimal.

The PRC has increased military spending by double-digit percentages nearly every year for more than a decade (18 percent in 2007) in order to modernize its armed forces and raise the pay of military personnel. China said that it spent $45 billion on defense in 2007. Many analysts think that the PRC vastly understates its defense budget. They estimate that it is really closer to two or three times the official figures. Still, China spends much less in total and vastly less per capita on military expenditures than does the United States, which spent over $500 billion on defense in 2007.

The key organizations in charge of the Chinese armed forces are the Military Commissions (CMC) of the CCP and PRC. On paper, these are two distinct organizations. In fact, they overlap entirely in membership and function. The chair of the state Military Commission is "elected" by the National People's Congress, but is always the same person as the chair of the party CMC. The CMC chair is, in effect, the commander-in-chief of China's armed forces. This position has almost always been held by the most powerful party leader. Hu Jintao is the current chair of China's Central Military Commission.

China's internal security apparatus consists of several different organizations. The Ministry of State Security is responsible for combating espionage and gathering intelligence at home and abroad. A 1.5-million-strong People's Armed Police guards public officials and buildings and carries out some border patrol and protection. It also quells serious public disturbances, including worker or peasant unrest. The Ministry of Public Security is responsible for the maintenance of law and order, the investigation of crimes, and the surveillance of Chinese citizens and foreigners in China suspected of being a threat to the state. Local Public Security Bureaus are under the command of central ministry authorities in Beijing. In effect, China has a national police force stationed throughout the country. There are also local police forces, but they do little more than supervise traffic.

In addition to a regular prison system, the Ministry of Public Security maintains an extensive system of labor reform camps for people convicted of particularly serious crimes, including political ones. These camps, which are noted for their harsh conditions and remote locations, are estimated to have millions of prisoners. Public Security Bureaus have the authority to detain indefinitely people suspected of committing a crime without making a formal charge. They can also use administrative sanctions (penalties imposed outside the court system) to levy fines or sentence detainees for up to three years of "re-education through labor." A special system of more than 300 camps holds such detainees (estimated at 300,000). They include prostitutes, drug users, and petty criminals, as well as some who might be considered political prisoners.

China's criminal justice system works swiftly and harshly. Great faith is placed in the ability of an official investigation to find the facts of a case. The outcome of cases that actually do come to trial is pretty much predetermined. The conviction rate is 98–99 percent for all criminal cases. Prison terms are long and subject to only cursory appeal. A variety of offenses in addition to murder—including, in some cases, rape and especially major cases of embezzlement and other "economic crimes"—are subject to capital punishment. All death penalty sentences must be approved by the country's Supreme Court. But such appeals are handled very quickly. Capital punishment cases do not linger in the courts for years, or even months. Execution is usually by a single bullet in the back of the convicted person's head, although the country is moving toward lethal injection. Amnesty International said that China led the world in the application of the death penalty in 2006, with about 1100 executions that it could verify, followed by Iran (177), Pakistan (82), Iraq (65), Sudan (61), and the United States (53). However, death penalty statistics are officially a state secret in the PRC, and Amnesty estimates that the actual number of executions in China was in the 7000–8000 range.

China has a four-tiered "people's court" system. It reaches from a Supreme People's Court down through higher (provincial-level), intermediate (city-level), and grassroots (county- and township-level) people's courts. The Supreme People's Court supervises the lower courts and the application of the country's laws. It hears few cases and does not exercise judicial review over government policies.

There are now more than 100,000 lawyers in China (compared to about a million in the United States). Legal advisory offices throughout the country provide citizens and organizations with legal assistance. Many laws and regulations have been enacted, including new criminal and civil codes, to make the legal system much fairer than it was during the Maoist period.

Although the PRC constitution guarantees judicial independence, China's courts and other legal bodies remain under party control. The appointment of judicial personnel is subject to party approval. The CCP is still able to bend the law to serve its interests. Legal reform in China has been undertaken because China's leaders are well aware that economic development requires detailed laws, professional lawyers and judicial personnel, predictable legal processes, and binding documents such as contracts.

Subnational Government

China is not a federal system (like Brazil, Germany, India, Nigeria, and the United States) that gives subnational governments considerable policy-making autonomy. Provincial and local authorities in the PRC operate "under the unified leadership of the central authorities" (Article 3 of the state constitution). This makes China a unitary state like France and Japan. The national government in Beijing exercises a high degree of control over other levels of government.

There are four main layers of state structure beneath the central government in China: provinces, cities, counties, and rural towns. There are also four very large centrally administered cities (Beijing, Shanghai, Tianjin, and Chongqing) and five autonomous regions (areas of the country with large minority populations, such as Tibet and Mongolia). Each of these levels has a representative people's congress that meets infrequently, and plays a limited, but increasingly active, role in managing affairs in its area. Executive officials, such as governors and mayors, have much greater authority than they did in the recent past, but they, too, are always subject to supervision by the central government and the Communist Party organization at their level.

Beneath the formal layers of state administration are China's 700,000 or so rural villages. These are home to the majority of the country's population. These villages, with an average population of roughly 500–1,000 each, are technically self-governing and are not formally responsible to a higher level of state authority. In recent years, village leaders have been directly and competitively elected by local residents. Village representative assemblies have become more vocal. These trends have brought an important degree of grass-roots democracy to village government (see Section 4). However, the most powerful organization in the village is the Communist Party committee, and the single most powerful person is the local Communist Party leader (the party secretary).

FOCUS QUESTIONS

How does the CCP exercise control of the policy-making process?

What other factors influence the policy-making process in China?

The Policy-Making Process

Political power in China has become much more decentralized and institutionalized than during the Maoist era. Policies now evolve from a complex process of cooperation, conflict, and bargaining among actors and organizations at various levels of the system. Provincial and local governments have a lot more clout in the policy process. The national focus on economic development has also given growing influence to nonparty experts and organizations in the policy loop.

Nevertheless the Chinese Communist Party still ultimately controls policy-making in China. The top two dozen or so party leaders wield nearly unchecked power. The CCP uses a weblike system of organizational controls to make sure that the government bureaucracy complies with the party's will in policy implementation Almost all key government officials (such a mayors and provincial governors) are also party members. Various party organizations keep a careful eye on government agencies. The CCP exercises control over appointments to millions of positions in the government and elsewhere, including universities, banks, trade unions, and newspapers.

In recent years, "leading small groups" have become very important in policy-making at the national level. These groups are made up of leaders from different organizations who coordinate decision making on important issues that may cut across bureaucratic boundaries. Some are more-or-less permanent, such as the National Security Leading Small Group, while others are set up to deal with a short-term crisis, like a natural disaster or an epidemic. Since most of the members are high-ranking CCP officials, they are also meant to insure party supervision of policy in that particular area.

guanxi a Chinese term that means "connections" or "relationships," and describes personal ties between individuals based on such things as common birthplace or mutual acquaintances.

Any account of the policy process in China must also note the importance of ***guanxi*** ("connections"). These are personal relationships and mutual obligations based on family, friendship, school, military, professional, or other ties. The notion of *guanxi* has its roots in China's traditional Confucian culture. It has long been an important part of political, social, and economic life. In the bureaucracy, personal ties are often the key to getting things done. *Guanxi* can either cut red tape and increase efficiency or stiffen organizational rigidity and feed corruption.

The power of the Communist Party is the most basic fact of political life in the People's Republic of China. But the policy-making process still "wriggles with politics" of many kinds, both formal and informal.[8] It is important to look at how various influences, including policy disagreements, bureaucratic interests, *guanxi*, and even citizen input (discussed in the next section) shape the decisions ultimately made by Communist Party leaders and organizations.

Summary

China is a communist party-state. It is one of the few remaining countries in the world that is still ruled by a communist party. Even though the Chinese Communist Party (CCP) has moved China in the direction of a capitalist, free market economy, it proclaims that it is following communist ideology (Marxism-Leninism) and that its goal is to create a socialist China. The CCP insists that it is the only political party that can lead the country toward this goal, and it prohibits any serious challenge to its authority. Power in China is highly concentrated in the top two dozen or so leaders of the Communist Party, presided over by the general secretary of the CCP, who are chosen through secretive inner-party procedures. The government of the People's Republic of China (the "state") is technically separate from the CCP, and political reform in China has brought a degree of autonomy to government institutions, such as the national legislature and the judiciary. But, in fact, the state operates only under the close supervision of the Communist Party and almost all high-ranking government officials are also members of the Communist Party.

SECTION 4

Representation and Participation

socialist democracy the term used by the Chinese Communist Party to describe the political system of the People's Republic of China.

The People's Republic of China says that it is a **socialist democracy** under the leadership of the Chinese Communist Party, which is, in turn, said to represent the interests of the overwhelming majority of the people. Socialist democracy is claimed by the PRC to be different from democracy in capitalist countries like the United States where big business and the rich are able to influence politics in their favor to the disadvantage of working people.

Although power in China is highly concentrated in the hands of the top leaders of the Chinese Communist Party, representation and participation do play important, if limited, roles in the China's political system. Legislatures, elections, and organizations like labor unions provide citizens with ways of influencing public policy-making and the selection of some government leaders.

FOCUS QUESTIONS

What powers does the National People's Congress have? How does the CCP control the NPC?

In what ways is it becoming more active and independent?

The Legislature

China's constitution grants the National People's Congress (NPC) the power to enact and amend the country's laws, approve and monitor the state budget, and declare and end war. The NPC is also empowered to elect (and recall) the president and vice president, the chair of the state Central Military Commission, the head of China's Supreme Court, and the procurator-general (something like the U.S. attorney general). The NPC has final approval over the selection of the premier and members of the State Council. On paper, China's legislature certainly looks to be the most powerful branch of government. In fact, these powers, which are not insignificant, are exercised only as allowed by the Communist Party.

The National People's Congress is elected for a five-year term and meets for only about two weeks every March. There are nearly 3,000 members (called "deputies") in the NPC. Deputies are not full-time legislators, but remain in their regular jobs and home areas except for the brief time when the congress is in session. All deputies, except those from the People's Liberation Army, are chosen on a geographic basis from China's provinces, autonomous regions, and major municipalities. There are representatives from China's two indirectly ruled Special Administrative Regions, the tiny former Portuguese colony and now gambling haven of Macau and the former British colony and now bustling commercial city of Hong Kong. To symbolize China's claim to Taiwan, deputies representing the island are chosen from among PRC residents with Taiwanese ancestry or other ties.

About 73 percent of the deputies elected in 2003 were members of the CCP. The others belonged to one of China's eight noncommunist (and powerless) political parties (see below) or had no party affiliation.

Workers and farmers made up about 18 percent of the deputies elected in 2003. Intellectuals and professionals made up another 21 percent. Government and party cadres accounted for a little under a third. Nine percent were from the

Hong Kong: From China to Britain—and Back Again

Hong Kong became a British colony in three stages during the nineteenth century as a result of what China calls the "unequal treaties" imposed under military and diplomatic pressure from the West following the Opium War. Two parts of Hong Kong were given *permanently* to Britain in 1842 and 1860. But the largest part of the small territory was given to Britain in 1898 with a ninety-nine-year lease. The anticipated expiration of that lease led to negotiations between London and Beijing in the 1980s. In December 1984, Britain agreed to return all of Hong Kong to Chinese sovereignty on July 1, 1997. On that date, Hong Kong became a Special Administrative Region (SAR) of the People's Republic of China.

Britain ruled Hong Kong for more than one hundred years in a traditional, if generally benevolent, colonial fashion. A governor from London presided over an administration in which British rather than local people exercised most of the power. There was a free press, a fair and effective legal system, and other important features of a democratic system. In the last years of their rule, the British appointed more Hong Kong Chinese to higher administrative positions. They also expanded the scope of elections for choosing some members of the colony's executive and representative bodies. The British, were criticized for taking steps toward democratization only on the eve of their departure from the colony. They allowed only a small number of Hong Kong residents to emigrate to the United Kingdom before the start of Chinese rule.

Hong Kong flourished economically under the free-market policies of the British. It became one of the world's great centers of international trade and finance. It now has the highest standard of living in Asia other than Singapore. Hong Kong is also characterized by extremes of wealth and poverty. When China took over Hong Kong in 1997, it pledged not to impose its political or economic system on the SAR for fifty years. The PRC has a strong motivation not to do anything that might destroy the area's economic dynamism.

Although the PRC took over full control of Hong Kong's foreign policy and has stationed troops of the People's Liberation Army in Hong Kong, Beijing has generally fulfilled its promise that the SAR will have a high degree of political as well as economic autonomy. Civil liberties, the independence of the judiciary, and freedom of the press have largely been maintained.

Nevertheless, China has made sure that it keeps a grip on power in Hong Kong. The SAR is headed by a chief executive, who along with other top civil servants must be approved by the PRC. Politicians favoring democracy in Hong Kong have a strong presence in the SAR's elected legislature, but the legislature itself is relatively powerless to make policy. In a telling example of the tug of war over the direction of Hong Kong's political future, the PRC's plan to implement a law prohibiting "any act of treason, secession, sedition, subversion against the Central People's Government [in Beijing], or theft of state secrets" was withdrawn in 2004 after large-scale protests by those who worry that British colonialism in Hong Kong might be replaced by Chinese authoritarianism. ❖

Hong Kong

Land area	401.5 sq mi/1,092 sq km (about six times the size of Washington, D.C.)
Population	7 million
Ethnic composition	Chinese, 95%; other, 5%
GDP at purchasing power parity (US$)	$293 billion, which ranks it 41st in the world and close to Austria and Norway
GDP per capita at purchasing power parity (US$)	$42,000, which ranks it above Switzerland and Canada

military. The remainder represented other occupational categories, such as business people. These numbers reflect the NPC's shift of emphasis from representing the working classes to taking economic development as its top priority. Women made up 20 percent of NPC deputies and ethnic minorities 14 percent.

Despite great fanfare in the press as examples of socialist democracy at work, legislation is passed and state leaders are elected in the National People's Congress by overwhelming majorities and little substantive debate. Nevertheless, some dissent does occur. In 1992, about a third of NPC deputies either voted against or abstained from voting on the hugely expensive ($70 billion) and ecologically controversial Three Gorges dam project now nearing completion on the Yangtze River. On very rare occasions, government legislative initiatives have even been defeated or tabled. But the NPC never takes up politically sensitive issues. The CCP also monitors the election process to make sure that no outright dissidents are elected as deputies.

Legislatures in communist party-states used to be called rubber stamps, meaning they automatically and without question approved party policies. But as economics has replaced ideology as the main motivation of China's leaders, the NPC has become a much more significant and lively part of the Chinese political system. Many NPC deputies are now chosen because of their ability to contribute to China's modernization rather than simply on the basis of political loyalty. Some have even become more assertive on issues like corruption and environmental problems. Debate and discussion can influence the final shape of legislation. The NPC is still not part of an independent branch of government in a system of checks and balances; but it also is no longer merely a rubber stamp of the Chinese Communist Party.

Political Parties and the Party System

FOCUS QUESTIONS

How has the CCP changed over time? How has it adapted to China's emphasis on economic development and modernization? What role do China's noncommunist parties play?

The Chinese Communist Party

With about 73 million members, the CCP is by far the largest political party in the world. But its membership makes up a very small minority of the population (about 8 percent of those over eighteen, the minimum age for joining the party). This is consistent with the party's view that it is a "vanguard" party that admits only those who are truly dedicated to the communist cause.

The social composition of the CCP's membership has changed considerably since the party came to power in 1949. In the mid-1950s, peasants made up nearly 70 percent. In 2007, "farmers, herdsmen, and fishermen" made up 31 percent of party members, while only 10.8 percent were industrial workers. The majority of CCP members are party-state officials, office workers, enterprise managers, military personnel, and professionals, including scientists, technical experts, and academics. The party now claims that rather than representing just workers and peasants, it represents the interests of the overwhelming majority of people in China and is open to all those who are committed to promoting national development and are willing to accept party leadership in achieving that goal.

The CCP has recently encouraged owners and employees of private businesses ("entrepreneurs") to join the party. It has also established party organizations in many private firms. This is quite a change from the Maoist era when any hint of capitalism was crushed. It is also recognition of the increasing importance of the private sector in China's economy. It is a strategy by which the party hopes to prolong its rule by adapting to a rapidly modernizing society.

Women make up only 20 percent of the CCP membership as a whole and just 6 percent of full members of the Central Committee (and 14 percent of alternates) elected in 2007. The Politburo has one female member, Liu Yandong, who has extensive experience working with youth and noncommunist organizations to help them articulate their interests and to make sure that they stay in line with party policies. No women serve on the party's most powerful organization, the Politburo Standing Committee.

Even though many Chinese believe that communist ideology is irrelevant to their lives and the nation's future, being a party member still provides unparalleled access to influence and resources. It remains a prerequisite for advancement in many careers, particularly in government. More than two million people join the CCP each year, most of them college graduates under the age of thirty-five.

China's Noncommunist "Democratic Parties"

China is usually called a one-party system because the country's politics are so thoroughly dominated by the Chinese Communist Party. In fact, China has eight political parties in addition to the CCP. These are officially referred to as China's "democratic parties," which is said to be another example of socialist democracy in the PRC. Each noncommunist party represents a particular group in Chinese society. For example, the Chinese Party for the Public Interest draws on overseas Chinese who have returned to live in China. But these parties, all of which were established before the founding of the PRC in 1949 and accept the "guidance" of the CCP, have a total membership of only a little over a half a million. They do not contest for power or challenge CCP policy. Their function is to provide advice to the CCP and generate support within their particular constituencies for CCP policies. Individual members of the parties may assume important government positions. But politically these parties are relatively insignificant. They certainly do not function as an opposition to the ruling communist party.

New political parties are not allowed to form. When a group of activists who had been part of the 1989 Tiananmen protests tried to establish a China Democracy Party in 1998 to promote multiparty politics, they were arrested or forced into exile abroad, and the party was banned.

FOCUS QUESTIONS

How are elections carried out in China? How have they become more democratic?

Elections

Elections in the PRC are basically mechanisms to give the communist party-state greater legitimacy by allowing large numbers of citizens to participate in the political process under very controlled circumstances. But elections are becoming a bit more democratic and more important in providing a way for citizens to express their views and hold some officials accountable.

Most elections in China are "indirect." In other words, it is the members of an already elected or established body that elect, mostly from among themselves, those who will serve at the next highest level in the power structure. For example, it is the deputies of a provincial people's congress, not all the eligible citizens of the province, who elect delegates to the National People's Congress.

Direct elections are elections in which all the voters in the relevant area get to cast a ballot for candidates for a particular position. Direct elections are most common in China at the village level, although there have been a few experiments with letting all voters choose officials and representatives at the next rung up the administrative ladder (the township). The authorities have been very cautious in expanding the scope of direct elections. The CCP wants to prevent them from becoming a forum for dissent or a vehicle to form an opposition party. The most powerful positions in the government, such a city mayors and provincial governors, are appointed, not elected.

Many direct and indirect elections now have multiple candidates, with the winner chosen by secret ballot. Any group of more than ten voters can nominate candidates for an election. A significant number of independently nominated candidates have defeated official nominees, although even independent candidates basically have to be approved by the CCP.

The most noteworthy progress toward real democratic representation and participation in China has occurred in the rural villages. Laws implemented since the late 1980s have provided for direct election of village leaders. These elections are generally multicandidate with a secret ballot. Villagers have used them to remove from office leaders they think are incompetent or corrupt.

The village CCP committee closely monitors such grass-roots elections. As noted in the previous section, the most powerful village leader is the head of the local Communist Party, and that is not an elected position. However, in many cases, the Communist Party leader has been chosen to serve simultaneously as the village head in a competitive election. This is often because the Communist Party leader is a well-respected person who has the confidence and support of the villagers. Only 1 percent of the leaders in China's 700,000 villages are women.

Village representative assemblies have members chosen from each household or group of households. The assemblies have taken a more active role in supervising the work of local officials and decision making in matters affecting community finances and welfare. Some outside observers believe such direct grass-roots elections and the representative assemblies are seeds of real democracy. Others believe they are merely a facade to appease international critics and give the rural population a way to express discontent with some officials without challenging the country's fundamental political organization.

Rural residents vote in a village election in China. In recent years, such grassroots democracy has become widespread in the countryside, although it is always closely monitored by the Chinese Communist Party. *(Getty Images)*

Recent electoral reform has certainly increased popular representation and participation in China's government. But elections in the PRC still do not give citizens a means by which they can exercise effective control over the party officials and organizations that have the real power in China's political system. Top Chinese communist leaders, from Mao to now, have repeatedly claimed that multiparty democracy is unsuited to China's traditions and conditions and would lead to chaos. In a major speech in June 2007, Chinese president and Communist Party leader, Hu Jintao, reaffirmed his support for the continuing development of socialist democracy in China, but he also noted "We must uphold the party's leadership" and that "unswervingly upholding the party's basic line is the most reliable safeguard ensuring that our cause is capable of standing the test and potential dangers and that we can smoothly arrive at our destination"[9]

Political Culture, Citizenship, and Identity

FOCUS QUESTIONS

What is replacing communist ideology as a source of values, beliefs, and identity in China?

How is the CCP responding to this change?

How large is China's ethnic minority population, and where do most of them live?

From Communism to Consumerism

Marxism-Leninism is still important in Chinese politics since the Communist Party proclaims that it is China's official ideology. Serious challenges to that ideology or the party are not permitted. The CCP also tries to keep communist ideology viable and visible by continued efforts to influence public opinion and values and limit opposition. For instance, the party ultimately controls the media, the arts, and education.

China's media are much livelier and more open than during the Maoist period when they were totally under CCP domination and did little other than convey party messages. However, freedom of the press is still quite limited.

What is their relationship to the Chinese communist party-state?

Reduced political control of the media has largely meant only the freedom to publish more entertainment news, human interest stories, local coverage, and some nonpolitical investigative journalism in areas that are consistent with party objectives. For example, in the summer of 2007, the news media helped expose the use of slave labor (including many children) in thousands of brick kilns and coal mines in two provinces in central China.

The arts are generally the area of life that has seen the greatest political change in China in recent years. There is much less direct (but not totally absent) censorship. The Chinese film industry has emerged as one of the best in the world.

Educational opportunities have expanded enormously in China since 1949. Primary school enrollment is close to 100 percent of the age-eligible population (ages six to eleven), but it drops to about 75 percent in middle and high school (ages eleven to eighteen) and 20 percent in college. Political study is still a required but now relatively minor part of the curriculum at all levels. Much greater attention goes to urging students to gain the skills and knowledge they need to further their own careers and help China modernize. More than 80 percent of China's students between the ages of seven and fourteen belong to the Young Pioneers, an organization designed to promote good social behavior, community service, patriotism, and loyalty to the party.

Internet access is exploding in China, with more than 200 million users by the end of 2007. Web connections are available even in some quite remote towns. The government worries about the influence of e-mail and electronic information it cannot control. It has blocked access to certain foreign websites and shut down unlicensed cyber cafés, which it likened to opium dens. It has arrested people it has accused of disseminating subversive material over the Internet.

Web access in China is tightly controlled by the licensing of just a few Internet Service Providers. They are responsible for who uses their systems and how. A special state organization, with an estimated 50,000 employees, polices the Internet. The government is investing huge sums to develop (with technical assistance from western companies) stronger firewalls and monitoring systems. Human rights organizations have criticized Microsoft, Yahoo, and Google for agreeing to political restrictions on websites, news sources, chat rooms, and blogs in exchange for the right to do business in China. The Chinese party-state knows that cutting-edge technology is critical to its modernization plans. Even the CCP has its own websites. The party wants citizens to become computer literate. As with so much else in China, however, the party-state wants to define the way and dictate the rules.

Alternative sources of socialization and belief are growing in importance in China. These do not often take expressly political forms, however, because of the threat of repression. In the countryside, peasants have replaced portraits of Mao and other Communist heroes with statues of folk gods and ancestor worship tablets. The influence of extended kinship groups such as clans often outweighs the formal authority of the party in the villages. In the cities, popular culture, including gigantic rock concerts, shapes youth attitudes much more profoundly than party propaganda. Consumerism ("buying things") is probably the most widely shared value in China today. Many observers have spoken of a moral vacuum in the country. This is not uncommon for societies undergoing such rapid, multifaceted change.

Organized religion, which was ferociously suppressed during the Mao era, is attracting an increasing number of adherents. Buddhist temples, Christian churches, and other places of worship operate more freely than they have in decades. However, despite the fact that freedom of religion is guaranteed by the PRC constitution (as is the freedom not to believe in any religion), religious life is strictly controlled and limited to officially approved organizations and venues. Clergy of any religion who defy the authority of the party-state are still imprisoned. Clandestine Christian communities, called house churches, have sprung up in many areas among people who reject the government's control of religious life and are unable to worship in public. Although local officials sometimes tolerate these churches, in numerous cases house church leaders and lay people have been arrested and the private homes where services are held have been bulldozed. The Chinese Catholic Church is prohibited from recognizing the authority of the pope, although there have been recent signs of a thaw between Beijing and the Vatican.

Citizenship and National Identity

The views of China's citizens about what ties them to the state—their sense of national identity—is going through a profound and uncertain transformation. Party leaders realize that most citizens are skeptical or dismissive of communist ideology and that appeals to socialist goals and revolutionary virtues no longer inspire loyalty. The CCP has turned increasingly to patriotic themes to rally the country behind its leadership. The official media put considerable emphasis on the greatness and antiquity of Chinese culture. They send the not-so-subtle message that it is time for China to reclaim its rightful place in the world order—and that only the CCP can lead the nation in achieving this goal.

In the view of some, such officially promoted nationalism could lead to a more aggressive foreign and military policy—especially with the country's growing need for energy resources—toward areas such as the potentially oil-rich South China Sea, where the PRC's historical territorial claims conflict with those of other countries including Vietnam and the Philippines.

It is, of course, the cultural tie of being "Chinese" that is the most powerful collective identity that connects people to the nation. The Chinese people are intensely proud of their ancient culture and long history. Their enthusiasm for hosting the 2008 Olympics in Beijing reflected this cultural pride. They can also be very sensitive about what they consider slights to their national dignity. Many Chinese feel that Japan has not done enough to acknowledge or apologize for the atrocities its army committed in China during World War II. This has been a strain in relations between the two countries and has sometimes led to spontaneous anti-Japanese demonstrations by Chinese students.

China's Non-Chinese Citizens

The PRC calls itself a multinational state with fifty-six officially recognized ethnic groups, one of which is the majority Han people (named after an early dynasty). The Han make up 91.5 percent of the total population. The defining elements of a minority group involves some combination of language, culture (including religion), and race that distinguish them from the Han. The fifty-five non-Han minorities number a little more than 100 million, or about 8.5 percent of the total population. These groups range in size from 16 million (the Zhuang of southwest China) to about 2,000 (the Lhoba in the far west). Most of these minorities have come under Chinese rule over many centuries through the expansion of the Chinese state rather than through migration into China.

China's minorities are highly concentrated in the five autonomous regions of Guangxi, Inner Mongolia, Ningxia, Tibet, and Xinjiang. Only in the last two, however, do minority people outnumber Han Chinese, who have been encouraged to migrate to these regions. The five autonomous regions are sparsely populated, yet they occupy about 60 percent of the total land area of the PRC. Some of these areas are resource rich. All are located on strategically important borders of the country, including those with Vietnam, India, and Russia.

The Chinese constitution grants these autonomous areas the right of self-government in certain matters, such as cultural affairs. But minority regions remain firmly under the control of the central authorities. Minority peoples enjoy some latitude to develop their local economies as they see fit. Religious freedom is generally respected, and the use of minority languages in the media and literature is encouraged, as is, to a certain extent, bilingual education. In order to keep the already small minority populations from dwindling further, China's stringent family planning policy is applied much more loosely among minorities, who are often allowed to have two or more children per couple rather than the one-child prescribed limit for most Chinese.

The most extensive ethnic conflict in China has occurred in Tibet. Tibet is located in the far west of China and has been under Chinese military occupation since the early 1950s. Tibetans practice a unique form of Buddhism and most are fiercely loyal to the Dalai Lama, a priest they believe is the incarnation of a divine being. China has claimed authority over Tibet since long before the Communist Party came to power. Tibetans have always disputed that claim and resisted Chinese rule, sometime violently, including in 1959, when the Dalai Lama fled to exile in India following the failure of a rebellion by his followers.

During the Maoist era, traditional Tibetan culture was suppressed by the Chinese authorities. Since the late 1970s, Buddhist temples and monasteries have been allowed to reopen, and Tibetans have gained a significant degree of cultural freedom; the Chinese government has also significantly increased investment in Tibet's economic development. However, China still considers talk of Tibetan political independence to be treason, and Chinese troops have crushed several anti-China demonstrations in Lhasa, the capital of Tibet.

There are more than 20 million Muslims in China. They live in many parts of the country and belong to several different ethnic minority groups. The highest concentration of Muslims is in the far west of China in the Ningxia Hui and Xinjiang Uyghur autonomous regions. The latter borders the Islamic nations of Afghanistan and Pakistan and the Central Asian states of the former Soviet Union.

The more secular Hui are well assimilated into Han Chinese society. But there is growing unrest among Uyghurs in Xinjiang. The Chinese government has clashed with Uyghur militants who want to create a separate Islamic state of "East Turkestan" and have sometimes used violence, including bombings and assassinations, to press their cause. The PRC became an eager ally of the United States in the post–9/11 war on terrorism in part because China could then justify its crackdown on the Xinjiang-based East Turkestan Islamic Movement (ETIM). Washington has included this group on its list of organizations connected to al Qaeda.

China's minority population is relatively small and geographically isolated. Ethnic unrest has been limited, sporadic, and easily quelled. Therefore, the PRC has not had the kind of intense identity-based conflict experienced by countries with more pervasive religious and ethnic cleavages, such as India and Nigeria. But it is possible that domestic and global forces will make ethnic identity a more visible and volatile issue in Chinese politics.

Interest Groups, Social Control, and Citizen Protest

FOCUS QUESTIONS

What is the difference between "mass organizations" and "nongovernmental organizations"?

How does the CCP monitor and control the way in which citizens express their interests?

What kinds of protests have been increasing in China?

Truly independent interest groups and social movements are not permitted to influence the political process in any significant way. The CCP supports official "mass organizations" as a means to provide a way for interest groups to express their views on policy matters—within strict limits.

Total membership of mass organizations in China reaches the hundreds of millions. Two of the most important are the All-China Women's Federation, the only national organization representing the interests of women in general, and the All-China Federation of Trade Unions (ACFTU), to which about 90 million Chinese workers belong. Neither constitutes an autonomous political voice for the groups they are supposed to represent. But they do sometimes act as an effective lobby in promoting the nonpolitical interests of their constituencies. For example, the Women's Federation has become a strong advocate for women on issues ranging from domestic violence to economic rights. The Trade Union Federation has pushed for legislation to reduce the standard workweek from six to five days. The ACFTU also represents individual workers with grievances against management, although its first loyalty is to the Chinese communist party-state.

Since the late 1990s, there has been a huge increase in the number of nongovernmental organizations (NGOs) less directly subordinate to the CCP than the official mass organizations. There is an enormous variety of national and local NGOs. These include ones that deal with the environment (such as the China Green Earth Volunteers), health (for instance, the China Foundation for the Prevention of STDs and AIDS), charitable work (such as the China Children and

Teenagers Fund), and legal issues (for instance, the Beijing Center for Women's Law Services). These NGOs, which must register with the government, have considerable latitude to operate within their functional areas without direct party interference *if* they steer clear of politics and do not challenge official policies.

Although China has certainly loosened up politically since the days of Mao Zedong, the party-state's control mechanisms still prevent the formation of movements that might defy the CCP's authority. In rural areas, the small-scale, closely knit nature of the village facilitates control by the local party and security organizations. Residents' committees are one of the major instruments of control in urban China. These neighborhood-based organizations, each of which covers 100 to 1,000 households depending on the size of the city, effectively extend the unofficial reach of the party-state down to the most basic level of urban society. They used to be staffed mostly by appointed retired persons (often elderly women). But now their functions are shifting from surveillance to service. Many are led by younger and better-educated residents. In some places neighbors elect committee members. The growth of private enterprise, increasing labor and residential mobility, and new forms of association (such as discos and coffeehouses) and communication (for example, cell phones, e-mail, fax machines) are just some of the factors that are making it much harder for the party-state to monitor citizens as closely as in the past.

Protest and the Party-State

The Tiananmen massacre of 1989 showed the limits of protest in China. The party leadership was particularly alarmed at signs that a number of independent student and worker grass-roots organizations were emerging from the demonstrations. The brutal suppression of the democracy movement was meant to send a clear signal that neither open political protest nor the formation of autonomous interest groups would be tolerated.

There have been few large-scale political demonstrations in China since 1989. Pro-democracy groups have been driven deep underground or abroad. Known dissidents are continuously watched, harassed, imprisoned, or expelled from the country, sometimes as a conciliatory diplomatic gesture.

Repression has not stopped all forms of citizen protest. The Falun Gong (literally, "Dharma Wheel Practice") has carried out the biggest and most continuous demonstrations against the party-state in recent years. The Falun Gong (FLG) is a spiritual movement with philosophical and religious elements drawn from Buddhism and Taoism along with traditional Chinese physical exercises (similar to *tai chi*) and meditation. It claims 70 million members in China and 30 million in more than seventy other countries. Its promise of inner tranquility and good health has proven very appealing to a wide cross-section of people in China as a reaction to some of the side effects of rapid modernization. The authorities began a crackdown in 1999, which intensified after approximately 10,000 Falun Gong followers staged a peaceful protest in front of CCP headquarters in the center of Beijing. The authorities have destroyed FLG books and tapes, jammed Web sites, and arrested thousands of practitioners. Despite a few small FLG demonstrations in recent years, the crackdown seems to have been successful.

Labor unrest is becoming more frequent, with reports of thousands of strikes and other actions in recent years. Workers have carried out big demonstrations at state-owned factories. They have protested the ending of the iron rice bowl system, layoffs, the nonpayment of pensions or severance packages, and the arrest of grass-roots labor leaders. Workers at some foreign-owned enterprises have gone on strike against unsafe working conditions or low wages. Most of these actions have remained limited in scope and duration, so the government has usually not cracked down on the protesters. On occasion, it has actually pressured employers to meet the workers' demands.

In mid-2007, the Chinese government implemented a new, rather sweeping labor law, which was largely designed to protect workers' rights. The law requires that employers, even foreign companies, give workers written contracts and regulates the use of temporary laborers. Workers cannot be fired without due process. Some observers see this as an effort to stem the tide of labor unrest. Others see it also as part of Hu Jintao's political platform to create a "harmonious society."

China's farmers have found ways to resist party-state policies that they believe hurt their interests. One such example is rural resistance to China's strict one-child population control policy.

The countryside has also seen a sharp increase of protest over other issues. In the poorer regions of the country, farmers have attacked local officials and rioted over corruption, exorbitant taxes and extralegal fees, and the government's failure to pay on time for agricultural products it has purchased. In areas benefiting from China's economic growth, people have protested environmental damage by factories whose owners care only for profit. Protests have also attacked illegal land seizures by greedy local officials working in cahoots with developers who want to build factories, expensive housing, or even golf courses.

These protests have not spread beyond the locales where they started. They have focused on the protestors' immediate material concerns, not on grand-scale issues like democracy. They have usually been contained by the authorities through a combination of coercion and concessions to some of the farmers' demands.

Grass-roots protests in both the countryside and cities most often target corrupt local officials or unresponsive employers, not the Communist Party. By responding positively to farmer and worker concerns, the party-state can win support and turn what could be regime-threatening activities into regime-sustaining ones.

The overall political situation in China remains rather contradictory. Although people are much freer than they have been in decades and most visitors find Chinese society quite open, repression can still be intense. Public political dissent is almost nonexistent. But there are many signs that the Chinese Communist Party is losing or giving up some of its ability to control the

China's One-Child Policy

As noted earlier, China and the United States are about the same size in terms of total area. But China has more than four times the population of the United States. This difference is reflected in the population density of each country: the United States has 31 people per square kilometer (80 per square mile); China has 137 per square kilometer (355 per square mile). The most heavily populated part of New York City (Manhattan) has 25,849 people per square kilometer (66,949 per square mile); in Shanghai, the Huangpu area has 126,500 per square kilometer (327,633 per square mile). Furthermore, the United States has more arable land (land that can be used to produce food) than does China. In the United States, much farmland goes unused (the government even pays some farmers *not* to grow crops); in China, literally every inch of land that can be used to produce food is under cultivation.

This should give you a sense of why China's government has long felt a need to control the growth of its population.

China experienced a huge surge in the size of its population beginning in the mid-eighteenth century. In fact, the economic pressures caused by this surge were one of the reasons for the collapse of China's imperial system and the revolution that brought the Communist Party to power in 1949. Mao Zedong did not promote population control because he believed that people were China's most precious resource and source of support for his radical policies.

By the 1970s, China's population exceeded 800 million. Greatly improved health conditions had allowed it to grow at about 2.8 percent per year, which is a very high rate of population increase. The Chinese population would double in just twenty-five years. Cutting the birthrate came to be seen by the country's post-Mao leaders as a major requirement to economic development. Since the 1980s, the Chinese government has enforced a strict population control policy that has, over time, used various means to encourage or even force couples to have only a single child. This is called the "One-Child Policy."

Intensive media campaigns laud the patriotic virtues and economic benefits of small families. Positive incentives such as more farmland or preferred housing have been offered to couples with only one child. Fines or demotions have punished violators. In some places, workplace medics or local doctors monitor contraceptive use and women's fertility cycles, and a couple must have official permission to have a child. Defiance has sometimes led to forced abortion or sterilization.

The combination of the one-child campaign, the modernizing economy, and a comparatively strong record in improving educational and employment opportunities for women have brought China's population growth rate to about 0.6 percent per year. This is even lower than the rate in the United States, which is 0.9 percent per year. China's rate of population increase is *very* low for a country at its level of economic development. India, for example, has also had some success in promoting family planning. But its annual population growth rate is 1.4 percent. Nigeria's is 2.4 percent. These may not seem like big differences, but consider this: at these respective growth rates, it will take 116 years for China's population to double, whereas India's population will double in about fifty years and Nigeria's in just twenty-nine years! India is projected to pass China as the country with the world's largest population sometime in the decade 2030–2040—and with only about one-third of the land.

However, the compulsory, intrusive nature of China's family planning program and the extensive use of abortion as one of the major means of birth control have led to much international criticism. Because their family income now depends on having more people to work, many farmers have evaded the one-child policy by not reporting births and other means. Furthermore, the still widespread belief that male children will contribute more economically to the family and that a male heir is necessary to carry on the family line causes some rural families to take drastic steps to make sure that they have a son. Female infanticide and the abandonment of female babies have increased dramatically. Ultrasound technology has led to large number of sex-selective abortions of female fetuses. As a result, China has an unusual gender balance among its young population. One estimate suggests that there are 70 million more males in China than females. Such a surplus of males (India has a similar situation) may cause a number of serious social problems, including the abduction and selling of young girls as "wives"; some scholars have even argued that it could lead the country to become more militarily aggressive.

Partly in response to rural resistance and international pressure, the Chinese government has relaxed its population policies. Forced abortion and infanticide is now infrequent, although sex-selective abortion is not. Rural couples are often allowed to have two children. The government is also offering special pensions to those who have only one son or two daughters so they will be less dependent on their children for support in their old age. In the cities, where there has been more voluntary compliance with the policy because of higher incomes and limited living space, the one-child policy is still basically in effect. ❖

movements and associations of its citizens and can no longer easily limit access to information and ideas from abroad. Some forms of protest also appear to be increasing and may come to pose a serious challenge to the authority of the party-state.

Summary

Representation of citizen interests and political participation are important parts of China's "socialist democracy." But they are carried out under the watchful eye of the Chinese Communist Party. The National People's Congress, the legislature of the PRC, has become more active and independent as the country's focus has shifted from revolutionary politics to economic development. Elections, particularly at the local level, have become more open and democratic. The Communist Party has also changed significantly, not just welcoming workers, peasants, and political activists into its ranks, but even recruiting members from among China's growing capitalist class of private business owners. Although they are much more open than during the Maoist era, the media, the arts, and education are still ultimately under party supervision. Communist ideology is declining as a unifying force for the country, and the ability of the communist party-state to control and influence its citizens is weakening. The Internet, religion, consumerism, and popular culture are growing in influence. These all present a challenge to the CCP, which now emphasizes Chinese nationalism and pride as sources of citizen identity. Some of the greatest political tensions in China are in parts of the country with high concentrations of non-Chinese ethnic minorities, such as in Tibet and the Muslim areas of the northwest. Protests by farmers and industrial workers with economic grievances have been on the increase, but these have not become large-scale or widespread.

SECTION 5

Chinese Politics in Transition

FOCUS QUESTIONS

What has been the political impact of China's rapid economic development?

What are the major political challenges facing the CCP?

What factors will influence the future of the democratic idea in China?

Political Challenges and Changing Agendas

Scenes from the Chinese Countryside[10]

China has become a lot more modern and urban in recent years. But it is still largely a rural country with a majority of its people living in the countryside. However, depending on where you look in its vast rural areas, you will see a very different China. Take, for example, the following:

Huaxi, Jiangsu Province. This rural village looks much like an American suburb: spacious roads lined with two-story townhouses, potted plants on doorsteps, green lawns, and luscious shade trees. Homes are air-conditioned with leather living room furniture, studies with computers, and exercise rooms. Most families have at least one car. Huaxi has grown rich by developing a number of industrial and commercial enterprises. These have replaced agriculture as the main source of income.

Nanliang, Shaanxi Province. This village is in one of the areas known as China's Third World. Persistent poverty is still the common lot. Per capita income is less than fifty dollars a year. Most families live in one-room, mud-brick houses with no running water that they often share with pigs or other farm animals. One muddy waterhole is used for bathing—by both people and livestock. There are no paved roads. The children, dressed in grimy clothes and ragged cloth shoes, are not starving. But they do not seem to be flourishing either. Education, professional health care, and other social services are minimal or nonexistent. The poor quality land barely supports those who work it.

Beihe, Shandong Province. This may be a typical Chinese village, nowhere near as wealthy as Huaxi nor as poor as Nanliang. Per capita income is about $600 per year. Most people work in small, privately owned factories. Many residents have mobile phones and own consumer electronics. But they are worried. The local enterprises are struggling to survive fierce market competition. The village-owned malt factory has gone bankrupt. Many hope to revive village fortunes by leasing out land to expanding businesses.

Daolin, Hunan Province. A few years ago, thousands of angry farmers marched on the township government headquarters to protest excessive taxes and fees and the gross corruption of local officials. One farmer was killed and dozens injured when the police used clubs and tear gas to disperse the crowd. Shortly afterward, nine people suspected of being ringleaders of the protests were arrested. But the national government did step in and ordered a reduction in financial burdens. It punished some of the most corrupt local officials.

Beiwang, Hebei Province. This was one of the first villages to establish a representative assembly and hold democratic elections for local officials. Among the first decisions made by the elected officials and the assembly was to give just a few families contracts to tend the village's 3000 pear trees rather giving each family an equal number to look after. They believed that this would lead to better pear farming and would cause the non–pear-tending families to develop other kinds of economic activity. The local Communist Party branch objected that this would lead to too much inequality. The party leaders eventually agreed, under pressure, to go along with the new policy. In a short time, pear production zoomed. The new system proved to be beneficial not only to the few families who looked after the trees but also to the village as a whole because of economic diversification and the local government's share of the increased profits.

These scenes reflect the enormous diversity of the Chinese countryside: prosperity and poverty, mass protests and peaceful politics. It is worth remembering that about 60 percent of China's population—that's more than 600 million people—still live in the rural parts of the country. What happens in the rural towns and villages will have a tremendous impact on China's political and economic future.

Beiwang reminds us that not all politics rises to national or international significance. The question of who looks after the village pear trees may matter more to local residents than what happens in the inner sanctums of the Communist Party or U.S.-China presidential summit meetings. The victory of the Beiwang representative assembly and elected officials on the pear tree issue shows that even in a one-party state, the people sometimes prevail against those with power, and democracy works on the local level—as long as the basic principle of party leadership is not challenged.

The Huaxi scene shows the astonishing improvement in living standards in much of rural China. But huge pockets of severe poverty, like Nanliang, still persist, especially in inland regions far removed from the more prosperous coastal regions. Most of rural China falls between the extremes. And it is in these in-between areas, such as Beihe and Daolin, where the combination of new hopes brought about by economic progress and the tensions caused by blatant corruption, growing inequalities, stagnating incomes, and other frustrations may prove to be politically explosive.

Economic Management, Social Tension, and Political Legitimacy

China's rural areas illustrate a larger challenge facing the leaders of the PRC: how to sustain and effectively manage the economic growth on which the CCP's legitimacy as the ruling party is now largely based. The party is gambling that continued solid economic performance will literally buy it legitimacy and that most citizens will care little about democracy or national politics if their material lives continue to get better. So far this gamble seems to have paid off.

But failure to keep inequality under control, especially between city and countryside, or failure to continue providing opportunities for advancement for the less well off could lead to social instability and become a liability for a political party that still espouses socialist goals. One of the government's most formidable tasks will be to create enough jobs not only for the millions of workers who are expected to be laid off by the closure or restructuring of state-owned enterprises, but also for the twenty million or so new entrants to the labor force each year. This situation will very likely be compounded by those displaced from companies that are no longer competitive in China's increasingly globalized economy.

The collapse of China's welfare system under the pressures of market reforms and globalization poses a serious challenge to China's technocratic leadership. The public health system is in a shambles, with AIDS and other infectious diseases spreading rapidly. China also has a rapidly graying population, that is, the percentage of elderly people in the population is growing. The country lacks any kind of adequate pension or social security system to meet the needs of its senior citizens. As mentioned before, these kinds of problems are the target of Hu Jintao's emphasis on building a "harmonious society." It remains to be seen whether the Chinese government will be able to translate this ideal into action.

The considerable autonomy from the central government gained by China provinces has had important economic benefits. It has also fostered regionalism. This is a potential threat to the CCP's political control and government efforts to have a coordinated national economic policy. China's Communist Party leaders must also decide how to further nurture the private sector, which is the most dynamic part of the economy. Business owners and investors still face significant restrictions. Corruption affects the lives of most people more directly than does political repression. It is probably the single most corrosive force eating away at the legitimacy of the Chinese Communist Party.

China and the Democratic Idea

China has evolved in recent decades toward a system of what has been called "Market-Leninism,"[11] a combination of increasing economic openness (a market economy) and continuing political rigidity under the leadership of a Leninist ruling party that adheres to a remodeled version of communist ideology.

However, as the people of China become more secure economically, better educated, and more aware of the outside world, they will also likely become more politically active. The steadily expanding class of private business owners may want political clout to match their wealth. Scholars, scientists, and technology specialists may become more outspoken about the limits on intellectual freedom. The many Chinese who travel or study abroad may find the political gap between their party-state and the world's democracies to be increasingly intolerable.

China's long history of authoritarian rule going back to its imperial system and the hierarchical values of Confucian culture, which is still deeply influential, seem to be mighty counterweights to democracy. The political legitimacy of the CCP may be relatively weak, and some aspects of its social control have broken down. But the party-state's coercive power remains formidable. The PRC's relatively low per capita standard of living, large rural population, vast areas of extreme poverty, and state-dominated media and means of communications also hinder democratization. Finally, many people are apathetic about politics or fearful of the violence and chaos that radical political change of any kind, even democracy, might unleash.

But Taiwan, which also has a deeply rooted Confucian heritage, has enjoyed impressive success in democratization in the past two decades. This includes free and fair multiparty elections from the local level up to the presidency. Taiwan's political development strongly suggests that the values, institutions, and process of democracy are not incompatible with Confucian culture.

Student demonstrators erected a statue called the "Goddess of Democracy" in Beijing's Tiananmen Square in late May 1989 to symbolize their demands for greater political freedom in China. In the background is an official portrait of former Chinese Communist Party leader Mao Zedong. Chinese troops toppled and destroyed the statue after they occupied the square on June 4, 1989, a process that also resulted in the death of many protestors. *(Source: AP Images)*

Furthermore, China has a higher literacy rate, more extensive industrialization and urbanization, a faster rate of economic growth, and a larger middle class than most countries at its level of economic development. These conditions are widely seen by political scientists as favorable to democracy.

A number of significant political changes in China may also be planting the seeds of democracy: the decentralization of political and economic power to local governments; the setting of a mandatory retirement age and term limits for all officials; the coming to power of younger, better educated, and more worldly leaders; the greater role of the National People's Congress in the policy-making process; the introduction of competitive elections in rural villages; the strengthening and partial depoliticization of the legal system; tolerance of a much wider range of artistic, cultural, and religious expression; the increasing activity and influence of nongovernmental organizations; and the important freedom (unheard of in the Mao era) for individuals to be apolitical.

Furthermore, the astounding spread of the democratic idea around the globe since the 1980s has created a trend that will be increasingly difficult for China's leaders to resist. The PRC has become a major player in the world of states. Its government must be more responsive to international opinion in order to continue the country's deepening integration with the international economy and growing stature as a responsible and mature global power.

FOCUS QUESTIONS

Why has the Chinese communist-party state survived while the Soviet Union and most other regimes of that type collapsed more than a decade ago?

In what ways is China still a developing country and a Third World state?

What lessons might be drawn about China from the development experience of other East Asian countries, such as South Korea?

totalitarianism a political system in which the state attempts to exercise total control over all aspects of public and private life, including the economy, culture, education, and social organizations.

Chinese Politics in Comparative Perspective

China as a Communist Party-State

Dramatic economic restructuring and rapidly rising living standards have saved the CCP from the kinds of economic crises that greatly weakened and led to the collapse of other Communist systems, including the Soviet Union. China's current leaders believe that the last Soviet party chief, Mikhail Gorbachev, went much too far with political reform and not far enough with economic change. They believe their reverse formula is a key reason that they have not suffered the same fate.

The Chinese Communists won power through an indigenous revolution with widespread popular backing. They did not need foreign military support for their victory. This sets China apart from most of the East-Central European communist parties, which depended on the Soviet Union. Despite its very serious mistakes in governing China over the last six decades, the CCP has a deep reservoir of historical legitimacy among the Chinese people.

But China still has much in common with other past and current communist party-states, including some of the basic features of a totalitarian political system. **Totalitarianism** (a term also applied to fascist regimes such as Nazi Germany) describes a system in which the ruling party prohibits all forms of meaningful political opposition and dissent, insists on obedience to a single state-determined ideology, and enforces its rule through coercion and terror. Such regimes also seek to bring all spheres of public activity (including the economy and culture) and even many parts of its citizens' private lives (including reproduction) under the total control of the party-state in the effort to modernize the country and, indeed, to transform human nature.

China is much less totalitarian than it was during the Maoist era. The CCP appears to be trying to save communist rule in China by moderating or abandoning many of its totalitarian features. To promote economic development, the CCP has relaxed its grip on many areas of life. Citizens can now pursue their interests without interference by the party-state as long as they avoid sensitive political issues. Bold economic and social reform may, in time, nurture a slow transition to democracy. But so far these reforms have helped to sustain a political system that is basically still a partly totalitarian communist party dictatorship.

China as a Third World State

In 1949, China was a desperately poor country, with an economy devastated by a century of civil strife and world war. It occupied a very weak position in the international system. The PRC has made remarkable progress in improving the well-being of its citizens, building a strong state, and enhancing the country's global role.

Why has China been more successful than so many other nations in meeting some of major challenges of economic development? Third World governments have often served narrow class or foreign interests more than the national interest. Many political leaders and governments in Africa, Asia, and Latin

America have been a drain on development rather than a stimulus. Third World states have often become defenders of a status quo built on extensive inequality and poverty rather than agents of needed change. In contrast, the PRC's recent rulers have successfully created a **developmental state**, in which government power and public policy effectively promote national economic growth.

developmental state a nation-state in which the government carries out policies that effectively promote national economic growth.

Much of the Third World seems to be heading toward political democracy without economic development—or at best very slow development. China, however, seems to be following the reverse course. The harsh political rule of the party-state contrasts sharply with its remarkable accomplishments in improving the material lives of the Chinese people. This contrast makes it difficult to settle on a clear evaluation of the overall record of communist rule in China, particularly in the post-Mao era. It is also hard to predict the future of the Chinese Communist Party. The regime's economic achievements could continue to provide it with the support, or at least compliance, it needs to stay in power despite its serious political shortcomings.

In keeping firm control on political life while allowing the country to open up in other important ways, CCP leaders believe they are wisely following the model of development pioneered by the newly industrializing countries (NICs) of East Asia such as South Korea and Taiwan. The lesson that the CCP draws from the NIC experience is that only a strong authoritarian government can provide the political stability and social peace required for rapid economic growth. According to this view, democracy—with its open debates about national priorities, political parties contesting for power, and interest groups squabbling over how to divide the economic pie—is a recipe for chaos, particularly in a huge and still relatively poor country.

However there is another lesson that can be drawn from the East Asian NICs. Economic development, social modernization, and globalization create powerful pressures for political change both from below and from abroad. In both Taiwan and South Korea, authoritarian governments that had presided over economic miracles in the 1960s and 1970s gave way in the 1980s and 1990s to democracy, largely in response to domestic demands from their own populations.

China's dynamic economic expansion and social transformation over the last quarter century suggest that the PRC is in a period of growth and modernization that will lead it to NIC status. However, in terms of the extent of industrialization, per capita income, the strength of the private sector of the economy, and the size of the middle and professional classes, China's development is still far below the level at which democracy succeeded in Taiwan and South Korea. Nevertheless, economic reform in China has already created groups and processes and given rise to interests and ideas that are likely to evolve as sources of pressure for more and faster political change. The experience of the NICs and other developing countries suggests that such pressures will intensify as the economy and society continue to modernize. At some point in the not-too-distant future, the Chinese Communist Party is very likely to face the challenge of the democratic idea once again. How China's new generation of leaders responds to this challenge is perhaps the most important and uncertain question about Chinese politics in the early twenty-first century.

Summary

What happens in China's countryside, where 600 million people still live, will have an enormous impact on the nation's future. Dealing with very serious rural problems is one of the major challenges facing China's current leaders. Economic development has created other major challenges: growing inequalities, rising unemployment, pervasive corruption, and loss of control over lower levels of government, to name just a few. The Communist Party is also very likely to face increasing demands for a political voice from different sectors of society as its citizens become more prosperous, well-educated, and worldly. In comparative perspective, China has proven more economically successful and politically adaptable than other communist party-states, including the Soviet Union, which collapsed in 1991. China has also been much more successful than most other developing countries in promoting economic growth but so far has not been part of the wave of democratization that has spread to so many other parts of the world.

Key Terms

communist-party state
Marxism-Leninism
autonomous regions
newly industrializing country (NIC)
authoritarian
guerrilla warfare
collectivization
socialism
Great Leap Forward
communism
Great Proletarian Cultural Revolution
technocrats
command economy
household responsibility system
iron rice bowl
sustainable development
martial law
cadres
guanxi
socialist democracy
totalitarianism
developmental state

Suggested Readings

Bergsten, Fred, et al. *China The Balance Sheet: What the World Needs to Know Now About the Emerging Superpower.* New York: Public Affairs, 2006.

Blecher, Marc J. *China Against the Tides: Restructuring Through Revolution, Radicalism, and Reform*, 2nd ed. London: Continuum, 2003.

Chang, Jung. *Wild Swans: Three Daughters of China.* New York: Simon & Schuster, 1991.

Cheek, Timothy. *Living with Reform: China Since 1989.* New York: Palgrave McMillan, 2007.

Denoon, David, ed. *China: Contemporary Political, Economic, and International Affairs.* New York: New York University Press, 2007.

Economy, Elizabeth C. *The River Runs Black: The Environmental Challenge to China's Future.* Ithaca: Cornell University Press, 2004.

Gao Yuan. *Born Red: A Chronicle of the Cultural Revolution.* Stanford, Calif.: Stanford University Press, 1987.

Goldman, Merle. *From Comrade to Citizen: The Struggle for Political Rights in China.* Cambridge, Mass.: Harvard University Press, 2006.

Grasso, June et al. *Modernization and Revolution in China*, 3rd ed. Armonk, N.Y.: M. E. Sharpe, 2004.

Hessler, Peter. *Oracle Bones: A Journey Between China's Past and Present*. New York: Harper Collins, 2006.

Kynge, James. *China Shakes the World: A Titan's Rise and Troubled Future—and the Challenge for America*. Boston: Houghton Mifflin, 2006.

Lampton, David M. *Same Bed, Different Dreams: Managing U.S.-China Relations, 1989–2000.* Berkeley: University of California Press, 2001.

McFarquhar, Roderick, and Michael Schoenhals. *Mao's Last Revolution*. Cambridge, Mass.: Harvard University Press, 2006.

Pei Minxin, *China's Trapped Transition: The Limits of Developmental Autocracy.* Cambridge, Mass: Harvard University Press, 2006.

Pomfret, John. *Chinese Lessons: Five Classmates and the Story of the New China.* New York: Henry Holt, 2006.

Spence, Jonathan. *Mao Zedong.* New York: Viking, 1999.

Notes

[1]See, Jonathan Spence, *The Gate of Heavenly Peace: The Chinese and their Revolution, 1895–1989* (New York: Viking Press, 1981).

[2]Mao Zedong, "Report on an Investigation of the Peasant Movement in Hunan," March 1927, in *Selected Readings from the Works of Mao Tsetung* (Beijing: Foreign Languages Press, 1971), 24.

[3]David Bachman, *Bureaucracy, Economy, and Leadership in China: The Institutional Origins of the Great Leap Forward* (Cambridge: Cambridge University Press, 1991), 2.

[4]See, for example, Nicholas D. Kristof and Sheryl WuDunn, *China Wakes: The Struggle for the Soul of a Rising Power* (New York: Time Books, 1994); and James Kynge, *China Shakes the World: A Titan's Rise and Troubled Future—and the Challenge for America* (Boston: Houghton Mifflin, 2006).

[5]Deng Xiaoping first expressed his "cat theory" in 1962 in a speech, "Restore Agricultural Production," in the aftermath of the failure and famine of the Great Leap Forward. In the original speech, he actually quoted an old peasant proverb that refers to a "yellow cat or a black cat," but it is most often rendered "white cat or black cat." See *Selected Works of Deng Xiaoping (1938–1965)* (Beijing: Foreign Languages Press, 1992), 293.

[6]Emily Honig and Gail Herschatter, *Personal Voices: Chinese Women in the 1980s* (Stanford, Calif.: Stanford University Press, 1988), 337.

[7]Li Cheng and Lynn White, "The Thirteenth Central Committee of the Chinese Communist Party: From Mobilizers to Managers, *Asian Survey*, vol. 28, no. 4 (Apr., 1988), pp. 371–399; and Kaiser Kuo, Made in China: The Revenge of the Nerds," Time.com, Jun. 27, 2001, http://www.time.com/time/world/article/0,8599,165453,00.html.

[8]Gordon White, *Riding the Tiger: The Politics of Economic Reform in Post-Mao China* (Palo Alto, Calif.: Stanford University Press, 1993), 20.

[9]For a report on this speech, see Joseph Kahn, "China's Leader Vows to Uphold One-Party Rule," *New York Times*, June 27, 2007.

[10]The following scenes are extrapolated from Jonathan Watts, "In China's richest village," *The Guardian*, May 10, 2005; Wang Zhe, "Behind the Dream of a Village," *Beijing Review*, June 14, 2001, 13–16; Lu Xueyi, "The Peasants Are Suffering, the Villages Are Very Poor," *Dushu* (Readings), January 2001, in U.S. Embassy (Beijing, China), PRC Press Clippings, http://www.usembassy-china.org.cn/sandt/peasantsuffering.html; Hannah Beech, "In Rural China, It's a Family Affair" Time/Asia, May 27, 2002; "The Silent Majority: A Rare Look inside a Chinese Village," *The Economist*, April 7, 2005; Erik Eckholm, "Heated Protests by Its Farmers Trouble Beijing," *New York Times*, February 1, 1999, A; Susan V. Lawrence, "Democracy, Chinese-Style: Village Representative Assemblies," *Australian Journal of Chinese Affairs*, no. 32 (July 1994): 61–68.

[11]Nicholas D. Kristof, "China Sees 'Market-Leninism' as Way to Future," *New York Times*, September 6, 1993.

Glossary

accommodation an informal agreement or settlement between the government and important interest groups that is responsive to the interest groups' concerns for policy or program benefits.

African South African usage refers to black Bantu language speakers, the demographic majority of South African citizens.

Afrikaner descendants of Dutch, French, German, and Scots settlers speaking a language (Afrikaans) derived heavily from Dutch and politically mobilized as an ethnic group through the twentieth century.

Amerindian original peoples of North and South America; indigenous people.

ancien régime the monarchical regime that ruled France until the Revolution of 1789, when it was toppled by a popular uprising. The term is also used to describe long-established regimes in other countries ruled by undemocratic elites.

anticlericalism opposition to the power of churches or clergy in politics. In some countries, for example, France and Mexico, this opposition has focused on the role of the Catholic Church in politics.

apartheid in Afrikaans, "separateness." First used in 1929 to describe **Afrikaner** nationalist proposals for strict racial separation and "to ensure the safety of the white race." Declared government policy after 1948 but dropped from the official lexicon in the 1980s. Elaborated thereafter into a program of hierarchically arranged administrative and representative institutions for each racial and ethnic group in which a central **state** under exclusive white control predominated.

Assembly of Experts nominates and can remove the **Supreme Leader** in Iran. The assembly is elected by the general electorate but almost all its members are clerics.

authoritian/authoritarianism a system of rule in which power depends not on popular legitimacy but on the coercive force of the political authorities. Hence, there are few personal and group freedoms. Authoritarian regimes are also characterized by near absolute power in the executive branch and few, if any, legislative and judicial controls.

autonomous *okrug* one of originally 10 territorial units of the Russian Federation defined in the 1993 constitution to be among the eighty-nine members of the federation, but reduced to 4 by 2008, as some of these small ethnically-based units have been merged with the ***oblast*** or ***krai*** in which they are located.

autonomous region in the People's Republic of China, a territorial unit equivalent to a province that contains a large concentration of ethnic minorities. These regions, for example, Tibet, have some autonomy in the cultural sphere but in most policy matters are strictly subordinate to the central government.

ayatollah literally, "sign of God." High-ranking clerics in Iran. The most senior ones—often no more than half a dozen—are known as grand ayatollahs.

bazaar an urban marketplace where shops, workshops, small businesses, and export-importers are located.

boer literally farmer, modern usage is a derogatory reference to Afrikaners.

brahmin highest caste in the Hindu **caste system** of India.

bureaucracy an organization structured hierarchically, in which lower-level officials are charged with administering regulations codified in rules that specify impersonal, objective guidelines for making decisions. In the modern world, many large organizations, especially business firms and the **executive** branches of **states**, are organized along bureaucratic lines.

cabinet the body of officials (ministers, secretaries, etc.) who direct **executive** departments presided over by the chief executive (prime minister, president, etc.) In parliamentary systems, the cabinet and high-ranking subcabinet ministers (also known as the government) are considered collectively responsible to parliament.

cabinet government a system of government in which most **executive** power is held by the **cabinet**, headed by a prime minister.

cadre a person who occupies a position of authority in a **communist party-state;** cadres may or may not be Communist Party members.

capitalism an economic system, and the **ideology** behind it, that is based on private property, the profit motive, competition, and a free market in which the **state** plays a limited role. See also **laissez-faire**.

caste system India's Hindu society is divided into castes. According to the Hindu religion, membership in a caste is determined at birth. Castes form a rough social and economic hierarchy. See also **Brahmin; untouchables**.

causal theories an influential approach in comparative politics that involves trying to explain why "If X happens, then Y is the result." In other words, how does X (the

independent variable) cause, or influence, Y (the **dependent variable**).

civil society refers to the space occupied by voluntary associations outside the **state**, for example, professional associations (lawyers, doctors, teachers), trade unions, student and women's groups, religious bodies, and other voluntary association groups. The term is similar to *society*, although *civil society* implies a degree of organization absent from the more inclusive term *society*.

clientelism (or **patron-client networks**) an informal relationship in which a powerful patron (for example, a traditional local boss, government agency, or dominant party) offers resources such as land, contracts, protection, or jobs in return for the support and services (such as labor or votes) of lower-status and less powerful clients; corruption, preferential treatment, and inequality are characteristic of clientelist politics.

cohabitation the term used by the French to describe the situation in the Fifth Republic when a president and prime minister belong to opposing political coalitions.

Cold War the hostile relations that prevailed between the United States and the Soviet Union from the late 1940s until the demise of the USSR in 1991. Although an actual (hot) war never directly occurred between the two superpowers, they clashed indirectly by supporting rival forces in many wars occurring in the Third World.

collectivization a process undertaken in the Soviet Union under Stalin from 1929 into the early 1930s and in China under Mao in the 1950s, by which agricultural land was removed from private ownership and organized into large **state** and collective farms.

collective identities the groups with which people identify, including gender, **social class**, race, region, and religion, and which are the "building blocks" for social and political action. Any given individual has a variety of identities, for example, a Muslim woman who is a member of the Kurdish ethnic group of northern Iraq. There is enormous variation regarding which collective identities are uppermost for particular individuals, which ones are influential within particular countries, and how effectively political systems process conflicts among collective identities. This question is among the most important issues studied in comparative politics.

command economy A form of **socialist** economy in which government decisions ("commands") rather than market mechanisms (such as supply and demand) are the major influences in determining the nation's economic direction; also called central planning.

communism a system of social organization based on the common ownership and coordination of production. According to Marxism (the theory of German philosopher Karl Marx, 1818–1883), communism is a culminating stage of history, following **capitalism** and **socialism**. In historical practice, leaders of China, the Soviet Union, and other states that have proclaimed themselves seeking to achieve communism have ruled through a single party, the Communist Party, which has controlled the **state** and society in an authoritarian manner, and have applied **Marxism-Leninism** to justify their rule.

communist party-state a type of **nation-state** in which the Communist Party attempts to exercise a complete monopoly on political power and controls all important **state** institutions. See also **communism**.

comparative politics the study of the domestic politics, political institutions, and conflicts of countries. Often involves comparisons among countries and through time within single countries, emphasizing key patterns of similarity and difference.

comparativist a political scientist who studies the similarities and differences in the domestic politics of various countries. See also **comparative politics**.

conditionality the requirement that certain commitments be made by receiving governments in exchange for credits or other types of assistance provided by international or foreign agencies, to ensure that the goals of the donor agency are respected.

conservative the belief that existing political, social, and economic arrangements should be preserved. Historically, this has involved a defense of the inequalities (of class, race, gender, and so on) that are part of the existing order; often used to identify the economic and social policies favored by right-of-center parties.

consolidated democracies democratic political systems that have been solidly and stably established for an ample period of time and in which there is relatively consistent adherence to the core democratic principles.

constitutional monarchy system of government in which the head of **state** ascends by heredity, but is limited in powers and constrained by the provisions of a constitution.

co-optation incorporating activists into the system while accommodating some of their concerns.

corporatist state a system in which important interests, such as unions and business associations, are formally included in government decision-making processes.

Corruption Perception Index a measure developed by Transparency International that "ranks countries in terms of the degree to which corruption is perceived to exist among public officials and politicians. It is a composite index, drawing on corruption-related data in expert surveys carried out by a variety of reputable institutions. It reflects the views of businesspeople and analysts from around the world, including experts who are locals in the countries evaluated." Range: 10 (highly clean) to 0 (highly corrupt). See *http://www.transparency.org*.

country a territorial unit controlled by a single **state**. Countries vary in the degree to which groups within them have a common culture and ethnic affiliation. See also **nation-state.**

coup d'état a forceful, extra-constitutional action resulting in the removal of an existing government, usually carried out by the military.

decentralization policies that aim to transfer some decision-making power from higher to lower levels of government, typically from the central government to subnational governments, such as states or provinces.

democracy from the Greek *demos* (the people) and *kratos* (rule). A type of political system that features the following: selection to important public offices through free and fair elections based on universal suffrage (the right of all adults to vote); political parties that are free to organize, offer their ideas, present candidates for public office, and compete in elections; an elected government that develops policy according to specified procedures that are fair and relatively open to public scrutiny; all citizens possess political rights and civil liberties; an independent judiciary (court system); civilian control of the military.

democratic centralism a system of political organization developed by V. I. Lenin and practiced, with modifications, by all **communist party-states**. Its principles include a hierarchal party structure in which (1) party leaders are elected on a delegate basis from lower to higher party bodies; (2) party leaders can be recalled by those who elected them; and (3) freedom of discussion is permitted until a decision is taken, but strict discipline and unity should prevail in implementing a decision once it is made. In practice, in all Communist parties in China, the Soviet Union, and elsewhere, centralizing elements tended to predominate over the democratic ones.

democratization transition from **authoritarian** rule to a democractic political order. In South Africa the term usually refers to the period of negotiated political transition between 1900 and 1994; between the ending of official bans on the liberation movements and the general elections. Also called a democratic transition.

demokratizatsiia the policy of democratization identified by former Soviet leader Mikhail Gorbachev in 1987 as an essential component of ***perestroika***. The policy was part of a gradual shift away from a vanguard party approach toward an acceptance of democratic norms. Initially, the policy embraced multicandidate elections and a broadening of political competition within the Communist Party itself; after 1989, it involved acceptance of a multiparty system.

dependent variable an important part of social (and natural) scientific research. The outcome or result to be measured or explained and which is dependent on other factors (**independent variables**). The effect in a cause-and-effect question.

deregulation the process of dismantling state regulations that govern social and economic life. Deregulation increases the power of private actors, especially business firms.

developmental state a **nation-state** in which the government carries out policies that effectively promote national economic growth.

dictatorship a non-democratic form of government in which political power is highly concentrated in individuals or organizations that are not acountable to citizens through elections or other means. See **authoritarianism; totalitarianism**.

dirigisme a French term denoting that the **state** plays a leading role in supervising the economy. In contrast to **socialism** or **communism**, firms remain privately owned under a system of *dirigisme*. At the other extreme, *dirigisme* differs from the situation where the state has a relatively small role in economic governance.

distributional politics the use of power, particularly by the **state**, to allocate some kind of valued resource among competing groups.

dual society a society and economy that are sharply divided into a traditional, usually poorer, and a modern, usually richer, sector.

economic deregulation the lifting or relaxation of government controls over the economy, including the reduction of import taxes (tariffs) and the phasing out of subsidized prices for producers and consumers.

economic liberalization the removal of government control and regulation over private enterprise.

ejidatario recipient of ***ejido*** land grant in Mexico.

ejido land granted by Mexican government to an organized group of peasants.

Emergency (1975–1977) the period when Indian Prime Minister Indira Gandhi suspended many formal democratic rights and ruled in an **authoritarian** manner.

Environmental Performance Index a measure of how close countries come to meeting specific benchmarks for national pollution control and natural resource management. See *http://www.yale.edu/epi*.

European Union (EU) an organization of European countries created in 1958 to promote economic integration and political cooperation among European **states**. At first, the EU's mandate was primarily to reduce tariff barriers among West European states. Since then, more countries throughout Europe have joined the EU, and its powers have vastly expanded to include promoting common policies on immigration, technical standards, and economic and monetary regulation.

executive the agencies of government that implement or execute policy. The highest levels of the executive in most countries are a president or prime minister and cabinet. The top executive officeholders supervise the work of administrative departments and bureaus.

Expediency Council a committee set up in Iran to resolve differences between the ***Majles*** (parliament) and the **Guardian Council**.

failed states states in which the government no longer functions effectively. A **state** may fail when its leaders violate the rule of law and prey on the population or when forces within the country become more powerful than the government.

Farsi Persian word for the Persian language. Fars is a province in Central Iran.

fatwa a pronouncement issued by a high-ranking Islamic cleric.

foreign direct investment ownership of or investment in cross-border enterprises in which the investor plays a direct managerial role.

Foundation of the Oppressed a clerically controlled foundation set up after the **revolution** in Iran.

free trade international commerce that is relatively unregulated or unconstrained by tariffs (special payments imposed by governments on exports or imports).

Freedom in the World Rating an annual evaluation by Freedom House of the level of freedom in countries around the world measured according to political rights and civil liberties through "a multi-layered process of analysis and evaluation by a team of regional experts and scholars." Countries are ranked in .5 gradations between 1.0 and 7.0, with 1.0–2.5 being "Free"; 3.0–5.0, "Not Free"; and 5.5–7.0, "Not free."

fundamentalism a term recently popularized to describe extremist religious movements throughout the world.

fusion of powers a constitutional principle that merges the authority of branches of government, in contrast to the principle of **separation of powers**. In Britain, for example, Parliament is the supreme legislative, **executive**, and judicial authority. The fusion of legislature and executive is also expressed in the function and personnel of the **cabinet**.

gender gap politically significant differences in social attitudes and voting behavior between men and women.

glasnost Gorbachev's policy of "openness" or "publicity," which involved an easing of controls on the media, arts, and public discussion, leading to an outburst of public debate and criticism covering most aspects of Soviet history, culture, and policy.

Global Gender Gap a measure of "the extent to which women in 58 countries have achieved equality with men in five critical areas: economic participation, economic opportunity, political empowerment, educational attainment, and health and well-being." See *www.weforum.org*.

globalization the intensification of worldwide interconnectedness associated with the increased speed and magnitude of cross-border flows of trade, investment and finance, and processes of migration, cultural diffusion, and communication.

grandes écoles prestigious and highly selective schools of higher education in France that train top civil servants, engineers, and business executives.

grands corps elite networks of graduates of selective training schools in France.

Great Leap Forward a movement launched by Mao Zedong in 1958 to industrialize China very rapidly and thereby propel it toward communism. The Leap ended in economic disaster in 1960, causing one of the worst famines in human history.

Great Proletarian Cultural Revolution the political campaign launched in 1966 by Chairman Mao Zedong to stop what he saw as China's drift away from **socialism** and toward **capitalism**. The campaign led to massive purges in the Chinese Communist Party, the widespread persecution of China's intellectuals, and the destruction of invaluable cultural objects. The Cultural Revolution officially ended in 1976 after Mao's death and the arrest of some of his most radical followers.

green revolution a strategy for increasing agricultural (especially food) production, involving improved seeds, irrigation, and abundant use of fertilizers.

gross domestic product (GDP) the total of all goods and services produced within a country that is used as a broad measure of the size of its economy.

gross national product (GNP) a broad measure of the size of an economy. Similar to **gross domestic product**, but also takes into account income received from foreign sources. The World Bank started using the term *gross national income* rather than *gross national product* in its reports and statistics in 2002.

guanxi a Chinese term that means "connections" or "relationships," and describes personal ties between individuals based on such things as common birthplace or mutual acquaintances. *Guanxi* are an important factor in China's political and economic life.

Guardian Council a committee created in the Iranian constitution to oversee the ***Majles*** (the parliament).

guerrilla warfare a military strategy based on small bands of soldiers (the guerrillas) who use hit-and-run tactics to attack a numerically superior and better-armed enemy.

hegemonic power a **state** that can control the pattern of alliances and terms of the international order, and often shapes domestic political developments in countries throughout the world.

hezbollahis literally "partisans of God." In Iran, the term is used to describe religious vigilantes. In Lebanon, it is used to describe the **Shi'i** militia.

hojjat al-Islam literally, "the proof of Islam." In Iran, it means a medium-ranking cleric.

homelands areas reserved for exclusive African occupation, established through the provisions of the 1913 and 1936 land legislation and later developed as semi-autonomous ethnic **states** during the apartheid era. At their fullest extent they represented 13 percent of South Africa's land surface, though at one stage they accommodated more than half the national population.

household responsibility system the system put into practice in China beginning in the early 1980s in which the major decisions about agricultural production are made by individual farm families based on the profit motive rather than by a **people's commune** or the government.

Human Development Index (HDI) a composite number used by the United Nations to measure and compare levels of achievement in health, knowledge, and standard of living. HDI is based on the following indicators: life expectancy, adult literacy rate and school enrollment statistics, and **gross domestic product** per capita at **purchasing power parity**.

ideology a set of fundamental ideas, values, or beliefs about how a political, economic, or social system should be organized. Examples of ideology include **capitalism, communism**, and **socialism**.

imam jum'ehs prayer leaders in Iran's main urban mosques. Appointed by the **Supreme Leader**, they have considerable authority in the provinces.

import substituting industrialization (ISI) a strategy for industrialization based on domestic manufacture of previously imported goods to satisfy domestic market demands.

independent variable an important part of social (and natural) scientific research. A factor that influences the outcome or result (the **dependent variable**) to be measured or explained. The cause in a cause-and-effect question.

Industrial Revolution A period of rapid and destabilizing social, economic, and political changes caused by the introduction of large-scale factory production, originating in England in the middle of the eighteenth century.

Indian Administrative Service (IAS) India's civil service, a highly professional and talented group of administrators who run the Indian government on a day-to-day basis.

indicative planning a term that describes a national plan identifying desirable priorities for economic and social development. Indicative planning can be distinguished from plans developed under command economies.

indigenous groups population of **Amerindian** heritage in Mexico.

influx control a system of controls in South Africa that regulated **African** movement between cities and between towns and the countryside, enforcing residence in the homelands and restricting African choice of employment. Administered through the pass laws dating from the early nineteenth century and abolished in 1986.

informal sector (economy) economic activities outside the formal economy that are unregulated by economic or legal institutions.

insider privatization a term used in relation to Russia to refer to the transformation of formerly **state**-owned enterprises into **joint-stock companies** or private enterprises in which majority control of the enterprise is in the hands of employees and/or managers of that enterprise.

iron rice bowl a feature of China's socialist economy during the Maoist era (1949–76) that provided guarantees of lifetime employment, income, and basic cradle-to-grave benefits to most urban and rural workers. Economic reforms beginning in the 1980s that aimed at improving efficiency and work motivation sought to smash the iron rice bowl and link employment and income more directly to individual effort.

jihad literally "struggle." Although often used to mean armed struggle against unbelievers, it can also mean spiritual struggle for more self-improvement.

joint-stock company a business firm whose capital is divided into shares that can be held by individuals, groups of individuals, or governmental units. In Russia, formation of joint-stock companies has been the primary method for privatizing large **state** enterprises.

judicial review the prerogative of a high court (such as the U.S. Supreme Court) to nullify actions by the **executive** and legislative branches of government that in its judgment violate the constitution.

jurist's guardianship Khomeini's concept that the Iranian clergy should rule on the grounds that they are the divinely appointed guardians of both the law and the people.

Keynesianism named after the British economist John Maynard Keynes, an approach to economic policy in which **state** economic policies are used to regulate the economy in an attempt to achieve stable economic growth. During recession, state budget deficits are used to expand demand in an effort to boost both consumption and investment and create employment. During periods of high growth when inflation threatens, cuts in government spending and a tightening of credit are used to reduce demand.

krai one of the six territorial units in the Russian Federation that are defined by the constitution of 1993 to be among the eighty-nine members of the federation, with a status equal to that of the republics and ***oblasts***. Like the *oblasts* during the Soviet period, the *krai* were defined purely as territorial-administrative units within a particular **republic** of the Soviet Union. A *krai* differed from an *oblast* in that part of its border was on an external boundary of the USSR or it included a mixture of diverse ethnic territories (or both). Generally a *krai* is a geographically large unit, but relatively sparsely populated.

laissez-faire a term taken from the French, which means "to let be," in other words, to allow to act freely. In political economy, it refers to the pattern in which the **state** management is limited to such matters as enforcing contracts and protecting property rights, while private market forces are free to operate with only minimal state regulation.

legitimacy a belief by powerful groups and the broad citizenry that a **state** exercises rightful authority. In the contemporary world, a state is said to possess legitimacy when it enjoys consent of the governed, which usually involves democratic procedures and the attempt to achieve a satisfactory level of economic development and equitable distribution of resources.

Lok Sabha the lower house of parliament in India where all major legislation must pass before becoming law.

macroeconomic policy government policy intended to shape the overall economic system at the national level by concentrating on policy targets such as inflation and growth.

mafia a term borrowed from Italy and widely used in Russia to describe networks of organized criminal activity that pervade both economic and governmental securities in that country and activities such as the demanding of protection money, bribe taking by government officials, contract killing, and extortion.

maharajas India's traditional rulers—monarchs—who retained their positions during the colonial period but were removed from power when the Indian republic was established.

Majles the Iranian parliament; from the Arabic term for "assembly."

maquiladora factories that produce goods for export, often located along the U.S.-Mexican border.

Mandal Commission a government-appointed commission in India headed by J. P. Mandal to consider seat **reservations** and quotas to redress **caste** discrimination.

market reform a strategy of economic transformation begun by the Yeltsin government in Russia in the 1990s and the Deng Xiaoping government in China in the 1980s that involves reducing the role of the **state** in managing the economy and increasing the role of market forces. In Russia, market reform is part of the transition to postcommunism and includes the extensive transfer of the ownership of economic assets from the state to private hands. In China, market reform has been carried out under the leadership of the Chinese Communist Party and involves less extensive privatization.

martial law a period of time during which the normal procedures of government are suspended and the executive branch enforces the law with military power.

Marxism-Leninism the theoretical foundation of **communism** based on the ideas of the German philosopher, Karl Marx (1818–1883), and the leader of the Russian Revolution, V. I. Lenin (1870–1924). Marxism is, in essence, a theory of historical development that emphasizes the struggle between exploiting and exploited classes, particularly the struggle between the bourgeoisie (capitalists) and the proletariat (the industrial working class). Leninism emphasizes the strategy and organization to be used by the communist party to overthrow **capitalism** and seize power as a first step on the road to communism.

maslahat Arabic term for "expediency," "prudence," or "advisability." It is now used in Iran to refer to what is best for the Islamic Republic.

mestizo a person of mixed white, indigenous (Amerindian), and sometimes African descent.

migrant labor workers in **apartheid** South Africa who were denied permanent residence rights in towns under the system of **influx control** and who would be employed on annual contracts that denied them job security. More generally, refers to laborers who move to another location to take a job, often a low-paying, temporary one.

middle-level theory seeks to explain phenomena in a limited range of cases, in particular, a specific set of countries with particular characteristics, such as parliamentary regimes, or a particular type of political institution (such as political parties) or activity (such as protest).

monetarism an approach to economic policy that assumes a natural rate of unemployment, determined by the labor market, and rejects the instrument of government spending to run budgetary deficits for stimulating the economy and creating jobs.

mosque Muslim place of worship, equivalent to a church, temple, or synagogue.

most different case analysis the logic of most different case analysis is that, by comparing cases that differ widely, one seeks to isolate a factor or factors (termed the **independent variable** or variables) that both cases share—despite their differences in other respects—that might explain an outcome (or **dependent variable**).

nationalization the policy by which the **state** assumes ownership and operation of private companies.

nation-state distinct, politically defined territory with its own **state**, relatively coherent culture, economy, and ethnic and other social identities. See also **country**.

neoliberalism a term used to describe government policies that aim to promote private enterprise by reducing government economic regulation, tax rates, and social spending.

newly industrializing countries (NICs) a term used to describe a group of countries that achieved rapid economic development beginning in the 1960s largely stimulated by robust international trade (particularly exports) and guided by government policies. The core NICs are usually considered to be Taiwan, South Korea, Hong Kong, and Singapore, but other countries, including Argentina, Brazil, Malaysia, Mexico, and Thailand, are often included in this category.

nomenklatura this is a system of personnel selection used in the Soviet Union and China under which the Communist Party maintained control over the appointment of important officials in all spheres of social, economic, and political life.

nonaligned bloc countries that refused to ally with either the United States or the USSR during the **Cold War** years.

North American Free Trade Agreement (NAFTA) a treaty among the United States, Mexico, and Canada implemented on January 1, 1994, that largely eliminates trade barriers among the three nations and establishes procedures to resolve trade disputes. NAFTA serves as a model for an eventual Free Trade Area of the Americas zone that could include most Western Hemisphere nations.

oblast one of forty-nine territorial units in the Russian Federation defined by the constitution of 1993 to be among the eighty-nine members of the federation, with a status equal to that of the republics and ***krai***. An *oblast* generally lacks a non-Russian national/ethnic basis. During the Soviet period, the *oblasts* were defined purely as territorial-administrative units located within a particular **republic** of the Soviet Union. See also **autonomous *okrug*; republic**.

oligarchs a small group of powerful and wealthy individuals who gained ownership and control of important sectors of Russia's economy in the context of the privatization of **state** assets in the 1990s.

OPEC Organization of Petroleum Exporting Countries. Founded in 1960 by Iran, Venezuela, and Saudi Arabia, it now includes most oil-exporting countries with the notable exceptions of Mexico and former members of the Soviet Union. It tries to regulate prices by regulating production.

other backward classes the middle or intermediary **castes** in India that have been accorded reserved seats in public education and employment since the early 1990s. See also **reservations**.

panchayats in India, elected bodies at the village, district, and state levels that have development and administrative responsibilities.

para-statals state-owned, or at least **state**-controlled, corporations, created to undertake a broad range of activities, from control and marketing of agricultural production to provision of banking services, operating airlines, and other transportation facilities and public utilities.

parity law a French law passed in 2000 that directs political parties to nominate an equal number of men and women for most elections.

parliamentary democracy system of government in which the chief executive is answerable to the legislature and may be dismissed by it. Parliamentary democracy stands in contrast to a presidential system, in which the chief executive is elected in a national ballot and is independent of the legislative branch.

parliamentary sovereignty a constitutional principle of government (principally in Britain) by which the legislature reserves the power to make or overturn any law without recourse by the **executive**, the judiciary, or the monarchy. Only Parliament can nullify or overturn legislation approved by Parliament; and Parliament can force the **cabinet** or the government to resign by voting a motion of no confidence.

pasdaran Persian term for guards, used to refer to the army of Revolutionary Guards formed during Iran's Islamic Revolution.

pass laws laws in **apartheid** South Africa that required **Africans** to carry identity books in which were stamped the permits they were required to have to travel between the countryside and the cities. The identity books also included the details of their employment. Failure to carry such books was an offense and during the 1960s, 300,000 "pass offenders" were imprisoned annually.

patrimonial state a system of governance in which a single ruler treats the **state** as personal property (patrimony). Appointments to public office are made on the basis of unswerving loyalty to the ruler. In turn, state officials exercise wide authority in other domains, such as the economy, often for their personal benefit and that of the ruler, to the detriment of the general population.

patronage system a political system in which government officials appoint loyal followers to positions rather than choosing people based on their qualifications. May also involve the exchange of favors between an office holder and a particular group, often trading something the group wants for political support.

People of the Book the Muslim term for recognized religious minorities, such as Christians, Jews, and Zoroastrians.

perestroika the policy of restructuring embarked on by Gorbachev when he became head of the Communist Party of the Soviet Union in 1985. Initially, the policy emphasized decentralization of economic decision making, increased enterprise autonomy, expanded public discussion of policy issues, and a reduction in the international isolation of the Soviet economy. Over time, restructuring took on a more political tone, including a commitment to ***glasnost*** and ***demokratizatsiia.***

political economy the study of the interaction between the **state** and the economy, that is, how the state and political processes affect the organization of production and exchange (the economy) and how the organization of the economy affects political processes.

power sharing constitutional arrangements to ensure that the major political parties share executive authority. These can include mandatory coalitions and allocation of senior official positions between parties.

power vertical a term used by Russian president Vladimir Putin to describe a unified and hierarchical structure of executive power ranging from the federal level to the local level, which can be reinforced by various mechanisms such as appointments by higher level officials and oversight of activities by higher organs over lower ones.

prefects French administrators appointed by the minister of the interior to coordinate **state** agencies and programs within the one hundred French departments or localities. Prefects had enormous power until decentralization reforms in the 1980s transferred some of their responsibilities to elected local governments.

privatization the sale of **state**-owned enterprises to private companies or investors. Those who support the policy claim that private ownership is superior to government ownership because for-profit entities promote greater efficiency. Privatization is a common central component of structural adjustment programs to curtail the losses associated with these enterprises and generate state revenue when they are sold.

privatization voucher a certificate worth 10,000 rubles issued by the government to each Russian citizen in 1992 to be used to purchase shares in **state** enterprises undergoing the process of **privatization.** Vouchers could also be sold for cash or disposed of through newly created investment funds.

proportional representation (PR) a system of political representation in which seats are allocated to parties within multimember constituencies, roughly in proportion to the votes each party receives. PR usually encourages the election to parliament of more political parties than single-member-district winner-take-all systems, such as in the United States.

purchasing power parity (PPP) a method of calculating the value of a country's money based on the actual cost of buying certain goods and services in that country rather than how many U.S. dollars they are worth. PPP is widely considered to be a more accurate indicator for comparing standards of living, particularly in countries at very different levels of economic development.

pyramid debt a situation when a government or organization takes on debt obligations at progressively higher rates of interest in order to pay off existing debt. In some cases, a structure of pyramid debt can result in a default on the entire debt obligation if interest owed becomes unmanageable.

quangos acronym for quasi-nongovernmental organizations, the term used in Britain for nonelected bodies that are outside traditional governmental departments or local authorities. They have considerable influence over public policy in areas such as education, health care, and housing.

Qur'an the Muslim Bible.

Rayja Sabha India's upper house of parliament; considerably less significant politically than the ***Lok Sabha.***

referendum an election in which citizens are asked to approve (or reject) a policy proposal.

regulations the rules that explain the implementation of laws. When Congress passes a law, it sets broad principles for implementation, but how the law is actually implemented is determined by regulations written by executive branch agencies. The regulation-writing process allows interested parties to influence the eventual shape of the law in practice.

rentier state a country that obtains much of its revenue from the export of oil or other natural resources.

republic in contemporary usage, a political regime in which leaders are not chosen on the basis of their inherited background (as in a monarchy). A republic may, but need not be, democratic. For Russia, a republic is one of twenty-one territorial units in the Russian Federation that are defined by the constitution of 1993 to be among the eighty-nine members of the federation and named after the indigenous non-Russian population group that inhabits the republic. A republic generally was originally formed in recognition of the presence of a non-Russian national or ethnic group residing in the territory. In the Soviet period, most of these units were called **autonomous republics**.

reservations jobs or admissions to colleges reserved by the government of India for specific social groups, particularly underprivileged groups.

revolution the process by which an established political regime is replaced (usually by force and with broad popular participation) and a new regime established that introduces radical changes throughout society. Revolutions are different from **coups d'état** in that there is widespread popular participation in revolutions, whereas coups d'état are led by small groups of elites.

sanctions international embargoes on economic and cultural contracts with a particular country; applied selectively to South Africa by various governments and the United Nations from 1948 until 1994.

scheduled castes the lowest caste groups in India; also known as the untouchables. See also **caste system** and **untouchables**.

secularism a doctrine that mandates maintaining a separation between church and **state**. Secularism requires that the state be neutral toward religious faiths and that public policy not be dictated by the teaching of any particular religion. A cause of conflict in regimes committed to secularism often involves where to draw the boundary between religion and the public sphere.

Sepoy Rebellion an armed uprising by Indian princes against expansion of British colonialism in India in 1857. Following the failure of this rebellion—also known as the Indian Mutiny of 1857—Britain assumed full control of India, which it ruled until 1947.

settler state colonial or former colonial administrations controlled by the descendants of immigrants who settled in the territory. Settler states often feature large-scale alienation of land from indigenous inhabitants as well as elaborately organized racial discrimination.

sexenio the six-year administration of Mexican presidents.

shari'a Islamic law derived mostly from the **Qur'an** and the examples set by the Prophet Muhammad.

Shi'i/Shi'ism a branch of Islam. It literally means "the followers or partisans of Ali." The other branch is known as Sunni, or the followers of tradition.

shock therapy a variant of **market reform** that involves the **state** simultaneously imposing a wide range of radical economic changes, with the purpose of "shocking" the economy into a new mode of operation. Shock therapy can be contrasted with a more gradual approach to market reform.

Sikhs a minority religious community in India whose members practice Sikhism. Sikhs constitute less than 2 percent of the Indian population and 76 percent of the state of Punjab.

siloviki derived from the Russian word *sil*, meaning "force." Russian politicians and government officials drawn from security and intelligence agencies (such as the Soviet KGB or its contemporary counterpart, the FSB), special forces, or the military, many of whom were recruited to important political posts under Vladimir Putin.

single-member plurality district an electoral system in which candidates run for a single seat from a specific geographic district. The winner is the person who receives the most votes, whether or not that is a majority. These systems, unlike systems of proportional representation, increase the likelihood that two national coalition parties will form.

social class a group whose members share common economic status determined largely by occupation, income, and wealth. Members of the same social class often share similar political attitudes.

socialism in a socialist regime, the **state** plays a leading role in organizing the economy, and most business firms are publicly owned. A socialist regime, unlike a **communist party-state**, may allow the private sector to play an important role in the economy and be committed to political pluralism. In **Marxism-Leninism**, socialism refers to an early stage in the development of **communism**. Socialist regimes can be organized in a democratic manner, in that those who control the state may be chosen according to democratic procedures. They may also be governed in an undemocratic manner when a single party, not chosen in free competitive elections, controls the state and society.

socialist democracy the term used by the Chinese Communist Party to describe the political system of the People's Republic of China. Also called the *people's democratic dictatorship*. The official view is that this type of system, under the leadership of the Communist Party, provides **democracy** for the overwhelming majority of people and suppresses (or exercises dictatorship over) only the enemies of the people. Socialist democracy is contrasted to bourgeois (or capitalist) democracy, which puts power in the hands of the rich and oppresses the poor.

social movements large-scale grass-roots action that demands reforms of existing social practices and government policies. Social movements are less formally organized than interest groups. An example would be the civil rights movement in the United States that began in the 1960s.

social security a national system of contributory and noncontributory benefits to provide assistance for the elderly, sick, disabled, unemployed, and others similarly in need of assistance. The specific coverage of social security, a key component of the **welfare state**, varies by country.

special relationship refers to relations between the United States and Britain (the United Kingdom) and meant to convey not only the largely positive, mutually beneficial nature of the relationship, but also the common heritage and shared values of the two countries.

state a unified, geographically defined political entity. The state comprises a country's most powerful political institutions, including the **executive**, legislative, and judicial branches of government as well as the police and armed forces, which claim the right to make the laws and enforce them through the use of coercion, if necessary. See also **civil society**.

state capitalism a strategy of economic development in which the **state** guides industrial, agricultural, and financial policy and aims to create the political conditions for its success. Unlike **socialism** or **communism**, the state does not own major parts of the economy; rather the state works in partnership with owners of private property to promote national economic growth.

state formation the historical development of a **state**, often marked by major stages, key events, or turning points (critical junctures) that influence the contemporary character of the state.

statism the doctrine that advocates firm **state** direction of the economy and society.

state-led economic development the process of promoting economic development using governmental machinery.

Supreme Leader head of the Islamic Republic of Iran.

sustainable development an approach to promoting economic growth that seeks to minimize environmental degradation and depletion of natural resources. Advocates of sustainable development believe that policies implemented in the present must take into account the impact on the ability of future generations to meet their needs and live healthy lives.

technocrats Career-minded bureaucrats who administer public policy according to a technical rather than a political rationale. In Mexico and Brazil, these are known as the *técnicos*.

theocracy a **state** dominated by the clergy, who rule on the grounds that they are the only interpreters of God's will and law.

totalitarianism a political system in which the **state** attempts to exercise total domination of all aspects of public and private life, including the economy, culture, education, and social organizations, through an integrated system of ideological, economic, and political control. The term has been applied to both **communist party-states** and fascist regimes such as Nazi Germany.

township South African usage refers to a segregated residential area reserved for **Africans**, during **apartheid** tightly controlled and constituted mainly by public housing.

township and village enterprises (TVEs) nonagricultural businesses and factories owned and run by local governments and private entrepreneurs in China's rural areas. TVEs operate largely according to market forces and outside the **state** plan.

transitional democracies countries that have moved from an **authoritarian** government to a democratic one. Also referred to as newly established democracies.

typology a method of classifying by using criteria that divide a group of cases into smaller numbers. For example, in this book, we use a typology of countries that distinguishes among established democracies, transitional democracies, and nondemocracies, or **authoritarian** regimes.

Umkhonto we Sizwe Zulu and Xhosa for "Spear of the Nation," the armed wing of the African National Congress, established in 1961 and integrated into the South African National Defence Force in 1994.

unitary state in contrast to the federal systems of Mexico, India, Canada, or the United States, where power is shared between the central government and state or regional governments, in a unitary **state** (such as Britain or China) no powers are reserved constitutionally for subnational units of government.

untouchables the lowest caste in India's **caste system**, whose members are among the poorest and most disadvantaged Indians.

vanguard party a political party that claims to operate in the "true" interests of the group or **social class** it purports to represent, even if this understanding doesn't correspond to the expressed interests of the group itself. The Communist parties of the Soviet Union and China are examples of vanguard parties.

voortrekkers pastoralist descendants of Dutch-speaking settlers in South Africa who moved northwards from the British controlled Cape in 1836 to establish independent republics; later regarded as the founders of the **Afrikaner** nation.

welfare state not a form of **state**, but rather a set of public policies designed to provide for citizens' needs through direct or indirect provisions of pensions, health care, unemployment insurance, and assistance to the poor.

Westminster model a form of **democracy** based on the supreme authority of Parliament and the accountability of its elected representatives; named after the Parliament building in London.

zamindars landlords who served as tax collectors in India under the British colonial government. The *zamindari* system was abolished after independence.

About the Editors and Contributors

Ervand Abrahamian is Distinguished Professor of History at Baruch College and the Graduate Center of the City University of New York. His publications include *Khomeinism: Essays on the Islamic Republic* (University of California Press, 1993) and *Tortured Confessions: Prisons and Public Recantations in Modern Iran* (University of California Press, 1999). His most recent book is *A History of Modern Iran* (Cambridge University Press, 2008).

Amrita Basu is Paino Professor of Political Science and Women's and Gender Studies and Associate Dean of Faculty at Amherst College. Her main areas of interest are social movements, religious nationalism, and gender politics in South Asia. She is the author of *Two Faces of Protest: Contrasting Modes of Women's Activism in India* (University of California Press, 1992) and several edited books, including *Localizing Knowledge in a Globalizing World, Community Conflicts and the State in India* (with Atul Kohli), *Women's Movements in Global Perspective; The Challenge of Local Feminism*, and *Appropriating Gender: Women's Activism and Politicized Religion in South Asia.*

Joan DeBardeleben is Professor of Political Science and of European, Russian, and Eurasian Studies at Carleton University in Ottawa, Ontario. She has published widely on Russian politics, with a focus on Russian federalism, public opinion, and elections. Recent articles have been published in *Europe-Asia Studies, Sotsiologicheskie issledovaniia (Sociological Research)*, and *Party Politics.* She is a contributing author to *Microeconomic Change in Central and East Europe* (Carol S. Leonard, ed., Palgrave Macmillan, 2002) and *The Struggle for Russian Environmental Policy* (Ilmo Masso and Veli-Pekka Tynkkynen, eds., Kikimora, 2001). Dr. DeBardeleben is also Director of Carleton University's Centre for European Studies.

Merilee S. Grindle is Edward S. Mason Professor of International Development at the John F. Kennedy School of Government and Director of the David Rockefeller Center for Latin American Studies, Harvard University. She is a specialist on the comparative analysis of policymaking, implementation, and public management in developing countries and has written extensively on Mexico. Her most recent book is *Going Local: Decentralization, Democratization, and the Promise of Good Governance* (Princeton University Press, 2007).

William A. Joseph is Professor of Political Science at Wellesley College and an Associate of the Fairbank Center for East Asian Research at Harvard University. His research focuses on contemporary Chinese politics and ideology. He is the editor of *China Briefing: The Contradictions of Change* (M.E. Sharpe, 1997), coeditor of *New Perspectives on the Cultural Revolution* (Harvard University Press, 1991), and contributing editor of *The Oxford Companion to Politics of the World* (Oxford University Press, 2nd ed., 2001).

Mark Kesselman is Professor of Political Science at Columbia University. A specialist on the French and European political economy, his recent publications include contributions to *The Mitterrand Era: Policy Alternatives and Political Mobilization in France* (Macmillan, 1995), *Mitterrand's Legacy, Chirac's Challenge* (St. Martin's Press, 1996), and *Diminishing Welfare: A Cross-National Study of Social Provision* (Greenwood, 2002). He is the coauthor of *A Century of Organized Labor in France* (St. Martin's Press, 1997) and *The Politics of Power: A Critical Introduction to American Politics* (Wadsworth, 2005), coeditor of *Readings in Comparative Politics* (Houghton Mifflin, 2006) and *European Politics in Transition* (Houghton Mifflin, 2008); and editor of *Politics of Globalization: A Reader* (Houghton Mifflin, 2007).

Atul Kohli is the David K. E. Bruce Professor of International Affairs and Professor of Politics and International Affairs at Princeton University. His principal research interests are in the areas of comparative political economy with a focus on the developing countries. He is the author of *State-Directed Development: Political Power and Industrialization in the Global Periphery* (winner of the 2005 Charles Levine Award of the International Political Science Association); *Democracy and Discontent: India's Growing Crisis of Governability*; *The State and Poverty in India*; and the editor of six volumes: *The State and Development in the Third World*; *India's Democracy; State Power and Social Forces*; *Community Conflicts and the State in India*; *The Success of India's Democracy*; and *States, Markets and Just Growth.* His current research focuses on the topic of imperialism and the developing world. He is the chief editor of *World Politics* and has received grants and fellowships from the Social Science Research Council, Ford Foundation, and Russell Sage Foundation.

Joel Krieger is Norma Wilentz Hess Professor of Political Science at Wellesley College. His publications include *Globalization and State* Power (Pearson Longman, 2005), *Blair's War*, coauthored with David Coates (Polity Press, 2004), *British Politics in the Global Age: Can Social Democracy*

Survive? (Polity Press, 1999), and *Reagan, Thatcher, and the Politics of Decline* (Oxford University Press, 1986). He is also editor-in-chief of *The Oxford Companion to Politics of the World* (Oxford University Press, 1993; 2nd ed., 2001).

Tom Lodge is Professor of Peace and Conflict Studies at the University of Limerick, Ireland. Between 1978 and 2005 he held posts at the University of the Witwatersrand in Johannesburg. His most recent book is *Nelson Mandela: A Critical Life* (Oxford University Press, 2006).

Index

*Page numbers in boldface indicate the page where a key term is defined.